HISTORY OF MY LIFE

GIACOMO CASANOVA

Chevalier de Seingalt

HISTORY OF MY LIFE

FIRST TRANSLATED INTO ENGLISH IN ACCORDANCE
WITH THE ORIGINAL FRENCH MANUSCRIPT

by Willard R. Trask

VOLUMES 3 AND 4

THE JOHNS HOPKINS UNIVERSITY PRESS
Baltimore and London

English translation copyright © 1967 by Harcourt, Brace &
World, Inc.
All rights reserved
Printed in the United States of America on acid-free paper

Originally published as *Histoire de Ma Vie,* Edition intégrale, by
Jacques Casanova de Seingalt, Vénitien, by F. A. Brockhaus,
Wiesbaden, Librairie Plon, Paris, 1960. © F. A. Brockhaus,
Wiesbaden, 1960.

This edition originally published in the United States as a Helen and
Kurt Wolff book by Harcourt, Brace & World, Inc.
Johns Hopkins Paperbacks edition, 1997
9 8 7 6 5 4 3

The Johns Hopkins University Press
2715 North Charles Street
Baltimore, Maryland 21218-4363
www.press.jhu.edu

Library of Congress Catalog Card Number 97-70304

A catalog record for this book is available from the British Library.

ISBN 0-8018-5663-9 (pbk.: Vols. 3 and 4)

TRANSLATOR'S NOTE

In this and the succeeding volumes Mr. Piero Chiari and Mr. Mondadori have kindly allowed me to include in the notes certain additions and rectifications appearing in the notes prepared by Mr. Chiari for the new Italian translation of Casanova by Giancarlo Buzzi: Giacomo Casanova, *Storia della mia vita* (6 vols., Verona, Arnoldo Mondadori, 1964-1965).

W. R. T.

HISTORY OF MY LIFE
Volume 3

CONTENTS

Volume 3

Contents

LIST OF PLATES

Volume 3

VOLUME 3

CHAPTER I

I attempt my magical operation. A terrible
storm comes up. My fear. Genoveffa remains
pure. I give up, and sell the sheath to
Capitani. I meet Giulietta again, with the
pretended Count Celi, now Count Alfani.
I decide to go to Naples. What puts me on a
different road.

Anno 1748,[1]
the 23rd of my age.

IT WAS on the next night that I was to perform the
great operation, for otherwise we should have had to wait
for the full moon of the following month. I was supposed
to compel the gnomes to bring the treasure to the surface at the place where I would put my conjurations on
them. I knew that the operation would fail, but that it
would be easy for me to explain the reason; meanwhile
I must continue to give a flawless performance in my
role of magician, which I very much enjoyed. I made
Genoveffa work all day at sewing together a circle of
thirty sheets of paper on which I had painted characters
and terrifying figures in black. This "Great Circle,"[2]
as I called it, had a diameter of three paces. I had made
a sort of scepter from the olive branch which Giorgio
Francia had brought me. So, having everything I needed,
I warned Genoveffa that at midnight, when I came out

of the circle, she must be ready for anything. She could not wait to give me such a proof of her obedience; but that did not lessen my feeling that I was still in her debt.

So, having instructed her father Giorgio and Capitani to station themselves on the balcony, not only to be ready to carry out my orders if I called to them but also to prevent the household from seeing what I was about to do, I take off all my profane garments; I put on the great surplice which had been touched only by the pure hands of the innocent Genoveffa; then I let my long hair hang loose, I set the seven-pointed crown on my head and take the great circle on my shoulders, and with one hand holding the scepter and the other the very knife with which St. Peter once cut off Malek's ear, I go down to the courtyard and, after spreading out my circle on the ground and walking around it three times, I jump into it.

After crouching inside it for two or three minutes, I rise and stand motionless, watching a heavy black cloud which was coming up on the western horizon while thunder rumbled violently in the same direction. How I should have been admired if I had dared to predict it! The lightning grew more frequent as the cloud ascended, leaving the celestial vault without a glimmer of light; that from the lightning was enough to make the terrible darkness brighter than day.

As all this was perfectly natural, I had no reason to be surprised at it; nevertheless a beginning of terror made me wish I were in my room, and I began to shudder when I heard and saw the thunder and lightning which were following one another with the greatest rapidity. The flashes, which were all about me, froze my blood. In the terror which overtook me I persuaded myself that if the flashes of lightning I saw did not strike me down it was because they could not enter the circle. For this reason I did not dare leave it and take to my heels. But for my false belief, which was only the product of fear,

I should not have remained in the circle for as long as a minute, and my flight would have convinced Capitani and Francia that, far from being a magician, I was an utter coward. The force of the wind, its frightful howling, my fear, and the cold combined to set me shaking like a leaf. My philosophical system, which I thought was proof against any assault, was gone. I recognized an avenging God who had lain in wait for me there to punish me for all my misdeeds and thus end my unbelief by death. What convinced me that my repentance was of no avail was that I absolutely could not move.

But now down comes the rain, I hear no more thunder, I see no more lightning, I feel my old courage reborn. But what a rain! It was a torrent falling from the sky through the air, which would have flooded everything if it had lasted for more than a quarter of an hour. When the rain ended both the wind and the darkness were gone. High in the absolutely cloudless sky I saw the moon, more beautiful than ever. I gathered up my circle, and after ordering Capitani and Francia to go to bed without speaking to me, I went to my room, where one glance showed me Genoveffa looking so beautiful that she frightened me. I let her dry me off without looking at her, and then in piteous tones told her to get into her bed. She said in the morning that, seeing me shivering despite the heat of the season, she had felt afraid for me.

After sleeping for eight hours I was sick of the comedy. When Genoveffa appeared I was astonished that she seemed a different person. She no longer seemed to be of a different sex from mine, since I no longer felt that mine was different from hers. At the moment an idea whose superstitiousness took nothing from its power made me believe that the girl's innocence was protected and that I should be struck dead if I dared to assail it. In the resolve which I made I had no other thought than that her father Francia would be less gulled and she less unhappy, unless, that is, the same thing happened to her which had happened to poor Lucia at Pasiano.

As soon as Genoveffa became an object of sacred terror in my eyes I determined to leave immediately. What made my resolve irrevocable was a panic yet very reasonable terror. Some peasants might have seen me in the circle and, convinced that the storm had been the effect of my magical operation, might go and accuse me to the Inquisition,[3] which would lose no time in seizing my person. Shaken by the possibility, which would have destroyed me, I sent for Francia and Capitani and told them in Genoveffa's presence that I had to put off the operation because of an agreement I had made with the seven gnomes who guarded the treasure, of which they had given me as full an account as I could wish. I left it with Francia in writing, drawn up in the following terms, and the same as the one I had given Capitani in Mantua:

"The treasure which lies here at seventeen and one half fathoms underground has been there for six centuries. It consists of diamonds, rubies, and emeralds, and a hundred thousand pounds of powdered gold. All this is contained in one chest, which is the same one which Godfrey of Bouillon took from Matilda Countess of Tuscany in the year 1081, when he went to help the Emperor Henry IV win his battle against that princess.[4] He buried the chest where it now is before he went to besiege Rome. Gregory VII,[5] who was a great magician, having learned where the chest was buried, determined to go and recover it in person; but he died before he could carry out his plan. In the year 1116, immediately upon the death of the Countess Matilda, the gnome who is the Genius presiding over hidden treasures gave it seven guardians."

After giving him this document I made him swear to wait for me, or to believe no one who did not give him an account of the treasure exactly like the one I was leaving him. I had the crown and the circle burned, ordering him to keep the other things until I should return, and I sent Capitani to Cesena at once to wait at the Albergo della Posta for the man whom Francia would send him with all our baggage.

Seeing that Genoveffa was inconsolable, I took her aside and assured her that she would see me soon. Some scruples of conscience made me feel obliged to tell her that, since her innocence was no longer necessary to the raising of the treasure, she was under no further obligation and was free to marry if the opportunity arose.

I went on foot to Cesena and to the inn, where I found Capitani ready to return to Mantua after having visited the fair at Lugo.[6] He shed tears as he told me that his father would be in despair when he saw him come back without St. Peter's knife. I gave it to him, and offered him the sheath as well if he would buy it for the 500 Roman scudi stipulated in the bill of exchange he had given me; and considering it a very good bargain he agreed at once and I gave him back the bill. I made him sign an agreement by which he undertook to return my sheath to me whenever I sent him the same sum of 500 Roman scudi.[7]

I had no use for the sheath, and no need of money; but I thought that to let him have it for nothing would dishonor me and give him an idea that I set no value on it. Chance decreed that we should not see each other until long afterward and when I was not able to give him the 250 zecchini.[8] So, as it turned out, my escapade made me the richer by that amount, while at the same time it never entered Capitani's head to complain or to believe that I had gulled him; for, with the sheath in his possession, he believed that he was master of all the treasures which might be hidden in all the Papal States.

Capitani left the next day, and for my part I would have set off for Naples without losing any time, had not something immediately happened which caused me to put off following my plan.

The innkeeper handed me a printed bill announcing

four public performances of Metastasio's *Didone*[9] at the Teatro Spada.[10] Reading the names of the actresses and actors and seeing that none of them is known to me, I decide to wait and see the first performance and to leave at dawn the next morning by the post. A nagging fear of the Inquisition still urged me to be off, and I felt that I already had spies on my track.

I enter the theater before the opera begins and see the actresses dressing, and the leading lady strikes me as most attractive. She was from Bologna and went by the name of Narici.[11] After making her a bow I ask her if she is at liberty; she answers that her only engagement is to the managers, Rocco and Argenti. I ask her if she has a lover, she answers that she has not; for politeness' sake I offer myself; she laughs at me and invites me to subscribe two zecchini for four tickets to the four performances. I give her two zecchini, I take the four tickets, and I give them to the girl who was dressing her hair and who was prettier than she was. After that I leave; she calls me back, and I pay no attention. I go to the door; I take a parterre ticket, and go and sit down. After the first ballet, having found everything bad, I am thinking of leaving, when to my great astonishment I see in the principal box the Venetian Manzoni[12] with Giulietta, "La Cavamacchie," whom my reader may remember. Seeing that I am not noticed, I ask the man beside me the name of the beautiful lady who shone more than her diamonds. He answers that she is Signora Querini, a Venetian lady, whom General Count Bonifazio Spada,[13] the owner of the theater, whom I saw beside her, had brought from Bologna and from Faenza, her native city. Delighted to learn that Signor Querini had finally married her, I have no thought of approaching her. I should have had to address her as "Your Excellency," I did not wish to be known; then, too, I might be badly received. The reader may remember our falling out when she made me dress her as an abate.

But at the very moment when I am leaving she sees me and beckons to me with her fan. I go to her and say in a whisper that, as I do not wish to be known, I am using the name of Farussi.[14] Signor Manzoni likewise whispers to me that I am speaking to Signora Querini. I tell him that I knew it from a letter I had received from Venice.

Giulietta, who is waiting for me, instantly creates me a baron and presents me to Count Spada. The nobleman invites me into his box, and after inquiring whence I had come and where I was going asks me to supper.

Ten years earlier[15] he had been Giulietta's lover in Vienna, at the time when the Empress Maria Theresa, seeing the bad influence exercised by her charms, had turned her out. She had later renewed her acquaintance with him in Venice, where she had induced him to take her to visit Bologna; Signor Manzoni, her erstwhile fancy man, who told me all this, was traveling with her so that he could certify her good conduct to Signor Querini. At Venice she tried to make everyone believe that he had married her secretly; but fifty leagues from home she did not feel constrained to secrecy. The General had already announced her as Signora Querini Papozze[16] to the entire nobility of Cesena. In any case, Signor Querini would have been wrong to be jealous of the General, for it was an old acquaintance. Women maintain that any current lover who says he is jealous of an old acquaintance must be an utter fool. Giulietta had quickly called me over, fearing that I would be indiscreet; but seeing that I must be equally afraid that she would be so, she felt reassured. I at once began to treat her with all the respect which was due to her rank.

I found a large company at the General's, and some quite pretty women. I look in vain for Giulietta; Signor Manzoni tells me she is at the faro table, where she is losing her money. I go there and see her sitting at the left of the banker, who, seeing me, turns pale. It was the self-styled Count Celi.[17] He immediately offers me

cards,[18] which I politely refuse, at the same time accepting Giulietta's offer to go halves with her. She had fifty
zecchini in front of her. I give her another fifty and take
a place beside her. At the end of the deal she asks me if
I know the banker, and I see that he has heard her; I
answer no, and the lady who was seated on my left tells
me that he is Count Alfani. A half hour later Signora
Querini, who was losing, had a *sept et le va*[19] for ten
zecchini; it was crucial. I rise and fix my eyes on the
banker's hands; but it makes no difference: he cheats,
and the Signora loses her card. Just then the General
comes to take her to supper, and she stops, leaving the
rest of her money on the table. At dessert she returns to
the game and loses it all.

The amusing stories with which I enlivened supper
gained me everyone's friendship, but especially that of
the General, who, having heard me say that I was only
going to Naples to satisfy an amorous fancy, begged me
to spend a month with him instead; but in vain for, my
heart being empty, I could not wait to be with Teresa
and Donna Lucrezia, whose charming faces I could only
remember dimly after five years. However, I consented
to remain in Cesena to pay my respects to him for the
four days he had decided to stay there.

The next morning while my hair was being dressed, I
see the swindler Alfani. I receive him with a smile, saying that I expected him. He does not answer, for the hair-
dresser is there; but no sooner is he gone than he asks
me what reason I could have to expect him.

"My reasons were probabilities which you shall hear
at length after giving me back a hundred zecchini this
instant."

"Here are fifty. You cannot ask more."

"I accept them on account; but warning you out of
the kindness of my heart not to come to the General's this
evening, for you will not be admitted, and the company
will have me to thank for it."

"I hope that before you do anything so malicious you will think it over."

"I have already thought it over. Now go, and quickly."

What may also have made him leave was a visit from the first castrato of the opera, who came to ask me to dine at La Narici's. The invitation having set me laughing, I accepted it. His name was Niccolò Peretti,[20] he claimed to be descended from a natural son of Sixtus V. We shall speak of this mountebank, whom I met again in London fifteen years later, when we come to that time.

Arriving at La Narici's for dinner, I see Count Alfani, who certainly did not expect to see me there. He at once asked me to let him speak with me in private.

"If I give you another fifty zecchini," he said, "as a man of honor you cannot take them except to give them to Signora Querini, and you cannot give them to her without telling her that you made me give them back to you. You see what the consequences will be."

"I will give them back to her when you are no longer here; in the meanwhile I will be discreet; but take care that you do not improve upon fortune in my presence, for I will do you a bad turn."

"Double my bank, and you shall have a half share."

His proposal made me laugh. He gave me the fifty zecchini, and I promised to say nothing. The company at La Narici's was largely made up of young men, who after dinner lost all their money. I did not play. She had invited me only because she thought I was of the same stamp as the others. Remaining a spectator, I saw how wise Mohammed was in forbidding games of chance in his Koran.

After the opera he made the bank, and I played and lost two hundred zecchini; but I had nothing to complain of except fortune. Signora Querini won. The next day before supper I almost broke his bank; and after supper I went to bed.

The next morning, which was my last day, I learned at the General's that his Adjutant had thrown the cards in his face and was to meet him at midday somewhere to receive or give him a sword thrust. I went to his room to offer him my company, assuring him at the same time that no blood would be shed. He thanked me; and when I came to dinner he told me with a laugh that I had prophesied rightly. Count Alfani had left for Rome. I promised the distinguished company that I would make a bank for them myself. But this is what Signora Querini answered me when, taking her aside, I tried to give her the fifty zecchini which in honor I owed her, after telling her how I had made the scoundrel return them to me.

"By means of this fairy tale," she said, "you wish to make me a present of fifty zecchini; but permit me to tell you that I do not need your money, and besides I am not such a fool as to let myself be cheated."

Philosophy forbids the wise man to repent of having performed a good action; but he is at liberty to regret it when a malevolent interpretation makes it appear a bad one.

After the opera, of which this was the last performance, I dealt at the General's, as I had promised to do, and I lost a little; but I was liked. That is sweeter than to win, when need does not drive the player to be on the watch for money.

Count Spada invited me to go to Brisighella[21] with him, but to no avail, for I could not wait to set off for Naples. I promised him I would pay him my respects again the next day at dinner.

The next morning at daybreak I am awakened by an extraordinary uproar in the public room and almost at the door of my bedroom. A minute later I hear the noise in the room next to mine. I get out of bed and quickly open my door to see what is going on. I see a troop of *sbirri*[22] at the open door of the room and in the room I see a decent-looking man sitting up in bed and shouting in Latin at the ruffians and at the innkeeper, who was there and who had dared to open his door for them. I ask the innkeeper what it was all about.

"This gentleman," he answers, "who apparently speaks only Latin, is in bed with a young woman, and the Bishop's constables have come to find out if she is his wife. It is perfectly simple: if she is, he has only to prove it to them by some certificate, and the thing will be over; but if she is not, he must put up with going to prison with the girl; but that won't happen to him, for I will undertake to patch the matter up for two or three zecchini. I will speak to their captain, and they will all go away. If you speak Latin, go in and make him see reason."

"Who forced the door of his room?"

"It was not forced; I opened it myself; it is my duty."

"It is the duty of a highway robber."

Surprised by such infamous proceedings, I cannot refrain from interfering. I enter, and I tell the man in the nightcap all the circumstances of the intrusion. He answers, with a laugh, that in the first place no one could know if whoever was in bed with him was a girl, for the person had been seen only in male attire, and that in the second place he considered that no one on earth had the right to force him to declare whether it was his wife or his mistress, always supposing that the person in bed with him was indeed a woman.

"Furthermore," he said, "I am determined not to spend a single paolo[23] to end the matter, and not to get out of bed until my door has been shut. As soon as I have dressed I will show you a pretty ending to this comedy. I will send all these robbers running with my saber."

I then see in the corner of the room a saber and a Hungarian coat which looked as if it belonged to a uniform. I ask him if he is an officer, and he answers that he had written his name and rank in the innkeeper's

register. Absolutely astounded at this extraordinary state
of affairs, I question the inkeeper,[24] who says that it is
true, but that the ecclesiastical tribunal nevertheless had
the right to inquire into any scandalous conduct.

"The insult you have just offered this officer," I tell
him, "will cost you dear."

In answer to my threat they all laughed in my face.
Much annoyed at being mocked by such riffraff, I ask
the officer if he dares entrust his passport to me; he says
that, since he has two, he can very well entrust me with
one of them and, so saying, he takes it from a portfolio
and hands it to me to read. It was from Cardinal Albani.[25] I see the officer's name and his rank as captain
in a Hungarian regiment of the Empress-Queen. He tells
me that he has come from Rome and is on his way to
Parma to deliver to Monsieur Dutillot,[26] Prime Minister
of the Infante the Duke of Parma, a package entrusted
to him by Cardinal Alessandro Albani.

Just then a man enters the room asking me to tell the
Signore in Latin that he wished to leave at once and had
not time to wait for him; so that he should either settle
matters with the constables immediately or pay him. He
was the *vetturino*.[27]

Seeing it was obviously a plot, I asked the officer to
leave the whole matter to me, assuring him that I would
bring him off with honor. He told me to do whatever I
pleased. I told the *vetturino* that he had only to bring
up the Signore's trunk and he would receive his money.
He brought up the trunk and received the eight zecchini
from my hands, giving a receipt to the officer, who spoke
only German, Hungarian, and Latin. The *vetturino* left
at once; and the *sbirri* likewise, in great alarm, except
for two, who remained in the public room.

I then advised the officer not to get out of bed until
I returned. I said that I was going to the Bishop to tell
him that he owed him the most complete satisfaction, and
he had no doubt of it when I told him that General Spada

was in Cesena; he answered that he knew him, and that if he had known he was there he would have blown out the innkeeper's brains for opening the door of his room to the *sbirri*. I quickly put on my redingote and not stopping to undo my curl-papers I went to the Bishop's palace and, raising a row, was conducted to the Bishop's room. A lackey told me he was still in bed; but not having time to wait I go in and I tell the prelate the whole story, exclaiming over the iniquity of such proceedings and railing at a police force which violated the law of nations.

He does not answer me. He calls, and orders me taken to the Chancellor's room.

I repeat the facts to the Chancellor, not measuring my words[28] and using a style calculated to irritate and not to gain favors. I threaten; I say that if I were the officer I would demand exemplary satisfaction. The priest smiles and, after asking me if I have a fever, tells me to go and talk with the captain of the *sbirri*.

Delighted that I had irritated him and so brought the matter to the point where only the authority of General Spada could, and must, end it to the honor of the insulted officer and the confusion of the Bishop, I go to the General's. I am told that he cannot be seen until eight o'clock, and I return to the inn.

The ardor with which I had embraced the affair appeared to spring from my innate sense of decency, which could not bear to see a foreigner treated in such a fashion; but what made me so hot in it was a far stronger motive. I imagined that the girl in bed beside him was very attractive; I could not wait to see her face. Shame had never permitted her to expose her head. She had heard me, and I was sure that I had made a good impression on her.

As the door of the room was still open, I enter and give the officer an account of all that I had done, assuring him that in the course of the same day he would be free to leave at the Bishop's expense, after receiving complete satisfaction at the behest of the General. I say that I cannot see him until eight o'clock. He expresses his gratitude; he tells me that he will not leave until the next day, and he pays me the eight zecchini I had given the *vetturino*. I ask him of what nationality his traveling companion was, and he answers that the person is French and understands no language but his own.

"Then you speak French?"

"Not a word."

"That's odd. Then you never talk to each other except by gestures?"

"Exactly."

"I am sorry for you. May I hope to breakfast with you?"

"Ask him if he wishes it."

So I address my request to him, and I see a tousled head appear from under the covers, revealing a smiling, fresh, attractive face which leaves me in no doubt of its sex, though the hair is cut like a man's.

Enchanted by the lovely apparition, I say that having taken up her cause without seeing her, the sight of her could only have increased my eagerness to be of use to her and my zeal. She refutes my reasoning as prettily as possible and with all the wit of her nation. I go out to order coffee and to give her time to sit up; for it had been settled that neither of them would get out of bed so long as the door of their room remained open.

The waiter having come, I go back, and I see the Frenchwoman in a blue redingote and with her hair awkwardly arranged like a man's. I am surprised by her beauty and sigh for the moment when I shall see her up. She drank coffee with us, never interrupting the officer, who was talking to me and to whom I did not listen in the ecstasy into which I was thrown by the face of this creature who did not look at me and whom the *pudor infans* ("silent shame")[29] of my dear Horace kept from uttering a single word.

At eight o'clock I go to the General's and I tell him the circumstances, exaggerating as much as possible. I say that if he does not deal with the situation, the officer considered that he must send an express to his patron the Cardinal. But my eloquence was not needed. Count Spada, after reading the officer's passport, said that, comedy though it was, he would treat it as a matter of the gravest importance. He ordered his Adjutant to go to the posthouse inn at once and invite the officer to dinner together with his companion, whose sex no one had been able to discover; and then to go and inform the Bishop officially that the officer would not leave until he had obtained whatever satisfaction he wished and whatever sum of money he considered proper as damages.

How I enjoyed witnessing this gratifying scene, of which, filled with justifiable vanity, I considered myself the author!

The Adjutant, preceded by me, waits on the Hungarian officer, gives him back his passport, and invites him to dinner with his companion; then tells him to put in writing the kind of satisfaction he wishes and what sum he asks in recompense for the time he has lost. I hurried to my room to provide him with ink and paper; and the brief document, in passable Latin for a Hungarian, was ready at once. The *sbirri* had vanished. The good Captain would ask for only thirty zecchini, despite all that I said to persuade him to ask for a hundred. On the score of satisfaction he was also too lenient. He insisted only upon seeing the innkeeper and all the *sbirri* asking his pardon together on their knees in the public room and in the presence of the General's Adjutant. Otherwise, if this was not done within two hours, he would send an express to Rome to Cardinal Alexander and would remain in Cesena until the answer came, with the Bishop paying his expenses at the rate of ten zecchini a day.

The Adjutant set off at once to take the document to the Bishop. A moment later in comes the innkeeper to tell the officer that he is free; but he left as fast as his legs could carry him when the officer told him he owed him a caning. After that I left them and went to my room to have my hair dressed and to change my clothes, as I was to dine with them at the General's. An hour later I saw them before me, well dressed in uniform. The lady's was simulated, and very elegant.

It was at this moment that I decided to leave for Parma with them. The girl's beauty reduced me to slavery on the spot. Her lover appeared to be sixty years of age; I thought their union very incongruous; and I imagined that I could settle everything amicably.

The Adjutant came back with a priest from the Bishop's palace, who told the officer that he would have all the satisfaction he desired in half an hour; but that he must be content with fifteen zecchini, since the journey to Parma took only two days. The officer answered that he would reduce none of his demands, and he was given the thirty zecchini, for which he refused to sign a receipt. So the matter was settled, and the welcome victory having been the fruit of my efforts, it gained me the unalloyed friendship of the couple. To see that the girl was not a man one had only to examine her figure. Any woman who thinks she is beautiful because, when she is dressed as a man, everyone takes her for a man, is not a beautiful woman.

When, toward the dinner hour, we entered the drawing room where the General was, he took pains to introduce the two officers to the ladies who were present and who laughed as soon as they saw the masquerader; but having already heard the whole story, they were surprised, for they had not expected to have the pleasure of dining with the heroes of the play. The women saw fit to treat the

young officer as if he were a man, and the men paid
him the homage they would have paid him if he had
declared that he was a girl. The only woman who sulked
was Signora Querini, for finding that she was receiving
less attention, she thought that she was outshone. She
addressed him only to show off her French, which she
spoke fairly well. The only person who never spoke was
the Hungarian officer, for no one cared to speak Latin,
and the General had almost nothing to say to him in
German.

An old abate who was at the table tried to justify the
Bishop by assuring the General that the constables and
the innkeeper had acted as they had done only by order
of the Holy Office of the Inquisition. That, he told us,
was why there were no bolts in rooms in inns, because
foreigners were not permitted to lock themselves in. Nor
were two persons of different sex permitted to sleep together unless they were husband and wife.

Twenty years later[30] in Spain I found that all rooms
in inns had a bolt on the outside, so that foreigners who
slept in them could be to all intents and purposes imprisoned.

CHAPTER II

*I buy a fine carriage and leave for Parma
with the old Captain and the young Frenchwoman. I see Genoveffa again and present her
with a fine pair of gold bracelets. My per-
plexities concerning my female traveling
companion. Monologue. Conversation with the
Captain. Private interview with the Frenchwoman.*

"IT IS strange," said Signora Querini to the masquerader, "that you can live together and never speak
to each other."

"Why strange, Signora? We understand each other
none the worse, for speech is not necessary in the business we do together."

This answer, which the General translated into good
Italian for the whole company at the table, provoked a
burst of laughter; but Signora Querini affected the
prude: she thought it too revealing.

"I do not know," she said to the pretended officer,
"of any business in which speech, or at least writing, is
not necessary."

"I beg your pardon, Signora. Is not gaming a business?"

"Then you do nothing but play cards?"

"Nothing else. We play faro, and I keep the bank."

This time the laughter lasted until everyone was out

of breath; and Signora Querini could not help laughing too.

"But does the bank," asked the General, "win a great deal?"

"Hardly. The stakes are so small that it's not worth counting up."

No one took the trouble to translate this answer for the worthy officer. Late in the afternoon the company broke up, and everyone wished the General, who was leaving, a good journey. He likewise wished me a good journey to Naples; but I told him that I wanted first to see the Infante, the Duke of Parma, and at the same time serve as interpreter to the two officers who could not understand each other: he answered that if he were in my place he would do the same. I promised Signora Querini that I would let her hear from me at Bologna, not intending to keep my promise.

The officer's mistress had begun to interest me when she was hidden under the bedclothes; she had attracted me when she put her head out, and far more when I saw her up; but she added the finishing touch at dinner, when she displayed a kind of wit which I greatly admired, which is seldom found in Italy and often found in France. As her conquest seemed to me no difficult matter I considered how to go about achieving it. Assuming, without the least conceit, that I was better suited to her than the officer, I did not imagine that I should find him making any difficulties. I thought him one of those natures who, considering love a trifle, yield easily to circumstances, adapt themselves, and accept whatever compromises chance may offer. Fortune could not possibly provide me with a better opportunity to push my attack than making me the couple's traveling companion. There was no likelihood that I would be refused; indeed, I thought my company would be very welcome to them.

As soon as we were back at the inn I asked the officer if he intended to go to Parma by post or by carriage. He answered that, having no carriage of his own,[1] he would prefer to go by post.

"I have a carriage," I said, "and a very comfortable one; and I offer you the two back seats in it, if my company is not distasteful to you."

"It falls out perfectly. Please propose your excursion to Henriette."[2]

"Will you, Madame Henriette, grant me the honor of conducting you to Parma?"

"I should be delighted, for we will talk; but your part will not be easy since you will often have to play a lone hand."

"I shall do so with the greatest pleasure, only regretting that our journey is a very short one. We will discuss it at supper. In the meanwhile permit me to go and finish some business."

The "business" was a carriage, which I owned only in imagination. It was to the Caffè della Nobiltà[3] that I immediately went to ask where there might be a good carriage for sale. I at once heard that there was an English carriage for sale at Count Dandini's[4] and that no one would buy it because the price was too high. He asked two hundred zecchini for it, and it was only a two-seater, with a folding seat. It was just what I wanted. I find someone to guide me to the coach house, the carriage is to my liking; the Count had gone out to supper, I promise to buy it the next day, and I return to the inn well satisfied. During supper I talked to the officer only to settle it that we would leave the next day after dinner and would each pay for two horses. The long dialogues were between Henriette and myself on any number of pleasant topics, in which I admired a wit in her which was entirely new to me, for I had never conversed with a Frenchwoman. Finding her always charming and unable to suppose her anything but an adventuress, I was surprised to find her entertaining sentiments which I thought could only be the fruit of a most refined education; but when the idea came to me I dismissed it. Every time I tried to make her talk about her lover the officer she evaded my question, but in the most gracious way possible. The only question I asked her to which she felt it necessary to give me an answer was that he was neither her husband nor her father. The good man had fallen asleep. When he woke I wished them good night, and I went off to bed very much in love and very much delighted with the promising adventure, which I imagined would be full of charm and whose demands upon me I was certain that I could meet, since I had plenty of money and was completely my own master. What crowned my happiness was that I was sure I should see the culmination of the intrigue within two or three days.

The next morning very early I went to Count Dandini's. Passing a jeweler's shop, I bought a pair of gold bracelets made with Spanish links[5] such as are worn in Venice, five ells long and unusually fine. I at once thought that I would make Genoveffa a present of them.

When Count Dandini saw me he recognized me. He had seen me at Padua, in the house of his father, who, when I was a student in the university there, held the chair of Roman Civil Law. I bought the carriage, which must have cost twice as much, on condition that he would at once send for a harness maker who would bring it to me at the inn door in perfect order an hour after noon.

From there I went to Francia's, where I delighted Genoveffa beyond measure by giving her the bracelets, of which no girl in Cesena had a pair as beautiful. By this present I paid ten times more than all the expenditure the good man had made during the ten or twelve days I had passed in his house. But a present of far greater value which I gave him was to make him swear to wait for me and never trust any other magicians to bring up the treasure, even if ten years should pass before he saw me again. I assured him that at the first operation undertaken by another philosopher,[6] the guardian gnomes

would make it go down twice as far, and that at thirty-
five fathoms even I should find it ten times as difficult
to bring it up. I said frankly that I could not tell him
exactly how soon he would see me again; but that he
must wait for me, for it was decreed that only I could
bring up his treasure. I accompanied his oath with mal-
edictions which, if he broke it, would bring certain ruin
to his whole family. Thus, far from having to reproach
myself with having deceived the good man, I became his
benefactor. He did not see me again, for he died; but I
am sure that his descendants are still waiting for me, for
the name of Farussi by which they knew me must have
remained immortal in their house.

Genoveffa saw me off to within thirty paces of the city
of Cesena, and in the course of hearty embraces with
which I took leave of her I saw that my fear of lightning
had only had a temporary effect on me; but I was too
glad not to have committed that particular piece of vil-
lainy to think of returning to it. The present I made her
in twenty words was of greater consequence than the
bracelets. I told her that if I put off coming back for
more than three months she could set about finding herself a husband without any fear that her marriage would
prevent acquiring the treasure, which I could not bring
up until the Great Science should allow me to. After
shedding a few tears she assured me that she would act in
accordance with what I had just told her.

So ended the business of the Cesena treasure, in which
instead of being a swindler I was a hero; but I dare not
boast of it when I consider that if I had not been master
of a purse full of gold I would have ruined poor Francia
with a light heart; and I believe that any young man
with a modicum of intelligence would have done the same
thing. As for Capitani, to whom I sold the sheath for
St. Peter's knife at rather too high a price, I have never
felt any remorse over it, and I should consider myself
the stupidest of men if I repented of it now; for Capitani

himself thought that he had gulled me when he accepted it as security for the two hundred and fifty zecchini he gave me; and the canonical commissary, his father, valued it to his dying day more than he would have valued a diamond worth a hundred thousand scudi. Dying in that conviction, the man died rich; and I shall die poor. I leave it to the reader to decide which of us was better off.

Back at the inn I arranged everything for the short journey, the thought of which was enough to make me happy. Each time Henriette said anything to me I thought her more charming, and her intelligence enslaved me more than her beauty. I had the impression that the officer was well pleased that I should fall in love with her; and I thought I saw very clearly that the girl asked nothing better than to change lovers. I could assume as much without conceit, for aside from the fact that on the physical side I had all that an acceptable lover could have in order to hope to please, I also appeared to be very rich, even though I had no servant. I told her that, to have the pleasure of not having one, I spent twice as much and that by serving myself I was always sure to be well served; in addition, I was sure I should not be robbed and should not have a spy at my heels. Henriette understood me perfectly; and in short my future happiness intoxicated me.

The worthy officer was determined to give me the money which his share of the posts to Parma would have cost him. We dined, had our trunks put on and securely tied, and then set off after a contest of politeness over the seat beside Henriette, which he wanted me to take. He did not see that the folding seat was the one which my budding love could not but prefer to his; but I had no doubt that Henriette saw it perfectly. Seated facing her, my eyes saw her without my having to turn my head to give them that pleasure, which is certainly the greatest a lover can have among those which he cannot be denied.

In a happiness which I felt to be so great I had to endure one trial. When Henriette said amusing things which made me laugh, seeing the Hungarian distressed because he could not laugh at them too I undertook to explain the joke to him in Latin; but it often turned out that I explained it so badly that it became flat. The officer did not laugh, and I was mortified, for Henriette must suppose that I did not speak Latin as well as she spoke French; and it was the truth. In all the languages in the world what one learns last is their wit; and it is very often idiom which makes the joke. I did not begin to laugh over reading Terence, Plautus, and Martial [7] until I was thirty.

Some repair being needed to my carriage, we stopped at Forlì.[8] After a very gay supper I insisted on going to sleep in another room. During the day's journey the girl had struck me as so unpredictable that I was afraid she would leave her lover's bed and get into mine. I did not know how the Hungarian, who seemed a man of strict honor, might have taken it. I wished to obtain possession of Henriette in peace and quiet, as the result of an amicable and honorable arrangement. The girl had nothing but the male attire she was wearing, not a scrap of woman's clothing, not even a shirt. When she changed hers, she put on a fresh one of her lover's. This was something as new to me as it was puzzling.

It was at Bologna, when we were in high spirits over our supper, that I asked her by what strange chance she had become the mistress of this worthy man, whom one would expect to hear was her father rather than her husband. She answered with a smile that I should get him to tell me the story himself, in all its circumstances and perfectly truthfully. I at once told him that I was curious to hear it, and that she was willing. After making certain that it would not distress her, and making her say again that he should tell me everything, he addressed me as follows:

"An officer who was a friend of mine in Vienna having to go to Rome on a mission, I obtained a six months' leave and went with him. I eagerly availed myself of the opportunity to see the great city, assuming that the Latin language must be at least as well known there as it is in Hungary. But I was very much mistaken, for even among churchmen no one speaks it more than badly. Those who know it only claim to be able to write it; but it is true that they write it purely.

"After a month Cardinal Alessandro Albani gave my friend dispatches for Naples; and we parted; but before he left he introduced me to the Cardinal, giving me such a good recommendation that His Eminence told me that within a few days he would give me a packet and a letter addressed to Monsieur Dutillot, Minister to the Infante, the new Duke of Parma, Piacenza, and Guastalla, paying me, of course, for the journey. As I wanted to see the port which the ancients called 'Centum cellae'[9] and which is now called 'Civitavecchia,' I decided to devote these days to it and went there with my guide, who spoke Latin.

"Visiting the port, I saw an old officer disembark from a tartan[10] with this girl, dressed as you see her. She made a great impression on me. But I should not have thought of her again if the same officer had not arrived with her and put up not only in the same inn where I was lodging but in a room so situated that from my windows I saw the whole inside of it. The same evening I saw the girl eat supper with him without ever seeing them exchange a single word. At the end of their supper I saw the girl get up and leave the table, while the officer never raised his eyes from a letter he was reading. A quarter of an hour later he closed his windows, and when I saw the room in darkness I supposed he had gone to bed. The next morning I saw him go out; and this girl here, left alone in the room with a book in her hand, interested me even more strongly. I went out, and coming back an hour later, I saw the officer speaking to her, while she only answered him by a word or two at intervals, in great dejection. At that I ordered my guide to go and tell the girl masquerading as an officer that if she could give me only an hour's meeting I would give her ten zecchini. Doing my errand at once, he came back and told me that she had answered in French that she was leaving for Rome after having eaten something, and that at Rome it would be easy for me to find out how I could arrange to talk with her. My guide assured me that he would learn where she would lodge from the *vetturino* who was driving her. She left after breakfasting with the same officer; and I left the next day.

"Two days after I returned to Rome I received from the Cardinal the packet, the letter for Monsieur Dutillot, and a passport with the money for my journey, which I was free to pursue at my leisure. So I took a carriage which was going back to Parma, for eight zecchini.

"I was really no longer thinking of the girl when, two days before my departure, my guide told me that he knew where she was lodging with the same officer. I told him to try to make her the same proposal, informing her that I was leaving on the next day but one and so the thing must be done quickly. He answered me the same day that, if she knew the hour of my departure and the gate by which I would leave, she would be on my road two hundred paces outside the city and that, if I were alone, she could get into my carriage, in which we could go somewhere and talk.

"Thinking this a very happy arrangement, I sent her word of the hour and the place, which would be outside the Porta del Popolo in the direction of the Ponte Molle.[11]

"She kept her promise in every detail. As soon as I saw her I stopped the carriage, and she seated herself beside me, saying that we should have plenty of time to talk since she had decided to come and dine with me.

You cannot imagine what efforts it took before I could understand her and how hard she tried to make herself comprehensible. It was by gestures. I agreed, and with great pleasure.

"So we dined together; and she refused me nothing I could ask of her; but she surprised me not a little when she would not take the ten zecchini I tried to give her, managing to make me understand that she would rather go with me to Parma, where she had something to do. Finding the adventure very much to my liking, I consented, only regretting that I could not warn her that, if she had been followed to force her to return to Rome, I was not in a position to protect her against such an attempt; I also regretted that, in our mutual ignorance of each other's language, I could not hope to entertain her with amusing talk nor entertain myself by learning of her adventures. Hence I can tell you nothing about her situation. All I know is that she wishes to be called Henriette, that she must be a Frenchwoman, that she is as gentle as a lamb, that she seems to have had a most excellent education, that she is in perfect health, and that she must be both intelligent and courageous, as appears from the examples of those qualities which she gave me in Rome and you at the General's table in Cesena. If she will tell you her story and allow you to translate it into Latin for me, say to her that she will give me the greatest pleasure, for I find that in these few days I have become sincerely her friend. To tell the truth, I shall be very much distressed when we have to part in Parma. Say to her that, instead of the ten zecchini I owe her, I will give her the thirty which, but for her, I should never have received from the Bishop of Cesena. Tell her that, if I were rich, I would give her a great deal more. Be so good as to make all this clear to her in her language."

After asking him if a faithful translation of all that he had just said to me would satisfy him and hearing him answer that he wished it to be perfectly faithful in every detail, I repeated to her word for word all that the officer had said to me.

Henriette, with a noble frankness in which there was, however, a trace of shame, substantiated everything. As for satisfying our curiosity by relating her vicissitudes to us, she asked me to tell him that he must excuse her.

"Tell him," she said, "that the same principle which forbids me to lie does not allow me to tell the truth."

As for the thirty zecchini which he had decided to give her when he left her, she asked me to tell him that she absolutely would not accept a single scudo and that he would distress her if he tried to insist.

"I want him," she said, "to let me go and lodge by myself wherever I see fit, and so far to forget me that he will not try to find out what has become of me in Parma and will pretend not to know me if he happens to meet me anywhere."

After speaking these terrible words to me in a tone as serious as it was gentle, and without any emotion, she embraced the old man in a way which expressed far more compassion than love. The officer, who did not know what words had led to the embrace, was greatly mortified when I translated them to him. He asked me to tell her that, to be willing to obey her order, he must be sure that in Parma she would have whatever she might need. Her only answer was to tell me to ask him not to feel any anxiety about her.

After this declaration we all became equally sad. We stayed there a good quarter of an hour, not only without speaking but without looking at one another. Getting up from the table to leave and wishing them good night, I saw that Henriette's face was fiery red.

As I went to bed I began talking to myself, as I always do when something by which I am greatly interested excites me. Silent thought is not enough for me. I must speak; and possibly at such moments I believe I am conversing with my demon. Henriette's unequivocal declarations confused me completely. "Who can this girl be," I asked the air, "who combines the finest feelings with an appearance of the greatest libertinism? In Parma she insists upon becoming her own mistress, and I have no reason to flatter myself that she will not impose the same law on me that she has decreed for the officer to whom she has already given herself. Farewell my hope! Who can she be? Either she is sure she will find her lover, or she has a husband in Parma, or respectable relatives, or, in a wild spirit of unbridled libertinism, she means to defy fortune to plunge her into the most terrible abyss if it will not raise her to the pinnacle of happiness by bringing her a lover who can lay a crown at her feet: that would be the project of a madwoman or a woman in despair. She has nothing, and as if she needed nothing she refuses to take anything from the officer from whom she could, without blushing, accept a small sum which in a manner of speaking he owes her. Since she does not blush for the favors she granted him without being in love with him, what shame can she feel at receiving thirty zecchini? Can she believe that it is less base to yield to the passing fancy of a man whom she does not know than to receive assistance of which she is absolutely in need to save her from destitution and the risk of finding herself in the street in Parma? Perhaps she thinks that her refusal will justify her misstep in the officer's eyes. She wants him to conclude that she took it only to escape from the man who had her in his power in Rome; and the officer could not think otherwise, for he could not suppose that he had made her fall irretrievably in love with him when he saw her at the window in Civitavecchia. So she might be right and believe that she has justified herself in his eyes; but not in mine. With her intelligence, she must have known that if she had not made me fall in love with her I would not have set off with her, and she could not have been unaware that she had only one means of deserving my forgiveness too. She might have virtues; but not the virtue which could have prevented me from claiming the usual reward which a woman owes to the desires of a lover. If she thought she could play the prude with me and make me her dupe, I ought to show her that she was mistaken.''

After this monologue I decided, before I fell asleep, that I would have it out with her no later than the following morning, before we left. ''I will ask her,'' I said to myself, ''to grant me the same favors that she has granted the officer; and if she refuses I will avenge myself by showing her the most humiliating contempt even before we reach Parma.'' I thought it obvious that she could not refuse me tokens of real or feigned affection except by flaunting a virtue which she did not possess, and if her virtue was feigned I ought not to fall victim to it. As for the officer, I was certain, after what he had said to me, that he could have no reason to take offense at my declaration. As a sensible man, he could only be neutral.

With my mind both filled with this reasoning and convinced by it, for I thought it was framed and dictated by the ripest wisdom, I fall asleep and, in a dream which fell nothing short of the charms of reality, Henriette appears before me all smiles and, to my great surprise, with her hair dressed as a woman's. She pleads her case, and proves me wrong, in the following terms: ''To demolish all the insulting sophisms you have heaped up, I have come to tell you that I love you and to prove it to you. I know no one in Parma, I am neither mad nor desperate, and I want to be only yours.'' After uttering these words she does not disappoint me; she yields to my amorous transports, which hers aroused.

In dreams of this sort the dreamer usually wakes an instant before the crisis. Nature, zealous for truth, will not let illusion go so far. A sleeping man is not wholly alive, and he must be alive at the moment when he can give life to a being like himself. But, oh miracle! I did not wake, and I spent the whole night with Henriette in my arms. But what a long dream! I could not know it was a dream until my waking at daybreak made it vanish. I lay there for a good quarter of an hour motionless and stupefied, going over the details of it in my astonished memory. I remembered that I had several times said in my sleep: "No, I am not dreaming"; and I should still have thought that I had not been dreaming if I had not found the door of my room bolted from inside. But for that, I should have believed that Henriette had left before I waked, after spending the night with me.

After this blissful dream I found that I was helplessly in love, and it could not be otherwise. Anyone who badly needs to eat and goes to bed without supper must, if he spends the night dreaming he is eating, wake in the morning ravenously hungry. I dressed quickly, determined to make certain of possessing Henriette before I got into the carriage, or to remain in Bologna, though letting her go on to Parma with the officer in my carriage. In order not to commit the slightest breach of good manners, I saw that before having it out with her I must talk frankly with the Hungarian Captain. I seem to hear even an intelligent reader laugh and exclaim: "Can anyone attach so much importance to such a trifle?" That reader, since he cannot be, and can never have been, in love, is right. For him it can be only a trifle.

After dressing I enter my traveling companions' room and after bidding them good morning and rejoicing with them over the good health which I saw depicted in their faces, I inform the officer that I have fallen in love with Henriette. I ask him if he would be offended if I tried to persuade her to become my mistress.

"If what obliges her," I said, "to ask you to leave her as soon as we reach Parma, and not even to inquire about her, is a lover she may have in that city, I flatter myself, if you will permit me to talk with her for half an hour alone, that I can persuade her to sacrifice her lover to me. If she refuses me I will remain here. You will go to Parma with her and leave my carriage at the posthouse, sending me a receipt here from the post master with which I can recover it at my convenience."

"After we have breakfasted," he replied, "I will go to see the Institute;[12] you will be left here alone with her; you shall speak to her. I hope that when I return in a couple of hours you will be able to tell me that you have persuaded her to do whatever you wish. If she persists in her resolve I can easily find a *vetturino* here; in that way you will keep your carriage with you. I should be infinitely happy to leave her in your custody."

Delighted to have accomplished half of the business and to find that I am not far from the end of the play, I ask Henriette if she is curious to see what is worth seeing in Bologna, and she answers that she would like to if she were dressed as a woman; but that she did not care to go about showing herself to the whole city in men's clothes. We breakfast, then the officer leaves. I tell Henriette that he is leaving me alone with her until his return because I had told him that I needed to speak with her in private.

"The order," I said, after sitting down facing her, "which you gave the Captain yesterday to forget you as soon as you have left him in Parma, to make no inquiries about you, and to pretend not to know you if he sees you anywhere—does it apply to me too?"

"It was not an order but an urgent request which I made of him, a favor which my circumstances forced me to ask of him and which, since he has no right to refuse it, I never supposed for a moment that he would make any difficulties about granting me. As for you, I would certainly not have failed to ask you to do me the same favor, if I could have supposed you were thinking of making indiscreet inquiries about me. You have shown me tokens of friendship and you can imagine that if, my circumstances being what they are, the protection which the Captain still wished to extend to me after my request to him would cause me distress because it might harm me, yours would harm me even more. If you were my friend, you should have understood all this.''

''Since I am your friend, you should likewise understand that I cannot possibly leave you alone, with no money and nothing you can sell, in the middle of the street in a city in which you cannot even converse. Do you suppose that a man whose friendship you have won can abandon you after he has become aware of your situation and has heard of it from your own lips? If you believe that, you have no notion of friendship; and if the man grants you the favor you ask of him, he is not your friend.''

''I am sure that the Captain is my friend, and you heard what he said. He will forget me.''

''I know neither of what nature the Captain's friendship for you may be, nor how much he can rely on his own will; but I know that if he can so easily grant you the favor you asked of him the friendship he feels for you is of an entirely different nature from mine. I am prepared to tell you that not only is it not easy for me to do you the strange favor of abandoning you in the state in which I see you, but that it is impossible for me to do what you wish if I come to Parma; for not only do I feel friendship for you, I love you, and I love you in such a way that it is absolutely necessary either that complete possession of your person should make me happy or that I should remain here, letting you go to Parma with the officer; for if I come to Parma, I should become the most unhappy of men, whether I see you with a lover, or a husband, or in the bosom of a respectable family, or, finally, if I cannot discover what has become of you. 'Forget me' is quickly said. Know, Madame, that a Frenchman may be able to forget, but that an Italian, to judge by myself, has no such strange power.

In short, I tell you that you must speak out now. Shall I come to Parma? Shall I remain here? One or the other. Decide. If I stay here that is the end of it. I will leave tomorrow for Naples; and I am sure that I shall be cured of the passion you have aroused in me. But if you tell me to accompany you to Parma you must, Madame, assure me that you will make me happy in the posses- sion of your heart—no less. I wish to be your only lover, on condition, however, if you wish, that you will not make me worthy of your favors until I have been able to deserve them by my services and my attentions and by all that I will do for you with a submission of which you will never have seen the equal. Choose, before that worthy and only too fortunate man returns. I have al- ready told him all.''

''How did he answer you?''

''That he would be delighted to leave you in my care. What is the meaning of that sly laugh?''

''Let me laugh, I beg you, for I have never in my life conceived of a declaration of love being made in anger. Do you understand what it is to say to a woman in a declaration of love, which should be all tenderness: 'Madame, one or the other, choose this instant'?''

''I understand it very well. It is neither sweet nor touching as it ought to be in a novel; but this is history, and history which could not be more serious. I have never felt such an urgency. Do you realize the excruciating condition of a man in love at the moment when he must choose a course which can determine his very life? Con- sider that, despite all my passion, I treat you with perfect respect; that the course I will take if you persist in your resolve is not a threat but a heroic act which makes me worthy of all your esteem. The word 'choose' cannot sound harsh to you; on the contrary, it honors you, for it leaves you to decide your fate and mine. To be con- vinced that I love you must you see me come like an idiot weeping to you to have pity on me? No, Madame.

Sure that I have qualities to deserve your heart, I refuse to ask you for pity. Go where you will; but let me leave. If, prompted by a humane feeling, you want me to forget you, permit me, by going far from you, to make it less difficult for me to recover an unhappy mastery over myself. If I come to Parma I shall go mad. Consider now, I beg you, that you would be doing me an unforgivable wrong if you said to me at this moment: 'Come to Parma, even though I ask you not to try to see me.' Do you understand that in all decency you cannot say that to me?''

"I certainly understand it, if it is true that you love me.''

"Thank God! Be sure that I love you. So choose. Decide.''

"Still the same tone! Do you know that you appear to be in a rage?''

"Forgive me. I am not in a rage, but in a violent paroxysm, and at a decisive moment. I cannot but resent my too freakish destiny and the accursed *sbirri* of Cesena who waked me; were it not for them I should not have seen you.''

"Then you are sorry you met me?''

"Have I not reason to be?''

"None whatever, for I have not yet chosen.''

"I begin to breathe. I wager you tell me to come to Parma.''

"Yes—come to Parma.''

*I set out from Bologna a happy man. The
Captain leaves us at Reggio, where I spend
the night with Henriette. Our arrival in
Parma. Henriette resumes the dress of her
sex; our mutual happiness. I encounter some
of my relatives, but do not make myself
known.*

IT WAS then that the scene changed. I fell at her
feet, I clasped her knees, kissing them a hundred times;
no more anger, no more harsh tones, tender, submissive,
grateful, ardent, I swear that I will never even ask to
kiss her hands until I have deserved her heart. The
divine woman, who was amazed to see me pass from
despair to the utmost tenderness, tells me in a tone even
more tender than mine to rise. She said that she was sure
I loved her, and that she would do everything in her
power to keep me faithful. If she had said that she loved
me as much as I loved her, she would have said no more.
I had my lips pressed to her beautiful hands when the
Captain came in. He congratulated us. I told him happily
that I would go and order the horses, and left him with
her. We set off together, all three of us well satisfied.

Halfway through the post before reaching Reggio,[1]
he put it to me that we ought to let him go on to Parma
alone. He told us that if he arrived with us he would give

occasion for talk, that he would be questioned, and that there would also be much more gossip about us if we arrived with him. We thought his view most prudent. We immediately decided to spend the night at Reggio and to let him go on to Parma alone in a postchaise. We acted accordingly. After having his trunk untied and put on the small carriage he left us, promising that he would come and dine with us the next day.

This procedure on the worthy man's part could not be as pleasing to Henriette as it was to me, for a certain delicacy, partly founded on prejudice, was felt on either side. After the new arrangement, how could we have lodged at Reggio? In all decency Henriette would have had to sleep in a bed alone, yet she could not have kept herself, or kept us, from realizing how absurd such a reserve would be, and the absurdity was unfortunately of a kind which would have made us all blush. Love is a divine child, to whom shame is so abhorrent that if he gives way to it he feels disgraced, and feeling disgraced makes him lose at least three quarters of his dignity. Neither Henriette nor I could feel perfectly happy unless we dismissed the worthy Captain's memory.

I at once ordered supper for Henriette and myself, finding the intensity of my happiness too much for my faculties; nevertheless I seemed downcast, and since Henriette seemed as downcast as I, she could not reproach me for it. We ate very little supper and talked scarcely at all, for our remarks seemed dull to us both; we vainly changed from one subject to another to find something interesting. We knew that we were going to sleep together; but we would have thought it indiscreet to say so to each other. What a night! What a woman she was, this Henriette whom I loved so greatly, who made me so happy!

It was not until three or four days after our union that I asked her what she would have done, without a scudo and knowing no one in Parma, if when I declared my love I had not gone on to tell her that I had decided to leave for Naples. She answered that in all likelihood she would have been in the most disastrous situation; but that, having been certain that I loved her, she could not but be equally certain that, unable to abandon her, I would have spoken my mind. She added that, impatient to make sure of what I thought of her, she had made me translate her resolution to the officer, knowing that he was not in a position either to oppose it or to continue to keep her with him. She said that, not having included me in the favor of forgetting her which she asked of the officer, she considered it impossible that I should not ask her if I could be of use to her, merely out of a feeling of friendship, and that then she would have made up her mind in accordance with the feelings she found that I entertained. She ended by saying that if she had gone wrong, her husband and her father-in-law were the cause of it. She called them monsters.

Entering Parma, I kept the name of Farussi; it was my mother's family name. Henriette herself wrote the name she took: "Anne d'Arci, Frenchwoman." Just as we were telling the customs officers that we had nothing new, a smart-looking young Frenchman offers me his services and says that instead of stopping at the post-house inn I would do better to let him show me the way to D'Andremont's,[2] where I would find everything French —apartment, cooking, and wines. Seeing that Henriette was pleased with the proposal I accept, and we go on to Andremont's, where we find that we are very well lodged. After engaging by the day the lackey who had taken us there, and concluded a detailed arrangement for everything with the proprietor, I went with him to put my carriage in a coach house.

After telling Henriette that we would meet again at dinnertime, and the hired lackey to wait for me in the anteroom, I went out by myself. Certain that in a city

under a new government[3] spies must be everywhere, I
wanted to go out alone, despite the fact that the city,
my father's birthplace, was entirely unknown to me.

I did not feel that I was in Italy: everything seemed
ultramontane. I heard passers-by speaking together in
French or in Spanish, those who spoke neither talked in
low tones. Going here and there at random, on the watch
for a shop where linen was sold and not wanting to ask
where I could find it, I see one in which I notice the fat
proprietress sitting in a corner behind her counter.

"Madame, I want to buy all kinds of linen."

"Monsieur, I will send for someone who speaks
French."

"There is no need, for I am Italian."

"God be praised! Nothing is so unusual nowadays."

"Why unusual?"

"Don't you know that Don Filippo has arrived? And
that Madame de France,[4] his wife, is on the way?"

"I congratulate you. Money is bound to flow, and
everything will be in good supply."

"True enough, but everything is expensive, and we
can't get used to these new ways. It's a mixture of
French freedom and Spanish jealousy, which makes us
dizzy. What do you want in the way of linen?"

"I warn you to begin with that I don't haggle; so
beware. If you overcharge me I will not come to your
shop again. I need fine linen to make twenty-four chemises for a woman, dimity to make petticoats and corsets,
muslin, handkerchiefs, and other things which I hope
you have, for, being a foreigner, God knows into what
hands I may fall."

"You will be in good hands if you trust to me."

"I think I may believe you; so I beg you to help me.
I must also find seamstresses who will work in the lady's
room, for she needs to have everything necessary made
as quickly as possible."

"Dresses too?"

"Dresses, hats, mantles, in short everything, for as a woman you can imagine her stark naked."

"If she has money I promise you she shall lack nothing. I will see to it myself. Is she young?"

"She is four years younger than I am, and she is my wife."

"Ah! May God bless you! Have you children?"

"Not yet, my good woman."

"How fortunate I am! I will send out at once for the pearl of seamstresses. Meanwhile, you shall choose."

After having chosen the best she had among all the various things I asked her for, I paid the price and the seamstress arrived. I told the proprietress that I was staying at D'Andremont's, and that if she would send me a merchant with materials she would be doing me a favor.

"Are you dining at home?"

"Yes."

"That is all I need to know. Trust to me."

I told the seamstress, who was with her daughter, to follow me, carrying my linen. I stop only to buy both silk and cotton stockings, and as I enter my apartment I bring in the shoemaker, who was at the door. That was the moment of true pleasure! Henriette, to whom I had said nothing beforehand, watches everything being laid out on the table with a look of the most complete contentment, but with no other show of her satisfaction except in the praise she bestowed on the fine quality of the articles I had chosen. No heightened gaiety because of it, no base thanks or expressions of gratitude.

The hired valet had gone into my room in the apartment when I arrived with the seamstresses, and Henriette had quietly told him to go back to the anteroom in readiness to come when he was called. The linens are spread out, the seamstress begins cutting to make chemises, the shoemaker takes her measure, and I tell him to bring us up the slippers first, and he leaves. A quarter of an hour later he comes up with slippers for Henriette and for me, and the hired valet comes in with him unsummoned. The shoemaker, who spoke French, was telling Henriette comic stories. She interrupts him to ask the hired valet, who was standing there beside us, what he wanted.

"Nothing, Madame; I am here only to receive your orders."

"Didn't I tell you that when you were needed we would call you?"

"I want to know which of you is my master."

"Neither," I said, laughing; "here is your day's pay. Go."

Henriette went on laughing with the shoemaker, who, seeing that she spoke only French, proposes a language teacher. She asks him what his nationality is.

"Flemish. He is learned. His age is fifty. He is a wise man. He lodges at Bornisa's.[5] He charges three Parmesan lire[6] for a lesson if it lasts an hour and six for two hours; and he wants to be paid each time."

"Do you wish me to engage him?" she asked me.

"Please engage him; it will keep you occupied."

The shoemaker promised to send him to her the next morning at nine o'clock. While the elder seamstress was cutting, her daughter began to sew; but as only one could not do much sewing I told the woman that she would do us a favor if she would get another who could speak French. She promised to have her come the same day. At the same time she offered me her son as a hired valet, saying that he was already beginning to make himself understood in French and was neither a thief nor a gossip nor a spy. Henriette having told me that she thought I would do well to engage him, she immediately ordered her daughter to go and fetch him and also to fetch the seamstress who spoke French. So here was company to entertain my dear wife.

The woman's son was a lad of eighteen who had been

to school; he was modest, and he looked honest. When I
asked him his name I was much surprised to learn that
it was Caudagna.

The reader knows that my father was a native of
Parma, and he may remember that a sister of my father's
had married a Caudagna.[7] "It would be odd," I said
to myself, "if this seamstress were my aunt and if my
valet were my cousin. Not a word!" Henriette asked me
if I wanted the seamstress to dine with us; but I begged
her not to mortify me in future by deferring to me in
such trifling matters. She laughed and promised that she
would not. I then put fifty zecchini in a small purse and
gave it to her, saying that with it she could herself buy
all the little things which I might have failed to divine
that she needed. She accepted it, saying that the gift
gave her the greatest pleasure.

A moment before we sat down at the table we saw the
Hungarian Captain come in. Henriette ran and embraced
him, calling him "Papa"; she begged him to come to
dinner with us every day. The worthy man, seeing all
the women at work, was delighted to find that he had
placed his adventuress so well, and his joy knew no
bounds when I embraced him and told him I owed him
my happiness.

We dined most choicely. Andremont's cook was excellent. I discovered that Henriette was an epicure and the
Hungarian a glutton; I was something of both. So, trying
several of our host's wines, we ate a very enjoyable
dinner. My young hired valet pleased me by serving
his mother no less respectfully than he did the rest.
Giannina, his sister, was sewing with the Frenchwoman.
They had already dined.

At dessert I saw the proprietress of the linen shop
arrive with two other women, one of whom, who was a
milliner, spoke French. The other had samples for all
kinds of dresses. I let Henriette choose whatever she
wished in the way of caps, bonnets, and trimmings from

the first; but I insisted on taking a hand in the choice of dresses, though adapting my taste to that of my beloved. I made her choose materials for four dresses, and it was I who was grateful for her willingness to accept them. The more I bound her heart to me, the more I felt that I was increasing my happiness. Thus we spent the first day, in which it was impossible to do more than we did. In the evening at supper, as she seemed to me not to be as gay as usual, I asked her why.

"My dear, you are spending a great deal of money for me, and if you are spending it to make me love you more, you are throwing it away, for I love you no more than I did day before yesterday. All that you do can please me only as I know more and more surely that you are worthy to be loved; but I have no need to be convinced of that."

"So I believe, dear Henriette; and I congratulate myself if you feel that your fondness cannot grow stronger; but know that I do as I do simply in order to love you the more; I want to see you shine in the finery of your sex, only regretting that I cannot make you shine still more. And if that pleases you, must it not delight me?"

"Certainly it pleases me; and in a way, since you have called me your wife, you are justified; but if you are not very rich you cannot but feel how I must reproach myself."

"Ah, dear Henriette! let me, I beg you, think that I am rich, and be sure that you cannot possibly be the cause of my ruin: you were born but to make me happy. Think only of never leaving me, and tell me if I may hope it."

"I wish it, my dearest; but who can be certain of the future? Are you free? Are you dependent?"

"I am free in the fullest sense of the word; and I am dependent on no one."

"I congratulate you and it rejoices my soul; no one can take you from me. But alas! you know that I cannot say as much. I am certain that I am being sought; and I know that if they catch up with me they can easily find means to gain possession of me. If they tear me from your arms I shall be wretched.''

''And I will kill myself. You make me tremble. Have you reason to think this misfortune can befall you here?''

''I have reason to think it only if someone who knows me contrives to see me.''

''Is it likely that the 'someone' is in Parma?''

''I think it scarcely possible.''

''Then let us not frighten our love with fears, I beg you; and above all be gay, as you were at Cesena.''

''Yet at Cesena I was unhappy, and I am happy now; but do not fear that you will find me gloomy, for gaiety is natural to me.''

''I imagine that at Cesena you must have been constantly afraid that the French officer with whom you were living in Rome would catch up with you.''

''Not in the least. He was my father-in-law, who, I am sure, did not make the slightest effort to find out where I had gone once he no longer saw me at the inn. He can only have felt very glad to be rid of me. What made me unhappy was being a burden to a man whom I did not love and with whom I could not converse. Add that I could not have the solace of thinking I was giving happiness to the man I was with, for I had only inspired a passing desire in him, which he had considered worth ten zecchini, and, when I had satisfied it, I could not but believe that I had become a burden to him, for it was obvious that he was not rich. I was unhappy for another and most painful reason. I thought it my duty to bestow caresses on him and since he had in all decency to return them, I was afraid that he was sacrificing his health to consideration: the idea distressed me, for, as we did not love each other, we were both doing violence to ourselves out of mere politeness. We lavished on courtesy what is due only to love. Another thought troubled me even more. I could not bear it that anyone should believe the good man was keeping me for his profit. That is why you cannot have been aware that you attracted me as soon as I saw you.''

''What! Was it not rather because of your own self-respect?''

''No, truly; for you could have no opinion of me but the one I deserved. I made the misstep of which you know because my father-in-law was going to put me in a convent. But I beg you, do not be curious about my story.''

''I will not press you, my angel. Let us love each other now, and let no fear of the future trouble our peace.''

We went to bed in love, only to rise in the morning even more in love. I spent three months with her, always as much in love and constantly congratulating myself that I was so.

The next morning at nine o'clock I saw the language teacher. He was a respectable-looking man, well-mannered, modest, speaking little and well, guarded in his answers, and learned in an old-fashioned way. He began by setting me laughing when he said that the Copernican system[8] could be accepted by a Christian only as an ingenious hypothesis. I answered that it could not but be God's system since it was Nature's, and that Scripture was not the book from which Christians could learn physics. His laughter made me think him a Tartufe;[9] but if he could amuse Henriette and teach her Italian it was all I wanted. She told him at once that she would give him six lire every day, since she wanted a two-hour lesson. Six Parmesan lire are worth thirty French sous.[10] After her lesson she gave him two zecchini to buy her new novels which were already praised.

While she was taking her lesson I chatted with the dressmaker Caudagna to find out if we were relatives. I asked her what her husband's occupation was.

"My husband is major-domo to the Marchese Sissa."

"Is your father still living?"

"No, Signore. He is dead."

"What was his family name?"

"Scotti."

"And are your husband's father and mother alive?"

"His father is dead, and his mother is still living with Canon Casanova, his uncle."

That was all I needed to know. The woman was my first cousin once removed, and her children my third cousins. Since my cousin Giannina was not pretty I kept her mother chattering. I asked her if the Parmesans were pleased to have become the subjects of a Spaniard.

"Pleased? It has put us all in a perfect maze; everything is upside down, we don't know where we are. Happy days, when the house of Farnese[11] reigned, you are no more! Day before yesterday I went to the theater,[12] and Arlecchino[13] had everybody laughing fit to burst; but guess what—Don Filippo, who's our new Duke, tried so hard to keep from laughing that he made faces; and when he couldn't hold in any longer he put his hat in front of his face so no one could see him roaring. Somebody told me that laughing spoils the grave countenance of an Infante of Spain, and that if he let it be seen they'd write to his mother[14] in Madrid and she would think it dreadful and unworthy of a great prince. What do you think of that? Duke Antonio[15]—God rest his soul!—was a great prince too; but he laughed so heartily you could hear it in the street. We're brought to such confusion as nobody would believe. For the last three months there's not a soul in Parma who knows what time of day it is.[16]

"Since God made the world the sun has always set at half past twenty-three, and at twenty-four o'clock people have always said the Angelus; and all decent people knew that was the time to light their candles. The way things are now is unbelievable. The sun has gone mad—it sets every day at a different time. Our peasants no longer know at what hour to come to market. They call it a regulation—but do you know why? Because now everyone knows that dinner is at twelve o'clock. A fine regulation! In the days of the Farnese people ate when they were hungry, and that was much better.''

Henriette had no watch; I went out to buy her one. I brought her gloves, a fan, earrings, and various knick-knacks, all of which pleased her. Her teacher was still there; he praised her aptitude.

''I could,'' he said, ''have taught Madame heraldry, geography, chronology, the sphere; but she knows all that. Madame received a superior education.''

The man's name was Valentin de La Haye.[17] He told me that he was an engineer and a professor of mathematics. I shall have much to say of him in these memoirs, and my reader will learn his character better from his actions than from any portrait of him that I might draw.

We dined gaily with our Hungarian. I could not wait to see my dear Henriette in women's clothes. She was to be brought a simple dress the next day, and petticoats and a few chemises had already been made for her.

Henriette's intelligence was as sparkling as it was subtle. The milliner, who was from Lyons, enters our room the next morning saying:

''Madame et Monsieur, I am your servant.''

''Why,'' Henriette asks her, ''don't you say 'Monsieur et Madame'?''

''I have always,'' the woman answered, ''seen the first honors paid to the ladies.''

''But by whom do we hope such honors will be paid us?''

''By men.''

''And don't you see that women become absurd if they do not pay men the same honors as men's politeness renders them?''

They who believe that a woman is incapable of making a man equally happy all the twenty-four hours of a day have never known an Henriette. The joy which flooded my soul was far greater when I conversed with her during the day than when I held her in my arms during the night. Having read a great deal and having natural taste, Henriette judged rightly of everything and, though not learned, she reasoned like a geometrician. Since she did not pretend to intellect, she never said anything important except with a laugh which, by giving it the color of frivolity, put it within the capacity of the entire company. In this way she bestowed intelligence on those who did not have it themselves, and who adored her for it. After all, a beautiful woman without a mind of her own leaves her lover with no resource after he has physically enjoyed her charms. An ugly woman of brilliant intelligence makes a man fall so much in love that she leaves him feeling no lack. So what must I have been with Henriette, who was beautiful, intelligent, and cultivated? It is impossible to conceive the extent of my happiness.

Ask a beautiful woman who is not very intelligent if she would give some small part of her beauty for a little more intelligence. If she is frank she will say that she is satisfied with what she has. Why is she satisfied? Because, having only a little, she can have no notion of the intelligence she lacks. Ask an ugly but intelligent woman if she would change places with the other. She will answer no. Why? Because, having a great deal of intelligence, she knows that it serves her for everything.

The intelligent woman who cannot make a lover happy is the bluestocking. In a woman learning is out of place; it compromises the essential qualities of her sex; then, too, it never goes beyond the limits of what is already known. No scientific discoveries have been made by women. To go *plus ultra* ("farther") requires a vigor which the female sex cannot have. But in simple reasoning and in delicacy of feeling we must yield to women. Hurl a sophism at an intelligent woman: she cannot un-

Magicians during a Conjuration

Two Freemasons

ravel it; but she is not the dupe of it; she tells you she is not taken in by it, and she rejects it. The man who finds it insoluble accepts it at face value, as does the bluestocking. What an intolerable burden for a man is a woman with the mind of Madame Dacier[18] for example! God preserve you from it, my dear reader!

When the seamstress arrived with the dress Henriette said that I must not be present at her metamorphosis. She told me to go out for a walk until I could come back to the house and find her no longer in disguise.

It is a great pleasure to do whatever the object of one's love commands. I went to the French bookseller's shop, where I found an intelligent hunchback. Nothing, by the way, is more uncommon than a stupid hunchback. Since all intelligent men are not hunchbacks, and all hunchbacks are intelligent, I long ago concluded that it is not intelligence which produces rickets but rickets which produces intelligence. The hunchback, with whom I at once struck up an acquaintance, was named Dubois-Chatellerault.[19] He was an engraver by profession, and director of the Duke-Infante's mint, for it was planned at the time to strike coins; but it was never done.

After spending an hour with this intelligent man, who showed me several of his engravings, I went back to my lodging, where I found the Hungarian Captain waiting for the door of Henriette's room to be opened. He did not know that she was to receive us undisguised. The door opened at last, and there she was. She receives us with perfect composure, dropping us a graceful curtsy in which there was no trace of either the overbearingness or the freedom of the soldier. It was we whom surprise and her new appearance had put out of countenance. She makes us sit down on either side of her; she looks at the Captain in a friendly way; her manner to me expresses tenderness and love, but with none of the show of familiarity which a young officer can make without dishonoring love but which is unsuitable in a well-bred woman. Her new bearing forces me to conform to it with complete good grace, for Henriette was not playing a part. She was actually the character she was representing.

In an ecstasy of admiration I take her hand to kiss it; but she draws it away, and offers me her lips, saying:

"Am I not the same?"

"No. And so little the same that I can no longer say *tu* to you. You are no longer the officer who answered Signora Querini that you played faro 'keeping the bank and the stakes are so small that it's not worth counting up.'"

"It is certain that, dressed as I am, I should not have dared say such a thing. But I am none the less Henriette, who has made three missteps in her life, the last of which, but for you, would have ruined me. Delightful misstep, the cause of my knowing you!"

These sentiments affected me so profoundly that I was on the point of throwing myself at her feet to ask her to forgive me if I had not shown her more respect, if I had taken it all too lightly, if I had conquered her too cavalierly.

Henriette, charming as ever, put an end to this too emotional scene by shaking the Captain, who seemed turned to stone. His obvious air of mortification arose from the shame he felt at having treated such a woman as an adventuress, for he could not believe that she was not what she appeared to be. He looked at her in amazement, he made her bow after bow; he seemed to be assuring her of his respect and his repentance; he was confounded. For her part, she seemed to be telling him, without a trace of reproach: "I am very glad that you know me now."

She began that same day to do the honors of the table like a woman who was accustomed to it. She treated the Captain as her friend and me as her favorite. At one moment she seemed my mistress, at another my wife.

The Captain asked me to tell her that if he had seen her disembark from the tartan dressed as she now was he would not have dared to send his guide to her.

"Oh, I am sure of that," she answered him; "but it is strange that a uniform is less worthy of respect than a simple dress."

I begged her not to think ill of her uniform, for I owed it my happiness.

"As I owe mine," she answered, "to the *sbirri* of Cesena."

It is a fact that I spent that whole day in Arcadian courtship; and that when we went to bed together it seemed as if it were for the first time.

CHAPTER IV

I take a box at the opera despite Henriette's
reluctance. Monsieur Dubois comes to call, he
dines with us; trick which my mistress plays
on him. Henriette reasons on happiness. We
call on Dubois; extraordinary talent which
my wife displays there. Monsieur Dutillot.
The court gives a magnificent entertainment
in the palace gardens; our disastrous en-
counter there. I have an interview with Mon-
sieur d'Antoine, the Infante's favorite.

MADAME DE FRANCE, the Infante's wife, having arrived, I told Henriette that I would engage a box for every day. She had said several times that her ruling passion was music. As she had never seen an Italian opera I was surprised to hear her answer me coldly:

"You mean you want us to go to the opera every day?"

"I even think we should get ourselves talked about if we did not go; but if you will not enjoy going, my dear, you know that you are under no obligation to put yourself out. I prefer our conversations in this room to all the music in the universe."

"I am mad about music, my dear; but I cannot help trembling at the very thought of going out."

"If you tremble, I shudder; but we must go to the opera, or leave for London or somewhere else. You have only to command."

"Take a box that is not too conspicuous."

I took a box in the second tier; but as the theater was small a pretty woman could not fail to be noticed in it. I told her so, and she replied that she did not think she was in danger of being recognized, since none of the names in the list of foreigners then in Parma which I had given her to read was known to her.

So Henriette came to the opera; but in the second tier, without rouge and without a candle. It was an *opera buffa*,[1] the music to which, by Buranello,[2] was as excellent as the actors. She used her opera glass only for them, never turning it either on the boxes or the parterre. No one seemed to be curious about us; so we went home well satisfied, in the bosom of peace and love. As the finale of the second act had pleased her greatly, I promised it to her. It was to Monsieur Dubois that I went to obtain it; and thinking that she might play the harpsichord, I offered her one. She answered that she had never learned to play the instrument.

The fourth or fifth time we went to the opera Monsieur Dubois came to our box. Not offering him my seat, since I did not want to introduce him, I asked him what I could do for him. He then gave me the *spartito*[3] of the finale, for which I paid him what it had cost him. As we were opposite to the sovereigns I asked him if he had engraved them, and when he replied that he had already made two medallions of them I asked him to bring them to me in gold. He promised that he would do so, and left. Henriette did not even look at him; and this was as it should be, since I had not introduced him to her; but the next day when we were still at table he was announced. Monsieur de La Haye, who was dining with us, immediately congratulated us on our having made the acquaintance of so celebrated an artist. It was he who took the liberty of introducing him to his beautiful pupil, who then treated him to the polite remarks which it is customary to make to all new acquaintances. After thanking him for the *spartito* she asked him to procure several other arias for her. He said that he had taken the liberty to call on me to bring me the medallions in which I had shown an interest; and so saying he took from his portfolio the two which he had made. On one of them was the Infante with the Infanta, on the other the Infante. As everything about the medallions was beautiful, we praised them.

"The workmanship is priceless," said Henriette, "but the gold can be reimbursed."

He answered modestly that they weighed sixteen zecchini, and she paid him for them, thanking him and asking him to come some other day at suppertime. Coffee was brought.

As Henriette was about to put sugar into Dubois's cup, she asked him if he liked it very sweet.

"Madame, your taste is mine."

"Then you must know that I like it without sugar; and I am very glad that my taste is the same as yours."

So saying, she puts no sugar in his cup and after putting some in De La Haye's cup and in mine she puts none at all in hers. I wanted to burst out laughing, for the minx, who usually liked it very sweet, drank it bitter that day to punish Dubois for the insipid compliment he had paid her by saying that his taste was the same as hers. However, the clever hunchback would not retract. Drinking it with every appearance of pleasure, he maintained that it should always be drunk bitter.

After they left, and after laughing for a long time with Henriette over the trick she had played, I told her that she would be the victim of it, for in future she would always have to take her coffee bitter whenever Dubois was present. She said she would pretend that her doctor had ordered her to drink it sweet.

At the end of a month Henriette was speaking Italian. It was the result of practicing with Giannina, who served her as chambermaid, more than of the lessons she received from De La Haye. Lessons serve only to teach the rules of languages; to speak them, practice is necessary. We had been to the opera a score of times without making any acquaintances. We were happy in the fullest sense of the word. I never went out except with her in a carriage, and neither of us would receive callers. I knew no one, and no one knew me. After the Hungarian left, the only person who came to dine with us, when we invited him, was Dubois, for De La Haye dined with us every day.

Dubois was very curious about us; but he was intelligent enough to conceal it. One day he talked to us of how brilliant Don Filippo's court had become since Madame's arrival and of the great number of foreigners of both sexes who had attended it that day.

"Most of the foreign ladies we have seen there," he said, addressing Henriette, "are unknown."

"Perhaps if they were known they would not have put in an appearance."

"Perhaps; but I can assure you, Madame, that even if their attire or their beauty made them conspicuous, the wish of the Sovereign is entirely in favor of freedom. I still hope, Madame, to have the honor of seeing you there."

"It is very unlikely, for you cannot imagine what a ridiculous figure I think a woman cuts who goes to court without being presented, especially if she is of a station which gives her the right."

The hunchback was at a loss for an answer, and Henriette nonchalantly changed the subject. After he left she laughed with me over his thinking that he had concealed his curiosity. I told her that in all conscience she should forgive any man whose curiosity she aroused, whereupon she came to me all smiles and caressed me. Living together in this fashion, and tasting the delights of true happiness, we scoffed at the philosophy which denies that happiness can be perfect, because, it maintains, it is not enduring.

"What do they mean," Henriette said one day, "by that word 'enduring'? If they mean 'perpetual,' 'immortal,' they are right. But since man is not so, happiness cannot be so; apart from that, all happiness is enduring, for to be so it needs only to exist. But if by perfect happiness they mean a series of varied and uninterrupted pleasures, they are wrong too; for by putting between our pleasures the calm which must follow each of them after we enjoy it, we gain the time to recognize the reality of our happiness. Man can be happy only when he recognizes that he is so, and he can recognize what he is only in a state of calm. Hence, without periods of calm, he would never be happy. Hence pleasure, to be such, has to end. So what do they mean by the word 'enduring'? Every day we reach the point when, desiring sleep, we set it above all other pleasures; and sleep is the true image of death. We can only be grateful to it after it has left us.

"Those who say that no one can be happy all his life talk to no purpose too. Philosophy teaches the means to compound such happiness, if he who wishes to achieve it remains free from disease. Lifelong happiness could be compared to a bouquet composed of various flowers which would make a combination so beautiful and so harmonious that one would take it for a single flower. Is it impossible that we should spend all our lives here as we have spent a month, always in good health and lacking nothing? To crown our happiness we could, when we are very old, die together, and then our happiness would have been perfectly enduring. Death would not interrupt it but would only end it. We could be unhappy only if we assumed that we should continue to exist after our existence ended, which I think implies a contradiction. Do you agree with me?''

It was thus that my divine Henriette gave me lessons in philosophy, reasoning better than Cicero in his *Tusculans*;[4] but she admitted that such enduring happiness could be realized only in the case of two people who, living together, were in love with each other, healthy, intelligent, sufficiently wealthy, with no duties except to themselves, and having the same tastes, more or less the same character, and the same temperament. Happy the lovers whose minds can take the place of their senses when their senses need rest! Sweet sleep follows, not to end until it has restored all their faculties to equal vigor. On waking, the first to revive are the senses, eager to set the mind to work again. Man and the universe share the same condition. We could say that there is no difference between them, for if we discount the universe there is no more man, and if we discount man there is no more universe, for who could have an idea of it? Thus if we take away space we cannot imagine the existence of matter, nor, taking away the latter, can we imagine the former.

I was very happy with Henriette, and she was no less happy with me: never a moment of ill-humor, never a yawn, never did a folded rose petal come to trouble our content.

The day after the closing of the opera,[5] Dubois, after dining with us, told us that he was having the two leading singers, male and female, to dinner the next day, and that we had only to wish it and we could hear the finest pieces they had sung at the theater in the vaulted drawing room of his country house, where music lost nothing. Henriette, first thanking him heartily, answered

that her health was so poor that she could make no en-
gagements from one day to the next; and she at once
turned the conversation to other subjects.

As soon as we were alone I asked her why she did not
wish to allow herself the diversion of going to Dubois's
house.

"I would go, my dear, and with great pleasure; but I
am afraid that I may find someone at his dinner who
would recognize me and so put an end to our happiness."

"If you have some new reason for being afraid, you
are right; but if it is only a groundless fear, my angel,
why do you take it upon yourself to give up a real pleasure? If you knew what joy I feel when I see you ravished
and as if in ecstasy when you hear some beautiful piece
of music!"

"Very well. I do not want you to think I have less
courage than you. We will go to Dubois's directly after
dinner. The singers will not sing before then. Besides,
it is likely that, since he will not be counting on us, he
will not have invited anyone who is curious to speak
with me. We will go without telling him and without his
expecting us. He said that he is at his country house,
and Caudagna knows where it is."

In accordance with her reasoning, to which she had
been inspired by prudence and love, which so seldom
agree, the next day at four in the afternoon we went
to his house. We were surprised to find him alone with a
pretty girl, whom he introduced to us, saying that she
was his niece, whom private reasons prevented him from
letting everyone see.

Professing to be delighted to see us, he said that as
he did not expect us he had changed his dinner to a
small supper party, which he hoped we would honor him
by attending, and that the *virtuosi*[6] would soon arrive.
So it was that we were obliged to stay for supper. I ask
him if he has invited many people, and he answers triumphantly that we shall be in company worthy of us,

and that he only regretted that he had not invited any ladies. Henriette made him a little curtsy and smiled. I saw her looking carefree and content; but she was forcing herself. Her noble soul refused to show uneasiness; but in any case I did not believe she had any real cause for fear. I would have believed it if she had told me her whole story; and I would certainly have taken her to England, and she would have been very glad to go.

A quarter of an hour later the two singers arrived: they were Laschi[7] and La Baglioni,[8] who in those days was very pretty. Then all the people whom Dubois had invited arrived. They were all Spaniards or Frenchmen, and all at least middle-aged. There was no question of introductions, in which I admired the hunchback's tact; but since all the guests were seasoned courtiers, the breach of etiquette did not prevent them from paying Henriette all the honors of the gathering, which she received with an ease unknown anywhere but in France, and indeed only in the most exalted circles, except for certain provinces where haughtiness is too often displayed.

The concert began with a magnificent symphony;[9] then the singers performed a duet, then a pupil of Vandini's[10] played a concerto for violoncello, which was much applauded. But now for what caused me the greatest surprise. Henriette rises and, praising the young man who had played the *a solo,* she takes his violoncello from him, telling him modestly and calmly that she would do it even better justice. She sits down in his place, takes the instrument between her knees, and asks the orchestra to begin the concerto over again. Most profound silence descends on the company, and deathly fear on me; but—thank God!—no one was looking at me. For her part, she did not dare. If she had raised her beautiful eyes to mine she would have lost courage. But seeing her merely strike the pose of being ready to play, I thought it was only a joke which would end with this really charming tableau; but when I saw her make the first stroke of the bow, I thought the excessive palpitation of my heart would strike me dead. Knowing me well, Henriette had no resource but never to look at me.

But what was not my state when I heard her play the *a solo,* and when after the first movement the applause almost deafened the orchestra? The transition from fear to a satisfaction as excessive as it was unexpected produced such a paroxysm in me as the most violent fever could not do at its height. The applause had not the slightest effect on Henriette, at least visibly. Without raising her eyes from the notes, which she knew only from having followed the entire concerto while the professor was playing, she did not rise until after she had played alone six times. She did not thank the company for having applauded her; but turning to the professor she told him, with an air of gracious and noble courtesy, that she had never played a better instrument. After thus complimenting him, she smilingly told the audience that they must forgive the vanity which had induced her to increase the length of the concert by half an hour.

This compliment having put the finishing touch to my astonishment, I vanished to go and weep in the garden, where no one could see me. Who can this Henriette be? What is this treasure whose master I have become? I thought it impossible that I should be the fortunate mortal who possessed her.

Lost in these reflections, which increased the pleasure of my tears, I should have stayed there for a long time if Dubois himself had not come to look for me and had not found me despite the darkness of the night. He summoned me to supper. I relieved his anxiety by telling him that a momentary dizziness had obliged me to come out to cure it by taking the air.

On the way I had time to dry my tears, but not to restore their normal color to the whites of my eyes.

However, no one noticed me. Only Henriette, seeing me reappear, told me by a sweet smile that she knew what I had gone to do in the garden. At table my place was opposite her.

The hunchbacked Dubois-Chatellerault, director of the Infante's mint, had assembled the most agreeable noblemen of the court at his house, and the supper which he gave them, of few but well-chosen dishes, was exquisite. Henriette being the only woman present, it was natural that all attention should be paid to her; but even if there had been others she was such as to eclipse them all. If she had astonished the entire company by her beauty and talent, she conquered them completely by her wit at table. Monsieur Dubois never said a word; considering himself the author of the play, he was proud of it and thought it his part to remain modestly silent. Henriette had the tact to be equally gracious to everyone and the intelligence never to say anything witty without including me. On my side, it was in vain that I pretended submission and the most profound respect for the goddess; she wanted everyone to understand that I was her oracle. The company might well think that she was my wife; but none of them could be sure of it from the manner in which I behaved toward her. The conversation having turned to the merits of the Spanish and French nations, Dubois was stupid enough to ask her which she preferred. The question could not have been more tactless, for half of the guests were Spanish and the other half French; for all that, she talked so well that the Spaniards wished they were French and the Frenchmen wished they were Spanish. Dubois, unquelled, asked her what she thought of the Italians, and at that I felt alarmed. A Monsieur de La Combe,[11] who was at my right, shook his head in disapproval of the question; but Henriette did not let it go unanswered.

"Concerning the Italians," she said uncertainly, "I can say nothing, for I know only one Italian, and a single example is not enough to put one nation above all others.''

I should have been the stupidest of men if I had shown the least sign that I had heard Henriette's magnificent answer, and even more stupid if I had not at once dismissed the odious subject by asking Monsieur de La Combe some banal question about the wine with which our glasses were filled.

The talk turned to music. A Spaniard asked Henriette if, besides the violoncello, she played any other instrument, and she answered that it was the only one for which she had ever felt any inclination.

''I learned in the convent,'' she said, ''in the hope of pleasing my mother, who plays it quite well; however, without a downright order from my father, supported by the Bishop, the Mother Abbess would never have allowed me to study.''

''And what reasons could the Abbess allege for refusing?''

''Pious bride of Our Lord that she was, she insisted that I could not hold the instrument except by assuming an indecent posture.''

At this dictum of the Abbess I saw the Spaniards bite their lips, but the Frenchmen roared with laughter. After a silence of a few minutes, Henriette having made a gesture which seemed to ask permission to rise, everyone rose, and a quarter of an hour later we left. Dubois attended her to the step of our carriage, thanking her endlessly.

I could not wait to clasp the idol of my soul in my arms. I did not give her time to answer all the questions I asked her.

''You were right,'' I said, ''not to want to go, for you were certain to make me enemies. At this moment I must be mortally hated; but you are my universe. Cruel Henriette! You very nearly killed me with your violoncello! As I could not believe that you would have kept it a secret, I thought you had gone mad, and as soon as I heard you I had to go out to dry the tears which you forced from my heart. Tell me now, I beg you, what other accomplishments you have which you are hiding from me and in which you excel, so that when they are manifested to me for the first time they will not make me die of terror or surprise.''

''No, my dear love, I have no others, I have emptied my sack, and now you know your Henriette completely. If you had not told me a month ago that you had no liking for music, I would have told you that I can play the instrument. If I had told you so, you could have got me one, and I do not wish to amuse myself with something which may bore you.''

No later than the next day I went and found her a violoncello; and she was very far from boring me with it. It is impossible for a man who has no marked passion for music not to become a passionate devotee of it when the person who performs it to perfection is the object of his love. The human voice of the violoncello, which is superior to that of any other instrument, went to my heart when Henriette played it, and she was convinced of it. She offered me the pleasure every day, and I suggested to her that she should give concerts; but she was prudent enough never to consent. Despite that, the course of destiny was not to be halted. *Fata viam inveniunt* (''Fate will find the way'').[12]

The day after his charming supper the ill-omened Dubois came to thank us, and at the same time to receive the praises which we bestowed on his concert, his supper, and the persons he had invited.

''I foresee, Madame, the difficulty I shall have in resisting the importunity with which I shall be asked for introductions to you.''

''You will not find it very difficult, Monsieur, since your answer can be put in a very few words. You know that I receive no one.''

He no longer dared speak of introductions. About this time I received a letter from the younger Capitani in which he told me that, being in possession of St. Peter's knife in its sheath, he had gone to Francia's with two learned men who were certain that they could bring up the treasure and had been surprised to find that he would not receive him. He asked me to write to him, and to go there myself, if I wanted to have my share. I did not answer him. I rejoiced that the good peasant, mindful of my instructions, was safe from the fools and the impostors who would have ruined him.

After Dubois's supper we spent three or four weeks lost in happiness. In the sweet union of our hearts and our souls not one empty moment ever came to show us that dreary specimen of misery known as a yawn. Our only outside diversion was a drive out of the city when the weather was fine. As we never left the carriage and never went anywhere, no one, either of the court or the city, had been able to make our acquaintance, despite the general curiosity about us and the desires which Henriette had inspired in all the men who had been present at Dubois's supper. She had become more courageous, and I more confident, after we found that no one had recognized her either at the theater or at the supper. She had no fear of finding the person who could reveal her identity except among the nobility.

One day when we were driving outside the Porta di Colorno,[13] we met the Infante and the Duchess on their way back to Parma. Fifty paces farther on we met a carriage in which we saw a nobleman with Dubois. Just as we would have drawn beyond them one of our horses fell. The nobleman who was with Dubois cried "Stop!" to send help to our coachman, who might need assistance. With dignified politeness he at once addressed the appropriate compliment under the circumstances to Henriette, and Dubois did not lose a moment in saying to her, "Madame, this is Monsieur Dutillot."[14] The usual bow was her answer. The horse got up, and in a minute we were on our way again. This perfectly simple meeting should have had no consequences; but it had one.

The next morning Dubois came to breakfast with us. He began by saying at once that Monsieur Dutillot, delighted with the fortunate chance which had given him the pleasure of making our acquaintance, had commissioned him to ask our permission to call on us.

"On Madame, or on me?" I answered instantly.

"On both."

"Very well," I replied; "but one at a time; for Madame, as you see, has her room, as I have mine. So far as I am concerned, it will be I who will hasten to wait on His Excellency if he has any order to give me or anything to communicate to me, and I beg you to tell him so. As for Madame, there she is, speak with her. I am only, my dear Monsieur Dubois, her most humble servant."

Thereupon Henriette calmly and with the utmost politeness told Monsieur Dubois to thank Monsieur Dutillot and at the same time to ask him if he knew her.

"I am certain, Madame, that he does not know you."

"You see? He does not know me, and he wants to call on me. You must admit that if I received him I should stamp myself an adventuress. Tell him that though no one knows me, I am not an adventuress; and that hence I cannot have the pleasure of receiving him."

Dubois, realizing the mistake he had made, said nothing more; and during the following days we did not ask him how the Minister had received our answer.

Another three or four weeks later, the court being at Colorno, a magnificent entertainment[15] was given—I forget on what occasion—during which everyone was allowed to walk about the gardens, which were to be illuminated all night. Dubois having frequently spoken of the entertainment, which was public, we were tempted to go to it, and Dubois himself accompanied us in our example, a woman of profound intelligence who one day asked me why the Italian alphabet contained *con rond*.[18] I laughed, and did not know how to answer.''

"I think they are abbreviations used in the old days.''

After making punch we amused ourselves eating oysters, exchanging them when we already had them in our mouths. She offered me hers on her tongue at the same time that I put mine between her lips; there is no more lascivious and voluptuous game between two lovers, it is even comic, but comedy does no harm, for laughter is only for the happy. What a sauce that is which dresses an oyster I suck in from the mouth of the woman I love! It is her saliva. The power of love cannot but increase when I crush it, when I swallow it.

She said that she was going to change her dress and come back with her hair ready for the night. Not knowing what to do I amused myself looking at what she had in her desk, which was open. I did not touch her letters but, opening a box and seeing some condoms,[19] I quickly wrote the following verses and substituted them for what I had stolen:

> *Enfants de l'amitié, ministres de la peur,*
> *Je suis l'amour, tremblez, respectez le voleur,*
> *Et toi, femme de Dieu, ne crains pas d'être mère*
> *Car si tu fais un fils, il se dira son père.*
> *S'il est dit cependant que tu veux te barrer*
> *Parle; je suis tout prêt, je me ferai châtrer.*

> ("Children of friendship, ministers of fear, I am
> Love, tremble, and respect the thief. And you,
> wife of God, do not fear to become a mother, for
> if you bear a son he will say he is its father. Yet if
> you are determined to bar your door, speak; I am
> ready, I will have myself gelded.")

M. M. reappeared in a new guise. She had on a dressing gown of India muslin embroidered with flowers in gold thread, and her nightcap was worthy of a queen.

I asked her if she had pretended not to know Monsieur d'Antoine.

"It was not a pretense. I know his name. It is a family well known in Provence; but I do not know him."

"Is it possible that he knows you?"

"He may possibly have seen me; but he has certainly never talked with me, for I should have recognized him."

"The meeting makes me uneasy, and it seems to me that you are not unconcerned over it. Let us leave Parma, if you will, and go to Genoa; and when my business is settled we will go to Venice."

"Yes, my dear, we shall be more at ease then. But I think we have no need to hurry."

The next day we saw the masquerades, and on the day after that we went back to Parma. Two or three days later my young valet Caudagna handed me a letter, saying that the messenger who had brought it was waiting outside for the answer.

"This letter," I say to Henriette, "makes me uneasy."

She takes it from me and, after reading it, hands it back, saying that she believes that Monsieur d'Antoine is a man of honor and that hence we have nothing to fear. Here is the letter:

"Either at your lodging, Monsieur, or at my house, or wherever you please, at whatever hour you appoint, I ask you to enable me to tell you something which should be of great interest to you. I have the honor to be your very humble and obedient etc. D'Antoine. To Monsieur de Farussi."

"I think," I said, "that I should hear what he has to say. But where?"

"Neither here nor at his house, but in the palace garden. Your answer should contain nothing but the hour at which you wish to meet him."

In accordance with her advice I wrote him that I would be in the first walk of the ducal garden at half past eleven, asking him to set another hour if the one I had named was inconvenient for him. After dressing and waiting until the time, I went to the place I had appointed for the meeting. We could not wait to know what it was all about.

At half past eleven I found Monsieur d'Antoine alone in the walk I had indicated.

"I have been compelled," he said, "to request the honor which you are doing me because I could find no safer means of conveying this letter to Madame d'Arci. I ask you to deliver it to her, and not to be offended if I give it to you sealed. If I am mistaken, it is a matter of no consequence, and my letter will not even deserve the trouble of an answer; but if I am not mistaken, only the lady herself should have the power to let you read it. That is why it is sealed. If you are truly the lady's friend, its contents cannot but be of no less interest to you than to her. May I be certain that you will deliver it to her?"

"Monsieur, I give you my word of honor that I will do so."

CHAPTER V

Henriètte receives Monsieur d'Antoine. I lose
that charming woman, whom I accompany as
far as Geneva. I cross the Saint Bernard Pass
and return to Parma. Letter from Henriette.
My despair. De La Haye pursues my acquaint-
ance. Unpleasant adventure with an actress;
its consequences. I become a bigot. Bavois. I
hoax a bragging officer.

AFTER HAVING repeated to Henriette, word for
word, what Monsieur d'Antoine had said to me, I handed
her the letter, which filled four pages. After she had
read it she said that the honor of two families did
not permit her to let me read it, and that she was now
obliged to receive Monsieur d'Antoine, who, as she had
just learned, was related to her.

"So now," I said, "the last act begins. Miserable
wretch that I am! What a final scene! Our happiness is
coming to its end. Why did we have to stay so long in
Parma? What blindness on my part! Under the present
circumstances there was not a place in all Italy more to
be feared than this, and I chose it above all the rest of
the earth, for, except in France, I believe, no one would
have been likely to recognize you anywhere. And I am
all the more a wretch because it is entirely my fault!—
for you had no other will than mine; and you never concealed your fears. Could I have made a more stupid

mistake than to permit Dubois to visit us? I should have
foreseen that the man would manage to satisfy his curiosity in the end, a curiosity which is too natural for me
to blame him for it and which in any case would not
have existed if I had not first aroused it and then increased it by letting him visit us freely. But what use
is it to think of all this now that it is too late? I foresee
the most painful outcome that I can imagine.''

"Alas, my dear! I beg you to foresee nothing. Let us
only prepare ourselves to be superior to whatever may
happen. I will not answer this letter. It is you who must
write him to come here tomorrow at three o'clock in his
carriage and to send in his name. You shall be with me
when I receive him; but a quarter of an hour later you
shall retire to your room on some excuse. Monsieur
d'Antoine knows my whole story and in what I have done
wrong, but he knows, too, in what I have done right,
which obliges him, as a man of honor, to protect me from
any affront, and he will do nothing except with my consent, and if he sees fit to depart from the conditions I
will lay down I will not go to France: we will go and
spend the rest of our days together wherever you choose.
Yes, my dear. But remember that inevitable circumstances may compel us to consider our separation our
best course, and that then we must adopt that course in
such a way that we may hope not to be unhappy. Trust
in me. Be sure that I shall find a way to assure myself of
all the happiness that can be supposed possible if I am
reduced to accepting the idea of living without you. You
must take the same precaution for your future, and I
am sure you will succeed; but meanwhile let us banish
sadness so far as we can. If we had left here three days
ago we might have made a mistake, for Monsieur d'Antoine might have decided to give my family a proof of
his zeal by making inquiries into my whereabouts which
would have exposed me to violent proceedings which

your love could not have tolerated; and then God knows
what would have happened."

I did all that she asked; but from that moment our
love began to grow sad, and sadness is a disease which
in the end kills love. We often spent an hour looking at
each other and not saying a word.

The next day when Monsieur d'Antoine arrived I followed her instructions to the letter. I spent six very boring hours alone, pretending that I was writing. Since
my door was open the same mirror by means of which
I saw them might also enable them to see me. They spent
the six hours writing, often interrupting what one or the
other of them was setting down by remarks which must
have been crucial. I could foresee nothing but the saddest of outcomes.

After Monsieur d'Antoine left, Henriette came to my
table, and she smiled when she saw that I was looking at
her eyes, which were swollen.

"Tell me," she asked, "shall we go away tomorrow?"

"Yes indeed. Where shall we go?"

"Wherever you please; but we must be back here in
two weeks."

"Here?"

"Alas, yes. I gave my word that I would be here when
the answer comes to the letter I wrote. I can assure you
that we need fear no violence. But, my dear, I can no
longer bear this city."

"Alas, I loathe it! Shall we go to Milan?"

"Excellent! To Milan, then."

"And since we have to return here, Caudagna and his
sister can come with us."

"Excellent."

"Leave it to me. They shall have a carriage to themselves, in which they will take your violoncello; but it
seems to me you must let Monsieur d'Antoine know
where you are going."

"On the contrary, it seems to me that I should tell him nothing about it. So much the worse for him if he can doubt that I will return. It is quite enough that I promised him I would be here."

The next morning I bought a trunk, into which she put whatever she thought she needed, and we set off, followed by our servants, after telling Andremont to lock up our apartment.

At Milan we spent two weeks, concerned with nothing but ourselves, never going out, and seen only by a tailor, who made me a coat, and a seamstress, who made her two winter dresses. I also gave her a lynx pelisse, of which she was very fond. An instance of Henriette's delicacy which greatly pleased me was that she never asked me the slightest question concerning the state of my purse. My own delicacy prompted me never to give her reason to believe that my purse was exhausted. When we returned to Parma I still had three or four hundred zecchini.

The day after our return Monsieur d'Antoine came to dine with us uninvited, and after coffee I retired as I had the first time. Their conference continued as long as the one in which Henriette had made her decision, and after the Chevalier's departure she came and told me that it was over, that her destiny decreed that we must part.

"When?" I asked her, clasping her in my arms and mingling my tears with hers.

"As soon as we reach Geneva, to which you will take me. You must set about tomorrow finding a respectable-looking woman with whom I will travel to France and the city to which I must go."

"Then we shall be together for a few days more? But I know no one except Dubois who can find you a woman of decent appearance, and I am troubled by the thought that the same woman may satisfy his curiosity concerning what you would not have him know."

"He will know nothing, for in France I will find another."

Dubois accepted the commission as a great honor, and three or four days later himself brought Henriette a middle-aged woman, passably well dressed, who considered herself fortunate to have found an opportunity to return to France. She was the widow of an officer who had recently died. Henriette told her to be in readiness to leave as soon as Monsieur Dubois sent her word. On the day before our departure Monsieur d'Antoine, after dining with us, gave Henriette a letter to read, addressed to Geneva, which he afterwards sealed and which she put in her pocket.

We set out from Parma at nightfall, and we stopped at Turin for only two hours to engage a manservant to wait on us as far as Geneva. The next day we ascended Mont Cenis[1] in sedan chairs, then descended to La Novalaise by sledge.[2] On the fifth day we reached Geneva and put up at the "Scales."[3] The next day Henriette gave me a letter addressed to the banker Tronchin,[4] who had no sooner read it than he told me he would come to the "Scales" in person to bring me a thousand louis.[5]

We were still at table when he appeared to discharge the obligation and at the same time to tell Henriette that he would give her two men for whom he would vouch. She told him that she would leave as soon as he should bring them to her and she should have the carriage she needed, as he must have learned from the letter I had delivered to him. After assuring her that she would have everything the next day, he left and we remained alone together, gloomy and pensive, as one is when the most profound sorrow weighs on the mind.

I broke the silence to say that the carriage which Tronchin would furnish her could not possibly be more comfortable than mine, and, that being so, she would be doing me a favor by keeping it for herself and letting me have the one the banker would give her; and she assented. At the same time she gave me five rolls of a hundred louis each, herself putting them in my pocket. A poor consolation for my heart, only too oppressed by so cruel a parting. During the last twenty-four hours the only eloquence we could muster was that which sighs, tears, and the tenderest embraces bestow on two happy lovers who have come to the end of their happiness and are forced by stern reason to accept the fact.

Henriette held out no illusory hopes to assuage my grief. She asked me not to make any inquiries about her and to pretend that I did not know her if, traveling in France, I should ever meet her anywhere. She gave me a letter to deliver to Monsieur d'Antoine in Parma, forgetting to ask me if I intended to return there; but I instantly resolved to do so. She asked me not to leave Geneva until after I had received a letter from her which she would write me from the first place at which she stopped to change horses. She left at daybreak, with her waiting-woman beside her and a footman on the coachman's seat and another ahead on horseback. I did not go back upstairs to our room until after I had followed the carriage with my eyes and long after I lost it from sight. After ordering the waiter not to enter my room until the horses with which Henriette was traveling should have returned, I went to bed, hoping that sleep would come to the aid of my grief-stricken soul, which my tears could not relieve.

The postilion returning from Châtillon[6] did not arrive until the following day. He gave me a letter from Henriette, in which I found only one word: "Farewell." He told me that no accident had befallen her and that she had continued her journey, taking the road to Lyons. Since I could not leave until the next morning, I spent one of the saddest days of my life alone in my room. On one of its two windows I saw written: "You will forget Henriette too." She had written the words with the point of a small diamond, set in a ring, which I had given her.

The prophecy was not of a nature to console me; but in how absolute a sense had she used the word "forget"? She could really mean no more than that the wound would heal, and since that was only natural she need not have gone to the trouble of making me a distressing prophecy. No. I have not forgotten her, and it is balm to my soul every time I remember her. When I consider that what makes me happy in my present old age is the presence of my memory, I conclude that my long life must have been more happy than unhappy, and after thanking God, cause of all causes and sovereign contriver—we know not how—of all combinations, I congratulate myself.

The next day I set out for Italy with a servant whom Monsieur Tronchin gave me. Despite the unfavorable season, I took the route through the Saint Bernard, which I crossed in three days on the seven mules required for ourselves, my trunk, and the carriage intended for my beloved. A man overwhelmed by a great sorrow has the advantage that nothing seems painful to him. It is a kind of despair which also has a certain sweetness. I felt neither hunger nor thirst nor the cold which froze all nature in that terrible part of the Alps. I reached Parma in reasonably good health, purposely going to lodge in a bad inn at the end of the bridge, where I was not at all pleased to find Monsieur de La Haye lodged in a small room next to the one which the innkeeper gave me. Surprised to see me there, he addressed me a long compliment intended to make me talk; but I answered only that I was tired and that we would see each other.

The next day I did not go out except to deliver Henriette's letter to Monsieur d'Antoine. Finding, when he unsealed it, that it contained a letter addressed to me, he gave it to me without reading it. But as it was not sealed he thought that Henriette must have intended that he should read it, and he asked me for permission to do so after I had read it to myself in a murmur. Handing it back to me, he said that he and all his credit were at my disposal on any occasion. Here is a copy of the letter Henriette wrote me:

"It is I, my only love, who had to forsake you. Do not add to your grief by thinking of mine. Let us imagine that we have had a pleasant dream, and let us not complain of our destiny, for never was an agreeable dream so long. Let us boast of having succeeded in being happy for three months on end; there are few mortals who can say as much. So let us never forget each other, and let us often recall our love to renew it in our souls, which, though parted, will enjoy it even more intensely. Do not inquire for me, and if chance brings you to know who I am, be as if you did not know it. Rest assured, my dear, that I have so ordered my affairs that for the rest of my life I shall be as happy as I can be without you. I do not know who you are; but I know that no one in the world knows you better than I do. I will have no more lovers in all my life to come; but I hope that you will not think of doing likewise. I wish you to love again, and even to find another Henriette. Farewell."

The reader will see where, and under what circumstances, I met Henriette again fifteen years later.[7]

As soon as I was alone in my room all I could do was go to bed after locking my door, without even bothering to order something to eat. Such is the effect of a great sorrow. It stupefies; it does not make its victim want to kill himself, for it stops thought; but it does not leave him the slightest ability to do anything toward living. I found myself in a like state six years later—but not on account of love—when I was put under the Leads,[8] and again twenty years later, in 1786 at Madrid, when I was imprisoned at Buen Retiro.[9]

At the end of twenty-four hours I found my state of inanition not unpleasant; even the thought that, by increasing, it might cost me my life did not strike me as consoling, but it did not frighten me. I was glad to see that no one came to my room to disturb me by asking if I did not want to eat something. I was glad that, immediately after I arrived, I had dismissed the servant who had attended me when I crossed the Alps. After twenty-four hours of fasting my prostration was marked.

In these straits it was De La Haye who came and knocked at my door. I would not have answered him had he not said as he knocked that someone had the most urgent reasons for talking with me. I get up and open my door for him, then go back to bed.

"A foreigner," he says, "who needs a carriage wishes to buy yours."

"I do not want to sell it."

"Then please excuse me; but you seem very ill."

"Yes; I need to be left in peace."

"From what illness are you suffering?"

He approaches, he has difficulty in finding my pulse, he is disturbed, he asks me what I had eaten the day before; and upon learning that nothing had entered my stomach for two days, he guesses the truth and becomes alarmed. He entreats me to take some broth, with such solicitude that he persuades me. Then, never mentioning Henriette, he preaches me a sermon on the life to come and on the vanity of this mortal life, though it is our duty to preserve it since we have not the right to deprive ourselves of it. I answer nothing; but determined not to leave me, he orders a light dinner three or four hours later and, when he saw me eat it, he was exultant and he entertained me all the rest of the day with the latest news.

The next day I asked him to keep me company at dinner; and considering that I owed him my life I gave him my friendship; but in a very short time my fondness for him became unbounded because of the event which I will now recount to my reader in detail.

Two or three days later Dubois, to whom De La Haye had told the whole story, came to see me, and I began going out. I went to the theater, where I made the acquaintance of some Corsican officers who had served in the Royal Italian Regiment in the service of France,[10] and of a young Sicilian named Paterno, who was the pattern of recklessness. Being in love with an actress who scorned him, the young man kept me entertained with his description of her adorable qualities and at the same time of her cruelty toward him, whom she received in her house but whom she repulsed whenever he tried to give her evidence of his love. She was ruining him by making him spend a great deal on dinners and suppers which were shared by her numerous family but for which she gave him no credit.

After attentively examining the woman on the stage and finding that she had some merit, I became curious about her, and Paterno was glad to take me to her house. Finding her decidedy approachable and knowing that she was poor, I had no doubt that I could obtain her favors at the cost of fifteen or twenty zecchini. I imparted my plan to Paterno, who laughed and said that she would no longer receive me if I dared make her such a proposal. He gave me the names of several officers whom she had declined to see again after they had made her proposals of the same sort; but he said he would be delighted if I made the attempt and afterwards would tell him frankly what had happened. I promised that I would tell him everything.

It was in her dressing room at the theater that, being alone with her and hearing her admire my watch, I offered it to her as the price of her favors. Handing it back to me, she replied in accordance with the catechism of her trade:

"A man of honor," she said, "can make such proposals only to whores."

I left her, saying that to whores I offered only a ducat.

When I told the story to Paterno I saw that he was triumphant; but his urgings were of no avail; I refused to attend any more of his suppers—utterly boring suppers at which, even as they were eating them, the actress's whole family laughed at the stupidity of the dupe who was paying for them.

A week or so later Paterno told me that the actress had related the incident to him exactly as I had reported it and had added that I no longer went to call on her for fear she would take me at my word if I made her the same proposal again. I asked the young scapegrace to tell her that I would call on her again, being certain not only that I would not make her the same proposal but also that I would not want her even if she were ready to give herself to me for nothing.

My young friend repeated my words so well that the actress, cut to the quick, charged him to tell me that she challenged me to visit her. Thoroughly determined to convince her that I despised her, I went to her dressing room again at the end of the second act of a play in which she had finished her role. After dismissing someone who was with her, she said she had something to say to me.

She locked her door; then, sitting on my knees, she asked me if it was true that I despised her so greatly. My answer was brief. I went to the point and, without a thought of bargaining, she surrendered at discretion. Yet duped, as I always am, by compassion, which is forever out of place when an intelligent man has to do with women of this sort, I gave her twenty zecchini, which she much preferred to my watch. Afterwards we laughed together at the stupidity of Paterno, who did not know how such challenges were bound to end.

I told him the next day that I had been bored and that I would not call on her again; and, as I was no longer curious about her, this was my intention; but the reason which compelled me to keep my promise to him was that three days later I found that the wretched woman had made me the same sort of present that I had been treated to by the prostitute at O'Neilan's. Far from feeling that I had cause to complain, I considered myself justly punished for having so basely abandoned myself after having belonged to an Henriette.

I thought it best to confide in Monsieur de La Haye, who dined with me every day, making no secret of his poverty. The worthy man, who deserved respect both for his age and his appearance, put me into the hands of a surgeon named Frémont,[11] who was also a dentist. Certain symptoms which he recognized decided him to put me through the great cure.[12] Because of the season the cure compelled me to spend six weeks in my room.

1749.[13]

But during those six weeks De La Haye's company infected me with a disease far worse than the pox,[14] and one to which I thought I was immune. De La Haye, who only left me for an hour in the morning to say his prayers in church, turned me into a bigot, and to such an extent that I agreed with him that I should consider myself fortunate to have caught a disease which had brought salvation to my soul. I sincerely thanked God for having made use of Mercury[15] to lead my mind, until then wrapped in darkness, to the light of truth. There is no doubt that this change in my method of reasoning proceeded from the mercury. That impure and always very dangerous metal so weakened my mind that I thought I had reasoned most erroneously until then. I came to the point of deciding to lead an entirely different life after I was cured. De La Haye often wept with me in his satisfaction at seeing me weep as a result of the genuine contrition which, with incredible skill, he had implanted in my poor, sick soul. He talked to me of Paradise and of the things of the next world as if he had been there in person, and I did not laugh at him. He had accustomed me to renounce my reason, where to renounce it one had to be a fool. No one knew, he said to me one

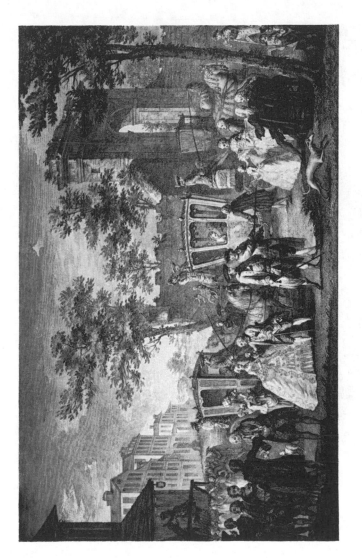

Traveling Carriages at a City Gate

Milliner in the Boudoir of a Young Frenchwoman

day, whether God created the world at the spring or at the autumn equinox.

"Granted creation," I answered, despite the mercury, "the question becomes puerile, for the season cannot be determined except in relation to some part of the earth."

De La Haye persuaded me that I must stop reasoning in this fashion, and I surrendered. He had been a Jesuit; but not only would he not admit it, he would not allow the subject to be raised with him. Here is the discourse with which he one day put the finishing touch to his seduction of me:

"After being educated at school, cultivating the sciences and the arts with some success, and spending twenty years at the University of Paris, I served in the army in the corps of engineers, and I published books, though without putting my name to them, which are still used in every school for the instruction of youth. Not being rich, I undertook the education of several youths who now shine in the world even more by their conduct than by their abilities. My last pupil was the Marchese Botta.[16] Being now without employment, I live, as you see, trusting in God. Four years ago I met the Baron de Bavois,[17] a young Swiss, a native of Lausanne, son of the general of the same name, who had a regiment in the service of the Duke of Modena,[18] and who later had the misfortune to give occasion to too much talk.[19] The young Baron, a Calvinist like his father, having no liking for the idle life he could have led at home, asked me to teach him what I had taught the Marchese Botta so that he could pursue a military career. Delighted that I could foster his honorable predilection, I left every other occupation to devote myself to him. In the conversations I had with the young man I discovered that he knew that in the matter of religion he lived in error. He remained in it only because of the consideration which he owed his family. After wringing his secret from him I easily brought him to see that it was

a matter of paramount concern, since his eternal salvation depended on it. Impressed by this truth, he abandoned himself to my affection. I took him to Rome and
presented him to Benedict XIV, who, after his abjura-
tion, procured him a post in the Duke of Modena's forces,
in which he is now serving with the rank of lieutenant.
But since my dear proselyte, who is now only twenty-five,
receives only seven zecchini a month, he has not enough
to live on. His change of religion results in his receiving
nothing from his parents, who are horrified by his
apostasy. He would have no choice but to go back to
Lausanne if I did not assist him. But alas! being myself
poor and without employment, I can only assist him by
the pittance I obtain for him from the purses of the
charitable souls whom I know. Having a grateful heart,
my pupil would like to know his benefactors; but they
do not wish to be known, and they are right, for charity
ceases to be a meritorious action if he who distributes it
cannot keep it free from all vanity. For my part—thank
God!—I have no cause for vanity. I am only too happy to
be able to serve as father to a young predestinate, and
to have had a share, as a weak instrument, in the salvation of his soul. This good, handsome youth trusts only
in me. He writes to me twice a week. Discretion forbids
me to give you his letters to read, but you would weep if
you read them. It was to him that I yesterday sent the
three louis which I had from you.''

At the end of this speech De La Haye rose and went to
the window to blow his nose and hurriedly dry his tears.
Feeling moved and admiring so much virtue in De La
Haye and in his pupil the Baron, who, to save his soul,
had reduced himself to living on charity, I wept too. In
my budding piety I told the apostle that not only did I
not want the Baron to know that it was I who was helping him but I did not even want to know how much I
was giving him, and that I therefore begged him to take

from my purse whatever he might need, without rendering any account to me. At that, De La Haye came to my bedside with open arms and said as he embraced me that by thus obeying the Gospels to the letter, I was following the one sure road to the Kingdom of Heaven.

The mind obeys the body. With my stomach empty, I became a fanatic; the mercury must have made a hollow in the region of my brain, in which enthusiasm had taken its seat. Unknown to De La Haye, I began writing Signor Bragadin[20] and my two other friends letters about the man and his pupil which communicated all my fanaticism to them. My reader knows that this disease of the mind is infectious. I urged it upon them that the greatest good of our little society depended upon our adding these two persons to it. "It is God's will," I said, "that you should employ all your resources to find some honorable employment in Venice for Monsieur de La Haye and in the army for young Bavois."

Signor Bragadin wrote me that De La Haye could stay with us in his palace, and that Bavois could write to his patron the Pope asking him to recommend him to the Venetian Ambassador,[21] a letter from whom to the Senate conveying the Holy Father's wish would, as things now stood, assure him of a post. The affair of the Patriarchate of Aquileia[22] was then being negotiated, and the Republic, which was in possession of it, as well as the House of Austria, which claimed the *jus eligendi*,[23] had appointed Benedict XIV to arbitrate it. It was clear that the Senate would accord the greatest attention to the wish of the Pontiff, who had not yet handed down his decision.

When I received this crucial answer I informed De La Haye of all that I had done in the matter; and I saw that he was astonished. He instantly grasped all the force and the truth of old Senator Bragadin's reasoning, and he sent his dear Bavois a magnificent letter in Latin to copy and send at once to His Holiness, in the certainty that he would be granted the favor he asked. After all, it was only a recommendation.

While this matter was being pursued and we were waiting for a letter from Venice which would tell us the effect of the Pontiff's recommendation, a comic adventure which befell me will perhaps be not unentertaining to my reader.

At the beginning of April, completely cured of the wounds of Venus and restored to my original vigor, going all day to churches and sermons with my converter, I also went with him to spend the evenings at a coffee-house, where we found good company in the persons of several officers. The one who kept everyone amused by his boasting was a Provençal in uniform who narrated the military exploits which had distinguished him in the service of several powers and chiefly of Spain. To keep him talking, everyone pretended to believe him. Once as I was looking at him closely he asked me if I knew him.

"By Heaven," I said, "how could I fail to know you, since we were together at the Battle of Arbela?" [24]

Hearing this, the whole company burst out laughing; but the braggart said petulantly that there was nothing to laugh at, for he had been there and was beginning to think he recognized me. He then told me the name of the regiment in which we served, and after embracing we ended by mutual congratulations on the good fortune we had had to meet again in Parma. Having had my fun, I went back to my inn with De La Haye.

The next morning I was still at table with him in my room when I saw the braggart come in and address me without taking off his hat:

"Monsieur d'Arbela, I have something important to say to you, so hurry and let us go out together; and if you are afraid, bring anyone you please along with you—I am good for a dozen."

I quickly rise, and snatching up a pistol I tell him that no one has the right to come and disturb me in my room, so I order him to leave.

My man then draws his sword, daring me to murder him; but De La Haye, by stamping on the floor, brought up the innkeeper, who warned the officer that he would send for the guard if he did not leave. He left, saying that I had insulted him in public and that he would see to it that the satisfaction I owed him would be public. After he left, seeing that the joke could have tragic consequences, I discussed with De La Haye how best to set things right, but we did not need to talk long. A half hour later an officer of Don Filippo's came to order me to go at once to the main guardpost, where Signor Bartoloni,[25] the Town Major, had something to say to me. I asked De La Haye to come with me, as a witness both to what I had said in the coffeehouse and to the way the man had come to attack me in my own room.

I found the Town Major with four or five officers, among whom I saw the one in question. Signor Bartoloni, who was a wit, smiled slightly when he saw me, then with the utmost seriousness told me that since I had publicly made fun of the officer whom I saw present, he was justified in demanding public satisfaction, and that he, as Town Major, was in duty bound to oblige me to give it to him so that the whole affair would be amicably settled.

"There is no question of satisfaction, Major, since it is not true that I insulted him by ridiculing him. I told him that I thought I had seen him at the Battle of Arbela, and I no longer doubted it when he told me not only that he had been present at it but that he recognized me."

"Yes," said the officer, interrupting me, "but I heard Rodela,[26] not Arbela, and everyone knows I was there. But you said Arbela, and you can only have said it to ridicule me, for it is more than two thousand years since that battle was fought, whereas the Battle of Rodela, in Africa, is of our own time—I served in it under the Duke of Montemar."[27]

"If you tell me so, I believe you; and it is I who demand satisfaction from you if you dare to deny that I was at the Battle of Arbela. I was aide-de-camp to Parmenio,[28] and I was wounded at it. I cannot show you the scar for, as you can imagine, I had a different body. As I stand before you, I am only twenty-three years old."[29]

"All this strikes me as madness; but in any case I have witnesses that you ridiculed me, for you said that you saw me and, by God! you cannot have seen me because I was not there. I demand satisfaction."

"I also have witnesses that you told me you had seen me at Rodela, though I was not there either."

"I may have been mistaken."

"And so may I; hence we have no claims on each other."

The Major, who could no longer contain his laughter, seeing the serious air with which I had been trying to convince the officer that he was wrong, told him that he could not demand the least satisfaction, since I admitted that I might have been mistaken.

"But," he answered, "is it credible that he was at Arbela?"

"He leaves you at liberty to believe it or not to believe it, just as he is at liberty to say that he was present at it. Will you maintain against him, sword in hand, that he is lying?"

"God forbid! I prefer to consider the matter settled."

The Major thereupon invited us to embrace each other, which we did with the best of grace, and the next day the Rodomonte[30] came and asked me to dinner. Signor Bartoloni invited us to dinner too; but as I did not feel like laughing I declined.

CHAPTER VI

*I receive good news from Venice, to which I
return, taking De La Haye and Bavois with
me. Excellent reception from my three friends,
and their surprise at finding me a model of
devotion. Bavois leads me back to my former
life. De La Haye a true hypocrite. Adventure
with the Marchetti girl. I win in the lottery. I
meet Balletti again. De La Haye leaves the
Palazzo Bragadin. I set off for Paris.*

DURING THESE days I received word from Venice
that the cases against me[1] had been forgotten, and at
the same time a letter from Signor Bragadin in which
he told me that the Savio di Settimana[2] had written
the Ambassador that he could assure the Holy Father
that when the Baron de Bavois presented himself steps
would be taken to give him a post in the troops of the
Republic, which would enable him to live honorably and
to entertain the highest hopes from his own merit.

With this letter in my hand, I rejoiced the heart of
De La Haye, who, seeing at the same time that since
my difficulties had been resolved I would return to my
native country, determined to go to Modena to have a
talk with Bavois and decide on the new course of action
which he should adopt in Venice in order to enter upon
the road to fortune. He could have no doubt either of my
sincerity or my friendship or my loyalty; he saw that

I had become a fanatic and he knew that it is usually
an incurable disease when the causes which have produced it remain in operation, and, by himself coming to
Venice, he hoped to keep them active. So he wrote to
Bavois that he was coming to see him; and two days later
he took leave of me, melting into tears, praising my soul
and my virtues, calling me his son, and assuring me that
he had not become attached to me until after he had seen
the divine mark of predestination stamped on my physiognomy. Such was his language.

Two or three days later I went to Ferrara and from
there to Venice by way of Rovigo, Padua, and Fusina,[3]
where I left my carriage. After a year's absence my
friends received me as if I were an angel come from
Heaven to make them happy. They showed the greatest
impatience to witness the arrival of the two sainted souls
whom I had promised them in my letters. A lodging for
De La Haye was already prepared, and two furnished
rooms for Bavois had also been found in the neighbor-
hood, for political considerations did not permit Signor
Bragadin to give lodging in his palace to a foreigner[4]
who was not yet admitted into the service of the Republic.

But their surprise was extreme when they could not
but observe the wonderful change in the life I led. To
mass every day, often to sermons, my assiduity in attending the "forty hours,"[5] no casinos, a coffeehouse
where the company consisted only in men of known
prudence, and continual study in my room when their
duties kept them out of the house. My new behavior
compared with my old habits made them adore Divine
Providence and its incomprehensible ways. They blessed
the crimes which had obliged me to spend a year far
from my country. What further astonished them was
that I began by paying all my debts, without asking a
soldo from Signor Bragadin, who, not having sent me
anything for a year, had taken care of all my money.

They were delighted to see that I had become averse to any kind of gaming.

At the beginning of May I received a letter from De La Haye in which he told me that he was about to embark with the dear son of his soul to put himself under the orders of the respectable persons to whom I had announced him.

Making sure of the hour at which the *barca corriere*[6] from Modena would arrive, we all went to meet him, except Signor Bragadin, who was at the Senate that day. He found all five of us at his palace and welcomed the two strangers as warmly as they could wish. De La Haye at once told me countless things; but I listened to him only with my ears, for Bavois engrossed my entire attention; I saw in him an entirely different person from the one I expected from the description of him which he had given me. I spent three days studying him before I could resolve upon a genuine attachment, for this is a portrait of the youth, who was twenty-five years of age:

Of middle height, handsome, very well built, blond, gay, always equable, speaking well and wittily, and expressing himself modestly and respectfully. His features were agreeable and regular, he had fine teeth, a good head of hair, elegantly curled and exhaling the scent of the excellent pomade with which he dressed it. This individual, who in neither substance nor form resembled the one De La Haye had portrayed for me, also surprised my friends. However, they were no less cordial to him on that account, nor did they form any judgment prejudicial to the good opinion they were bound to have of his morals.

As soon as I saw Monsieur de La Haye well settled in his room it fell to me to conduct the Baron de Bavois to his apartment, not very far from the Palazzo Bragadin, whither I had already had his few pieces of baggage carried. As soon as he found that he was excellently lodged in the house of a worthy citizen and his wife, who,

having been well schooled beforehand, began by showing
him a thousand attentions, he embraced me affectionately,
assuring me of his entire friendship and of the profound
gratitude he felt for all that I had done for him without
knowing him and of which Monsieur de La Haye had
informed him in full. I replied that I did not know to
what he was referring; and I turned the conversation to
the kind of life he wished to lead in Venice until the
time when a post would give him an obligatory occupation. He answered that he hoped we would amuse ourselves very pleasantly, since he believed that his tastes
were not different from mine. What I noticed at once
was that he immediately attracted the hostess's two
daughters, who were neither pretty nor ugly, but whom
he at once flattered with an affability which could not
but make them believe they had attracted him. I thought
it common politeness. For the first day I only took him
to the Piazza San Marco and to a coffeehouse until suppertime. It went without saying that he would dine and
sup every day at Signor Bragadin's. At table he made
an impression with apt remarks; and Signor Dandolo[7]
appointed the hour on the following morning at which
he would call for him to present him to the Savio for
War.[8] After supper I took him to his lodging, where I
left him in the hands of the two daughters of the household, who said they were delighted that the young Swiss
nobleman whose arrival we had announced to them had
no servant, as they had feared he might, for they undertook to convince him that he could do without.

The next morning I went to call for him with Signor
Dandolo and Signor Barbaro, who were to introduce him
to the Savio. We found the young Baron at his toilet
under the delicate hands of the elder daughter of the
house, who was dressing his hair and whose skill he
praised. His room was fragrant with pomade and scented
waters. My friends were in no way scandalized; but I

observed their surprise, for they did not expect to see so great a show of worldliness in the convert. What almost made me burst out laughing was that, upon Signor Dandolo's remarking that if we did not hurry we should not have time to go to mass, the Baron asked him if it was a feast day. He answered that it was not, without adding any comment; but in the days that followed there was no longer any question of mass. I let them go, and we met again at dinner, where the talk was of the reception the Savio had given him; and in the afternoon my friends took him to visit their patrician relatives of the female sex, who were all pleased to see the charming young man. Thus in less than a week he had edged into society and was in no danger of being bored; but during the same week I became thoroughly acquainted with his character and his way of thinking. It would not have taken me so long if I had not entertained contrary preconceptions: Bavois loved women, gambling, and spending money, and, since he was poor, women were his chief resources. As for religion, he had none; and since he had the shining virtue of not being a hypocrite, he did not hide it from me.

"How," I asked him one day, "did you manage, being what you are, to deceive De La Haye?"

"Heaven preserve me from deceit! De La Haye knows the system I follow and my way of thinking, he knows me *funditus* ('thoroughly'). Pious as he is, he fell in love with my soul, and I let him. He has done me good; I am grateful to him, and I love him, and the more so because he never bores me by talking dogma and eternal salvation to me. It is all settled between us."

The amusing part of the business is that in the same week Bavois not only restored my mind to the state it was in when I parted from Henriette but made me blush to have been duped by De La Haye, who, though he played the role of thorough Christian to perfection, could nevertheless be nothing but a thorough hypocrite. Bavois opened my eyes, and I quickly resumed all my old ways. But let us return to De La Haye.

A man who at bottom cared for nothing but his own well-being, well on in years, and with no inclination for the sex, he was precisely the person to enchant my friends. Talking to them of nothing but God, angels, and eternal glory, always going to one church or another with them, they adored him, and they could not wait for the moment when he would reveal himself, for they imagined he was a Rosicrucian,[9] or at least the hermit of Carpegna[10] who, teaching me the cabala, had made me a present of the immortal Paralis.[11] They were distressed that, by the very words of the oracle, I had forbidden them ever to speak of my science in De La Haye's presence. This left me free to enjoy all the time I should have had to devote to their pious curiosity; and in any case I could not but fear De La Haye, for, such as I saw him to be, he would never have lent himself to my nonsense and he would probably even have tried to disabuse my friends in order to supplant me.

In the short space of three weeks I saw him obtain such an ascendancy over their minds that he was foolish enough to think not only that he had no further need of me to maintain his standing but that he had standing enough to knock me head over heels if he felt so inclined. I saw this from the different tone in which he talked to me and from the difference in his behavior. He began having private secrets with the three of them, and he had persuaded them to introduce him in houses which I did not frequent. He began giving himself airs, though always with a smile, and complaining, though in honeyed words, when I spent the night no one knew where. It began to annoy me that, when he preached me his gentle sermons at table in the presence of my friends and his proselyte, he appeared to regard me as one who was leading him astray. He did it as if in jest; but I was not taken in. I put an end to his game by going to call on him in his room and telling him frankly that, as a votary of the Gospels, I would now tell him in private what on another occasion I would say to him in public.

"What is it, my dear friend?"

"Take care in future not to treat me to any more of your jibes about the life I lead with Bavois, in the presence of my three friends. Privately, I will always listen to you gladly."

"You are wrong to take a certain jesting seriously."

"Why do you never aim at the Baron? Be prudent in future, or fear that, no less in jest, I may treat you to a reply which I spared you yesterday but which I will not spare you at the first opportunity."

During these same days I spent an hour with my three friends giving them instructions from the oracle never to do anything which Valentin (it was by his baptismal name that the oracle named him) might suggest to them without first consulting me. I had no doubt that they would obey the order. De La Haye, who did not fail to see a certain change, began to behave more sensibly. Bavois, whom I informed of my action, praised it. I was already thoroughly convinced that De La Haye had been of service to him only out of weakness—in other words, that he would have done nothing for him if he had not had a pretty face, though Bavois would never admit it. He did not have experience enough to admit it. The young man, seeing that giving him a post was constantly put off, entered the service of the French Ambassador;[12] which compelled him not only to cease visiting Signor Bragadin but also to stop seeing De La Haye because he was lodging in that nobleman's house. This is one of the most inviolable laws of the sovereign guardians of the Republic. Neither patricians nor their households may have the slightest connection with the households of foreign envoys.[13] But the step which Bavois took did not prevent my friends from soliciting a post for him; and they succeeded, as will be seen later in these memoirs.

Carlo,[14] the husband of Cristina, whom I never went to see, urged me to go to the casino to which his aunt went with his wife after her confinement. I found her charming and speaking Venetian like her husband. At the casino I met a chemist who made me wish to take a course in chemistry. Going to spend the evening at his house with him, I became curious about a girl who, living in a house next to his, came in to keep his old wife company. At the first hour of night[15] a servingwoman would come to fetch her and she would leave. I had spoken to her of the inclination she had inspired in me only once, and that in the presence of the chemist's old wife, when I was surprised to see no more of her and said so. She answered that apparently her cousin the Abate, with whom she lived, having learned that I visited her house, had become jealous and would no longer allow her to come.

"A cousin who is an abate, and jealous?"

"Why not? He lets her out only on feast days to go to the first mass at Santa Maria Mater Domini,[16] which is only twenty paces from his house. He let her come to my house because he knew that no one visited here; and apparently it was the servingwoman who told him she had seen you."

Jealous men being my abhorrence even as my own amorous vagaries are my delight, I write the girl that if she would leave her cousin for me I would set her up a house in which she would be mistress and in which, living with her as her lover, I would provide her with an enjoyable circle of acquaintances and see that she had all the pleasures which a girl like herself should enjoy in a city like Venice. In the same letter, which I gave her in the church to which she went to mass, I said that she would see me on the next feast day to give me an answer.

She answered that since the Abate was her tyrant, she would think herself happy if she could escape from his hands; but that she could not resolve to do so unless I was willing to marry her. She ended her letter by saying that if I had that honorable intention I had only to speak to Giovanna Marchetti, her mother, who lived at Lusia. This town is thirty miles from Venice.

Her letter annoyed me because I thought she had written it in concert with the Abate. Convinced that they meant to trap me, and in any case considering the proposal that I should marry her both absurd and impudent, I decided to avenge myself; but as I needed to know everything I went to Lusia to call on the widow Giovanna Marchetti, the girl's mother.

The woman was greatly flattered, after reading the letter her daughter had written me, to hear me say that I felt inclined to marry her, but that I could never bring myself to do so as long as she continued to live with the Abate.

"The Abate," she replied, "who is distantly related to me, owned and lived alone in the same house in Venice in which he is now living with my daughter. Two years ago he told me that he urgently needed a housekeeper and that he was inclined to take my daughter, who could easily find a good opportunity to marry, once she was in Venice. He offered me an engagement in writing in which he undertook to give her, when she married, his furniture, valued at a thousand ducati correnti,[18] and to make her his heir to an estate he owns here which brings him in a hundred ducati a year. As I thought the bargain a good one, and my daughter was satisfied with it, he gave me the stipulated deed in the presence of a notary; and my daughter went with him. I know that he keeps her like a slave; but it was her own wish. You can well imagine that all I want in the world is to see her married."

"Then come with me to Venice; remove her from the Abate's keeping, and, receiving her from you, I will marry her; never otherwise. If I received her from him, marrying her would dishonor me."

"Not at all, for he is her cousin, though in the fourth degree; what is more, he is a priest and says mass every day."

"You make me laugh. Take her back with you; otherwise you will never see her married."

"If I take her back he will never give her his furniture and he may sell his estate."

"Leave it to me. I will have her out of his custody and restored to your arms with all the furniture, and when she is my wife I will have her landed property. If you knew me you would have no doubt of it. Come to Venice, and I assure you that in four or five days you will be back here with her."

She read the letter her daughter had written me through again, she thought for a little, then said that she was a poor widow and had no money either for the journey to Venice or to stay there.

"At Venice you will have whatever you need; but in any case here are ten zecchini."

"Ten zecchini? I can come with my sister-in-law."

"Come with anyone you please. Let us go at once to spend the night at Chioggia, and we will dine tomorrow in Venice."

We slept in Chioggia, and the next day at seventeen o'clock[19] we reached Venice. I lodged the two women in Castello[20] in a house in which the second story was completely unfurnished. I left them there, taking the priest's deed with me, and after dining with my friends, to whom I explained that I had spent the night in Chioggia to settle an important matter, I called on the advocate Marco da Lezze,[21] who, after hearing the whole story, told me that if the mother would present a petition in person to the heads of the Council of Ten,[22] she would at once be given the authority and the necessary assistance to remove her daughter from the priest's custody together with all the furniture in his house, which she could have carried wherever she might please. I told him to draw up the petition, which I would come to fetch the following morning, accompanied by the mother, who would sign it.

So she came with me to the advocate's, and from there we went to the Bussola,[23] where she presented the petition to the heads of the Ten. A quarter of an hour later a *fante*[24] of the tribunal was ordered to accompany the woman to the priest's house and put her in possession of her daughter, who was to leave the house with all the furniture she wished to take.

The order was carried out to the letter. I was present with the mother in a gondola at the quay of the piazza near the house and with a large boat into which I saw the *sbirri* load all the furniture in the house, and finally I saw the girl get into the gondola, very much surprised to see me there. Her mother embraced her and told her that I was to become her husband the next day. She answered that she was sure of it and that she had left her tyrant only a bed and his clothes.

We reached Castello, where I had all her furniture unloaded and where I dined with the three women, persuading them to go and wait for me in Lusia, where they would see me again as soon as I had put my affairs in order. I spent the whole afternoon with my intended in most amusing talk. She told us that her cousin the Abate was dressing when the *fante* entered. He showed him the deed, and as soon as he had admitted it was his, he was ordered on pain of death to do nothing to oppose the girl's going or the removal of all the furniture. The Abate went off to say his mass, and everything was carried out to the letter. The same *fante* had told her that her mother was waiting for her in a gondola which was at the quay, in which she was very much surprised to see me because she could not believe that the thing was my doing. I told her that it was the first sample I was giving her of my affection.

I ordered a choice supper for four, with exquisite wines, and after spending two hours at table in joy and peace, I spent four more laughing with my intended.

The next morning after breakfast I sent for a peota,[25] into which I had all the furniture loaded to be transported to Lusia, and after giving the mother ten more zecchini I wished them a good journey. Victorious, proud, and triumphant, I went home.

The business had made such a stir that it could not remain unknown to my good friends, who when they saw me showed that they were saddened and surprised. Monsieur de La Haye embraced me with an air of the greatest grief; it was a role which he played to perfection. Only Signor Bragadin laughed heartily and told the three others that they did not understand it at all and that the whole thing had been done only to bring about a greater piece of work which was known only to the higher intelligences. For my part, not knowing through which of its particulars they believed they were acquainted with the whole story, which they could not really know, I laughed with Signor Bragadin, but said nothing. With nothing to fear, I resolved to amuse myself by listening to whatever was said. We sat down at table. Signor Barbaro was the first to say to me in a friendly tone that he had not expected to see me the day after my marriage.

"Are people saying that I am married?"

"Everyone says so, and everywhere. Even the heads of the Council of Ten believe it and have reason to believe it."

"They are all mistaken. I like to do good at the expense of my money, but not at the expense of my freedom. When you want to know my business it is from me that you should learn it. The public voice is fit only to amuse fools."

"But," said Signor Dandolo, "you spent the night with the girl who is said to be your wife."

"No doubt, but I am not obliged to account to anyone for what I did last night. Do you not agree with me, Monsieur de La Haye?"

"I beg you not to ask my opinion, for I know nothing about it. However, I will say to you that you should not hold the public voice in so little esteem. The tender affection which I feel for you is the reason why what is being said pains me."

"How is it that what is being said pains neither Signor Bragadin nor me?"

"I respect you, but I have learned at my own expense to fear slander. It is said that to obtain possession of a girl who was living with her uncle, a worthy priest, you paid a woman to say she was her mother and to go as such to demand the use of force from the heads of the Council of Ten to get her for you. The *fante* of the Council of Ten himself swears that you were in the gondola with the pretended mother when the girl got into it. It is said that the deed of gift by virtue of which you carried off the good priest's furniture is forged; and you are accused of having made the tribunal the instrument of these crimes. It is said, finally, that even if you have married the girl, which must be the case, the heads of the Ten will have much to say concerning the means you had the effrontery to employ to gain your end."

I answered him coldly that *a wise man who has heard a story told in which there are criminal circumstances ceases to be wise if he repeats it to others, for if it is slanderous he thus becomes an accomplice of the slanderer.*

After this maxim, which made him blush and whose

wisdom my friends admired, I asked him never to worry about me, to believe that I knew honor only to follow its commands, and to let people talk, just as I myself did when I heard evil tongues speaking evil of him.

The incident furnished the story which kept the city amused for five or six days; then it was forgotten.

Three months later, however, as I had never gone to Lusia and never answered the letters which the Signorina Marchetti wrote me or paid their bearers the money she demanded of me, she determined on a course which might have had consequences, but which had none.

Ignazio,[26] *fante* of the redoubtable tribunal of the State Inquisitors, appeared before me at a moment when I was still at table with Signor Bragadin, my two other friends, De La Haye, and two strangers. He told me politely that the Cavaliere Contarini dal Zoffo[27] wished to speak to me and that he would be at his house in Santa Maria dell'Orto[28] the next day at such-and-such an hour. I answered, rising, that I would not fail to obey His Excellency's[29] order. He left at once; I could not imagine what such a great personage could want of my small person. However, the message could not but put us all in a kind of consternation, for the man who was summoning me was a State Inquisitor. Signor Bragadin, who had been one himself in the days when he was a Councilor,[30] and knew their procedures, told me calmly that I had nothing to fear.

"Ignazio," he said, "being dressed in country clothes, did not come as a messenger of the tribunal, and Signor Contarini himself wishes to speak to you only as a private citizen, since he sends you word to wait on him at his palace and not in the sanctuary.[31] He is a severe old man, but just, and one to whom you must speak clearly and above all admit the truth if, by denying it, you run the risk of making matters worse."

His advice pleased me, and I needed it. I presented

myself in the nobleman's antechamber at the appointed hour.

I am announced and am not kept waiting. I enter, and His Excellency, who was seated, spends a minute looking me up and down without saying a word. He rings and tells the footman who enters to show in the two persons who were in the next room. I was not at all surprised to see the Marchetti woman and her daughter come in. The nobleman asks me if I know them.

"I cannot but know them, Monsignore, since the Signorina is to be my wife as soon as she has proved to me by her conduct that she is worthy to be."

"Her conduct is good; she lives with her mother at Lusia; you have deceived her; why do you put off marrying her; why do you not go to see her; you do not answer her letters, and you leave her in want."

"I cannot marry her without having something to live on, and that will come three or four years hence from a post which I shall obtain through the patronage of Signor Bragadin, my only support. In the meanwhile she will live in God's grace. I will not marry her until I am convinced of it and, above all, that she does not see the Abate her cousin in the fourth degree. I do not go to see her because my confessor and my conscience forbid me to."

"She wishes you to make her a formal promise of marriage and to give her enough to live on."

"Nothing obliges me to make her such a promise, and as I have nothing to live on myself it is impossible for me to give her anything. In her mother's house she cannot die of starvation."

"When she was with my cousin," her mother interrupted, "she lacked nothing. She shall go back there."

"If she goes back there," I said, "I will not again take the trouble to deliver her; and then His Excellency will see that I am right in putting off marrying her until I am sure that her behavior has become what it should be.''

His Excellency told me that I might leave, and it was all over. I heard nothing more of the matter, and my account of the dialogue amused Signor Bragadin's dinner table.

1750.

At the beginning of the Carnival I won a *terno*[32] which brought me three thousand ducati correnti. Fortune made me the present at a moment when I did not need it. I had spent the autumn at cards every day, but making the bank. It was at a small casino for members, to which no Venetian nobleman dared to come because one of the members was an officer of the Duke of Montealegre, the Spanish Ambassador.[33] The presence of noblemen is embarrassing to private citizens in an aristocratic government, where equality exists only among members of the government. I put a thousand zecchini in Signor Bragadin's hands, intending to make a journey to France after the Ascension Day fair. With this idea in mind I had the firmness to spend the Carnival without ever risking my money punting. A very obliging patrician had accorded me a quarter share in his bank, and on the first day of Lent we found ourselves the winners by a sufficient sum.

In the middle of the Carnival my friend Balletti, who had produced the ballets at Mantua for the second time, came to Venice under contract to produce them at the Teatro San Moisè[34] during the fair. I was delighted to see him with Marina, who, however, did not lodge with him. She immediately found an English Jew named Mendex,[35] who spent a great deal of money on her. This Jew, with whom she invited me to dine, gave me news of my dear Teresa-Bellino, telling me that he had been in love with her and had left her pleasant recollections. The news pleased me. I congratulated myself that Henriette had prevented me from going to see her when I had intended to, for I could easily have fallen in love with her again, and God knows what would have happened.

At this same time the Baron de Bavois was appointed a captain in the service of the Republic; he had a most successful career, as I will narrate in its proper place.

De La Haye undertook the education of a young man named Felice Calvi and a year later took him to Poland with him. I will narrate in its proper place how I met him in Vienna three years later.

At the same time that I was arranging to go to the fair at Reggio,[36] then to Turin, where, on the occasion of the marriage of the Duke of Savoy[37] to an Infanta of Spain, daughter of Philip V, all Italy was present, then to Paris, where, Madame la Dauphine[38] being pregnant, magnificent festivals were in preparation in the expectation of a prince, Balletti was also arranging to make the same journey. His father and his mother, who was the famous actress Silvia,[39] were summoning him back to the bosom of his family. He was to dance at the Théâtre Italien[40] and to play the first lover's roles there. I could not choose company more agreeable and more apt to procure me countless advantages in Paris and a quantity of brilliant acquaintances.

So I took leave of Signor Bragadin and my two other friends, promising them that I would return at the end of two years. I left my brother Francesco studying under the battle painter Simonetti,[41] known as Il Parmigiano, promising him that I would think of him when I was in Paris, where in those days genius was certain to make its way to fortune. The reader will see how I kept my word to him.

I also left in Venice my brother Giovanni, who had returned there with Guarienti[42] after making the tour of Italy. He was about to leave for Rome, where he remained for fourteen years studying under the Cavaliere

Mengs.[43] He returned to Dresden in 1764 and died there in 1795.

So I set out from Venice after Balletti, who had gone on to wait for me in Reggio. It was the first day of June in the year 1750. I set out well equipped, with plenty of money, and certain not to be in want of it if I behaved properly.

A four-oared peota put me ashore at Pontelagoscuro[44] twenty-four hours after I embarked. It was noon. I immediately took a calèche to convey me to Ferrara for dinner.

The 25th year of my age.

CHAPTER VII[1]

My stay in Ferrara and comic adventure which
befalls me there. My arrival in Paris, 1750.

I DISEMBARK from a peota at noon at Pontelagoscuro; I take a chaise to hurry on to Ferrara for
dinner. I put up at the Albergo San Marco,[2] and I go
upstairs, preceded by a valet to show me to my room.
A sound of merriment coming from an open room
prompts me to see what it might be. I see ten or twelve
people at table; it is nothing unusual; and I was going
on, but I am halted by a "There he is!" spoken by a
pretty woman, who rises and runs to me with open arms,
embraces me, and says:

"*Set a place for my dear cousin at once, and have his
trunk put in the room next to this one.*"

A young man comes toward me, and she says to him:

"*Didn't I tell you he would arrive today or tomorrow?*"

She makes me sit down beside her, and the entire
company, who had risen in my honor, return to their
places.

"You are sure to be hungry," she says to me, treading on my foot; "there is my fiancé, whom I introduce to you, and there are my father-in-law and my mother-in-law. These ladies and gentlemen are friends of the family. How is it that my mother did not arrive with you?"

The moment had come when I must speak.

"Your mother, my dear cousin, will be here in three or four days."

I look at the minx closely, and I recognize her as Cattinella,[3] a very well-known dancer, to whom I had never spoken in my life. I see that she is making me play a false role for the sake of a play of her own composition, and one which she needed to bring on its dénouement. Curious to know if I really had the talent with which she credited me, I gladly fall in with her scheme, certain that she will reward me at least with her favors in secret. What was required of me was the skill to play my role well yet not to compromise myself. In the meanwhile, on the pretext that I wanted to eat, I gave her all the time we needed to fill me in. She gave me a good example of her quick wit by explaining the whole working of the plot to me through remarks which she made, while I was eating, now to one member of the company, now to another. I gathered that her marriage could not take place until the arrival of her mother, who was to bring her her clothes and her diamonds, and that I was the *maestro* who was going to Turin to compose the music of the opera for the marriage of the Duke of Savoy. Certain that she could not prevent me from leaving the next day, I saw that I risked nothing by playing the role. Except for the nocturnal reward which I promised myself, I would have told the company that she was mad. Cattinella might be thirty years of age, she was extremely pretty, and famous for her intrigues.

The supposed mother-in-law, who was seated across from me, filled a glass for me and, as I had to reach out

my arm to take it, she noticed my hand, which I held as
if it were sprained.

"What's that?" she asked.

"A little sprain which will soon be cured."

Cattinella burst out laughing and said that she was
very sorry, for now they could not hear me at the
harpsichord.

"I am surprised that you laugh at it."

"I laugh because I remember a sprain I pretended I
had suffered two years ago to avoid dancing."

After coffee the mother-in-law said that Signorina
Cattinella must have family matters to discuss with me
and that we should be left to our own devices; so at last
I found myself alone with the schemer in the room next
to hers, which she had arranged that I should have.

She sank onto a sofa to succumb to laughter which she
could not contain. She said that she felt sure of me,
though she knew me only by sight and by name, and
she ended by saying that I would do very well to leave
the next day.

"I have been here," she said, "for two months without
a soldo; I have nothing but some dresses and linen, which
I should have had to sell to live on if I had not managed
to inspire a passion in the innkeeper's son, whom I
flattered into believing that I would become his wife and
bring him a dowry of twenty thousand scudi in diamonds,
which I am supposed to have in Venice and which my
mother is supposed to be bringing me. My mother has
nothing, knows nothing about the plot, and will not stir
from Venice."

"Pray tell me what end this farce will have: I foresee
that it will be tragic."

"You are wrong. Very comic. I am waiting here for a
lover, who is Count Ostein,[4] brother to the Elector of
Mainz. He wrote to me from Frankfurt, he has left there,
and he must now be in Venice. He will come for me to

take me to the fair at Reggio. If my supposed fiancé
decides to make difficulties, he will certainly give him a
beating, at the same time paying him my bill; but I
want him neither to beat him nor pay him. As I leave,
I will whisper to him that I will come back, and all will
go smoothly, for I will assure him that I will marry him
on my return.''

''It is perfect; you are as clever as an angel; but I will
not wait until your return to marry you, that must be
done at once.''

''What madness! At least wait until tonight.''

''Not a bit of it, for I seem to hear your Count's
horses already. If he doesn't arrive we'll be none the
worse off for tonight.''

''So you love me?''

''Madly; but what of it? Your play deserves my
adoring you and making you sure of it. Let us be quick.''

''Wait. Lock the door. You are right. It is an episode,
but a very pretty one.''

Toward nightfall they all joined us upstairs, and there
was talk of going to take the air. We were just about to
do so, when a carriage drawn by six post horses was
heard to arrive. Cattinella looks out of the window and
tells everyone to leave, since it was a prince coming for
her, she was sure of it. Everyone left, and she pushes me
into my room and locks me in. Sure enough, I see the
berlin[5] stop in front of the inn, I see a nobleman four
times my size emerge from it supported by two servants.
He comes upstairs, he enters the bride's room, and I had
nothing left to entertain me except my ability to hear
everything they said and to see through a crack everything that Cattinella did with his enormous bulk. But
the entertainment finally bored me, for it went on for
five hours. They were devoted to packing all Cattinella's
belongings, loading them on the berlin, supping, and
emptying several bottles of Rhine wine. At midnight
Count Ostein left as he had arrived, taking the bride

away from the bridegroom. No one ever came to my room during all this time, and I avoided summoning anyone. I was afraid I should be discovered and I did not know how the German prince might take it if he knew that he had a hidden witness to his demonstrations of love, which did no honor to either of the persons who were concerned in them. I made sundry reflections on the miserable estate of the human race.

After the heroine's departure I saw the innkeeper's son through the crack; I knocked to get him to open the door for me, and he told me in a plaintive voice that the lock would have to be broken since the Signorina had carried off the key. I asked him to do it at once since I was hungry; and it was done. He kept me company at table. He told me that the Signorina had found a moment to assure him that she would return in six weeks; he told me that she had wept as she gave him the assurance and that she had embraced him.

"Did the Prince pay her bill?"

"No indeed. We would not have accepted it if he had offered to. My intended would have taken offense, for you cannot imagine how nobly she thinks."

"What does your father say about her going?"

"My father always thinks the worst; he says that she will not come back, and my mother is more of his opinion than of mine. But you, Signor Maestro, what do you think?"

"That if she told you so, she will undoubtedly return."

"If she had not intended to come back, she would not have assured me of it."

"Exactly. Your reasoning is faultless."

My supper was the remains of what the Count's cook had prepared, and I drank a bottle of Rhenish which Cattinella had filched as a present for him.[6] After supper I took the post, and I left after assuring him that I would persuade my cousin to return as soon as she could. I wanted to pay; but he would take nothing. I reached

Bologna a quarter of an hour after Cattinella and lodged at the same inn. I found an opportunity to tell her of the conversation I had had with her stupid lover.

I reached Reggio before her, but I was never able to speak to her, for she never left her Count. I spent the whole fair there without anything happening to me which is worth recording. I left Reggio with Balletti, and reached Turin, which I was eager to see. When I had been there with Henriette I had stopped only long enough to change horses.

At Turin I found everything equally fine—the city, the court, the theater, and the women, who were all beautiful beginning with the Duchesses of Savoy.[7] I laughed when I was told that the city was well policed and saw the streets full of beggars. Yet the efficiency of the police was the principal concern of the King[8] himself, who was highly intelligent, as everyone knows from history. But I was silly enough to be astonished by the monarch's appearance. Never having seen a king in my life, a spurious idea made me believe that a king should have something rarely beautiful or majestic in his physiognomy, not shared by the rest of mankind. As a young, thinking republican, my idea was not entirely stupid; but I soon got rid of it when I saw the King of Sardinia ugly, hunchbacked, morose, and common even in his manners. I heard La Astrua[9] and Gafarello[10] sing, and I saw La Geoffroi[11] dance, whom a very gentlemanly dancer named Bodin married at about this time. No amorous inclination disturbed the peace of my soul in Turin, except for the daughter of a washerwoman, with whom there befell me an accident which I record only because it taught me a lesson in physiology.

After doing everything I could to obtain an interview with the girl in my lodging or in hers or anywhere at all and not succeeding, I resolved to have her by using a little violence at the foot of the concealed staircase down which she usually went when she left my lodging. I hid at the foot of it, and when I saw that she was within reach I sprang on her and, partly by persuasion, partly by swift action, I subjugated her on the last steps; but at the first thrust of our union a most extraordinary sound, proceeding from the place next to the one I was occupying, stayed my fury for a moment, and the more so because I saw the victim put her hand over her face to hide the shame she felt at her indiscretion.

I reassure her by a kiss and make to continue, but lo! a second sound, louder than the first; I proceed, and now comes the third, then the fourth, and so regularly that it was like the bass of an orchestra giving the time for a piece of music. This aural phenomenon, together with the embarrassment and confusion which I saw in my victim, suddenly took possession of my soul; all together they presented so comical an idea to my mind that, laughter having overpowered all my faculties, I had to let go. She seized the moment to run away. From that day on she did not dare to enter my sight. I remained there sitting on the stairs for more than a quarter of an hour before I could shake off the comedy of the thing, which makes me laugh every time I think of it. I reflected afterward that the girl perhaps owed her virtuous behavior to her infirmity. It might also be due to a certain configuration of the organ, and in that case she ought to thank eternal Providence for a gift which an ungrateful feeling perhaps prompted her to consider a defect. I believe that three out of four loose women would cease to be so if they were subject to this phenomenon, unless they were sure that their lovers were subject to it too, for then the strange symphony might become one more charm of a happy union. It might even be easy to hit on a device which could be applied to the sluice gate and which would make the explosions odor-

iferous, for one sense should not suffer when another
sense is enjoying; and the sense of smell plays no small
part in the pleasures of Venus.

Gambling at Turin avenged me for the wrong it had
done me at Reggio, and I was easily persuaded by my
friend Balletti to go with him to Paris, where magnificent festivals were being prepared in expectation of the
birth of a Duke of Burgundy.[12] Everyone knew that
Madame la Dauphine was near the end of her pregnancy.
So we set out from Turin, and on the fifth day we arrived in Lyons. We spent a week there.

Lyons is a very fine city, in which not even three or
four noble houses are open to foreigners; but to make up
for it there are a hundred belonging to businessmen,
merchants, manufacturers, and commission agents far
richer than manufacturers, in which there is excellent
society. The tone is considerably below that of Paris, but
one gets used to it, and one enjoys life more methodically.
What makes Lyons rich is taste and low prices. The
divinity to which the city owes its prosperity is fashion.
It changes every year, and a stuff for which thirty is
paid because of its new pattern fetches only twenty the
next year and is sent to foreign countries, where the
buyers sell it as something brand-new. Lyons pays high
fees to designers who have taste; that is the secret. Low
prices come from competition, whose soul is freedom.
Hence a government which wishes to see the state pros-
pering by commerce has but to leave commerce completely free, only being watchful to prevent frauds which
private interest may invent to the detriment of the
general interest. The sovereign should hold the scales,
and allow his subjects to load them as they please.

At Lyons I found the most celebrated of all Venetian
courtesans. Her name was Ancilla.[13] Her beauty was
astonishing. Everyone said that her equal had never
been seen. Those who saw her could not help wanting to
enjoy her, and she could refuse no one, for if all men

Don Philip of Spain, Duke of Parma

Scenes in Antique Style

loved her individually, she loved the male sex in general. Those who had not the small amount of money which the law demanded that they give her to obtain her favors obtained them for nothing as soon as they could acquaint her with their desires.

Venice always had courtesans more famous for their beauty than for their intelligence; the chief of these among my contemporaries were this same Ancilla and another named Spina;[14] both daughters of gondoliers; both dead at an early age after deciding to enter a profession which they thought would raise their standing. Ancilla at the age of twenty-two became a dancer; and Spina tried to become a singer. The man who made Ancilla a dancer was a dancer named Campioni,[15] a Venetian who, dancing serious roles, taught her all the graces of which her beautiful form was capable, and married her. Spina learned music from a castrato who called himself Beppino della Mammana,[16] who could not marry her; but she was always less than mediocre and continued to live on what she earned by her charms. Ancilla danced in Venice until two years before her death, of which I will speak at the proper time.

I found her at Lyons with her husband. They had just come from London, where they had been applauded at the Haymarket Theater.[17] She had stopped at Lyons with her husband purely for her own pleasure, and she had at her feet all the fashionable and rich young men of the city, who went to call on her every evening and did whatever she wanted to please her : outings by day, great suppers, and faro all night. The banker was a certain Don Giuseppe Marcati,[18] the same man whose acquaintance I had made in the Spanish army eight years earlier, where he was called Don Bepe il cadetto, and who some years later made known his real name of Afflisio and who came to such a bad end. His bank won three hundred thousand francs in a few days. In a country with a court such a sum would not have been talked about, but in a city of merchants it alarmed all the heads of families, and the Italian contingent thought of leaving.

A respectable personage whom I met at the house of Monsieur de Rochebaron[19] procured me the privilege of being admitted[20] into the company of those who see the light. I became an apprentice *Freemason.* Two months later at Paris I received the second degree,[21] and some months later the third, which is the mastership. It is the highest. All the other titles which were conferred on me in the course of time are pleasing fictions which, though symbolic, add nothing to the dignity of Master.

There is not a man on earth who succeeds in knowing everything; but every man should aspire to know everything. Every young man who travels, who wishes to know society, who does not wish to be inferior to another and excluded from the company of his equals in the age in which we live, should be initiated into what is called Freemasonry, if only to acquire a superficial knowledge of what it is. However, he must be careful to make the right choice of the lodge of which he wishes to become a member, for though evil company cannot act in the lodge, it may be present in it, and the candidate must beware of dangerous connections. Those who decide to become Masons only to learn the secret may well be deceiving themselves, for a man can be a Master Mason for fifty years and never learn the secret of the brotherhood.

The secret of Masonry is inviolable by its own nature, since the Mason who knows it, knows it only because he has divined it. He has learned it from no one. He has discovered it by virtue of going to the lodge, observing, reasoning, and deducing. When he has arrived at it, he takes great care not to share his discovery with anyone, were it his best friend and a Mason, because if he has not had the ability to find it out, he will by the same token not have the ability to profit by it if he learns it by word of mouth. The secret, then, will always be a secret.

Whatever one does in lodge must be kept secret; but those who, in their dishonest indiscretion, have not scrupled to reveal what is done there have not revealed the heart of the matter. How could they reveal it if they did not know it? If they had known it they would not have revealed the ceremonies.

The same impression which the Brotherhood of Masons produces today on many who have not been initiated into it was produced in ancient times by the great mysteries which were celebrated at Eleusis[22] in honor of Ceres. They aroused the interest of all Greece, and the greatest men in the world aspired to be initiated into them. That initiation was of far greater significance than initiation into modern Freemasonry, among whose members some are rascals and the dregs of human society. Impenetrable silence was long preserved concerning everything that took place in the Eleusinian mysteries, because of the veneration which they inspired. Someone dared, for example, to reveal the three words which the hierophant[23] addressed to the initiates when he dismissed them at the conclusion of the mysteries; but what did that accomplish? Only to dishonor him who had revealed them, for the three words were in a barbarian language unknown to the profane. I have somewhere read that the three words meant: "Watch, and do no evil." The initiation lasted for nine days, the ceremonies were most imposing, the company was of the worthiest. We read in Plutarch[24] that Alcibiades was sentenced to death and that all his property was confiscated because he had dared to ridicule the great mysteries in the privacy of his house with Polytion and Theodoros, contrary to the laws of the Eumolpides.[25] In consequence of his sacrilege he was sentenced to be cursed by the priests and priestesses, but the curse was not pronounced; a priestess[26] opposed it, giving as her reason that she was a priestess "to bless, not to curse," a most noble lesson which our Most Holy Father the Pope scorns. Nothing is important today.

Botarelli[27] publishes all the practices of the Freemasons
in a pamphlet, and no one says anything except that he
is a scoundrel. It was already common knowledge. At
Naples a Prince and Monsieur Hamilton[28] perform the
miracle of San Gennaro[29] at home. The King shuts his
eyes and does not remember that he wears on his royal
breast an order on which, around the effigy of San
Gennaro, are the three words: *In sanguine foedus* ("In
the blood of the covenant").[30] Everything nowadays is
inconsequential and there is nothing which has any
significance. The present trend will be defended and
pursued; but everything will go from bad to worse if
it stops halfway.

We engaged two places in the diligence which would
take us to Paris in five days; Balletti informed his family
of the time of his departure, so they knew the hour at
which we should arrive.

We were eight in the conveyance, which is called a
"diligence";[31] we were all seated, but all uncomfortably,
for it was oval; no one had a corner seat since it had
no corners. I thought this poorly considered; but I said
nothing, for as an Italian it was my part to consider
everything in France admirable. An oval coach: I
bowed to the fashion, and I cursed it, for the strange
movement of the vehicle made me want to vomit. It was
too well sprung. I should have found a jolting less trying.
The very force of its speed over the fine road made it
rock; hence it was called a "gondola"; but the true Venetian gondola propelled by two oarsmen goes smoothly
and does not cause a nausea which turns one inside out.
My head was spinning. The swift motion, which at least
did not jolt me in the slightest, affected my intestinal
vapors and made me throw up everything I had in my
stomach. My fellow passengers thought me bad company,
but none of them said so. All that anyone said was that
I had eaten too much supper, and a Parisian Abbé spoke
up in my defense, saying that I had a weak stomach,

and there was an argument. Out of patience, I put a stop to it by saying:

"*You are both wrong, for I have an excellent stomach and I did not eat supper.*"

An elderly man who had a boy of twelve or thirteen years with him said to me in honeyed tones that I should not tell the gentlemen that they were "wrong," but that I could have told them that they were "not right," thus imitating Cicero, who did not tell the Romans that Catiline[32] and the other conspirators were dead but that they "had lived."

"Is it not the same thing?"

"I beg your pardon, Monsieur, the one is impolite and the other is polite."

He then delivered a magnificent dissertation on politeness, which he concluded by saying to me, with a smile:

"I wager that Monsieur is Italian."

"Yes, but may I make bold to ask you from what you guessed it?"

"Oh, from the attention with which you honored my lengthy prattle."

The whole company then burst out laughing, and I began making up to the eccentric, who was tutor to the youth beside him. I made use of him through all those five days to give me lessons in French politeness, and when we had to part he called me aside and said that he wished to make me a small present.

"What is it?"

"You must forget and renounce the particle *non* which you use without mercy in season and out of season. *Non* is not a French word. Say *pardon,* it comes to the same thing and does not offend. *Non* is a contradiction. Give it up, Monsieur, or be prepared to draw your sword in Paris every moment."

"I thank you, Monsieur, and I promise never to say *non* again as long as I live."

At the beginning of my stay in Paris it seemed to me

that I had become the guiltiest of men, for I did nothing but beg pardon. One day I even thought that I had brought a quarrel on myself by begging it out of season. It was at the theater that a young dandy trod on my foot by mistake.

"Pardon me, Monsieur," I said quickly.

"It is for you to pardon."

"For you."

"For you."

"Alas, Monsieur, let us pardon each other and embrace."

So ended our quarrel.

One day when I was sleeping quite soundly sitting up in the gondola-diligence, which was making great speed, my neighbor suddenly shakes me to wake me up.

"What is it?"

"Ah, Monsieur, look at that château, I beg you."

"I see it. It is not much. What do you consider remarkable about it?"

"Nothing—if we were not forty leagues from Paris. Will my gawking fellow citizens believe me when I tell them I have seen such a fine château forty leagues from the capital? How ignorant one is when one has not traveled a little!"

"You are quite right."

The man was a Parisian himself, an inveterate gawker, like a Gaul in the days of Caesar.

But if the Parisians go gawking about from morning to night, being amused by everything and admiring everything, a foreigner like myself should be even more of a curiosity-seeker. The difference between them and myself was that, being accustomed to seeing things as they are, I was surprised to see them under a mask which changed their nature, whereas the Parisians' surprise is due to their often being led to suspect what is under the mask.

What greatly pleased me was the beauty of the high-

road, the immortal work of Louis XV, the cleanliness
of the inns, the fare which they supplied, the promptness with which we were served, the excellence of the
beds, the modest manner of the person who served us at
table, who was usually the most accomplished daughter
of the house and whose bearing, cleanliness, and manners
were enough to check any licentiousness. Who among us
in Italy takes pleasure in seeing the waiters in our
inns with their effrontery and their insolence? In those
days in France overcharging was unknown; France was
the home of foreigners. Is it now the home of the French?
There was the disadvantage of often seeing an odious
despotism consisting in *lettres de cachet*.[33] It was the
despotism of kings. We shall see what is the despotism
of a raging, ferocious, uncontrollable people who flock
together, hang, cut off heads, and murder those who, not
being of the people, dare to speak their minds.[34]

We slept at Fontainebleau, and an hour before reaching Paris we saw a berlin coming from it.

"That is my mother," said Balletti, "stop, stop!"

We got out; and after the usual ecstasies between
mother and son he introduces me, and his mother, who
was the celebrated actress Silvia, greets me only with:

"I hope, Monsieur, that my son's friend will be so
good as to sup with us tonight."

So saying she gets into her carriage with her son and
her daughter, who was nine years old. I return to the
gondola.

On arriving in Paris I find one of Silvia's servants
waiting with a hackney coach; he attended to everything
and conducted me to a lodging[35] which I found very
clean. After leaving my trunk and all my possessions
there he took me to his mistress's house, which was fifty
paces away. Balletti introduced me to his father, who was
named Mario,[36] and who was convalescing. Mario and
Silvia were the names they bore in the comedies which
they improvised. The French never called the Italian

actors any other names in society than those by which they were known on the stage. "Bonjour, Monsieur Arlequin; bonjour, Monsieur Pantalon"—so the actors who played those parts were addressed at the Palais-Royal.[37]

CHAPTER VIII

*My apprenticeship in Paris. Portraits. Odd-
ities. Things many and various.*

SILVIA CELEBRATED her son's arrival by inviting her relatives to supper at her house. I was delighted to have reached Paris in time to make their
acquaintance. Mario, Balletti's father, did not come to
the table because he was recovering from an illness, but
I met his elder sister, who was called by her stage name
of Flaminia.[1] She was known in the Republic of Letters[2]
for some translations; but what made me want to know
her well was the story, which was current all over Italy,
of the sojourn[3] which three famous men had made in
Paris. The three men were the Marchese Maffei,[4] the
Abate Conti,[5] and Pier Giacomo Martelli.[6] They became
enemies, the story went, because of the preference to
which each of them aspired in the actress's good graces,
and as men of learning they fought with their pens.
Martelli wrote a satire on Maffei, in which he gave him
the anagrammatic name of ''Femia.''

As I was presented to Flaminia as a candidate in the
Republic of Letters, she saw fit to honor me with her

conversation. I found her repulsive in her face, her tone, her style, and even her voice; she did not quite say it, but she gave me to understand that, famous herself in the Republic of Letters, she was talking to an insect; she acted as if she were laying down the law and she considered that, at the age of seventy, she had every right to do so toward a youth of twenty-five who had added nothing to any library. To flatter her, I talked of the Abate Conti, and in a certain connection I cited two lines by that profound writer. She corrected me affably enough on the word *scevra,* which means separated, which I pronounced with the consonantal *u,* which is *v.*[7] She said that it should be pronounced as a vowel, and that I should not take it amiss to have learned the fact in Paris on my first day there.

"I am certainly eager to learn, Madame, but not to unlearn. It should be pronounced *scevra,* and not *sceura,* because it is a contraction of *scévera.*"

"It remains to be seen which of us is wrong."

"You are, Madame, according to Ariosto, who rhymes *scevra* with *persevra.*"

She was going on when her husband, who was eighty years old,[8] told her that she was mistaken. She said no more, and from that time on she told everyone that I was an impostor. Her husband was Lodovico Riccoboni, known as Lelio, the same man who had brought the Italian troupe to Paris in the year sixteen in the service of the Duke-Regent.[9] I was aware of his merit. He had been very handsome, and he rightly enjoyed the esteem of the public both for his talent and for his morals. During supper my principal concern was to study Silvia, who was praised to the skies. I found her above everything that was said of her. Her age was fifty, her figure elegant, her bearing distinguished, as were her manners; she was easy, affable, pleasant, well-spoken, obliging to everyone, full of wit yet completely unpretentious. Her face was an enigma, it was interesting and it pleased everyone, yet on examination it could not be considered beautiful; but by the same token no one had ever dared to pronounce it ugly. She could not be said to be neither beautiful nor ugly, for the fascination of her character made an instantaneous impression. So what was she? Beautiful—but in accordance with laws and proportions unknown to all except those who, feeling an occult power drawing them to love her, had the courage to study her and the capacity to discover them.

This actress was the idol of all France, and her talent was the mainstay of all the comedies which the greatest authors wrote for her, and especially Marivaux.[10] But for her, their comedies would never have come down to posterity. An actress capable of replacing her has never been found, and never will be found, for she would have to combine in herself all the aptitudes which Silvia possessed in the too difficult art of the theater—action, voice, countenance, intelligence, bearing, and knowledge of the human heart. Everything in her was nature; the art which accompanied and had perfected it all was not allowed to appear.

To be unique in every respect, she added to those which I have just mentioned a quality even without which she would have risen to the pinnacle of fame as an actress. Her life was pure. She was ready to make friends of men, but never lovers—scorning a privilege which she could have enjoyed but which would have made her base in her own estimation. For this reason she gained a reputation for respectability at an age when it would have seemed absurd and almost insulting to all women of her profession. For this reason several ladies of the highest rank honored her with their friendship even more than with their patronage. For this reason the capricious Parisian groundlings never dared to hiss her in a role which they did not like. By general and unanimous consent, Silvia was a woman above her profession.

Since she did not consider that her good conduct could

be placed to her credit, for she knew that she practiced it only for the sake of her self-esteem, no pride, no show of superiority was ever seen in the relations she was obliged to have with her fellow actresses, who, content to shine by their talents, were not concerned to make themselves conspicuous by their virtue. Silvia loved them all, and she was loved by them, she did them justice publicly, and she praised them. But she was right: she had nothing to fear, none of them could cast the slightest shadow on her.

Nature cheated this unique woman out of ten years of her life. She became consumptive at the age of sixty, ten years after I met her. The climate of Paris plays these tricks on Italian women. Two years before her death I saw her play the role of Marianne in Marivaux's comedy,[11] in which she seemed to be only Marianne's age. She died in my presence, holding her daughter in her arms and giving her her last advice five minutes before she expired. She was honorably buried at Saint-Sauveur[12] without the slightest opposition from the parish priest, who said that her profession[13] of actress had never prevented her from being a Christian.

Excuse me, reader, if I have delivered Silvia's funeral oration ten years before reaching her death. When I come to that, I will spare you another.

Her only daughter, the principal object of her affection, was seated beside her at this same supper. She was only nine years old. Entirely taken up by the mother's excellences, I did not pause to make any observations on the daughter. That was to come only later. Well satisfied with my first evening, I returned to my lodgings in the house of Madame Quinson. Such was the name of my hostess.

When I woke, Mademoiselle Quinson came to tell me that there was a manservant outside, who had come to offer me his services. I see a very short man; this I find distasteful, and I tell him so.

"My shortness, Prince, will assure you that I will not wear your clothes to go gadding in."

"Your name?"

"Whatever name you please."

"What? I am asking you what your name is."

"I have none. Each master whom I serve gives me one, and in the course of my life I have had more than fifty. I will take the name you give me."

"Come now, you must have a name of your own, your family name."

"Family? I never had a family. I had a name in my youth, but in the twenty years that I have been a servant, always changing masters, I have forgotten it."

"I will call you L'Esprit."

"You do me great honor."

"Go get me change for this louis."

"Here it is."

"I see you are rich."

"Entirely at your service, Monsieur."

"Who will give me information about you?"

"The agency for servants, and Madame Quinson as well. Everyone in Paris knows me."

"That will do. I will give you thirty sous a day. I do not provide your clothing, you will sleep at home, and you will be at my orders every morning at seven o'clock."

Balletti came to see me and asked me to come to dinner and supper every day. I had L'Esprit show me the way to the Palais-Royal [14] and left him at the gate. Eager to satisfy my curiosity concerning a promenade which was so highly praised, I began by observing everything. I saw a rather fine garden, walks bordered by big trees, fountains, the whole surrounded by *high houses,* many men and women strolling, benches here and there, from which *new pamphlets,* scented waters, toothpicks, and trinkets were sold; I saw cane chairs which were rented for a sou, newspaper readers sitting in the shade, light women and men breakfasting alone and in company; coffeehouse waiters hurrying up and down a small concealed staircase behind beds of shrubbery. I sit down at a small empty table, a waiter asks me what I will have, I ask for chocolate without milk, and he brings me some which is horrible in a silver cup. I let it stand and tell the waiter to bring me coffee if it is good.

"Excellent, I made it yesterday myself."

"Yesterday? I don't want it."

"The milk in it is excellent."

"Milk? I never drink it. Make me a cup of coffee made with water, at once."

"With water? We make that only after dinner. Would you like a bavaroise? [15] Would you like a decanter of orgeat?" [16]

"Yes, orgeat."

I find it an excellent beverage, and I decide to make it my regular breakfast. I ask the waiter if there is anything new, and he answers that the Dauphine has given birth to a prince; an abbé tells him he is mad: it is a princess she has borne. A third man comes forward and says:

"I have just come from Versailles, and the Dauphine has borne neither a prince nor a princess."

He tells me that he gathers I am a foreigner, and I answer that I am an Italian, arrived in Paris the day before. He then talks to me of the court, of society, of the theater; he offers to introduce me everywhere, I thank him, I leave, and the Abbé accompanies me and tells me the names of all the light women who are strolling about. A gentleman of the robe[17] meets him, he embraces him, and the Abbé introduces him to me as learned in Italian literature; I address him in Italian, he answers wittily, and I laugh at his style and tell him the reason: he spoke exactly in the style of Boccaccio. My remark pleases him, I persuade him that it is not the way

to speak, though that ancient writer's language is perfect. In less than a quarter of an hour we become fast
friends, finding that we have the same inclinations. He
a poet, I a poet, he interested in Italian literature, I in
French, we give each other our addresses and promise to
exchange visits.

I see many men and women crowded together in one
corner of the garden, looking up. I asked my new friend
what was remarkable there. He said that they were
watching the meridian line, each with his timepiece in
his hand, waiting for the moment when the shadow of the
style would show exactly noon, when they would set their
timepieces.

"But aren't there meridians everywhere?"

"Yes, but the most celebrated is the one in the Palais-
Royal."

At that I could not help laughing.

"Why are you laughing?"

"Because it is impossible that all meridians are not
the same; so this is the height of gawking."

He thought a little and then laughed too; and he gave
me the courage to criticize the good Parisians. We leave
the Palais-Royal by the main gate, and I see to my right
a crowd in front of a shop whose sign was a civet cat.[18]

"What's this?"

"Now you will really laugh. All these people are waiting to buy snuff."

"Is it sold only in this shop?"

"It is sold everywhere; but for the last three weeks
no one will have any snuff in his snuffbox except what
comes from the Civet Cat."

"Is it better than others?"

"Not at all; it may even be worse; but since the
Duchess of Chartres[19] made it fashionable no one will
have anything else."

"What did she do to make it fashionable?"

"She stopped her carriage two or three times outside

the shop, buying only enough to fill her snuffbox and openly telling the young woman who sells it that it was the best snuff in Paris; the gawkers who crowded around her told others, and everyone in Paris knew that if one wanted good snuff one had to buy it at the Civet Cat. The woman will make her fortune, for she sells over a hundred crowns' worth of it a day.''

''The Duchess of Chartres probably does not know she has made the woman's fortune.''

''On the contrary, the Duchess, who is very intelligent, contrived the whole thing herself; being fond of the woman, who was recently married, and considering what she could do to help her, she decided that the thing to do was just what she has done. You cannot imagine what good souls the Parisians are. You are in the only country in the world in which intelligence can make its way to fortune either if it displays itself in genuine contributions, in which case it is welcomed by intelligence, or if it imposes what is specious, in which case it is rewarded by stupidity; stupidity is characteristic of the nation, and what is astonishing is that it is the daughter of intelligence, so that it is no paradox to say that the French nation would be wiser if it were less intelligent.

''The gods who are worshiped here, though no altars are raised to them, are novelty and fashion. A man has but to run, and all those who see him run after him. They would not stop until he was found to be mad; but to find that out is to count the sands: we have madmen here who have been mad from birth and they are still accepted as wise. The snuff from the Civet Cat is a very small example of what a flock of sheep our citizens are. Our King, out hunting, came to the Pont de Neuilly[20] and wanted a drink of ratafia.[21] He stopped at the tavern there; he asked for it, and by some strange chance the poor tavernkeeper had a flagon of it, and the King, after drinking a glass, saw fit to say to those around him that it was an excellent drink and asked for another.

That was all it took to make the tavernkeeper's fortune. In less than twenty-four hours the whole court and the whole city knew that the ratafia at Neuilly was the best drink in Europe, for the King had said so. The most fashionable people flocked to Neuilly at midnight to drink ratafia, and in less than three years the tavern-keeper was a rich man and had a house built on the same spot, on which you will see the inscription *Ex liquidis solidum* ('From liquids, a solid'), which is quite amusing and which was given him by one of our Academicians. What saint must the fellow thank for his swift rise to a brilliant fortune? Stupidity, flightiness, love of a joke.''

"It seems to me," I said, "that this approbation of the views of the King and the princes of the blood comes from an unconquerable affection in the nation, which adores them; it is so great that they believe them to be infallible.''

"True. Everything that happens in France makes foreigners believe that the nation adores its King; but those among us who think see that this love of the nation for the monarch is only tinsel. How can one base anything on a love which has no basis? The court does not rely on it. The King comes to Paris, and everyone cries: 'Long live the King' because some idler has begun shouting it. It is a cry which comes from high spirits, or perhaps from fear, and which the King himself, believe me, does not take seriously. He cannot wait to get back to Versailles, where there are twenty-five thousand men to protect him from the fury of the same populace which, grown wise, might take it into their heads to cry: 'Death to the King.' Louis XIV knew them. And his knowledge cost several councilors of the Great Chamber[22] their lives when they ventured to talk of assembling the States-General [23] when the country was threatened with calamity. France has never loved her Kings, except St. Louis[24] for his piety, Louis XII,[25] and Henri IV [26] after his death. The King who now reigns said with perfect sincerity during his convalescence: *'I am amazed at these great rejoicings because I have recovered my health, for I cannot see any reason why I should be so much loved.'* This remark of our monarch's has been praised to the skies. He was actually using his reason. A philosophical courtier should have told him that he was so much loved because his surname was 'the Well Beloved.' ''

"Are there any philosophers among the courtiers?"

"No—for as a courtier, a man cannot be a philosopher; but there are intelligent men who, in deference to their own interests, only champ the bit. Not long ago the King, in conversation with a courtier whom I will not name, extolled the pleasures he enjoyed when he spent the night with Madame la M.,[27] and said that he did not believe there was another woman on earth who could furnish their equal. The courtier answered that His Majesty was of that opinion because His Majesty had never been to a bordello.[28] The courtier was banished to his estate.''

"The Kings of France are right, I believe, to shun summoning the States-General, for then they are in the same situation as a Pope who summons a Council."

"Not quite, but very nearly. The States-General would be dangerous if the people, who are the third estate, could counterbalance the votes of the nobility and the clergy; but that is not the case,[29] and it never will be, for it is not to be believed that policy will put the sword in the hands of madmen. The people would be glad to acquire the same influence, but there will never be either a King or a minister who will grant it to them. Such a minister would be a fool or a traitor.''

The young man who, so discoursing, at once gave me a just idea of the nation, of the Parisian populace, of the court, and of the monarch, was named Patu.[30] I shall have occasion to speak of him. Still talking in the same vein, he took me to Silvia's door and congratulated me on my having the entrée to such a house.

I found the amiable actress in brilliant company. She introduced me to all her guests, telling me who each of them was as she introduced me. The name which struck me was Crébillon.[31]

"What, Monsieur!" I said to him. "Am I so quickly fortunate? For eight years you have charmed me. Listen, I beg you."

Thereupon I recite him the finest scene in his *Zénobie et Rhadamiste*,[32] in my blank verse translation. Silvia was delighted to see the pleasure which Crébillon, at the age of eighty, took in hearing himself rendered into a language which he loved more than his own. He recited the same scene in French, and he politely pointed out the places in which he said I had improved it. I thanked him, but was not taken in by his compliment. We sat down at table and, asked what I had seen of interest in Paris, I told them everything I had seen and heard, except Patu's discourse. After I had talked for at least two hours Crébillon, who had seen more clearly than any of the others the course I was taking to learn both the good and the bad of his nation, addressed me as follows:

"For a first day, Monsieur, I think you promise very well. You will make rapid progress. You tell your story excellently. You speak French in a way which is perfectly comprehensible; but all that you said, you put in Italian constructions. You make people listen to you, you arouse interest, and the novelty of your language renders your listeners doubly attentive; I will even say that your idiom is just the thing to gain their approval, for it is odd and new, and you are in the country where everything odd and new is sought after; nevertheless, you must begin tomorrow, and no later, to make every effort to learn to speak our language well, for in two or three months the same people who now applaud you will begin laughing at you."

"I believe it, and I fear it; so my principal purpose in coming here was to apply myself entirely to the French language and French literature; but how, Monsieur, am I to go about finding a teacher? I am an intolerable pupil, always questioning, curious, demanding, insatiable. I am not rich enough to pay such a teacher, even supposing that I find him."

"For fifty years now, Monsieur, I have been looking for a pupil such as you describe yourself to be, and it is I who will pay you if you will come to me for lessons. I live in the Marais,[33] in the Rue des Douze Portes, I have the best Italian poets, whom I will make you translate into French, and I will never find you insatiable."

I accepted, at a loss to express all my gratitude. Crébillon was six feet tall, overtopping me by three inches; he ate well, told stories amusingly but without laughing himself, and he was famous for his witticisms. He spent his life at home, going out very seldom, and seeing almost no one because he always had a pipe in his mouth and was surrounded by eighteen or twenty cats with which he played for the greater part of the day. He had an old housekeeper, a cook, and a valet. His housekeeper saw to everything, handled his money, and, since she never let him want for anything, he never asked her to render an account. It is a remarkable fact that Crébillon's face resembled a lion's, or a cat's, which is the same thing. He was a royal censor,[34] and he told me it entertained him. His housekeeper read him the works which were brought to him, and paused in her reading when she thought something called for his criticism; and I often laughed over his quarrels with the woman when he was of a different opinion. One day I heard her turn away someone who had come to receive his corrected manuscript:

"Come next week," she said, "for we haven't had time to look over your work yet."

I visited Crébillon three times a week for a year, and I

learned from him all the French I know, but I have never been able to rid myself of Italianisms; I recognize them when I find them in others; but when they come from my pen I do not recognize them, and I am sure I shall never learn to recognize them, just as I have never known what fault in Latinity Livy[35] is taxed with.

I composed an octet in irregular measure on a certain subject and took it to Crébillon for him to correct. After reading my eight lines attentively he addressed me as follows:

"Your thought is fine and very poetic; your language is flawless; your verses are good and exactly measured; nevertheless your octet is bad."

"How can that be?"

"I have no idea. What is lacking is the 'certain something.'[36] Imagine that you see a man and find him handsome, well built, pleasing, witty, and in short perfect in your most severe judgment. A woman comes up, she looks at him, and after considering him thoroughly she leaves, telling you that he does not please her. 'But, Madame, tell me what fault you find in him.' 'I don't know.' You go back to the man, you consider him more carefully, and you find that he is a castrato. 'Ah!' you say, 'now I see the reason why the woman did not find him to her taste.'"

It was by this comparison that Crébillon made me realize why my octet could not please.

At table we talked a great deal about Louis XIV,[37] to whom Crébillon had paid court for fifteen years, and he told us some very curious anecdotes which no one knew. He assured us that the Siamese Ambassadors[38] were rogues in the pay of Madame de Maintenon. He said that he had never finished his tragedy entitled *Cromwell*[39] because the King himself had one day told him not to waste his pen portraying a scoundrel.

He talked to us of his *Catilina*,[40] and said that he considered it the weakest of all his plays, but that he would

not have wanted it to be good if, to make it so, he had
had to bring Caesar on the stage, for Caesar as a young
man would arouse laughter, as Medea[41] would do if she
were brought on the stage before she knew Jason. He
praised Voltaire's talent highly, at the same time accusing him of theft, for he had stolen the Senate scene[42]
from him. He said that, to do him justice, he was born
with every talent for writing history but that he falsi-
fied it and filled it with fairy tales to make it interesting.
According to Crébillon the Man in the Iron Mask [43] was
a fairy tale, and he said that he had been assured of it
by Louis XIV himself.

The play being given at the Théâtre Italien that day
was *Cénie*,[44] by Madame de Graffigny.[45] I went early to
get a good place in the amphitheater.[46] The ladies covered with diamonds who were entering the first-tier boxes
interested me, and I observed them attentively. I had a
fine coat, but since the sleeves of it were open and it had
buttons all the way down everyone who saw me recognized me as a foreigner; the fashion no longer existed
in Paris. While my attention was thus occupied a richly
dressed man three times my size approaches me and
politely asks if I am a foreigner. I say that I am, and
he immediately asks me if I like Paris. I reply by praising it; and at the same moment I see entering the box
at my left a woman covered with jewels but immensely
stout.

"Who on earth," I ask my fat neighbor, "is that fat
sow?"

"She is the wife of this fat pig."

"Ah, Monsieur, I ask a million pardons."

But the man was in no state for me to beg his pardon
for, far from being angry, he was choking with laughter.
I was in despair. After having a good laugh, he rises,
leaves the balcony, and a moment later I see him in the
box speaking to his wife. I see them both laugh, and I

was on the verge of leaving when I hear him calling me:
"Monsieur, Monsieur."

I cannot refuse without being impolite, and I approach
the box. Now perfectly serious, he begs my pardon with
the greatest dignity for having laughed so much and
most graciously invites me to come to supper at his house
that evening. I thank him and tell him that I already
have an engagement. But he insists and his wife joins in,
and to convince them that it is not a pretext I tell them
that I am invited to Silvia's.

"I am certain," he says, "that I can obtain your release, if you have no objection; I will go to her myself."

I yield, he goes; he comes back later with Balletti,
who gives me a message from his mother that she is delighted to have me make such excellent acquaintances
and that she expects me for dinner the next day. Balletti
tells me privately that it is Monsieur de Beauchamp,[47]
Receiver-General of Finances.

After the play I gave my hand to Madame and got into
her carriage. In their house I found the lavishness which
was the rule among all people of their sort in Paris: a
great crowd of guests, a great many parties at cards,
and great gaiety at table. We rose from supper an hour
after midnight, and I was driven home. The house was
open to me during all the time I stayed in Paris, and
it was very useful to me. Those who say that all foreigners who go to Paris are bored for at least the first
two weeks are right, for it takes time to make one's way
in. For my part, I know that in twenty-four hours I
was already kept occupied and was sure that I would
enjoy myself there.

The next morning Patu appeared at my lodging and
presented me with the prose eulogy he had composed on
the Maréchal de Saxe.[48] We set out together and went to
breakfast at the Tuileries, where he introduced me to
Madame du Boccage.[49] Speaking of the Maréchal de
Saxe, the lady made a witty remark.

"It is strange," she said, "that we cannot say a *De profundis* for the man who has made us sing so many *Te Deums*." [50]

Afterward he took me to call on a famous actress of the Opéra whose name was Le Fel,[51] a favorite of all Paris and a member of the Royal Academy of Music.[52] She had three small and charming children, who fluttered about the house.

"I adore them," she said.

"The beauty of their faces," I said, "is of a different sort in each of the three."

"And well it may be. The eldest is the son of the Duke of Aneci,[53] that one is by Count Egmont,[54] and the youngest is the son of Maisonrouge,[55] who has just married La Romainville."

"Oh, oh. Excuse me, I beg you. I thought you were the mother of all three of them."

"And so I am."

So saying she looks at Patu, and she and he together burst out laughing, which makes me blush to the ears. I was a novice. I was not used to hearing a woman usurp the rights of men in this way. Mademoiselle Le Fel was not shameless, she was frank, and superior to all prejudices. The noblemen to whom these little bastards belonged left them in their mother's care and paid her a pension for bringing them up, and the mother lived in luxury. My inexperience of Parisian customs led me into many such awkward blunders. Mademoiselle Le Fel would have laughed at anyone who told her that I had wit after the interrogation through which I had put her.

Another day, calling on Lany,[56] the ballet master at the Opéra, I saw four or five girls, each accompanied by her mother, to whom he was giving dancing lessons. They were all between thirteen and fourteen years old, and had the modest manner which comes from being well brought up. I said flattering things to them, and they replied by lowering their eyes. One of them had a headache, and I made her smell Eau des Carmes;[57] her little friend asks her if she had slept well.

"It is not that," the child answers; "I think I am pregnant."

At this unexpected reply I say, like a fool:

"I should never have thought that Madame was married."

She looks at me, then turns to her friend, and they both fall to laughing with all their hearts. I went away covered with shame and determined that in future I would never impute virtue to young women of the theater. They pride themselves on not having it, and they laugh at the stupidity of those who impute it to them.

Patu introduced me to all the women of pleasure who enjoyed some reputation in Paris; he loved the fair sex as much as I did, but unfortunately for him he did not have as strong a constitution as mine and he paid for it with his life. If he had lived he would have taken Voltaire's place. He died at the age of thirty, at Saint-Jean-de-Maurienne,[58] on his way back from Rome to France. It was from him that I learned a secret which a number of young French writers use to make sure that their prose is perfect when they have to write something which demands the most beautiful prose possible, for example eulogies, funeral orations, letters of dedication. I got the secret out of Patu himself, by surprise.

One morning at his house I saw on his table loose sheets filled with unrhymed alexandrines;[59] I read a dozen verses and told him that, though they were well turned, they gave me more vexation than pleasure, and I added that what I had read in the verses had pleased me much more in the prose eulogy he had composed on the Maréchal de Saxe.

"My prose would not have pleased you if I had not first written everything I say in it in unrhymed alexandrines."

"That is going to a great deal of trouble for nothing."

"No trouble, since unrhymed verses require no effort. One writes them as if one were writing prose."

"Then you believe that your prose becomes more beautiful when you copy it from your own verses?"

"I believe it because there is no doubt of it; it becomes more beautiful, and in addition I make sure that my prose has not the fault of being full of hemistichs, which come from a writer's pen without his being aware of it."

"Is it a fault?"

"A great one, and unforgivable. Prose interlarded with chance verses is worse than prosaic poetry."

"It is true that involuntary verses which occur in an oration must make a bad impression and indeed be bad."

"Certainly. Take the example of Tacitus, whose history begins with *Urbem Romam a principio reges habuere* ('In the beginning the city of Rome was ruled by kings').[60] It is a very bad hexameter,[61] which he certainly did not write intentionally and which he did not notice afterward, for he would have constructed his sentence differently. Is not your Italian prose in which involuntary verses occur faulty?"

"Very faulty. But I will tell you that several writers of little genius put verses into their prose intentionally, to make it more sonorous; it is tinsel, but they flatter themselves that it will pass for gold and that their readers will not notice the difference. But I think you are the only writer who is willing to go to so much trouble."

"The only one? You are mistaken. All those to whom verses come without effort, as is the case with me, do it when the thing they are writing is to be copied by themselves. Ask Crébillon, the Abbé de Voisenon,[62] La Harpe,[63] anyone you please, and they will tell you what I am telling you. Voltaire was the first to make use of the art in the little pieces in which his prose is enchanting. His epistle to Madame du Châtelet[64] is one of them; it is superb; read it, and if you find a single hemistich, say that I am wrong.''

I asked Crébillon, and he told me the same thing; but he assured me that he had never done it himself.

Patu could not wait to take me to the Opéra to see the impression which the spectacle would make on me, for an Italian cannot but find it extraordinary. The opera being given was entitled *Les Fêtes vénitiennes.*[65] An interesting title. We take places in the parterre, paying forty sous; one stands[66] there, and one finds good company. The spectacle is the delight of the nation. *Solus Gallus cantat* (''Only the cock [or: the Gaul] sings'').[67]

After an overture which was very beautiful in its kind, performed by an excellent orchestra, the curtain goes up and I see a set representing the Piazzetta seen from the little island of San Giorgio Maggiore; but I am surprised to see the Doge's Palace on my left and the Procuratie and the great campanile on my right. This too ridiculous mistake—a disgrace to my century—begins by making me laugh, and Patu, whom I enlighten, has to laugh too. The music, though beautiful in the old style, entertains me for a time because of its newness, then bores me, and the recitative distresses me because of its monotony and its senseless shrieks. The French claim that this recitative of theirs replaces both the melopoeia of the Greeks and our *recitativo,* which they detest and which they would not detest if they understood our language.

As for the error in the stage setting, I attribute it to the crass ignorance of the painter, who had made a botch of copying a print. If he had found men wearing swords at their right sides he would not have understood that if he sees them on the right they should be on the left.

The action took place on a day during the Carnival,

when the Venetians walk about masked in the great
Piazza San Marco, and the scene represented gallants,
procuresses, and women entering into and carrying on
intrigues; everything in the way of costumes was false
but amusing. But what really made me laugh was seeing
the Doge and twelve Councilors come out of the wings in
bizarre robes and fall to dancing a passacaglia.[68] Suddenly I hear the parterre clapping at the appearance of
a tall, well-built masked dancer in a black wig with long
curls which reached halfway to his waist and wearing a
robe which was open in front and came down to his heels.
Patu told me in devout and earnest tones that I was
seeing the great Dupré.[69] I had heard him talked of, and
I am all attention. I see the fine figure advance with
rhythmical steps and, reaching the edge of the orchestra pit, slowly raise its arms in a circle, move them
gracefully, extend them to the full, draw them in again,
move its feet, take small steps, execute some mid-leg
battements, then a pirouette, and disappear, backwards,
into the wings. This whole dance of Dupré's lasted only
thirty seconds. The clapping from the parterre and the
boxes was universal; I ask Patu what it means, and he
answers seriously that the applause was for Dupré's
grace and the divine harmony of his movements. He was,
he said, sixty years of age, and he was the same as he
had been forty years earlier.

"What! He never danced differently?"

"He cannot have danced better; for the performance
you saw is perfect. Is there anything above perfection?
He always does the same thing, and we always find it
new; such is the power of the beautiful, the good, the
true, it speaks to the soul. This is true dancing; it is a
song; you have no notion of it in Italy."

At the end of the second act out comes Dupré again
with his face, needless to say, covered by a mask, and
dances to a different air but, so far as I could see, the
same thing. He advances toward the orchestra pit, halts

for a moment, striking—I admit—a very fine pose; and suddenly I hear a hundred voices in the parterre whispering:

"Oh my God, my God! he is stretching, he is stretching."

And to tell the truth he appeared to be an elastic body which, by stretching, became larger. I granted Patu that there was grace in it all, and I saw that he was pleased. Immediately after Dupré I see a female dancer who rushes all over the stage like a madwoman, making *entrechats* to right and left in rapid succession, but scarcely rising, and violently applauded.

"She is the famous Camargo,[70] my friend, whom you have come to Paris in time to see. She is sixty years old too. She is the first woman dancer who dared to leap, before her they did not, and the wonderful thing is that she does not wear drawers."

"I beg your pardon, I saw."

"What did you see? It was only her skin, which, to tell the truth, is not white."

"La Camargo," I answered penitently, "does not please me; I prefer Dupré."

An admirer, a very old man, who was on my left, said that when she was young she did the *saut de basque* and even the *gargouillade*[71] and that he had never seen her thighs even though she danced without drawers.

"But if you never saw her thighs how can you swear that she did not have on drawers?"

"Oh, that sort of thing is easy to find out. I see that Monsieur is a foreigner."

"You are right about that."

A thing which pleased me at the French opera was the scene changes at the command of the whistle. Likewise the orchestra attacking at the stroke of the bow; but the originator of the music with scepter in hand indulging in violent movements to right and left, as if he had to make all the instruments work by strings, offended me.

What pleased me too was the silence of all the spectators. In Italy one is rightly scandalized by the insolent noise made during the singing, and one cannot but laugh afterward when one observes that silence is maintained during the performance of the ballet. There is not a place on earth where the observer does not note aberrations if he is a foreigner, for if he is a native of the country he cannot discern them.

I was delighted at the Comédie Française.[72] My great pleasure was to go there on the days when something old was being given and there were not two hundred spectators. I saw *Le Misanthrope, L'Avare, Le Joueur, Le Glorieux,*[73] and I pretended that I was seeing their first performances. I arrived in time to see Sarrazin, his wife Grandval, La Dangeville, La Dumesnil, La Gaussin, La Clairon, Préville,[74] as well as several actresses who had retired from the stage and were living on their pensions, among them La Levasseur.[75] I talked with them with pleasure, for they told me the most savory anecdotes. In addition they were very helpful. A tragedy was being performed in which a pretty actress played the mute role of a priestess.

"How pretty she is!" I said to one of these matrons.

"Yes, delicious. She's the daughter of the actor who played the confidant. She is very agreeable in company and shows a great deal of promise."

"I should very much like to make her acquaintance."

"Lord! that's not difficult. Her father and mother are civility itself, and I am sure they will be delighted if you ask them to invite you to supper, and they will not be in your way; they will go off to bed and leave you at table with the girl for as long as you please. You are in France, Monsieur, where people know what life is worth and try to make the most of it. We love pleasures and count ourselves happy if we can be the cause of them."

"Your way of thinking is divine, Madame; but how

could I have the effrontery to ask an invitation to supper of respectable people who do not know me?''

"Lord, what are you saying? We know everyone. You see how I treat you. Would anyone think I did not know you? After the play I will introduce you.''

"I will ask you, Madame, to do me the honor some other day.''

"Whenever you please, Monsieur.''

CHAPTER IX

*My blunders in French, my successes, my
numerous acquaintances. Louis XV. My
brother comes to Paris.*

ALL THE Italian actors in Paris wanted to show
me how lavishly they lived. They invited me to meals,
they entertained me. Carlino Bertinazzi,[1] who played
Arlecchino, and whom everyone in Paris adored, reminded me that he had seen me at Padua thirteen years
earlier, when he had come from Petersburg with my
mother. He gave me a fine dinner in the house of Madame
de La Caillerie,[2] where he was lodging. The lady was in
love with him. She had four children, who fluttered about
the house; I complimented her husband on their childish
charm, and her husband replied that they were Carlino's.

"That may be so, but in the meanwhile it is you who
take care of them, and it is you whom they should recognize as their father, whose name they will bear."

"Yes, that would be so in law; but Carlino is too decent a man not to look after them when I take it into
my head to get rid of them. He knows very well that
they are his, and my wife would be the first to complain
if he did not admit it."

Choral Service in the Basilica di San Marco, Venice

Stage Set for a Gala Performance

Thus did this honest man think, and thus did he express himself with the utmost calm. He loved Carlino as much as his wife loved him, with only the difference that the consequences of his fondness were not those which result in children being born. Affairs of this kind are not uncommon in Paris among people of a certain sort. Two of the greatest noblemen of France changed wives quite calmly and had children who bore the names not of their real fathers but of their mothers' husbands; this happened not a century ago (Boufflers and Luxembourg),[3] and the descendants of their children go under the same names today. Those who know about the matter laugh, and they are right. The privilege of laughing and being right is one which belongs only to those who know how a matter stands.

The richest of the Italian actors was Pantalone,[4] he was the father of Corallina and Camilla; in addition he knew and practiced the art of lending against pledges. He invited me to dinner with his family. The two sisters enchanted me. Corallina was being kept by the Prince of Monaco,[5] son of the Duke of Valentinois,[6] who was still alive, and Camilla was in love with the Count of Melfort,[7] the favorite of the Duchess of Chartres, who had recently become the Duchess of Orléans by the death of her father-in-law.

Corallina was less animated than Camilla, but she was prettier; I began paying my court to her at odd hours, as a person of no importance; but odd hours, too, belong to the proprietor; so I would sometimes be there at the time the Prince came to see her. On the first few of these occasions I bowed and left, but later I was asked to stay, for princes alone with their mistresses usually do not know what to do. The three of us would sup together, and their part would be to look at me, listen to me, and laugh; while mine was to eat and talk.

I thought it my duty to pay my respects to the Prince at the Hôtel de Matignon in the Rue de Varenne.

"I am very glad," he said to me one morning, "that you have come, for I promised the Duchess of Ruffec[8] that I would bring you to call on her, and we will go at once."

Another Duchess! I asked nothing better. We get into a *diable*,[9] a carriage then fashionable, and by eleven o'clock in the morning we are being received by the Duchess. I see a woman of sixty with a face covered with rouge, a blotchy complexion, thin, ugly, and faded, sitting immodestly on a sofa, who as soon as I appear cries:

"*Oh, what a handsome young man!* Prince, you are charming. Come and sit here, young man."

I obey, thoroughly astonished, and am immediately repelled by an unbearable stench of musk. I see a hideous bosom, which the virago displayed in its entirety, and pimples, not visible because they were covered with patches, but palpable. Where am I? The Prince leaves, saying that he will send his *diable* back for me in half an hour and will wait for me at Corallina's.

Scarcely is the Prince gone before the harpy surprises we with two drooling lips which offer me a kiss I should perhaps have put up with, but at the same time she extends a gaunt arm to the place to which her hellish fury bound her ugly soul saying:

"*Let's see if you have a fine . . .*"

"Oh, my God! Madame la Duchesse!"

"You draw back? You are acting like a child."

"Yes, Madame. Because . . ."

"What?"

"I have . . . I can't . . . I don't dare . . ."

"What's the matter with you?"

"I have the clap."[10]

"Filthy creature!"

She rises in anger, and so do I, and I make for the door and leave the house, very much afraid that the porter will stop me. I take a hackney coach, and I go and tell the infamous adventure in so many words to Corallina, who laughed heartily but at the same time agreed that the Prince had played me a foul trick. She praised the presence of mind with which I had escaped from the nasty situation; but she did not give me the opportunity to convince her that I had deceived the Duchess. Nevertheless I did not despair. I knew that she did not consider me enough in love.

At supper three or four days later I talked to her so eloquently and demanded my dismissal in such clear terms that she promised me the reward of my love on the following day.

"The Prince of Monaco," she said, "will not return from Versailles until day after tomorrow. Tomorrow we will go to the warren,[11] we will dine together in private, have a hunt with a ferret, and come back to Paris satisfied."

"Very good."

The next morning at ten o'clock we get into a cabriolet and are soon at the Vaugirard barrier.[12] Just as we are going through, along comes a *vis-à-vis*[13] with a foreign livery: "Stop, stop!"

It was the Chevalier de Württemberg, who, not condescending to give me even a look, begins flattering Corallina, then, thrusting out his whole head, whispers to her; she answers in the same manner, he speaks to her again, she thinks for a moment, then, taking my hand and with her face all smiles, says:

"I have important business with the Prince; go to the warren, my dear friend, dine there, hunt, and come to see me tomorrow."

So saying, she steps out, gets into the *vis-à-vis*, and abandons me.

Any of my readers who has found himself in a situation like mine has no need for me to explain the kind of anger with which I was fired at that outrageous moment. I am powerless to explain it to those who have not been so situated. I could not bear to remain in the accursed cabriolet a single instant; I told the driver to go to the devil, I took the first hackney coach I found, and went to see Patu, to whom I told the story in a fury. Patu found my adventure comical, not new, and quite within the rules.

"Within the rules?"

"Within the rules, for there is not a fancy man to whom something of the sort is not bound to happen, and who, if he is intelligent, is not willing to put up with it. For my part, I envy such a hitch; I would sign a note to have one like it tomorrow. I congratulate you. You are certain to have Corallina tomorrow."

"I don't want her any more."

"That's another matter. Shall we go dine at the Hôtel du Roule?[14]

"Yes indeed. It's an excellent idea. Let us go."

The Hôtel du Roule was celebrated in Paris. In the two months that I had spent there I had not yet seen it and I was most curious to do so. The capable woman who had rented it had furnished it very well and had twelve or fourteen choice girls there. She had a good cook, good wines, excellent beds, and she welcomed all who came to visit her. She was known as Madame Paris, she was protected by the police;[15] she was at some distance from Paris, hence she was certain that those who came to her establishment were people of means, for it was too far to go on foot. Her business was excellently organized; pleasures were charged for at a set price, which was not high. One paid six francs to breakfast with a girl, twelve francs to dine there, and a louis to sup and spend the night. It was an orderly house, and people spoke of it with admiration. I could not wait to be there, and I decided that it was better than the warren.

We get into a hackney coach. Patu says to the driver:

"To the Porte Chaillot."[16]

"I understand, Your Honor."

He is there in half an hour. He stops at a porte-

cochère, on which I read "Hôtel du Roule." The door
was closed. A mustachioed servant, emerging from a door
at the rear, comes and looks at us. Satisfied with our appearance, he opens. We dismiss our coach, we enter; and
he shuts the door. A well-dressed, polite woman, with
one eye missing, who seemed to be about fifty, asks us
if we have come to dine there and to see the young ladies
of her household. We answer yes, and she conducts us
to a drawing room where we see fourteen girls wearing
identical dresses of white muslin, with their sewing in
their hands, sitting in a semicircle; when we appear they
all rise and simultaneously make us a deep curtsy. They
all had their hair nicely dressed, were all about the same
age, and all pretty—some tall, others of middle height,
others short, some were brunettes, some blondes, some
auburn-haired. We pass them all in review, saying a
few words to each, and just as Patu was choosing his
I take hold of mine. Our two choices cry out joyously,
throw themselves on our necks, hurry us out of the room
to show us the garden while we wait to be called for dinner. Madame Paris leaves us, saying:

"*Take a stroll in my garden, gentlemen, enjoy the
good air and the peace and silence which reign in my
house, and I answer to you for the good health of the
girls you have chosen.*"

After a short stroll each of us takes his partner to a
room on the ground floor. The girl I had chosen looked
rather like Corallina, so I immediately paid her my respects. We were summoned to table, where we dined mod-
erately well, but we had scarcely finished our coffee when
the one-eyed dame appeared, watch in hand, to tell us
that our turn was over, but that by paying another six
francs we could amuse ourselves until evening. Patu says
that he agrees but wants to choose another partner, and
I am of the same mind.

"It is for you to say, gentlemen."

So we go back to the seraglio, we choose again, and go

out for a stroll. As might be expected, this second combat
made us find the time too short. We were informed that
it was up at an unpleasant moment, but we had to yield
and obey the regulations. I took Patu aside, and after our
philosophical considerations we concluded that these
pleasures measured out by the hour fell short of perfection.

"Let us go back to the seraglio," I said, "and choose a
third partner and assure ourselves that she will be in
our power until tomorrow."

Patu liked my plan, and we went and imparted it to
the abbess, who confessed that we thereby proved ourselves men of discernment. But when we entered the
room to make a third choice, and the girls we had already
had found that they were rejected, all the others laughed
at them, and they avenged themselves by booing at us
and saying that we were awkward.

But I was astonished when I saw my third, who was
a beauty. I thanked Heaven that she had escaped me, for
I was now sure that I would have her for fourteen hours.
Her name was Saint-Hilaire;[17] she was the girl who,
under the same name, became notorious a year later with
an English nobleman who took her to England. She
looked at me with an air of pride and scorn. It took me
more than an hour's walk with her to calm her. She considered me unworthy to sleep with her because I had
presumed not to take her either the first or the second
time. But when I showed her that my inadvertence would
now make us both the gainers, she began to laugh and she
became charming to me. The girl had intelligence, cul-
ture, and everything necessary to make her fortune in
the profession she had entered. While we were supping
Patu said to me in Italian that I had forestalled him only
by a moment, but he insisted on having her five or six
days later. He assured me in the morning that he had
spent the whole night sleeping; but I did not imitate him.
La Saint-Hilaire was very well satisfied with me, and

boasted of it to her companions. I returned to Madame Paris's more than ten times before I left for Fontaine-bleau, and I did not have the heart to take another girl. Saint-Hilaire was proud of having been able to hold me.

The Hôtel du Roule was the reason why I cooled off in my pursuit of Corallina. A Venetian musician named Guadagni,[18] handsome, well versed in his art, and a man of quick intelligence, succeeded in ingratiating himself with Corallina two or three weeks after I fell out with her. The handsome young fellow, who had only the appearance of virility, aroused Corallina's curiosity, and he was the cause of her breaking with the Prince of Monaco, who caught her in the act. But Corallina managed to patch it up with the Prince a month later, and to such effect that nine months later she gave him a child. It was a girl, whom she named Adélaïde[19] and whom the Prince dowered. Then the Prince left her after the death of the Duke of Valentinois to marry Signorina Bri-gnole,[20] of Genoa, and Corallina became the mistress of Count de La Marche, who is now Prince of Conti.[21] Corallina is no longer living, nor is a son whom the Prince had by her and to whom he gave the title of Count of Montréal.[22] But to return to myself.

At this time Madame la Dauphine gave birth to a princess,[23] who at once received the title of Madame de France. In August I saw at the Louvre the new paintings which the members of the Royal Academy of Painting[24] were exhibiting to the public, and seeing no battle pieces I formed the plan of bringing my brother Francesco to Paris; he was in Venice and was talented in the genre. Parosselli,[25] the only French battle painter, being dead, I thought that my brother could make his fortune; I wrote to Signor Grimani and to my brother himself, and I persuaded them, but he did not reach Paris until the beginning of the next year.

King Louis XV, who was passionately fond of hunting, was in the habit of spending six weeks of the autumn of every year at Fontainebleau.[26] He was always back at Versailles by the middle of November. The journey cost him five millions; he took with him everything that could contribute to the enjoyment of all the foreign envoys and his whole court. The French and Italian comedians and his actors and actresses of the Opéra were commanded to follow him. During these six weeks Fontainebleau was far more brilliant than Versailles. Even so, the great city of Paris was not left without spectacles. Opera and the French and Italian players continued nevertheless, for there were so many actors that substitutes could be found for those who were absent.

Mario, Balletti's father, who had completely recovered his health, was to go there[27] with his wife Silvia and his whole family; he invited me to go with them, offering me a lodging in a house which he had rented, and I accepted. I could not have enjoyed a better opportunity to become acquainted with all the court of Louis XV and all the foreign envoys. So I at once waited on Signor Morosini,[28] now Procurator of San Marco, then Ambassador of the Republic to the King of France. The first day on which opera was given he permitted me to escort him; it was a piece by Lully.[29] I was seated in the parquet, exactly under the box occupied by Madame de Pompadour,[30] whom I did not know. In the very first scene the famous Lemaure[31] comes out of the wings and at her second line gives a shriek so loud and so unexpected that I thought she had gone mad; I give a little laugh, in all innocence, never imagining that anyone would think it out of place. A Blue Ribbon,[32] who was in attendance on the Marquise, asks me curtly from what country I come, and I answer curtly that I am from Venice.

"When I was in Venice I often laughed at the recitative in your operas too."

"I believe you, Monsieur, and I am equally certain

that no one there ever thought of preventing you from laughing.''

My rather sharp answer brought a laugh from Madame de Pompadour, who asked me if I really came from ''down there.''

''From where?''

''From Venice.''

''Venice, Madame, is not down; it is up.''

This answer of mine was thought even odder than my first, and the whole box falls to deciding whether Venice was down or up. Apparently it was concluded that I was right, and I was not attacked again. I listened to the opera without laughing, and since I had a cold I blew my nose too often. The same Blue Ribbon, whom I did not know, and who was the Maréchal de Richelieu,[33] remarked to me that apparently the windows of my room were not tightly closed.

''Beg pardon, Monsieur; they are even *calfoutrées*.''

There was general laughter, and I was mortified because I realized that I had mispronounced the word *calfeutrées*.[34] I looked thoroughly humiliated. A half hour later Monsieur de Richelieu asks me which of the two actresses pleased me better in the way of beauty.

''That one.''

''She has ugly legs.''

''One does not see them, Monsieur, and in any case in assessing the beauty of a woman the first thing I put apart[35] is her legs.''

This witticism, which I had uttered by chance and of whose implication I was unaware, gave me standing and made the company in the box curious about me. The Maréchal learned who I was from Signor Morosini himself, who told me that he[36] would be pleased to have me wait on him. My witticism became celebrated, and the Maréchal de Richelieu received me graciously. The foreign envoy on whom I waited most assiduously was Lord

Keith,[37] Marshal of Scotland, who was Ambassador from the King of Prussia. I shall have occasion to speak of him.

It was on the day after I arrived in Fontainebleau that I went to court alone. I saw the handsome King on his way to mass, the whole royal family, and all the court ladies, who surprised me by their ugliness as those at the court of Turin had surprised me by their beauty. But seeing a surprising beauty among so much ugliness, I asked someone what the lady's name was.

"She is Madame de Brionne,[38] Monsieur, who is even more virtuous than beautiful, for not only is there not a single story about her but she has never given the slightest occasion for slander to invent one."

"Perhaps nothing became known."

"Oh, Monsieur, at court everything becomes known."

I went on alone, prowling everywhere, even into the royal apartments, when I saw ten or twelve ugly ladies who looked as if they were running rather than walking and so awkwardly that they seemed about to fall flat on their faces. I asked where they were coming from and why they were walking so awkwardly.

"They are coming from the apartment of the Queen, who is about to dine, and they walk so awkwardly because their slippers have heels half a foot high, which makes them walk with their knees bent."

"Why do they not wear lower heels?"

"Because they think these make them look taller."

I enter a gallery and I see the King pass supporting himself with one arm around Monsieur d'Argenson's[39] shoulders. Louis XV's head was ravishingly beautiful and set on his neck to perfection. Not even a most skillful painter could draw the attitude the monarch gave it when he turned to look at someone. One felt instantly forced to love him. I thought that I saw the majesty for which I had looked in vain in the face of the King of Sardinia. I felt certain that Madame de Pompadour had already fallen in love with that countenance when she contrived to make his acquaintance. Perhaps it was not true, but the face of Louis XV[40] compelled the observer to think so.

I enter a room in which I see ten or twelve courtiers walking up and down, and a table prepared for dinner, big enough for twelve, but set only for one.

"For whom is that table?"

"For the Queen, who is about to dine. There she is."

I see the Queen of France,[41] without rouge, wearing a large bonnet, looking old and pious, thanking two nuns who set on the table a plate containing fresh butter. She sits down; the ten or twelve courtiers who were walking about station themselves before the table in a semicircle ten paces away, and I join them in the deepest silence.

The Queen begins to eat, looking at no one and keeping her eyes fixed on her plate. She had eaten some of a dish and, finding it to her taste, she returned to it, but as she returned to it she cast her eyes over the company, apparently to see if she saw anyone to whom she should justify her epicureanism. She found him and she addressed him, saying:

"Monsieur de Lowendal." [42]

At the name I see a handsome man two inches taller than myself, who, bowing and taking three steps toward the table, answers:

"Madame."

"I believe that the best ragout of all is a fricassee of chicken."

"I am of that opinion, Madame."

After this answer, which was delivered in the most serious tone, the Queen eats and the Maréchal de Lowendal falls back three steps and resumes his previous station. The Queen said no more, finished dining, and returned to her apartments.

Curious as I was to make the acquaintance of the celebrated soldier who had taken Bergen-op-Zoom,[43] I am enchanted to have done so on this occasion. Consulted by the Queen of France on the excellence of a fricassee, and giving his opinion in the same tone in which a death sentence is pronounced at a court-martial. Enriched by the anecdote, I go to regale Silvia's table with it at an elegant dinner at which I found the choicest of agreeable company.

A week or ten days later I am in the gallery at ten o'clock, forming a line with everyone else to have the ever fresh pleasure of seeing the King go by on his way to mass and the singular pleasure of seeing the nipples of Mesdames de France[44] his daughters, who were so dressed that they displayed them to everyone, together with their completely bare shoulders, when I am surprised to see La Cavamacchie, Giulietta,[45] whom I had left in Cesena under the name of Signora Querini. If I was surprised to see her, she was no less so to see me in such a place. Giving her his arm was the Marquis de Saint-Simon,[46] first gentleman of the bedchamber to Prince de Conti.[47]

"Signora Querini at Fontainebleau?"

"You here? I remember Queen Elizabeth,[48] who said: *Pauper ubique jacet*" ("The poor man makes his bed everywhere").[49]

"The comparison is excellent, Madame."

"I am joking, my friend; I have come here to see the King, who does not know me, but the Ambassador will present me tomorrow."

She takes her place in the line five or six paces above me in the direction from which the King was to come. The King enters, with Monsieur de Richelieu by his side, and I see him immediately look at the supposed Madame Querini, and as he walks along I hear him address *his friend* exactly in these words:

"We have prettier women here."

After dinner I go to the Venetian Ambassador's, and I find him at dessert with a large company, seated be-

side Signora Querini, who, on seeing me, says the most
gracious things possible, which was extraordinary in such
a nitwit who had no reason either past or present to like
me, for she was aware that I knew her through and
through and had been able to make her do as I wished.
But I understand the reason for it all, and I make up
my mind to do everything to please her and even to serve
her as a false witness if that should be what she needed.

She comes round to speaking of Signor Querini, and
the Ambassador congratulates her on his having rendered
justice to her merit by marrying her.

"Strangely enough," said the Ambassador, "I did
not know of it."

"Yet it happened more than two years ago," said
Giulietta.

"It is a fact," I said to him, "for it was two years
ago that General Spada introduced the Signora by the
name of Querini to all the nobility in Cesena, where I
had the honor to be."

"I do not doubt it," said the Ambassador, looking at
me, "since Querini himself writes me of it."

When I made to leave, the Ambassador took me into
another room on the pretext of showing me a letter. He
asked me what was said in Venice on the subject of the
marriage, and I answered that no one knew of it and
that, in fact, people were saying that the heir of the
house of Querini was to marry a Grimani.[50]

"I will write the news to Venice day after tomorrow."

"What news?"

"That Giulietta is really Querini, since Your Excellency will present her as such to Louis XV."

"Who told you that I shall present her?"

"She herself."

"She may have changed her mind by now."

I thereupon repeated to him the exact words I had
heard from the King's lips, which showed him the reason
why Giulietta no longer wished to be presented. Monsieur

de Saint-Quentin,[51] the minister who secretly carried out
the monarch's private commands, had gone in person
after mass to tell the beautiful Venetian that the King of
France had poor taste, since he had not thought her more
beautiful than several other ladies at his court. Giulietta
left Fontainebleau early the next morning. I discussed
Giulietta's beauty at the beginning of these memoirs;[52]
her countenance had extraordinary charms, but they had
lost their power by the time I saw her at Fontainebleau;
then, too, she painted her face white, an artifice which
the French cannot forgive; and they are right, for white
paint conceals nature. Yet women, whose business is to
please, will continue to use it, for they always hope to
find a man who is taken in by it.

After my journey to Fontainebleau I saw Giulietta
again at the Venetian Ambassador's; she laughed and
told me that she had been joking when she called herself Madame Querini and that in future she would be
obliged to me if I would call her by her real name of
Countess Preati;[53] she told me to come and see her at
the Hôtel du Luxembourg, where she was staying. I
went there very often to amuse myself by observing her
intrigues, but I never entered into them. During the four
months which she spent in Paris she drove Signor Zanchi
out of his mind. He was secretary of the Venetian Embassy, an amiable, upright, and well-read man. She made
him fall in love with her, he said he was ready to marry
her, she flattered him, and then she treated him so badly
and made him so jealous that the poor wretch lost his
reason and died soon afterward. Count Kaunitz,[54] Ambassador of the Empress-Queen, was attracted by her,
and so was Count Zinzendorf.[55] The intermediary in
these brief affairs was an Abbé Guasco,[56] who, not being rich and being extremely ugly, could aspire to her
favors only by becoming her confidant. But the man on
whom she set her heart was the Marquis de Saint-Simon.
She wanted to become his wife, and he would have mar-

ried her if she had not given him false addresses for him
to obtain information about her birth. The Preati family,
of Verona, which she had appropriated, disowned her,
and Monsieur de Saint-Simon, who despite his love had
managed to keep his common sense, had the strength of
mind to leave her. She did not come off well in Paris,
and she left her diamonds in pawn there. Back in Venice,
she managed to marry the son of the same Signor
Uccelli[57] who sixteen years earlier had taken her out of
poverty and put her on the stage. She died ten years ago.

In Paris I still went to take lessons from the elder
Crébillon; nevertheless my speech, which was full of
Italianisms, often made me say in company what I did
not mean to say, and my remarks almost always produced
very odd jokes which were repeated afterward; but my
gibberish did not prevent people from forming a favorable opinion of my wit; on the contrary, it gained me
some choice acquaintances. Several women who mattered
asked me to come and teach them Italian, adding that it
would give them the pleasure of correcting my French,
and in the exchange I gained more than they did.

Madame Préaudeau,[58] who was one of my pupils, received me one morning still in bed and saying that she
did not feel like taking a lesson because she had taken
medicine the night before. I asked her if during the
night she had *déchargé*[59] well.

"What a question! What curiosity! You are intolerable."

"Lord, Madame, why does one take a medicine if it
is not to *décharger*?"

"A medicine purges, Monsieur, and does not make one
décharger, and let this be the last time in your life that
you use the word."

"I know very well, now that I think of it, that I can
be misinterpreted; but say what you will, it is the right
word."

"Would you like some breakfast?"

"No, Madame, I've had it. I drank a *café* with two Savoyards[60] in it."

"Good God! I am lost. What a madman's breakfast! Explain yourself."

"I drank a *café*, as I drink one every morning."

"But that is nonsense, my friend; a *café* is the shop in which it is sold, and what one drinks is a cup of it."

"Do you drink the cup? In Italy we say *un caffè*, and we have brains enough to understand that we didn't drink the shop."

"He refuses to be wrong. And the two Savoyards—how did you swallow them?"

"Dipped in the coffee. They were no bigger than those you have there on your night table."

"You call those Savoyards? Say *biscuits*."

"We call them Savoyards in Italy, Madame, for the fashion for them came from Savoy, and it is not my fault if you thought I ate two of those porters who stand at street corners to serve the public and whom you call Savoyards,[61] while they may be from some other country. In future I will say that I have eaten *biscuits*, to conform to your usage; but permit me to tell you that the term *Savoyards* fits them better."

In comes her husband; she tells him of our disagreements; he laughs and says that I am right. Her niece enters. She was a girl of fourteen, well behaved, intelligent, and extremely modest; I had given her five or six lessons, and since she liked the language and applied herself earnestly she was beginning to speak. Here is the fatal compliment which she addressed to me:

"*Signore, sono incantata di vi vedere in buona salute*" ("Sir, I am delighted to see you in good health").

"I thank you, Mademoiselle, but to translate 'I am delighted' you must say *ho piacere*. And again, to translate 'to see you,' you must say *di vidervi*, not *di vi vedere*."

"I thought, Monsieur, that the *vi* should be put in front."

"No, Mademoiselle, we put it *derrière*" ("behind").[62]

Monsieur and Madame are dying with laughter, the young lady smiling, and I speechless and in despair at having made so gross a blunder; but it was done. I take up a book, sulking and wishing in vain that their laughter would end; but it lasted more than a week. My shameless *double-entendre* spread all over Paris and made me furious; but I at last learned the power of words and for the time being my credit diminished. Crébillon, after laughing heartily, told me that I should have said *après* instead of *derrière*. But if the French laughed over the mistakes I made in speaking their language, I took my revenge by pointing out some absurd usages of theirs.

"Monsieur," I ask, "how is Madame your wife?"

"You do her great honor."

"Her honor has nothing to do with it; I am asking after her health."

A young man in the Bois de Boulogne falls from his horse; I run to pick him up, but he is on his feet and full of life.

"Have you come to any harm?"

"On the contrary, Monsieur."

"Then I take it the fall did you good."

I am calling on Madame la Présidente Charon[63] for the first time; her nephew makes a brilliant entrance; she presents me and tells him my name and country.

"What! You are an Italian, Monsieur? On my word, you make such a good appearance that I would have wagered you were French."

"Monsieur, when I saw you I very nearly fell into the same error—I would have wagered that you were Italian."

"I did not know that I looked Italian."

I was at table at Lady Lambert's,[64] someone remarked

on a cornelian I had on my finger on which the head of Louis XV was engraved to perfection. My ring makes the round of the table, everyone finds the likeness striking; a young Marquise hands me back the ring, saying:

"*Is it really an antique?*"

"You mean the stone? Yes, Madame, it is."

Everyone laughs, and the Marquise, who had the reputation of being intelligent, does not see fit to ask why people are laughing. After dinner the conversation turns to the rhinoceros which was being shown at the fair at Saint-Germain[65] for twenty-four sous a head. "Let us go see it, let us go see it!" We get into a carriage, stop at the fair, and take several turns through the walks, looking for the one in which the rhinoceros was. I was the only man, I had a lady on either arm, the intelligent Marquise was preceding us. At the end of the walk where we had been told the animal was, its master was sitting at the gate to take their money from people who wished to go in. It is true that he was dressed in African costume, enormously fat, and looked like a monster; but the Marquise ought at least to have recognized that he was a man. Not a bit of it.

"Are you the rhinoceros, Monsieur?"

"Step in, Madame, step in."

She sees us choking with laughter, and, seeing the real rhinoceros, she feels obliged to apologize to the African, assuring him that she had never in her life seen a rhinoceros and so he must not be offended if she had made a mistake.

In the greenroom of the Comédie Italienne, where during the intermissions the greatest noblemen are to be found, for they go there to get warm in winter and at all seasons to amuse themselves by talking with the actresses who sit there waiting for their turns in the parts they are playing, I was sitting beside Camilla, Corallina's sister, keeping her laughing by flirting with her. A young councilor, who did not like my monopolizing her attention, attacked me in a conceited tone on an account I had given of an Italian play and showed his ill-humor only too clearly by unjustly criticizing my country. I answered him in a way which he did not expect, keeping my eyes on Camilla, who laughed; and everyone present was intent on the encounter, which, as it was only a duel of wits, had nothing so far to make it disagreeable. But it seemed to become serious when the fop, changing the subject to the police of the city, said that for some time it had been dangerous to walk at night in Paris.

"In the last month," he said, "Paris has seen seven hanged men in the Place de Grève[66] and five of them were Italians. It is astonishing."

"Not at all astonishing," I replied, "for right-thinking people go and get themselves hanged outside their own countries—in proof of which sixty Frenchmen were hanged last year between Naples, Rome, and Venice. Five times twelve makes sixty, and you see that it is only a fair exchange."

The laughter was all on my side, and the young councilor left. An agreeable nobleman who thought I had answered well came up to Camilla and asked her in a whisper who I was, and the acquaintance was made. He was Monsieur de Marigny,[67] brother of Madame la Marquise, whom I was delighted to know so that I could present my brother to him, for I was expecting him from day to day. He was overseer of the royal buildings, and the whole Academy of Painting was under his jurisdiction. I mentioned my brother to him at once, and he promised me that he would be his patron. Another young nobleman struck up a conversation with me, asked me to come to see him, and told me that he was the Duke of Maddaloni.[68] I told him that I had seen him when he was still a child, eight years earlier in Naples, and that Don Lelio Caraffa, his uncle, had been my benefactor. The young Duke was delighted, and, he having repeatedly insisted that I come to see him, we became good friends.

My brother arrived in Paris in the spring of 1751, lodged with me at Madame Quinson's, and began working successfully for private individuals; but since his main idea was to paint a picture for the Academy to judge, I presented him to Monsieur de Marigny, who received him graciously and encouraged him by promising him his protection. So he set to work making sketches, in order not to fail in his purpose.

Signor Morosini, having completed his embassy, had gone back to Venice, and Signor Mocenigo[69] had come in his place. I had been recommended to him by Signor Bragadin and he opened his house to me, as he did to my brother, whom he was concerned to patronize as a Venetian and as a young man who was seeking to make his fortune in France by his talent.

Signor Mocenigo was completely unassuming; he loved gambling, and he always lost; he loved women, and he was unsuccessful because he did not know how to go about it. Two years after he came to Paris he fell in love with Madame de Colande;[70] she would have none of him, and the Venetian Ambassador killed himself.

Madame la Dauphine gave birth to a Duke of Burgundy,[71] and the rejoicings which I witnessed become incredible today when we see what the very same nation is doing against its King.[72] The nation wants to free itself; its ambition is noble and reasonable, and it will bring its enterprise to fulfillment under this same monarch, who, by a strange and unique coincidence, has a soul without ambition, the successor to sixty-five kings, all of them more or less ambitious and jealous of their authority. But is it likely that his soul will pass into the body of his successor?

France has seen her throne occupied by several other monarchs who were indolent, who hated work, avoided difficulties, and were concerned only with their own peace of mind. Secluded at the center of their palace, abandoning despotism to their deputies, who acted in their names, they always remained kings and true monarchs; but the world has never seen a king like this one, who has in good faith put himself at the head of the nation which has assembled to dethrone him. He seems delighted that he has at last reached the point of not having to think of anything except obeying. Hence he was not born to reign, and it seems certain that he regards as his personal enemies all those who, animated by a genuine regard for his interests, do not subscribe to the decrees of the Assembly, all of which are calculated to degrade the King's majesty.

A nation which revolts to cast off the yoke of despotism, which it calls and will always call "tyranny," is not unusual, for it is natural; the proof is that the monarch always expects it and is careful not to drop the reins, for he is certain that the nation will not fail to take the bit in its teeth. What is unusual, unique, and unexampled is a monarch who puts himself at the head of twenty-three millions of his subjects and asks nothing of them except that they leave him the empty name of king and leader, not that he may command them but to execute their orders. "Be legislators," he says to them, "and I will see that all your laws are carried out, provided that you will give me armed assistance against the unruly who will not obey; moreover you will be free to pursue them tooth and claw and tear them to pieces without any sort of legal proceedings; for who could oppose your will? You will actually occupy my place. Those who will object to this will be the nobles and the priests, but they are only one against twenty-five. It is for you to clip their physical and moral wings so that they will have no power to set bounds to your authority or to harm you. To achieve this you will break the pride of the priests by giving ecclesiastical dignities to your equals and by giving them only such stipends as are necessary to support them. As for the nobility, you do not need to impoverish it; you will have done enough if you cease to respect it for its empty titles of birth; there will be no more nobles; follow the example of the wise Turkish regulations;[73] when these gentlemen find that they are no longer dukes or marquises they will moderate their ambition, and the only pleasure which will remain to them will be to spend their money on ostentation, and so much the better for the nation, for their expenditures will pour their money into it, and it will make their money circulate and increase by commerce. As for my ministers, they will be discreet in the future, for they will depend upon you and it will not be for me to judge of their capability; I will choose them myself for form's sake; but I will dismiss as many of them as you please. I shall thus at last see an end to the tyranny under which they oppressed me, by making me do whatever they wished, by very frequently compromising me, and by always burdening the State with debt in my name. I said nothing, but I could bear it no longer. Now at last I am delivered. My wife, and in time my children, my brothers, my cousins who call themselves princes of the blood, will condemn me, I know, but only in their hearts, for they will not dare to speak out to me. I shall instill more fear in them now under your high protection than I did when my only defense was my household, the uselessness of which I have myself helped you demonstrate to the public.

"Those who are discontented and have gone to live outside of the kingdom will return to it one day or another if they feel so inclined, and if not, they must be left to do as they please; they say that they are my true friends, and they make me laugh, for I cannot have any true friends except those who are willing to think as I do. The only important thing in the world, according to them, is the ancient rights of our house to royalty and its concomitant despotism; the only important thing in the world, according to me, is first my peace, second the extirpation of the tyranny which my ministers exercised over me, and third that you should be content. I could also tell you, if I were a charlatan, that what concerns me is the wealth of the kingdom, but I am indifferent to it; it is for you to think of it, it concerns only you, since the kingdom is no longer mine; I am no longer, thanks be to God, King of France; but I am, as you very well put it, King of the French. All that I ask of you is that you make haste, and let me go hunting at last, for I am tired of being bored.''

This historic and completely authentic harangue proves, I believe, that the counterrevolution cannot take place. But it also proves that it will take place when the King changes his way of thinking; and there is no likelihood of that, as there is no likelihood that he can have a successor who will resemble him.

The National Assembly will do whatever it pleases, despite the nobility and the clergy, because it has at its service the unbridled people, the blind executor of its orders. At the present moment the French nation can be regarded as like gunpowder, or like chocolate; both are composed of three ingredients; their goodness could not, and cannot, depend upon anything but the proportions. Time will show us which ingredients were in excess before the Revolution, or which ingredients are in excess now. All I know is that the stench of sulphur is deadly and that vanilla is a poison.

As for the people, the people is the same everywhere: give a thief six francs to shout "Long live the King,'' he will do you the favor, and for three livres[74] he will shout "Death to the King'' a minute later. Put a rabble-rouser at its head and in one day it will destroy a citadel of marble. It has neither laws, nor system, nor religion; its gods are bread, wine, and idleness, it believes that liberty means impunity, that aristocrat means tiger, that demagogue means loving shepherd of his flock. The people, in short, is only an enormous animal which does not reason. The prisons of Paris are overflowing with

prisoners who were all members of the people in revolt.
Let anyone go and say to them, ''I will open the doors
of your prison if you will promise to blow up the hall
in which the Assembly sits,'' they will agree and go at
once. Every people is a union of executioners. The French
clergy knows this; hence the clergy counts on nothing
but the people if it can succeed in inspiring them with
religious zeal, which is perhaps even stronger than zeal
for liberty, which is known only by a process of abstrac-
tion of which material minds are incapable.

It is possible, moreover, not to believe that there is a
single member of the National Assembly who is solely
animated by his country's good. The soul of each of them
is his own self-interest; and there is not one among them
who, if he were king, would have imitated Louis XVI.

The Duke of Maddaloni introduced me to the Roman
Princes Don Marcantonio and Don Giovanni Battista
Borghese[75] who were amusing themselves in Paris and
living without ostentation. I observed that when these
Roman princes are presented at the French court they
are received only under the title of Marquis. For the
same reason the Russian princes who were presented
were not accorded the title of Prince; they were called
Knez.[76] It made no difference to them, for the word
means ''Prince.'' The French court was always scru-
pulously particular in the matter of titles. Simply reading the gazette is enough to show it. The title ''Monsieur''
—which is commonly given everywhere—is used very
sparingly; ''Sieur'' is the form of address to the un-
titled. I noticed that the King called none of his bishops
''Bishop,'' he called them ''Abbé.'' He also affected not
to know any nobleman of his kingdom whose name he did
not find inscribed among those who were in his service.
Yet the haughtiness of Louis XV had only been inculcated into him by his upbringing, it was not natural
to him. When an ambassador presented someone to him,
the person so presented went home certain that the King

of France had seen him, but that was all. He was the most polite of Frenchmen, especially toward ladies and toward his mistresses in public; he dismissed from his favor anyone who dared to fail in respect to them, even in the slightest; and no one more than he possessed the royal virtue of dissimulation, faithfully keeping a secret and delighted when he was sure that he knew something of which everyone else had no inkling. Monsieur d'Éon's being a woman[77] is a small example. The King alone knew, and had always known, that he was a woman, and the whole altercation between the false Chevalier and the Foreign Office was a comedy which the King allowed to play itself out simply because it amused him.

Louis XV was great in everything, and he would not have had a failing if flattery had not forced failings upon him. How could he know that he was at fault when he was always being told that he was the best of kings? About this time the Princess of Ardore gave birth to a son.[78] Her husband, who was the Neapolitan Ambassador, wanted Louis XV to stand godfather to it, and the King consented. The present he gave his godson was a regiment. The new mother would have none of it, because she did not like soldiers. The Maréchal de Richelieu told me that he had never seen the King laugh so much as when he was informed of her refusal.

At the Duchess of Fulvy's[79] I made the acquaintance of Mademoiselle Gaussin,[80] known as Lolotte, who was the mistress of Lord Albemarle,[81] the English Ambassador, a man of brilliant and most noble parts and very generous, who, one night when he was out walking with Lolotte, chided her for praising the beauty of the stars she saw in the sky, since he could not give them to her. If His Lordship had been the English envoy in France at the time of the break between his nation and the French he would have patched things up, and the unhappy war which caused France to lose the whole of Canada[82] would not have occurred. There is no doubt that the harmony between two nations most often depends upon the respective envoys whom they have at the courts which are on the verge or in danger of falling out.

As for his mistress, all who knew her had the same opinion of her. She had all the qualities to deserve to become his wife, and the greatest houses in France did not consider that she needed the title of Lady Albemarle in order to be admitted into their society, and no woman was offended to find her seated at her side because it was common knowledge that she had no title except that of His Lordship's mistress. She passed from her mother's arms into His Lordship's at the age of thirteen, and her conduct was always irreproachable; she had children, whom His Lordship recognized, and she died Countess of Érouville. I will speak of her in due course.

At this same time I met at the house of the Venetian Ambassador Signor Mocenigo a Venetian lady,[83] the widow of the English baronet Wynne, who had just come from London with her children. She had gone there to make sure of her dowry and the estate of her late husband, which could not pass to her children unless they declared that they were of the Anglican religion. She had accomplished this, and she was returning to Venice satisfied with her journey. She had with her her eldest daughter,[84] who was only twelve years old but whose character was already delineated to perfection in her beautiful face. She now lives in Venice, the widow of the late Count Rosenberg, who died in Venice as Ambassador from the Empress-Queen Maria Theresa; she shines in her native country by her discreet behavior, her wit, and her social virtues, which are of the highest. Everyone says of her that her only failing is not being rich. It is true, but no one can complain of it; she feels how great a failing it is only when it prevents her from being generous.

At this time I had some little difficulties with the French guardians of the law.

CHAPTER X

*I run foul of the law in Paris. Mademoiselle
Vesian.*

THE YOUNGEST daughter of my landlady Madame
Quinson often came to my room unsummoned, and
having perceived that she loved me I should have
thought it strange in me if I had taken it into my head to
be cold to her—the more so as she was not without qualities, she had a pretty voice, she read all the new publica-
tions, and rattled away about everything with a vivacity
which was charming. Her age was an ambrosial fifteen
or sixteen.

For the first four or five months there was nothing between us but childish trifling; but happening one night
to come in very late I found her asleep on my bed.
Curious to see if she would wake, I undressed by myself,
I got in, and the rest goes without saying. At daybreak
she went downstairs and got into her own bed. Her name
was Mimi. Two or three hours later chance would have
it that a milliner came with a young girl to see if I
would offer them a breakfast. The girl was pretty, but

having worked too hard with Mimi I told them to go away after spending an hour chatting with them. As they were leaving my room, in comes Madame Quinson with Mimi to make my bed. I sit down to write, and I hear her say:

"Oh, the sluts!"

"To whom do you refer, Madame?"

"The riddle is easily answered; these sheets are ruined."

"I am sorry; excuse me; say nothing and change them."

"Say nothing? Just let the hussies come back!"

She goes downstairs for fresh sheets, Mimi remains, I reproach her for her imprudence, she laughs and says that Heaven has protected the innocence of our doings. From that day on Mimi stood on no ceremony; she came to sleep with me when she felt the need, and I, no less unceremoniously, sent her away when I did not want her, and our little household was as harmonious as possible. Four months after our union Mimi told me she was pregnant; I answered that I did not know anything to do about it.

"Something must be thought of."

"Then think."

"What am I to think of? What will happen, will happen. As for me, I will not give it another thought."

By the fifth or sixth month Mimi's belly leaves her mother in no doubt of the state of things; she takes her by the hair, beats her, forces her to admit it, insists on knowing who is responsible for her girth; and Mimi tells her—and perhaps truthfully—that it is I.

Madame Quinson comes upstairs and enters my room raging. She flings herself into an armchair, recovers her breath, relieves her anger by insulting me, and ends by saying that I must prepare to marry her daughter. At this ultimatum I understand what is afoot, and I reply that I am married in Italy.

"Then why did you go and give my daughter a baby?"

"I assure you I had no such intention, and besides, who told you that it is I?"

"She did, Monsieur, she is certain of it."

"I congratulate her; for my part, I am ready to swear that I am not certain of it."

"Then what?"

"Then nothing. If she is pregnant, she will bear a child."

She goes downstairs threatening me, and from my window I see her get into a hackney coach. The next day I am summoned before the district commissary;[1] I go, and find Madame Quinson in battle array. After asking my name, how long I had been in Paris, and various other things, and writing down all my answers, the commissary asks me if I admit having done the wrong of which I was accused to the daughter of the lady there present.

"Be good enough, Monsieur le Commissaire, to write down my answer word for word."

"Very well."

"I have done no wrong to Mimi, daughter of Madame Quinson here present, and I refer you to Mimi herself, who has always shown me the same friendship that I have shown her."

"She says that you made her pregnant."

"It is possible, but it is not certain."

"She says it is certain, since she has seen no man but you."

"If that is true, she is unfortunate, for a man cannot trust anyone in such a matter except his wife."

"What did you give her to seduce her?"

"Nothing, for it was she who seduced me, and we were of one mind in an instant."

"Was she a virgin?"

"I was not concerned about that either before or afterward; so I have no idea."

"Her mother demands reparation from you, and the law is against you."

"I have no reparation to make to her, and as for the law, I will gladly submit to it when I have seen it and am convinced that I have broken it."

"You have already admitted that. Do you maintain that a man who gets a decent girl with child in a house of which he is an inmate does not transgress the laws of society?"

"I agree, if the mother is deceived; but when she sends her daughter to my own room, must I not suppose that she is prepared to suffer all the consequences of the frequentation without complaining?"

"She sent her to you only to serve you."

"And she served me, even as I served her in the needs of human nature; and if she sends her to me this evening I may do the same, if Mimi is willing, but nothing by force, or outside of my room, for which I have always punctually paid the rent."

"You can say what you please, but you will pay the fine."

"I will pay nothing, for there cannot be a fine to pay when no violation of law has occurred, and if I am found guilty I will appeal to the last jurisdiction and until equity does me justice, for I know that such as I am I shall never have the ill grace to refuse my caresses to a girl who attracts me and who comes to my own room to submit to them, especially when I am certain that she has come with her mother's consent."

Such, or very nearly such, was my interrogation, which I read and signed and which the commissary transmitted to the Lieutenant-General of Police,[2] who summoned me to a hearing and who, after examining the mother and daughter, acquitted me and sentenced the imprudent mother to pay the costs. Nevertheless I yielded to Mimi's tears and defrayed her mother for her lying-in. She gave birth to a boy, whom I allowed to go to the Hôtel-Dieu[3] for the benefit of the nation. After all this Mimi ran away from her mother's house to appear on the stage of the comic opera[4] at the Saint-Laurent fair[5] under Monnet.[6] As she was not known she had no trouble finding a lover who thought her a virgin. I was delighted when I saw her on the stage at the fair. I thought her very pretty.

"I did not know," I said to her, "that you were a musician."

"Like all the rest of us here. The girls at the Paris Opéra don't know a note either; but they sing just the same. All one needs is a good voice."

I asked Mimi to have Patu to supper and he thought her charming. But later she got into trouble. She fell in love with a violinist named Bérard[7] who ran through everything she had, and she disappeared.

The Italian players were then allowed to give parodies of operas and tragedies on their stage, and I made the acquaintance of the famous Chantilly[8] who had been the mistress of the Maréchal de Saxe,[9] and who was known as Favart because the poet Favart[10] had married her. She sang the part of Tonton in the parody of Monsieur de Fontenelle's[11] *Thétis et Pélée*,[12] to tremendous applause. Her charms and her talent won the heart of a man of the greatest merit, whom all France knew by his works. He was the Abbé de Voisenon,[13] with whom I became as intimately acquainted as I had been with Crébillon. All the plays which are generally supposed to be by Madame Favart and which bear her name are by the celebrated Abbé, who was elected to the Academy[14] after my departure. I made his acquaintance, I cultivated it, and he honored me with his friendship. It was from me that he conceived the idea of writing oratorios in verse, which were sung for the first time at the Concert Spirituel[15] at the Tuileries during the few days of the year when religion commands that the theaters be closed. The Abbé, secretly the author of several comedies, was a man whose health was as precarious as his person was small; he was all sparkle and grace, famous for his witticisms, which were cutting and which nevertheless offended no one. He could not have enemies, for his criticism only grazed the skin and did not sting.

"The King was yawning," he told me one day when he had just come back from Versailles, "because he has to go to the Parlement tomorrow to hold a bed of justice." [16]

"Why is it called a 'bed of justice'?"

"I don't know. Perhaps because justice sleeps in it."

I found the image of the Abbé at Prague in the person of Count Franz Hartig,[17] now Minister Pleni- potentiary of the Emperor at the electoral court of Saxony. It was the Abbé who introduced me to Monsieur de Fontenelle, who was then ninety-three years of age and who was not only a wit but also a profound natural scientist, famous too for his epigrams, of which a collec- tion could be made. He could not pay a compliment without enlivening it with wit. I told him that I had come from Italy *expressly* to visit him. He answered, pouncing upon the meaning of the word "express":

"Confess that you have kept me waiting a long time."

A courteous and at the same time a critical answer, for it shows the mendaciousness of my compliment. He presented me with his works.[18] He asked me if I liked French theatrical performances, and I answered that I had seen *Thétis et Pélée* at the Opéra; it was by him, but when I praised it to him he said it was a *tête pelée*.[19]

"Friday at the Théâtre Français," [20] I said, "I saw *Athalie*." [21]

"It is Racine's masterpiece, Monsieur, and Voltaire was wrong when he accused me of criticizing him by attributing to me an epigram of which no one has ever discovered the author and the last two lines of which are very bad:

Garden of the Palais-Royal, Paris

Conversation in the Ladies' Drawing Room

> *Pour avoir fait pis qu'Esther*[22]
> *Comment diable as-tu pu faire?"*

("How the devil did you manage to compose something worse than *Esther?*")[23]

I was told that Monsieur de Fontenelle had been the lover of Madame de Tencin[24] and that Monsieur d'Alembert[25] had been the fruit of their intimacy. Le Rond was the name of his foster father. I met D'Alembert at Madame de Graffigny's.[26] That great philosopher had in the highest degree the talent of never seeming learned when he was in an agreeable company of people who were not scientists. He also had the art of imparting intelligence to those who argued with him.

The second time I returned to Paris, on my flight from the Leads,[27] I looked forward to seeing Fontenelle again, and he died two weeks after I arrived, at the beginning of the year 1757.

The third time[28] I returned to Paris, intending to stay there until my death, I counted on the friendship of Monsieur d'Alembert, and he died just two weeks after the day I arrived, toward the end of the year 1783. I shall not see Paris again, nor France; I am too much afraid of the executions of an unbridled people.

Count Loss,[29] Ambassador of the King of Poland and Elector of Saxony[30] in Paris, ordered me in this year 1751 to translate into Italian a French opera which would allow for great transformation scenes and for great ballets connected with the subject of the opera, and I chose *Zoroastre*[31] by Monsieur de Cahusac. I had to fit the Italian words to the French music of the choruses. The music remains beautiful, but the Italian poetry did not come off well. Nevertheless I received from the generous monarch a handsome gold snuffbox, and greatly pleased my mother.[32]

At this same time Mademoiselle Vesian[33] came to Paris

with her brother, in the first flush of her youth, well born, well brought up, very pretty, completely unspoiled, and as charming as possible. Her father, who had served in the army in France, had died in Parma, his native country; left an orphan, and having nothing to live on, his daughter followed the advice someone gave her to sell everything and make her way as best she could to Versailles with her brother to move the Minister of War[34] to pity and obtain something. Leaving the diligence, she told a coachman to take her to a furnished room near the Théâtre Italien, and the coachman took her to the Hôtel de Bourgogne[35] in the Rue Mauconseil, where I was lodging.

I was told the next morning that the room on the rear of my floor was occupied by two young Italians, a brother and sister who had just arrived, both very handsome but having with them only what could be contained in a small traveling bag. Italians, just arrived, good-looking, poor, and my neighbors were five reasons for my going in person to see what it was all about. I knock, I knock again, and a youth in his shirt comes and opens the door, begging my pardon for being in his shirt.

"It is I who must ask your pardon. I come as an Italian and your neighbor to offer you my services."

I see a mattress on the floor, on which, as the brother of the pair, the youth had slept, and I see a bed hidden by curtains in which I suppose the sister must be, and I say to her without seeing her that if I had thought she would still be in bed at nine o'clock in the morning I would not have made bold to knock at her door. She answers, without appearing, that she had slept longer than usual because she had gone to bed exhausted by the journey and that she would get up if I would be so kind as to give her time.

"I will go to my room, Mademoiselle, and you will be so good as to have me called as soon as you consider yourself fit to be seen. I am your neighbor."

A quarter of an hour later, instead of sending for me she arrives herself and making me a pretty curtsy says that she has come to return my visit and that her brother will come as soon as he is ready. I thank her, I ask her to be seated, I at once inform her candidly of the interest she inspires in me, she is delighted, and she does not wait for many questions to tell me the whole short and simple story which I have just described; she ends it by saying that she must try that day to find a cheaper lodging, for she has only six francs left and nothing to sell. She had to pay a month in advance for the room she was occupying. I ask her if she has any letters of recommendation, and she draws from her pocket a parcel of papers in which I soon see seven or eight testimonials to her father's services, baptismal certificates for him, herself, and her brother, death certificates, testimonials to good conduct and poverty, and passports. That is all.

"I will wait, with my brother," she says, "on the Minister of War, and I hope that he will take pity on us."

"You know no one?"

"No one. You are the first person in France to whom I have told my story."

"We are fellow countrymen. You are commended to me by your situation and your face, and I will be your adviser, if you are willing. Give me your papers and let me make inquiries. Tell no one that you are in want, do not leave this house, and here are two louis which I lend you."

She accepts them, overcome with gratitude.

Mademoiselle Vesian was a brunette sixteen years of age with every attraction, though not a perfect beauty. Speaking French well, she told me her pitiful situation without groveling and without the timidity which seems to come from fear that the listener is disposed to take advantage of the distress which is being confided to him.

She seemed neither humiliated nor bold; she was not without hope, and she did not boast of her courage; with a noble bearing, and with no sign that she was trying to make a parade of virtue, she yet had something which discouraged the libertine; and the proof is that though her eyes, her fine figure, her white, fresh complexion, her dishabille all tempted me, from the very first moment she summoned up my better feelings and not only did I make no attempt on her but I promised myself that I would not be the first to set her on the wrong road. I put off until another time a speech by which I should learn her attitude in that respect and which would perhaps make me adopt a different course of conduct; but on this first occasion I told her only that she had come to a city in which her destiny was bound to declare itself and in which all the qualities she possessed, and which appeared to be gifts of nature to help her make her fortune, might be the causes of her irreparable ruin.

"You have," I said, "come to a city in which rich men scorn all light women except those who have sacrificed their virtue to them. If you have virtue and are resolved to keep it, prepare to suffer poverty, and if you feel that you have a mind above prejudice and ready to consent to anything to secure you a comfortable position, at least try not to let yourself be deceived. Put no trust in the gilded words which a man full of ardor will address to you to obtain your favors; believe him when deeds will have preceded words, for after enjoyment the fire goes out, and you will find that you are betrayed. Beware, too, of assuming disinterested feelings in those whom you see overwhelmed by your charms: they will give you false coin in abundance to persuade you to give them good. Do not be compliant. For my part, I am sure that I will do you no harm, and I hope I shall do you good; and to reassure you, I will treat you like my sister, for I am still too young to treat you as a father:

I would not be talking to you in this way if I did not find you charming.''

Her brother then entered, and I saw a handsome youth of eighteen years, very well built, but entirely lacking in style, speaking very little, and with a countenance that promised nothing. We breakfasted, and when I tried to learn from him what course he wished to take, he answered that he was ready to do anything to earn an honest living.

''Have you any particular talent?''

''I write fairly well.''

''That is something. If you go out, beware of everyone; you must not go to a coffeehouse, and you must speak to no one in the street. Eat in your room with your sister, and arrange at once to have a small room for yourself on the fourth floor. Write something in French today to give to me tomorrow morning, and hope. As for you, Mademoiselle, here are books, choose among them. I have your papers, I shall have something to tell you tomorrow, for I come home very late.''

She chose some books and took her leave in the most well-bred manner, after saying that she had complete confidence in me.

Very much inclined to be of use to the girl, I talked of her situation wherever I went all that day, and everywhere I heard both men and women say that if she was pretty some good fortune could not fail to befall her, and that in the meanwhile she should take what steps she could; as for the brother, I was told that if he could write a place would be found for him in some office. I considered finding a woman of station in a position to recommend her to Monsieur d'Argenson and to introduce her to him. It was the best course; I felt that I could support her meanwhile, and I asked Silvia to mention the matter to Madame de Monconseil,[36] who had great influence with the Minister of War. She prom-

ised me she would do so, and she asked to see the young
lady first.

I got home at eleven o'clock, and seeing a light in
Mademoiselle Vesian's room I knocked and she opened
the door, saying that she had not gone to bed in the
hope of seeing me. I told her all that I had done for
her, and I found her ready for anything and overwhelmed with gratitude. She talked of her situation with
an air of noble indifference which was maintained only
to restrain tears which she would not allow to flow; but
I saw her eyes, which the gathering tears made brighter,
the sight wrung a sigh from me, and I felt ashamed.
Our talk continued for two hours. In the course of the
conversation I managed decorously to bring it out that
she had never loved and so was worthy of a lover who
would recompense her properly if she sacrificed her
virtue to him. It was absurd to suppose that the recompense should be marriage; the girl had never taken the
false step, but she did not play the prude by telling me
that she would not have taken it for all the money in
the world; her one hope was that she would not give
herself inconsiderately or for very little.

I sighed as I heard her speaking so sensibly and with
a sincerity beyond her years, and I burned. I remembered poor Lucia at Pasiano, my remorse, and the wrong
I had done in acting toward her as I had acted, and I
saw myself now sitting beside a lamb who was bound
to be the prey of some hungry wolf and who had not
been brought up to end so and whose education had
given her sentiments which deserved to be fostered by
virtue and honor. I sighed because I was in a position
neither to provide her with a competence by taking her
illegitimately, nor to be her safeguard. I even saw that
by becoming her protector[37] I should have done her
more harm than good and that instead of helping her
to a respectable competence I should perhaps have contributed to her ruin. There she was, sitting beside me;

and there was I, talking sentiment to her and never love, kissing her hand too often and even her arm, and never proceeding to a decision or a beginning which would too quickly have reached its end and which would then have obliged me to keep her; after that, there would be no good for which she could hope or any way for me to get rid of her. I have loved women even to madness, but I have always preferred my freedom to them. When I have been in danger of sacrificing it, only chance has saved me.

It was three hours after midnight when I took leave of Mademoiselle Vesian, who, since she could not suppose that my restraint was the result of my virtue, must have attributed it either to shame or to impotence or to some secret malady; but not to a lack of inclination, for my amorous fire had sufficiently shown itself in my eyes and in the absurd avidity with which I kissed her hands and her arms. Such was I forced to be with that charming girl, only to repent of it afterward. As I wished her a happy slumber, I said that we would dine together the next day.

We dined in high spirits, and her brother went for a walk after dinner. The windows of my room, from which we saw the whole of the Rue Française, also permitted us to see all the carriages which were arriving at the entrance to the Théâtre Italien, where there was a great crowd that day. I ask my fellow countrywoman if she would be pleased to let me take her to the play; she begs me to do so; I find her a place in the amphitheater and I leave her there, saying that we would meet again at the house at eleven o'clock. I did not want to stay with her, in order to avoid all the questions I should be asked, for the more simply she was dressed the more interest she aroused.

After supping at Silvia's I go home, and at the door I see a most elegant carriage; I am told that it belongs to a young nobleman who had supped with Mademoiselle

Vesian and who was still there. So she was launched. What do I care? I go to bed.

I get up the next morning, I see a hackney coach stop at the door, a young man in morning dress gets out, comes upstairs, and I hear him enter my neighbor's room. It is nothing to me. I dress to leave, and in comes Vesian to tell me that he is not going to his sister's room because the same nobleman who had taken them to supper was with her.

"That is to be expected."

"He is rich, and extremely well-mannered. He wants to take us to Versailles himself, and to get me a position at once."

"Who is he?"

"I have no idea."

I put her papers in an envelope, which I seal, and give it to him to deliver to his sister, and I go out. I come back at three o'clock, and the hostess hands me a note which the young lady, who had gone, had told her to give me. I go to my room, I open the note, and I find two louis and these words: "I return the money you lent me, and I thank you. The Count of Narbonne[38] is concerned for me and certainly wishes only to help me, as he does my brother, and I will write you everything from the house in which he wishes me to live and where he will see that I want for nothing; but I have the highest regard for your friendship and I beg you to continue it toward me. My brother remains in the small room on the fourth floor, and my room is mine for the whole month, for I have paid for everything."

Her leaving her brother tells the story. She moved very fast. I decide to have nothing more to do with it, and I repent of having left her untouched for the young Count, who will make God knows what of her. I dress to go to the Français and to find out what I could about Narbonne, for, though I was angry, I felt some interest in learning the whole story. At the Comédie Française the first comer tells me that Narbonne is the son of a rich father on whom he is dependent, that he is riddled with debt, and that he frequents all the light women in Paris.

I went to two or three theaters every day, more to see Narbonne, whom I was curious to know, than for the sake of La Vesian, whom I thought I despised, and a week having gone by without my having managed to learn anything or even to see the young nobleman, I was beginning to forget the incident when Vesian came to my room at eight in the morning to tell me that his sister was in hers and that she wished to speak with me. I go without losing a moment, and I find her very sad and with her eyes swollen. She told her brother to go out for a walk, and she spoke to me as follows:

"Monsieur de Narbonne, whom I believed to be upright because I needed him to be so, sat down beside me where you left me, told me that my face interested him, and asked who I was. I told him all that I told you. You promised me that you would think about my situation; but Narbonne said there was no need to think and that he would see to everything immediately. I believed him; I was his dupe; he deceived me; he is a scoundrel."

As she could no longer hold back her tears I went to the window to give her time to shed them unobserved, and a few minutes later I returned to her side.

"Tell me everything, my dear Vesian, and unburden yourself freely. Do not think that you are guilty toward me, for when all is said and done I am the cause of your misfortune. You would not feel the grief which is rending your soul if I had not been so thoughtless as to take you to the theater."

"Alas, Monsieur, do not say that; am I to hold it against you that you believed me virtuous? To be brief: He promised to do everything for me on condition that I give him a proof of the confidence which he deserved that I should place in him; the proof was that I should go to lodge with a woman of station in a small house which he rented, and above all without my brother, for spite could think him my lover. Alas for me! Could I go there without asking your advice? He told me—and he lied to me—that the respectable woman to whose house he was taking me would herself escort me to Versailles, where he would arrange for my brother to be, so that we could be presented to the Minister together. After supper he left, saying that he would come for me the next morning in a hackney coach, and he gave me two louis and a gold watch, which I thought I could accept without putting myself under any obligation to a rich nobleman who said that he wished to do me good without any other design.

"When we reached his small house he introduced me to a woman whose appearance did not seem to me respectable, and he kept me there all this week, coming, going, leaving, returning, but never reaching a decision; when at last today, at seven o'clock in the morning, the woman told me that for family reasons the Count had been obliged to go to the country and that there was a hackney coach at the door to take me to the Hôtel de Bourgogne, from which he had brought me and where he would come to see me on his return. She told me, pretending regret, that I must leave the gold watch he had given me with her, for she had to return it to the watchmaker, whom the Count had forgotten to pay for it. I handed it to her instantly, answering not a word; I wrapped what I had brought with me in a kerchief, and returned here half an hour ago."

A minute later I asked her if she hoped to see him again on his return from the country.

"See him again! Speak to him again! Not I!"

I quickly went back to the window to give her tears scope again, for she was choking. Never did an unhappy girl in a lamentable situation so touch me. Pity took the place of the love she had inspired in me a week earlier, and though she did not accuse me of it I recognized that I was the chief cause of her misfortune; hence I felt obliged to show her the same friendship. Narbonne's infamous proceedings so disgusted me that if I had known where to find him alone there is no doubt that, without saying anything to La Vesian, I would have gone and attacked him.

I took care not to ask her for the detailed story of the week she had spent in the small house. It was a story which I knew by heart without needing to reduce her to humiliation by indirectly forcing her to tell it to me. In the return of the watch I saw the infamy, the low deceit, the miserliness, the shame of the base Narbonne. She left me at the window for more than a quarter of an hour; I returned to her when she called me, and I found her less sad. In great sorrow the relief of tears is an infallible remedy. She begged me to have the heart of a father toward her, assuring me that she would not again be unworthy of it, and to tell her what she should do.

"As things now stand," I said, "you must not only forget Narbonne's crime, you must also forget the error you made in enabling him to commit it. What is done is done, my dear Vesian; you must love yourself again and recover the expression which lightened your beautiful face a week ago. Honesty, frankness, good faith were visible in it then, and the noble self-assurance which arouses sympathy in those who appreciate its charms. All this must appear in your face again, for only this commands the interest of decent people, and you need their interest now more than ever. As for me, my friendship can do little, but I promise you the full extent of it when I tell you that you have a claim upon it which you did not have a week ago. I promise you that I will never leave you until you are certain of a secure future. At this moment I do not know what more to say; but be sure that I will take thought for you."

"Ah, my dear friend, if you promise me that, I ask no more. Alas, there is no one who takes thought for me!"

The reflection affected her so much that I saw her chin tremble and the onslaught of anxiety which made her faint away. I took care of her without summoning anyone, until I saw her restored and calm. I told her true or improvised stories about the snares set by those whose only occupation in Paris was to deceive girls; I told her amusing stories to cheer her, and I ended by saying that she ought to thank Heaven for what had happened to her with Narbonne, for she needed the misfortune to teach her once and for all to be more circumspect in future.

Throughout this conversation, by which I instilled true balm into her soul, I had no difficulty in abstaining from taking her hand and showing her signs of love, for to tell the truth the only feeling which animated me was pity. It was with genuine pleasure that, at the end of two hours, I saw her convinced and with courage enough to bear her misfortune like a heroine. She suddenly rises; she looks at me with an expression between confidence and doubt, and she asks me if I have any pressing business to attend to that day; I answer no.

"Then," she says, "take me somewhere outside of Paris, where breathing the country air will give me back the appearance which you consider I must have in order to enlist the interest of those who see me. If I can manage to sleep peacefully this coming night, I feel that I can be happy again."

"I thank you for your confidence in me; I will dress, and we will go somewhere; in the meanwhile your brother will come back."

"What does my brother have to do with it?"

"Remember, my dear friend, that you must make Narbonne ashamed and miserable all his life by your conduct. Consider that if he ever learns that on the very day on which he sent you away you went to the country alone with me, he will exult and say that he treated you as you deserved. But accompanied by your brother, and going with me your fellow countryman, you will give malice no ground and slander no occasion."

The docile child blushes and agrees to wait for her brother; he came back a quarter of an hour later, and I at once sent for a hackney coach. Just as we were getting into it Balletti turns up to call on me. After introducing him to the young lady I invite him to join the party; he accepts, and we go to Le Gros Caillou[39] to eat eel stew, boiled beef, an omelet, and boned and broiled pigeons; the gaiety which I managed to inspire in the young lady made up for the rather helter-skelter dinner.

After dinner Vesian went for a walk by himself, and his sister remained alone with us. I saw with pleasure that Balletti thought her agreeable, and without consulting her I determine to persuade my friend to teach her to dance. I inform him of her situation, of her reason for leaving Italy, the slight hope she had of obtaining a pension at court, and of her need for some employment suitable to her sex and by which she could live decently. Balletti reflects and says that he is ready to do anything, and after carefully considering the young lady's figure and frame of mind, he assures her that he will find a way to induce Lany[40] to take her for the ballets at the Opéra.

"Then," said I, "you must begin giving her lessons tomorrow. Mademoiselle is staying in the room next to mine."

The extemporized plan thus quickly decided upon, La Vesian burst out laughing at the idea of becoming a dancer, a thing which had never entered her head.

"But can one learn to dance so quickly? I can only dance the minuet, and I have a good ear for quadrilles; but I don't know a single step."

"The ballet girls at the Opéra," Balletti answers, "know no more than you do."

"And how much shall I ask from Monsieur Lany, for I do not think I can expect much?"

"Nothing. For ballet girls are not paid at the Opéra."

"Then what will I live on?"

"Don't worry about that. Such as you are, you will immediately find ten rich noblemen who will offer you their homage. Your part will be to choose wisely. We shall see you covered with diamonds."

"Now I understand. One of them will take me and keep me as his mistress."

"Exactly. It's much better than a pension of four hundred francs, which you will perhaps only obtain after a great deal of effort."

In her astonishment she looked at me to find out if all this was serious; and Balletti having gone off, I assured her that it was the best course she could take unless she preferred the dreary position of chambermaid to some great lady whom we might find for her. She answered that she would not be a chambermaid to the Queen herself.

"And a ballet girl at the Opéra?"

"Better that."

"You are laughing?"

"It's enough to make anyone die laughing. Mistress of a great nobleman, who will cover me with diamonds! I will choose the oldest."

"Right you are, my dear friend; but take care you do not cuckold him."

"I promise you I will be true to him. He will find a post for my brother."

"Of course."

"But until I get into the Opéra and my old lover appears, who will give me enough to live on?"

"I, Balletti, and all my friends—and all of us for no other reward than to see your beautiful face, to be sure that you are behaving as you should, and that we are contributing to your happiness. Are you convinced?"

"Completely convinced; I will do nothing but what you tell me to do. Only be always my friend."

We returned to Paris at nightfall. I left La Vesian at the Hôtel de Bourgogne and went off to sup with my friend, who at table made his mother promise to speak to Lany. Silvia said it was better than begging a wretched pension from the War Ministry. The talk then turned to a plan which was being considered by the management of the Opéra and which consisted in putting up for sale all the appointments for ballet girls and chorus girls; the intention, in fact, was to set a high price on them, for the more expensive they were the more the girls who bought them would be esteemed. This project, which was part of the general dissoluteness of the times, nevertheless had an appearance of wisdom. It would in a way have ennobled a breed of women who continue to be contemptible.

In those days at the Opéra I noticed a number of girls, both dancers and singers, who were ugly and untalented, yet all of whom were living comfortably; for it is inevitable that a girl who is there must, by her position, renounce what the lower classes call "virtue," for if one of them tried to live virtuously she would die of starvation. But if a new girl is clever enough to remain virtuous for a month her fortune is made, for then the noblemen who try to conquer such an exemplary virtue are among the most eminent. A great nobleman is delighted if the audience names him when the girl appears. He even forgives her some infidelities provided she does not throw away what he gives her and that she does not cuckold him too brazenly; the nobleman who keeps her seldom objects to her fancy man, and in any case he never goes to sup with his mistress without letting her know in advance. What chiefly makes French noblemen eager to have a girl at the Opéra to their credit is the fact that all the girls there belong to the King as members of his Royal Academy of Music.

I came home at eleven o'clock, and seeing Vesian's door ajar I went in. She was in bed.

"I'll get up, for I want to talk with you."

"Stay in bed, and you can talk with me just as well. I find you more beautiful."

"Then I am glad."

"What do you want to say to me?"

"Nothing—just to talk about the profession I am entering. I am about to practice virtue in order to find a man who loves it only to destroy it."

"That is it exactly; and believe me, everything in this life is much the same. We refer everything to ourselves, and each of us is a tyrant. That is why the best of mortals is he who is tolerant. I am happy to see you becoming a philosopher."

"How does one do that?"

"By thinking."

"How long?"

"All one's life."

"Then it's never over?"

"Never; but one learns what one can and gains all the share of happiness of which one is capable."

"And this happiness—in what effect is it felt?"

"It is felt in all the pleasures which the philosopher can procure for himself, and when he considers that he has procured them by his own efforts and by overriding all prejudices."

"What is pleasure, and what is prejudice?"

"Pleasure is immediate sensual enjoyment; it is a

complete satisfaction which we grant to our senses in all that they desire; and when, exhausted or wearied, our senses want rest, whether to catch breath or to revive, pleasure becomes imagination; imagination takes pleasure in reflecting on the happiness which its tranquillity procures it. The philosopher is he who refuses no pleasure which does not produce greater pains and who knows how to create pleasures.''

''And you say this depends on overriding prejudices. What is prejudice, and how can we override it and where can we find the strength to do so?''

''There is no greater question in moral philosophy, my dear friend, than the one which you ask me; hence it is a study which lasts all our lifetime. But I will tell you briefly that prejudice means every so-called duty for which we find no reason in nature.''

''Then the principal occupation of the philosopher must be to study nature?''

''It is the only thing he must do. The wisest man is he who is least mistaken.''

''Who, according to you, is the philosopher who has been least often mistaken?''

''Socrates.''

''But he was sometimes mistaken.''

''Yes, in metaphysics.''

''Oh, that's no matter. I think he could get on without that.''

''You are wrong; for ethics itself is the metaphysics of natural science, since everything is nature. For which reason I allow you to call any man a fool who comes and tells you that he has made a new discovery in metaphysics. But now I must be becoming obscure to you. Think, be guided by maxims which follow from sound reasoning, always have your happiness in view, you will be happy.''

''I like the lesson you have given me much better than

the dancing lesson Balletti is to give me tomorrow, for I foresee that I will be bored, and I am not bored in your company now.''

''What tells you that you are not bored?''

''The desire I feel that you should not leave me.''

''May I perish, my dear Vesian, if a philosopher ever defined boredom better than you have done. What a pleasure! How is it that I want to prove it to you by kissing you?''

''It is because our souls cannot be happy except when they are in harmony with our senses.''

''What do I hear, divine Vesian? Your mind is giving birth.''

''It is you, my divine friend, who are the midwife, and I am grateful to you for it, and so much so that I feel the same desire that you do.''

''Then let us satisfy our desire, my dear, and embrace each other without restraint.''

In such considerations we spent the whole night, and what assured us at dawn that our joy had been perfect was that it never occurred to us that the door of the room was open—proof that we never thought we had any reason to go and shut it.

Balletti gave her a few lessons, she was accepted at the Opéra, and she appeared there only two or three months, always governing herself by the precepts which I had inculcated in her and which her intelligence made her realize were golden. She refused all who came to conquer her, because they all in some way resembled Narbonne. The one she chose was a nobleman different from all the rest because he did for her what none of them would ever have done. He made her give up the stage at once. He took a small box for her, which she occupied every day there was a performance at the Opéra and in which she received her patron and all his friends. He was the Count de Tressan, if I am not mistaken, or de Trean,[41] for the name wavers in my memory. She remained with him until his death, always happy and making him happy. She still lives in Paris, dependent upon no one, for her lover settled an income on her. No one talks of her now, for in Paris a woman of fifty-six is as if she no longer existed. After she left the Hôtel de Bourgogne I did not speak to her again; when I saw her covered with diamonds, our souls greeted each other. Her brother was given a post, but the only profession he practiced was being married to La Piccinelli,[42] who may be dead by now.

CHAPTER XI

The beautiful O-Morphi. Imposture by a
painter. I practice cabalism for the Duchess
of Chartres. I leave Paris. My stay in Dresden
and my departure from there.

AT THE Saint-Laurent fair my friend Patu took a
notion to sup with a Flemish actress named Morphy[1]
and invited me to join him; I accepted. La Morphy did
not tempt me; but that did not matter—a friend's pleasure is motive enough. So he offered her two louis, which
were at once accepted, and after the opera we went to
the beauty's house in the Rue des Deux Portes Saint-
Sauveur. After supper Patu wanted to sleep with her,
and I asked for a couch for myself in some corner of
the house. La Morphy's younger sister, a pretty, ragged,
dirty little creature, said she would give me her bed but
wanted a half écu;[2] I promised it to her. She takes me
to a closet in which I see only a mattress on three or
four boards.

"Do you call that a bed?"

"It's my bed."

"I don't want it, and you shan't have the half écu."

"Were you going to undress for bed?"

"Of course."

"What an idea! We haven't any bedclothes."

"Then you sleep with your clothes on?"

"Certainly not."

"Very well, go to bed yourself and you shall have the half écu. I want to see you."

"All right, but you mustn't do anything to me."

"Not a thing."

She undresses, lies down, and covers herself with an old curtain. She was thirteen years old. I look at the girl; I send every prejudice packing; I see her neither slovenly nor in rags, I find her a perfect beauty. I make to examine her completely, she refuses, she laughs, she resists; but a whole écu makes her as mild as a lamb, and since her only fault is being dirty I wash her all over with my own hands; my reader knows that admiration is inseparable from another kind of appreciation, and I find the little Morphy willing to let me do whatever I please, except what I did not want to do. She warns me that she will not permit that—for that, according to her elder sister, was worth twenty-five louis.[3] I tell her we will haggle about it some other time; and thereupon she gives me every indication of her future consent by consenting most freely to everything I could want.

The little Helen[4] whom I had enjoyed, though leaving her a virgin, gave her sister the six francs and told her what she hoped from me. She calls me aside before I leave and says that, since she needs money, she will come down a little. I answer that I will return and talk to her the next day. I wanted Patu to see the girl as I had seen her, to make him admit that it was impossible to see a more consummate beauty. Helen, white as a lily, had everything that nature and the art of the painter could combine in the way of perfect beauty. In addition she had a beauty of countenance which instilled the most delicious peace into the soul which beheld her. She was blonde. I went there that evening, and not having reached a suitable price, I gave her twelve francs in exchange for her sister's lending her her bed, and I finally came to an agreement to keep giving her twelve francs each time until I decided to pay the six hundred. The rate of interest was usurious, but La Morphy was a Greek[5] by nature, and she had no scruples in the matter. It is certain that I would never have brought myself to pay the twenty-five louis, for I should have thought that I was the loser by it. The elder Morphy thought me the greatest of dupes, since in two months I had spent three hundred francs for nothing. She attributed it to my stinginess. Stinginess indeed! I paid six louis to have her painted naked by a German painter,[6] who produced a living likeness. She was lying on her stomach, resting her arms and her bosom on a pillow and holding her head as if she were lying on her back. The skillful artist had drawn her legs and thighs in such a way that the eye could not wish to see more. I had him write under it *O-Morphi*.[7] The word is not Homeric, but it is Greek none the less. It means "beautiful."

But what are not the secret paths of all-powerful destiny! My friend Patu wanted a copy of the portrait. Can one refuse such a thing to a friend? The same painter made it, went to Versailles, and showed it, with several other portraits, to Monsieur de Saint-Quentin,[8] who showed them to the King, who became curious to know if the portrait of the "Greek Girl" was a true likeness. If it was, the monarch claimed the right to sentence the original to quench the fire which it had kindled in his heart.

Monsieur de Saint-Quentin asked the painter if he could bring the original of the "Greek Girl" to Versailles, and he answered that he thought it perfectly possible. He called on me to tell me of the proposal, and I thought it excellent. La Morphy jumped for joy when I told her that she was to go to court with her sister under conduct of the painter and there submit to the decrees of Providence. So one fine morning she cleaned up her little sister, dressed her decently, and went to Versailles with the painter, who told her to stroll in the park until he came back.

He came back with the Groom of the Bedchamber, who told him to go to the inn and wait for the two sisters, whom he took to a garden house and shut them in. I learned the next morning from La Morphy herself that a half hour later the King came, alone, asked her if she was Greek, drew the portrait from his pocket, looked carefully at her younger sister, and said:

"I have never seen a better likeness."

He sat down, took her on his knees, caressed her here and there, and, after his royal hand had assured him that she was a virgin, gave her a kiss. O-Morphi looked at him and laughed.

"What are you laughing at?"

"Because you are as like a six-franc piece[9] as two peas."

At this ingenuousness the monarch burst out laughing and asked her if she would like to stay at Versailles; she answered that he must arrange it with her sister, and her sister told the King that nothing could make her happier. The King then left, locking them in. A quarter of an hour later Saint-Quentin came and let them out, put the younger sister in an apartment on the ground floor in the custody of a woman, and went off with the elder sister to find the German, to whom he gave fifty louis for the portrait, but nothing to La Morphy. He only took her address, assuring her that she would hear from him. She received a thousand louis, which she showed me the next day. The honest German gave me twenty-five louis for my portrait and made me another, copying it from the one Patu had. He offered to paint for me, gratis, all the pretty girls whose portraits I might wish to have. What gave me the most pleasure was seeing the joy of the worthy Flemish girl, who, gazing at five hundred double louis,[10] thought she was rich, and who considered me the first cause of her good fortune.

"I didn't expect so much, for it's true that Helen is pretty but I didn't believe what she told me about you. Is it possible, my dear friend, that you left her a virgin? Tell me the truth."

"If she was, I can assure you that she did not cease to be by my doing."

"She certainly was, for you're the only one I gave her to. What a man of honor! She was destined for the King. Who would have thought it? God disposes. I admire your virtue. Come here and let me kiss you."

O-Morphi (for so the King always called her) pleased him even more by an ingenuousness of which the monarch had no notion than by her beauty, though it was as perfect as possible. He put her in an apartment in the Parc aux Cerfs,[11] where His Majesty kept nothing short of a seraglio and which no one was allowed to enter except ladies presented at court. At the end of a year[12] the girl bore a son, who became no one knows what, for Louis XV would never hear anything about his bastards as long as Queen Marie was alive.

O-Morphi fell into disgrace after three years. The King gave her four hundred thousand francs, which she brought as a dowry to a staff officer[13] in Brittany. I saw a son from this marriage at Fontainebleau in the year 1783. He was twenty-five years of age, and he did not know the story of his mother, whose living image he was. I asked him to give her my compliments and wrote my name on his tablets.[14]

The cause of the beauty's disgrace was the malice of Madame de Valentinois,[15] sister-in-law of the Prince of Monaco. During a visit to the Parc aux Cerfs, that lady, who is well known in Paris, told O-Morphi to make the King laugh by asking him how he treated his old wife.[16] O-Morphi, who was too simple-minded, asked the King the impertinent and insulting question, which so astonished the monarch that, rising and looking daggers at her,

"You miserable wretch," he said, "who got you to ask me that question?"

O-Morphi tremblingly told him the truth; the King turned his back on her and never saw her again. The Countess of Valentinois was not seen at court again until two years later. Louis XV, who knew that he failed his wife as a husband, wanted at least to make it up to her as King. Woe to anyone who dared fail in respect to her!

Despite all the wit of the French, Paris is and will always be the city in which impostors will succeed. When an imposture is discovered everyone shrugs and laughs, and the impostor laughs even more, for he has already become rich, *recto stat fabula talo* ("the play is a hit").[17] This characteristic which makes the nation fall into a trap so easily comes from the supreme influence which fashion exercises over it. The imposture is new; so it becomes fashionable. It is enough if the thing has the power to surprise by being out of the ordinary, and everyone welcomes it for everyone fears he will look foolish if he says "It is impossible." In France alone is it true that only natural philosophers know that between the possibility and the act there is infinity, whereas in Italy the meaning of the axiom is firmly fixed in everyone's mind. A painter had a great success for a time by announcing that he could paint a person's portrait without seeing him; all that he asked was full information from the person who ordered the portrait; he had to describe the countenance to him so precisely that the painter could not possibly go wrong. The result was that the portrait was even more to the informant's credit than to the painter's; it also followed that the informant had to say that the portrait was a perfect

likeness, for if he said anything else the painter alleged
the most legitimate excuse: he said that if the portrait
was not a good likeness the fault lay with the person
who had not been able to describe the subject's countenance to him. I was surprised at Silvia's when someone
retailed this piece of news, but—be it noted—without
ridiculing it or casting doubt on the skill of the painter,
who, so he had heard, had already painted over a hundred portraits, all excellent likenesses. Everyone said
it was brilliant. I alone, choking with laughter, said it
was an imposture. The man who had told the story took
offense and offered to wager me a hundred louis; but
I laughed again, because it was a question on which one
could not wager without running the risk of being
duped.

"But the portraits are likenesses."

"I do not believe it; and if they are likenesses there
is trickery."

Only Silvia, who was of my opinion, accepts his proposal to go and dine at the painter's with him and myself. We go, and we see a quantity of portraits, all said
to be likenesses; but since we did not know the originals
it meant nothing.

"Could you paint my daughter's portrait for me,
Monsieur," Silvia asked him, "without seeing her?"

"Yes, Madame, if you are sure you can describe her
countenance to me."

We exchanged a look, and that was the end of it.
Politeness forbade us to say more. The painter, whose
name was Sanson,[18] gave us a good dinner, and his niece,
who was intelligent, pleased me extremely. As I was in
a good humor I held her attention by making her laugh
a great deal. The painter told us that his favorite meal
was supper and that he would be honored if we would
often give him the pleasure of our company at it. He
showed us more than fifty letters from Bordeaux, Toulouse, Lyons, Rouen, Marseilles, the writers of which

ordered portraits from him, giving him descriptions of the faces they wanted him to paint; I read three or four of them with the greatest pleasure. He was paid in advance.

Two or three days later at the fair I saw his pretty niece, who reproached me for not coming to supper at her uncle's. The niece was very attractive and, flattered by her reproach, I went there the next day, and in a week or so the business became serious. I fell in love with her, and the niece, who was intelligent and was not in love, granted me nothing. Nevertheless I hoped, and I saw that I was snared.

I was drinking coffee alone in my room and thinking of her when I am visited by a young man whom I cannot place. He tells me he has had the honor to sup with me at the house of the painter Sanson.

"Ah yes, excuse me, Monsieur, I did not place you"

"That is only natural; at table you had eyes for no one but Mademoiselle Sanson."

"That may well be, for you must admit she is charming."

"It is not hard for me to admit it since, unfortunately, I know it only too well."

"Then you are in love with her."

"Alas, yes."

"Then win her love."

"That is what I have been trying to do for a year, and I was beginning to hope when you appeared and reduced me to despair."

"Who, Monsieur, I?"

"Yes, you."

"I am very sorry; but at the same time I fail to see what I can do about it."

"Yet it would not be very difficult, and if you will permit me I will myself suggest what you could do to oblige me."

"Please tell me."

"You could never set foot in her house again."

"I agree that it is the only thing I could do if I wanted very much to oblige you; but do you think that, if I did it, she would love you?"

"Oh, that is up to me. Meanwhile, do not go there again, and I will see to the rest."

"I admit that I may do you this extraordinary favor, but permit me to say that I think it strange you should have counted on it."

"Yes, Monsieur, after giving it much thought I saw that you were a man of great intelligence. I therefore made bold to conclude that you would be able to put yourself completely in my place, that you would consider the matter rationally, and that you would not wish to fight to the death with me for a young lady whom you, I imagine, do not wish to marry, whereas in my love my only object is that bond."

"And if I, too, were thinking of asking for her hand?"

"Then we should both deserve to be pitied, and I more than you, for as long as I am alive Mademoiselle Sanson will never be the wife of another."

This well-built young man, pale, serious, cold as ice, and in love, standing there in my own room deliberately saying such things to me with amazing calm, gave me occasion to think. I walked up and down for a good quarter of an hour to weigh the two courses of action dispassionately and see which of them would prove me the more courageous and the more worthy of my own esteem. I saw that the one which would best prove me the more courageous was the one which would prove to my rival that I was wiser than he.

"What will you think of me, Monsieur," I asked him firmly, "if I never set foot in Mademoiselle Sanson's house again?"

"That you pity an unhappy wretch who will always be ready to shed all his blood to show you his gratitude."

"Who are you?"

"I am Garnier,[19] only son of Garnier the wine merchant in the Rue de Seine."

"Very well, Monsieur Garnier, I will cease to visit
Mademoiselle Sanson. Be my friend."

"Until death. Good-by, Monsieur."

A moment after he was gone, in comes Patu, to whom
I tell the story and who declares me a hero; he embraces
me, he thinks, and he says that he would have done the
same in my place, but not in Garnier's place.

The Count of Melfort, then Colonel of the Orléans
regiment, asked me through Camilla, sister of Corallina
(the latter I no longer saw), to answer two questions
by means of my cabala. I make up two answers which
are very obscure but full of meanings, I seal them and
give them to Camilla, who the next day asks me to go
with her to a place which she will not name. She takes
me to the Palais-Royal and we go up a narrow staircase
to the apartment of the Duchess of Chartres,[20] who
comes in a quarter of an hour later, showers the little
beauty with caresses, and thanks her for having brought
me to her. After a short preamble, all dignity and
graciousness but without ceremony, she begins telling
me all the difficulties she had found in the two answers
I had given and which she had in her hand. After
showing some surprise that the questions had been Her
Highness's, I tell her that I know how to operate the
cabala but that I am no good at interpreting it, so she
must go to the trouble of asking further questions likely
to produce clearer answers. So she writes down everything she could not understand and everything she
wanted to know; I tell her that she must separate the
questions, since one could not ask the oracle two things;
she tells me to prepare the questions myself; I answer
that she must write the whole with her own hand and
imagine that she is interrogating an intelligence which
knew all her secrets. She writes down everything she
wanted to know in seven or eight questions; she reads

them over to herself, and says with great dignity that she wishes to be sure that no one except myself will ever see what she has just written. I promise it on my word of honor; I read, and I see not only that she was right but that by putting them in my pocket to return them to her the next day with the answers I was in danger of compromising myself.

"I need only three hours, Madame, to do all this, and I want Your Highness to feel no anxiety. If Your Highness has anything to do, Your Highness can go and leave me here, provided that no one interrupts me. When I have finished I will seal everything; I need only know to whom I am to deliver the packet."

"To me, or to Madame de Polignac,[21] if you know her."

"Yes, Madame, I know her."

With her own hands the Duchess gave me a tinderbox so that I could light a small candle when I needed to seal, and she left and Camilla with her. I remained there, locked in; and three hours later, just as I was finishing, Madame de Polignac entered and I handed her the package and left.

The Duchess of Chartres, daughter of the Prince of Conti, was twenty-six years of age. She had in abundance the kind of intelligence which makes every woman who possesses it adorable, she was extremely animated, without prejudices, gay, witty in conversation, loving pleasure and preferring it to the hope of a long life. "Short and sweet" was an expression which was forever on her lips. In addition she was kind, generous, patient, tolerant, and constant in all her affections. With all that, she was very pretty. She carried herself awkwardly, and she laughed at the dancing teacher Marcel when he tried to correct her. She danced with her head bent forward and her toes turned in; even so, she was charming. A prime defect, which troubled her greatly and marred her beauty, was pimples, which were believed to be due to her liver but which in fact came from an impurity of the blood which finally caused her death and against which she struggled to her last breath.

The questions she put to my oracle were directed to matters which concerned her heart, and among other things she wanted to know a remedy to rid her beautiful skin of the small pimples which distressed everyone who saw her. My oracles were obscure concerning everything whose particulars I did not know; but they were not obscure concerning her malady, and it was this which made my oracle precious and necessary to her.

The next day after dinner Camilla, as I expected, wrote me a letter in which she asked me to drop everything and be at the Palais-Royal at five o'clock, in the room to which she had taken me. I went, and an old valet, who was waiting for me, set off at once and five minutes later I saw the charming Princess.

After complimenting me briefly but most graciously, she took all my answers from her pocket and asked me if I was busy; I assured her that my only business was to serve her.

"Good! I will not go out either and we will work."

She thereupon showed me all the new questions she had already prepared on all sorts of subjects and especially concerning the remedy to make her pimples disappear. What had given her confidence in my oracle was something it had told her which no one could know. I guessed, and my guess was right; if I had not, it would have made no difference. I had had the same malady, and I was physician enough to know that a forced cure of a cutaneous disease by local remedies could kill the Princess. I had already answered that she could not be cured of the marks of the malady on her face in less than a week, and that it would take at least a year of dieting to cure it radically, but that in a week she would appear to be cured. We now spent three hours finding out all that she must do. Fascinated by what my oracle knew, she submitted to everything, and a week later all her pimples disappeared. I purged her every day, I prescribed what she should eat, I forbade her any pomades, advising her instead only to wash before going to bed and in the morning with plantain water.[22] My modest oracle told the Princess to use the same wash wherever she wanted to produce the same result, and enchanted with the Intelligence's discretion, the Princess obeyed.

I purposely went to the Opéra on the day when the Princess appeared there with her complexion completely clear. After the performance she walked in the great promenade of her Palais-Royal, followed by all the principal ladies, and flattered by everyone; she saw me and honored me with a smile. I felt I was the happiest of men. Camilla, Monsieur de Melfort, and Madame de Polignac alone knew that I had the honor to be the Princess's oracle. But the day after she went to the Opéra, small pimples returned to mar her face, and I was summoned to appear at the Palais-Royal in the morning. The old valet, who did not recognize me, showed me into a delightful little room next to another in which there was a bathtub, and the Duchess came in looking rather sad, for she had pimples on her chin and her forehead. She was holding a question for the oracle, and since it was short I amused myself by making her obtain the answer herself, which surprised her when, translating the numbers into letters, she found that the angel reproached her with having broken the prescribed diet. She could not deny it. She had eaten ham and had drunk liqueurs. Just then one of her chambermaids came in and whispered something to her. She told her to wait outside for a moment.

"You will not take it amiss, Monsieur," she said, "to see someone here who is a friend of yours and discreet."

So saying, she puts all the papers which have nothing to do with her malady in her pocket and she calls. In

Madame de Pompadour

Louis XV of France

comes a person whom I really took to be a stable boy. It was Monsieur de Melfort.

"Look," she said, "Monsieur Casanova has taught me to operate the cabala," and she showed him the answer she had obtained. The Count did not believe it.

"Then," she said to me, "we must convince him. What do you want me to ask?"

"Whatever Your Highness pleases."

She thinks, she takes an ivory box from her pocket, and she writes: "*Tell me why this pomade no longer produces any effect on me.*"

She constructs the pyramid, the columns, and the keys as I had already taught her to do, and when she is ready to obtain the answer I show her how to make various additions and subtractions which appear to arise from the numbers but which are really arbitrary, then I tell her to translate the numbers into letters and I go out, alleging some necessity. I come back when I think the translation has been completed, and I see the Duchess beside herself with astonishment.

"Ah, Monsieur, what an answer!"

"It may be wrong; but that can happen."

"Not at all; it is divine. Here it is: '*It has no effect except on the skin of a woman who has not had children.*'"

"I see nothing astonishing in the answer."

"Because you do not know that the pomade is the one prescribed for me by the Abbé de Brosses,[23] which cured me five years and ten months ago before I gave birth to the Duke of Montpensier.[24] I would give everything I possess in the world to learn to operate this cabala myself."

"What!" said the Count. "It is the same pomade the history of which I know?"

"The very same."

"It is astonishing."

"I should like to ask another question about a woman whom I do not wish to name."

"Just say 'the woman I have in mind.'"

She then asks what the woman's malady is, and I make her obtain the answer that she wants to deceive her husband. At that the Duchess cried out in amazement.

It was very late, and I left with Monsieur de Melfort, who had first spoken privately to Her Highness. He told me that what the cabala had answered about the pomade was astonishing; and here is the story.

"The Duchess," he said, "pretty as you see her, had her face so full of pimples that the Duke, in disgust, could not bring himself to sleep with her, hence she would never have borne a child. The Abbé de Brosses cured her with this pomade, and in all her beauty she went to the Comédie Française in the Queen's box. As chance would have it, the Duke of Chartres goes to the theater, not knowing that his wife was there, and takes a place in the King's box. He sees his wife in the opposite box, he thinks her pretty, he asks who she is, he is told that she is his wife, he does not believe it; he leaves his box, goes to see her, compliments her on her beauty, then goes back to his box. At half past eleven we were all at the Duchess's apartment; she was playing cards. Suddenly—and contrary to all precedent—a page informs the Duchess that the Duke her husband is entering her apartment, she rises to receive him, and the Duke tells her that he had thought her so beautiful at the theater that, on fire with love, he has come to ask her to allow him to get her with child. Hearing this, we all left immediately; it was in the summer of the year '46, and in the spring of '47 she gave birth to the Duke of Montpensier, who is five years old and in good health. But after her lying-in the pimples came back and the pomade had no more effect."

After relating this anecdote the Count took from his pocket an oval tortoise-shell box with a very good likeness of the Duchess and gave it to me as a present from her, saying that if I wanted to have it set in gold she sent me the gold as well, and he handed me a roll of a hundred louis. I accepted it, begging him to express all my gratitude to the Princess; but I did not have the portrait set in gold, for I was greatly in need of money at the time. When the Duchess summoned me to the Palais-Royal after that there was no further question of curing her pimples, for she would never follow a diet; instead she made me spend five hours or six hours now in one corner now in another, leaving me, coming back again, having dinner or supper served to me by the old valet, who never spoke a word to me. The cabalas concerned only private matters of her own or of other people in whom she was interested, and she hit upon truths which I did not know I knew. She wanted me to teach her to operate the cabala, but she never pressed me to do it; she only had Monsieur de Melfort tell me that she would obtain me a post which would give me an income of twenty-five thousand livres if I would teach her the calculations. Alas, it was impossible. I was madly in love with her, but I never let her see the least sign of my passion. I thought such a conquest beyond me. I feared I should be humiliated by too scornful a refusal, and perhaps I was a fool. All I know is that I have always regretted that I did not speak out. It is true that I enjoyed several privileges which she might not have allowed me to enjoy if she had known that I loved her. I was afraid that I should lose them if I declared myself. One day she wanted the oracle to tell her if it was possible to cure a cancer which Madame La Pouplinière[25] had on one breast. I took it into my head to answer that the lady did not have a cancer and was in excellent health.

"What!" she said, "everyone in Paris believes it, and she consults every doctor; nevertheless, I believe the cabala."

She sees Monsieur de Richelieu at court and she tells

him she is sure that Madame La Pouplinière is shamming; the Marshal, who was in on the secret, told the Duchess she was wrong, and she offered to wager him a hundred thousand francs; when she told me this, I trembled.

"Did he accept your wager?"

"No. He seemed amazed, and you know that he ought to know."

Three or four days later she told me that Monsieur de Richelieu had admitted to her that the cancer was a ruse to excite pity in her husband, to whom she wanted to return, but that the Marshal had told her he would pay a thousand louis to find out how she had discovered it.

"If you want to earn them," she said, "I will tell him everything."

"No, no, Madame—I implore you."

I feared a snare. I knew the Marshal's character; and the story of the hole[26] in the fireplace wall by which that illustrious nobleman entered the lady's house was known all over Paris. Monsieur de La Pouplinière had himself made the thing common knowledge by refusing to see his wife, to whom he gave twelve thousand francs a year. The Duchess had composed some very pretty verses on the affair; but no one outside of her own circle had seen them except the King, who was very fond of her despite the fact that she occasionally treated him to cutting witticisms. One day she asked him if it was true that the King of Prussia was coming to Paris; and the King having replied that there was no truth in it, she retorted that she was sorry because she was dying to see a king.

My brother, who had already painted several pictures in Paris, decided to present one of them to Monsieur de Marigny. So one fine morning we went together to call on the nobleman, who lived in the Louvre,[27] where artists went to pay court to him. We were in the large room next to his apartment, and having been the first to arrive were waiting for him to come out. The picture was hanging there. It was a battle piece in the style of Bourguignon.[28]

In comes a man dressed in black, sees the picture, stops in front of it for a moment, and says, addressing no one:

"It is bad."

A moment later two more men come in, look at the picture, laugh, and say:

"It is by some student."

I glanced at my brother, who was sitting beside me, sweating profusely. In less than a quarter of an hour the hall is full of people, and the badness of the picture was the butt of all those who stood around it snickering and criticizing. My poor brother was almost expiring and kept thanking God that no one knew him.

As his state of mind provoked me to laughter, I got up and went into the next room. I told my brother, who followed me, that Monsieur de Marigny would come out presently and, by declaring his picture beautiful, would avenge him on all these people; but with great good sense he did not agree with me. We go downstairs as fast as possible, and get into our hackney coach, ordering our servant to go and fetch the picture. And so we went home, and my brother slashed his picture a good twenty times with his sword and instantly resolved to settle his affairs, leave Paris, and go elsewhere to study and master the art to which he had devoted himself. We decided to go to Dresden.

Two or three days before the end of my pleasant stay in the enchanting city of Paris, I dined alone at the Tuileries in the house of the Swiss at the Porte des Feuillants,[29] whose name was Condé. After dinner his wife, who was rather pretty, handed me a bill in which I found that everything was charged double; I tried to get it reduced, but she would not take off even a liard.[30] So I paid, and as the bill was receipted at the bottom by the words "femme Condé," I took the pen and added to the "Condé" a "Labré." [31] After which I left and walked toward the swing bridge.[32] When I had stopped thinking about the Swiss's wife who had overcharged me, I see a short man with his hat over one ear, an enormous bouquet in his buttonhole, and wearing a sword of which the hilt guard tierced two inches, who comes up to me with an insolent look and tells me in so many words that he has a mind to cut my throat.

"By jumping, since you are only a dwarf compared with me, who will cut off your ears."

"Hell and damnation, Monsieur!"

"That is enough from you. You have only to follow me."

I stride toward the Étoile,[33] where, seeing no one, I ask the insolent fellow what he wants with me and what reason he has to attack me.

"I am the Chevalier de Talvis.[34] You have insulted a respectable woman who is under my protection. Unsheathe."

So saying, he draws his sword. I instantly draw mine and, not waiting for him to guard his body, I wound him in the chest. He jumps back and says that I have wounded him treacherously.

"You lie; admit it, or I will cut your throat."

"You will do no such thing, for I am wounded; but I demand my revenge, and our meeting will be judged."

I left him there; but my thrust was legitimate, for he had his sword out before I did. If he did not guard his body, it was his own fault.

In the middle of August I set out with my brother from Paris, where I had stayed for two years and where I enjoyed all the pleasures of life without any drawbacks, except perhaps that I was often short of money. By way of Metz and Frankfurt we reached Dresden at the end of the month, and we saw our mother, who greeted us most affectionately in her delight at seeing the first two fruits of her marriage, whom she could not hope to see again. My brother devoted himself entirely to studying his art by copying the excellent battle pictures by the most famous painters in the celebrated gallery.[35] He spent four years there until he considered that he was ready to go back to Paris and face criticism. I will relate in due course how we returned there nearly at the same time; but before then my reader will see how I was treated by an alternately benignant and hostile Fortune.

The life I led at Dresden until the end of the Carnival in the following year, 1753, offers nothing out of the ordinary. The only thing I accomplished was to favor the actors with a tragicomedy in which I had two characters playing the role of Harlequin. My play was a parody of Racine's *Frères ennemis*.[36] The King laughed heartily at the comic incongruities with which my comedy was filled, and at the beginning of the Carnival I received a handsome present from the monarch, whose prodigality was seconded by a minister[37] whose equal in liberality Europe has nowhere seen. I said good-by to my mother, my brother, and my sister, who had married Peter August, the court harpsichordist, who died two years ago leaving his wife with a decent competence and his family happy.

I spent the first three months of my stay in Dresden making the acquaintance of all its mercenary beauties. I found them superior to those of Italy and France in physical endowments, but very inferior in grace, in wit, and in the art of pleasing, which chiefly consists in appearing to be in love with the man who has found them attractive and pays them. In consequence they have the reputation of being cold. What stopped me in this ruthless pursuit was a malady with which I was infected by a Hungarian girl in La Creps's[38] bevy. It was the seventh infection, and I got rid of it, as always, by dieting for six weeks. I have never done anything in my life except try to make myself ill when I had my health and try to make myself well when I had lost it. I have been equally and thoroughly successful in both, and today in that particular I enjoy perfect health, which I wish I could ruin again; but age prevents me. The malady which we call the "French disease" does not shorten life when one knows how to cure it; it merely leaves scars; but we are easily consoled for that when we consider that we gained them with pleasure, even as soldiers take pleasure in seeing the scars of their wounds, the proofs of their virtue and the wellsprings of their fame.

King Augustus, the Elector of Saxony, was fond of his Prime Minister Count Brühl because he spent proportionately more than his master and because he never let him think that anything was impossible. The King was an inveterate enemy of economy, laughing at those who robbed him and spending lavishly merely to find occasions for laughing. Not having wit enough to laugh at the political blunders of his fellow monarchs and the absurdities of people in general, he had in his service four buffoons, known in German as "fools," [39] whose function was to rouse laughter by outright scurrility, low jests, and impertinence. These gentlemen often obtained considerable favors from their master for those whose interests they undertook to advance. Hence they were often honored and cultivated by decent people who needed their patronage. Where is the man whom necessity does not drive to baseness? Agamemnon in Homer tells Menelaus that necessity commands them to be base.

Both the common voice and history are wrong today when they say that Count Brühl was the cause of what was then called the "ruin of Saxony." [40] The man was no more than his master's faithful minister; and all his children, who inherited nothing of all the wealth he was supposed to have accumulated, sufficiently justify their father's memory.

In short, I saw at Dresden the most brilliant court in Europe, and the arts which flourished at it. I saw no amorous intriguing, for King Augustus was not inclined that way, nor is gallantry in the nature of the Saxons unless their sovereign sets them the example.

On arriving in Prague, where I did not intend to stay, I only sent over a letter from Amorevoli[41] to Locatelli,[42] the manager of the opera, and went to see La Morelli.[43] She was an old acquaintance, who took the place of everything else for me during the three days I spent in that vast city. But just as I was about to leave, I ran into my old friend Fabris[44] in the street; he was now a colonel and he insisted on my going to dine with him. I embrace him and explain to him that I must leave.

"You shall leave this evening with a friend of mine and overtake the diligence."

I did as he wished, and I was delighted. He was longing for war, which came two years later,[45] and he won great glory in it.

As for Locatelli, he was an original character and well worth knowing. He ate every day at a table laid for thirty; the guests were his actors and actresses, his dancers and danseuses, and his friends. He presided himself over the excellent fare which he served, for good eating was his passion. I shall have occasion to speak of him when I come to my journey to Petersburg, where I saw him again and where he died not long ago at the age of ninety.[46]

CHAPTER XII

*My stay in Vienna. Joseph II. My departure
for Venice.*

SO HERE I am, in the capital of Austria for the
first time, at the flourishing age of twenty-eight. I had
a few possessions, but scarcely any money; so I had to
go slowly until the return of a letter of exchange which
I at once drew on Signor Bragadin. The only other letter
I had was one from the poet Migliavacca,[1] of Dresden,
introducing me to the celebrated Abate Metastasio,[2]
whose acquaintance I was most eager to make. I presented it to him on the next day but one, and in an hour's
conversation I found him even more learned than his
works proclaim him to be and with a modesty which at
first I could not believe was natural; but I very quickly
perceived that it was real when it vanished as soon as
he recited something of his own and himself pointed out
its beauties. I talked to him of his teacher Gravina,[3] and
he recited five or six stanzas which he had composed on
his death and which were not printed, and I saw him

shed tears, touched by the sweetness of his own poetry. After reciting them to me, he added these words:

"Ditemi il vero: si può dir meglio?" ("Tell me the truth: is it possible to write better?")

I answered that only he had the right to believe it impossible. I asked him if his beautiful lines cost him much effort, and he at once showed me four or five pages filled with erasures due to his trying to bring fourteen lines to perfection. He assured me that he had never been able to compose more lines than that in a day. He then substantiated a truth which I already knew, namely, that the lines which cost a poet the most labor are those which uninitiated readers think cost him none. I asked him which of his operas he liked the best, and he said it was his *Attilio Regolo*,[4] and he added:

"Ma questo non vuol già dire che sia il migliore." ("But that does not necessarily mean it is the best.")

I told him that all his works had been translated into French prose[5] at Paris, and that the publisher had gone bankrupt because it was impossible to read them, and that this showed the power of his beautiful poetry. He answered that some other fool had gone bankrupt in the previous century by translating Ariosto[6] into French prose, and he laughed heartily at those who maintained, and who maintain, that a work in prose has the right to be called a poem. On the subject of his ariettas, he said that he had never written one of them without setting it to music himself, but that he usually did not show his music to anyone; and he laughed heartily at the French for believing that it is possible to fit words to a tune composed beforehand. He made a very philosophical comparison:

"It is," he said, "as if you said to a sculptor: 'Here is a piece of marble, make me a Venus which will show her expression before you have carved her features.'"

At the Imperial Library[7] I found, to my great surprise, Monsieur de La Haye with two Poles and a young Venetian[8] whom his father had entrusted to him for a good education. I embraced him several times. I thought he was in Poland. He told me that he was in Vienna on business and that he would go back to Venice in the summer. We called on each other, and as soon as I told him I had no money he lent me fifty zecchini, for which I was grateful to him. The news he told me which gave me decided pleasure was that of his friend the Baron de Bavois, who was already a lieutenant-colonel in the Venetian service. He had had the good fortune to be chosen as adjutant-general by Signor Morosini, whom the Republic had appointed border commissioner[9] on his return from his embassy in France. I was delighted at the good fortune of those who could not but recognize me as first cause of it. I learned beyond doubt in Vienna that De La Haye had been a Jesuit; but no one was allowed to speak to him on the subject.

Not knowing where to go and wanting amusement, I went to the rehearsal at the opera,[10] which was to open after Easter, and I found Bodin, the premier danseur, who had married La Geoffroi. I had seen them both at Turin. I also found Campioni, the husband of the beautiful Ancilla, who told me that he had divorced her because she dishonored him. Campioni was a great dancer and a great gambler. I lodged with him.

Everything in Vienna was splendid, there was much money and much luxury; but there was great hardship for those who were votaries of Venus. Rascals turned spies, who were known as "Commissaries for Chastity,"[11] pitilessly persecuted all pretty girls; the Empress, who had all the virtues, had not the virtue of tolerance in the matter of illegitimate love between a man and a woman. That great and very religious sovereign hated mortal sin in general, and wishing to deserve well of God by extirpating it, she rightly thought that it must be persecuted in detail. So, taking into her royal hands the register of what are called mortal sins, she found that they numbered seven, and she thought she could hedge about six of them, but she considered lechery unforgivable, and it was against lechery that her zeal mustered all its forces and let loose.

"It is possible," she said, "not to recognize pride, for dignity bears its standard. Avarice is horrible, but one may be mistaken about it, for it may look like economy to him who loves money. As for anger, it is a disease which is murderous when the fit is on, but murderers are punished with death. Gluttony may be only love of choice food, which is considered a virtue in good society, and it is connected with appetite. So much the worse for those who die of indigestion! Envy is never admitted, and sloth is punished by boredom. But lust is what I cannot pardon. My subjects shall be free to find any woman beautiful in whom they see beauty, and women may do whatever they wish to the end of appearing so; let men and women desire one another as much as they please, I cannot prevent it; but I will never tolerate the base act which satisfies that desire and which is nevertheless inseparable from human nature and the cause of the reproduction of the species. Let people marry if they wish to have that pleasure, and let all those perish who wish to procure it for money, and let there be exile in Temesvar[12] for all the miserable women who live on what they suppose they can earn by their charms. I know that Rome is indulgent in the matter, to prevent, so they say, sodomy and incest and adultery; but my climate is different; my Germans don't have the devil in their bodies like the Italians, who have not, as we have here, the resource of the bottle; in addition, a watch will be kept for licentiousness of any consequence, and when I learn that a wife is unfaithful to her husband I will have her locked up too, despite the claim that her husband is her only master. This cannot be admitted in my dominions, for husbands here are too indolent. Fanatical husbands

who claim that I dishonor them by punishing their wives
may protest as much as they please. Are they not already
dishonored?''

''But, Madame, dishonor can be only in the thing
being known, and besides, you may be mistaken.''

''Be still!''

From this ferocious principle, the product of the only
fault which the great Maria Theresa had *sub specie recti*
(''under the appearance of rectitude''),[13] arose all the
injustices and all the violences committed by the murderous ''Commissaries for Chastity.'' At every hour of the
day any girl who was walking alone in the streets of
Vienna, even to earn an honest living, was seized and
haled off to prison. But how could it be known that these
girls were going to some man's house for solace or were
looking for some man to solace them? A spy followed
them at a distance; the police had five hundred of them
in their pay, and they were not in uniform. When the
girl entered a house the spy who had seen her, having no
way of knowing to what floor she had gone, waited downstairs for her and took her in charge to find out on whom
she had called and what she had done there, and at the
least obscurity in her answers, the villain haled her off
to prison, beginning by taking whatever money or jewels
she had, of which nothing more was ever heard. During
a disturbance in the street at Leopoldstadt a girl who
was running away, and whom I did not know, slipped
a gold watch into my hands, foreseeing that it would become the booty of those who were going to take her to
the Stockhaus.[14] A month later I returned it to her, after
hearing her story and by what sacrifices she had delivered herself from her torments. In short, all girls who
walked in the streets of Vienna were reduced to carrying
rosaries. Then they could not be arrested out of hand,
for they said they were going to church, and Maria
Theresa would have had the Commissary hanged. Vienna
was so encumbered with these blackguards that a man

who needed to make water could hardly find a place where no one would see him. I was greatly surprised one day when I was interrupted by a fellow in a round wig who threatened to have me arrested if I did not go and finish somewhere else.

"Why, if you please?"

"Because to your left there is a woman at a window who can see you."

I look and, sure enough, I see in a fourth-story window the face of a woman who, if she had had a spyglass, could have seen whether I was a Jew or a Christian. I obeyed, laughing at the incident, which I related to all and sundry; but no one thought it unusual.

I went to the "Sign of the Crawfish"[15] to dine with Campioni at the common table and I was surprised to see Bepe il cadetto, whom I had met at the time of my arrest by the Spanish army and had seen again at Venice and later at Lyons under the name of Don Giuseppe Marcati. Campioni, who had been his partner in Lyons, embraced him, spoke to him privately, and told me before we sat down at table that the gentleman had resumed his real name, which was Count Afflisio. He said that after dinner they would make a bank at faro, in which I would have a small share, and so I must refrain from playing. I agreed. The bank was made, Afflisio won, Captain Beccaria[16] threw the cards in his face; but Afflisio prudently disregarded it. Afflisio, Campioni, and I went to a coffeehouse with an engaging officer, who looked at me and smiled but not in such a way as to offend against good manners.

"I am smiling because you do not remember me."

"No, Monsieur, but it seems to me . . ."

"Nine years ago at Prince Lobkowitz's order I conducted you to the gate in Rimini."

"You are Baron Weiss."[17]

"The same."

He offered me his friendship and promised to procure

me all the pleasures in his power in Vienna. And that very evening he introduced me to a countess, at whose house I met the Abate Testagrossa,[18] whom everyone called Grossatesta, who was Ambassador from the Duke of Modena and well liked at court because he negotiated the marriage between the Archduke and the Princess Beatrice d'Este.[19] Among the guests I met a Count Roggendorf [20] and a Count Sarotin,[21] and several Fräuleins,[22] together with a baroness who had gone the pace but who was still attractive. Supper was served and I was made a baron; it was in vain that I said I had no title; I was told that in such a company I had to be something and I could not be less than a baron and I must agree to be one if I wanted to be received anywhere in Vienna. I gave in. The Baroness nonchalantly made me understand that I was to her taste and that she would be glad to receive my attentions; I paid her a visit the next day: she told me to come in the evening if I liked cards, and I met several players. It was there that I met Tramontini,[23] whose wife I already knew as Signora Tesi.[24] There I also met three or four Fräuleins who, quite unawed by the Commissaries for Chastity, were devoted to love and so kindly disposed that they had no fear of sullying their nobility by accepting money. After discovering the privileges enjoyed by these young ladies, I saw that the Commissaries were a hindrance only to people who did not frequent good houses.

The Baroness told me that I might introduce my friends to her if I had any, and after consulting Campioni, I brought Afflisio, Baron Weiss, and even Campioni, who, being a dancer, did not need a title. Afflisio played, held the bank, won, and Tramontini introduced him to his wife, who introduced him to her Prince Sachsen-Hildburghausen.[25] It was there that Afflisio began the triumphant career which ended so badly for him twenty-five years later. Tramontini, having become his partner in the great gambling sessions which he induced him to organize, easily got his wife to persuade the Prince to have him made a captain in the service of Their Imperial and Royal Austrian Majesties. It did not take long, for three weeks later I myself saw him in uniform. He was already in possession of a hundred thousand florins when I left Vienna, the Empress loved play, and the Emperor too, but not as a punter. He had someone hold a bank for him. He was a good prince, magnificent yet economical; I saw him in his role of Imperial Majesty and was surprised to find that he was dressed in the Spanish fashion.[26] I thought I was seeing Charles V, who established this etiquette, which still existed despite the fact that after him no Emperor was Spanish and Franz I had no connection with that nation. I saw the same thing, but with better reason, in Warsaw at the time of the coronation of Stanislas August Poniatowski,[27] who also indulged the whim of wearing Spanish dress. The costume brought tears to the eyes of the old courtiers, but they had to swallow the pill, for under the Russian despotism they were left with no power but the power to think.

The Emperor Franz I was handsome, and I should have known that his physiognomy promised good fortune even if I had not seen him a monarch. He treated his wife with the utmost consideration, he did not prevent her from being prodigal, for it was only Kremnitz ducats[28] which she staked at cards or gave away in pensions, and he let her put the State in debt because he had the skill to become its creditor himself. He favored commerce because he put into his coffers a good share of the profits which it produced. He was also given to gallantry, and the Empress, who always addressed him as "Master," pretended not to notice. Perhaps she did not want it known that her charms did not suffice her husband's nature, and the more so since everyone admired the beauty of her numerous family. I saw all her Archduchesses[29] and thought them all beautiful except the eldest; among the males I studied only her eldest son,[30] whose physiognomy I found unpromising, despite the contrary opinion of the Abate Grossatesta, who also prided himself on being a physiognomist.

"What do you see in it?"

"I see conceit and suicide."

I guessed rightly, for Joseph II killed himself; and despite the fact that he did not intend it, he killed himself none the less. His conceit was the reason for his not being aware of it. What he professed to know, and did not know, made what he did know useless, and the acuity he tried to have spoiled what acuity he had. He loved to talk to anyone who, dazzled by his reasoning, did not know how to answer him, and those whose sound arguments invalidated his own he called "pedants." He told me in Laxenburg[31] seven years ago, talking of a man who had spent a fortune to buy a patent of nobility, that he despised anyone who bought one. I replied that it would be better to despise the person who sold it. He turned his back on me and from then on did not consider me worthy to hear his voice. His passion was to see people laugh, at least in their sleeves, when he told some story, for he told them well and embroidered on the circumstances amusingly; and he considered those who did not laugh at his jokes lacking in intelligence. They were precisely the people who understood them best. He preferred the arguments of Brambilla,[32] who encouraged him to kill himself, to those of the doctors whose advice to him was *Principiis obsta* ("Resist from the beginning").[33] As for the art of ruling, he did not know it, for he had no knowledge of the human heart, he could neither dissimulate nor keep a secret; he showed the pleasure he took in punishing, and he had not learned to control his countenance. He so far neglected this art that when he saw someone he did not know he made a grimace which rendered him very ugly, when he could have used an eyeglass instead, for the grimace seemed to say, "Who can that creature be?"

He succumbed to a malady which was most cruel in that it left him his reason until the end and because, before killing him, it showed him that his death was inescapable. He must have known the unhappiness of repenting of everything he had done and the other unhappiness of being unable to undo what he had done, partly because it was impossible and partly because he would have thought it dishonorable, for his sense of his high birth must always have remained in his soul even when it was languishing. He had the greatest esteem for his brother,[34] who reigns in his stead today, yet he had not the strength of mind to follow the important advice which he more than once gave him. With great magnanimity he gave a large reward to the intelligent physician[35] who had pronounced his death sentence, but with no less pusillanimity he had some months earlier rewarded the physicians and the charlatan who had made him believe he was cured. He also had the unhappiness of knowing that he would not be regretted; it is a most grievous thought. Another misfortune he had was not to die before the Archduchess his niece.[36] If those who were about him had really loved him, they would have spared him the dreadful news, for he was already dying and there was no need to fear that he would so far recover as to punish discretion as indiscretion; but they were afraid that his successor would not be generous to the worthy lady, who at once obtained a hundred thousand florins. Leopold would have defrauded no one.

Delighted by my stay in Vienna and by the pleasures I procured with the beautiful Fräuleins whom I had met at the Baroness's, I was thinking of leaving, when Monsieur Weiss, encountering me at the wedding festivities for Count Durazzo,[37] invited me to a picnic at Schönbrunn. We went, and I did not stint myself in anything;

but I returned to Vienna with such a case of indigestion
that within twenty-four hours I was at the brink of the
grave.

I used what dregs of intelligence I had left to save my
life. At my bedside were Campioni, in whose house I was
lodging, Monsieur Roggendorf, and Sarotin. The latter,
who had become my staunch friend, had come with a
physician, though I had explained that I did not want
one. The physician, considering himself at liberty to employ the despotism of his art, had sent for a surgeon,
and I was about to be bled, without my consent and
against my will. Half dead, I do not know what inspira-
tion made me open my eyes, whereupon I saw the man
with his lancet about to pierce my vein. "No, no," I
said, and feebly drew back my arm; but according to
the doctor, the butcher was going to restore me to life
despite myself, and I see my arm grasped. I quickly
laid hold of one of the two pistols which I had on my
night table, and I fired it at the man who had sworn
to obey the doctor. The ball uncurled a lock of his hair,
and that was quite enough to send away the surgeon, the
physician, and everyone who was with me. Only the
chambermaid did not abandon me and gave me water to
drink whenever I asked for it, and in four days I was
in perfect health. The whole of Vienna heard the story,
and the Abate Grossatesta assured me that if I had killed
him nothing would have happened to me, for the two
noblemen who were present had been witnesses that I
was about to be bled by force. In addition everyone told
me that all the physicians in Vienna said that if I had
been bled I would be dead. However, it is true that I
had to beware of falling ill, for no physician would have
dared to visit me again. This incident made a stir. I went
to the opera, and many people wanted to make my acquaintance; I was admired as a man who had defended
himself against Death by firing a pistol at him. A miniature painter named Marolles,[38] a friend of mine, who had

died because he had been bled for indigestion, had impressed it on me that to recover from the indisposition one need only drink water and be patient. One is in a state of distress which one cannot define. One does not want to vomit, for vomiting does not cure. I shall never forget a jest from the lips of a man who never made one; it was Monsieur de Maisonrouge, who was being brought home dying of indigestion. A jam of carts forces his coachman to stop opposite the Quinze-Vingts.[39] A beggar comes up to his carriage and asks him for a sou for charity, saying that he is dying of hunger. Maisonrouge opens his eyes, looks at him, and says:

"You're a very lucky fellow."

At this same period I made the acquaintance of a Milanese dancer who, besides being pretty, had a taste for literature. Her receptions were frequented by people of distinction. There I met a Count Christoph Erdödy,[40] pleasant, rich, and generous, and a sparkling Prince Kinsky[41] who had all the graces of a Harlequin. The girl, who is still alive, I believe, inspired me with love, but in vain, for she had fallen in love with a dancer named Angiolini,[42] who had just arrived from Florence. I paid my court to her, but she would have none of me. A girl of the theater who is in love with some man is invincible unless one can conquer her by force of money. I was not rich. Nevertheless I did not despair and I continued to go there; my company entertained her because she showed me the letters she wrote and I pointed out their beauties; at the same time, sitting beside her, I enjoyed the beauty of her eyes. She showed me letters from her brother, who was a Jesuit and a preacher. She had been painted in miniature, and the portrait was a speaking likeness; on the eve of my departure, furious because I had not been able to obtain anything from the beauty, I resolved to steal her portrait, a poor compensation for one so unlucky as not to have obtained the original. So on the day I bade her good-by I took it without her

noticing it, and put it in my pocket. The next day I left
for Pressburg, to which Baron Weiss had invited me for
an outing with two Fräuleins.

We got out of our carriage at an inn, and the first
person I see is the Chevalier de Talvis, the very man
who had obliged me to give him a little wound with my
sword at the Étoile on the day I had written "Labré"
after "Condé" on the receipt from the wife of the Swiss
at the Tuileries. He no sooner sees me than he comes up
and says I owe him a revenge. I reply that I never leave
one company for another and that we shall meet again.

"That is enough," he answered. "Will you do me the
honor of introducing me to these ladies?"

"With pleasure, but not in the street."

We go upstairs, he follows us, and it occurs to me that
the man, who was certainly no coward, might amuse us,
and I introduce him. He had been lodging at the same
inn for two days, and he was dressed in mourning[43] and
wearing a shirt with frayed cuffs. He asks us if we are
going to the Prince-Bishop's[44] ball, of which we had
heard nothing, and Weiss answers that we are.

"One can go to it," he says, "without being presented,
and that is why I expect to go, for I have no acquaintances here."

A moment later he leaves, the innkeeper comes to take
our orders, he tells us about the ball, the Fräuleins want
to go to it; after eating something, we go, we see a great
many people, and, being known to no one, we walk about
freely.

We enter a room in which we see a large table surrounded by members of the nobility punting at faro; the
dealer was the Prince and we thought the sovereigns[45]
and ducats in the bank amounted to thirteen or fourteen
thousand florins. The Chevalier de Talvis was standing
between two ladies, to whom he was saying pretty things,
while Monsignore was shuffling. He offers the pack to be

cut, and takes it into his head to look at the Frenchman and tell him to stake on a card too.

"With pleasure, Monsignore—banco on this card."

"Banco," said the Bishop loftily, wanting to show that he was not afraid, whereupon the card appears at his left and the Chevalier indifferently gathers up all the money. The astonished Bishop says to the Gascon:

"If your card had lost, Monsieur, how would you have paid me?"

"Monsignore, that is not your business."

"Monsieur, you have more luck than sense."

Talvis left with his money in his pocket.

This astonishing incident gave rise to all sorts of talk, but everyone ended by saying that the foreigner must be either mad or desperate and that the Bishop was a fool.

A half hour later we return to the inn, we ask what has become of the winner, and are told that he has gone to bed. I tell Weiss that we ought to turn the incident to advantage by borrowing a small sum. We enter his room very early, I congratulate him and ask him to be so good as to lend me a hundred ducats.

"Most gladly."

"I will return them to you in Vienna. Shall I write you a receipt?"

"No, no."

He counts out a hundred Kremnitz ducats, and a quarter of an hour later leaves for Vienna by post. His entire luggage was a traveling bag, an overcoat, and a pair of boots. I faithfully divided the hundred ducats between the four of us, and we went back to Vienna the next day. We found that the story was on the lips of all our acquaintances, but no one knew either that we had received a hundred ducats or that the winner was the Chevalier de Talvis; furthermore until that moment not a soul in Vienna had been able to guess who the man was.

No one at the French Embassy[48] had any idea. I never learned if anything was heard of him again. I left by the diligence and on the fourth day reached Trieste, whence I at once took ship for Venice. I arrived there two days before Ascension Day in the year 1753.

CHAPTER XIII

*I return the portrait I had carried off from
Vienna. I go to Padua; incident during my
return; its consequences. I meet Teresa Imer
again. My acquaintance with Signorina C. C.*

DELIGHTED THAT I was back in my native country, which the greatest of prejudices endears to all
men, become the superior of several of my equals in respect to experience and to knowledge of the laws of honor
and good manners, I could not wait to resume my old
courses, but more systematically and with more reserve.
In the room where I slept and wrote I saw with pleasure
my papers shrouded in dust, certain proof that no one
had entered it for the past three years.

The next day but one after my arrival, just as I was
going out to accompany the *Bucentaur*,[1] in which the
Doge, according to custom, was going to marry the Adriatic, a gondolier brought me a note. I open it, and I find
that Signor Giovanni Grimani[2] asks me to come to his
house to receive a letter which he was instructed to deliver to me in person. This nobleman, aged twenty-three,
a rich patrician, had no right to summon me, but he
counted on my good manners. I went at once. After con-

gratulating me on my safe return, he hands me a small unsealed letter which he had received the previous day. I find this in it:

"After you left I looked everywhere in vain for my portrait in miniature. I am sure that it is in your possession, because, since I do not receive thieves, everything in my house is safe. You will deliver it to the person from whom you receive this letter.—Fogliazzi."

Very glad that I have the portrait in my pocket, I instantly hand it to the nobleman, who is all amiability. I see on his countenance an expression of surprise and satisfaction. He had had good reason to think that his task would be difficult.

"It is apparently love which induced you to commit this theft," he said; "but I congratulate you on its not being very strong. I deduce this from the promptness with which you return the jewel."

"I would not so easily return it to anyone else."

"In that case I beg you to count on my friendship in future."

"It is worth far more than the portrait, and than the original. Dare I hope that Your Excellency will send her my answer?"

"Of course. Here is paper. You need not seal it."

Here are the few lines I wrote: "*The pleasure which Casanova feels in ridding himself of this portrait is far greater than that which he enjoyed when an unworthy caprice prompted him to the folly of putting it in his pocket.*"

On the next day, bad weather having caused the postponement of the miraculous wedding until Sunday, I accompanied Signor Bragadin to Padua, to the quiet of which he was retiring during the days which the festivities in Venice made distasteful to him. A truly amiable old man leaves boisterous pleasures to the young. On Saturday, after dining with him, I kissed his hand and took a *barella*³ for Venice. If I had left Padua ten seconds earlier or later, everything that has happened to me in my life would be different; my destiny, if it is true that destiny is dependent upon coincidence, would have been changed. The reader shall judge.

Having, then, left Padua at this fateful moment, two hours later at Oriago[4] I meet a cabriolet, drawn by two post horses at full trot, in which there is a pretty woman on the right of a man in the German uniform. Eight or ten paces from me the cabriolet overturns in the direction of the river, the woman falls across the officer and is in obvious danger of falling into the Brenta.[5] I jump out of my small carriage without shouting "halt," and I stop the lady, quickly pulling down her skirts, which had exposed all her secret wonders to my eyes. Her companion comes running at the same moment, and she stands there in complete confusion and certainly less put out by her fall than by the indiscretion of her skirts, despite the beauty of all that they had displayed. In the course of her thanks, which continued for all the time that her postilion and mine took to right the carriage, she several times called me her "angel." After the two postilions had quarreled, each blaming the other as usual, the lady set off for Padua and I continued my journey. I had scarcely reached Venice before I masked and went to the opera.

The next morning I masked early to follow the *Bucentaur,* which, as the day was fair, was to go to the Lido without fail. This function, which is not only unusual but unique, depends upon the courage of the Admiral of the Arsenal,[6] since he must answer for the weather remaining fair on peril of his head. The least contrary wind could capsize the vessel and drown the Doge with the whole Serenissima Signoria, the Ambassadors, and the Nuncio of the Pope, founder and guarantor of the efficacy of this strange sacramental ceremony, which the Venetians rightly revere to the point of superstition. The crowning misfortune of such a tragic accident would

be that it would set all Europe laughing and saying that
the Doge of Venice had finally gone to consummate the
marriage.

I was drinking coffee unmasked under the Procuratie[7]
in the Piazza San Marco when a beautiful female masker
who was passing by gave me a playful blow on the
shoulder with her fan. Not knowing the masker, I pay
no attention. After drinking my coffee I put on my mask
and make my way to the Riva del Sepolcro, where Signor
Bragadin's gondola was waiting for me. Near the Ponte
della Paglia[8] I see the same masker who had struck me
with her fan staring at the picture of a caged monster[9]
which was shown to anyone curious enough to give ten
soldi to go in. I approached the masked lady and ask
her what right she had had to strike me.

"To punish you for not recognizing me after you saved
my life yesterday beside the Brenta."

I compliment her, I ask her if she intends to follow the
Bucentaur, and she answers that she would go if she had
a perfectly safe gondola; I offer her mine, which is of
the largest; she consults with the officer whom, though
he is masked, I recognize by his uniform, and she accepts.
We go aboard, I urge them to unmask, and they answer
that they have reasons not to reveal themselves. I then
ask them to tell me if they were connected with some
ambassador, in which case I must ask them to get out,
and they answer that they are Venetians. Since the
gondoliers wore the livery of a patrician, I should have
been in trouble with the State Inquisitors. We followed
the *Bucentaur.* As I am sitting on the bench beside the
lady, I take a few liberties under cover of her cloak; but
she discourages me by changing her position. After the
ceremony we return to Venice, we disembark at the
Colonne,[10] and the officer says that they would be happy
if I would dine with them at the "Wild Man," [11] I accept. I had become greatly interested in the woman, who
was pretty and of whom I had seen something more than

her face. The officer left me alone with her, going on ahead to order dinner for three.

I at once told her that I loved her, that I had a box at the opera, that I offered it to her, and that I would attend her throughout the fair if she would assure me that I would not be wasting my time.

"So if you intend," I said, "to be cruel to me, be so good as to tell me so frankly."

"Be so good as to tell me with whom you think you are."

"With a woman who is completely charming, be she a princess or a woman of the lowest condition. You will show me some signs of kindness today, or after dinner I will take a respectful leave of you."

"You will do as you please; but I hope that after dinner you will speak differently, for the tone you are taking is one to make you hated. It seems to me that such a matter can hardly be discussed until after people know each other. Do you not agree?"

"Yes—but I am afraid of being deceived."

"Poor man! And for that reason you want to begin where people end."

"I ask only a payment on account today; after that you will find me undemanding, obedient, and discreet."

"I think you are very amusing; I advise you to calm yourself."

We found the officer at the door of the "Wild Man" and went upstairs. When she unmasked I thought her even prettier than the day before. I still had to find out, for the sake of form and etiquette, whether the officer was her husband, her lover, her relative, or her procurer. Inured as I was to adventures, I wanted to know on what kind of adventure I had embarked.

We eat, we converse, and both she and he behave in such a way that I believe I must proceed cautiously. It was to him that I saw I should offer my box, and it was accepted; but since I did not have one I left them, on some pretext, to go and buy one, and I took it for the *opera buffa*[12] which was being given at the San Moisè and in which Laschi[13] and Pertici[14] were appearing with great success. After the opera I invited them to supper at an inn; then I took them to their lodging in my gondola, in which, under cover of the darkness, the beauty granted me all the favors which propriety permits a woman to grant when there is a third person to be considered. When we parted the officer said that I would hear from him the next day.

"Where and how?"

"I will see to it."

The next morning I was told that an officer had come to call. It was he. After thanking him for honoring me with a visit, I ask him to tell me his name and rank, congratulating myself on having made his acquaintance. He answers me as follows, speaking very fluently but not looking at me:

"My name is P. C.[15] My father is very well off and in excellent standing at the Exchange; but we do not get on well with each other. My house is on the Fondamenta di San Marco;[16] and the lady whom you have seen, whose maiden name was O.,[17] is the wife of the broker C. Her sister[18] is married to the patrician P. M. Signora C. is at odds with her husband over me, as I am at odds with my father over her. I wear this uniform by virtue of a captain's commission in the Austrian service; but I have never served. I am in charge of supplying the Venetian State with beef cattle,[19] importing them from Styria and Hungary. When the accounts are made up, this enterprise assures me of a clear ten thousand florins a year; but an unexpected slump, which I shall remedy, a fraudulent bankruptcy, and unusual expenditures now place me in financial difficulties. It is four years since, having heard of you, I wished to make your acquaintance; and you see that Heaven itself decreed that I should make it day before yesterday. I do not hesitate to ask you for a necessary favor which will unite us in the closest friendship. Become my backer *without risking anything yourself.* Honor these three bills of exchange, and do not fear that you will have to redeem them when they fall due, for I will give you these other three, which will be paid to you before the due date of yours. In addition, I will mortgage my cattle shipments to you for the whole of the present year, so that, if I should fail you, you could sequestrate all my cattle at Trieste, for they can only come to Venice from there."

Astonished by such a speech and such a proposition, which seemed to me chimerical and the source of countless difficulties which I loathed, and by the man's extraordinary notion that I would be taken in by it which had made him choose me in preference to a hundred other men he must know, I do not hesitate to reply that I will never honor the three bills of exchange. At that, his eloquence redoubled to convince me; but his ardor diminished when I told him that I was surprised he should have chosen me in preference to many others. He replied that, knowing that I was highly intelligent, he had felt certain that I would have no objection to raise.

"Then you know better by now," I said. "Indeed I am such a fool that I shall never get it through my head how, if I do it, I shall not risk being gulled by it."

He left, excusing himself and saying that he hoped to see me toward evening on the Liston[20] at the Piazza San Marco, where he and Signora C. would be. He left me his address, saying that, without his father's knowledge, he was still occupying his rooms. It was as much as to tell me that I must return his visit. If I had been wise, I would have dispensed with fulfilling this supposed obligation.

Disgusted with the man's designs on me, I was also disgusted with mine on Signora C. I thought I saw a plot; I thought I saw that I was being taken for an easy mark and, determined not to be one, I did not go to the Liston;

but the next morning I went to his house. I thought that a polite call could have no consequences.

A servant having conducted me to his room, he embraced me and reproached me in a friendly way for having made them wait for me in vain on the Liston. Immediately bringing up his business again, he showed me a mass of papers which bored me. If I would honor the three bills of exchange, he said that he would make me his partner in the provisioning enterprise. By this mark of extraordinary friendship he was enriching me by five thousand florins a year. My only answer was to ask him not to mention the matter to me again. I was about to leave, when he said he wished to introduce his mother and his sister to me.

He goes out and a moment later returns with them. I see a woman who looks both ingenuous and respectable, and a very young girl who strikes me as a prodigy. A quarter of an hour later the mother all too trustfully asks me to excuse her, and the girl remains. It took her no more than half an hour to enchant me by her bearing, her face, and by all that I saw was budding in her. What chiefly struck me was a lively and perfectly unspoiled nature brimming over with candor and ingenuousness, a gay and innocent vivacity, simple and noble feelings— in short, a combination of qualities which showed my soul the venerable portrait of virtue, which always had the greatest power to make me the slave of the object in which I believed I saw it.

Signorina C. C.[21] never went out except with her mother, who was pious and indulgent. She had read only the books in the library of her father, a serious man who possessed no novels; she was longing to know Venice; no one visited the house; she had never been told that she was a miracle of nature. The short time I remained there, while her brother wrote, I spent entirely in answering questions which she asked me, and to which I could not fully reply except by adding to her primitive

The Zwinger Palace in Dresden

An Enchanting Moment

stock of ideas others which she had not known she could entertain; her soul was still in chaos. I told her neither that she was beautiful nor that she interested me in the highest degree, because it was only too true and having lied on the subject to so many other women, I feared she would distrust me.

I left the house sad and pensive, only too impressed by the rare qualities I had discovered in the girl. I promised myself that I would not see her again. I regretted that I was not the man to ask her father for her hand in marriage. I thought her uniquely endowed to make me happy.

Having not yet seen Signora Manzoni,[22] I called on her, and I found her the same as she had always been toward me. The news she told me was that Teresa Imer, the same Teresa on whose account old Senator Malipiero had given me a caning thirteen years earlier, had just arrived from Bayreuth, where the Margrave[23] had made her fortune. As she was staying in the house across the way, Signora Manzoni, wishing to enjoy her surprise, sent a message to ask her to come to call. She appeared a quarter of an hour later with a boy eight years of age and as handsome as could be. It was her only son,[24] whom she had had by the dancer Pompeati,[25] who had married her; he had remained in Bayreuth.

Our surprise at seeing each other again was equaled by the pleasure we took in recollecting what had happened to us when we were leaving childhood. So all that we could remember was childish trifling. I offered her my congratulations on her good fortune, and, judging by appearances, she thought she must congratulate me on mine; but hers would have been more durable than mine if she had behaved herself later. She indulged her impulses far more than I did, and my reader will hear something of it five years hence. She had become a great musician; but her good fortune had not depended entirely on her talent; her charms had contributed to it more than anything else. She narrated her adventures to me at length, of course passing over those which her self-esteem did not allow her to tell me. The interview ended two hours later, after she had invited me to breakfast with her the next morning. The Margrave, she said, was having her watched; but as I was an old acquaintance I could not be suspect. This is the aphorism of all light women. She told me to go that evening to her box at the opera, where Signor Papafava[26] would be glad to see me. I went. He was her godfather. Very early the next morning I went to breakfast with her.

I found her in bed with her son, the principles of whose education taught him to get up as soon as he saw me sitting at his mother's feet. I spent three hours with her, of which the last was the one which counted. My reader will see its consequences five years hence. During the two weeks she spent in Venice I was with her one more time, and on her departure I promised to visit her at Bayreuth, but I did not keep my promise.

During these first days of my return to my native country I had to attend to the affairs of my posthumous brother, who having, or so he said, a divine vocation to become a priest, could not do so because he had no patrimony.[27] Ignorant and completely uneducated, with nothing in his favor but a handsome face, he thought that he could succeed only in the priesthood, counting chiefly on preaching, for which the women he knew told me he had a marked talent. I made all the applications he asked me to, and I succeeded in forcing the Abate Grimani to furnish him with a patrimony. He could not avoid it, since he was in debt to us for all the furniture in our house and had never accounted to us for it. He gave him a life interest in a house he owned, and two years later my brother took holy orders by title of patrimony. But the patrimony was fictitious, for the house was already mortgaged; the transaction was a stellionate. I shall speak of my unfortunate brother's conduct when it becomes connected with my own vicissitudes.

Two days after my visit to P. C. I met him in the street. He told me that his sister did nothing but talk of me, that she had remembered many of the things I had said to her, and that his mother was delighted that she had made my acquaintance. He said that she would be a good match for me, since she would bring me a dowry of ten thousand ducati correnti.[28] He asked me to come and drink coffee with her and her mother the next day, and I went despite the fact that I had promised myself I would not go there again. *It is always easy to break one's word to oneself.*

On this second visit three hours of nothing but conversation, which passed very quickly, sent me away so much in love that I realized I was incurable. Saying to her, as I left, that I envied the lot of the man whom Heaven had destined for her, I saw a flame from her very soul spread over her face. No one had ever said as much to her before.

On my way home I examined the nature of my budding passion, and I found it cruel. I could proceed with C. C. neither as an honorable man nor as a libertine. I could not delude myself into believing that I could obtain her hand, and I thought that I would kill anyone who dared to suggest that I seduce her. To turn my thoughts elsewhere I went to a gambling casino. Gambling is often a great palliative for a man in love.

Leaving the gambling den the winner by some hundred zecchini, I was suddenly approached in a solitary street by a man bent under the weight of years, whom I at once recognized as Count Bonafede.[29] After a short preamble he said that he was in dire want and reduced to despair by his obligation to support his numerous family.

"I do not blush," he said, "to ask you for a zecchino, which will keep me alive for five or six days."

I quickly gave him ten, preventing him from groveling to me to show his gratitude, but I could not prevent him from shedding tears. He told me as he left that his crowning misfortune was the state of his elder daughter, who, having become a beauty, would rather die than sacrifice her virtue to necessity.

"I can," he said with a sigh, "neither support her in her feelings nor reward them."

Understanding what he wanted, I took his address and promised to call on him. I was curious to see what the ten years since I had lost sight of it might have done to a virtue of which I had no high opinion. I went the next day. He lived in the Biria.[30] The almost bare house in which I found the daughter, for the father was not at home, did not surprise me. The young Countess, having seen my arrival from a window, came to the stairs to meet me. She was quite well dressed. I found her beautiful and lively, as I had known her at the fortress of Sant'Andrea. Her father had told her that I would come. Transported with joy, she embraced me; she could not have welcomed an adored lover more fondly. She showed me to her room, where, after telling me that her mother was ill in bed and unable to receive a visitor, she surrendered to fresh transports caused, she said, by her pleasure at seeing me again. The storm of kisses, which were given and received under the merest guise of friendship, so affected our senses that the thing which propriety defers to the end of a visit happened in the first quarter of an hour. After that our role, whether genuine or assumed, was to show our surprise. In all decency I could not but assure the poor Countess that what I had done was only the forerunner of a constant attachment; she believed it, as I believed it myself at the moment. In the calm which followed she told me of her family's poverty, of her brothers roaming the streets of Venice in rags, of her father who literally had nothing to feed them.

"Then you have not a lover?"

"A lover! What man would have the courage to be a lover in a house like this? As for profiting by my person, do you think me a woman to give myself for thirty soldi? There is no one in Venice who would set a higher price on me, seeing me in this wretched house. Besides, I do not feel that I was born to be a prostitute."

She now began to shed tears—which brought me to a standstill, mind, body, and soul. *The sad spectacle of misery revolts and frightens love.* She would not let me go until I had promised I would come to see her often. I gave her twelve zecchini, and the amount astonished her; she had never had so much money.

The day after this encounter P. C. called on me early to tell me in most cordial tones that his mother had given his sister permission to go to the opera with him, that she was delighted because she had never seen a theater, and that if I wished I could meet them somewhere.

"Does your sister know that you are so kind as to include me in the party?"

"She knows it, and she is delighted."

"And does your mother know it?"

"No; but when she hears of it she will not take it amiss, for she thinks highly of you."

"In that case I will try to get a box."

"Then kindly meet us at twenty-one o'clock[31] in the Campo dei Santi Apostoli." [32]

The scoundrel said no more about his bills of exchange. Seeing that I was not interested in his mistress, and aware that his sister had attracted me, he conceived the pretty plan of selling her to me. I felt sorry for the mother, who entrusted her daughter to him, and for the girl, who thus put herself in the hands of such a brother; but I was not virtuous enough to refuse the invitation. On the contrary, I thought that, since I loved her, I should be present to guard her against other snares. If I had refused he would have found some other man; and the idea was poison to my soul. I thought that with me she ran no risk.

I took a box for the *opera seria*[33] which was being given at San Samuele,[34] and, not bothering to eat dinner, waited for them at the time and place agreed upon. I saw C. C., ravishingly beautiful and elegantly masked. I made them get into my gondola, for P. C. in his uniform might be recognized and someone might have guessed that the pretty masker was his sister. He asked to be let out at his mistress's house, saying that she was ill, and promised to join us in our box, the number of which I told him. What surprised me was that C. C. seemed neither afraid nor reluctant to be left alone with me in the gondola. As for her brother's abandoning her to me, it did not surprise me. It was obvious that he hoped to profit by it. I told C. C. that until the hour for the Liston we would have the gondoliers row us about, and that since the day was very hot she could unmask. She did so instantly. As I was bound to respect her by the strict principle of conduct I had adopted, and seeing a noble assurance in her countenance and pure confidence and joy of soul shining in her eyes, my love became immense.

Not knowing what to say to her, for I naturally could not talk to her of anything but love and the subject was dangerous, I only kept my eyes on her face, not daring to let them stray to her young bosom for fear I should frighten her modesty. Cut too low in front, her bodice let me see the buds of her breasts through the lace of her *bautta*.[35] I had seen them only for an instant, and, terrified, I did not dare look at them again.

"Do speak to me," she said; "you only look at me and say nothing. You have sacrificed yourself today, for I am sure that my brother would have taken you to call on his lady, who, he says, is as beautiful and intelligent as an angel."

"I know your brother's lady. I have never gone to her

house, and I shall never go there; I am sacrificing nothing for you, and if I do not talk to you it is because my happiness and your beautiful confidence in me have me in ecstasies."

"I am delighted; but how could I fail to have confidence in you? I feel freer and safer than if I were with my brother. My mother herself says there is no mistaking it and that you are certainly one of the most honorable young men in Venice. Besides, you are not married. It's the first thing I asked my brother. Do you remember telling me that you envied the lot of the man who would marry me? At the very same moment I was saying to myself that the girl who gets you will be the happiest girl in Venice."

Hearing these words uttered with angelic sincerity, and not daring to print a kiss on the beautiful lips from which they had come, I pity the reader who does not know what sort of torment I endured at the same time that I felt the sweetest joy from knowing that I was loved by this angel incarnate.

"Our sentiments being the same," I said, "ought we not to be happy, my charming C., if we could be united forever? But I could be your father."

"You my father! What nonsense! Do you know that I am fourteen?"

"And I am twenty-eight."

"So there you are! What man of your age has a daughter like me? I laugh when I think that if my father were like you he would certainly never frighten me and I would hide nothing from him."

At the hour for the Liston we disembarked at the Piazzetta and the spectacle, which was new to her, occupied all her attention. Toward nightfall we ate ices, then went to the opera, where her brother joined us during the third act. I took them to supper at an inn,[36] where the pleasure of seeing the young lady in high spirits and eating with the greatest appetite made me forget that I had not dined. I scarcely spoke: I was sick with love and in a state of excitement which could not continue. When I said that I had a toothache they condoled with me and let me remain silent.

After supper P. told his sister that I was in love with her and that I would feel better if she would let me kiss her. Her only answer was to turn a smiling mouth to me. It would have been churlishness in me not to do my duty, but it was only a polite salute, a kiss on the cheek, and even a very cold one. *What prevented me from kissing her otherwise was crime not daring to sully innocence.*

"What a kiss!" said the scoundrel. "Come, give her a lover's kiss."

I did not stir, and the fellow's provocations annoyed me. Then his sister, turning her beautiful head away,

"Do not urge him," she said, "for I do not please him."

This conclusion startled me, pierced my soul, and determined me to act.

"What!" I said. "You do not attribute my reserve to my feeling for you? You think you do not please me? You are mistaken, heavenly C., and if a kiss is needed to tell you that I love you, this is how I must print it on your beautiful, smiling mouth."

With which, clasping her fondly to my bosom, I gave her the kiss which she deserved and which I was dying to give her. But the nature of my kiss showed the dove that she was in the talons of the hawk. She left my arms blushing crimson and as if stunned to have discovered my love in such a fashion. Her brother congratulated me, while she busied herself putting on her mask. I asked her whether she now doubted if she pleased me. She answered that I had convinced her, but that I need not have hurt her to undeceive her. This answer, which was dictated by the purity of her feeling, seemed nonsense to her wretched brother. After taking them home I went home myself, content, yet very sad.

CHAPTER XIV

Progress of my love affair with the beautiful
C. C.

ON THE next day but one P. C. came to call and told me triumphantly that his sister had told her mother that we loved each other and that, if she must marry, she could not be happy with anyone but me.

"I adore her," I answered; "but will your father give her to me?"

"I do not think so; but he is old. In the meanwhile, love. My mother is willing that she should go to the *opera buffa* with you today."

"Then we will go, my friend."

"I am obliged to ask you to do me a small favor."

"Command me."

"At the moment there is some excellent Cyprus wine for sale cheap. I can have a cask of it against a note payable in six months. I am sure I can resell it at once, and make a profit; but the merchant requires a guarantee, and is willing to accept yours. Will you sign my note?"

"With pleasure."

"Here it is."

I signed without hesitation. Who is the man in love who at that moment could have refused such a favor to one who, to revenge himself, could have made him miserable? After arranging to meet him at the same place at twenty o'clock,[1] I went to the Piazza San Marco to engage a box.[2] A quarter of an hour later I see P. C. masked and in a brand-new suit of clothes. I tell him he has done well to give up wearing his uniform and I show him the number of my box. We part. I go to the fair, I buy a dozen pairs of white gloves, a dozen pairs of silk stockings, and embroidered garters with gold clasps, which I at once put at the top of my own stockings. I am delighted to be giving this first present to my angel. After that, the hour being at hand, I hurry to the Campo dei Santi Apostoli, and I see them standing still and looking about for me; P. C. says that he has business which obliges him to leave us and that since he already knows the number of my box he will join us at the opera. I thereupon tell his sister that there is nothing for us to do but row about in a gondola until time for the Liston. She answers that she would like to go for a walk in a garden on La Giudecca,[3] I second her idea. Not having dined, as I found she had not, I tell her that we can get something to eat in the garden, and we go there in a ferry-gondola.

We go to a garden I know in San Biagio,[4] where a zecchino makes me lord and master of the place for the whole day. No one else was permitted to enter. We order what we want to eat, we go upstairs to the apartment, leave our disguises there, and go down to the garden for a walk. C. C. had on only a short taffeta bodice and a skirt of the same material; it was her entire costume. My amorous soul saw her naked, I sighed, I cursed duty and all feelings contrary to the nature which triumphed in the Golden Age.

As soon as we reached the long walk, C. C., like a young greyhound released from days of tedious confinement in its master's room and given the freedom of the fields at last—joyously obeying its instincts, it runs at top speed left and right, back and forth, returning every moment to its master's feet as if to thank him for allowing it to play so wildly—even so did C. C., who had never been granted the untrammeled freedom she was enjoying that day; she ran and ran until she was out of breath, and then laughed at the astonishment which kept me motionless and staring at her. After catching her breath and wiping her forehead she takes it into her head to challenge me to a race. The notion pleases me, I accept; but I insist on a wager.

"The loser," I say, "must do whatever the winner pleases."

"Agreed."

We set the goal of the race at the gate which gives on the Lagoon. The first to touch it will be the winner. I was certain to win; but I meant to lose to see what she would order me to do. We start. She uses all her strength, but I spare mine so that she touches the gate five or six paces ahead of me. She catches her breath, thinking up some pretty penalty to inflict on me, then she goes behind the trees and a minute later comes and says that she sentences me to find her ring, which she had hidden somewhere on her person, that I am free to look for it, and that she will think very little of me if I do not find it.

It was charming: there was mischief in it, but she was enchanting; and I must not take advantage of her, for her ingenuous confidence was something to be encouraged. We sit down on the grass. I search her pockets, the folds of her short bodice and her skirt, then her shoes, and I turn up her skirt, slowly and circumspectly, as high as her garters, which she was wearing above the knee; I unfasten them and I find nothing. I fasten them again, I draw down her skirt, and, since I am free to do anything, grope under her armpits. The tickling makes her laugh; but I feel the ring, and if she wants me to get it she has to let me unlace her bodice and touch the pretty breast over which my hand must pass to reach it; but just in time the ring drops lower, so that I had to take it from the waist of her skirt, thereby blessing both my hungry eyes and my hand, which she was surprised to see shaking.

"Why are you shaking?"

"With pleasure at finding the ring; but you owe me a revenge. You shall not beat me this time."

"We'll see."

At the beginning of the race the charming runner did not make much speed, and I was in no hurry to get ahead of her. I felt certain that I could gain the lead toward the finish and touch the gate before her. I could not suppose that she was up to the same trick; but she was. When she was thirty paces from the goal, she ran her best, and, realizing that I must lose, I fell back on an unfailing ruse. I let myself fall, crying:

"Oh, my God!"

She turns, she thinks I have hurt myself, and she comes to me. With her help I get up, groaning, and pretending that I could not stand on one foot, and she is perturbed. But as soon as I see that I am one step ahead of her, I look at her, I laugh, I run to the gate, I touch it, and I cry victory.

The charming girl was too amazed to understand what had happened.

"Then you didn't hurt yourself?"

"No—I fell on purpose."

"On purpose to fool me, counting on the kindness of my heart. I would not have believed you capable of it. It's against the rules to win by a trick, and you have not won."

"I won, because I got to the gate ahead of you, and, trick for trick, you must admit that you tried to trick me when you began running your best."

"But that's fair. Your trick, my dear friend, was outrageous."

"But it got me the victory.

> " *'Vincasi per fortuna o per inganno*
> *Il vincer sempre fu laudabil cosa.'* " [5]

> ("Whether victory be gained by luck
> or by ruse, winning has always been
> praiseworthy.")

"That's a maxim I have more than once heard from my brother but never from my father. But to cut it short, I admit that I lost. Pronounce my sentence, I will obey you."

"Wait. Let us sit down. I must think about it.

"I sentence you," I said thoughtfully, "to change garters with me."

"Garters? You saw mine. They're old and ugly, they're worth nothing."

"Never mind. I shall think of the object of my love twice a day, at the moment when it is always in the mind of a devoted lover."

"It is a pretty idea and it flatters me. I forgive you now for having tricked me. Here are my ugly garters."

"And here are mine."

"Oh, my dear deceiver, how beautiful they are! What a pretty present! How my dear mother will like them! They must be a present you have just received, for they are brand-new."

"No. They're not a present. I bought them for you, and I have racked my brains to find a way of persuading you to accept them. Love suggested making them serve as the forfeit for our race. Imagine my disappointment when I saw you on the verge of winning. It was love itself which suggested a trick based on what does you honor, for admit that if you had not come running to me at once it would have shown you were hardhearted."

"And I'm sure you wouldn't have played such a trick on me if you could have guessed how much it made me suffer."

"Then you feel a deep interest in me?"

"I would do anything on earth to convince you of it. As for these garters, I assure you I'll never wear any others and my brother shall never steal them from me."

"Is he capable of it?"

"Perfectly so, if this is gold."

"It is gold; but you shall tell him it is gilded copper."

"But you must show me how to fasten these pretty clasps, because my legs are thin there."

"Let us go and eat our omelette."

We needed the light repast. She became gayer, and I more in love and hence more to be pitied because of the restraint I had laid on myself. Impatient to put on her garters, she asked me to help her in perfect good faith, with no thought of evil and not a grain of coquetry. An innocent girl who, though she is fourteen years old, has never loved and never mingled with other girls knows neither the violence of desire nor exactly what excites it nor the dangers of being alone with a lover. When instinct makes her fall in love with a man she believes him worthy of all her trust, and she thinks she can only make him love her by showing him that she trusts him with no reservations. C. C. pulled her skirt up to her thighs and finding that her stockings were too short for her to put the garters on above the knee, she said that she would put them on with longer stockings; but I at once gave her the dozen pairs of pearl-gray stockings I had bought. In an ecstasy of gratitude, she sat on my lap, giving me the same sort of kisses she would have given her father when he made her such a present. I returned them, quelling the violence of my desires with a strength more than human. However, I told her that a single one of her kisses was worth more than a kingdom. C. C. took off her shoes and put on a pair of my stockings, which

reached halfway up her thigh; and, supposing that I
was in love with her, she thought not only that the sight
would please me but that, since it was of no consequence,
I would think her a fool if she attached any importance
to it. The more innocent I found her to be, the less I
could make up my mind to possess her.

We went downstairs again, and after strolling until
nightfall we went to the opera wearing our masks, for,
the theater being small, we might have been recognized.
C. C. was certain that she would no longer be allowed
to go out if her father discovered that she was given the
privilege.

We were surprised not to see P. C. At our left was the
Marchese di Montealegre,[6] the Spanish Ambassador, with
his mistress Signorina Bola, and at our right a masked
man and woman who, like ourselves, had never taken
off their masks. They watched us constantly, but C. C.,
whose back was toward them, could not be aware of it.
During the ballet she put the libretto of the opera on
the ledge of the box, and I saw the masked man reach
out and take it. Judging from this that it could only
be a person whom one of us knew, I mentioned it to C. C.,
who at once recognized her brother. The lady could be
none other than his C. Knowing the number of my box,
he had taken the one beside it, and I foresaw that he
intended to have his sister to supper with the woman.
I did not like it; but I could not avoid it except by a
direct challenge; and I was in love.

After the second ballet he came to our box with his
lady, and after the usual compliments the introduction
was made; and we had to go to supper at his casino.
After taking off their disguises the ladies embraced, and
C. fulsomely praised the beauties of my angel. At table
she affected to shower her with attentions, and she, having
no knowledge of the world, treated her with the utmost
respect. Yet I saw that C., despite all her art, was very
jealous of the budding charms which I had preferred

to hers. P. C., boisterously gay, minced no words in his
stupid jokes, at which only his lady laughed; my annoyance made me serious, and C. C., who understood
nothing of the situation, remained silent. Our supper
party was as depressing as possible.

At dessert, by which time he was drunk, he embraced
his lady, challenging me to do as much to mine; I answered calmly that since I loved the Signorina I would
not go so far until I had won rights over her heart. C. C.
thanked me, her brother said that he did not believe us,
and his lady told him to be still. At that I took from my
pocket the gloves I had bought and gave her six pairs
of them, presenting the other six to C. C. As I put them
on for her, I kissed her beautiful arm again and again as
if it were the first favor I had secured. Her brother
laughed derisively and got up from the table.

He threw himself on a sofa, bringing C., who had also
drunk too much, down with him and exposing her bosom
to our view, while she only pretended to resist; but
when he saw that his sister had turned her back on him
and gone to a mirror and that his lewd behavior disgusted me, he pulled up her skirts to display for my
admiration what I had already seen when she fell beside
the Brenta and had handled since. For her part she
slapped him in pretended punishment, but she was laughing. She wanted me to believe that her laughter deprived
her of the power to defend herself; but her efforts had
the contrary effect of revealing her completely. An accursed hypocrisy forced me to praise the shameless
creature's charms.

But now the libertine, apparently calmed, asks her to
forgive him, rearranges her dress, and changes her
position; then, without changing his, he displays his
bestial condition and adjusts the lady to himself, holding her astride him while she, still pretending that she
was powerless in his hands, lets him perform, and performs. At that I go and talk to C. C., standing between

her and them to hide the horror which she must already have seen in the mirror. Red as fire, she spoke to me of her beautiful gloves, which she folded on the mantelpiece.

After his brutal performance the scoundrel came and embraced me, and the lady embraced his sister, saying she was sure she had seen nothing. C. C. modestly answered that she did not know what there had been for her to see. But I saw that her beautiful soul was in the greatest perturbation. As for my own state, I leave it to the reader who knows the human heart to divine it. How could I bear this scene in the presence of an innocent girl whom I adored; and at the very moment when my soul was struggling between crime and virtue to defend her from myself? What torture! Anger and indignation set me trembling from head to foot. The infamous scoundrel believed that he had given me a great proof of his friendship. Reckoning as nothing the fact that he was dishonoring his lady and debauching and prostituting his sister, he was so blinded and infatuated that he did not understand that what he had done must have aggravated me to the point of very nearly drenching the scene in blood. I do not know how I restrained myself from cutting his throat. The only reasonable excuse he offered me two days later was that he could not imagine that when I had been alone with his sister I had not treated her just as he had treated C. After taking them home, I went to bed, hoping that sleep would calm my anger.

Upon awaking and finding that I was only indignant, my love became unconquerable. I thought C. C. was to be pitied only because I could not myself make her happy, for I was determined to do anything necessary to prevent the scoundrel from profiting in any way by her charms if I were forced to give her up. I felt I must lose no time. How horrible! What an unparalleled sort of seduction! What a strange way of winning my friendship! I seemed to be under the dire necessity of pretend-

ing to accept as tokens of friendship what could spring
only from the baseness of an unbridled libertinism ready
to sacrifice everything for the sake of its own continu-
ance. I had been told that he was deeply in debt, that he
had gone bankrupt in Vienna, where he had a wife and
children, and he had done the same in Venice, compromising his father, who had turned him out of the
house and who pretended not to know that he was still
living there. He had seduced C., whom her husband
refused to see, and after running through what money
she had, he wanted to keep her as his mistress despite
the fact that he did not know where to turn for a single
zecchino. His mother, who adored him, had given him
everything she possessed, even to her clothes. I expected
to see him come to ask me for money again or to stand
surety for him; but I was resolved to refuse him. I could
not bear either the thought that C. C. was to become the
cause of my ruin or the thought that she must serve as
her brother's tool in supporting his debauchery.

Guided by love, I called on him the next day and after
telling him that I adored his sister with the purest intentions, I made him realize what pain he had made me
feel during that infamous supper. I told him that I had
resolved to associate with him no longer, even if I had
to renounce the pleasure of seeing his sister; but that
I would find means to keep her from going out with him
if he flattered himself that he could sell her to someone
else.

He answered only that I must forgive him because he
had been drunk and that he did not believe I loved his
sister with a love which excluded possessing her. He embraced me with tears in his eyes, and just then his
mother came in with her daughter to thank me for the
pretty presents I had given her. I told her that I loved
her only in the hope that she would grant me her hand
and that to that end I would send someone to speak with
her husband after I had secured a sufficient income to

make her happy. So saying, I kissed her hand, unable to hold back my tears, which set hers flowing. After thanking me for the sentiments I had expressed to her, she withdrew, leaving me with her daughter and her son, who seemed turned to stone.

The world is full of mothers of this stamp, every one of them honest and endowed with all the virtues, the first of which being good faith they are nearly always the victims of the trust they repose in those whom they take to be people of probity.

My speech to the Signora astonished her daughter. But she was even more astonished when I repeated to her what I had said to her brother. After reflecting for a very short time, she told him that with any other man but myself she would have been ruined, and that she would not have forgiven him if she had been in the place of the lady he had dishonored even if she had been his wife.

P. C. wept. But the scoundrel could command his tears. The day being Whitsunday and the theaters not open, he asked me to meet him on the next day at the usual place, where he would bring his sister to me. He added, addressing us both, that since honor and love obliged him not to leave Signora C. alone, he would leave us in perfect freedom.

"I will give you my key," he said to me, "and you shall bring my sister back here after you have supped wherever you please."

He left us after giving me the key, which I had not strength of mind to refuse, and I left a moment later, telling C. C. that we would talk the next day in the garden on La Giudecca. She said that what her brother had now done was the most honorable decision he could take.

It was fulfilled the next morning; he left her with me and, burning with love, I foresaw what must happen. After engaging a box we went to our garden, where, it being Whitmonday, we found many people; but as the casino was unoccupied we asked nothing more.

We go upstairs and, certain that we should not dare take a walk, since ten or twelve parties were sitting at a number of tables in the garden, we decide to sup in the casino, not caring to go to the opera until the second ballet. So we ordered supper for later. We had seven hours before us; she said she was sure we would not be bored and, having taken off her disguise, she threw herself in my arms, saying that I had finally won her heart and soul during that terrible supper where I had been so considerate toward her. What we said was always accompanied by kisses, with which we deluged each other's faces. *But love kisses the face only to thank it for the desires it inspires; and since its desires have a different goal, love becomes irritated if that is not attained.*

"Did you see," she asked, "what my brother did to his lady when she got astride him as one rides a horse? I hurried to the mirror; but I could well imagine what was happening."

"Were you afraid I would do the same to you?"

"No, I assure you. How could I have feared such a thing, knowing how much you love me? You would have humiliated me so greatly that I could no longer have loved you. We will keep ourselves until we are married. Shall we not? You cannot imagine the joy of my soul when you spoke out to my mother. We will love each other forever. But, while I think of it, please explain the two verses on my garters."

"Are there two verses on them? I didn't know it."

"Please read them. They are in French."

As she was sitting on my lap, she unfastens one garter while I take off the other. Here are the two verses, which I ought to have read before I gave her the garters:

En voyant tous les jours le bijou de ma belle
Vous lui direz qu'amour veut qu'il lui soit fidèle.

("You who see my beauty's jewel every day, tell
it that Love bids it be true.")

The verses which, though naughty, I thought were
perfect, both funny and witty, made me burst out laughing and then laugh even more when I had to explain
them word by word to satisfy her. Since they depended
on two ideas both of which were new to her, she needed a
commentary which set us both on fire. The first thing I
had to tell her was that the ''jewel'' stood for her little
such-and-such, of which I could only obtain possession
by marrying her, and the second was that her garters
would have the privilege of seeing it constantly if they
had eyes. Blushing furiously, C. C. embraced me with
all her heart and said that her jewel did not need any
such flattering advice from her garters, since it knew
very well that it was only for her husband.

''I am only sorry,'' she said after thinking a moment,
''that I shall not dare show anyone my garters now.
Tell me what you are thinking.''

''I am thinking that those lucky garters have a privilege which I may never enjoy. Why am I not where they
are! I may die of the desire I feel, and I shall die unhappy.''

''No, my dear. I am in the same state as you, for you
must have jewels to interest me, too, and I am sure I
shall live. Besides, we can hasten our marriage. For my
part, I am ready to pledge you my faith tomorrow if you
wish. We are free, and my father will be obliged to consent.''

''Your reasoning is sound, for his honor would demand
that of him; yet I wish first to show him my respect by
making an application for your hand, and our household will soon be set up. It will be a matter of a week
or ten days.''

''So soon? You'll see that he will say I am too young.''

''And perhaps he will be right.''

"No; for I am young, but not too young. I am certain, my dear, that I could be your wife."

I was burning; I could no longer resist the compelling force of nature.

"My dear one," I said, holding her clasped in my arms, "are you sure that I love you? Do you think I could fail you? Are you certain you will never repent of marrying me?"

"I am more than certain of it, dear heart; I shall never believe you capable of making me unhappy."

"Then let us marry now before God, in his presence; we cannot have a truer and more worthy witness than our Creator, who knows our consciences and the purity of our intentions. We have no need of documents. Let us pledge our faith to each other; let us unite our destinies here and now and be happy. We will have a church ceremony when we can do everything publicly."

"So be it, my dear. I promise God and you that from this moment until my death I will be your faithful wife, and that I will say the same to my father, to the priest who will bless us in church, and to the whole world."

"I make you, my dear, the same vow, and I assure you that we are truly married and belong to each other. Now come to my arms. We will complete our marriage in bed."

"Now? Is it possible that I am so near to my happiness?"

Thereupon I went out and told the hostess not to bring us supper until we called and to leave us undisturbed, for we wanted to sleep until nightfall. C. C. had thrown herself on the bed with all her clothes on; but I laughed and told her that Love and Hymen went naked.

"Naked? And you too?"

"Of course. Leave it to me."

In less than a minute I had her before my avid and covetous eyes with no veil to hide the least of her charms from me. In an ecstasy of admiration which put me beside myself I devoured all that I saw with fiery kisses, hurrying from one spot to another and unable to stop anywhere, possessed as I was by the desire to be everywhere, regretting that my mouth must move less swiftly than my eyes.

"Your beauty," I said, "is divine; it will not let me believe at this moment that I am mortal."

C. C., white as alabaster, had black hair, and her puberty was apparent only in the down which, divided into little curls, formed a transparent fringe above the little entrance to the temple of love. Tall and slender, she was ashamed to let me see her hips, which the junction of her thighs set off to perfection and whose proportions she thought faulty, whereas if they had been less full and less prominent they would have been less beautiful. Her belly scarcely showed its contours, and her breasts left nothing for either my eyes or my hands to desire. Her large black eyes, under brows not given to anger,[7] bore witness to the joy of her soul in its delight at seeing the effect of her wonderful beauty in my admiration. Her rosy cheeks, which contrasted with her whiteness, showed only two small dimples except when a sweet smile added a fraction of an inch to the length of her coral lips, which at the same time showed teeth whose whiteness surpassed that of her bosom only because it was brightened by the sheen of their enamel.

Beside myself, I began to fear either that my happiness was not real or that it could not be made perfect by an even greater enjoyment. But at that most serious moment mischievous Love gave me occasion to laugh.

"Can it be the law," said C. C., "that the husband must not undress?"

"No, my angel. And even if such a barbarous law existed I would not submit to it."

Never have I undressed more quickly. Then it was her turn blindly to obey the promptings of instinct. She did not interrupt her transports and her ardors except to ask me if it was really true that I belonged to her. She said that the statue of Beauty her father possessed proved that the first sculptor had been a man, for a woman would have made it of the opposite sex from hers.

"Great power of love!" she cried. "I feel no shame. Would I have believed it ten days ago? Please don't tickle me there, it's too sensitive."

"Dear heart, I am going to hurt you more than that."

"I am sure of it; but let nothing stop you. What a difference between you and my pillow."

"Your pillow? Are you joking? Tell me what you mean."

"It's just silliness. These last four or five nights I couldn't get to sleep unless I held a big pillow in my arms and kissed it over and over and imagined it was you. I only touched myself there, dear, just for a moment at the end and very lightly. Then a pleasure for which there are no words left me motionless and as if dead; I fell asleep and when I woke eight or nine hours later I laughed to find the big pillow in my arms."

C. C. became my wife like a heroine, as every girl in love must do, for pleasure and the assuagement of desire make even pain delicious. I spent two whole hours without ever separating from her. Her continual swoons made me immortal. Nightfall bade me resolve to suspend our pleasures. We dressed and I called for lights and supper.

What a delicious repast, even though there was not much of it! We ate gazing at each other, and we did not speak because we did not know what more to say. We found our supreme happiness in the thought that it was we who had created it and that we would renew it whenever we wished.

The hostess came up to see if we wanted anything else, and she asked us if we were going to the opera and if it was true that it was such a fine spectacle.

"Have you never gone?" C. C. asked her.

"Never—it's too expensive for people like us. My

daughter is so curious about it that she would give—
God forgive me!—her maidenhead to go just once.''

C. C. burst out laughing and replied that she would be
paying too dearly to satisfy her curiosity, and just as
I was thinking of offering the woman the box I had
taken she said to me that we could make the girl happy
by giving her our key. I give it to her, swearing that I
had had the same idea.

"Here," she said to the hostess, "is the key to a box
at San Moisè, which cost two zecchini. Go to the opera at
once with your daughter, and tell her to keep her maidenhead for something better."

"And here are two more zecchini," I added, "to do
as you please with."

Amazed at such a liberal present, the good woman ran
to take it to her daughter, while we congratulated ourselves on having made it necessary for us to go back to
bed. The hostess comes back upstairs with her daughter,
a beautiful and quite savory blonde, who insists on
kissing the hands of her benefactors.

"She will be off at once," said her mother, "with her
lover, who is downstairs, but I won't let her go alone
because he's a strapping fellow. I shall go with them."

I told her to keep the gondola in which they came back,
and we would take it to return to Venice.

"Really? You mean to stay here until four o'clock?" [8]

"Yes, for we were married this morning."

"This morning? God bless you!"

She goes to the bed and, seeing signs worthy of veneration, she embraces my charming initiate, congratulating
her on her virtue; but what amused us extremely was a
sermon the woman preached to her daughter while she
pointed out what, according to her, did immortal honor
to C. C. and what Hymen very seldom saw on his altar.
The daughter replied, casting down her blue eyes, that
she was certain the same thing would happen when she
was married.

"I'm sure of it too, because I never let you out of my sight. Take the basin and get some water and bring it here, for the bride must need it."

She brought up water, then they left, and the comical scene diverted my angel exceedingly. After refreshing ourselves all over, we locked ourselves in and went back to bed, where four hours passed very quickly. The last combat would have gone on longer if my wife, already grown curious, had not taken it into her head to put herself in my place and me in hers. When she thus displayed herself before my soul in a state of obsession which pronounced her ravaged by Venus, the supreme degree of pleasure seized on my senses. Left as if dead, we fell asleep; but a moment later the hostess knocked to say that the gondola was at our service. I hurried to open the door, eager to laugh at what she would have to tell us about the opera; but she left it to her daughter while she went to make us coffee. The blonde helped C. C. to dress, occasionally giving me glances which showed me beyond doubt that her mother was greatly mistaken if she thought her inexperienced.

Nothing was more telltale than my angel's eyes, which had such dark circles that they looked as if they had been bruised. The poor child had sustained a combat which had literally left her another person. After drinking some very hot coffee we told the hostess that we wanted a choice dinner for the following day. By the light of early dawn we disembarked at the Campo di Santa Sofia[9] to evade the curiosity of the gondoliers. We parted content, happy, and certain that we were well and duly married. I went to bed resolved that, by an infallible oracle, I would compel Signor Bragadin to obtain the girl's hand for me. I slept until noon; I ate dinner in bed, and I spent the rest of the day gambling and losing.

CHAPTER XV

Continuation of my love affair with C. C.
Signor Bragadin asks for the young lady's
hand for me. Her father refuses and puts her
in a convent. De La Haye. I lose at cards.
Association with Croce, which replenishes my
purse. Various incidents.

THE NEXT day I saw P. C. in my room in high
spirits and taking an entirely new tone with me. He told
me in so many words that he was sure I had slept with
his sister and that he was delighted.

"She refuses to admit it," he said, "but that makes no
difference. I will bring her to you today."

"You will be doing me a kindness, for I love her, and
I shall arrange to have her father asked for her hand for
me in such a way that he will not refuse."

"I should like nothing better, but I doubt it. Meanwhile, I am under the necessity of asking you to do me
another favor. In exchange for a note payable in six
months, I can have a ring worth two hundred zecchini
which I am sure I can sell today for the same price;
but unless you will stand surety, the merchant, who
knows you, will not let me have it. Will you do me this
favor? I know that you lost three hundred zecchini
yesterday; I offer you a hundred, which you will repay
me when the note falls due."

How could I refuse the wretch what he asked of me?
I answered that I was ready; but that he was wrong in
thus abusing the affection which bound me to his sister.
We went to the merchant who had the ring and we completed the transaction. The man, whom I did not know,
thought he was paying me a great compliment when he
said that he was ready to give P. C. everything he had
on my surety. Such was the fashion in which the scoundrel went about Venice looking for the one man in a
hundred ill advised enough to grant me credit against
all reason, for I had nothing. And so C. C., who should
have brought me nothing but happiness, became the cause
of my ruin.

C. C.'s father having gone to Treviso on business, her
brother brought her to me at noon. To convince me that
he was honest he gave me back the note for the Cyprus
wine for which I had stood surety, insisting at the same
time that when next we met he would give me the hundred zecchini he had promised me.

On La Giudecca, where I at once had the garden closed,
we dined in a grape arbor. I thought C. C. had become
more beautiful. Friendship had been added to love, so
that our perfect contentment shone in our faces. The
hostess, who had found me generous, gave me game and
sturgeon. The blonde waited on us at table and came to
wait on us in our room when she learned that we were
going to bed. After helping my wife undress she offered
to take off my shoes; but I waved her away, pretending
not to see her bosom, which on the excuse of the hot
weather she displayed too lavishly. But could I have
eyes for anyone else when I was with C. C.?

She at once asked me what was the meaning of the
hundred zecchini her brother was to bring me, and I
told her the whole story. She said that in future I must
absolutely refuse him my signature, for, since the wretch
was sunk in debt, he would involve me in his ruin, which
was inevitable.

On this second occasion we found our amorous pleasures more substantial; we thought we relished them with more delicacy, we discussed them. She begged me to do everything possible to make her pregnant, for in case her father obstinately refused to let her marry so young he would change his mind when he saw her with a big belly. I had to give her a lecture on the rudiments to make her understand that her becoming a mother depended upon us only in part, but that it was likely it would happen on one occasion or another, especially when we reached the sweet ecstasy at the same time.

So, both applying ourselves sedulously and single-mindedly after two attempts which she said went very well, we spent four good hours sleeping. I called; candles were brought, and after drinking coffee we resumed our amorous labors in order to arrive together at that life-engendering death which was to ensure our happiness. But dawn having come to warn us that we must go back to Venice, we dressed in haste and left.

We did the same on Friday, but I think I should spare the reader the details of our communion, which, though always new to those who are in love, often does not seem so to those who hear it recounted. We arranged to go to the garden for the last time on Monday, the last day for masks. Death alone could prevent me from going, for it might be the last day of our amorous enjoyments.

So, having seen P. C. on Monday morning, when he confirmed the appointment for the same hour at the same place, I did not fail to be there. The first hour passes quickly, despite the impatience of him who waits; but after the first another passed, then a third, a fourth, and a fifth, and the couple for whom I was waiting did not appear. I could imagine only the most terrible disasters. But if C. C. had been unable to leave, her brother should have come to tell me so; but it was possible that some insurmountable obstacle had prevented him from going to fetch his sister. I could not go to their house for fear of missing them on the way.

It was finally on the stroke of the Angelus that I saw C. C. coming toward me, masked, but alone.

"I was sure," she said, "that you were here, and I let my mother say what she would. Here I am. You must be dying of hunger. My brother has not shown his face all day. Let us go to our garden quickly. I need to eat, and to have love console me for all that I have suffered today."

As she had told me everything I did not need to ask her any questions. We went to our garden, despite a very violent storm which, our gondola having only one oar, terrified me. C. C., who was unaware of the danger, frisked about, and the movement she imparted to the gondola put the gondolier in danger of falling into the water, which would have meant our death. I told her to keep quiet, though I did not tell her the danger we were in for fear of frightening her. It was the gondolier who shouted that if we did not sit still we were lost. We arrived at last, and the gondolier smiled when I paid him four times the fare.

We spent six hours there in a state of happiness which the reader can imagine. Sleep was not of our company. The only thought which clouded our joy was that, the season of masks[1] being over, we did not see how we could continue our amorous meetings. I promised that I would call on her brother on Wednesday morning, when she would join us as usual.

After taking leave of the kind hostess of the garden, who could not hope to see us again, we went to Venice and, after leaving C. C. at her door, I went home. The news with which I was greeted when I woke at noon was the return of De La Haye with his pupil Calvi. He was a very handsome boy, as I think I have said, but I laughed heartily at table when, encouraging him to speak, I found him a young De La Haye in miniature even to his gestures. He walked, he laughed, he looked about like him, he spoke De La Haye's French, which was correct but harsh. I thought this was going much too far. I considered it my duty to tell his tutor publicly that he must certainly rid his pupil of his affectations, for his aping him would expose him to bitter raillery. Baron Bavois came in, and after spending an hour with the boy he thought as I did. The promising boy died two or three years later. Two or three months after Calvi's death De La Haye, whose passion was forming pupils, became tutor to a young Cavaliere Morosini,[2] the nephew of the Morosini who had set Baron Bavois on the road to fortune and who was then Border Commissioner for the Republic to settle its boundary with the House of Austria, whose commissioner was Count Cristiani.[3]

In love as I was, I could no longer put off taking the step on which, as I thought, my happiness depended. After the company left I asked Signor Bragadin and his two faithful friends to grant me a hearing for two hours in our withdrawing room, where we were inaccessible. It was there that, making no exordium but *ex abrupto,* I told them that I was in love with C. C. and determined to elope with her if they could not induce her father to grant me her hand.

"It will be necessary," I said to Signor Bragadin, "to provide me with an income on which I can live and to guarantee the ten thousand ducats which the girl will bring me as her dowry."

Their answer was that if Paralis would give them all the necessary instructions they would obey. I asked nothing better. I thereupon spent two hours constructing all the pyramids they wished, and the upshot was that the intermediary who was to ask her father for the girl would be Signor Bragadin in person, because it was he who would have to guarantee the dowry by all his present and future possessions. As C. C.'s father was then in the country I told them that I would inform all three of them when he returned, since the three of them must be together when he was asked for her hand.

Well satisfied with what I had done in the matter, I called the next morning on P. C. An old woman told me that he was not at home but that the Signora would come to me at once. I see her a moment later with her daughter, both looking sad. C. C. tells me that her brother is in prison for debt and that it would be difficult to get him out since the amounts he owed were too great. Her mother weeps as she says she is in despair because she cannot support him in prison and shows me the letter he had written in which he asked her to give an enclosed letter to his sister. I ask her if I may read the letter he had written her, she hands it to me, and I find that he begs her to recommend him to me. I say, handing it back to her, that she can only write him that I can do nothing for him and at the same time I ask the mother to accept twenty zecchini, with which she could help him, sending him one or two at a time. She took them only at her daughter's urging.

After this mournful scene I tell them what I have done toward obtaining C. C. as my wife. The Signora said that my measures did them much honor and were well planned; but she added that I must not hope for anything, since her husband would not give her in marriage until she was eighteen, and then only to a merchant. He was to arrive that day. As I was going, C. C. slipped a note into my hand. She wrote me that, since I had the key to the small door, I could safely come to her at midnight, sure that I would find her in her brother's room. My joy was complete, for, despite their doubts, I hoped for everything. I go home and inform Signor Bragadin that Signor Ch.,[4] C. C.'s father, is expected at any moment. He writes the note in my presence. He asked him to appoint an hour at which he could come to discuss an important matter with him. I told him to wait until the next day to send it.

Conversation in Passing

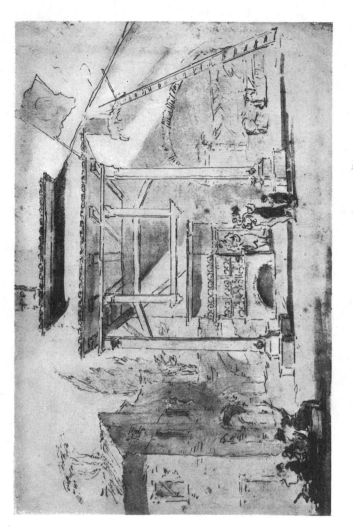

Country House of the Grimani Family, Padua

Having gone to C. C.'s house at midnight, I found her waiting for me with open arms in her brother's room. After she had assured me that I had nothing to fear, that her father had returned in perfect health, and that everyone was asleep, we gave ourselves up to love; but she trembled when I told her that her father would receive the fatal note the next day. She told me what she feared, and her reasoning was sound.

"My father," she said, "who now thinks of me only as a child, will look at me with new eyes and, once he begins examining my conduct, God knows what he will do. We are even happier now than we were when we were going to La Giudecca, for we can spend every night here together; but what will my father do when he finds out that I have a lover?"

"What can he do? If he refuses me I will carry you off, and the Patriarch[5] cannot refuse us the nuptial benediction. We shall belong to each other for the rest of our lives."

"It is all that I ask, and I am ready for anything; but I know my father and I am afraid."

Two hours later I left her, promising that I would return the next night. Signor Bragadin sent his note to her father about noon. He replied that he would himself go to his palace the following day to receive his orders. About midnight I told all this to my dear C. C., who said that her father was most curious to know what Signor Bragadin, to whom he had never spoken, could want with him. Uncertainty, fear, and delusive hope made the pleasures of love much less keen during these last two hours we spent together. I was certain that when Signor Ch. returned home after hearing Signor Bragadin's proposal he would have a long talk with his daughter, and, since she must expect it, I saw that she was terrified; the pity she aroused in me pierced my heart, I could think of no advice to give her, for I could not know how her father would take the matter; she must hide from him whatever circumstances might be injurious to her virtue, at the same time she must in general tell him the truth and show herself more than ready to obey his will. In the course of these reflections I repented that I had taken the great step, precisely because its consequences would be too decisive. I could not wait to escape from the cruel uncertainty which weighed on my soul, and I was surprised to see C. C. less anxious than I was. I felt certain that I would see her the next night. The contrary seemed to me impossible.

The next day after dinner Signor Ch. called on Signor Bragadin, and I did not show myself. He left after spending two hours with him and his two friends, and I learned at once that he had said what his wife had already told me, but with an addition which was most painful for me. He said that he would send his daughter to a convent for the four years which must pass before she married. He had ended by saying that if, at the expiration of that time, I had a well-established position, he might grant me her hand. I found his answer devastating, and in the despair with which it filled my soul I was not surprised at midnight to find the small door of C. C.'s house locked from inside. I went home neither dead nor alive. I spent twenty-four hours in the cruel indecision of one who must adopt a course and does not know what course to adopt. I thought that carrying her off would now be difficult, even as, with P. C. in prison, it would be difficult to correspond with my wife, for I considered her such by a far stronger bond than one we might have contracted before the Church and a notary.

It was about noon on the next day but one that I resolved to visit Signora C., ringing at the main door of the house. A maid came down and told me that the Signora had gone to the country and it was not known when she would return. At that moment I almost gave up hope. All ways of obtaining any information were closed to me. I tried to appear indifferent when I was with my three friends; but I was the most unhappy of men. Hoping to hear something, I was reduced to visiting P. C. in prison.

Surprised to see me, he expresses the greatest gratitude. He explains the state of his debts, he tells me any number of lies, which I pretend to believe; he assures me that he will be out of prison in ten or twelve days, and he asks me to forgive him for not having given me the hundred zecchini he had promised me; but he assures me that when the time comes he will honor the note for two hundred for which I had stood surety. After letting him talk I coldly ask him for news of the family. He knows nothing, and believes there is nothing new; he says that it will be my own fault if I do not call on his mother occasionally, where I will see his sister. I promised to go, and after giving him two zecchini I left.

I racked my brains for a way to find out what C. C.'s situation was. I imagined that she was unhappy, and aware that I was the cause of it I was in despair, I loathed myself. Soon I could neither eat nor sleep.

Two days after Signor Ch.'s refusal, Signor Bragadin and his two friends went to Padua for a month on the occasion of the Fair of St. Anthony. The state of my soul and my uncertain situation did not allow me to go with them. I was left alone in the palace; but I went there only to sleep. I spent the whole day at cards, I lost constantly, I had sold or pawned everything I owned, and I owed money everywhere; I could hope for help only from my faithful friends, who were in Padua, and shame kept me from writing to them.

In this situation, which was enough to bring thoughts of suicide (it was June 13th,[6] St. Anthony's Day), while I was shaving my valet announces a woman. She enters with a basket and a letter. She asks me if I am the person whose name I saw written in the address. I see the imprint of a seal which I had given to C. C. I thought I should drop dead. To calm myself, I told the

woman to wait, thinking that I would finish shaving, but
my hand was shaking. I put down the razor, turn my
back on the woman, unseal the letter, and read the following:

"Before writing you at length, I must be sure of this
woman. I am boarding in this convent, and very well
treated; and I am in perfect health, despite the anxiety
of my mind. The Mother Superior has orders not to let
me see anyone and not to allow me to correspond with
anyone; but I am already sure that I can write to you
despite her prohibition. I do not doubt your constancy,
my dear husband, and I am sure that you do not doubt
and will never doubt mine or my readiness to do whatever you command me to do; for I am yours. Answer
only a few words, until we are sure of the messenger.
Murano, June 12th."

All the letters I quote are faithful translations of the
originals, which I have always kept.

In less than three weeks the girl had become an ex-
pert in moral science; but her teacher must have been
love, which alone performs miracles. The moment during
which a man returns from death to life can only be a
moment of crisis; so I needed to sit down and spend four
or five minutes returning to myself.

I asked the woman if she could read.

"Oh, Signore, if I couldn't read I'd be in a bad way.
There are seven of us appointed to serve the blessed nuns
of XXX⁷ in Murano. Each of us takes her turn coming
to Venice on her day of the week; my day is Wednesday.
So a week from today I can come back and bring you the
answer to the letter which, if you wish, you can write
now. You can see that, since our principal errands are the
letters we're given to carry, we shouldn't be wanted unless we could read the addresses on those we're entrusted
with. The nuns want to be sure—and they're right—that
we won't give Peter a letter they write to Paul. They
are always afraid we'll make that very blunder. So

you'll see me a week from today at the same hour, but
give orders that you're to be waked if you're asleep, for
our time is measured out *like gold*. Above all, when you
deal with me you need fear no indiscretion. If I didn't
know how to hold my tongue, I'd lose my employment,
and what would I do then, being a widow with a son
eight years old and three pretty daughters, the eldest
sixteen and the youngest thirteen? You're welcome to
come and see them if you come to Murano. I live on the
ground floor ten paces from the bridge nearest the
church, on the garden side in the alley, and the door has
four steps outside and I'm always home or at the convent gate or in the visiting room or running errands, of
which there are plenty. The Signorina, whose name I
don't know, for she's only been with us for a week and
who—God keep her in health!—is really a perfect
beauty, gave me this letter, but so cleverly! . . . Oh,
she must be a sly one, for three nuns who were there
certainly never noticed it. She gave it to me with this
note for me, which I leave you too. She tells me to be
discreet. The poor child! I beg you to write her that
she can be sure of it and don't be afraid to vouch for
me, but not for the others, though I believe they're all
honest women, for God preserve me from thinking ill of
anyone; but, you see, they're all ignorant, and they
certainly chatter away at least to their confessors. As
for me—thank God!—I know I need account to him
only for my sins, and carrying a letter from a Christian woman to a Christian man isn't one; and besides,
my confessor is an old monk who—God forgive me!—
I think must be deaf, because he never answers me at
all; but if he's deaf, that's his business, not mine.''

So it was that the woman, whom I had not intended to
question, kindly saved me the trouble by telling me
everything I could wish to know, simply to persuade me
to use no one but herself in the intrigue. It would appear that her very chatter, which sticks in the mind,

contains a sublime eloquence which persuades and instills perfect confidence.

I at once answered my dear captive, intending to write only a few lines as she told me to do; but I did not have time enough to write her a short letter; it filled four pages and it perhaps said less than she had said to me in one. I told her that her letter had saved my life, since I knew neither where she was nor if she was alive or dead. I asked her if I could hope, if not to speak with her, at least to see her. I told her that I had given the bearer a zecchino, that she must have found one herself under the seal of my letter, and that I would send her as much money as she wished if she thought it might be necessary or useful to her. I begged her not to fail to write to me every Wednesday and never to fear that she was writing at too great length, telling me not only every detail of the life she was being forced to lead but also all her ideas on the subject of breaking all the chains and destroying all the obstacles which could stand in the way of our reunion, for I belonged to her just as she told me that she belonged to me. I impressed it upon her that she must use all her ingenuity to make herself loved not only by all the nuns but also by her fellow boarders, yet without confiding anything to them or showing any resentment at having been put where she was. After praising her ingenuity in finding a way to write to me despite the Mother Superior's prohibition, I impressed it upon her that she must take the greatest care never to be caught writing to me, for then her room and her chest of drawers and even her pockets would be searched and any papers she had would be confiscated. On this account I asked her to burn all my letters. I told her to apply all the powers of her mind to the consideration that she was obliged to go to confession frequently; being certain that she would well understand what I was trying to say to her. I ended by imploring her to tell me all her sufferings, assuring her that her sorrows were of even greater concern to me than her joys.

After sealing my letter in such a fashion that the zecchino under the wax would be neither seen nor felt, I gave another to the woman, assuring her that I would reward her in the same way each time she brought me a letter from the same young lady. She wept with gratitude. She said that, since she was free to come and go there, she would give my letter to the Signorina at a time when she found her alone. Here is the note which my dear C. C. had given the woman when she entrusted the letter to her:

"It is God, my good woman, who prompts me to rely on you rather than on any of the others. Take this letter to its address and, if the person is not in Venice, bring it back to me. You must deliver it into his own hands. I am sure that you will at once be given the answer, which you will deliver to me only when you are sure that no one sees you."

Love becomes imprudent only when it is impatient to enjoy; but when it is a matter of procuring the return of a happiness to which a baleful combination of circumstances has raised impediments, love sees and foresees all that the most subtle perspicacity can discover. My wife's letter filled my soul with joy, and in an instant I had passed from one extreme to the other. I felt certain that I could carry her off even if the walls of her convent were guarded with artillery. My first thought was to find some way of quickly passing the week at the end of which I was to receive her second letter. Only gambling could distract me, and everyone was in Padua. I quickly order my valet to pack my trunk and take it to the *burchiello*[8] which was about to leave, and I instantly set off for Padua, from where, at full gallop, in less than three hours I am at the door of the Palazzo Bragadin,[9] where I see its master going in to eat dinner. He embraced me and, seeing me covered

with sweat, said with a laugh that he was sure I was in
no hurry. I answered that I was dying of hunger.

I brought joy to the company and it increased when
I told them that I would spend six days with them.
After dinner I saw Signor Dandolo shut himself up in
his room with De La Haye. They spent two whole hours
there. Signor Dandolo came to my bedside to tell me
that I had arrived just in time to consult my oracle
about an important matter which concerned him, and
he gave me his question. He asked if he would do well
to accept the proposal which De La Haye had just made
to him. I produce the answer that he should reject it.
Signor Dandolo is surprised and returns with another
question. He asks what reasons he shall give him for
his refusal. I suggest that he answer that he had
thought he should ask my advice and, finding me opposed to the plan, wished to hear no more of it.
Pleased that he could put all the odium of his refusal
upon me, Signor Dandolo left. I did not know what it
was all about, but I did not care to know. My satisfaction
consisted in the fact that Signor Dandolo's curt refusal should teach De La Haye that he must not try to
make my friends do anything except through me.

I quickly masked and went to the opera. I sat down
at a faro bank, I played, and I lost all my money. Fortune showed me that she was not always on love's side.
After this ill-considered performance I went to bury my
sorrow in sleep.

On waking in the morning I see De La Haye, all
smiles. After professing the most exaggerated regard
for me, he asks me why I had dissuaded Signor
Dandolo from accepting the proposal he had made to
him.

"What proposal?"

"You know."

"I know nothing about it."

"He told me himself that you advised him against it."

"Very well, I advised him against it; but I did not dissuade him, for if he had been persuaded he would have had no need to ask my advice."

"As you please. May I ask your reasons?"

"First tell me what the proposal is."

"Did he not tell you himself?"

"Possibly. But if you want me to tell you my reasons I must hear the whole thing from you, for he spoke to me under my promise of secrecy. You would do the same in my place. I have always heard you say that in matters of secrecy one must always be on guard against being taken unawares."

"I am incapable of taking a friend unawares; but in general your maxim is sound. I like circumspection. Here is the story. You know that Signora Tiepolo[10] has been left a widow and that Signor Dandolo continues to court her assiduously after having courted her for ten whole years during the lifetime of her husband. The lady, who is still young, beautiful, and fresh, who has very good sense and is sweetness itself, wishes to become his wife. She chose me to confide in, and, seeing nothing that is not praiseworthy in the union, either temporally or spiritually, for you know that we are all human, I was much pleased to take the matter in hand. I even thought I saw that Signor Dandolo was inclined toward it when he said he would give me his answer today. I will tell you sincerely that I was not surprised that he should ask your advice, for it is the part of a sensible man to ask the advice of a prudent friend before he resolves upon an important and decisive step; but I was greatly astonished that such a marriage did not have your approval. Forgive me if, to improve my mind, I ask you to tell me the reasons which make your opinion so different from mine."

Delighted to have discovered everything and to have arrived in time to prevent my friend, who was goodness itself, from contracting a ridiculous marriage, I answered De La Haye that I loved Signor Dandolo and that, knowing his constitution, I was certain that marriage with a woman like Signora Tiepolo would shorten his life.

"That being so," I said, "you must admit that, as a true friend, I was bound to advise him against it. Do you remember telling me that you had never married for the same reason? Do you remember talking to me at great length in Parma in defense of bachelors? Consider too, if you please, that every man is something of an egoist, and that I am entitled to be one when I think that if Signor Dandolo should take a wife his wife's credit with him must have some weight and that whatever influence she gained over him would be at the expense of mine. So you see it would be going against nature if I should advise him to take a step which he could take only to my disadvantage. If you can show me that my arguments are beside the point or are sophistries, speak, and I will yield and make my recantation to Signor Dandolo. Signora Tiepolo will become his wife upon our return to Venice; but I warn you that I will not yield unless I am thoroughly convinced."

"I do not believe I have the power to convince you. I will write to Signora Tiepolo that it is to you that she must apply."

"Do not write that, for she will think you are making a fool of her. Do you think she is stupid enough to expect that I would consent? She knows that I do not like her."

"How can she know that you do not like her?"

"From seeing that I would never let Signor Dandolo take me to call on her. In short, as long as I live with my three friends they shall never have any wife but me. As for you, marry if you please, and I will raise no objection; but if you want us to remain friends give up your scheme of seducing them away from me.''

''You are caustic this morning.''

''I lost all my money last night.''

''Then I chose a bad time. Good-by.''

From that day De La Haye became my secret enemy; and he played no small part in my being imprisoned under the Leads two years later, not by calumniating me, for he was incapable of that, but by pious discourses to pious people. If my reader is fond of bigots, I advise him not to read these memoirs. There was no more talk of the marriage after we returned to Venice. Signor Dandolo continued to pay his court to the widow every day, and I made my oracle forbid me ever to set foot in her house.

Don Antonio Croce,[11] a young Milanese whose acquaintance I had made in Reggio, a great gambler and an old hand at rectifying bad luck, came to call on me just as De La Haye was leaving. He said that, having seen me lose my money, he had come to offer me a way of recouping if I would go halves with him in a faro bank which he would open in his house and at which the punters would be seven or eight rich foreigners, all of whom were paying court to his wife.

''You shall put three hundred zecchini in my bank,'' he said, ''and you shall be my croupier. I have three hundred myself; but it is not enough, for the punters play high. Come to dinner at my house today and you shall meet them all. We can play tomorrow, because it being Friday there is no opera. Be sure that we shall win very large sums, for a Swede named Gillenspetz[12] can lose twenty thousand zecchini all by himself.''

Certain that the celebrated swindler did not have designs on me and sure that he knew the secret of winning, I found that I was not conscientious enough to deny him my assistance as his partner and to refuse a half share in his winnings.

CHAPTER XVI

*I come into money again. My adventure at
Dolo. Analysis of a long letter from my mis-
tress. P. C. plays me a scurvy trick in Vicenza.
My tragicomic scene at the inn.*

THE DIFFICULTY was to find the money; but
in the meanwhile I wanted to make the acquaintance of
the gulls and of the idol to whom they did homage.
So we went to the Prato della Valle[1] where we found
Signora Croce at the coffeehouse, surrounded by foreigners. She was pretty. A secretary to Count Rosenberg,[2] the Imperial Ambassador, who was with her, was
the reason why no Venetian nobleman dared to appear
in her train. The ones who interested me were the
Swede Gillenspetz, a man from Hamburg, an English
Jew named Mendex,[3] whom I have already mentioned,
and three or four others whom Croce called to my attention. We went to dine and afterwards everyone
asked him to make a bank; but he excused himself,
which surprised me, for the three hundred zecchini he
said he had should have been enough for the skillful
player he was; but he cleared my doubt when, taking
me to a private room, he showed me fifty fine doblones

de a ocho,[4] which amounted to exactly five hundred
zecchini. On my promise that I would secure the same
amount, he invited them all to supper the next day.
Our agreement was that we would divide the winnings
before we parted, and that he would let no one play
on his word.

It was to Signor Bragadin that I turned to procure
the amount, for his money box was always empty. He
found a Jewish usurer who, against a note which my
benefactor signed, gave me a thousand Venetian ducati[5]
at five percent per month, payable at the end of a
month and with the interest deducted in advance. It
was the amount I needed. I went to supper, he dealt
until dawn, and our shares were eight hundred zecchini
each. On Saturday Gillenspetz alone lost two thousand
zecchini and the Jew Mendex a thousand. On Sunday
we did not play and on Monday the bank won four
thousand. On Tuesday he had the company to dinner,
because I had told him I must go to Venice. He made a
bank after dinner, and here is what happened at the
end of the afternoon.

An adjutant of the Podestà[6] entered and told him
that he had orders from His Excellency to speak to
him in private. They went out together and two minutes
later my associate came back looking rather embarrassed and told the company that he had just received
an order forbidding him to deal in his house. His lady
said she felt ill and withdrew, and all the players filed
out. After taking half of the money on the table, I left
too. He said we would meet again in Venice,[7] for he
had been ordered to leave within twenty-four hours.
I expected as much, for the young man was too well
known, but also for the still stronger reason that the
authorities wanted people to lose their money at the
gaming room in the theater, where most of the bankers
were Venetian noblemen.[8]

I set off at full gallop at nightfall in very bad

weather; but nothing could have held me back. I was to receive C. C.'s letter early the next morning.

Six miles from Padua my horse fell on its side, so that I was caught with my left leg under its belly. As my boots were soft, I feared that I had broken it. The postilion, who was riding ahead of me, comes running up, pulls me out, and I am delighted that I have suffered no injury; but my horse was lamed. I make use of my privilege and mount the postilion's horse, but the insolent fellow takes it by the bit and will not let me go. I prove to him that he is in the wrong; but it makes no difference; he holds me back, giving me a quantity of spurious arguments, and I have no time to lose. I fire my pistol at him point-blank, at which he makes off and I pursue my journey. At Dolo[9] I go into the stable and myself saddle a horse which the postilion, to whom I immediately gave a scudo, tells me is excellent. No one is surprised that my postilion has remained behind. It was an hour after midnight, a storm had damaged the road, and, the night being very dark, when I reached Fusina I saw the first light of dawn.

I was told that there would be another storm, but I made light of it, a four-oared boat dared the elements, and I reached home safe and sound, though roughly handled by the rain and the wind. A quarter of an hour later the woman from Murano brought me a letter from C. C., saying that she would come back in two hours for my answer.

The letter was a journal seven pages long, a translation of which would bore my reader; but here is the gist of it. Her father, returned home after talking with Signor Bragadin, had summoned her to his room with her mother and had gently asked her where she had made my acquaintance. She answered that she had talked with me five or six times in her brother's room, where I had asked her if she would consent to become my wife, to which she had replied that she was governed by her father and mother. He had then told her that she was too young to think of marrying and that in any case I had as yet no established position. After that he had gone to the room in which his son was living and had himself bolted the small door opening onto the alley and the door which gave access to his mother's room, ordering him to have me told that she had gone to the country if I came to call on her.

Two days later he told her at the bedside of her mother, who was ill, that her aunt would take her to a convent where she would remain as a boarder until she should receive a husband from the hands of her father and mother. She had answered that, being perfectly obedient to his will, she was very glad to go. He had then promised to visit her there and that when her mother was well she would go too. A quarter of an hour after this conversation she got into a gondola with her aunt, who was her father's sister and who took her to the convent in which she now was. Her bed and all her clothes had been brought the same day, and she was well pleased with her room and with the nun to whom the Abbess had entrusted her and under whose supervision she was. It was this nun who had told her that she was forbidden to receive visits and letters and to write letters, under pain of excommunication. However, the same nun had given her books and everything she needed to copy out the passages she liked; it was at night that she abused this favor by writing to me, having no fear of an excommunication which she considered unreasonable. She said that she thought the woman who carried her letters was discreet and trustworthy, and that she would remain so since, being poor, four zecchini a month would make her rich. She thanked me for the zecchino I had sent her, saying that she would let me know when she needed another from me. She told me, in a very amusing style, that the most beautiful nun in the convent loved her to distraction, that she

gave her French lessons twice a day, and had forbidden
her to make the acquaintance of her fellow boarders.
The nun was only twenty-two years old and, as she was
rich and generous, all the other nuns treated her with
deference. She said that when they were alone she gave
her kisses of which I could rightly be jealous if she were
of a different sex. As for my plan of eloping with her,
she said she did not think it would be difficult to execute it, but that it would be wiser to wait until she
could tell me all about the convent building. She urged
me to be true to her, saying that constancy depended
upon fidelity; and she ended her letter by asking me for
my portrait in a ring, but with a secret device so that
no one could see it. She said that I could easily send
it to her by her mother, who was well again and went
alone every day to the first mass at the church of the
P. S.[10] She assured me that her mother would be delighted if I would go there and speak with her. She
hoped, she said, that in five or six months she would
be in a condition which would scandalize and dishonor
the convent if she remained there.

I answered at once, not finishing my letter until I
saw the woman. Her name was Laura. After giving her
her zecchino I entrusted her with a package in which
were fine paper, sealing wax, and a tinderbox. She left,
assuring me that my cousin was growing more beautiful
every day. C. C. had told her that I was her cousin, and
Laura pretended to believe it. Not knowing what to do
in Venice, and my honor demanding that I go to Parma,
my hurried departure from which might have given rise
to such unfavorable conjectures as Croce's had done,
I drank a bouillon and set off, going myself to the
Roman post for a *bollettone*.[11] It was easy to foresee
that my pistol shot near Fiesso[12] and the lamed horse
could have put the post masters in a bad humor to the
point of refusing me horses; but they had to obey when
they saw what is called a *bollettone* in Italy. As for the

pistol shot, I had no fear because I knew I had missed the insolent fellow on purpose. But even if I had killed him nothing would have happened to me.

At Fusina I took a two-wheeled *barella,* being extremely tired and even in no condition to ride a horse. I reach Dolo, I am recognized at once, and I am refused horses. The post master comes out and threatens to have me arrested if I do not pay for the horse I had killed. I answer that if the horse is dead I will account for it to the post master in Padua, and I hand him my *bollettone* to read. He says that since I had nearly killed my postilion none of his will serve me. I say that in that case he shall serve me himself. He laughs in my face and goes off. I then go to a notary with two witnesses, I draw up a complaint, and I threaten him with a fine of ten zecchini an hour if he persists in refusing me horses.

At that he sends out a postilion with two rampaging horses; I clearly see that the plan is to have me upset, perhaps into the river. I coldly tell the postilion that the instant he overturns me I will blow out his brains. He goes back with the horses and tells the post master that he will not serve me. Just then a courier arrives at full gallop from Padua and orders six horses for a berlin and two saddle horses. I thereupon tell the post master that he shall give no one horses before me and that if an attempt should be made to use force blood will be shed, and so saying I show him my pistols. He curses and goes off; everyone around me says he is in the wrong.

Five or six minutes later who should appear but Croce in a fine six-horse berlin with his wife, a chambermaid, and footmen in his livery! He had on an imposing uniform. He gets out, we embrace, and I pull a long face and tell him that he will not leave before I do; I explain the reason, and he says I am right. He raises a row, everybody trembles, the post master had

taken to his heels, his wife comes down and orders that
I be served. Croce says that I am doing well to show
myself in Padua, for people were saying that I too had
left it by order. He tells me that Signor Gondoin,[13] a
colonel in the service of the Duke of Modena, who also
made a bank in his house, had likewise been compelled
to leave. I promised that I would go to see him in
Venice the following week. This man, who had come
into my life as if he had dropped from the sky, had
won ten thousand zecchini in four sessions, of which I
received four thousand nine hundred. I paid all my
debts and redeemed all the possessions I had pawned;
but what is more, he filled my purse.

On arriving in Padua I found all my friends greatly
alarmed except Signor Bragadin, to whose custody I
had entrusted my money box the day before. They believed a rumor which was going the rounds that the
Podestà had also sent me an order to leave. As I was
a Venetian, such an order could not be sent me. Instead
of going to bed I dressed in my best to go to the opera
unmasked. I told them that I must go to give the lie
to everything that evil tongues had been saying about
me.

"I am delighted," said De La Haye, "if everything
that is being said is false, but you have only yourself
to blame. Your hurried departure did you this injustice.
People want to know the reason for everything, and
when they do not know it they invent one. However, it
is certain that you tried to kill the postilion; give
thanks to God that you missed him."

"Another slander. Do you think that a pistol fired
point-blank can miss?"

"But the horse is dead, and you must pay for it."

"I will not pay for it, for the postilion was ahead
of me. Do you know the rules of the post? Besides, I
was in a hurry. I had promised a lady to breakfast with
her that morning."

He seemed annoyed when, after this dialogue, I returned to him all the money he had lent me in Vienna. A man can reason well only when he has money, unless a tumultuous passion makes him lose patience. Signor Bragadin said that I would do well to go to the opera unmasked.

On my appearance in the parterre I saw that everyone was astonished, and whoever spoke to me congratulated me, whether sincerely or not. After the first ballet I went to the gaming room and in three or four deals I won five hundred zecchini. Dying with sleep and hunger, I went home to boast of my victories. My dear Bavois borrowed fifty zecchini from me, which he never returned; but it is true that I never asked him for them.

Still thinking of C. C., I spent the whole next day having my portrait painted in miniature by a skillful Piedmontese who had come to the fair and who later made a great deal of money in Venice; he also painted me a St. Catherine[14] of the same size. A Venetian who was an excellent jeweler made the ring for me surpassingly well. The figure one saw was the saint. An almost invisible blue dot on the white enamel which surrounded her was to be pushed with the point of a pin. The saint sprang up and my portrait appeared, a very good likeness. He delivered it to me four days later, as he had promised.

On Friday, just as we were getting up from table, a letter was brought for me. I was surprised to see that it was P. C. asking me to come to him at once at the "Star" (this was the posthouse inn). He said that he had news to tell me which would interest me greatly. I thought it was something which concerned his sister and I went at once.

I found him, as I expected, with his mistress C. After congratulating him on being out of prison, I asked him what the interesting news was. He said he was certain that his sister was being boarded in a convent and assured me that he would be able to tell me the name of the convent as soon as he returned to Venice. I answered that he would be doing me a favor. But the news was only a means to get me to come and talk with him. The reason for his zeal was something else. He told me exultantly that he had sold a three-year lease on his right to supply cattle for fifteen thousand florins, and that the contracting party with whom he had made the transaction had got him out of prison by standing surety for him and had advanced him six thousand florins in the form of four bills of exchange. He at once showed them to me, all four of them honored by a name which I did not know but of whose excellent reputation he assured me.

"I want to buy," he went on, "six thousand florins' worth of silks from the manufactories in Vicenza, paying the makers by these notes, which are to my order and which I will make over to theirs. I am certain to sell the silks and make a profit of ten percent. Come with us, and I will give you silks to the value of two hundred zecchini; and thus you will be covered for the two hundred zecchini you guaranteed for me on the ring. It will take us only twenty-four hours to finish the whole business."

I should not have gone; but my wish to have the value of my guarantee in my hands overcame my judgment. I consented. "If I do not go," I said to myself, "he will sell the goods at once at a loss of twenty-five percent, and my money will be gone." So I promised to leave with them early the next day. He showed me letters of recommendation to the leading houses in Vicenza. An avariciousness which was not in my character made me fall into the trap.

So very early the next morning I am at the "Star." Four horses are harnessed. The innkeeper comes upstairs with the account and P. C. asks me to pay it; I see a bill for five zecchini, four of which had been paid

out by the innkeeper, for the Signore owed them to the
vetturino he had engaged at Fusina. I paid, with a little
laugh. The scoundrel had left Venice without a soldo.
We got into the carriage, we reach Vicenza in three
hours and put up at the "Sign of the Hat." [15] He orders a choice dinner, then leaves me with his lady while
he goes to talk with the cloth manufacturers.

Signora C. begins by treating me to reproaches
which I disdain. She says that it is eighteen years since
she began to love me, that we were both nine years old
when we saw each other for the first time in Padua. She
brings it back to me. She was the daughter of the Abate
Grimani's antiquarian friend who had put me to board
with the Slavonian woman. Her story makes me smile,
for I recollect that her mother was fond of me.[16]

But in come some shopboys, already bringing lengths
of goods. Signora C. is delighted. In less than two hours
the room is full of silks. P. C. arrives with two manufacturers whom he has invited to dinner. C. flirts with
them, we dine, there is a great plenty of fine wines.
After dinner more goods are brought; P. C. lists them,
with their prices; but he wants still more. He is promised that he shall have more the next day, though it is
a Sunday.

Toward nightfall several Counts arrive; for in Vicenza all noblemen are Counts.[17] P. C. had left his letters of introduction at their houses. There were a Count
Velo, a Count Sesso, and a very pleasant Count Trento;
they invite us to the casino which the nobility frequented. C. is admired there. After spending two hours
at the casino, P. C. invites them to sup with us. Gaiety
and profusion. I was bored to death; I said nothing;
no one spoke to me. I go to bed in a room on the third
floor, leaving them at the table. In the morning I come
down for breakfast, and until noon I see so many
lengths of goods that there must be enough. P. C. tells
me that the whole transaction will be completed during

the course of the next day and that we are invited to
a ball at which all the nobility will be present. The manufacturers with whom he had been dealing all came to
dinner with us. The same profusion.

At the ball that evening I really lost my patience.
Everyone talked with C. and with P. C., who said nothing worth hearing, and when I said anything no one
listened. I take a lady out to dance a minuet, she dances
it, but looking this way and that. A quadrille is made
up, and I find I am left out and that the same lady who
refused me is dancing with another man. If I had been
in good spirits I would not have put up with it; but
I preferred to return to the inn at once and go to bed,
at a loss to understand what reason the nobility of
Vicenza could have to treat me in such a fashion. Perhaps I was neglected because I was not named in the
letters which P. C. had presented; but the rules of
politeness could not be unknown to them. I possess my
soul in patience. We were to leave the next day.

The next day the tired couple slept until noon. After
dinner P. C. went out to pay for the goods he had
chosen. We were to leave the next day, Tuesday, early
in the morning. The Counts, whom C. had enchanted,
came to supper. I left them still at table, impatient for
the next day to come, for I must be in Venice early on
Wednesday.

In the morning the inn boy comes up and tells me
that breakfast is ready in the room downstairs; I delay
a little. He comes up again and tells me that my wife
asks me to hurry. At the word "wife" my hand strikes
the poor innocent's face while my feet kicking his belly
show him to the stairs, which he descends headlong at
the risk of breaking his neck.

I go down furious, I enter the room in which I am
awaited, and I ask P. C. who is the blackguard who has
announced me at the inn as the Signora's husband; and
just as he is answering that he knows nothing about it,

in comes the innkeeper with a knife in his hand and asks me why I had kicked his nephew downstairs. I ask him, pistol in hand, who had told him that I was the woman's husband. He replies that it was Captain P. C. himself who had registered the party. I thereupon seize the Captain by his coat collar, I push him against the wall, and it is the innkeeper who, dropping the knife, prevents me from breaking his head open with the butt of my pistol. The Signora, as always, appeared to be in a faint. The scoundrel did nothing but shout, *"It is not true, it is not true."* The innkeeper goes downstairs and quickly comes back with the register, and, with a murderous look, holds it under the villain's eyes, defying him to repeat that it was not he who had dictated: *"P. C., Captain in the Imperial Army, with Signor and Signora Casanova."* He answers that he had misunderstood him, at which the innkeeper hits him in the face with the book. When I see the coward swallow this insult without remembering that he had a sword and was wearing a uniform, I left the room and, going upstairs, told the innkeeper's nephew to order me a *barella* and two horses for Padua at once. Frothing with rage, I put my possessions in a traveling bag, realizing too late the unpardonable error a decent man commits when he associates with scoundrels. But in comes Signora C.

"Leave this room, for I am furious, and I should not respect your sex."

She drops into an armchair and, bursting into tears, says that she is innocent; she swears that when the shameless knave dictated the registration she was not present. The innkeeper's wife comes in and tells me the same. At that my anger begins to evaporate in words; and from my window I see the *barella* I had ordered standing ready at the door. I send for the innkeeper, to pay him whatever my share may be. He replies that, since I had ordered nothing, I owed him nothing. At this juncture in comes Count Velo.

"I wager, Signor Conte, that you thought this woman is my wife."

"The whole town knows it."

"Hell and damnation! I am astonished that you should have thought so when you know that I lodge alone in this room and when you saw me retire last night leaving her with you all."

"There are accommodating husbands."

"I am not one of them, and you are no judge of men of honor. Let us go outside and I will prove it to you."

The Count quickly made for the stairs and left the inn. C. was choking, and I felt no pity for her. But then it occurs to me that if I leave without paying anything people would laugh at the scene I had made and say I had had a share in the swindle. I order the innkeeper to bring me the bill, as I insisted on paying half of it. He goes for it at once, whereupon I am treated to a fresh surprise. Signora C., falling to her knees and weeping, says that if I abandon her she is lost, for she has neither money nor anything to pawn.

"What! Have you not four thousand scudi worth of goods?"

"They have all been taken away. Did you not know it? The bills of exchange which you saw and which we thought were as good as ready money only made the gentlemen laugh; they took back all the lengths of goods we had chosen. Is it possible?"

"The scoundrel foresaw everything, and that is why he got me to come here. But I am ashamed to complain. I did a stupid thing, and I must pay the penalty."

The bill which the innkeeper brought me came to forty zecchini, an enormous amount for three days; but the money he had paid out was included. I instantly realized that my honor demanded that I pay the whole of it, and I fulfilled the obligation on the spot, taking a receipt signed by two witnesses. I gave the innkeeper's nephew two zecchini to forgive me for having mis-

treated him, and I refused two to C., who sent the innkeeper's wife to ask me for them.

So ended this ugly affair, which taught me a lesson,
but one which I should not have needed. Two or three
weeks later I learned that Count Trento had packed off
the two wretches, with whom I refused to have any
further dealings. A month later P. C. was back in
prison, the man who had stood surety for him having
gone bankrupt. He had the effrontery to send me a
long letter asking me to come to see him; but I did not
even answer it. I did the same to Signora C., who was
reduced to poverty.

I stopped in Padua only to get my ring and to dine
with Signor Bragadin, who returned to Venice a few
days afterward.

C. C.'s letter, which Laura brought me punctually
the next morning, told me nothing new. In my answer
I gave her a detailed account of the trick her brother
had played on me, and I told her to expect her ring, explaining its secret to her.

So, following the instructions she had given me, at
dawn one morning I stationed myself at a place from
which I saw her mother enter the church. Kneeling
down beside her I said I must speak with her, and she
came to the cloister. After trying to console her and
assuring her that I would remain constant in my love
for her daughter until the day of my death, I asked
her if she went to visit her. She answered that she expected to go on Sunday and that she was sorry she
could not tell me in what convent she was. I said there
was no use in my knowing and that I only begged her
to tell her that my heart was hers alone and to give her
the ring, which I showed her.

"It is the likeness," I said, "of her patron saint,
without whose protection she will never become my
wife."

She was to keep it on her finger day and night, and

say a Paternoster and an Ave Maria to it every day. I said that I did the same with my patron San Giacomo, reciting a Credo to him every day.

Delighted that she could teach her daughter this new devotion, she took the ring and promised to deliver it to her. I left her, giving her two zecchini which her daughter might be glad to have to satisfy her small needs. She accepted them, at the same time assuring me that she did not lack anything she needed.

In the letter she wrote me the following Wednesday I found the quintessence of true love. She said that as soon as she was alone nothing was quicker than the point of the pin with which she made St. Catherine spring up. She then kissed my portrait a hundred times and did not leave off if someone came in, for she instantly made the cover drop over it. The nuns were all edified by her confidence in the protection of her blessed patron, whose features by some chance, all the convent said, resembled hers. She said that for that reason the nun who taught her French had offered her fifty zecchini for her ring—not for love of the saint, at whom she had laughed when she read her life, but because she looked like her. The two zecchini I had sent her were very precious to her for, since her mother had given them to her publicly, she could use them as she pleased without arousing idle speculation in those who, seeing her spending money, might wonder from where she could have received it. She liked to make "little presents" to her fellow boarders. She said that her mother had praised my Christian piety, and she ended her very long letter by asking me not to tell her any more news of her brother.

For three or four weeks her letters were about nothing but her St. Catherine, which made her shake with fear when it was in the hands of some nun who, being shortsighted, rubbed the enamel. "Where would I be," she wrote me, "if at such a moment the spring worked and the nun suddenly saw a face which certainly does not look like a saint's? Tell me what I should do.''

A month after P. C. was put in prison the merchant who had sold him the ring for two hundred zecchini gave me the note, reconciling himself to losing twenty. I sent it to the wretch in his prison, who kept writing me asking for money.

Croce was the talk of Venice. He kept a fine house; he dealt at faro and cleaned out the punters. Foreseeing what would happen sooner or later, I never set foot there; but his wife having given birth to a boy[18] and asking me to stand godfather to him, I went there and stayed for supper. From then on I never set foot in his house again.

CHAPTER I

1. *1748:* C. had not left Venice until December 1748. Various considerations lead to the conclusion that the following events took place in the summer of 1749.
2. *Great Circle:* Mathematical and astronomical concept, but here meaning a magician's circle.
3. *Inquisition:* Cesena was in the Ecclesiastical State, and Casanova feared the particularly strict Inquisition in the territories ruled by the Pope.
4. *Godfrey . . . princess:* Allusions to events in the course of the dispute over investitures between the Emperor and the Pope. Matilda of Tuscany, widow of Godfrey of Lorraine, was allied with Pope Gregory VII and the Emperor Henry IV. Henry's penance at Canossa (1077) only interrupted the struggle for a time.
5. *Gregory VII:* Pope from 1073 to 1085, educated at Cluny, the great reforming Pope of the medieval Church; he sought to subordinate secular to ecclesiastical power. He was canonized in 1606. From what source Casanova drew the allegation that Gregory was a great magician is unknown.
6. *Lugo:* A small city in the valley of the Po, between Ravenna and Bologna; at the period it belonged to the Ecclesiastical State.
7. *Scudi:* The Roman scudo was a silver coin which was minted at Rome from the time of Pope Sixtus V (1585-1590) to that of Pope Pius IX (1846-1878); its value was 10 paoli or 100 baiocchi.
8. *Zecchini:* The zecchino was a gold coin minted at Venice from the 15th century. Its value was 22 Venetian lire.
9. *Didone:* Metastasio's *Didone abbandonata* was first set to music by Domenico Sarri (1679-1744) and then, during the

course of the 18th century, by 34 other composers—ample
testimony to the extraordinary popularity of the story. It
was first staged at Naples in 1724.

10. *Teatro Spada:* From 1560 theatrical performances were
given at Cesena in the Palazzo Alidosi, which had come into
the possession of the Spada family. The official designation
"Teatro Spada" was not bestowed until 1797. The building
was demolished in 1843.

11. *Narici:* Barbara Narici, born in Bologna, documented
as singing at Naples in 1738-1739, at Bologna in 1742, at
Graz in 1745, at Venice in 1746, and at Padua in 1751.

12. *Manzonni:* Giovanni Maria Manzoni (1702-1786), Venetian
notary. In 1741 he had introduced C. to the courtesan and
singer Giulia Ursula Preato, called La Cavamacchie, in
Venice (cf. Vol. 1, Chap. IV).

13. *Spada:* Count Bonifazio Spada (died 1767), cavalry general
(cf. Vol. 1, Chap. IV).

14. *Farussi:* This was the maiden name of Casanova's mother
(cf. Vol. 1, Chap. I).

15. *Ten years earlier:* We are in 1749. Maria Theresa had
been reigning for only nine years (since 1740).

16. *Querini Papozze:* Properly Querini delle Papozze. A
branch of the Venetian patrician family of Querini; the
denominative is from the village of Papozzo, near Ferrara
(cf. Vol. 1, Chap. IV).

17. *Count Celi:* Also known as Count Alfani, adventurer and
professional gambler; he is documented at Milan in 1748
and at Cesena in 1749 (cf. Vol. 2, Chap. X).

18. *Cards:* Original, *un livret;* faro term: the thirteen cards
dealt to each of the banker's opponents.

19. *Sept et le va:* Often also *sept et lever,* faro term, meaning
seven times the original stake.

20. *Niccolò Peretti:* Italian castrato and singer, appeared at
Venice from 1745 to 1749, at Turin in 1750, and at London
in 1762. It is improbable that Pope Sixtus V (1585-1590),
whose civil name was Felice Peretti, had a son. But after
the death of his niece Maria Felice Damasceni, he adopted
her four children; so it is possible that Niccolò Peretti was
descended from one of them.

21. *Brisighella:* A village some seven miles south of Faenza, on the northern slope of the Apennines.

22. *Sbirri:* Policemen.

23. *Paolo:* A coin whose value was 11 soldi, minted from the time of Pope Paul III.

24. *Innkeeper:* In the 18th century officers were not required to register at inns.

25. *Albani:* At the time there were three Cardinals named Albani: Annibale Albani, Cardinal from 1711, his brother Alessandro, Cardinal from 1721, and their nephew Gian Francesco, Cardinal from 1747. Cardinal Alessandro Albani (1692-1779) was the "Protector Hungariae"; hence the Hungarian officer's connection with him.

26. *Dutillot:* Guillaume Léon Dutillot (or Du Tillot) (1711-1774), major-domo to the ducal house of Parma from 1749, Minister from 1756 to 1771.

27. *Vetturino:* Hire coachman.

28. *Not measuring my words:* Original, *parlant hors des dents,* one of C.'s more extreme Italianisms.

29. Horace, *Sat.,* I, 6, 57.

30. *Twenty years later:* C. was in Spain in 1767-1768, hence eighteen years after the events here narrated.

CHAPTER II

1. *Carriage of his own:* In addition to travel by mailcoach, it was possible at the period to travel in one's own carriage, horses and driver being furnished by the post.

2. *Henriette:* Obviously a fictitious name. According to recent research the woman whom C. so designates was probably Jeanne Marie d'Albert de Saint-Hippolyte (1718-1795), who married Jean Baptiste Laurent Boyer de Fonscolombe (died 1788) in 1744. She had separated from her husband, probably in 1749.

3. *Caffè della Nobiltà:* The name given to coffeehouses which principally catered to members of the nobility.

4. *Count Dandini:* Son of Count Ercole Francesco Dandini (1691-1747) of Cesena, from 1736 Professor of Jurisprudence at the University of Padua.

5. *Spanish links:* Chains composed of interlocking links of gold wire.
6. *Philosopher:* In accordance with 18th-century Italian usage, the word here means "alchemist."
7. *Terence, etc.:* Publius Terentius Afer (ca. 201-159 B.C.), born in Carthage, and Titus Maccius Plautus (ca. 250-184 B.C.), born in Umbria, the greatest Roman comic dramatists; Marcus Valerius Martialis (ca. 40-102), born in Spain, celebrated Roman epigrammatist.
8. *Forlì:* Town between Bologna and Rimini on the Via Emilia.
9. *Centum cellae:* In Roman times Civitavecchia was called "Centum cellae," after the many small basins for ships there; under the Emperor Trajan it received the name "Portus Traiani." The present name goes back only to the 9th century, when the inhabitants, after the town was destroyed by the Saracens, returned to the "old city."
10. *Tartan:* A small vessel used in the Mediterranean and carrying a mast with a lateen sail and two jibs.
11. *Ponte Molle:* The route from Rome northward was by the Via Flaminia, which left the city by the Porta del Popolo and then crossed the Tiber by the Ponte Molle (later Ponte Milvio).
12. *Institute:* The reference is to the Istituto delle Scienze (Accademia Benedettina) in Bologna.

CHAPTER III

1. *Reggio:* Town at the foot of the Apennines, between Bologna and Piacenza.
2. *D'Andremont:* No innkeeper of this name in Parma is documented in contemporary sources.
3. *New government:* By the Treaty of Aix-la-Chapelle (1748), which marked the end of the War of the Austrian Succession, the Infante Philip of Spain, second son of the Bourbon King Philip V of Spain and Elisabetta Farnese, received the duchies of Parma, Piacenza, and Guastalla. He entered Parma on March 7, 1749.
4. *Madame de France:* In France the King's eldest daughter was called "Madame"; "Mesdames de France" was the designation for the French Princesses. The reference here is

to Louise Elisabeth, eldest daughter of King Louis XV, who married Duke Philip (Don Filippo) and entered Parma on Nov. 23, 1749.

5. *Bornisa's:* An Osteria Bornisa still existed in Parma in the 19th century; it was in the section of the city across the River Parma.

6. *Lire:* The Parmesan lira was a silver coin whose value was 20 soldi.

7. *Caudagna:* Nowhere else in his memoirs does C. say that a sister of his father's had married a Caudagna.

8. *Copernican system:* The famous work by Nicolaus Copernicus (1473-1543) on the revolutions of the heavenly bodies (*De revolutionibus orbium coelestium libri VI,* Nuremberg, 1543) was on the Index of Forbidden Books from 1616 to 1757 because it replaced the geocentric by the heliocentric system.

9. *Tartufe:* A hypocrite; from the name of the leading character in Molière's comedy *Tartufe.*

10. *Sous:* The French sou was a copper coin first minted under Louis XV; its value was the twentieth part of a franc (which was also called "livre").

11. *Farnese:* The house of Farnese came to an end with Antonio Francesco, who died in 1731 leaving no male descendant.

12. *The theater:* The Teatro Ducale (built 1689) in Parma was open to the public. It was replaced by the Teatro Regio in 1829.

13. *Arlecchino:* One of the principal characters ("masks") of the *commedia dell'arte.*

14. *His mother:* Elisabetta Farnese, from 1714 second wife of King Philip V of Spain.

15. *Duke Antonio:* Antonio Francesco Farnese (1679-1731); became Duke of Parma in 1727.

16. *What time of day it is:* In Italy the hours of the day were reckoned from the first hour at the ringing of the Angelus (hence a half hour after sunset) and continuing to the twenty-third hour. The actual time of any given hour of course changed with the seasons. The decree abolishing the system was not issued until 1755; however, the French doubtless introduced the French system of reckoning into the Duchy of Parma in 1749.

17. *De La Haye:* According to C., Valentin de La Haye (ca. 1699-1772) was a Jesuit; however, his name does not appear as such in contemporary sources.

18. *Madame Dacier:* Anne Dacier, née Lefèvre (1654-1720), was married to the French philologist André Dacier (1651-1722); she was considered one of the most learned women of her time and was known especially for her translations from ancient writers.

19. *Dubois-Chatellerault:* Baron Michel Dubois-Chatellerault (1711-1776 or '77), ennobled by Frederick the Great, was an engraver in the service of the Duke of Parma; he reformed the Venetian coinage in 1755, became a member of the Reale Accademia di Belle Arti at Parma in 1757, and was appointed Director General of the Parmesan mint in 1766.

CHAPTER IV

1. *Opera buffa:* The reference is probably to the comic opera *L'Arcadia in Brenta,* with a libretto by Carlo Goldoni.

2. *Buranello:* Byname of the composer Baldassare Galuppi 1706-1785), who came from the island of Burano, near Venice.

3. *Spartito:* Score in parts.

4. *Tusculans:* Cicero wrote his *Tusculanae Disputationes* in 45-44 B.C. after the death of his daughter; it is a moral and philosophical discussion on death, suffering, and passion.

5. *Closing of the opera:* The reference is probably to the nineday suspension on account of the Christmas season.

6. *Virtuosi:* Musicians.

7. *Laschi:* Filippo Laschi, Italian singer, who appeared in opera in Italy, England, and Austria from 1743 to 1775.

8. *La Baglioni:* Presumably Giovanna Baglioni, Italian singer, whose four sisters, however, were also well-known singers. Giovanna is documented as appearing in Italy and in Vienna until 1772.

9. *Symphony:* Composition for orchestra (not a "symphony" in the modern sense).

10. *Vandini:* Antonio Vandini (died 1770), celebrated Italian

violoncellist, performed in Prague in 1723 but later resided principally in Padua.

11. *De La Combe:* Louis de La Combe (died 1757), intimate friend of Duke Philip of Parma.

12. After Vergil, *Aeneid*, III, 395 and X, 113.

13. *Porta di Colorno:* Later called Porta di San Barnabà, in the northern part of Parma, near the present railway station. Coiorno, some nine miles north of Parma, was the spring and summer residence of the Dukes.

14. *Dutillot:* See note 26 to Chap. I of this volume.

15. *Entertainment:* The events described took place in December 1749; it is improbable that a night garden-party was given at that time of year.

16. *Order of St. Louis:* Established by Louis XIV in 1693; in the 18th century it had about 16,000 members.

17. *D'Antoine:* Count François d'Antoine-Placas, Gentleman of the Bedchamber to the Duke of Parma and Chief Equerry to the Duchess Louise Elisabeth; he must have been an old man in 1749.

CHAPTER V

1. *Mont Cenis:* The Col du Mont Cenis, at an altitude of 6800 feet, had long served as a pass over the Alps for travelers from the Piedmont to Savoy.

2. *Sledge:* In the winter months the descent from the top of the pass was made in sledges. Casanova is in error regarding the name "La Novalaise." The modern Novalesa is south of the pass; the first community to the north is Lanslebourg.

3. *"Scales":* This inn ("À la Balance") was still considered the best hotel in Geneva in the 19th century. Goethe, Schopenhauer, and Stendhal lodged there. It no longer exists.

4. *Tronchin:* The reference appears to be only to the Genevan representative of the well-known banker Jean Robert Tronchin (1702-1788) of Lyons, possibly to his brother François Tronchin (1704-1798) or to their cousin Jacob Tronchin (1717-1801), both of whom long resided in Geneva.

5. *Louis:* French gold coin first minted under Louis XIII in the 17th century; value, 24 francs.

6. *Châtillon:* First post station on the road from Geneva to Lyons (some 28 miles from Geneva).

7. *Fifteen years later:* C. met Henriette again in 1763, but did not speak to her; he saw her once more in 1769, but did not recognize her.

8. *The Leads:* In 1755 (cf. Vol. 4).

9. *Buen Retiro:* Name of a royal palace in Madrid, with an extensive garden, built in the 17th century under Philip IV.

10. *Service of France:* Corsica, which had belonged to the Republic of Genoa since 1299, began to struggle for its independence early in the 18th century and was supported by France, which, however, bought the island in 1768. Hence in the War of the Austrian Succession Corsican officers were fighting in Italy on the side of France.

11. *Frémont:* Jacques Frémont was court surgeon and dentist to the Duke of Parma.

12. *Great cure:* Treatment with mercury.

13. *1749:* C. is mistaken in the date; the events he relates occurred in January 1750.

14. *The pox:* Here, as often in the memoirs, C. writes *v...,* for *vérole* ("the pox," "syphilis").

15. *Mercury:* A deliberate pun; Mercury both means the metal and is the Latin name for Hermes as guide of souls.

16. *Botta:* Jacopo Botta-Adorno (1729-1803), Austrian diplomat and Field Marshal.

17. *Bavois:* Louis de Saussure, Baron de Bavois (1729-1772), served the King of Naples until 1748, entered the service of the Venetian Republic in 1752. He was of Swiss extraction.

18. *Duke of Modena:* Francesco III Maria d'Este (1698-1780), from 1737 Duke of Modena, Reggio, and Mirandola.

19. *Too much talk:* The father of Louis de Saussure was David de Saussure, Baron de Bercher et Bavois (1700-1767), Commander of the Swiss regiment of the Duke of Modena; he was demoted in 1748 for serious derelictions.

20. *Bragadin:* Matteo Giovanni Bragadin (1689-1767), Venetian Senator and one of C.'s patrons (cf. especially Vol. 2).

21. *Ambassador:* The reference is either to Alvise Mocenigo, Venetian Ambassador in Rome until Feb. 28, 1750, or to his successor Pietro Andrea Capella, who was in Rome from Jan. 20, 1750.

22. *Aquileia:* The disputes between Venice and Austria over Aquileia were already long-standing, since the jurisdiction of the Patriarch, who was always chosen from among the Venetian patricians, extended into Austrian territory. In 1751 Pope Benedict XIV abolished the Patriarchate of Aquileia and created two archdioceses (Udine in Venetian territory, Görz in Austria).

23. *Jus eligendi:* The right to choose the Patriarch of Aquileia.

24. *Arbela:* City east of the Tigris (now Erbil, in Iraq). The Battle of Arbela, in which Alexander the Great defeated the Persian king Darius, was fought in 331 B.C.

25. *Bartoloni:* The Marchese Paolo Bartoloni, military officer in the service of the Duke of Parma.

26. *Rodela:* A place in North Africa, known for a battle which led to the Spanish reconquest of Oran (Algeria) in 1732.

27. *Duke of Montemar:* José Carillo de Albornoz (1663-1747), Duke of Montemar from 1735; from 1741 to 1743 Captain-General of the Spanish army in Italy.

28. *Parmenio:* Macedonian general who was put to death in Media in 330 B.C. by order of Alexander the Great.

29. *Twenty-three years old:* Early in 1750 C. was nearly twenty-five.

30. *Rodomonte:* A boastful knight in Ariosto's *Orlando furioso.*

CHAPTER VI

1. *Cases against me:* The two accusations which had been the cause of C.'s leaving Venice (cf. Vol. 2, Chap. X).

2. *Savio di Settimana:* Title of the ranking administrative official of the Venetian Republic, appointed for a term of one week (cf. Vol. 2, Chap. IX, n. 13).

3. *Fusina:* A small port on the mainland, south of Mestre.

4. *Foreigner:* As a patrician and a Senator of the Republic, Bragadin was forbidden to lodge foreigners in his house.

5. *Forty hours:* The Forty-hour Prayer, "Oratio quadraginta horarum" (commemorating the forty hours during which Christ lay in the tomb), at which the Holy Sacrament is exhibited, originated in 1527; in 1623 it was made obligatory in all churches, and was finally confirmed by Pope Clement XI in 1705.

6. *Barca corriere:* Packet boat.

7. *Signor Dandolo:* Marco Dandolo (1704-1779), younger brother of the Venetian patrician Enrico Dandolo and friend of Senator Giovanni Bragadin.

8. *Savio for War:* The Venetian Minister of War was officially entitled *Savio alla Scrittura* (cf. Vol. 1, Chap. VI, n. 36).

9. *Rosicrucian:* Member of a secret brotherhood with mystical and reformatory tendencies, founded by Johannes V. Andreae, who wrote a book on the legendary Christian Rosy Cross of the 15th century in 1605. Rosicrucian Brotherhoods existed in Germany, England, and France. In the 18th century an alchemistically oriented secret society appears to have sprung up under the same name. At the same period Masonic Lodges adopted many Rosicrucian concepts.

10. *Carpegna:* Monte Carpegna, a mountain in the Apennines, southwest of Rimini. Casanova had asserted that he was initiated into the occult sciences by a hermit who lived there (cf. Vol. 2, Chap. VII, n. 17).

11. *Paralis:* Name of the spirit from whom C. claimed to receive commands (cf. Vol. 2, Chap. VIII, n. 18).

12. *French Ambassador:* The reference is probably to the Envoy Extraordinary Paul François Galucci, Sieur de l'Hôpital, Marquis de Châteauneuf-sur-Cher, who was temporarily conducting his negotiations with Venice from Naples.

13. *Foreign envoys:* A law originally promulgated in 1481 and re-enacted on several occasions, most recently in 1717, forbade patricians to talk with foreign diplomats; conversations were permitted only on purely official business.

14. *Carlo:* Carlo Bernardi (cf. Vol. 2, Chap. IX, n. 16).

15. *First hour of night:* Old Italian reckoning; an hour and a half after sunset.

16. *Santa Maria Mater Domini:* Built in 960, destroyed in 1503, and rebuilt in the 16th century from plans by Pietro Lombardo; in the Sestiere della Croce.

17. *Lusia:* On the Adige, 7½ miles west of Rovigo.

18. *Ducati correnti:* Venetian money of account; value 6 lire, 4 soldi.

19. *Seventeen o'clock:* About 11 A.M. (cf. n. 15).

20. *Castello:* Fortified section of Venice, on the island of Olivolo, guarding the Lido; Latin "Castrum Olivoli."

21. *Da Lezze:* Venetian advocate, in whose office C. had been employed in 1744 and 1746 (cf. Vol. 2, Chap. IX, n. 2).

22. *Heads of the Council of Ten:* Capi del Consiglio dei Dieci, the three members of the Council of Ten who were charged with acting on all proposals (cf. Vol. 2, Chap. VII, n. 5).

23. *Bussola:* Anteroom of the Council of Ten and of the State Inquisitors, on the door of which there was a knocker (Italian, *bussola*).

24. *Fante:* Fante dei Capi, one of the six official assistants to the Council of Ten, who waited for orders in the Bussola.

25. *Peota:* A covered gondola (cf. Vol. 1, Chap. VII, n. 28).

26. *Ignazio:* Ignazio Beltrame (ca. 1690-1774), assistant to the Venetian State Inquisitors.

27. *Contarini dal Zoffo:* Zorzi Contarini dal Zoffo (1681 - ca. 1760), Venetian State Inquisitor. A branch of the house of Contarini had been given the title of a Count of Joppe or Jaffa (Palestine) in 1473; in Venetian the name became Zoffo.

28. *Santa Maria dell'Orto:* The district took its name from its 14th-century parish church which, though dedicated to St. Christopher, was known as La Madonna dell'Orto after a statue of the Virgin which had been transported to it from a garden. The church (in the Cannaregio quarter) was restored in the 19th century.

29. *Excellency:* In the 18th century only Venetian Senators had a right to this title; but it was also commonly given to all patricians.

30. *Councilor:* The Doge's Council was created in 1033, with two patricians as members; in 1179 its membership was increased to six Councilors (Consiglieri), who represented the six sections of the city for a year and advised the Doge on official business. One of the three State Inquisitors was chosen from among these six Councilors, who were also members of the Council of Ten.

31. *Sanctuary:* The reference is to the Bussola (cf. note 23).

32. *Terno:* A winning combination in the lottery. The lottery was introduced into Venice in the 16th century as the Lotto Genovese and was made a permanent institution, under the name of Lotto Publico, in 1734; it was abolished in Venice after the fall of the Republic, but still exists in Italy. The

player could stake on one or several numbers or on all five: Casanova had won with three correct numbers.

33. *Spanish Ambassador:* José Joaquín, Duke of Montealegre (died 1771), was Spanish Ambassador in Venice from 1749 to 1771.

34. *San Moisè:* The theater was built ca. 1640 and destroyed by fire in 1668; it was rebuilt and continued to be used into the 19th century.

35. *Mendex:* First name unknown, probably Joshua Mendes da Costa, English Jew of Spanish-Portuguese origin, who married a daughter of a certain Joseph Salvador, of London, in 1760.

36. *The fair at Reggio:* It lasted from April 22 to May 7.

37. *Duke of Savoy:* Vittorio Amadeo III (1726-1796), from 1773 King of Sardinia; married Maria Antonia Fernanda of Bourbon on May 31, 1750.

38. *La Dauphine:* Maria Josepha (1731-1767), daughter of the Elector Friedrich August II of Saxony, second wife (from 1747) of the Dauphin Louis, who predeceased his father Louis XV.

39. *Silvia:* Rosa Giovanna Balletti, née Benozzi, known as Silvia (1701-1758), actress with the Comédie Italienne in Paris, always played the *seconda amorosa* (the feminine counterpart of the *secondo amoroso*—"second lover"—usually in the subplot).

40. *Théâtre Italien:* There had been itinerant troupes of Italian actors in France from the reign of Henri III (1574-1589); in 1660 the first Italian troupe settled in Paris, where it alternated with Molière's troupe in giving performances at the Palais-Royal. From 1680 it began an independent existence in the Hôtel de Bourgogne, at first playing only pieces in Italian from the repertoire of the *commedia dell'-arte;* from 1684 French parts were added. The Italian actors were banished in 1697, at the instance of Madame de Maintenon. Under the regency of the Duke of Orléans they returned to Paris in 1716. In the middle of the 18th century they joined forces with French artists and gave comic operas or plays entirely in French.

41. *Simonetti:* C. is in error; the painter to whom he refers

was Francesco Simonini (1686-1753), who lived in Venice from 1740 to 1745.

42. *Guarienti:* Pietro Maria Guarienti (1676 or 1700-1753), Director of the Gallery of Fine Arts in Dresden (cf. Vol. 2, Chap. VIII, n. 9).

43. *Mengs:* Anton Raphael Mengs (1728-1779), born at Aussig (Bohemia), court painter to Augustus III of Saxony, Professor at the Capitoline Academy at Rome, founded by Pope Benedict XIV (cf. Vol. 2, Chap. VIII, n. 10).

44. *Pontelagoscuro:* A small port on the right bank of the Po, near Ferrara; it had considerable importance in the regular traffic by ship with Venice.

CHAPTER VII

1. The manuscript contains two versions of Chapters VII-XII; since the later version, which seems to have been written after January 1793, is incomplete, the Brockhaus-Plon edition gives only the earlier, which was probably begun in 1789, and which is translated here.

2. *Albergo San Marco:* This inn was on the square then called the Piazza della Pace (now Corso Martiri della Libertà), opposite the castle of the Dukes of Este.

3. *Cattinella*: Catterina Lazari, known as La Cattinella, Venetian dancer and courtesan, was banished from the city in 1746 but appears to have returned there later.

4. *Ostein:* Count Ludwig Wilhelm Johann Max von Ostein (1705-1757), Field Marshal and brother to the Elector Johann Friedrich Carl von Ostein (1689-1763). C. erroneously writes "Holstein."

5. *Berlin:* Four-seated covered traveling carriage; it is said to have been first manufactured in Berlin.

6. *Him:* I.e., the innkeeper's son.

7. *Duchesses of Savoy:* Eleonora Teresa (born 1728), Maria Luisa (born 1729), and Maria Felicita (born 1730), daughters of the King of Sardinia Carlo Emmanuele I and his wife Polixena, daughter of the Landgrave of Hesse-Rheinfels-Rotenburg.

8. *The King:* Carlo Emmanuele I (1701-1773), from 1730 King of Sardinia, endeavored to give his country a model political organization.

9. *La Astrua:* Giovanna Astrua (ca. 1720-1758), Italian singer, prima donna at the Berlin Opera from 1747 to 1756, sang at Turin in 1740 and 1750.

10. *Gafarello:* Gaetano Majorana or Majorano (1703-1783), known as Gafarello, also Caffarello, later became Duke of San Donato by inheriting the fief of that name; Italian soprano.

11. *La Geoffroi:* Louise Geoffroi, French dancer and actress, danced at Turin from 1748 to 1750, married to Pierre Bodin.

12. *Duke of Burgundy:* Title of the eldest son of the Dauphin.

13. *Ancilla:* Venetian dancer and courtesan (died 1755) (cf. Vol. 2, Chap. VIII).

14. *Spina:* Pasqua Spina, Venetian singer and courtesan.

15. *Campioni:* Vicenzo Campioni, a dancer of Venetian birth; his first wife was Ancilla (cf. note 13).

16. *Beppino della Mammana:* Byname of Giuseppe Ricciarelli (died after 1776), Italian castrato, who appeared in many European cities; he became a Freemason in London in 1774.

17. *Haymarket Theater:* The reference is probably to the King's Theater in the Haymarket (now Her Majesty's Theater), built in 1700; operas were performed there. The Little Theater (now the Haymarket Theater), built in 1720, was chiefly used for the production of comedies.

18. *Marcati:* Giuseppe Afflisio or Affligio, known as Don Bepe il cadetto or Don Giuseppe Marcati (died 1787), adventurer, professional gambler, and theatrical impresario, was sentenced to the galleys in 1779. His meeting with C. occurred in 1744 (cf. Vol. 2, Chap. II, n. 13).

19. *Rochebaron:* François de La Rochefoucauld, Marquis de Rochebaron (1677-1766), Lieutenant-General at Lyons.

20. *Admitted:* In Lyons there were then three Masonic Lodges ("Grande Loge Écossaise," "Amitié," and "Amis choisis"). Balletti, who, like all French actors of the period, was himself a Freemason, undoubtedly had a hand in C.'s admission.

21. *Degree:* The three degrees in French Lodges were: *Apprenti* (Apprentice), *Compagnon* (Companion), *Maître écoussé,* or *écossais* (Scotch master, but with no reference to Scotland). In his second version, C. adds that he became a

Companion in the Lodge of the Duke of Clermont; the Duke was the Grand Master of all French Lodges.

22. *At Eleusis:* The most famous of Greek mysteries, in honor of the earth-goddess Demeter in her temple at Eleusis, some 12 miles northwest of Athens. The sacred words have a meaning in Greek, but it is not that which C. attributes to them.

23. *Hierophant:* Greek, "he who shows the sacred things"; high priest or priestess, especially of the Eleusinian mysteries.

24. *Plutarch:* Greek biographer and moralist (ca. 46 - ca. 120). His account of Alcibiades' profanation of the mysteries and condemnation is in Chapters XIX and XXII of the biography of Alcibiades in his *Parallel Lives.*

25. *Eumolpides:* The Athenians Polytion and Theodoros were accused of sacrilege together with Alcibiades (cf. Plutarch, "Alcibiades," Chap. XIX). The Eumolpides, descendants of Eumolpos, founder of the Eleusinian mysteries, were always the hierophants of the Temple of Demeter.

26. *Priestess:* Theano, daughter of Menon (cf. Plutarch, "Alcibiades," Chap. XXII).

27. *Botarelli:* Giovanni Botarelli or Bottarelli, Sienese writer and adventurer, author of a book revealing the secrets of Freemasonry, *L'Ordre des francs-maçons trahi et le secret des Mopses dévoilé* (1745).

28. *Hamilton:* Sir William Hamilton (1730-1803), archaeologist and art collector, British Minister Plenipotentiary in Naples from 1767 to 1800.

29. *San Gennaro* (Januarius): Patron saint of the city of Naples. Two vials containing what is held to be his coagulated blood are kept under strict guard in the Cappella del Tesoro. The blood is believed to become liquid on the day of the saint's festival and whenever the city is in danger. In the 18th century the vials were constantly guarded by a deputation of twelve noblemen.

30. After Exodus 24, 8.

31. *Diligence:* The diligence from Lyons to Paris, which made the journey in five days in summer and in six in winter, was considered the most comfortable public coach in France.

32. *Catiline:* Lucius Sergius Catilina (ca. 108-62 B.C.), leader of a conspiracy to seize power as consul. The plot was re-

vealed by Cicero. The phrase which C. attributes to Cicero does not occur in the latter's orations against Catiline.

33. *Lettres de cachet:* Secret royal letters, especially orders for imprisonment, which were greatly abused during the Old Regime. They were abolished in 1789 (cf. Vol. 1, Chap. IX, n. 27).

34. *Uncontrollable people who . . . . :* Allusion to the excesses of popular rule during the French Revolution. Hence this part of the memoirs must have been written in 1793-1794, since Robespierre was overthrown in July 1794.

35. *A lodging:* In the house of a certain Madame Quinson in the Rue Mauconseil, near the Comédie Italienne (cf. Chap. X).

36. *Mario:* Giuseppe Antonio Balletti, called Mario (1692-1762), Silvia's husband, actor in the Comédie Italienne at Paris, always played the *secondo amoroso* (cf. note 39 to the previous chapter).

37. *Palais-Royal:* Built by Cardinal Richelieu from 1629 to 1634; he left it to the King after his death, hence Palais-Royal. Its garden, which was open to the public, was a favorite spot for walks and assignations.

CHAPTER VIII

1. *Flaminia:* Elena Virginia Riccoboni, née Balletti (1686-1771), sister of Mario, actress with the Comédie Italienne at Paris. She played the role of the *prima amorosa* Flaminia; hence her byname. As a writer and translator she was a member of several academies, among them the Arcadian Academy of Rome. She married the Italian actor and author Lodovico Andrea Riccoboni (see note 8, below).

2. *Republic of Letters:* As used in 18th-century France, the term included both writers and scholars.

3. *Sojourn:* The "three famous men" (see the three following notes) were said to have come to Paris only to compete for the favor of Elena Virginia Riccoboni. Their rivalry must already have begun in Italy, before the Italian troupe, including Flaminia, was summoned back to Paris in 1716.

4. *Maffei:* Marchese Scipione Maffei (1675-1755), Italian writer and literary critic; he composed his tragedy *Merope* for Flaminia in 1712.

5. *Conti:* Antonio Conti, known as the Abate Conti (1677-1749), Italian philosopher and poet, chiefly celebrated for his tragedies.

6. *Martelli:* Pier Giacomo Martelli (1665-1727), Italian poet; composed a virulent satire on Maffei in 1724.

7. *V:* The argument appears to be without foundation, since the question is at most one of orthography, not of pronunciation.

8. *Eighty years old:* Lodovico Riccoboni, known as Lelio (1677-1753), Italian actor, playwright, and writer on the theater, was 74 years old at the time.

9. *Duke-Regent:* After the death of Louis XIV (1715), Duke Philip of Orléans (1674-1723) assumed the Regency during the minority of Louis XV. Louis XIV had banished the Italian actors from Paris, at the instigation of Madame de Maintenon, in 1697; the Regent brought them back in 1716.

10. *Marivaux:* Pierre Carlet de Chamblain de Marivaux (1688-1763), celebrated author of plays and novels.

11. *Marivaux's comedy:* The reference is to his *Le Jeu de l'amour et du hasard* (1730).

12. *Saint-Sauveur:* Parish church, built in the 13th century, in the 2nd Arrondissement.

13. *Profession:* In France in the 18th century the Church still denied Christian marriage and burial in consecrated ground to actors. Voltaire protested hotly against this severity.

14. *Palais-Royal:* Cf. note 37 to Chap. VII.

15. *Bavaroise:* A beverage supposed to have been brought to Paris by Bavarian princes in the 18th century. It was made of strong tea sweetened with cane sugar, to which were added the yolk of an egg, milk, and kirsch.

16. *Orgeat:* A decoction of barley or almonds.

17. *Gentleman of the robe:* An advocate. Here Claude Pierre Patu (1729-1758), advocate at the Parlement (High Judicial Court) of Paris, and writer. He and C. soon became close friends.

18. *Civet cat:* La Civette, a well-known 18th-century tobacco

shop; at the time it was located opposite the Café de la Régence, near the Palais-Royal.

19. *Duchess of Chartres:* Louise Henriette (1726-1759), from 1743 Duchess of Orléans.

20. *Neuilly:* Earlier a small fishing port on the Seine, with a ferry; the first bridge there was built in 1606. The present Pont de Neuilly was built from 1768 to 1772.

21. *Ratafia:* A very sweet fruit liqueur, esteemed in the 18th century as a cure for stomach disorders.

22. *Great Chamber:* The Grande Chambre was the principal chamber of the Parlement (High Judicial Court).

23. *States-General:* Body created in 1302 to represent the three "estates" (clergy, nobility, third estate); it was supposed to be summoned by the King to discuss all important political questions with him. During the Age of Absolutism it was not once convoked (from 1614). The present National Assembly evolved from it during the French Revolution.

24. *St. Louis:* Louis IX (1215-1270), King of France from 1226, was canonized in 1297.

25. *Louis XII:* 1462-1515, King from 1498; he was called "the Father of the People."

26. *Henri IV:* 1553-1610, King of France from 1589; brought peace to the country after the Wars of Religion by enforcing tolerance through the Edict of Nantes (1598); wished every Frenchman to have "a chicken in the pot" on Sundays.

27. *Madame La M.:* The Marquise de Pompadour.

28. *Bordello:* The original has *b..d.l.*.

29. *Is not the case:* In the States-General the third estate (the people) had the same number of representatives as the clergy and the nobility; hence the two privileged estates together had twice as many votes.

30. *Patu:* See note 17 to this chapter.

31. *Crébillon:* Prosper Jolyot de Crébillon (1674-1762), dramatist and royal censor. Famous in his time, he was soon eclipsed by his son Claude, the novelist and short-story writer.

32. *Zénobie et Rhadamiste:* Correctly, *Rhadamiste et Zénobie,* a tragedy by the elder Crébillon (1711).

33. *Marais:* The Marais was then an aristocratic quarter, on the right bank of the Seine.

34. *Royal censor:* Censorship, which from the Middle Ages had been exercised by the theological faculty of the Sorbonne, began to be regularly practiced by the State from the time of Richelieu. But it was not until 1741 that permanent royal censors were appointed; of these, there were 79 in all, of whom 35 had jurisdiction over belles-lettres.

35. *Livy:* Titus Livius (59 B.C. - A.D. 17), famous Roman historian; he was a native of Padua and was criticized for using provincial expressions in his writings.

36. Original: le *je ne sais quoi.*

37. *Louis XIV:* Though he had died in 1715, he was much talked of at the time because of Voltaire's *Le Siècle de Louis XIV*, which was published in 1751.

38. *Siamese Ambassadors:* The King of Siam had sent ambassadors to the French court in 1682, 1684, and 1686, because he feared Dutch colonial policy; but there is nothing to substantiate C.'s allegation that Madame de Maintenon had a role in the missions.

39. *Cromwell:* Crébillon later used material from his forbidden *Cromwell* in his tragedy *Le Triumvirat* (1754).

40. *Catilina:* Tragedy by Crébillon, first performed in 1748.

41. *Medea:* In Greek legend, Medea was the daughter of the King of Colchis and married Jason; to punish her unfaithful husband she killed her children (tragedy by Euripides).

42. *The Senate scene:* Voltaire wrote his tragedy *Catilina* in 1752.

43. *Man in the Iron Mask:* In Chapter 24 of *Le Siècle de Louis XIV*, Voltaire states that the Man in the Iron Mask was a brother of the King. There is no doubt that he existed; he was Count Ercole Mattioli, Secretary of State to the Duke of Mantua.

44. *Cénie:* The play was performed June 25, 1750, but at the Théâtre Français, not at the Comédie Italienne.

45. *Madame de Graffigny:* Françoise de Graffigny (1695-1758), woman of letters, aunt of Helvétius.

46. *Amphitheater:* Accommodations for spectators in the French theaters of the period were: *théâtre* (on the stage

itself), *parterre* (standing room on the floor of the house), *loges* (first-tier boxes), *amphithéâtre* ("dress circle"), *loges hautes* (second-tier boxes), *loges du troisième rang* (third-tier boxes).

47. *Beauchamp:* A fictitious name; no Receiver-General of this name is documented at the period.

48. *Maréchal de Saxe:* Moritz (Maurice), Count of Saxony (1696-1750), son of Augustus II of Saxony, King of Poland; Marshal of France from 1744.

49. *Madame du Boccage:* Marie Anne Fiquet du Boccage (1710-1802), French poetess.

50. *Te Deums:* Both the *Te Deum* and the *De profundis* are chants of the Catholic Church; the former was often sung in thanksgiving for military victories, the latter is part of the Requiem Mass for the Dead. Since Maurice de Saxe was a Protestant, no Catholic requiem would be celebrated for him.

51. *Le Fel:* Marie Le Fel (1716-1804), French singer; documented as performing at Paris from 1733 to 1770.

52. *Royal Academy of Music:* Académie Royale de Musique; this was the official name of the Paris Opéra, founded in 1672 by Lully.

53. *Aneci:* Probably a slip for Ancenis: perhaps the Marquis Armand Joseph de Béthune, Duke of Ancenis (1685-1759). There was a contemporary French diplomat named Charles Joseph François d'Annecy, but he was only a baron.

54. *Egmont:* Original, Eguemont; probably the Marquis Casimir Pignatelli, Count Egmont (1727-1801).

55. *Maisonrouge:* Étienne de Masson de Maisonrouge (1702-1785), son of the tax farmer Masson, married the opera singer Rotisset de Romainville in February 1752.

56. *Lany:* Jean Barthélemy Lany (1718-1786), ballet master at the Paris Opéra.

57. *Eau des Carmes:* Aqua Carmelitarum, melissa cordial.

58. *Saint-Jean-de-Maurienne:* In Savoy.

59. *Alexandrines:* Verse of twelve syllables with caesura after the sixth syllable, the heroic verse of French classicism.

60. Tacitus, *Annals*, I, 1.

61. *Hexameter:* Antique meter of six metrical feet, the verse of the *Iliad* and the *Aeneid*.

62. *Voisenon:* Claude Henri de Fusée de Voisenon (1708-1775), French poet and short-story writer.

63. *La Harpe:* Jean François de la Harpe (1739-1803), poet and celebrated literary critic. C. is in error here, for La Harpe was only eleven years old at the time (1750).

64. *Madame du Châtelet:* The Marquise Gabrielle Emilie du Châtelet-Lomont (1706-1749), whose friendship with Voltaire began in 1733. Voltaire published a series of letters to her (1734-1736).

65. *Les Fêtes vénitiennes:* Ballet opera, with music by Campra (1660-1744) and ballets by Danchet. First performance 1710, revived in 1750.

66. *Stands:* The parterre provided only standing room until 1782 (see note 46 to this chapter).

67. Perhaps after Plautus, *Miles gloriosus,* 689, or after Horace, *Satires,* I, 1, 10. There is a pun on Gallus = cock and Gallus = Gaul.

68. *Passacaglia:* An ancient slow dance of Spanish origin.

69. *Dupré:* Louis Dupré (1697-1774), famous dancer of the period, retired from the stage in 1751.

70. *Camargo:* Marie Anne Cupis de Camargo (1710-1770), Spanish dancer, in Paris from 1726, retired in 1751.

71. *Gargouillade:* A fast dance, consisting chiefly of half pirouettes: in 18th-century ballets it was used for the entrances of demons and winds.

72. *Comédie Française:* Also known as the Théâtre Français, it was founded in 1680. In Casanova's time it performed in a tennis court in the Rue des Fossés-Saint-Germain, now the Rue de l'Ancienne Comédie (6th Arrondissement). Its present quarters in the Palais-Royal were not built until 1786-1790.

73. *Le Misanthrope,* etc.: *Le Misanthrope* ("The Misanthrope") and *L'Avare* ("The Miser"), by Molière; *Le Joueur* ("The Gambler") by Jean François Regnard; *Le Glorieux* ("The Boaster") by Philippe Néricault-Destouches.

74. *Sarrazin,* etc.: Celebrated players with the Comédie Française: Pierre Sarrazin (1689-1762), from 1729; Marie Geneviève Grandval (1711-1783), from 1734; Marie Anne Botot, known as La Dangeville (1714-1796), from 1730, a famous soubrette; Marie Françoise Marchand, known as

La Dumesnil (1713-1803), from 1737; Jeanne Catherine Gaussin or Gaussem (1711-1767), from 1731; Claire Hippolyte Josèphe Leyris de la Tude, known as La Clairon (1723-1803), from 1743; Pierre Louis Dubus, known as Préville (1721-1799), from 1750.

75. *La Levasseur:* Possibly Rosalie Levasseur (Le Vasseur), who danced in the ballet of the Comédie Française in 1759. But in that case C. is here confusing his first visit to Paris with his second (1759).

CHAPTER IX

1. *Bertinazzi:* Carlo Antonio Bertinazzi (1710-1783), known as Carlino, Italian actor; married the actress Françoise Suzanne Foulquier, of Nantes, in 1760.

2. *Madame de La Caillerie:* Nothing is known of her except that she collaborated with the actor Gandini on the outline of a comedy, *Le Songe vérifié*, first performed in 1751.

3. *Boufflers and Luxembourg:* C. refers to a notorious exchange of wives which had taken place earlier in the century. Duke Joseph Marie de Boufflers (1706-1747), who had married Marie Madeleine Angélique de Neufville-Villeroy (1707-1787) in 1721, exchanged wives with Duke Charles François Frédéric de Montmorency-Luxembourg (1702-1764), who was married to Marie Sophie Colbert de Seignelay.

4. *Pantalone:* The most celebrated performer of this role in Paris at the time was Carlo Veronese (1702-1762). His daughters Anna Maria and Giacoma Antonia were known by the names of the roles they played in the *commedia dell'arte;* Corallina was the name of a young servant girl (*servetta*), Camilla was one of Pantalone's two daughters.

5. *Prince of Monaco:* Charles Maurice Grimaldi, Count of Valentinois (1727-1790).

6. *Duke of Valentinois:* Jacques François Léonor Goyon-Matignon, Duke of Estouteville and Valentinois (1689-1751), married to Louise Hippolyte Grimaldi in 1715.

7. *Count of Melfort:* André Louis Hector, Count of Drum-

mond-Melfort (1722-1788), descendant of a Scotch family; he was an officer in the French army and a Freemason.

8. *Duchess of Ruffec:* Catherine Charlotte Thérèse, Duchess of Ruffec (1707-1755), mother-in-law of the Prince of Monaco (see note 5 above), who married her daughter Marie Christine in 1749. C.'s "woman of sixty" exaggerates her age by almost twenty years.

9. *Diable:* An elegant four-wheeled carriage with open sides but with a top.

10. *Clap:* Original, *la ch...*, for *chaudepisse*, slang for gonorrhea.

11. *Warren:* French *garenne*, a game preserve, but in the 18th century restricted to a preserve for wild rabbits. To which of the several *garennes* on the outskirts of Paris C. refers is not clear.

12. *Barrier:* Until 1859 Paris had 60 such barriers at streets leading out of the city; customs duties were collected there for certain goods brought in. Vaugirard was a small village, which later gave its name to the 15th Arrondissement.

13. *Vis-à-vis:* A light carriage with facing seats for two passengers.

14. *Hôtel du Roule:* House of prostitution in the Faubourg Saint-Honoré (from 1750); named after the village of Le Roule, which later became a suburb of Paris.

15. *Protected by the police:* However, the proprietress was arrested in 1752. The house passed into other hands and by the end of the 18th century served as a boarding school for children of the nobility.

16. *Chaillot:* In 1750 Chaillot was still a village outside of the city; it later became a suburb of Paris.

17. *Saint-Hilaire:* Professional name of Gabrielle Siberre, also known as Mademoiselle La Boissière (ca. 1729-1760).

18. *Guadagni:* Gaetano Guadagni, Italian musician and singer; documented as appearing in London, Dublin, and Paris from 1748.

19. *Adélaïde:* This daughter is mentioned in no contemporary source, though Corallina is known to have borne a daughter named Anne in 1755.

20. *Signorina Brignole:* Anna Brignole, née Balbi (1702-1774), married to the Marchese Brignole (died 1769), who was the

Genoese Ambassador in Paris from 1742 to 1754; she became Princess of Monaco in 1757.

21. *Prince of Conti:* Louis François Joseph, Prince of Conti (a branch of the Bourbon family) (1734-1814).

22. *Count of Montréal:* The natural son of the Prince of Conti and Corallina was a Count de Vauréal (1761-1785), not Montréal.

23. *A Princess:* The wife of the heir to the throne of France bore a girl child named Marie Zéphirine in 1750, but the little Princess lived only until 1755.

24. *Royal Academy of Painting:* The Académie Royale de Peinture, de Sculpture et de Gravure was founded under Louis XIV in 1648; it was abolished in 1793 and later incorporated into the Institut de France as the Académie des Beaux-Arts.

25. *Parosselli:* Charles Parrocel (1688-1752).

26. *Fontainebleau:* A favorite residence of the French Kings from the time of Louis XIII. In 1750 Louis XV stayed there from October 7 to November 17.

27. *There:* I.e., to Fontainebleau.

28. *Morosini:* Francesco II Lorenzo Morosini (1714-1793), Venetian patrician, Ambassador of the Republic in Paris 1748-1751, from 1755 Procuratore di San Marco.

29. *Lully:* Jean Baptiste Lully (1632-1687), French composer of Italian origin; director of the Paris Opéra (Académie Royale de Musique).

30. *Madame de Pompadour:* Jeanne Antoinette Poisson (1721-1764), married to Charles Guillaume Le Normand d'Étioles 1741; mistress of Louis XV, who created her Marquise de Pompadour in 1745 and a Duchess in 1752.

31. *Lemaure:* Catherine Nicole Lemaure or Le Maure (1703-1786), French opera singer.

32. *Blue Ribbon:* Knight of the Order of the Holy Ghost. The order was established in 1578 by Henri III in honor of his accession to the throne of France and his election as King of Poland. Both events took place on Whitsunday (the feast of the descent of the Holy Spirit), which accounts for the name of the order. The emblem of the order was worn on a blue ribbon. The Knight of the order to whom C. refers is the Duke of Richelieu. (See the following note.)

33. *Maréchal de Richelieu:* Louis François Armand, Duke of Richelieu and Fronsac (1696-1788), Marshal of France from 1747.

34. *Calfeutrées:* "Stopped up." C.'s mispronunciation involves the vulgarism *foutre* ("to have sexual intercourse").

35. *Put apart:* Original, *écarter,* which means both "to spread apart" and "to set aside."

36. *He:* I.e., Richelieu.

37. *Lord Keith:* George Keith, 10th Earl Marischal of Scotland (1693-1778), exiled as a Jacobin in 1716, lived in Berlin from 1745, was Prussian Ambassador in Paris 1751-1754. In Vol. 2, Chap. IV, C. says that he met him in Constantinople in 1745.

38. *Madame de Brionne:* Louise Julie Constance, Countess of Brionne (1734-1815), married to the Count of Brionne in 1748.

39. *Monsieur d'Argenson:* Marc Pierre de Voyer de Paulmy, Count of Weil-d'Argenson (1696-1764), from 1720 Lieutenant-General of Police, from 1742 Minister of War.

40. *The face of Louis XV:* The many portraits of Louis XV show him to have been, in fact, a very handsome man.

41. *The Queen of France:* Maria Leszczyńska, daughter of the dethroned King of Poland, Stanislaus Leszczyński, married to Louis XV in 1725.

42. *Monsieur de Lowendal:* Ulrik Frederik Volmar, Freiherr von Lowendal (1700-1755), Russian Count from 1738, Marshal of France from 1747.

43. *Bergen-op-Zoom:* The famous fortress of Bergen-op-Zoom in Brabant was captured by Lowendal in 1747 during the War of the Austrian Succession.

44. *Mesdames de France:* Title of the daughters of the reigning King of France. Here the daughters of Louis XV: Elisabeth (born 1727, married to the Duke of Parma in 1739, lived in Parma from 1749), Henriette (1727-1752), Adélaïde (born 1732), Victoire (born 1733), Sophie (born 1734), Louise (born 1737).

45. *Giulietta:* Giulia Ursula Preato, known as La Cavamacchie (1724-1790), Venetian singer and courtesan (cf. Chap. I of this volume).

46. *Marquis de Saint-Simon:* Maximilien Henri, Marquis de

Saint-Simon-Sandricourt (1720-1799), Adjutant-General to the Prince of Conti.

47. *Prince de Conti:* Louis François, Prince of Bourbon-Conti (1717-1776), Marshal of France and diplomat.

48. *Queen Elizabeth:* Elizabeth I of England (1533-1603).

49. Ovid, *Fasti,* I, 218. Giulietta refers to a well-known epigram addressed to Queen Elizabeth; but her memory of it is inaccurate, for the speaker is not the Queen but the poet: *In thalamis, Regina, tuis hac nocte iacerem / Si foret hoc verum, pauper ubique iacet* ("I should sleep in your bed tonight, O Queen, if it were true that the poor man makes his bed everywhere").

50. *Marry a Grimani:* The marriage did not take place until 1757.

51. *Monsieur de Saint-Quentin:* Nothing is known of this Gentleman of the Bedchamber to the King.

52. *Beginning of these memoirs:* See Vol. 1, Chap. IV.

53. *Countess Preati:* Giulietta, whose name was Preato, assumed the name of the noble Veronese family of Preati.

54. *Count Kaunitz:* Wenzel Anton, Count Kaunitz, from 1764 Prince of Kaunitz-Rietberg (1711-1794), was Austrian Ambassador in Paris from 1750 to 1753.

55. *Count Zinzendorf:* Ludwig Friedrich Julius, Count Zinzendorf (1721-1780), first served the Elector of Saxony, then entered the service of Austria; he was in Paris 1750-1752.

56. *Abbé Guasco:* Octavien de Guasco, Count of Clavières (1712-1780), of Piedmontese origin; Canon of Tours, member of the Academy of Inscriptions.

57. *Signor Uccelli:* Francesco Antonio Uccelli (born 1728), Venetian notary, later secretary to the Venetian Embassy in Vienna, married Giulietta Preato in 1752 (cf. Vol. 1, Chap. IV).

58. *Madame Préaudeau:* Catherine Étiennette Charlotte Préaudeau, née Gaulard, married Claude Jean Baptiste Préaudeau (died 1762) in 1751.

59. *Déchargé:* "Discharged, unloaded," but incorrectly used in C.'s context.

60. *Savoyards:* In Italian *savoiardo* is the name of a biscuit which originated in Savoy. In French *Savoyard* means a native of Savoy.

61. *Whom you call Savoyards:* In Paris porters, chimney
    sweeps, bootblacks, and the like, who offered their services
    in the streets, were called "Savoyards," since many of them
    came from Savoy.
62. *Derrière:* C. not only commits an error in French, as
    Crébillon explains to him in the next paragraph, but also
    perpetrates an obscenity, since Italian *vi* ("you") sounds
    exactly like French *vis* (slang for "penis").
63. *Charon:* C. added the name in his revision. The reference
    may be to the wife of the Councilor Élie Bochart de Saron.
64. *Lady Lambert:* Lady Mary Lambert (ca. 1717-1762) was
    married to the English baron and banker John Francis
    Lambert (died 1755).
65. *Fair at Saint-Germain:* The fair, which originated in the
    12th century, was held yearly from Feb. 3 to Palm Sunday
    in front of the Church of Saint-Germain-des-Prés.
66. *Place de Grève:* This square was the scene of executions
    (now Place de l'Hôtel de Ville).
67. *Monsieur de Marigny:* Abel François Poisson (1725-1781),
    brother of the Marquise de Pompadour; from 1746 Seigneur
    de Vandières, from 1754 Marquis de Marigny, from 1747
    director and manager of the royal buildings and gardens and
    of arts and manufactures.
68. *Duke of Maddaloni:* Carlo Caraffa, Duke of Maddaloni
    (Matalona) (1734-1765); Don Lelio Caraffa was his great-
    uncle (cf. Vol. 1, Chap. IX, nn. 11, 12).
69. *Signor Mocenigo:* Alvise II Zuan Mocenigo (1711-1756),
    Venetian Ambassador in Paris 1751-1756. He was killed by
    falling down a stairway in his house.
70. *Madame de Colande:* Marie Catherine, Marquise de
    Colande, wife of Alexandre Pierre Jacques Le Gendre,
    Marquis de Colande.
71. *Duke of Burgundy:* Title of the eldest son of the Dauphin;
    here Louis Joseph Xavier (Sept. 13, 1751-1761).
72. *Against its King:* C. must have written the following re-
    flections on the King of France before October 1789.
73. *Turkish regulations:* Turkey had no equivalent of the
    French nobility.
74. *Livres:* Livre is synonymous with franc.
75. *Borghese:* Marcantonio Niccolò, Prince Borghese (1730-

1800), and Giovanni Battista Francesco, Prince Borghese (born 1733).

76. *Knez:* "Prince" in Slavonic languages.

77. *Being a woman:* C. is mistaken; he was a man. Charles Chevalier d'Éon de Beaumont (1728-1810), French diplomat, from 1755 secret agent of Louis XV, lived in Paris as a woman from 1777 to 1785, and died in England.

78. *Gave birth to a son:* Erica, Princess of Ardore (1708-1766), bore a son named Luigi Maria at Paris in 1743; her husband was Neapolitan Ambassador in Paris from 1741 to 1753.

79. *Duchess of Fulvy:* C. probably refers to Hélène Louise Henriette Orry de Fulvy (died 1768), who was not a Duchess but the wife of an Intendant of Finances.

80. *Gaussin:* C. confuses La Gaussin (cf. Chapter VIII of this volume) with Louise Gaucher, called Lolotte (died 1765), actress and mistress of Lord Albemarle.

81. *Lord Albemarle:* William Anne Keppel, 2nd Earl of Albemarle (1702-1754), appointed English Ambassador in Paris in 1749.

82. *Canada:* France lost Canada to England by the French and Indian War, which ended in 1759 when the English took Quebec.

83. *Venetian lady:* Lady Anna Wynne, née Gazini (1713-1780), was married in 1739 to Sir Richard Wynne, whose mistress she had been and who died in 1751.

84. *Her eldest daughter:* Giustiniana Franca Antonia Wynne (1736 or '37-1791); in 1761 she married Philipp Joseph, Count Orsini-Rosenberg (1691-1765), who was Austrian Ambassador in Venice from 1754 to 1764.

CHAPTER X

1. *District commissary:* In Paris in the 18th century there were 48 police commissaries, two or three for each of the 21 districts into which the city was divided; they also served as examining magistrates.

2. *Lieutenant-General of Police:* One of the most important offices under the Old Regime. From 1747 to 1757 it was held by Nicolas René Berryer de Renouville (1703-1762).

3. *Hôtel-Dieu:* The largest hospital in Paris; it was originally a convent but became a hospital as early as the ninth century. C. doubtless means the Foundling Hospital (Hôpital des Enfants Trouvés), which had been built in 1670 opposite to the Hôtel-Dieu.

4. *Comic opera:* At the beginning of the 18th century all theaters except the Opéra and the Comédie Française were forbidden to give entire plays. Hence the theaters at fairs played only pantomimes, single scenes, and comic sketches with songs. Later on, comedies with popular songs interspersed were also permitted. Out of this grew the Opéra Comique, which was combined with the Comédie Italienne in 1762.

5. *Saint-Laurent fair:* This fair was held yearly during July and August on the site now occupied by the Gare de l'Est.

6. *Monnet:* Jean Monnet (1703-1785) was director of the Comédie Française in 1743 and again from 1752 to 1758.

7. *Bérard:* Born 1725; violoncellist at the Théâtre Italien.

8. *Chantilly:* Marie Justine Cabaret du Ronderay, called La Chantilly (1727-1772), dancer; she married Favart (see note 10) in 1744.

9. *Maréchal de Saxe:* See note 48 to Chap. VIII.

10. *Favart:* Charles Simon Favart (1710-1792), playwright and theater director, founder of the Opéra Comique.

11. *Fontenelle:* Bernard Le Bovier de Fontenelle (1657-1757), famous French writer; though a precursor of the Enlightenment, he wrote several works in the taste of his period.

12. *Thétis et Pélée:* Lyric tragedy by Fontenelle, music by Colasse, first performed in 1689. The parody was entitled *Les Amants inquiets* ("The Uneasy Lovers") and was written by Favart; first performance 1751, at the Comédie Italienne.

13. *Voisenon:* Claude Henri de Fusée de Voisenon (1708-1775), abbé and author of works in the lighter vein.

14. *Académie:* The Académie Française, founded by Richelieu in 1635, especially to guard the purity of the language. Among its members have been not only poets and prose writers but generals and statesmen. Voisenon was elected to it in 1762.

15. *Concert Spirituel:* Founded in 1729 by Philidor, these concerts of religious music had been given on holy days and

almost daily from Palm Sunday to the first Sunday after Easter, in the Salle des Cent Suisses at the Tuileries Palace.

16. *Bed of justice: Lit de justice.* Until the Revolution the French Parlements, both in Paris and the provinces, were only judicial institutions whose function was to register the King's edicts. When the King attended a solemn sitting of the Paris Parlement—usually only to enforce the registration of an edict—he sat under a baldaquin; hence the term *lit de justice.*

17. *Hartig:* Franz de Paula Anton, Count Hartig (1758-1797), Austrian Ambassador in Dresden 1787-1794.

18. *His works:* Probably the edition in six volumes, published at Paris in 1742.

19. *Tête pelée:* literally "baldpate," but used to mean "of no account," with an untranslatable echo of *Thétis et Pélée.*

20. *Théâtre Français:* The theater in which the Comédie Française played.

21. *Athalie:* A late tragedy of Racine's, with a Biblical subject, composed at the instance of Madame de Maintenon (1681).

22. *Esther:* Racine's second tragedy on a Biblical subject (1688).

23. The untranslatable point of the couplet consists in using the word *faire* in two senses: in the first line it means "compose," in the second it means "manage."

24. *Madame de Tencin:* Claude Alexandrine Guérin, Marquise de Tencin (1685-1749); her literary salon in Paris was one of the most celebrated from 1726 until her death.

25. *D'Alembert:* Jean d'Alembert (1717-1783), celebrated French man of science and one of the great thinkers of the Enlightenment. His father was not Fontenelle but probably a brother of the poet P. Destouches. As he was left on the steps of the Church of Saint-Jean-le-Rond, the Foundling Hospital gave him the name Le Rond.

26. *Madame de Graffigny:* See note 45 to Chap. VIII, above.

27. *The Leads:* I Piombi, the Venetian prison from which C. escaped in October 1756. See Vol. 4.

28. *Third time:* After his second long stay in Paris (1757-1759), C. visited the city several times (1761, 1763, 1767, 1783).

29. *Loss:* Johann Adolf, Count Loss (1690-1759), was Saxon Ambassador in Paris from 1741 to 1753.

30. *King . . . Elector:* Friedrich August II, Elector of Saxony, and King of Poland under the name of August III (1733-1763).

31. *Zoroastre:* The libretto (music by Rameau) was by Louis de Cahusac (1700-1759), who was an advocate at Toulouse; first performance, Paris, 1794. C.'s Italian version, with music by Johann Adam, who used some of Rameau's score, was performed in Dresden on Feb. 7, 1752.

32. *Pleased my mother:* C.'s mother was in Dresden and no doubt attended the performance.

33. *Mademoiselle Vesian:* Antoinette Louise Soleri de Vesian (ca. 1737-1804), born in Parma, appeared at the Comédie Italienne in Paris under the name of Camille Gabriac from 1753 to 1755 and from 1756 at the Opéra under her real name. Her brother was Antonio Francesco Soleri de Vesian.

34. *Minister of War:* The post was held by D'Argenson from 1742 to 1757 (see note 39 to Chap. IX of this volume).

35. *Hôtel de Bourgogne:* C. had obviously changed his lodgings after his quarrel with Madame Quinson. The Hôtel de Bourgogne is not the theater of that name but a house in which furnished rooms were let.

36. *Madame de Monconseil:* Cécile Thérèse Guinot de Monconseil (1707-1775), married Lieutenant-General Louis Étienne Antoine Guinot de Monconseil in 1725.

37. *Protector:* The manuscript has *producteur,* which the editor regards as a slip for *protecteur.* It is possible, however, that C. intended *producteur,* in which case the meaning would be: "If I were to be the one who brought her into notice . . ."

38. *Count of Narbonne:* Presumably Jean François, Count of Narbonne-Lara (died 1806).

39. *Le Gros Caillou:* Name of a popular resort on the left bank of the Seine; then a suburb of Paris, now part of the 7th Arrondissement.

40. *Lany:* See note 56 to Chap. VIII.

41. *Tressan . . . Trean:* The reference is to Jacques Robert d'Héricy, Marquis d'Etréhan; he lived with La Vesian only until 1767.

42. *La Piccinelli:* Anna Piccinelli, singer at the Comédie Italienne, married Vesian in 1762.

CHAPTER XI

1. *Morphy:* Victoire Morphy (born ca. 1734), actress in comic opera. She was the daughter of an Irishman, Daniel Morphy, but had acted in Flanders.
2. *Half écu: Petit écu,* coin worth 3 francs or livres; the *grand écu,* or *écu de six francs,* was worth twice as much.
3. *Twenty-five louis:* = six hundred francs.
4. *Helen:* C. calls her Helen because of her beauty. She was Marie Louise Morphy, known as Louison (1737 or '38-1815). Mistress of Louis XV from 1752 to 1755.
5. *A Greek:* Slang for "sharper."
6. *A German painter:* Probably the Swedish painter Gustaf Lundberg (1695-1786); but perhaps Johann Anton Peters (1725-1795), who lived in Paris from 1746 to after 1787, was ennobled by Louis XV in 1763, and who chiefly copied paintings by Boucher.
7. *O-Morphi:* Modern Greek ὄμορφη = "beautiful" (feminine).
8. *Monsieur de Saint-Quentin:* See note 51 to Chap. IX.
9. *Six-franc piece: Écu de six francs* (see note 2, above). It bore a portrait of Louis XV.
10. *Double louis:* Gold coin worth 48 francs.
11. *Parc aux Cerfs:* Originally a game preserve created by Louis XIII in Versailles. It later became a residential section of the city and, as such, kept its old name.
12. *At the end of a year:* The boy was probably born in the summer of 1753.
13. *Staff officer:* Jacques de Beaufranchet, Count of Ayat (died 1757), from the Auvergne.
14. *Tablets:* A portable set of leaves or sheets, used for writing, especially for memoranda; in the 18th century, often made of ivory.
15. *Madame de Valentinois:* Marie Christine Chrétienne Grimaldi, Countess of Valentinois, née De Rouvroi de Saint-Simon de Ruffec (1728-1774).
16. *Old wife:* See note 41 to Chap. IX.

17. Altered from Horace, *Epistles,* II, 1, 176.

18. *Sanson:* Possibly a descendant of the cartographer Nicolas Sanson, of Abbeville (1600-1667), and his son Adrien (died 1718).

19. *Garnier:* His father, Jean Garnier, long in the service of the Count of Argenson, made a fortune supplying the army; he became Major-Domo to the Queen in 1749.

20. *Duchess of Chartres:* Louise Henrietta, née Princess of Bourbon-Conti (1726-1759), married Louis Philippe, Duke of Chartres (later Duke of Orléans) in 1743. She was president of the women's Masonic Lodges in France.

21. *Madame de Polignac:* Marie, Marquise de Polignac, née Rioult de Courzay (died 1784).

22. *Plantain water:* In the 18th century plantain in various forms was much employed in medicine. The likelihood is that the Duchess's pimples were the result of a venereal disease.

23. *Abbé de Brosses:* Probably the Abbé Marcel de Brosses, for whose arrest the Parlement de Paris issued a warrant in 1761.

24. *Duke of Montpensier:* Louis Philippe II, from 1785 Duke of Orléans, best known as the "Citizen King" under the name of Philippe Égalité (1747-1793).

25. *Madame La Pouplinière:* Mimi Le Riche de La Pouplinière, née Boutinon des Hayes, earlier an actress under the name of Mimi Dancourt (ca. 1713-1756), married the tax farmer Alexandre Jean Joseph Le Riche de La Pouplinière in 1737.

26. *Hole:* Richelieu had rented an apartment in the house next door, from which he had access to Madame de La Pouplinière's bedroom through an opening in the fireplace. Her husband discovered it and left his wife. She died of cancer.

27. *Lived in the Louvre:* Not in the Louvre proper; he lived in the administration building in the Rue Saint-Thomas du Louvre.

28. *Bourguignon:* Jacques Courtois (Cortese), called Le Bourguignon (1621-1676), French painter of battle pictures, died at Rome.

29. *Porte des Feuillants:* One of the six entrances to the Tuileries; it gave access to the monastery of the Feuillants,

a branch of the Cistercian Order, whose Swiss guards and porters furnished food and drink.

30. *Liard:* A copper coin worth a quarter of a sou.

31. *Labré:* C.'s addition gives "Condé-Labré," which can also be read as *con délabré* ("dilapidated vagina").

32. *Swing bridge:* This bridge, which led from the Tuileries toward the present Place de la Concorde, was erected in 1716.

33. *Étoile:* This cannot be the present Place de l'Étoile; C. must mean some place near the Tuileries or in the garden itself.

34. *Talvis:* Michel Louis Gatien, Vicomte de Talvis (Tailvis, Taillevis, Taibris) de la Perrine, French army officer, later adventurer and professional gambler.

35. *Gallery:* The art in the Zwinger Palace in Dresden, founded 1722.

36. *Frères ennemis:* C.'s parody of Racine's earliest tragedy, *La Thébaïde ou les Frères ennemis* (1664), was a comedy in three acts entitled *La Moluccheide o sia i gemelli rivali*.

37. *Minister:* Heinrich, Count von Brühl (1700-1763), Saxon statesman; entered the service of Augustus the Strong in 1720, in 1746 appointed Minister to Augustus III, whom he completely controlled.

38. *Creps:* Presumably a misspelling for Krebs; the reference is clearly to some house of prostitution in Dresden, but the establishment is not mentioned in contemporary sources.

39. *Fools:* Their nicknames were Joseph Fröhlich ("Merry"), Baron Schwindel ("Swindle"), Saumagen ("Sowbelly"), and Leppert ("Silly").

40. *"Ruin of Saxony":* Von Brühl's anti-Prussian policy brought Saxony into the Seven Years' War.

41. *Amorevoli:* Angelo Amorevoli (1716-1798), Italian tenor, engaged to sing at Dresden in 1742.

42. *Locatelli:* Giovanni Battista Locatelli (between 1713 and '15-1785), born at Milan and died at St. Petersburg, man of letters and theatrical impresario.

43. *La Morelli:* Teresa Morelli (died after 1781), Venetian dancer.

44. *Fabris:* Domenico Tomiotti de Fabris, Count of Cassano (1725-1789), officer in the Austrian service. C. had first met him at Padua in 1747 (cf. Vol. 2, Chap. X).

45. *Two years later:* The Seven Years' War did not begin until three years later, in 1756.
46. *Ninety:* Locatelli died at the age of seventy or seventy-two.

CHAPTER XII

1. *Migliavacca:* Giovanni Ambrogio Migliavacca (born ca. 1718 at Milan), Italian poet, pupil of Metastasio; from 1752 court poet to the King of Poland at Dresden.
2. *Metastasio:* Pietro Antonio Metastasio (real name Trapasso; 1698-1782), celebrated Italian poet, best known for his opera librettos; from 1730 court poet at Vienna.
3. *Gravina:* Gian Vincenzo Gravina (1664-1718), professor of law at the University of Rome and well-known literary critic, founder of the Arcadian Academy, adoptive father of Metastasio.
4. *Attilio Regolo:* Tragedy with music (1740), first performed at Dresden in 1750.
5. *French prose:* The first French prose translation of Metastasio's works was published in 12 volumes by J. Richelet from 1751 to 1756.
6. *Ariosto:* Metastasio was presumably referring to the translation by F. de Rousset, published in 1615.
7. *Imperial Library:* The library, later the National Library, was founded by Maximilian I and enlarged by his successors. The splendid building which houses it on the Josefsplatz was built in 1721 by order of Karl VI, the father of Maria Theresa.
8. *A young Venetian:* Probably Felice Calvi, already mentioned in Chapter VI.
9. *Border commissioner:* As the result of a long series of boundary disputes between Austria and the Republic of Venice, a commission of plenipotentiaries from either side was set up in the 18th century: Francesco II Lorenzo Morosini (1714-1793) was a commissioner for Venice from 1752 to 1754.
10. *Opera:* Then still in the Burgtheater, built by Maria Theresa. The Kärntnertor theater, built in 1708, did not become the opera house until after the fire of 1781.

11. *Commissaries for Chastity:* The Keuschheits-Kommission ("Commission for Chastity") was established in 1751 and abolished under the Emperor Franz II (1792-1866).

12. *Temesvar:* Now Timisoara, in western Rumania. After the establishment of the Commission for Chastity, it became the place of exile for prostitutes. Deportations took place in May and October of each year until 1769.

13. After Horace, *De arte poetica,* 25.

14. *Stockhaus:* Old German term for prison.

15. *The Sign of the Crawfish:* An inn already well known in the 16th century, on the Hohe Markt in Vienna; it survived until the end of the 18th century.

16. *Beccaria:* Valerius de Beccaria (1692-1770), born at Padua; officer in the Austrian army.

17. *Baron Weiss:* Gottlieb von Weiss (died 1757), Lieutenant-Colonel in the Austrian army (cf. Vol. 2, Chaps. II and III).

18. *Testagrossa:* Antonio Testagrossa, also Grossatesta (died 1761), abate and diplomat in the service of the Duke of Modena; he was in Vienna from 1752 to 1753 negotiating the marriage between the Archduke Leopold and Princess Maria Beatrice d'Este. The marriage did not take place.

19. *Princess Beatrice d'Este:* Maria Riccarda Beatrice d'Este, Duchess of Massa and Carrara (1750-1829), heiress to the Duchy of Modena, married the Archduke Ferdinand (born 1754), son of Maria Theresa, in 1771.

20. *Roggendorf:* Ernst, Count Roggendorf (1714-1790).

21. *Sarotin:* Doubtless a misspelling of C.'s; the person referred to was probably a member of the Sarentein (Sarentheim) or the Zierotin family.

22. *Fräuleins:* C. writes *frailes*. The appellative was given to young ladies of station.

23. *Tramontini:* Giacomo Tramontini (ca. 1705-1785).

24. *Signora Tesi:* Vittoria Tesi-Tramontini, née Tesi (ca. 1690-1775), Florentine singer; called "the queen of song."

25. *Sachsen-Hildburghausen:* Josef Friedrich, Prince of Sachsen-Hildburghausen (1702-1787), Field-Marshal-General in the Imperial Army. Vittoria Tesi-Tramontini was his mistress.

26. *In the Spanish fashion:* Spanish dress, black with a white

ruff, was still considered a mark of distinction in Vienna in the 18th century.

27. *Poniatowski:* Stanislas II August Poniatowski (1732-1798), King of Poland from 1764 to 1795, was crowned at Warsaw on November 25, 1764.

28. *Kremnitz ducats:* Austrian gold coin, value four gulden; it was minted at Kremnitz, in Slovakia.

29. *Archduchesses:* Maria Anna (born 1738); Maria (born 1742); Elisabeth (1743); Maria Amalia (1746); Johanna (1750); Josepha (1751); Karoline (1752). Marie Antoinette, later married to Louis XVI of France, had not been born at the time of which C. writes.

30. *Eldest son:* Joseph II (1741-1790), Emperor from 1765, ruined his health by unremitting work, though he knew that his constitution was not equal to the strain.

31. *Laxenburg:* Summer palace near Vienna, favorite resort of Joseph II.

32. *Brambilla:* Gian Alessandro Brambilla (1728-1800), born in Pavia, physician-in-ordinary to Joseph II. Anton von Störck (1741-1803), physician-in-ordinary to Maria Theresa, was also in the service of Joseph II after the death of the Empress and did not conceal his serious condition from him. Presumably C. refers to him here.

33. Ovid, *Remedia amoris*, 91.

34. *His brother:* Leopold II (1747-1792), Emperor from 1790. Hence C. wrote this account after 1790 and before 1792 (accession of Franz II).

35. *The intelligent physician:* The reference is either to von Störck (cf. note 32) or to Joseph Quarin (1734-1814), from 1758 professor at the University of Vienna.

36. *His niece:* Elisabeth, Princess of Württemberg (1767-1790), married the Archduke Franz of Austria in 1788, died in childbed in 1790.

37. *Durazzo:* Giacomo, Count Durazzo (died 1794), of a Genoese patrician family, was Ambassador of the Republic of Genoa in Vienna from 1749 to 1752; he married Ernestine Aloysia Ungnade, Countess of Weissenwolf, in 1750.

38. *Marolles:* Antoine Alexandre Marolles (died 1751 or '52), French draftsman and illustrator.

39. *Quinze-Vingts:* Asylum for the blind, founded in 1260 by Louis IX; the name Quinze-Vingts ("Fifteen Score") comes from the fact that it accommodated 300 blind men and women. It was demolished in 1780.

40. *Erdödy:* Christoph, Count Erdödy (1726-1777), was married to Antonia, Countess Kinsky.

41. *Prince Kinsky:* Probably a relative of the Countess Erdödy, née Kinsky, mentioned in note 40.

42. *Angiolini:* Gasparo Angiolini (1723 - ca. 1796), Milanese dancer and ballet master, married the dancer Maria Teresa Fogliazzi.

43. *Dressed in mourning:* At the period wearing mourning could signify poverty.

44. *Prince-Bishop:* Nikolaus Csáky de Keresztszag (1698-1757), Archbishop of Gran, Primate of Hungary from 1751.

45. *Sovereign:* The sovereign, or sovrano, was an Austrian gold coin worth 13.33 gulden; minted from 1750 to 1758 and again from 1824 to 1857.

46. *French Embassy:* There was no French Ambassador in Vienna in the spring of 1753. C.'s reference must be to the French Chargé d'Affaires François Joseph Dumont, who had been in Vienna since 1752.

CHAPTER XIII

1. *Bucentaur:* Bucintoro, the state barge of Venice, in which on Ascension Day the Doge was rowed out into the Adriatic to throw a ring into the water to symbolize the marriage of the Republic with the sea. The ceremony dated from a visit to Venice by Pope Alexander III and the Emperor Barbarossa in 1177.

2. *Grimani:* At the time there were four Grimanis in Venice whose Christian name was Giovanni (Venetian, Zuan).

3. *Barella:* A two-wheeled post carriage.

4. *Oriago:* On the post road from Padua to Venice, some six miles from Venice.

5. *Brenta:* The post road from Padua to Venice ran along the Brenta, a small river which rises in the southern Dolomites and flows into the Venetian Lagoon.

6. *Admiral of the Arsenal:* Provveditore (or Ammiraglio) all' Arsenale, one of the three high Venetian officials charged with guarding the Arsenal; the *Bucentaur* was kept there.

7. *Procuratie:* Built in the 16th century as dwellings for the Procuratori di San Marco, the highest judicial officers of the Republic.

8. *Ponte della Paglia:* Bridge leading to the Riva del Sepolcro and the Riva degli Schiavoni.

9. *Monster:* Doubtless one of the wild animals from various countries which were commonly exhibited at fairs in the 18th century.

10. *Colonne:* There was a Rio delle Colonne near San Marco, but the name was also that of other places.

11. *"Wild Man":* An inn dating from the 14th century and not closed until 1870; variously known as Al Salvadego, Del Omo Salvadego, or Al Salvatico. The present Calle del Salvadego still bears its name.

12. *Opera buffa:* Comic opera.

13. *Laschi:* Filippo Laschi (died after 1775), Italian singer; appeared in Venice, London, Turin, Vienna, Leghorn.

14. *Pertici:* Pietro Pertici (1731 - after 1760), Italian singer and actor; appeared in Venice, London, Parma, Florence, Trieste.

15. *P. C.:* Recent research has shown that the initials do not stand for Pietro Campana, as was formerly thought, but for Pier Antonio Capretta (ca. 1721-1779), son of the Venetian merchant Christoforo Caprctta.

16. *Fondamenta di San Marco: Fondamenta* is the generic Venetian term for a quay at which ships could dock; there were several of them, bearing different names.

17. *O.:* Maria Ottaviani (ca. 1726 - after 1753), daughter of the chemist Carlo Ottaviani, of Padua, and married to the Venetian broker Angelo Colonda.

18. *Her sister:* Rosa Ottaviani (ca. 1727 - before 1790) married in 1757 to the patrician Piero Marcello (1719-1790), who in 1755 was sentenced to six years' imprisonment under the Leads.

19. *Beef cattle:* From the 16th century there were two Provveditori alle beccarie charged with supplying the State with

meat; they were members of the Senate and patricians. Capretta, as a *cittadino,* can at most have been their subordinate.

20. *Liston:* A fashionable promenade.

21. *C. C.:* Caterina Capretta (died after 1780), daughter of the Venetian merchant Christoforo Capretta; she married the advocate Sebastiano Marsigli in 1756.

22. *Signora Manzoni:* Caterina Manzoni, née Capozzi (1706-1787), wife of the notary Giovanni Maria Manzoni (1702-1786); she took a motherly interest in C. (cf. Vols. 1 and 2).

23. *Margrave:* Friedrich, Margrave of Bayreuth (1711-1763).

24. *Only son:* In 1753 Teresa Imer already had two children, a son (born 1746) and a daughter (born February 1753).

25. *Pompeati:* Angelo Francesco Pompeati (1701[?]-1768), Venetian dancer and ballet master; he married Teresa Imer about 1740.

26. *Papafava:* Annibale Papafava (born 1691), Venetian patrician.

27. *Patrimony:* According to a decree of the Lateran Council (1179), a bishop who consecrated a priest without at the same time being able to provide him with a benefice was obliged to supply him with an adequate income in the form of a patrimony if the priest had no income of his own.

28. *Ducati correnti:* Venetian money of account; value 6 lire, 4 soldi.

29. *Bonafede:* Count Giuseppe Bonafede (1682-1762), first in the service of the Tuscan court, then an officer in the Austrian army, later became a spy for the Venetian Republic (cf. Vol. 1, Chap. VII, n. 14).

30. *Biria:* The northwestern quarter of Venice, near the present railway station.

31. *Twenty-one o'clock:* Old Italian reckoning, about 3:00 P.M.

32. *Campo dei Santi Apostoli:* Square in front of the church of the same name, north of the Rialto bridge.

33. *Opera seria:* "Grand opera."

34. *San Samuele:* The Teatro San Samuele, near the church of the same name, was on the Grand Canal, about halfway between San Marco and the Rialto bridge.

35. *Bautta:* A sort of mantle worn by maskers (cf. Vol. 2, Chap. VIII, n. 27).

36. *An inn:* Original, *locande.* C. has a marginal note: "The Academy writes locante, but it is mistaken. The right form is locande." However, the form *locante* is nowhere found. In the 18th century the word designated a hostelry superior to an *albergo.*

CHAPTER XIV

1. *Twenty o'clock:* Old Italian reckoning, about 5:00 P.M.
2. *To engage a box:* There were already several shops in Venice at which theater tickets could be purchased.
3. *Giudecca:* Venetian, Zuecca. In the 18th century this island, to the south of the city proper, had many gardens and country houses; it was a favorite place for excursions.
4. *San Biagio:* The eastern part of the island, so called after the church of the same name (built in 1222, demolished in 1860).
5. Altered from Ariosto in Domenico Batacchi's *La Rete di Vulcano.*
6. *Montealegre:* José Joaquín, Duke of Montealegre, was Spanish Ambassador in Venice from 1748 to 1771.
7. *Brows not given to anger:* I.e., narrow eyebrows, according to the doctrine of Lavater (1741-1801), whose *Physiognomical Fragments* C. knew in the French translation by the author (published 1781-1785).
8. *Old Italian reckoning:* About midnight.
9. *Campo di Santa Sofia:* On the Grand Canal, a short disstance north of the Rialto bridge.

CHAPTER XV

1. *Season of masks:* In 1753 the fair, and with it the time during which masks might be worn, lasted from May 30 to June 12. Many of the dates given later in this chapter are erroneous, as is often the case with C.
2. *Morosini:* Francesco Morosini (born 1751), nephew of Francesco Lorenzo Morosini (1714-1793); for the latter, who was a hereditary Cavaliere della Stola d'Oro, see note 28 to Chap. IX of this volume.
3. *Cristiani:* Beltrame, Count Cristiani (also Christiani, 1702-

1758), Austrian privy councilor, Grand Chancellor of Austrian Lombardy.

4. *Ch.:* I.e., Christoforo, Christian name of Caterina Capretta's father.

5. *Patriarch:* The Bishop of Venice bore this title from 1451. The office of Patriarch of Venice was held by Alvise Foscari from 1741 to 1758.

6. *June 13th:* The Fiera del Santo, in honor of the saint whose feast it was, began in Padua on this day. There is another error in dates here (cf. note 1).

7. *XXX:* Recent research has led to the supposition that the convent was that of San Giacomo di Galizzia in Murano; but the convent of Santa Maria degli Angeli is also a possibility.

8. *Burchiello:* A vessel carrying passengers and freight, which made a daily round trip between Venice and Padua.

9. *Palazzo Bragadin:* Senator Bragadin owned a palace in the Santa Sofia quarter of Padua, in which he usually spent the summer and autumn with his friends.

10. *Signora Tiepolo:* Cornelia Tiepolo, née Mocenigo, married to the Venetian patrician Francesco Tiepolo (1697-1750) in 1722.

11. *Croce:* Antonio Croce, alias Della Croce, De La Croix, Santa Croce, Castelfranco, Crozin (died 1796), son of Giovanni Battista Croce, of Milan, adventurer; in Italy the title "Don" was given to priests, Roman noblemen, and noblemen of the provinces which had been under Spanish rule.

12. *Gillenspetz:* Swedish army officer, sentenced to death *in absentia* for fomenting rebellion, moved to Venice and became the lover of Marina Pisani, the wife of a patrician.

CHAPTER XVI

1. *Prato della Valle:* A large square in Padua; its present aspect dates only from 1775. Croce appears to have lived in a house on the square.

2. *Rosenberg:* Philipp Joseph, Count Orsini-Rosenberg (1691-1765), did not enter on his office as Austrian Ambassador in Venice until July 1754. C. doubtless refers to the Chargé

d'Affaires Stephan von Engel, later secretary to the Ambassador, who represented his country's interests until Rosenberg arrived.

3. *Mendex:* Probably an English Jew named Joshua Mendes da Costa, who settled in Venice in 1750.
4. *Doblones de a ocho:* Spanish gold coin, value 8 gold scudi.
5. *Venetian ducati:* Originally a gold coin minted in Venice from 1284, and which in the 16th century came to be called a zecchino. In the 17th century a new ducato was minted, with a value of 14 lire.
6. *Podestà:* In general the mayor of an Italian town; in the towns of the Venetian mainland possessions the podestà, as a high judicial officer, was almost always a Venetian patrician.
7. *In Venice:* According to contemporary sources, Croce had been banished from the territories of the Venetian Republic as early as November 7, 1753. However, this is contradicted by the birth of his child in Venice (cf. note 18).
8. *Venetian noblemen:* In the 18th century Venetian patricians were permitted to make bank for games of chance, but not to play themselves.
9. *Dolo:* On the post road from Padua to Venice, on the Brenta, some ten miles east of Padua.
10. *P. S.:* Perhaps for "Pères Somasques" (monks of the Somaschian Order; cf. Vol. 1, Chap. V, n. 7); if so, then the reference is to the Church of Santa Maria della Salute.
11. *Bollettone:* A sort of ticket which could be paid for in advance and which gave the holder priority at post stations.
12. *Fiesso:* Post station some eight miles east of Padua.
13. *Gondoin:* A professional gambler of this name, of Greek origin, was banished from Padua in July 1756.
14. *Catherine:* C. here gives away C. C.'s Christian name (Caterina).
15. *The "Sign of the Hat":* Al Cappello rosso; it was known as the best inn in Padua from the 15th century. Goethe lodged there in 1786.
16. *Her mother was fond of me:* Signora C. (Maria Colonda) was the daughter of Carlo Ottaviani of Padua. His wife Elisabetta, née Marcolini, had welcomed the nine-year-old C. most affectionately at Padua in 1734 (cf. Vol. 1, Chap. I).

17. *Counts:* In the 18th century there were some twelve families with a legitimate claim to the title of Count in Padua; there were also some 300 noble families which currently used the title.

18. *A boy:* Actually the child, which was born and baptized on March 15, 1754, was a girl, Barbara Giacoma Croce; C.'s name as one of her two godfathers appears in the register of the Church of Santa Maria Formosa in Venice.

HISTORY OF MY LIFE

Volume 4

CONTENTS

Volume 4

LIST OF PLATES

Volume 4

VOLUME 4

CHAPTER I

*Croce expelled from Venice. Sgombro. His
disgrace and death. Misfortune which befalls
my dear C. C. I receive an anonymous letter
from a nun and I answer it. Love intrigue.*

WHAT BROUGHT my dear partner the order to
leave the States of the Republic was not gaming, for
the State Inquisitors would have had too much to do if
they had tried to purge the State of swindling gamesters.
The cause of his exile was something very different and
very extraordinary.

A Venetian nobleman of the Gritti[1] family, surnamed
Sgombro,[2] fell in love with the man, contrary to nature,
and he, either for the fun of it or because it was his taste,
did not reject his advances. The great trouble was that
they did not conceal their monstrous love. The scandal
reached such a point that the wise government was forced
to order the young man to live elsewhere.

But soon afterward what happened to Sgombro had
even more serious consequences. Having fallen in love
with his two sons,[3] he reduced the handsomer of them
to needing the services of a surgeon. The poor boy confessed that he had not had the courage to disobey the

author of his existence. This submission to paternal affection rightly seemed of a sort which Nature must abhor. The State Inquisitors sent the tyrannical father to
the citadel of Cattaro,[4] where he died at the end of the
year,[5] poisoned by breathing the air of the place. The
deadly effect of its air is so well known to the Tribunal
that it sentences no one to breathe it except citizens who
have deserved death by committing crimes which policy
does not permit to be tried in public.

It was to Cattaro that the Council of Ten[6] some fifteen
years ago sent the celebrated advocate Contarini,[7] a
Venetian nobleman whose eloquence had given him control over the Great Council [8] and who was about to alter
the constitution. He died there at the end of a year. As
for his accomplices, it was thought the part of wisdom
to punish only the four or five leaders.

This noble Sgombro whom I have mentioned had a
charming wife, who, I believe, is still alive. She is
Signora Cornelia Gritti,[9] even more celebrated for her
wit than for a beauty superior to the ravages of age.
Finding herself her own mistress on her husband's death,
she laughed at all the men who came forward to persuade
her to sacrifice her freedom to them; but having never
been a resolute enemy of love she always accepted their
homage.

One Monday toward the end of July my valet woke
me at daybreak, saying that the woman who came every
Wednesday wished to speak with me. Here is the letter
which she gave me with a very sad countenance:

"Sunday evening. A misfortune which befell me this
morning is making me miserable because I have to hide it
from the whole convent. I am losing my blood, I do not
know how to stop the flow, and I have very little linen.
Laura told me that I need a great deal of it in case the
hemorrhage should continue, and I can trust no one. So
send me some linen, my only friend. You see that I have
had to confide in Laura, who can come to my room at

any hour. If the hemorrhage kills me the whole convent will know what I died of; but I think of you; and I tremble. What will you do in your grief? Ah, my dear! What a pity!''

I dress quickly, using the time to think the matter over. I ask Laura what kind of hemorrhage it is, and she says plainly that it is the result of a miscarriage, and that we must act with the greatest secrecy for the sake of the Signorina's reputation. She tells me that she needs only linen and that it will not come to anything. This is what such women always say. I am scarcely dressed before I have another oar put to my gondola, and I go with Laura to the Ghetto,[10] where I buy a Jew's whole stock of sheets and more than two hundred napkins, and after putting them in a bag I go to Murano with her. On the way I write to my dear one in pencil that she must have perfect confidence in Laura and I assure her that I will not leave Murano until her bleeding has stopped. As she got out of the gondola Laura persuaded me that, since I did not wish to be seen, I would do well to hide in her house. She left me in a room on the ground floor littered with rags and in which I saw two beds. After putting all the linen she could under her skirt she went off to the patient, whom she had seen at nightfall the day before. I hoped she would find her out of danger and I could not wait to hear it.

She came back an hour later and told me that, having lost much blood all night, she was in bed and very weak, and that we must commend her to God, for if the hemorrhage did not stop she would succumb within twenty-four hours. When I saw the linen which she took out from under her skirt I very nearly dropped dead. It was sheer butchery. She assures me that there is no fear that the secret will not be kept, but says there is everything to fear for the poor child's life. A strange sort of consolation! But at the moment her stupidity could not make me laugh. She told me that when she had read my note she had smiled and that after kissing it she had said that since I was so near her she was sure she would not die.

I shuddered when the woman showed me a little shapeless lump in among the blood. She said that she was going out to wash everything and that she would come back and go to the convent with linen for the patient when everyone there was at dinner.

"Has she had visitors?"

"Everyone in the convent; but no one has any idea what brought on her illness."

"But with the heat this time of year she can only be using a very light coverlet, and it is impossible that the great mound her napkins must make will not be noticed."

"There is no fear of that, for she is sitting up."

"What does she eat?"

"Nothing. She must not eat."

She then left, and so did I. I went to see a physician named Payton, where I wasted my time and the money I gave him for a long prescription which I did not use. It would have told the whole convent what my angel's trouble was, and the convent physician would himself have made it public, perhaps in revenge. After going home for a few things I needed I returned to my hiding place, where a half hour later I saw Laura looking very sad as she gave me a note in which C. C. wrote me:

"My dear, I have not the strength to write to you. I am still bleeding, and there is no remedy. God disposes; but my honor is safe. My only consolation is knowing that you are here."

Laura terrified me by showing me ten or twelve more napkins soaked with blood. She thought it would comfort me to tell me that a pound of it would soak a hundred napkins; but I was beyond comforting. I was really in despair. Seeing myself the murderer of this innocent girl, I did not feel that I could survive her. Overwhelmed, I stayed in bed for six whole hours, never saying a word until Laura came back from the convent with twenty soaked napkins. It was night, so she could not go back. She had to wait for the next morning. I waited for it too, without sleeping or eating or even letting Laura's daughters undress me, for, though they were pretty, they filled me with loathing. I saw them as the instruments of my horrible incontinence, which had made me the executioner of an angel incarnate.

The sun was appearing above the horizon when Laura entered and dolefully gave me the news that the poor girl was no longer bleeding. She thought she was thus preparing me to hear the news of her death the same day.

"She is exhausted," she said, "she has only just strength enough to keep her eyes open, she looks as if she were made of wax, her pulse is almost too weak to feel."

"But my dear Laura, this news is not bad. She must have something to eat now."

"The physician has been sent for. It is he who will prescribe what is to be given her; but to tell you the truth I have no hope. As you can imagine, she will not tell the physician the truth, so God knows what he will prescribe for her. I whispered to her not to take anything, and she understood."

"If she does not die of inanition before tomorrow I am sure she will live, and her physician will have been Nature."

"God grant it! I will go back to see her at noon."

"Why not sooner?"

"Because her room will be full of people."

Needing to hope, I thought of sustaining my own life, I ordered a meal prepared, and in the meanwhile I began a letter to C. C. against the time when she would be strong enough to read it. Moments of repentance are very gloomy. I was to be pitied. I badly needed to see Laura again to learn what the physician's oracle had been. I had good reason to laugh at all oracles; nevertheless I was badly in need of this physician's, and above all of hearing that it was favorable.

Laura's daughters brought me a dinner, but I could swallow nothing. They amused me by eating it all themselves with ravenous appetites. Her eldest daughter, the showpiece, never looked at me. I thought the two younger ones were free and easy; but I examined them only to feed my painful repentance.

Laura came at last and told me that the patient was still in the same state of inanition, that her extreme weakness had greatly surprised the physician, who did not know to what to attribute it. He had prescribed cordials and light broths, and he had prognosticated that she would recover her health if she could sleep. When he ordered a night nurse for her the patient had given Laura her hand; so she promised me she would not leave her again. Her mother had gone to see her, and I was glad to hear it. I saw very well that if she could sleep she would recover, so I longed for morning. I gave Laura six zecchini and her daughters one apiece, and ate some fish for supper. I also went to bed undressed, despite the badness of the bed. When Laura's daughters saw me in bed they undressed without further ado and lay down in another, which was beside mine. Their confidence pleased me. The eldest sister must have known what was what. She went off to bed in another room, for she had a lover who was to marry her in the fall.

Very early the next morning Laura came in looking cheerful and told me that the patient had slept well and that she was going back to the convent to take her a dish of soup. However, it was too soon to cry victory, for she still needed to regain her strength and replace the blood she had lost. I now felt sure that she would recover her health; and so she did. But I stayed there another week, unable to make up my mind to go until C. C. practically ordered me to do so in a four-page letter. When I left,

Laura wept for joy on finding herself rewarded by
nearly all the fine linen I had bought for her for the patient, and her two younger daughters cried too, apparently because they had not managed to persuade me to
give them at least a kiss during the ten days I spent in
their house.

In Venice I returned to my old occupations; but without a real and satisfying love affair I could not be happy.
The only pleasure I had was receiving every Wednesday
a letter from my little wife, who encouraged me to wait
instead of begging me to carry her off. Laura assured me
that she had become more beautiful. I was dying to see
her.

It was at the end of August that, Laura having told
me of a profession[11] which had the whole convent in
turmoil, I decided to give myself the pleasure of seeing
my beautiful angel. Since the visiting rooms were sure to
be full of people and the nuns would be receiving visitors at the convent gate, it was likely that the boarders
would appear and that C. C. would be there too. There
was no reason to fear that I would be noticed more than
anyone else on a day when there would be a crowd of
strangers. So I went, having neither said anything to
Laura nor announced my visit to C. C. in my last letter.

I thought I should die with pleasure when I saw her
four paces from me, staring at me in her surprise at
seeing me there. I thought she was taller and more de-
veloped, that her face was even more beautiful, which
I had considered impossible. I had eyes only for her, and
I did not go back to Venice until the gate was closed.

But the letter which she wrote me three days later
described her pleasure at seeing me too vividly for me
not to try to think of some way of giving it to her often.
I answered immediately that she would see me at mass
at her church on every feast day; and I began at once.
It cost me nothing. I did not see her; but as I knew that
she saw me, her pleasure was enough to make mine com-

plete. I had nothing to fear, for it was almost impossible that I should be recognized in a church to which no one went except the plain citizens of Murano and their womenfolk. After hearing one or two masses I got into a *traghetto* gondola,[12] whose gondolier could have no possible interest in knowing who I was. However, I remained on my guard. Knowing that her father's intention was to make C. C. forget me, I was sure that if he learned that I still put in an appearance he would confine her to another convent where I could have no contact with her.

Thus did I reason, but I was not well enough acquainted with the character of nuns or their peculiar kind of curiosity. Moreover it did not occur to me that, my person being noticeable and they seeing that I assiduously frequented their church, they would all conclude together that there must be some reason for it and would do their best to find it out.

After five or six feast days C. C. wrote me jocosely that I had become the puzzle of the entire convent, both nuns and boarders. The whole choir looked for me on the minute; they told one another when they saw me come in and take holy water; and it was observed that I never looked at the grating behind which all the recluses must be nor at any woman or girl who entered or left the church. The old nuns said that I must have some sorrow from which my only hope of being relieved was the protection of their Holy Virgin, in whom it was clear that I must have perfect trust; and the young ones said that I must be suffering from melancholia, a misanthrope who shunned the great world. My dear wife's writing me all this amused me. I wrote her that if she feared I might be recognized I would stop going, and she answered that she would be very sad if she were deprived of the pleasure of seeing me, which was her only happiness. Having learned of this general curiosity, however, I no longer dared to go to Laura's house. I was growing thin, I was

wearing myself out; I could not long survive this sort of
life. I was born to have a mistress and to live happily
with her. Not knowing what to do, I gambled and I won
nearly every day, yet for all that I was bored. After the
five thousand zecchini I had won in Padua through the
lucky hands of my partner I had followed Signor Bragadin's advice. I rented a casino,[13] where I dealt at faro
on half shares with a magnate who protected me against
the frauds of certain tyrannical aristocrats in competition
with whom a mere private citizen is always in the wrong
in my charming country.

1753.

On All Saints' Day, just as I was about to get into
my gondola to return to Venice after hearing mass, I
met a woman of the same type as Laura, who, after letting a letter drop at my feet, walked on. I pick it up and
I see the same woman, satisfied that she had seen me do so,
pursue her way. The letter was white and sealed with
wax the color of aventurine.[14] The imprint represented
a running knot. No sooner have I entered the gondola
than I unseal it and read the following:

"A nun who has seen you in her church every feast
day for the past two and a half months wishes you to
make her acquaintance. A pamphlet which you lost and
which has come into her hands assures her that you understand French. However, you may answer her in
Italian, for she desires clarity and precision. She does
not invite you to have her summoned to the visiting room,
because before you obligate yourself to speak with her
she wishes you to see her. So she will give you the name
of a lady whom you can accompany to the visiting room,
who will not know you, and hence will not be compelled
to introduce you if by any chance you do not wish to be
known.

"If this seems to you unsuitable, the same nun who
writes you this letter will give you the address of a

casino here in Murano where you will find her alone at
the first hour of the night on the day you indicate to her;
you can stay and sup with her, or leave a quarter of an
hour later if you have business.

"Would you prefer to offer her supper in Venice? Let
her know the day, the hour of the night, and the place to
which she is to go, and you will see her leave a gondola
masked, provided you are on the quay alone, without
a servant, masked, and holding a candle.

"Being certain that you will answer me, and as impatient as you can imagine to read your answer, I beg you
to deliver it tomorrow to the same woman who brought
you this letter. You will find her an hour before noon
in the Church of San Canziano[15] at the first altar on the
right.

"Consider that if I had not supposed you to be well
disposed and honorable, I should never have resolved to
take a step which might give you an unfavorable opinion
of me."

The tone of this letter, which I copy word for word,
surprised me even more than its contents. I had business,
but I dismissed everything to shut myself in my room
and answer. Making such a request was sheer madness,
yet I found a dignity in it which forced me to respect
her. I was at first inclined to believe that the nun might
be the one who was teaching C. C. French and who was
beautiful, rich, and a flirt, and that my dear wife might
have been indiscreet yet know nothing about this un-
heard-of step on her friend's part, and for that reason
had been unable to notify me of it. But I dismissed the
suspicion precisely because it pleased me. C. C. had
written me that the nun who taught her French was not
the only one who had a good command of the language.
I could not doubt C. C.'s discretion and the candor with
which she would have confessed it to me if she had confided anything at all to the nun. However, since the nun
who had written me might be C. C.'s beautiful friend

or might be someone else, I wrote her an answer in which I straddled the ditch as far as good manners permitted me to do so; here it is:

"I hope, Madame, that my answer in French will detract nothing from the clarity and precision which you demand and of which you set me an example.

"The subject is most interesting; it seems to me of the greatest moment under the circumstances, and obliged to give an answer without knowing to whom, do you not understand, Madame, that, not being a conceited fool, I must fear a snare? It is honor which obliges me to be on my guard. If it is true, then, that the pen which writes to me is that of a respectable lady who does me the justice to suppose me possessed of a soul as noble and a heart as well disposed as her own, she will find, I hope, that I can answer her only in the following terms:

"If you have thought me worthy, Madame, of making your acquaintance personally, your opinion of me being based only on my appearance, I consider it my duty to obey you if only to disabuse you should I by chance have involuntarily led you into error.

"Of the three arrangements which you have been so generous as to propose to me, I dare choose only the first, on the conditions which your very clear foresight has stipulated. I shall accompany to your visiting room a lady whom you will name to me and who will not know me. Hence there will be no question of introducing me. Be indulgent, Madame, to the specious reasons which oblige me not to name myself. In exchange, I promise you on my honor that your name will become known to me only that I may do you homage. If you see fit to speak to me I will answer you only with the most profound respect. Permit me to hope that you will be alone at the grating and to tell you for form's sake that I am a Venetian and free in the fullest sense of the word. The only reason which prevents me from deciding on the two other arrangements which you propose to me and which do me infinite honor is, permit me to repeat, my fear of being trapped. Those happy meetings can take place as soon as you have become better acquainted with me and no doubts trouble my soul, which abhors falsehood. Very impatient in my turn, I will go tomorrow at the same hour to San Canziano to receive your answer.''

Having found the woman at the appointed place, I gave her my letter and a zecchino. The next morning I returned there and she came up to me. After giving me back my zecchino she handed me the following answer, asking me to go and read it and to come back afterward to tell her if she should wait for an answer. After reading it I went and told her that I had no answer to give her. This is what the nun's letter to me said:

''I believe, Monsieur, that I have been mistaken in nothing. Like yourself, I abhor falsehood when it can have consequences; but I consider it only a trifle when it harms no one. Of my three proposals you have chosen the one which does most honor to your perception. Respecting the reasons you may have for concealing your name, I write the Countess S.[16] what I ask you to read in the note herewith. You will seal it before having it delivered to her. She will be forewarned of it by another note. You will go to her house at your convenience; she will appoint an hour and you will accompany her here in her own gondola. She will not interrogate you, and you need give her no explanations. There will be no question of an introduction; but since you will learn my name, it will rest with you to come to see me masked whenever you wish, asking for me in the name of the same Countess. Thus we shall become acquainted without your being obliged to sacrifice any of the evening hours which may be precious to you. I have ordered the woman who brings this to wait for your answer in case you should be known to the Countess and hence unwilling to make this use of her. If my choice is agreeable to you tell the woman that you have no answer to send; whereupon

she will take my note to the Countess. You may take the
other to her at your convenience.''

I told the woman that I had no answer to send when
I was certain that I was not known to the Countess,
whose name I had never heard. Here is the wording of
the note I was to deliver to her:

''I beg you, my dear friend, to come and speak with
me when you have time, and to name your hour to the
masker who brings you this note so that he can accompany you. He will be punctual. You will greatly
oblige your loving friend.''

The address was to the Countess S., Riva del Rio
Marin.[17] I thought the note a masterpiece of the spirit
of intrigue. There was something lofty in this way of
proceeding. I was made to play the role of a person who
was being granted a favor. I saw it all clearly.

In her last letter the nun, showing no interest in who
I was, approved my choice and tried to appear indifferent to nocturnal meetings; but she expected, and even
seemed certain, that I would come and have her called
to the visiting room after I had seen her. Her certainty
increased my curiosity. She had reason to hope that I
would do it if she was young and pretty. It was perfectly
possible for me to delay for three or four days and find
out from C. C. who the nun might be; but aside from its
being an underhanded action, I was afraid I should spoil
my chances and be sorry. She told me to call on the
Countess at my convenience; her dignity demanded that
she should not seem eager; but she knew that I must
be so. She seemed too much at home in intrigue for me
to believe her a novice and inexperienced; I feared I
would repent of having wasted my time; and I prepared to laugh if I found I was with some old woman.
In short, it is certain that I would not have gone had
I not felt curious to see what sort of face a woman of
this kind would put upon a meeting with me after she
had offered to come to supper with me in Venice. Then,

too, I was much surprised at the great freedom enjoyed by these holy virgins, who could so easily violate their rule of enclosure.

At three in the afternoon I sent a note in to the Countess S. She came out a minute later from the room in which she was entertaining guests and said that she would be glad if I would call at her house the next day at the same hour; and after dropping me a fine curtsy she withdrew. She was a domineering woman, beginning to fade a little but still beautiful.

The next morning, which was a Sunday, I went to mass at my usual hour, in my finest clothes and with my hair elegantly dressed, and already unfaithful in imagination to my dear C. C., for I was more concerned with displaying myself to the nun, be she young or old, than to her.

After dinner I mask and at the appointed hour go to call on the Countess, who was waiting for me. We go down, get into a commodious two-oared gondola, we arrive at the convent of the XXX[18] without having talked of anything but the beautiful autumn we were enjoying. She asks to see M. M.[19] The name astonishes me, for the bearer of it was celebrated. We go into a small visiting room, and five minutes later I see M. M. appear, go straight to the grating, open four square sections of it by pressing a spring, embrace her friend, then close the ingenious window again. The four sections made an opening eighteen inches square. Any man of my stature could have passed through it. The Countess sat down facing the nun and I on the other side in a position from which I could examine this rare beauty of twenty-two or twenty-three years at my ease. I decide at once that she must be the same nun whom C. C. had praised to me, the one who loved her dearly and was teaching her French.

Very nearly beside myself with admiration, I heard nothing of what they said. As for me, not only did the

nun not once speak to me, she did not condescend to
give me a single look. She was a perfect beauty, tall,
so white of complexion as to verge on pallor, with an air
of nobility and decision but at the same time of reserve
and shyness, large blue eyes; a sweet, smiling face,
beautiful lips damp with dew, which allowed a glimpse
of two magnificent rows of teeth; her nun's habit did
not let me see any hair; but whether she had it or not,
its color must be light chestnut; her eyebrows told me
as much; but what I found admirable and surprising
were her hand and forearm, which I saw to the elbow:
it was impossible to see anything more perfect. No veins
were visible, and instead of muscles I saw only dimples.
Despite all this I did not regret having refused the two
meetings over a supper which the divine beauty had
offered me. Sure that I should possess her in a few days,
I enjoyed the pleasure of paying her the tribute of
desiring her. I could not wait to be alone with her at
the grating, and I thought I should have committed the
worst of offenses if I had waited any longer than the
next day to assure her that I had accorded her qualities
all the justice they deserved. She continued not to look
at me; but in the end it pleased me.

Suddenly the two ladies lowered their voices and put
their heads together; as this indicated that I was one too
many, I slowly walked away from the grating and looked
at a painting. A quarter of an hour later they bade each
other good-by, after embracing at the movable window.
The nun turned away without giving me an opportunity
even to bow to her. On the way back to Venice the
Countess, perhaps tiring of my silence, remarked with
a smile:

"*M. M. is beautiful, but her mind is even more extraordinary.*"

"I have seen the one and I believe the other."

"She did not say a word to you."

"Since I did not wish to be introduced to her, she

wished to ignore my being there. It was her way of punishing me.''

The Countess having made no reply, we arrived at her house without opening our mouths again. I left her at her door, because it was there that she dropped me the fine curtsy which means, ''Thank you. Good-by.'' I went elsewhere to muse over the strange adventure, whose inevitable consequences I was eager to see.

CHAPTER II

Countess Coronini. Wounded feelings.
Reconciliation. First meeting. Philosophical
digression.

SHE HAD not spoken to me, and I was glad of it.
I was so overwhelmed that I might not have answered
anything worth saying. I saw that she had no need to
fear the humiliation of a refusal; yet it takes great
courage in such a woman to run the risk of it. So much
boldness at her age surprised me and I was at a loss to
understand so much freedom. A casino at Murano! Able
to go to Venice! I decided that she must have an
acknowledged lover who was happy to make her happy.
The idea set bounds to my sense of triumph. I saw that
I was on the verge of becoming unfaithful to C. C.;
but I did not feel restrained by any scruple. I thought
that an infidelity of this kind, even if she were to discover it, could not offend her, because it would only be
meant to keep me alive and so to preserve me for her.

The next morning I went to call on Countess Coronini,[1]
who chose to live in the convent of Santa Giustina.[2] She
was an old woman with a long experience of all the courts

of Europe and who had made a reputation by taking a hand in their affairs. The desire for repose which follows disgust had made her choose the convent as her retreat. I had been introduced to her by a nun who was a relative of Signor Dandolo. This former beauty, finding that she no longer wished to exercise her considerable intelligence in the machinations of royal self-interest, kept it entertained with the frivolous gossip with which the city in which she lived supplied her. She knew everything and, as was only to be expected, always wanted to know more. She received all the ambassadors at her grating, and in consequence every foreigner was introduced to her, and several grave Senators from time to time paid her long visits. Curiosity was always the mainspring of these visits on either side; but it was concealed under the veil of the interest which the nobility may be expected to take in whatever is going on. In short, Signora Coronini knew everything and took pleasure in giving me very entertaining lessons in morals when I went to see her. As I was to call on M. M. in the afternoon I thought that I should succeed in learning something about the nun from the well-informed Countess.

As I found it perfectly easy, after some other subjects, to bring the conversation around to that of the convents in Venice, we were soon discussing the intelligence and reputation of a nun of the Celsi[3] family, who, though ugly, exercised great influence in whatever quarter she pleased. We then spoke of the young and charming nun of the Micheli family[4] who had taken the veil to prove to her mother that she was the more intelligent of the two. Speaking of several other beauties who were said to indulge in love affairs, I named M. M. and said that she must be of the same stamp, but that she was an enigma. The Countess smiled and answered that she was not an enigma to everybody but that she must be so to people in general.

"But what really is an enigma," she added, "is her

suddenly having taken the veil when she is rich, highly intelligent, very cultivated, and, so far as I know, a freethinker. She became a nun for no reason, either physical or moral. It was sheer caprice.''

''Do you think she is happy, Signora?''

''Yes, if she has not repented and if repentance does not overtake her—which, if she is wise, she will keep to herself.''

Convinced by the Countess's mysterious tone that M. M. must have a lover, but resolved not to let it trouble me, I mask after dining without appetite, I go to Murano, I ring at the gate, and, with my heart racing, I ask for M. M. in the name of Countess S. The small visiting room was closed. I am shown the one I am to enter. I take off my mask, put it on my hat, and sit down to wait for the goddess. She was long in coming, but instead of making me impatient the wait pleased me; I feared the moment of our interview and even its effect. But an hour having gone by very quickly, such a delay seemed to me unnatural. Surely she had not been informed. I rise, resuming my mask, go back to the gate, and ask if I have been announced to Mother M. M. A voice answers yes, and that I had only to wait. I returned to my chair, a little thoughtful, and a few minutes later I see a hideous lay sister, who says:

''Mother M. M. is occupied the whole day.''

The words were scarcely spoken before she was gone.

Such are the terrible moments to which a pursuer of women is exposed; there is nothing more cruel. They degrade, they distress, they kill. In my revulsion and humiliation, my first feeling was contempt for myself, a dark contempt which approached the limits of horror. The second was disdainful indignation toward the nun, on whom I passed the judgment she appeared to deserve. She was mad, a wretched creature, shameless. My only consolation was to think her such. She could not have acted toward me as she had done unless she was the most

impudent of women, the most lacking in common sense;
for her two letters, which were in my possession, were
enough to dishonor her if I wanted to avenge myself, and
what she had done cried for vengeance. She could only
defy it if she was more than mad; her behavior was that
of a raving maniac. I would already have thought her
out of her mind, if I had not heard her talk rationally
with the Countess.

Yet in the tumult which shame and anger aroused in
my soul *affixa humo* ("fastened to the earth")[5] I was
encouraged by discerning lucid intervals. I saw clearly,
laughing at myself, that if the nun's beauty and stately
bearing had not dazzled me and made me fall in love,
and if a certain amount of prejudice had not entered in
as well, the whole thing would not amount to much. I
saw that I could pretend to laugh at it, and that no one
would be able to guess that I was only pretending.

Aware, despite all this, that I had been insulted, I
saw that I must take my revenge, but that there must be
nothing base in it; and no less aware that I must not give
her the least opportunity to crow over having played a
practical joke on me, I saw that I must not show any
vexation. She had sent me word that she was engaged,
and that was all. I must pretend indifference. Another
time she would not be engaged; but I defied her to trap
me another time. I thought I ought to convince her that
her behavior had only made me laugh. I must, of course,
send her back the originals of her letters, but enclosed
in a short and sufficient one from me. What greatly annoyed me was that I must certainly stop going to mass at
her church, for since she had no idea that I went there
for C. C., she might have supposed that I would be going only in the hope that she would make some apology
and would again offer me the opportunities to meet her
which I had rejected. I wanted her to be certain that I
scorned her. For a moment I believed that the meetings
she had proposed were merely figments to deceive me.

I fell asleep about midnight with this plan in mind, and on waking in the morning I found it ripe. I wrote a letter and after writing it I put it aside for another twenty-four hours to see if, when I read it over, it would show even a trace of the wounded feelings which were tormenting me.

I did well, for when I read it over the next morning I thought it unworthy of me. I quickly tore it up. There were expressions in it which revealed that I was weak, pusillanimous, and in love, and so would have made her laugh. There were others which betrayed anger, and others which showed that I was sorry to have lost all hope of possessing her.

The next day I wrote her another, after writing to C. C. that serious reasons forced me to stop going to hear mass at her church. But the next morning I thought my letter laughable, and I tore it up. It seemed to me that I had lost my ability to write, and I did not realize the reason for my difficulty until ten days after she had insulted me. I had one.

Sincerum est nisi vas, quodcumque in fundis acescit.

("Unless the vessel is clean, whatever is put in it turns sour.")[6]

M. M.'s face had made an impression on me which could not be effaced by the greatest and most powerful of abstract beings—by Time.

In my ridiculous situation I was tempted again and again to go and tell my troubles to Countess S.; but—thank God!—I never went any farther than her door. The thought coming to me at last that the harebrained nun must be living in terror because of her letters, with which I could ruin her reputation and do the greatest harm to the convent, I resolved to send them to her with a note in the following terms. But it was not until ten or twelve days after the incident.

"I beg you to believe, Madame, that it was by an oversight that I did not immediately send you your two letters, which you will find herewith. I have never thought of departing from what I am by taking a base revenge. I am obliged to forgive you for two pieces of folly, whether you committed them naturally and unthinkingly or to mock me; but I advise you not to act in the same manner toward some other man in the future, for not everyone is like me. I know your name; but I assure you it is as if I did not know it. I tell you this though it is possible that you care nothing for my discretion; but if that is the case I am sorry for you.

"You will no longer see me in your church, Madame, and it will cost me nothing, for I will go to another; yet I think it proper that I should tell you the reason. I consider it likely that you have committed the third folly of boasting of your exploit to some of your friends, and so I am ashamed to put in an appearance. Forgive me if despite my being, as I suppose, five or six years older than you, I have not yet trampled upon all prejudices; believe me, Madame, there are some which should never be shaken off. Do not take it amiss if I give you this little lesson, after the only too substantial one which you apparently gave me only in mockery. Be certain that I will profit by it all the rest of my life."

I felt that my letter was the gentlest treatment I could give the giddy nun. I went out and, calling aside a Friulian,[7] who could not recognize me under my mask, I gave him my letter, which contained the two others, and gave him forty soldi to take it at once to its address in Murano, promising him another forty when he should come back to tell me he had faithfully done his errand. The instructions I gave him were that he should deliver the packet to the portress, then leave without waiting for an answer even if the portress told him to wait. But it would have been a mistake on my part to wait for him. In our city the Friulians are as reliable and trustworthy as the Savoyards[8] were in Paris ten years ago.

Five or six days later, as I was coming out of the

opera, I see the same Friulian carrying his lantern. I call him and, not taking off my mask, ask him if he knows me; after looking at me attentively he says he does not. I ask him if he had done the errand in Murano on which I sent him.

"Ah, Signore! God be praised! Since it is you I have something urgent to tell you. I took your letter as you ordered me to, and after delivering it to the portress I left despite her telling me to wait. When I got back I did not find you, but what of it? The next morning a Friulian of my acquaintance, who was at the gate when I delivered your letter, came and woke me to tell me I must go to Murano, because the portress insisted on talking to me. I went, and after making me wait for a time she told me to go into the visiting room, where a nun wished to speak with me. The nun, who was as beautiful as the morning star, kept me for an hour and more, asking me countless questions all directed to learning, if not who you are, at least some way of my discovering where I could find you; but it was all to no avail since I knew nothing about you.

"She left, ordering me to wait, and two hours later she reappeared with a letter. She gave it to me and said that if I could manage to deliver it to you and bring her the answer she would give me two zecchini; but that if I did not find you I should go to Murano every day and show her her letter, promising me forty soldi for each trip I made. Up to now I have earned twenty lire; but I am afraid she will get tired of it. You have only to answer her letter and I will earn the two zecchini." [9]

"Where is it?"

"Locked up where I live, for I am always afraid of losing it."

"Then how am I to answer it?"

"Wait for me here. You will see me back with the letter in a quarter of an hour."

"I will not wait for you, for I have no interest in answering it; but tell me how you persuaded the nun to believe that you could find me. You are a rascal. It is not likely that she would have entrusted her letter to you if you had not given her reason to expect you to find me.''

''That is so. I described your coat to her, and your buckles, and your height. I assure you that for the last ten days I have looked carefully at every masker of your height, but in vain. It is your buckles there that I recognized; but I should not have recognized you by your coat. Alas, Signore! It will cost you nothing to answer only a line. Wait for me in that coffeehouse.''

Unable any longer to overcome my curiosity, I decide not to wait for him but to go with him to his lodging. I did not think I was obliged to answer more than: ''I have received your letter. Farewell.'' The next morning I would have changed buckles and sold the coat. So I go to his door with the Friulian, he goes for the letter, hands it to me, and I take him with me to an inn where, to read the letter at leisure, I engage a room, have a fire lighted, and tell him to wait for me outside. I unseal the packet, and the first thing which surprises me is the two letters she had written me and which I had thought I should return to her to set her heart at rest. At the sight I am seized by a palpitation which already heralds my defeat. Besides the two letters I see a short one signed ''S.'' It was addressed to ''M. M.'' I read it, and I find:

''The masker who escorted me to the convent and home again would never have opened his lips to say a word to me if I had not taken it into my head to tell him that the charms of your mind are even more winning than those of your face. He answered that he wished to become acquainted with the former and that he was certain of the latter. I added that I did not understand why you had not spoken to him; and he answered with a smile that you wanted to punish him and that since he had not wished to be introduced to you, you in your turn wished to ignore his presence. I wanted to send you this note this morning; but I could not. Farewell. S. F.''

After reading the Countess's note, which neither added nor subtracted an iota from the truth, and which might be a piece of evidence for the defense, my heart beat less violently. Delighted to discover that I am on the verge of being convinced that I was wrong, I pluck up my courage, and this is what I find in the letter from M. M.:

''From a weakness which I consider thoroughly excusable, curious to know what you might have found to say about me to the Countess on your way to visit me and when you took her back home, I seized the moment when you were walking up and down in the visiting room to ask her to inform me. I told her to send me word at once, or at latest the next morning, for I foresaw that in the afternoon you would certainly come to pay me a duty call. Her note, which I send you and which I ask you to read, reached me a half hour after you were sent away. First fatal mishap. Not having received her letter when you asked to see me, I did not have the courage to receive you. Second fatal weakness, for which I can easily be forgiven. I ordered the lay sister to tell you that I was 'ill the whole day.' A perfectly legitimate excuse whether it is true or false, for it is a polite lie in which the words 'the whole day' convey all. You had already left and I could not send someone running after you when the idiotic old woman came and reported to me what she had told you, not that I was 'ill,' but that I was 'occupied.' Third fatal mishap. You cannot imagine what I wanted to say, and to do, to the lay sister in my righteous anger; but here one can neither do nor say anything. One can only be patient, dissimulate, and thank God when mistakes arise from ignorance rather than from malice. I at once foresaw in part what did indeed happen, for human reason could never have foreseen it all. I guessed that, believing you had been duped, you would be disgusted, and I felt the blackest misery since I saw no way to let you know the truth until the feast day. I was certain that you would come to our church. Who could have guessed that you would take the thing with the extraordinary violence which your letter set before my eyes? When I did not see you appear in church my grief began to be unbearable, for it was mortal, but it drove me to despair and pierced my heart when I read, ten days after the event, the cruel, barbarous, unjust letter which you wrote me. It made me wretched, and I will die of it unless you come to justify yourself immediately. You thought you had been duped—that is all you can say, and you are now convinced that you were mistaken. But even believing that you were duped, you must admit that to take the course you did and to write me the terrible letter you sent me, you must imagine me a monster not to be found among women who, like myself, are well born and have been well brought up. I send you back the two letters which you sent back to me to soothe my fears. Know that I am a better physiognomist than you are, and that what I did I did not do out of 'folly.' I have never thought you capable of a base action, even if you were certain that I had brazenly duped you; but in my countenance you have seen only the soul of shamelessness. You will perhaps be the cause of my death, or at least you will make me wretched for all the rest of my life, if you do not wish to justify yourself; since, for my part, I believe I am justified completely.

"Consider that, even if my life is of no concern to you, your honor demands that you come to talk with me at once. You must come in person to recant all that you have written me. If you do not realize the terrible effect your infernal letter must have on the soul of an innocent woman, and one who is not out of her mind, permit me to feel sorry for you. You would not have the slightest knowledge of the human heart. But I am sure you will come, if the man to whom I am entrusting this letter finds you. M. M.''

I did not need to read her letter twice to be in despair. M. M. was right. I at once masked to go out of the room and speak to the Friulian. I asked him if he had spoken with her that morning and if she looked ill. He replied that he thought she looked more dejected every day. I went back, telling him to wait.

I did not finish writing to her until daybreak. Here, word for word, is the letter which I wrote to the noblest of all women, whom, drawing the wrong conclusion, I had most cruelly insulted.

''I am guilty, Madame, and as unable to justify myself as I am completely convinced of your innocence. I cannot live except in the hope of your forgiveness, and you will grant it to me when you reflect upon what made me commit my crime. I saw you, you dazzled me, and, thinking of my honor,[10] it seemed to me chimerical; I thought I was dreaming. I saw that I could not be rid of my doubt until twenty-four hours later, and God alone knows how long they seemed to me. They passed at last, and my heart palpitated when I was in the visiting room counting the minutes. At the end of sixty—which, however, as the result of a kind of impatience entirely new to me, went by very quickly—I see an ill-omened figure which, with odious brevity, tells me that you are 'occupied' for the whole day; then it makes off. Imagine the rest! Alas, it was nothing short of a thunderbolt, *which did not kill me and did not leave me alive.* Dare I tell you, Madame, that if you had sent me, even by the hands of the same lay sister, two lines traced by your pen, you would have sent me away if not satisfied at least unperturbed. This is the fatal mishap, which you forgot to cite to me in your charming and most powerful justification. The effect of the thunderbolt was the fatal one which made me see myself as duped, mocked. It revolted me, my self-esteem cried out, dark shame overwhelmed me. I loathe myself and am forced to believe that under the countenance of an angel you fostered a fiendish soul. I leave in consternation, and in the course of eleven days I lose my common sense. I wrote you the letter of which you are a thousand times justified in complaining; but —can you believe it?—I thought it courteous. It is all over now. You will see me at your feet an hour before noon. I shall not go to bed. You shall pardon me, Madame, or I will avenge you. Yes, I myself will be your avenger. The only thing I ask of you, as a great favor, is that you will burn my letter or say nothing about it tomorrow. I sent it to you only after having written you four which I tore up after reading them, because I found expressions in them from which I feared you would read the passion which you have inspired in me. A lady who had duped me was not worthy of my love, were she an angel. I was not wrong but . . . wretched! Could I believe you capable of it after I had seen you? I will now lie down for three or four hours. My tears will flood my pillow. I order the bearer to go to your convent at once, so that I may be sure you will receive this letter when you wake. He would never have found me if I had not approached him as I left the opera. I shall have no more need of him. Do not answer me.''

After sealing my letter I gave it to him, ordering him to go to the convent gate and to deliver it only into the hands of the nun. He promised to do so, I gave him a zecchino, and he set off. After spending six hours in impatience I masked and went to Murano, where M. M. came down as soon as I was announced. I had been shown into the small visiting room in which I had seen her with the Countess. I went down on my knees before her; but she hurriedly told me to get up, for I could be seen. Her face was instantly suffused by a fiery blush. She sat down, I sat down before her; and so we spent a good quarter of an hour looking at each other. I finally broke the silence by asking her if I could count on being forgiven, and she put her beautiful hand out through the grating; I bathed it with my tears and kissed it a hundred times. She said that our acquaintance having begun with such a fierce storm should make us hope for an eternal calm.

"It is the first time," she said, "that we are talking together; but what has happened to us is enough for us to believe that we know each other perfectly. I hope that our friendship will be equally tender and sincere, and that we can be indulgent toward each other's failings."

"When may I convince you of my feelings, Signora, outside these walls and in all the joy of my soul?"

"We will sup at my casino whenever you please—I need only know two days in advance—or with you in Venice, if that is not inconvenient for you."

"It would only increase my happiness; I must tell you that I am in easy circumstances and that, far from fearing to spend money I delight in it and that all I have belongs to the object I adore."

"I welcome both the fact and the confidence. I, too, can tell you that I am tolerably rich and that I feel I could refuse nothing to my lover."

"But you must have one."

"Yes, I have; and it is he who makes me rich and who is completely my master. For this reason I never leave him in ignorance of anything. Day after tomorrow at my casino you shall know more."

"But I hope that your lover—"

"Will not be there? You may be sure he will not. And have you a mistress?"

"Alas! I had one, but she has been torn from me. For six months I have lived in perfect celibacy."

"But you still love her."

"I cannot remember her without loving her; but I foresee that the seduction of your charms will make me forget her."

"If you were happy I am sorry for you. She was torn from you; and you have been consumed with grief, shunning society—I divined it. But if it falls out that I take her place, no one, my dear friend, shall tear me from your heart."

"But what will your lover say?"

"He will be delighted to see me in love and happy with a lover like you. Such is his nature."

"Admirable nature! Heroism beyond my strength."

"What sort of life do you lead in Venice?"

"Theaters, society, casinos, where I defy Fortune and find her sometimes kind and sometimes not."

"At the houses of foreign ambassadors too?"

"No, because I am too closely connected with certain patricians; but I know them all."

"How can you know them if you do not see them?"

"I met them in foreign countries. In Parma I knew the Duke of Montealegre,[11] the Spanish Ambassador; in Vienna Count Rosenberg;[12] in Paris the French Ambassador,[13] about two years ago."

"My dear friend, I advise you to leave, for it is about to strike noon. Come day after tomorrow at the same hour, and I will give you the necessary instructions so that you can sup with me."

"Alone?"

"Of course."

"Dare I ask you for a pledge? For this good fortune is so great."

"What pledge do you wish?"

"To see you stand at the small window, with myself in the place where Countess S. was."

She rose and with the most gracious smile pressed the spring, and after a kiss whose harshness must have pleased her as much as its sweetness, I left her. She followed me to the door with her amorous eyes.

Joy and impatience absolutely prevented me from eating and sleeping during the whole two days. It seemed to me that I had never been so happy in love and that I was to be so for the first time. In addition to M. M.'s birth, her beauty, and her intelligence, which together constituted her true worth, bias entered in to make the extent of my happiness incomprehensible. She was a vestal.[14] I was to taste a forbidden fruit. I was to infringe on the rights of an omnipotent husband, snatching from his seraglio the most beautiful of his sultanas.

If at the time my reason had not been enslaved I should have seen very well that my nun could not be essentially different from all the pretty women I had loved in the thirteen years I had been skirmishing on the fields of love; but what man in love dwells on such a thought? If it comes into his mind he rejects it with disdain. M. M. must be absolutely different from all the women in the universe and more beautiful.

Animal nature, which chemists call the "animal kingdom," instinctively secures the three means necessary to perpetuate itself. They are three real needs. It must feed itself, and in order that doing so shall not be a labor, it has the sensation called "appetite"; and it finds pleasure in satisfying it. In the second place it must preserve its own species by generation, and certainly it would not perform that duty—despite what St. Augustine[15] says—if it did not find pleasure in doing it. In the third place it has an unconquerable inclination to destroy its enemy; and nothing is better contrived, for since it must preserve itself it must hate whatever achieves or desires its destruction. Under this general law, however, each species acts independently. These three sensations— hunger, appetite for coitus, hate which tends to destroy the enemy—are habitual satisfactions in brute beasts, let us not call them pleasures; they can only be such comparatively speaking; for they do not reason about them. Man alone is capable of true pleasure, for, endowed with the faculty of reason, he foresees it, seeks it, creates it, and reasons about it after enjoying it. My

dear reader, I beg you to follow me; if you drop me
at this point, you are not polite. Let us examine the
thing. Man is in the same condition as the beasts when
he yields to these three instincts without his reason entering in. When our mind makes its contribution, these
three satisfactions become pleasure, pleasure, pleasure:
the inexplicable sensation which makes us taste what we
call happiness, which we cannot explain either, although
we feel it.

The voluptuary who reasons disdains greediness, lust,
and the brutal vengeance which springs from a first im-
pulse of anger; he is an epicure; he falls in love but he
does not wish to enjoy the object he loves unless he is
sure that he is loved; when he is insulted, he will not
avenge himself until he has coldly arrived at the best way
to relish the pleasure of his revenge. In the result he is
more cruel, but he consoles himself by the knowledge that
he is at least reasonable. These three operations are the
work of the soul, which, to procure itself pleasure, becomes the minister of the passions *quae nisi parent im-
perant* ("which, if they do not obey, command").[16] We
bear hunger in order to savor culinary concoctions better; we put off the pleasure of love in order to make it
more intense; and we defer a vengeance in order to make
it more deadly. Yet it is true that people often die of
indigestion, that we deceive ourselves or allow ourselves
to be deceived in love by sophisms, and that the object
we wish to exterminate often escapes our vengeance; but
we run these risks willingly.

CHAPTER III

*Continuation of the preceding chapter. First
assignation with M. M. Letter from C. C. My
second assignation with the nun in my superb
casino in Venice. I am happy.*

NOTHING CAN be dearer to the thinking man
than life; yet the greatest voluptuary is he who best
practices the difficult art of making it pass quickly. He
does not want to make it shorter; but he wants amusement to render its passing insensible. He is right, if he
has not failed in any duty. They who believe that they
have no duty save that of pleasing their senses are wrong,
and Horace may have been wrong too in the passage
where he told Julius Florus[1]: *Nec metuam quid de me
judicet heres, Quod non plura datis inveniet* (''Nor will
I fear my heir's judgment of me because he does not find
more than I received'').[2]

The happiest of men is he who best knows the art of
being happy without infringing on his duties; and the
unhappiest is he who has adopted a profession in which
he is under the sad necessity of foreseeing the future
from dawn to dark of every day.

Certain that M. M. would not break her word, I went

to the visiting room two hours before noon. My expression made her instantly ask me if I was ill.

"No," I answered; "but I may look so in the uneasy expectation of a happiness too great for me. I have lost appetite and sleep; if it is deferred I cannot answer to you for my life."

"Nothing is deferred, my dear friend; but how impatient you are! Let us sit down. Here is the key to the casino³ to which you will go. There will be people there, for we have to be served; but no one will speak to you and you need speak to no one. You will be masked. You are not to go there until half past the first hour of night,* ⁴ no sooner. You will go up the stairs opposite the street door and at the top of the stairs you will see, by the light of a lantern, a green door, which you will open to enter an apartment which you will find lighted. In the second room you will find me, and if I am not there you will wait for me. I will not be more than a few minutes late. You may unmask, sit by the fire, and read. You will find books. The door to the casino is in such-and-such a place."

Since her description could not be more precise, I express my delight that I cannot go wrong. I kiss the hand which gives me the key and the key as well before putting it in my pocket. I ask her if I will see her in secular clothes or dressed as a saint as I now saw her.

"I leave here dressed in my habit, but at the casino I put on secular clothes. There I have everything I need in the way of masking attire too."

"I hope that you will not put on secular clothes this evening."

"Why, if I may ask?"

"I love you so much in your coif, as you are now."

"Ah, I understand. You imagine that I have no hair,

* According to the Italian reckoning this is two hours after sunset. (C.'s note.)

so I frighten you; but let me tell you that I have a wig which could not be better made.''

''Good God! What are you saying? The very name of 'wig' undoes me. But no. No, no; never doubt it—I will think you charming even so. Only be careful not to put it on in my presence. I see that you are mortified. Forgive me. I am in despair that I mentioned it to you. Are you certain that no one will see you leaving the convent?''

''You will be certain of it yourself when, making the circuit of the island in a gondola, you will see where the little quay is. It gives onto a room of which I have the key, and I am sure of the lay sister who waits on me.''

''And the gondola?''

''It is my lover who vouches to me for the fidelity of the gondoliers.''

''What a man your lover is! I imagine he is old.''

''Certainly not. I should be ashamed. I am sure he is not forty. He has everything, my dear friend, to deserve love. Good looks, wit, a gentle nature, and perfect manners.''

''And he forgives you your caprices.''

''What do you mean by 'caprices'? He took me a year ago. Before him I knew no man, as before you I knew no one who inspired me with a fancy. When I told him everything he was rather surprised, then he laughed and only read me a short lecture on the risk I was running by putting myself in the power of a man who might be indiscreet. He wanted me to know who you are before I went any further; but it was too late. I vouched for you, and he laughed again at my vouching for someone I did not know.''

''When did you confide it all to him?''

''Day before yesterday; but completely truthfully. I showed him copies of my letters and of yours, reading which made him say he thought you were French despite your having told me that you were Venetian. He is curious to know who you are, and that is all; but since I am not curious about it you need have no fear. I give you my word of honor that I will never make the slightest attempt to find out.''

''Nor I to find out who this man is, who is as extraordinary as yourself. I am in despair when I think of the bitter sorrow I caused you.''

''Let us say no more about it; but console yourself, for when I think about it I conclude that you could have acted otherwise only if you were a conceited fool.''

When I left she repeated the pledge of her love to me at the little window and she remained there until I was out of the visiting room.

That night at the appointed hour I found the casino without any difficulty, I opened the door and, following her instructions, I found her dressed in secular clothes of the utmost elegance. The room was lighted by candles in girandoles in front of mirrors and by four other candelabra on a table on which there were some books. M. M. seemed to have a beauty entirely different from that which I had seen in the visiting room. Her hair appeared to have been done in a chignon which emphasized its abundance, but my eyes merely glanced at it, for nothing would have been more stupid at the moment than a compliment on her fine wig. To fall on my knees before her, to show her my boundless gratitude by constantly kissing her beautiful hands, were the forerunners of transports whose outcome ought to be a classical amorous combat; but M. M. thought her first duty was to defend herself. Ah! those charming refusals! The strength of two hands repelling the attacks of a respectful and tender lover who is at the same time bold and insistent, played very little part in them; the weapons she used to restrain my passion, to moderate my fire, were arguments delivered in words as amorous as they were energetic and reinforced every moment by loving kisses which melted my soul. In this struggle, as sweet as it was painful to us both, we spent two hours. At the end of the combat we congratulated ourselves on each having carried off the victory; she in having been able to defend herself against all my attacks, I in having kept my impatience in check.

At four o'clock[5] (I am still using the Italian reckoning) she said she was very hungry and that she hoped she would not find me differing from herself. She rang, and a well-dressed woman who was neither young nor old and whose appearance betokened respectability came in and laid a table for two, and after putting everything we needed on another beside us, she served us. The service was of Sèvres porcelain.[6] Eight made dishes composed the supper; they were set on silver boxes filled with hot water which kept the food always hot. It was a choice and delicious supper. I exclaimed that the cook[7] must be French, and she said I was right. We drank only Burgundy, and we emptied a bottle of "oeil de perdrix" champagne[8] and another of some sparkling wine for gaiety. It was she who dressed the salad; her appetite was equal to mine. She rang only to have the dessert brought, together with all the ingredients for making punch. In everything she did I could not but admire her knowledge, her skill, and her grace. It was obvious that she had a lover who had taught her. I was so curious to know who he was that I said I was ready to tell her my name if she would tell me that of the happy man whose heart and soul she possessed. She said we must leave it to time to satisfy our curiosity.

Among her watch charms she had a little rock-crystal flask exactly like the one I had on my watch chain. I showed it to her, praising the essence of rose which it contained and with which a small piece of cotton was soaked. She showed me hers, which was filled with the same essence in liquid form.

"I am surprised," I said, "for it is very rare and it costs a great deal."

"And it is not for sale."

"That is true. The creator of the essence is the King of

France; he made a pound of it, which cost him ten thousand écus."

"It was a present to my lover, who gave it to me."

"Madame de Pompadour sent a small flask of it two years ago to Signor Mocenigo,[9] the Venetian Ambassador in Paris, through the A. de B.,[10] who is now the French Ambassador here."

"Do you know him?"

"I met him that day, having the honor to dine with him. As he was about to set out on his journey here, he had come to take his leave. He is a man whom Fortune has favored, but a man of merit and great wit and of distinguished birth, for he is a Count of Lyons.[11] His handsome face has won him the nickname of 'Belle-Babet';[12] we have a little collection of his poems,[13] which do him honor."

Midnight had struck and, since time was beginning to be precious, we leave the table, and before the fire I become insistent. I said that if she would not yield to love she could not refuse nature, which must be urging her to go to bed after such a fine supper.

"Are you sleepy, then?"

"Not in the least; but at this hour people go to bed. Let me put you to bed and sit by your side as long as you wish to stay there, or else permit me to retire."

"If you leave me you will make me very unhappy."

"No more unhappy than I shall feel at leaving you; but what are we to do here in front of the fire until dawn?"

"We can both sleep in our clothes on the sofa you see there."

"In our clothes? So be it. I can even let you sleep; but if I do not sleep will you forgive me? Beside you, and uncomfortable in my clothes, how could I sleep?"

"Very well. Besides, this sofa is a real bed. You shall see."

With that she rises, pulls the sofa out at an angle, ar-

ranges pillows, sheets, and a blanket, and I see a real
bed. She tucks my hair under a large handkerchief and
hands me another so that I can do her the same service,
saying that she has no nightcap. I set to work, concealing
my distaste for her wig, when something totally unexpected gives me the most agreeable surprise. Instead of
a wig, I find the most beautiful head of hair. She tells
me, after laughing heartily, that a nun's only obligation
is not to let the outside world see her hair, and after saying so she throws herself down at full length on the
couch. I quickly take off my coat, kick my feet out of
my shoes, and fall more on her than beside her. She clasps
me in her arms, and subjecting herself to a tyranny
which insults nature, she considers that I must forgive
her all the torments which her resistance cannot but
inflict on me.

With a trembling and timid hand and looking at her
with eyes which begged for charity, I undo six wide rib-
bons which fastened her dress in front and, ravished with
joy because she does not stop me, I find myself the fortunate master of the most beautiful of bosoms. It is too
late: she is obliged, after I have contemplated it, to let
me devour it; I raise my eyes to her face, and I see the
sweetness of love saying to me: "Be content with that,
and learn from me to bear abstinence." Driven by love
and by omnipotent nature, in despair because she will
not let my hands move elsewhere, I make every imaginable effort to guide one of hers to the place where she
could have convinced herself that I deserved her mercy;
but with a strength greater than mine she refuses to remove her hands from my chest, where she could have
found nothing to interest her. Nevertheless, it was there
that her mouth descended when it detached itself from
mine.

Whether from need or from the effect of lassitude, having passed so many hours unable to do anything but constantly swallow her saliva mixed with mine, I sleep in her

arms, holding her clasped in mine. What woke me with a start was a loud chiming of bells.

"What is that?"

"Let us dress quickly, my dear, my love; I must get back to the convent."

"Then dress. I am going to enjoy the spectacle of seeing you disguised as a saint again."

"Gladly. If you are not in any hurry you can sleep here."

She then rang for the same woman, who I realized must be the great confidante of all her amorous mysteries. After having her hair done up, she took off her dress, put her watches, her rings, and all her secular ornaments in a desk, which she locked, put on the shoes of her order, then a corset in which, as in a prison, she confined the pretty children which alone had fed me on their nectar, and finally put on her habit. Her confidante having gone out to summon the gondolier, she flung herself on my neck and said that she would expect me the next day but one to decide on the night she would come to spend with me in Venice, where, she said, we would make each other completely happy; and she left. Very well pleased with my good fortune, though full of unsatisfied desires, I put out the candles and slept deeply until noon.

I left the casino without seeing anyone, and, well masked, went to call on Laura, who gave me a letter from C. C. which ran as follows:

"Here, my dear husband, is a good example of my way of thinking. You will find me ever more worthy to be your wife. You must believe that, despite my age, I can keep a secret and that I am discreet enough not to take your silence in bad part. Sure of your heart, I am not jealous of what can divert your mind and help you to bear our separation patiently.

"I must tell you that yesterday, going through a corridor which is above the small visiting room and wanting to pick up a toothpick I had dropped, I had to take a stool away from the wall. Picking it up, I saw through an almost imperceptible crack where the floor meets the wall your own person very much interested in conversing with my dear friend Mother M. M. You cannot imagine either my surprise or my joy. Yet those two feelings instantly gave place to my fear of being seen and making some babbling nun curious. After quickly putting the stool back in its place, I left. Ah, my dear! I beg you to tell me everything. How could I love you and not be curious about the whole story of this remarkable occurrence? Tell me if she knows you, and how you made her acquaintance. She is my dear friend, of whom I told you, and whom I did not think it necessary to name to you. It is she who has taught me French and she has given me books in her room which have enlightened me on a very important matter of which few women have any knowledge. Know that but for her the terrible illness which almost killed me would have been discovered. She gave me linen and sheets; I owe her my honor; and so she learned that I have had a lover, as I have learned that she has had one too, but we were never curious about our respective secrets. Mother M. M. is an incomparable woman. I am certain, my dear, that you love her and that she loves you, and since I am not in the least jealous of her I deserve that you should tell me all about it. But I am sorry for you both, for all that either of you can do can only serve, I believe, to excite your mutual passion. The whole convent believes that you are ill; I am dying to see you. So come at least once. Farewell.''

The letter made me uneasy, for I felt very sure of C. C., but the crack might betray us to others. In addition, I now had to tell my darling a lie, for honor and love forbade me to tell her the truth. In the answer which I immediately sent her I said that she must at once inform her friend that she had seen her through the crack, talking to a masker. As for my having made the nun's acquaintance, I said that having heard of her rare quali-

ties I had had her called to the grating, announcing myself under a false name, and that consequently she must
refrain from talking about me, for she had recognized me
as the same man who went to hear mass at her church.
As for love, I assured her that there was no such thing
between us, though I agreed that she was a charming
woman.

On St. Catherine's Day,[14] which was C. C.'s name day,
I went to mass in her church. Going to the *traghetto* to
take a gondola, I observe that I am followed. I needed
to make sure of it. I see the same man also take a gondola and follow me; this could be natural; but to make
certain I disembark in Venice at the Palazzo Morosini del
Giardino,[15] and I see the same man disembarking too.
After that I am in no more doubt. I come out of the
palace, I stop in a narrow street near the Flanders post,[16]
and, knife in hand, I force him into the corner of the
street and, putting the point to his throat, I insist on his
telling me at whose order he is following me. He would
perhaps have told me all if someone had not happened
to enter the street. At that he got away, and I learned
nothing. But seeing that it was only too easy for a busy-
body to know who I was if he persisted in trying to
find out, I resolved not to go to Murano again except
masked or at night.

The next day, which was the one on which M. M. was
to let me know how she would arrange to come to supper
with me, I went to the visiting room very early. I saw
her before me, displaying on her face the signs of the
contentment which flooded her soul. The first compliment
she paid me was on my appearing at her church after
three weeks during which I had not been seen there. She
told me that the Abbess had been very pleased, because
she said she was sure she knew who I was. I thereupon
told her the story of the spy, and my resolve not to go to
mass in her church again. She replied that I would do
well to show myself in Murano as little as possible. She

then told me the whole story of the crack in the old flooring and said that it had already been stopped up. She said she had been warned by a boarder at the convent who was fond of her, but she did not name her.

After these few remarks I asked her if my happiness was deferred, and she answered that it was deferred only for twenty-four hours because the new lay sister had invited her to supper in her room.

"Such invitations," she said, "come seldom, but when they do one cannot refuse except at the cost of making an enemy of the person who extends the invitation."

"Can one not say one is ill?"

"Yes, but then one must receive visitors."

"I understand, for if you refuse you may be suspected of slipping away."

"No, no—slipping away is not considered possible."

"Then you are the only one who can perform the miracle?"

"You may be sure that I am the only one, and that gold is the powerful god who performs it. So tell me where you will wait for me tomorrow precisely at the second hour of the night."

"Could not I wait for you here[17] at your casino?"

"No, for the person who will take me to Venice is my lover."

"Your lover?"

"Himself."

"That is something new! Well then, I will wait for you in the Piazza dei Santi Giovanni e Paolo, behind the pedestal of the equestrian statue of Bartolomeo da Bergamo."[18]

"I have never seen either the statue or the square except in an engraving; but I will not fail to be there. You have told me enough. Nothing but terribly bad weather could keep me from coming; but let us hope for good. So good-by. We will talk much tomorrow evening, and if we sleep we shall go to sleep more content."

I had to act quickly, for I had no casino. I took a second rower, so that I was in the San Marco quarter in less than a quarter of an hour. After spending five or six hours looking at a number of them, I chose the most elegant and hence the most expensive. It had belonged to Lord Holderness,[19] the English Ambassador, who had sold it cheaply to a cook on his departure. He rented it to me until Easter for a hundred zecchini in advance, on condition that he himself would cook the suppers and dinners I might give.

The casino had five rooms, furnished in exquisite taste. It contained nothing that was not made for the sake of love, good food, and every kind of pleasure. Meals were served through a blind window which was set back into the wall and filled by a revolving dumb-waiter which closed it completely. The masters and the servants could not see one another. The room was decorated with mirrors, chandeliers, and a magnificent pier glass above a white marble fireplace; and the walls were tiled with small squares of painted Chinese porcelain, all attracting interest by their representations of amorous couples in a state of nature, whose voluptuous attitudes fired the imagination. Some small armchairs matched the sofas which were placed to left and right. Another room was octagonal and walled with mirrors, with floor and ceiling of the same; the counterposed mirrors reflected the same objects from innumerable points of view. The room was next to an alcove, which gave by concealed doors onto a dressing room on one side and on the other a boudoir in which were a bathtub and an English-style water closet. All the wainscoting was embossed in ormolu or painted with flowers and arabesques. After telling him not to forget to put sheets on the bed and candles in all the chandeliers and in the candelabra in each room, I ordered him to prepare a supper for two for that evening, warning him that I wanted no wines except Burgundy and champagne and no more than eight made dishes, leaving the choice to him regardless of expense. He was to see to the dessert too. Taking the key to the street door I warned him that when I came in I wished to see no one. The supper was to be ready at the second hour[20] of night and was to be served when I rang. I observed with pleasure that the clock in the alcove had an alarm, for despite my love I was beginning to succumb to the power of sleep.

After giving these orders I went to a milliner's to buy a pair of slippers and a nightcap trimmed with a double ruffle of Alençon point.[21] I put it in my pocket. Since I was to give supper to the most beautiful of all the sultanas of the Master of the Universe, I wanted to make sure the evening before that everything would be in order. Having told her that I had a casino, I must not appear to be a novice in any respect.

It was the cook who was surprised when he saw me at the second hour all alone. I instantly berated him for not having lighted candles everywhere, when, as I had told him the hour, he could be in no doubt about it.

"I will not fail to do so another time."

"Then light up and serve."

"You told me it would be for two."

"Serve for two. Remain present at my supper this first time, so that I can point out to you everything I find good or bad."

The supper came in the dumb-waiter in good order, two dishes at a time; I commented on everything; but I found everything excellent in Saxon porcelain.[22] Game, sturgeon, truffles, oysters, and perfect wines. I only reproached him with having forgotten to set out hardboiled eggs, anchovies, and prepared vinegars on a dish, to make the salad. He rolled up his eyes with a contrite look, accusing himself of having committed a great crime. I also said that another time I wanted to have bitter oranges to give flavor to the punch and that I wanted rum, not arrack. After spending two hours at table I

told him to bring me the account of all that he had spent.
He brought it a quarter of an hour later, and I found it
satisfactory. After paying him and ordering him to bring
me coffee when I should ring, I retired to the excellent
bed which was in the alcove. The bed and the good supper won me the most perfect sleep. But for them, I
should not have been able to sleep for thinking that on
the next night I should have my goddess in my arms in
that very bed. On leaving in the morning I told my man
that for dessert I wanted all the fresh fruits he could
find and, above all, ices. To keep the day from seeming
long I gambled until nightfall and I did not find Fortune
different from my love. Everything went just as I wished.
In the depths of my soul I gave thanks for it to the powerful Genius of my beautiful nun.

It was at the first hour[23] of night that I took up my
post by the statue of the heroic Colleoni. She had told
me to be there at the second hour, but I wanted to have
the sweet pleasure of waiting for her. The night was
cold, but magnificent, and without the least wind.

Exactly at the second hour I saw a gondola with two
rowers arrive and disembark a masker, who, after speaking to the gondolier at the prow, came toward the statue.
Seeing a male masker, I am alarmed, I slip away, and I
regret not having pistols. The masker walks around the
statue, comes up to me, and offers me a peaceable hand
which leaves me in no more doubt. I recognize my angel
dressed as a man. She laughs at my surprise, clings to
my arm, and without a word between us we make our
way to the Piazza San Marco, cross it, and go to the
casino, which was only a hundred paces from the Teatro
San Moisè.

Everything is as I have ordered. We go upstairs, I
quickly unmask, but M. M. gives herself the pleasure of
walking slowly through every corner of the delicious
place in which she was being received, delighted that I
should see all the graces of her person in every profile

and often in full face and admire in her clothing what kind of man the lover who possessed her must be. She was surprised at the magic which everywhere showed her her person from a hundred different points of view at the same time even when she stood still. The multiplied portraits of her which the mirrors offered her by the light of all the candles expressly placed for the purpose were a new spectacle which made her fall in love with herself. Sitting on a stool I attentively examined all the elegance of her attire. A coat of short-napped rose velvet edged with an embroidery of gold spangles, a matching hand-embroidered waistcoat, than which nothing could be richer, black satin breeches, needle-lace ruffles, buckles set with brilliants, a solitaire of great value on her little finger and on her other hand a ring which showed only a surface of white taffeta covered by a convex crystal. Her *bautta*[24] of black blond-lace was as beautiful as possible in both design and fineness. So that I could see her even better she came and stood in front of me. I search her pockets and I find a snuffbox, a comfit box, a phial, a case of toothpicks, a pair of opera glasses, and handkerchiefs exhaling scents which sweetened the air. I attentively examine the richness and workmanship of her two watches and of her fine seals hung as pendants from chains covered with small diamonds. I search her side pockets and I find flintlock pistols with a spring firing mechanism, of the finest English manufacture.

"All that I see," I say, "is beneath you, but permit my astonished soul to do homage to the adorable being who wishes to convince you that you are really his mistress."

"That is what he said when I asked him to take me to Venice and leave me there, adding that his wish was that I should enjoy myself there and become ever more convinced that he whom I was about to make happy deserved it."

"It is unbelievable, my dear. Such a lover is one of a

kind, and I can never deserve a happiness by which I am already dazzled.''

"Let me go and unmask by myself."

A quarter of an hour later she appeared before me with her beautiful hair dressed like a man's but unpowdered and with side locks in long curls which came down to the bottom of her cheeks. A black ribbon tied it behind, and it fell to her knees in a hanging plait. M. M. as a woman resembled Henriette,[25] and as a man a Guards officer named *L'Étorière*[26] whom I had known in Paris; or rather she resembled the youth Antinoüs,[27] whose statues are still to be seen, if her French clothes had permitted the illusion.

Overwhelmed by so many charms, I thought I felt ill. I threw myself on the sofa to support my head.

"I have lost all my confidence," I said; "you will never be mine; this very night some fatal mishap will tear you from my desires; perhaps a miracle performed by your divine spouse in his jealousy of a mortal. I feel prostrated. In a quarter of an hour I may no longer exist."

"Are you mad? I am yours this moment if you wish. Though I have not eaten I do not care about supper. Let us go to bed."

She felt cold. We sit down before the fire. She tells me that she has no vest on. I unfasten a diamond brooch in the shape of a heart which kept her ruffle closed, and my hands feel before my eyes see what only her shirt defended against the air, the two springs of life which ornamented her bosom. I become ardent; but she needs only a single kiss to calm me, and two words: "After supper."

I ring, and seeing her alarm I show her the dumb-waiter.

"No one will see you," I say; "you must tell your lover, who may not know of this device."

"He knows of it; but he will admire your thoughtfulness and will say that you are no novice in the art of pleasing and that clearly I am not the only woman who enjoys the delights of this little house with you."

"And he will be wrong. I have neither supped nor slept here except alone; and I hate deceit. You are not my first passion, my divine love; but you will be my last."

"I am happy, my dear, if you will be faithful. My lover is so; he is kind, he is gentle; but he has always left my heart empty."

"His must be so too, for if his love were like mine he would not permit you an absence of this kind. He could not put up with it."

"He loves me, as I love you; do you believe that I love you?"

"I must believe it; but you would not put up with—"

"Say no more; for I feel that, if you will not keep anything from me, I will forgive you everything. The joy which I feel in my soul at this moment is due more to my certainty that I shall leave you wanting nothing than to my certainty that I shall spend a delicious night with you. It will be the first in my life."

"Then you have not spent nights with your worthy lover?"

"Yes, but those nights were inspired only by friendship, gratitude, and compliance. Love is what counts. Despite that, my lover is like you. He has a natural vivacity and his wit is always ready, like yours; besides which both his face and his person are attractive, though he does not resemble you in looks. I also think he is richer than you are, though this casino might make one conclude the opposite. But do not imagine that I consider you less deserving than he because you confess that you are incapable of the heroism of permitting me an absence; on the contrary, if you told me that you would be

as indulgent as he is to one of my caprices, I should know
that you do not love me as I am very glad that you do
love me.''

"Will he wish to know the details of this night?''

"He will believe that it will please me if he asks me
about it, and I shall tell him everything except some circumstances which might humiliate him.''

After the supper, which she found choice and exquisite, as she did the ices and the oysters, she made
punch, and in my amorous impatience, after drinking
several glasses of it, I begged her to consider that we
had only seven hours before us and that we should be
doing very wrong not to spend them in bed. So we went
into the alcove, which was lighted by twelve flaming
candles, and from there to the dressing room, where,
presenting her with the fine lace cap, I asked her to
dress her hair like a woman. After saying that the cap
was magnificent she told me to go and undress in the
outer room, promising that she would call me as soon
as she was in bed.

It took only two minutes. I flung myself into her
burning arms, on fire with love and giving her the most
lively proofs of it for seven continuous hours which were
interrupted only by as many quarters of an hour devoted to the most feeling talk. She taught me nothing
new so far as the physical side of the performance was
concerned, but any quantity of new things in the way of
sighs, ecstasies, transports, and unfeigned sentiments
which find scope only at such moments. Each discovery
I made elevated my soul to Love, who furnished me
with fresh strength to show him my gratitude. She was
astonished to find herself capable of so much pleasure,
for I had shown her many things which she thought were
fictions. I did what she did not think she was entitled
to ask me to do to her, and I taught her that the slightest
constraint spoils the greatest of pleasures. When the
alarm chimed she raised her eyes to the Third Heaven[28]

like an idolator, to thank the Mother and the Son[29] for having so well rewarded her for the effort it had cost her to declare her passion to me.

We dressed in haste, and seeing me put the beautiful cap in her pocket she assured me that it would always be most dear to her. After taking coffee we hurried to the Piazza dei Santi Giovanni e Paolo, where I left her, assuring her that she would see me on the next day but one. After watching her get into her gondola I went home, where ten hours of sleep restored me to my normal state.

CHAPTER IV

*Continuation of the preceding chapter. Visit
to the convent and conversation with M. M.
Letter which she writes me and my answer.
Another meeting at the casino in Murano in
the presence of her lover.*

ON THE next day but one I went to the visiting room
after dinner. I send for her, and she comes at once and
tells me to leave, for she is expecting her lover, but that
I must come without fail on the following day. I leave.
At the end of the bridge I see a poorly masked masker
getting out of a gondola the gondolier of which I knew
and had good reason to believe was then in the service of
the French Ambassador. He was not in livery, and the
gondola was plain, like all gondolas belonging to Venetians. I turn and see the masker going to the convent.
I feel no more doubt, and I go back to Venice delighted
to have made the discovery and pleased that the Ambassador was my senior partner. I resolve to say nothing
about it to M. M.

I go to see her the next day and she tells me that her
friend had come to take leave of her until the Christmas
holidays.

"He is going to Padua," she says, "but everything is arranged for us to sup at his casino if we wish."

"Why not in Venice?"

"No, not in Venice, until he is back. He asked me not to. He has great judgment."

"Very well. When shall we sup at the casino?"

"Sunday, if you like."

"Let it be Sunday; I will go to the casino at dusk and will read while I wait for you. Did you tell your friend that you were not uncomfortable in my casino?"

"My dear, I told him everything; but one thing greatly troubles him. He wants me to beg you not to expose me to the danger of a big belly."

"May I die if it ever entered my mind. But don't you run the same risk with him?"

"Never."

"Then we must be very careful in future. I think, since there is no masking[1] during the nine days before Christmas, I shall have to go to your casino by water, for if I go by land I could easily be recognized as the same man who went to your church."

"That is very prudent. I can easily point out the quay to you. I think you can come during Lent too, when God wants us to mortify our senses. Isn't it odd that there is a time when God approves of our amusing ourselves and another when we can only please him by abstinence! What can an anniversary have in common with the divinity? I do not understand how the action of the creature can influence the creator, whom my reason can only conceive as independent. It seems to me that if God had created man with the power to offend him, man would be justified in doing everything he forbade him to do, if only to teach him how to create. Can one imagine God being sad during Lent?"

"My divine one, you reason perfectly; but may I ask you where you learned to reason, and how you managed to break away?"

"My friend gave me good books, and the light of truth quickly dissipated the clouds of superstition which were oppressing my reason. I assure you that when I reflect on myself I think I am more fortunate in having found someone who has enlightened my mind than unfortunate in having taken the veil, for the greatest happiness of all is to live and die at peace, which we cannot hope to do if we believe what the priests tell us."

"You are very right; but permit me to wonder at you, for enlightening an extremely prejudiced mind such as yours must have been could not be the work of a few months."

"I should have seen the light much less quickly if I had been less steeped in error. What separated the true from the false in my mind was only a curtain; reason alone could draw it; but I had been taught to scorn reason. As soon as I was shown that I should set the greatest store by it I put it to work; it drew the curtain. The evidence of truth appeared with the utmost clarity, my stupid notions disappeared; and I have no reason to fear that they will reappear, for I strengthen my defenses every day. I can say that I did not begin to love God until after I had rid myself of the idea of him which religion had given me."

"I congratulate you. You were more fortunate than I. You have gone further in a year than I in ten."

"Then you did not begin by reading what Lord Bolingbroke[2] has written. Five or six months ago I was reading Charron's[3] *La Sagesse,* and I don't know how our confessor found it out. He dared to tell me at confession that I must stop reading it. I answered that since my conscience was not troubled by it, I could not obey him. He said that he would not absolve me, and I answered that I would go to communion nevertheless. The priest went to Bishop Diedo[4] to ask what he should do, and the Bishop came to talk with me and gave me to understand that I should be guided by my confessor. I

answered that my confessor's business was to absolve me,
and that he did not even have the right to advise me
unless I asked him for advice. I told him outright that,
since it was my duty not to scandalize the entire convent,
if he persisted in refusing me absolution I would go to
communion nevertheless. The Bishop ordered him to
leave me to my conscience. But I was not satisfied. My
lover procured me a brief from the Pope which author-
izes me to confess to anyone I choose. All my sisters are
jealous of the privilege; but I used it only once, for the
thing is not worth the trouble. I always confess to the
same priest, who has no difficulty in absolving me, for
I tell him absolutely nothing of any importance."

So it was that I came to know her as an adorable freethinker; but it could not be otherwise, for she had an
even greater need to quiet her conscience than to satisfy
her senses.

After assuring her that she would find me at the
casino I went back to Venice. On Sunday after dinner
I had myself rowed around the island of Murano in a
two-oared gondola, to see where the quay for the casino
was and also the small one by which she left the convent;
but I could make out nothing. I did not find the quay
for the casino until during the novena,[5] and the small
quay for the convent six months later at the risk of my
life. We shall speak of it when we come to that time.

About the first hour of night I went to the temple of
my love and, waiting for my idol to arrive, I amused
myself by looking at the books which made up a small
library in the boudoir. They were few but choice. They
included all that the wisest philosophers have written
against religion and all that the most voluptuous pens
have written on the subject which is the sole aim of love.
Seductive books, whose incendiary style drives the reader
to seek the reality, which alone can quench the fire he
feels running through his veins. Besides the books there
were folios containing only lascivious engravings. Their

great merit lay in the beauty of the drawing far more than in the lubricity of the poses. I saw engravings for the *Portier des Chartreux*,[6] made in England, and others for Meursius,[7] or Aloisia Sigea Toletana, than which I had never seen anything finer. In addition the small pictures which decorated the room were so well painted that the figures seemed to be alive. An hour went by in an instant.

The appearance of M. M. in her nun's habit wrung a cry from me. I told her, springing to embrace her, that she could not have come in better time to prevent a schoolboy masturbation to which all that I had seen during the past hour would have driven me.

"But in that saintly dress you surprise me. Let me adore you here and now, my angel."

"I will put on secular clothes at once. It will take me only a quarter of an hour. I do not like myself in these woolens."

"No, no. You shall receive the homage of love dressed as you were when you brought it to birth."

She answered only with a *Fiat voluntas tua* ("Thy will be done") delivered with the most devout expression as she let herself fall on the commodious sofa, where I treated her with caution despite herself. After the act I helped her take off her habit and put on a plain robe of Pekin muslin which was the height of elegance. I then played the role of chambermaid while she dressed her hair and put on a nightcap.

After supper, before going to bed we agreed not to meet again until the first day of the novena when, the theaters being closed for ten days, masks are not worn. She then gave me the keys to the door giving onto the quay. A blue ribbon fastened to the window above it was to be the signal which would show it to me by day, so that I could later go there by night. But what filled her with joy was that I went to stay in the casino and never left it until her lover returned. During the ten days I stayed there I had her four times and thereby convinced her that I lived only for her. I amused myself reading, or writing to C. C., but my love for the latter had grown calm. The chief thing which interested me in the letters she wrote me was what she told me about her dear friend Mother M. M. She said that I had done wrong not to cultivate her acquaintance, and I answered that I had not pursued it for fear of being recognized. In this way I made her even more obliged to keep my secret inviolably.

It is not possible to love two objects at once, and it is not possible to keep love vigorous if one either gives it too much food or none at all. What kept my passion for M. M. always at the same pitch was that I could never have her except with the greatest fear of losing her. I told her it was impossible that, one time or another, some nun would not need to speak with her at a time when she was neither in her room nor in the convent. She maintained that it could not happen, since nothing was more respected in the convent than a nun's privilege of shutting herself up in her room and denying herself even to the Abbess. She had nothing to fear but the fatal circumstance of a fire, for then, when everything was in confusion and it was not natural that a nun would remain calm and indifferent, her absence must necessarily become known. She congratulated herself on having been able to win over the lay sister, the gardener, and another nun whom she always refused to name. Her lover's tact and his money had done it all, and he vouched for the fidelity of the cook and his wife, who together took care of the casino. He was sure of his gondoliers, too, despite the fact that one of them must certainly be a spy for the State Inquisitors.

On Christmas Eve she told me that her lover was about to arrive, that she was to go with him to the opera[8] on St. Stephen's Day and sup with him at the casino on the third day of Christmas. After saying that she would

expect me for supper on the last day of the year she gave
me a letter, asking me not to read it until I was at home.

An hour before dawn I packed my things and went
to the Palazzo Bragadin, where, impatient to read the
letter she had given me, I immediately locked myself
in my room. It ran as follows:

"You nettled me a little, my dear, when day before
yesterday, on the subject of my having to keep everything
about my lover from you, you said that, satisfied with
possessing my heart, you leave me mistress of my mind.
Dividing heart and mind is a sophistical distinction, and
if it does not seem so to you, you must admit that you do
not love the whole of me, for it is impossible that I can
exist without a mind and that you can cherish my heart
if it is not in accord with it. If your love can be content
with the contrary, it does not excel in delicacy.

"But since circumstances may arise in which you could
convict me of not having acted toward you with all the
sincerity which true love demands, I have resolved to
reveal a secret concerning my lover to you, despite the
fact that I know he is certain I will never reveal it, for
it is treachery. Yet you will not love me the less for it.
Reduced to choosing between the two of you, and obliged
to deceive one or the other, love has conquered in me;
but not blindly. You shall weigh the motives which had
the power to tip the scales to your side.

"When I could no longer resist my desire to know
you intimately I could not satisfy it except by confiding
in my friend. I had no doubt of his willingness. He
conceived a very favorable idea of your character when
he read your first letter, in which you chose the visiting
room, and he thought you showed yourself a man of
honor when, after we became acquainted, you chose the
casino in Murano in preference to your own. But as
soon as he learned of it he also asked me to do him the
favor of allowing him to be present at our first interview ensconced in a perfect hiding place from which he

would not only see all that we did without himself being seen but also hear all that we said. It is a closet whose existence cannot even be guessed. You did not see it during the ten days you spent in the casino; but I will show it to you on the last day of the year. Tell me if I could refuse him the favor. I granted it; and nothing was more natural than to keep it a secret from you. So now you know that my friend witnessed all that we said and did the first time we were together. But do not take it amiss, my darling; you pleasesd him, not only by everything you did but also by all the amusing things you said to me. I felt very anxious when our conversation turned to the nature my lover must have to be so excessively tolerant; but fortunately all that you said could only be flattering to him. This is the complete confession of my treachery, which, as a sensible lover, you must forgive me, and the more so since it did you no harm. I can assure you that my friend is most curious to know who you are. That night you were natural and very likable; if you had known that you were being watched God knows what you would have been. If I had told you the thing it is even possible that you would not have consented, and you would perhaps have been right.

"But now I must risk everything for the sake of everything and make myself easy, knowing that I have done nothing for which I can be reproached. Know, my dear, that on the last day of the year my friend will be at the casino, and that he will not leave it until the next day. You will not see him, and he will see everything. Since you are not supposed to know, you understand how natural you must be in everything, for if you were not, my friend, who is very intelligent, might suspect that I have betrayed the secret. The principal thing you must be careful about is what you say. He has all the virtues except the theological one called faith, and on that subject you have free rein. You can talk of literature, travel, politics, and tell as many anecdotes as you please, and be sure of his approval.

"The question remains whether you are willing to let a man see you during the moments when you surrender to the furies of love. This uncertainty is now my torment. Yes or no: there is no middle course. Do you understand how painful my fear is? Do you feel how difficult it must have been for me to take this step? I shall not sleep tomorrow night. I shall have no rest until I have read your answer. I will then decide on a course in case you answer that you cannot be affectionate in someone's presence, especially if the 'someone' is unknown to you. Yet I hope that you will come nevertheless, and that if you cannot play the role of lover as you did the first time no bad consequences will ensue. He will believe, and I will let him believe, that your love has cooled."

Her letter surprised me greatly; then, after thinking it over, I laughed. But it would not have made me laugh if I had not known what sort of man it was who would witness my amorous exploits. Certain that M. M. must be very uneasy until she received my answer, I answered her at once, in the following terms:

"My divine angel, I want you to receive my answer to your letter before noon. You shall dine perfectly easy.

"I will spend the night of the last day of the year with you and I assure you that your friend, as our spectator, will see and hear nothing which can lead him to suppose that you have revealed his secret to me. Be sure that I will play my role perfectly. If man's duty is to be ever the slave of his reason, if he must, so far as he is able, permit himself nothing without taking reason as his guide, I can never understand how a man can be ashamed of letting a friend see him at a moment when he is giving the greatest proofs of love to a very beautiful woman. Such is my situation. Yet I must tell you that if you had forewarned me the first time you would have done wrong. I would have refused absolutely. I should have thought that my honor was involved; I should have thought that, in inviting me to supper, you were only the willing accomplice of a friend, a strange man dominated by this strange taste, and I would have formed such an unfavorable opinion of you that it would perhaps have cured me of my love, which at that time was only beginning to bud. Such, my charmer, is the human heart; but at present the case is different. Everything you have told me about your worthy friend has shown me his character, I consider him my friend too, and I love him. If a feeling of shame does not keep you from letting him see you fond and loving with me, how—far from being ashamed of it—can I fail to be proud of it? Can a man blush at what makes him proud? I cannot, my dear, either blush over having conquered you or over letting myself be seen in moments when I flatter myself I shall not appear unworthy of your conquest. Yet I know that, by a natural feeling which reason cannot disapprove, most men feel a repugnance to letting themselves be seen at such moments. Those who cannot give good reasons for their repugnance must have something of the cat in their nature; but they can have good reasons for it and yet feel under no obligation to explain them to anyone. The chief reason is probably that a third person who is looking on and whom they see cannot but distract them, and that any distraction can only lessen the pleasure of intercourse. Another important reason could also be considered legitimate, that is, if the actors knew that their means of obtaining pleasure would appear pitiable to those who should witness them. Such unfortunates are right in not wishing to arouse feelings of pity in the performance of an act which would seem more properly to arouse jealousy. But we know, my dear, that we certainly do not arouse feelings of pity. Everything you have told me makes me certain that your friend's angelic soul must, in seeing us, share our pleasures. But do you know what will happen, and what I shall be very sorry for, since your lover can only be a most likable man? Seeing us will drive him frantic, and he will either run away or have to come out of his hiding place and go down on his knees to me, begging me to give you up to the violence of his amorous desires in his need to calm the fire which our transports will have kindled in his soul. If that happens I will laugh and give you up to him; but I will leave, for I feel that I could not remain the unmoved spectator of what some other man might do to you. So good-by, my angel; all will be well. I hasten to seal this letter, and I will take it to your casino this instant."

I spent these six holidays with my friends and at the Ridotto,[9] which at that period was opened on St. Stephen's Day. As I could not deal, since only patricians wearing the official robe[10] were allowed to make bank there, I played day and night, and I constantly lost. Whoever punts cannot but lose. The loss of four or five thousand zecchini, which was my entire wealth, only made my love stronger.

At the end of the year 1774 a law issued by the Great Council forbade all games of chance and caused the closing of the Ridotto, as it was called. The Great Council was amazed when it saw, on counting the ballots, that it had passed a law which it could not pass, for at least three quarters of those who had cast ballots had not wanted it, and yet three quarters of the ballot proved that they had wanted it. The voters looked at one another in astonishment. It was a visible miracle of the glorious Evangelist St. Mark, who had been invoked by Signor Flangini, then First Corrector,[11] now a Cardinal, and by the three State Inquisitors.

On the appointed day I arrived at the casino at the usual hour, and there was the beautiful M. M. dressed as a woman of fashion, standing with her back to the fire-place.

"My friend," she said, "has not yet come; but as soon as he is here I will give you a wink."

"Where is the place?"

"There. Look at the back of that sofa against the wall. All the flowers in relief which you see have holes in their centers which go through to the closet behind. There is a bed, a table, and everything a man needs to stay there for seven or eight hours entertaining himself by watching what is done here. You shall see it when you wish."

"Did he have it built himself?"

"Certainly not, for he could not foresee that it might be of use to him."

"I understand that the spectacle may give him great pleasure; but since he cannot have you when nature will give him the greatest need of you, what will he do?"

"That is his concern. Besides, he is free to go if he is bored, and he can sleep, but if you are natural he will enjoy it."

"I shall be, except that I shall be more polite."

"No politeness, my dear, for you will at once become unnatural. Where did you ever hear of two lovers in the fury of love thinking of being polite?"

"You are right, dear heart; but I will be delicate."

"That you may, just as you always are. Your letter pleased me. You treated the subject thoroughly."

M. M. was wearing nothing over her hair, but it was negligently dressed. A sky-blue quilted dress was her only attire. She had on ear-buttons studded with brilliants; her neck was completely bare. A fichu of silk gauze and silver thread, arranged in haste, half revealed the beauty of her bosom and displayed its whiteness where her dress opened in front. She had on slippers. Her shy and modestly smiling face seemed to be saying: "This is the person you love." What I found most unusual and what pleased me excessively was her rouge, which was applied as the court ladies apply it in Versailles. The

charm of such painting lies in the carelessness with which
it is placed on the cheeks. The rouge is not meant to look
natural, it is put on to please the eyes, which see in it
the tokens of an intoxication which promises them amorous transports and furies. She said that she had put
on rouge to please her lover, who liked it. I answered
that such a taste led me to think him French. When I
said this she winked at me: her friend had arrived. So
it was then that the comedy was to begin.

"The more I look at your face, the more angry I am
at your spouse."

"They say he was ugly."

"It has been said: so he deserves to be cuckolded, and
we shall work at it all night. I have lived in celibacy for
the past week, but I need to eat, for I have nothing in my
stomach but a cup of chocolate and the whites of six
fresh eggs which I ate in a salad dressed with Lucca
oil[12] and Four Thieves vinegar." [13]

"You must be ill."

"Yes; but I shall be well when I have distilled them
one by one into your amorous soul."

"I did not know that you were in need of *frustratoires*." [14]

"Who could need them with you? But my fear is
reasonable, for if I miss you, I will blow out my brains."

"What does 'miss' mean?"

"In the figurative sense it means 'fail in one's purpose.' Literally it means that when I want to shoot my
pistol at my enemy, the priming doesn't catch. I *miss*
him."

"Now I understand you. And it would be a misfortune,
my dark-haired love, but not enough to make you blow
out your brains."

"What are you doing?"

"I am taking off your cloak. Give me your muff,[15] too."

"That will be difficult, for it is nailed."

"Nailed?"

"Put your hand in it. Try."

"Oh, the wretch! Is it the egg whites that gave you such a nail?"

"No, my angel, it is your whole charming person."

At that I picked her up, she held me around the shoulders to make less weight for me, and, having dropped my muff, I grasped her by the thighs and she steadied herself on the nail; but after a turn around the room, fearing what would follow I set her down on the carpet, then sat down myself and made her sit on me, whereupon she had the kindness to finish the job with her beautiful hand, collecting the white of the first egg in the palm of it.

"Five to go," she said; and after cleaning her beautiful hand in a potpourri of aromatic herbs, she gave it to me to kiss again and again. Calmed, I spent an hour telling her amusing stories; then we sat down at table.

She ate for two, but I for four. The service was of porcelain but at dessert of silver gilt, as were the candelabra, each of which held four candles. Seeing that I admired their beauty she said they were a present her friend had made her.

"Did he give you snuffers too?"

"No."

"Then I conclude that your lover must be a great lord, for great lords know nothing of snuffing."

"The wicks of our candles do not need snuffing."

"Tell me who taught you French, for you speak it too well for me not to be curious to know."

"Old La Forêt, who died last year. I was his pupil for six years; he taught me to compose verses too; but I have learned words from you which I never heard pass his lips: *à gogo, frustratoire, dorloter*.[16] Who taught them to you?"

"Good society in Paris, Madame de Boufflers[17] for

example, a woman of profound intelligence who one day asked me why the Italian alphabet contained *con rond*.[18] I laughed, and did not know how to answer.''

''I think they are abbreviations used in the old days.''

After making punch we amused ourselves eating oysters, exchanging them when we already had them in our mouths. She offered me hers on her tongue at the same time that I put mine between her lips; there is no more lascivious and voluptuous game between two lovers, it is even comic, but comedy does no harm, for laughter is only for the happy. What a sauce that is which dresses an oyster I suck in from the mouth of the woman I love! It is her saliva. The power of love cannot but increase when I crush it, when I swallow it.

She said that she was going to change her dress and come back with her hair ready for the night. Not knowing what to do I amused myself looking at what she had in her desk, which was open. I did not touch her letters but, opening a box and seeing some condoms,[19] I quickly wrote the following verses and substituted them for what I had stolen:

> *Enfants de l'amitié, ministres de la peur,*
> *Je suis l'amour, tremblez, respectez le voleur,*
> *Et toi, femme de Dieu, ne crains pas d'être mère*
> *Car si tu fais un fils, il se dira son père.*
> *S'il est dit cependant que tu veux te barrer*
> *Parle; je suis tout prêt, je me ferai châtrer.*

("Children of friendship, ministers of fear, I am Love, tremble, and respect the thief. And you, wife of God, do not fear to become a mother, for if you bear a son he will say he is its father. Yet if you are determined to bar your door, speak; I am ready, I will have myself gelded.")

M. M. reappeared in a new guise. She had on a dressing gown of India muslin embroidered with flowers in gold thread, and her nightcap was worthy of a queen.

I threw myself at her feet to beg her to yield to my desires then and there; but she ordered me to hold my fire until we were in bed.

"I do not want," she said with a smile, "to be bothered with keeping your quintessence from falling on the carpet. You shall see."

With that she goes to her desk, and instead of the condoms she finds my six verses. After reading them, then reading them over again aloud, she calls me a thief and, giving me kiss after kiss, she tries to persuade me to restore the stolen goods. After reading my verses slowly aloud once more, pretending to reflect on them, she goes out on the pretext of looking for a better pen, then comes back and writes the following answer:

Dès qu'un ange me f..., je deviens d'abord sûre
Que mon seul époux est l'auteur de la nature.
Mais pour rendre sa race exempte des soupçons
L'amour doit dans l'instant me rendre mes condoms.
Ainsi toujours soumise à sa volonté sainte
J'encourage l'ami de me f... sans crainte.

("When an angel f...s me I am at once sure that my only husband is the author of nature. But to make his lineage free from suspicion Love must instantly give me back my condoms. Thus always obedient to his sacred will, I encourage my friend to f... me without fear.")

I thereupon returned them to her, giving a very natural imitation of surprise; for really it was too much.

Midnight had struck, I showed her her little Gabriel, who was sighing for her, and she made the sofa ready, saying that as the alcove was too cold, we would sleep there. The reason was that in the alcove her friend could not see us.

While waiting I tied up my hair in a Masulipatam[20] kerchief which, going round my head four times, gave me the redoubtable look of an Asiatic despot in his seraglio. After imperiously putting my sultana in the state of nature and doing the same to myself, I laid her down and subjugated her in the classic manner, delighting in her swoons. A pillow which I had fitted under her buttocks and one of her knees bent away from the back of the sofa must have afforded a most voluptuous vision for our hidden friend. After the frolic, which lasted an hour, she took off the sheath and rejoiced to see my quintessence in it; but finding, even so, that she was wet with her own distillations, we agreed that a brief ablution would restore us *in statu quo*. After that we stood side by side in front of a large upright mirror, each putting one arm around the other's back. Admiring the beauty of our images and becoming eager to enjoy them, we engaged in every kind of combat, still standing. After the last bout she fell onto the Persian carpet which covered the floor. With her eyes closed, her head to one side, lying on her back, her arms and legs as if she had just been taken down from a St. Andrew's cross,[21] she would have looked like a corpse if the beating of her heart had not been visible. The last bout had exhausted her. I made her do the "straight tree,"[22] and in that position I lifted her up to devour her chamber of love, which I could not reach otherwise since I wanted to make it possible for her, in turn, to devour the weapon which wounded her to death without taking her life.

Reduced after this exploit to asking her to grant me a truce, I set her on her feet again; but a moment later she challenged me to give her her revenge. It was my turn to do the "straight tree" and hers to grasp me by the hips and lift me up. In this position, steadying herself on her two diverging pillars, she was horrified to see her breasts splattered with my soul distilled in drops of blood.

"What do I see?" she cried, letting me fall and herself falling with me. Just then the alarm chimed.

I called her back to life by making her laugh.

"Have no fear, my angel," I said, "it is the yolk of the last egg, which is often red."

I myself washed her beautiful breasts, which human blood had never soiled before that moment. She was very much afraid that she had swallowed some drops of it; but I easily persuaded her that even if it were so, it would do no harm. She dressed in her habit and then left, after imploring me to go to bed there and to write and tell her how I was before I went back to Venice. She promised to do as much for me the next day. The caretaker would have her letter. I obeyed. She did not leave until a half hour later, which she certainly spent with her friend.

I slept until evening, and scarcely had I waked before I wrote her that I was well. I went to Venice, where, to fulfill my promise, I looked up the same painter who had made my portrait for C. C. He needed only three sittings. I had him make it a little larger than the first, because M. M. wanted it in a medallion concealed under some sacred image which would hide it from everyone, she alone possessing the secret of uncovering it. It was the jeweler's task to produce a secret device different from the first. The same painter made me an Annunciation, in which the Angel Gabriel appeared as dark-haired and the Holy Virgin as a blonde, opening her arms to the divine messenger. The famous painter Mengs used the same idea in the Annunciation[23] which he painted at Madrid twelve years later.

CHAPTER V

I give M. M. my portrait. Her present to me.
I go to the opera with her. She gambles and
replenishes my purse. Philosophical conversa-
tion with M. M. Letter from C. C. She knows
all. Ball at the convent: my exploits as Pier-
rot. C. C. comes to the casino instead of M. M.
I spend an absurd night with her.

1754.

ON THE second day of the year, before going to the
casino I went to Laura's house to give her a letter for
C. C. and to receive one which made me laugh. M. M.
had initiated the girl not only into the mysteries of
Sappho,[1] but also into pure metaphysics. She had become
a freethinker. She wrote that, not wishing to give an account of her doings to her confessor but at the same time
not wanting to lie to him, she had stopped telling him
anything. "He told me," she wrote, "that perhaps I
confessed nothing to him because I did not examine my
conscience well, and I answered that I had nothing to tell
him, but that if he liked I would commit some sin on
purpose, so that I could have something to tell him."

Here is a copy of the letter from M. M. which I found
at the casino:

"I am writing to you in bed, my dark-haired dear,
because I feel as if my hips were completely out of joint;

Faro Players in a Casino

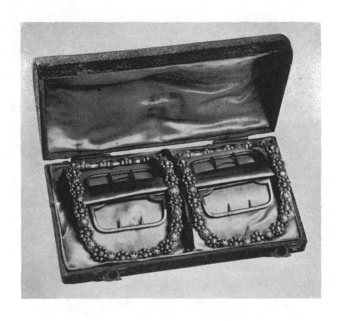

Pair of Shoe Buckles in Case

but it will go away, for I am eating and sleeping well. What brought balm to my blood was the letter in which you assured me that the loss of yours had no ill effect. I shall be certain of it on Twelfth-night in Venice. Write me if I can count on that. I want to go to the opera. I forever forbid you egg whites in salad. In future when you go to the casino you must ask if anyone is there, and if you are told there is, you must go away; my friend will do likewise; so you will never meet; but it will not be for long, for he is mad about you and determined that you shall make his acquaintance. He says he did not believe there was a man of your vigor in the universe; but he insists that, making love as you do, you are defying death, for he maintains that the blood you spurted out must have come from the brain. But what will he say when he learns that you think nothing of it? But here is something to make you laugh: he wants to eat salads of egg whites, and I am to ask you to give me some of your Four Thieves vinegar; he says he knows it exists, but it is not to be had in Venice. He told me he spent a sweet and cruel night, and he expressed a certain uneasiness for me, too, for he thought my efforts were beyond the delicacy of my sex. That may well be; but in the meanwhile I am delighted at having outdone myself and having been put to such a noble test of my strength. I love you to adoration; I kiss the air, thinking that you are there; and I cannot wait to kiss your portrait. I hope that mine will be as dear to you. I believe we are born for each other, and I curse myself when I think that I have put a barrier between us. The key which you see here is to my jewel-box. Search it; take whatever you see addressed 'To my Angel.' It is a small present which my friend wanted me to give you in exchange for the nightcap you gave me. Farewell.''

The small key which I found in the letter was to a casket in the boudoir. Impatient to see the nature of the present which her friend had inspired her to give me,

I go and open the little casket, and I undo the packet. I find a letter and a shagreen case. Here is the letter:

"What will make this present dear to you, my loving friend, is my portrait, of which our friend, who has two, is happy to deprive himself when he thinks that you will become its owner. In this box you will find my portrait twice concealed by two different secret devices. You will see me as a nun if you remove the bottom of the snuffbox lengthwise; and if you push the corner of it you will see a hinged cover open, under which I appear as you have made me. It is impossible, my dear, that any woman has ever loved you as I love you. Our friend encourages my passion. I cannot decide if I am more fortunate in my friend or in my lover, for it is beyond my powers to imagine anything better than either."

In the case I found a gold snuffbox, which a few traces of Spanish snuff showed had been used Following the instructions I found her at the bottom of it, dressed as a nun, standing, and in half profile. Raising the false bottom showed her to me lying naked on a black silk mattress in the pose of Correggio's Magdalen.[2] She was looking at a Cupid who had his quiver at his feet and was seated on her nun's habit. It was a present of which I did not think myself worthy. I wrote her a letter in which she could not but find the deepest gratitude truly depicted. In the same small casket I saw all her diamonds in drawers and four purses filled with zecchini. Handsome behavior being one of my great admirations, I shut the casket and went back to Venice, happy if I could only have found the will and the means to escape from the sway of Fortune by ceasing to gamble.

The jeweler gave me the medallion of the Annunciation just as I wished it to be. It was made to be worn hanging from the neck. A link through which the neck cord was to pass contained the secret device. If it was pulled hard, the Annunciation sprang up and revealed my portrait. I attached it to a gold chain of Spanish

links six ells long, which made it a most noble present.
I put it in my pocket and in the evening of Epiphany
Day I posted myself at the foot of the fine statue which
the grateful Republic had erected to the hero Colleoni
after having him poisoned,[3] if backstairs history tells
true. *Sit divus, modo non vivus* ("Let him be a god so
long as he is not alive")[4] is a saying of the enlightened
monarch which will endure as long as there are monarchs.

At exactly two o'clock[5] I saw M. M. get out of the
gondola dressed, and very well masked, as a woman. We
went to the opera at San Samuele, and at the end of the
second ballet we went to the Ridotto, where she greatly
enjoyed looking at all the patrician ladies, whose rank
gives them the privilege of sitting down with their faces
unmasked. After walking about for half an hour we
went to the room set apart for the great bankers. She
stopped at Signor Momolo Mocenigo's[6] bank; at that
time he was the handsomest of all the young patrician
gamesters. As there was no play at his table, he was
lolling easily in front of two thousand zecchini, with his
head bent toward the ear of a masked lady sitting beside
him. She was Signora Marina Pisani,[7] whose adoring
cavalier he was.

M. M. having asked me if I wished to play, and I
having answered no, she said that she was taking me for
her partner and, not waiting for me to reply, she draws
out a purse and puts a roll of coins on a card. The banker,
moving only his hands, shuffled, then cut, and M. M.
won her card and then the paroli. The Signore pays,
takes a new pack of cards, and begins whispering to
the lady beside him, quite indifferent to four hundred
zecchini which M. M. had already put on the same card.
The banker continuing his conversation, M. M. said to
me in good French: "Our stakes are not high enough
to interest the Signore; let us go." So saying, she takes
away her card and moves on. I pick up the money without
answering the Signore, who says:

"Your masker is too intolerant."

I rejoin my beautiful gamester, who was surrounded. She stops at the bank of Signor Piero Marcello,[8] another charming young man, at whose side was Signora Venier,[9] Signor Momolo's sister. She plays, and loses five rolls one after the other. Having no more money, she takes coins by handfuls from the pocket in which I had the four hundred zecchini, and in five or six deals she has the bank at death's door. She stops, and the noble banker congratulates her on her luck. After pocketing all the money she had won I give her my arm and we go downstairs and set off to have supper. Noticing that several busybodies were following us I took a *traghetto* gondola, and had it land where I wished. This is the way to escape from busybodies in Venice.

After eating a good supper I emptied my pockets. For my share I found I was in possession of nearly a thousand zecchini; she asked me to do hers up in rolls and put them in her little casket and keep the key to it. I finally gave her the medallion containing my portrait, whereupon she reproached me for not having done her the favor sooner. After having tried in vain to discover the secret, she was delighted to learn it, and she thought me a very good likeness.

Remembering that we had only three hours before us I urged her to undress.

"Yes," she said; "but be careful; for my friend maintains that you may die on the spot."

"And why does he think you are not in equal danger, since your ecstasies are more frequent than mine?"

"He says that the liquid which we women distill cannot come from the brain, since the womb has no connection with the seat of understanding. It follows, he says, that the child is not the mother's son in respect to the brain, which is the seat of reason, but the father's; and I think it is true. According to this system woman has at most only the quantity of reason which she needs;

she has none over to give a portion of it to the fetus.''

''Your lover is wise. According to this system we must forgive women all the follies they commit for love's sake, and men none. That is why I shall be in despair if I find that you have become pregnant.''

''I shall know that in a few weeks, and if I am pregnant so much the better. I have decided what course I shall take.''

''And what course is that?''

''To entrust myself entirely to my friend and to you. I am certain that neither of you will let me be brought to bed in the convent.''

''That would be a stroke of fate which would determine our destiny. I should have to carry you off and take you to England and marry you.''

''My friend thinks that it would be possible to bribe a physician who would declare that I was suffering from some malady of his own invention and order me to go and drink mineral waters at the springs, which the Bishop might allow. At the watering place I would be cured, then I would come back here; but I would far rather that we united our destinies until death. Could you live comfortably anywhere, as you do here?''

''Alas, no! But with you could I be unhappy? We will talk of this when it becomes necessary. So now let us go to bed.''

''Let us. If I bear a son my friend will take care of him as his father.''

''Could he believe that he is?''

''You can both take the credit; but some resemblance will show me the truth.''

''Yes—for example if in time to come he writes pretty verses you can conclude that he is his.''

''Who told you that he can write verses?''

''Admit that he wrote the six in answer to mine.''

''I will not admit it. Good or bad, they are mine, and I mean to convince you of it on the spot.''

"No, no. Let us go to bed, or Love will challenge Apollo to a duel."

"An excellent idea! Take this pencil and write. At the moment I am Apollo."

She then dictated the following four lines:

> *Je ne me battrai pas. Je te cède la place.*
> *Si Venus est ma sœur, commune est notre race.*
> *Je sais faire des vers. Un moment de perdu*
> *Ne pourra pas déplaire à l'amour convaincu.*

> (I will not fight. I yield the ground to you. If Venus is my sister, we are kindred. I can write verses. A moment lost cannot offend a confident Love.")

I thereupon asked her pardon on my knees, admitting that she was also versed in mythology; but could I suppose that a Venetian lady of twenty-two who had been brought up in a convent could be so talented? She said that she had an insatiable desire to convince me that she deserved my heart, and she asked me if I thought her a shrewd gamester.

"Shrewd enough to make the banker tremble."

"I do not always play so high, but having taken you as my partner I defied Fortune. Why did you not play?"

"Because having lost four thousand zecchini during the last week of the year, I had no money left; but I will play tomorrow and Fortune will favor me. Meanwhile here is a little book I took from your boudoir. It is Pietro Aretino's postures. In these three hours I want to try some of them."

"That is very like you. But some of them are impossible and even silly."

"True, but four are very interesting."

It was in these labors that we spent the three hours. The chimes of the clock put an end to our celebration. After escorting her back to her gondola I went home to bed; but I could not sleep. I got up and went to pay some pressing debts. One of the greatest pleasures a wastrel can enjoy is that of paying certain debts. The money M. M. had won for me brought me luck all night, and I reached the end of the Carnival having won every day.

Going to the casino in Murano three days after Twelfth-night to put ten or twelve rolls in M. M.'s casket, I found the caretaker's wife with a letter from her for me. I had just received one from C. C. by Laura. After giving me as good news of her health as I could wish, M. M. asked me to find out if the same jeweler who had set her medallion had by any chance set a ring which displayed a St. Catherine which must also conceal a portrait; she wanted to know the secret of it. She said that it was a boarder of whom she was fond who had the ring, that it was very thick, and that the girl did not know that there must be a secret device for opening it. I answered that I would obey all her commands. But here is C. C.'s letter, which is amusing because of the quandary in which it put me. The letter from C. C. was of very recent date; M. M.'s had been written two days earlier.

"Oh, how happy I am! You love my dear friend Mother M. M. She has a medallion as thick as my ring. She can have received it only from you; it must contain your portrait. I am sure that the painter who painted her Annunciation is the same one who painted my patron saint; the jeweler must be the same one too. I feel very sure that it was you who gave it to her. Content to know all, I did not want to risk grieving her by telling her that I had discovered her secret. But my dear friend, being either more frank or more curious, did not do likewise. She told me she was certain that my St. Catherine served to cover a portrait, which must be that of the person who had given it to me. I answered that it was true my ring came from my lover, but that I did not know it could contain his portrait. She replied that if such was the case, and I was willing, she would try to find out the secret and afterward she would reveal hers to me too. Certain that she could not find the secret, I gave her my ring, saying that discovering it would please me. The nun who is my aunt sending for me just then, I left my ring with her, and she gave it back to me after dinner, saying that she had been unable to discover anything, but she was still certain the portrait must be in it. She is convinced of it, but I assure you that in this respect she will not find me obliging, for if she saw you she would guess everything and then I should have to tell her who you are. I am sorry that I must keep something from her, but I am not at all sorry either that you love her or that she loves you, and I pity you so much for being cruelly reduced to making love at a grating that I would gladly let you take my place. I should make two people happy at one stroke. Farewell.''

I answered that she had guessed rightly that my portrait was in M. M.'s medallion; but I urged her to continue to keep my secret, assuring her that the fancy I had taken for her dear friend in no way detracted from the constancy of my passion for her. Thus did I equivocate, to keep up the intrigue, which I yet saw coming to its end in the closeness of their friendship.

Having learned from Laura that on such-and-such a day a ball was to be given in the large visiting room of the convent, I made up my mind to go to it masked in such a way that my two dear friends could not recognize me. I was certain that I should see them. During the Carnival in Venice nuns are allowed to have this innocent pleasure. There is dancing in the visiting room, and they remain inside, watching the festivities from behind their wide gratings. At the end of the day the festivities are over, everyone leaves, and they retire well satisfied to have been present at one of the pleasures of the laity. The ball was to take place on the day on which M. M. had invited me to sup at her casino; but that did not prevent me from going masked to the visiting room, where I was sure to see my dear C. C. as well.

Wanting to make certain that my two friends would not recognize me, I decided to mask as Pierrot.[10] There is no costume better fitted to disguise a person, provided he is neither a hunchback nor lame. The wide tunic of a Pierrot, the long, very wide sleeves, the wide trousers which come down to the heels, conceal everything distinctive in his figure by which someone who knew him intimately could recognize him. A cap which covers his whole head, his ears, and his neck hides not only his hair but also the color of his complexion, and a piece of gauze in front of the eyes of his mask prevents anyone from seeing whether they are black or blue.

So, having eaten a dish of soup, I mask after this fashion and, heedless of the cold (for the whole costume being of white linen, one cannot be more lightly clad), I board a gondola, have it drop me at a *traghetto,* and there take another gondola which conveys me to Murano. I had no cloak. In my trouser pockets I had only a handkerchief, the keys to the casino, and my purse.

I go down to the visiting room, which was full, but everyone makes way for the strange mask, whose characteristics were unknown in Venice. I walk on, assuming the gait of a booby as the nature of the mask demands, and I enter the circle of dancers. I see Punches, Scaramouches, Pantaloons, Harlequins. At the gratings I see all the nuns and all the boarders, some seated, others standing, and though I do not let my eyes linger on any of them I see M. M. and, on the opposite side, my loving C. C., who was standing up to enjoy the spectacle. I proceed around the entire circle, walking as if I were drunk, looking everyone up and down, but more looked at and studied. Everyone was trying to make me out.

I stop in front of a pretty girl disguised as a female Harlequin and rudely take her hand to make her dance a minuet with me. Everyone laughs and draws back to make room for us. The Harlequiness dances in perfect character with her costume, and I with mine: I amused the company vastly by constantly appearing to be on the verge of falling, though I always kept my balance. Each time the general apprehension was followed by laughter.

After the minuet I danced twelve furlanas[11] with extraordinary energy. Out of breath, I let myself drop and pretended to sleep, and when my snores were heard everyone respected Pierrot's slumbers. Next there was a contradance which lasted an hour and in which I thought it best not to join; but after the contradance up comes a Harlequin who, with the impertinence permissible to his character, spanks me with his lath. This is Harlequin's weapon. Having, as Pierrot, no weapon, I catch him by the belt and run about the room carrying him, he meanwhile continuing to hit me with his lath on my behind. His Harlequiness, who was the charming girl who had danced with me, comes running to rescue her friend and also hits me with her lath. At that I put the Harlequin down, snatch his lath, and take the Harlequiness on my shoulders, hitting her on the behind and running at full speed all over the room to the laughter of the company and the frightened cries of the girl, who was afraid that if I fell she would show her thighs or her drawers. But an impertinent Punch put a sudden end to the whole comical struggle. He came up behind me and tripped me so hard that I could not keep from falling. Everyone booed him. I quickly got up and, very much annoyed, began an out-and-out wrestling match with the insolent fellow. He was as tall as I am. Since he was awkward and had no resources but his brute strength, I made him bite the dust and I handled him so roughly that his coat came unbuttoned, whereupon he lost his hump and his false belly. To the sound of the clapping and laughter of all the nuns, who had perhaps never enjoyed such a spectacle, I seized the moment, dashed through the crowd, and escaped.

Dripping with sweat, I called a gondola, shut myself up in it, and had it take me to the Ridotto to avoid catching a chill. Night was falling, I was not to be at the casino in Murano until two o'clock, and I could not wait to see M. M.'s surprise when she saw Pierrot before her. So I spent the two hours playing at all the small banks, going from one to another, winning, losing, indulging in all sorts of antics in complete freedom of body and soul, sure that no one recognized me, enjoying the present and snapping my fingers at the future and at all those who are pleased to exercise their reason in the dreary task of foreseeing it.

But two o'clock strikes and reminds me that love and a delicious supper await me to bring me new pleasures. With my pockets full of silver I leave the Ridotto, I hurry to Murano, go to the casino, and enter the bedroom, where I think I see M. M. in her habit standing with her back to the fireplace. I approach to see the effect of the surprise on her face, and I am turned to stone. What I see is not M. M., but C. C. in a nun's habit; even more surprised than I am, she neither speaks nor moves. I drop into an armchair to give myself time to get over my astonishment and recover my intellectual faculties.

When I saw C. C. I was as if struck by lightning. My soul was left as motionless as my body, lost in an inextricable labyrinth.

"It is M. M.," I said to myself, "who is playing this trick on me; but how did she manage to find out that I am C. C.'s lover? C. C. has betrayed my secret. But if she has betrayed me how dare she appear before me? If M. M. loves me how can she have deprived herself of the pleasure of seeing me and sent me her rival? It cannot be meant as a favor for no one carries doing favors to such lengths. It is meant to be a stinging, scornful insult."

My self-esteem did not fail to produce strong arguments to refute the possibility, but in vain. Shivering in
the cold gloom of my disappointment, I alternately saw
that I was tricked, deceived, trapped, scorned.

In this fashion I spent half an hour, bleak and silent,
keeping my eyes fixed on C. C.'s face while she, too,
looked at me without a word, more embarrassed and non-
plussed than I, for she could at most recognize me as the
same masker who had cut such capers in the visiting
room.

Being in love with M. M., and having gone there only
for her sake, I did not have the easy recourse open to
the so-called reasonable man—I could not make the best
of the situation by substituting the one for the other,
despite the fact that I was far from scorning C. C., whose
merits were at least as great as M. M.'s. I loved her,
I adored her; but at that moment she was not the one
for me to have. It would have been an outright denial of
love, which could not but rouse my reason to indignation.
It seemed to me that if I settled for doing the honors to
C. C. I should be contemptible; it seemed to me that
honor forbade me to lend myself to such deceit; in addition, I was glad both to gain the opportunity of reproaching M. M. with an indifference very far from love and
of refraining from acting in a way which would ever
lead her to suppose that she had done me a favor. Add
that during all this time I was inclined to believe that she
was in the hiding place and her friend with her.

I had to resolve on a course, for I could not think of
spending the whole night there masked as I was and saying nothing. I considered deciding to leave, the more so
because neither M. M. nor C. C. could be certain that the
Pierrot was I; but I dismissed the idea with horror when
I thought of the intense mortification C. C.'s beautiful
soul would suffer if she ever learned that I was the Pierrot; it was with the greatest grief that I thought that
she might even now suspect it. I was her husband; I was

the man who had seduced her. These reflections lacerated my soul.

I suddenly begin to imagine that M. M. is in the secret closet and that, if she is, she will show herself when she considers the time is ripe. With this thought in mind, I decide to remain. I untie the handkerchief which bound the white mask of Pierrot to my head, and I relieve my charming C. C. from anxiety by showing her my face.

"It could only be you," she says, "but I breathe again. You seemed surprised to see me. Did you not know that you would find me here?"

"You may be sure I knew nothing about it."

"If you are displeased, I am in despair; but I am innocent."

"My adorable love, come to my arms. How can you suppose that I could be displeased to see you? You are always my better half; but I beg you to release my soul from the cruel labyrinth in which it is lost, for you could not be here unless you have betrayed our secret."

"I! I could never have done that, even if it cost me my life."

"Then how can you be here? How did your dear friend manage to discover everything? No one on earth can have told her that I am your husband. Perhaps Laura—"

"Laura is loyal. My dear love, I cannot even guess."

"But how were you persuaded to put on this disguise, to come here? You are able to leave the convent, and you have never told me so important a secret?"

"Can you believe that I would not have told you anything so important if I had ever left it? Today was the first time—two hours ago; and nothing is so simple or so natural as what made me do what I have done."

"Tell me about it, my love; my curiosity is boundless."

"Your curiosity is dear to me, and I will tell you everything. You know how fond M. M. and I are of each other; our affection could not be greater; you must be

sure of it from all that I have written to you. Well, then
—two days ago M. M. asked the Abbess and my aunt to
let me sleep in her room instead of the lay sister, who had
a bad cold and had gone to cough in the infirmary. She
was given permission, and you cannot imagine how
happy we were to find ourselves free for the first time
to sleep together in the same bed.

"Today, a moment after you left the visiting room
where you made us laugh so much, and where neither
M. M. nor I could ever have imagined that it was you,
she went out. I followed her, and as soon as we were
alone she said she needed me to do her a service on which
her happiness depended. I replied that she had only to
tell me what it was. She thereupon opened a drawer and
to my great surprise dressed me as you see me now. She
kept laughing, and I laughed too, not knowing where
the joke might end. When she saw that I was all dressed
she said that she was going to trust me with a great secret, which she fearlessly confided to my loyalty. 'Know,
my dear friend,' she said, 'that I was going to leave the
convent tonight and not come back until tomorrow morning. But now it has been decided that it is not I who will
go, but you. You have nothing to fear, and you need no
instructions, for I am sure that in your situation you will
not be at a loss. In an hour a lay sister will come here, I
will speak to her privately, then she will tell you to follow her. Accordingly, you will go out with her by the
small door and cross the garden until you reach the room
which gives on the little quay. There you will get into a
gondola, saying nothing to the gondolier except, "To the
casino." You will be there in five minutes, you will get
out, and you will enter a small room in which you will
find a fire burning. You will be all alone there, and you
will wait.' 'Wait for whom?' I said. 'No one. That is all
you are to know. Nothing will happen to you which will
offend you. Trust to me. At the casino you will eat supper and go to bed, too, if you wish, for no one will dis-

turb you. I beg you not to ask me any further questions, for I cannot tell you more.'

"Tell me, my dear, what I could do after hearing this, and after having promised her that I would do whatever she asked? Begone, base suspicion! I laughed, and expecting only something pleasant, as soon as the lay sister came I followed her, and here I am. After being bored for three quarters of an hour, I saw Pierrot.

"I can assure you on my honor that the very moment I saw you appear my heart told me that it was you; but the next moment, when I saw you start back after looking at me closely, I knew just as clearly that you felt that you had been tricked. You sat here in such a gloomy silence that I should have thought it very wrong if I had been the first to break it, and the more so since, despite what my heart told me, I could not but fear that I was mistaken. Pierrot's mask might hide someone else —but certainly no one who could be dearer to me than you after eight months during which only force has kept me from embracing you. Now that you must be sure I am innocent, let me congratulate you on your knowing this casino. You are fortunate, and I wish you happiness. M. M. is the only woman, after me, who is worthy of your affection, the only woman with whom I can be content to share it. I pitied you; I pity you no more, and your happiness makes me happy. Kiss me."

I should have been an ingrate and a barbarian if I had not then clasped to my breast with unfeigned signs of the most sincere affection the angel of goodness and beauty who was there only for friendship's sake. But after convincing her that I considered her entirely justified, I did not fail to express my tender feelings and then to launch into theories equally reasonable and unreasonable to account for M. M.'s extraordinary behavior, which I considered very dubious and next to impossible to interpret to her credit. I told her in so many words that, apart from the pleasure it gave me to see her, it was obvious that her friend had played a vile trick on me which I could not but resent for its patent offensiveness.

"I do not see that," C. C. replied. "My dear friend must have contrived to find out, though I don't know how, that you were my lover before you met her. She might well have believed that you still love me, and she believed—for I know her soul—that she was giving us a sacred proof of perfect friendship by procuring us, without forewarning, the highest happiness for which two lovers can hope. I cannot but love her for it."

"You are right, my dear one; but your situation is very different from mine. You have no other lover, and, unable to live with you, I could not resist M. M.'s charms. I have fallen madly in love with her; she knows it; and, with her intelligence, she cannot have done what she has done except to show me her scorn for me. I admit that I feel it most keenly. If she loved me as I love her she could never have done me the excruciating favor of sending you here in her stead."

"I do not agree with you. Her soul is as great and noble as her heart is generous, and just as I am not displeased to know that you love her and are loved by her and that you have made each other happy, as appearances tell me you have, so she is not displeased to know that we love each other and indeed is delighted to have an opportunity to convince us that she approves of it. She wants you to understand that she loves you for yourself, that your pleasures are hers, and that she is not jealous of me, who am her dearest friend. To convince you that you should not be displeased that she has discovered our secret, she tells you, by sending me here, that she is satisfied that you should share your heart between her and me. You know that she loves me, and that I am often her wife or her fond husband; so, just as you do not object to my being your rival and to my often making her happy, she does not want you to suppose that her love is like hate, for such is the love of a jealous heart.''

"You plead your friend's cause like an angel, my dear wife, but you do not see the thing in its true light. You have intelligence and a pure soul; but you have not my experience. M. M. loves me only to amuse herself, knowing perfectly well that I am not such a fool as to be taken in by what she has now done. I am miserable, and it is she who makes me so.''

"Then I, too, should have cause to complain of her. She has shown me that she has all power over my lover and that, having made him her own, she finds no difficulty in giving him back to me. On top of that, she shows me that she scorns the affection I feel for her, by putting me in a position to show it to someone else.''

"Now your argument is getting shaky. The case between her and you is entirely different. The love you and she indulge in is only a game by which you delude your senses. The pleasures you enjoy do not exclude others; what could make you jealous of each other would be a love of the same kind between women; but M. M. could not feel offended that you had a lover, just as you could not if she had one—provided in either case that the lover was not the other's.''

"But that is precisely our case, and you are wrong. We are not a bit offended that you love us both. Didn't I write you that I wished I could give you my place? Does that make you think I scorn you too?''

"Your wish, my dear, to give me your place when you did not know that I was her lover arose from the fact that your love had changed into friendship, and for the time being I must be glad of it; but I have good reason to be offended if M. M. entertains the same sentiment, for I love her now and I am certain that I can never marry her. Do you understand that, my angel? Being sure that you will become my wife I am equally sure of our love, which will have time enough to be rekindled; but M. M.'s love will not return. Is it not humiliating for me if all I

have done and all I have been able to do is to make
myself an object of contempt? As for you, you cannot
but adore her. She has initiated you into all her mysteries; you owe her eternal gratitude and friendship.''

Such is the substance of our discussion, which continued until midnight, when the tactful caretaker brought
us an excellent supper. I could not eat, but C. C. had a
good appetite. Despite my gloom I had to laugh when
I saw a salad of egg whites. She said that I was right to
laugh, because the yolks, which were the best part, had
been removed. I took pleasure in admiring the increase
in her beauty, though I felt not the least desire to show
her my feeling. I have always held that there is no merit
in being faithful to a person one truly loves.

Two hours before dawn we went back to sit in front of
the fire. C. C., seeing me sad, showed the most delicate
respect for my situation—not a trace of provocation, no
posture which deviated from the strictest decency. Her
words were loving and tender, but she never once dared
to reproach me for my coldness.

Toward the end of our long conversation she asked me
what she was to say to M. M. when she returned to the
convent.

''She expects,'' she said, ''to see me perfectly happy
and full of gratitude for her generous gift of this night.
What shall I tell her?''

''The plain truth. You must not keep one word of our
conversation from her, or one of my thoughts if you can
remember them. You must tell her that she has made me
unhappy for a long time to come.''

''I should distress her too much if I told her that, for
she loves you, and the medallion which contains your
portrait is her dearest possession. I will do my very best
to make it up between you quickly. I will send you a
letter from me by Laura, unless you assure me that you
will go to her house for it tomorrow.''

''Your letters will always be dear to me; but you will

see that M. M. will not want to have things out. There is one point on which she may not believe you.''

''Yes, I know—the strength of mind we had to spend eight hours together like brother and sister. If she knows you as I know you she will think it impossible.''

''In that case tell her the opposite if you wish.''

''No, no! It would be a very ill-timed lie. I can dissimulate a little; but I shall never learn to lie. I love you, too, because all through this night you have not pretended that you still love me.''

''Believe me, my angel, I am sick with grief. I love you with all my soul; but now I am in a situation to be pitied.''

''You weep, my dear; I beg you to spare my heart. I cannot forgive myself for having said that to you; but believe that I had no intention of reproaching you. I am sure that in a quarter of an hour M. M. will be weeping too.''

When the hour struck, having no more hope that M. M. would appear to justify herself, I kissed C. C., I resumed my disguise to cover my head and so shelter myself from a very strong wind whose whistlings I heard, and I hurried down the stairs after giving C. C. the key to the casino and telling her to return it to M. M.

CHAPTER VI

I am in great danger of perishing in the lagoons. Illness. Letters from C. C. and M. M. Reconciliation. Assignation at the casino in Murano. I learn the name of M. M.'s friend, and I consent to have him to supper at my casino with our common mistress.

I RUN to the *traghetto,* expecting to find a gondola, and I find none.

According to Venetian police regulations this can never happen, for at all hours each *traghetto* is required to have at least two gondolas ready for the public service; nevertheless, it sometimes happens, though rarely, that there is none. This was one of the times. There was a very strong wind from the west, and the disgusted gondoliers had apparently gone home to bed. What was I to do at the end of the quay an hour before daylight and almost naked? I might have gone back to the casino if I had had the key. The wind was blowing me off my feet, and there was no house I could enter to take shelter from it.

I had in my pockets at least three hundred filippi[1] which I had won at the Ridotto, and a purse full of gold; I had reason to fear the robbers of Murano, very dangerous and determined cutthroats who enjoy and abuse a number of privileges which the policy of the government grants them in return for the work they do in the glass factories with which the island abounds; to keep them from emigrating the government grants all of them Venetian citizenship. I expected to encounter a pair of them, who would have stripped me to my shirt, for I did not even have in my pocket the usual knife which all honest men in Venice carry to defend their lives. Unfortunate predicament! I was to be pitied and I was shaking with cold.

Through the cracks in the blinds of a wretched one-story house I see light. I decide to knock modestly at the door of the little house. Someone calls:

"Who is knocking?"

The blind is opened.

"What do you want?" says a man who is amazed to see me in such a costume. I beg him to let me in, giving him a filippo, a coin which was worth eleven lire, telling him my perilous situation in a few words. He comes and opens the door, and I ask him to go and fetch me a gondola which will take me to Venice for a zecchino. He quickly dresses, thanking Providence and assuring me that he will get me one immediately. He puts on his cloak and leaves me in his bedroom, where I see his whole family in one bed, all amazed at my appearance. A half hour later in comes my man and tells me that a two-oared gondola is at the quay, but that the gondoliers insisted on having the zecchino in advance. I agree, I thank him, and I leave, fearing nothing, for I see that the two gondoliers are stout fellows.

We make good progress as far as San Michele;[2] but scarcely have we passed the island before the wind increases with such fury that I see I am in danger of perishing if I go on; for though I was a good swimmer I was sure neither of my own strength nor of the possibility of resisting the current. I order the gondoliers to tie up to the island; but they answer that I am not in the

hands of cowards and to have no fear. Knowing the character of our gondoliers I decide to say nothing; but the
gusts of wind redoubled, the foaming waves were coming
in over the side of the gondola, and my men, despite their
strong arms, could not drive it forward.

We were only a hundred paces from the mouth of the
Rio dei Gesuiti[3] when a furious gust of wind knocked
the man at the poop into the water, but he caught hold of
the gondola and had no difficulty getting aboard again.
Having lost his oar he took another; but the gondola,
going about, had already traveled two hundred paces to
my left and broadside on in one minute. The situation
was desperate. I shout to them to abandon the *felce** [4]
to the sea, throwing a handful of silver pieces on the carpet of the gondola. I was instantly obeyed, whereupon
my two hearties, using all their energy, showed Aeolus[5]
that his strength must yield to theirs. In less than four
minutes we entered the Rio dei Mendicanti,[6] and, praising them, I ordered them to take me to the quay of the
Palazzo Bragadin in Santa Marina,[7] where I had no
sooner arrived than I got into bed under blankets to recover my natural heat; a good sleep would have restored
me to my usual state, but nothing I could do would bring
it. Five or six hours later Signor Bragadin and the other
two inseparables came to see me and found me in the
throes of fever; but that did not keep Signor Bragadin
from laughing when he saw my Pierrot costume on the
couch. After congratulating me on having escaped safe
and sound, they left me to myself. Toward evening I began to sweat so profusely that my bed had to be changed
during the night, and in the morning I had a recurrence,
accompanied by delirium. The next morning I ached all
over. The stiffness kept me from moving. The fever having abated, I could hope to recover my health only by
a good diet.

---

* What envelops the gondola. (C.'s note.)

Very early on Wednesday I saw Laura. I told her that I could neither write nor read, but asked her to come back the next day. She put on my night table what she had brought for me, and she left having seen enough of my condition to tell C. C. how I was.

It was not until evening that, feeling a little better, I had my servant lock my door so that I could read what C. C. had written me. The first thing which pleased me was the key to the casino, which she returned to me, for I already very much regretted having left it. I already felt that I had done wrong, and having the key in my hands again was balm to my blood. In the packet I see a letter from M. M., and I read it avidly.

"The details which you have read, or will soon read, in C. C.'s letter will, I hope, make you forget the wrong I did when I hoped to give you the pleasantest of surprises. I saw and heard everything, and you would not have gone off without the key if I had not fallen asleep an hour before you left. So keep the key which C. C. is sending back to you and use it to return to the casino tomorrow evening, since Heaven has preserved you from the storm. Your love perhaps entitles you to complain, but not to ill-treat a woman who has certainly shown you no sign of scorn."

Here is C. C.'s long letter, which I translate only because I think it is interesting:

"I beg you, my dear husband, not to send this key back to me unless, become the most cruel of men, you take pleasure in grieving two women whose only love you are. Knowing your heart, I am certain that you will go to the casino tomorrow night, and that you will make it up with M. M., who cannot go there this evening. You will see that you can insist you are right only if you are stupid. Meanwhile, here is all that you do not know and must be very glad to learn.

"As soon as you left in that terrible storm, which kept me very uneasy, just as I was about to go downstairs to return to the convent I was greatly surprised to see M. M. before me. She said dejectedly that from a place where we could not see her she had seen and heard everything. She had several times been tempted to appear; but she had never made up her mind to it because she was always afraid of arriving at the wrong moment and particularly at the moment when her presence would have prevented the reconciliation which must take place between two people who could not but be in love with each other. Yet she would have decided upon it toward the end of our conversation if she had not fallen asleep. She woke as the clock chimed, just when, after giving me a key of which I knew nothing, you left as if you were fleeing from some den of infamy. M. M. said that she would tell me everything in her room and we left in a terrible storm and in great distress, thinking of you, who, she said, if you had been sensible should have stayed in the casino. As soon as we were in her room we undressed, I to resume my secular clothing and she to go to bed. I sat down by her bedside, and here, almost in her own words, is the account she gave me: 'When you left your ring with me to go and see what your aunt wanted, I examined it so carefully that I suspected the little blue dot. As it had nothing to do with the white enamel border around the arabesque I saw that the secret might be in it. So I took a pin and pushed it. Imagine my surprise and my great satisfaction when I discovered that we loved the same man, and at the same time the grief I felt at the thought that I was keeping him from you. Delighted with my discovery and instantly resolving to make use of it to procure you the pleasure of supping with him, I quickly pushed down your St. Catherine and gave it back to you pretending to have discovered nothing. What joy! At that moment I felt that I was the happiest of women. Acquainted with your heart, knowing that you knew that your lover loved me, since I had let you see his portrait in my medallion, and seeing that you were not jealous, I should have considered myself contemptible if I could have entertained sentiments different from yours—and the more so since your right over him could not but be stronger than mine. As for the care you always took to keep your lover's name a dead secret from me, I at once guessed that it could only be at his order, and I admired the beauty of your soul in your fidelity. Your lover, I judged, must be afraid that he would lose us both if we should discover that neither of us possessed his heart entirely. You cannot believe what pity I felt for you when I reflected that you continued to appear indifferent even after seeing his portrait in my possession must have made you certain that he did not love you alone. Enchanted with the soundness of my reasoning, I gave myself up to it heart and soul, determined to act accordingly and in a manner to convince you both that M. M. deserves your love, your friendship, and your esteem. My satisfaction was unimaginable when I considered that all three of us would be a hundred times happier when there were no more secrets between us. With this thought in mind, I arranged everything to play such a trick on you both as could not but bring the affection you feel for me to the highest pitch. I substituted you for myself, thus perfecting my scheme, which I thought the masterpiece of human intelligence in its kind. You let me dress you as a nun, and, with a readiness which bespoke the greatest confidence in me, you went to my casino not knowing where you were going; after taking you there, the gondola came back for me and I secreted myself where, sure that I could not be seen, I could not fail to see and hear whatever took place between you. Being the author of the play, it was only natural that I should give myself the pleasure of being its audience. I was sure that I did not risk seeing anything unpleasant.

" 'I reached the casino a quarter of an hour after you, and you cannot imagine my delighted surprise when I

saw the same Pierrot who had amused us in the visiting
room and whom neither you nor I had been clever enough
to recognize. But his appearance as Pierrot was the only
surprise in the play which I enjoyed. My fear, my uneasiness, and my disappointment began at once, and I contrived my own unhappiness. Our lover misconstrued
everything, he left in despair, he still loves me; but his
only thought is to be cured of his passion, and he will be.
His returning this key is enough to tell me that he will
not come back to the casino. Accursed night—in which,
intending only to make three people happy, I have made
three people unhappy, and which will cost me my life if
you do not bring him to see reason, for I feel that I
cannot live without him. You certainly have some way of
writing to him, you know him, you know where you can
send this key back to him with a letter which will persuade him to come to the casino tomorrow evening or the
next to talk with me at least once; and I have hope.
Sleep today, my dear friend, and tomorrow write him
the whole truth, take pity on your poor friend and forgive her if she loves your lover. I will write him a short
letter too, which you will enclose in yours. I am the reason why he no longer loves you, you ought to hate me,
and you still love me, I adore your soul, I saw his tears,
I saw how much and how he loves me, I know him now;
I did not know there were men who loved as he does.
I have spent a night in hell. Do not think that I am
angry, my dear friend, because I heard you confide to
him that we loved each other as husband and wife; it
does not displease me; it is not an indiscretion to have
told it to him, whose mind is as free from prejudice as
his heart is good.'

"Her words ended in tears. I tried to comfort her by
promising to write to you and I retired to my own bed,
where I slept for four good hours; but M. M. could not
sleep. However, she got up in the morning; we found the
convent full of sad news which could not but greatly con-

cern us. We heard that an hour before dawn a fishing boat had gone down in the Lagoon, that two gondolas had capsized, and that the people in them had drowned. Imagine our anxiety; we did not dare to ask questions. An hour before dawn was just the time you had left. M. M. returned to her room, I followed her and took care of her when she fainted for fear you had perished. More courageous than she, I told her that you could swim; but chills heralding a fever obliged her to go back to bed. We were in this state when, a half hour later, my aunt, who is always merry, came in laughing and said that in the storm before dawn the same Pierrot who had made us laugh so much had very nearly been drowned. 'Poor Pierrot!' I said. 'Tell us all about it, my dear aunt. I am very glad he was saved. Who is he? Does anyone know?' 'Yes,' she answered, 'the whole story is out, for the gondola which took him home is ours. The prow gondolier has just told us that Pierrot spent the night at the Briati ball,[8] and that, wanting to go back to Venice and finding no gondolas at the *traghetto,* he gave ours a zecchino to take him home. The poopman, his companion, fell into the Lagoon; but do you know what our fine Pierrot did then? He threw all the money he had on the *zenia** and threw the *felce* of the gondola into the sea, and then, the wind being west, they took him home, entering Venice by the Rio dei Mendicanti. The gondoliers happily divided thirty filippi in silver which they picked up from the carpet, and then went back and recovered the *felce.* Pierrot will remember Murano and the Briati ball. The gondolier says he is the son of Signor Bragadin, the brother of the Procuratore; they took him to the palace nearly dead with fright and cold, for he was dressed in linen and had no cloak.'

"After this account my aunt left and we remained there looking at each other as if we had returned from

---

* The carpet of a gondola. (C.'s note.)

death to life. M. M. asked me, smiling, if it was true
that you were Signor Bragadin's son. I could only answer her that it might possibly be so, but that your name
did not show that you were his bastard, still less his legitimate son, for the Signore had never married. M. M.
answered that she would be very sorry if you were a
Bragadin. I then felt I must tell her your real name,
and about Signor Bragadin's attempting to obtain me
as your wife and the result of it, which was putting me
in the convent. And so, my dear, your little wife has no
more secrets to hide from M. M. I hope that you will not
accuse me of indiscretion, for it is better that our loving
friend should know the pure and simple truth than
truth mixed with falsehood. What amused us and made
us really laugh was the assurance with which everyone
says that you spent the night at the Briati ball. When
people do not know something which is needed to round
out a story, they make it up; and the probable often substitutes very nicely for the true. What I can tell you is
that the news brought balm to the soul of our dear friend,
she slept very well last night, and has regained her
beauty only from the hope that you will come to the
casino at once. She has read this letter three times and
kissed me more than thirty. I could not be more eager
than I am to give her the letter which you will write her.
Laura will wait. Perhaps I shall see you again at the
casino, and in a better humor, I am sure. Farewell.''

It was more than enough to bring me to my senses.
When I finished reading I admired C. C. and adored
M. M.; but I was ill and stiff, though I had no fever.
Being certain that Laura would come back early the next
morning, I could not keep from writing to them both—
only a little, but enough to assure them that I was myself
again. I wrote C. C. that she had done well to tell her
friend my name, and the more so because, having ceased
to appear in the church, I no longer had any good reason
to conceal my identity. For the rest, I assured her that

I admitted I was at fault and that I would give M. M.
the greatest possible assurances of it as soon as I was fit
to leave my bed. Here is a copy of the letter I wrote to
M. M.:

"I left the key to the casino with C. C. to give back
to you, my charmer, because I believed I was deliberately
tricked, scorned, and dishonored by you. In this self-
delusion, I felt it impossible to let you see me, and despite
my love I trembled with horror at the thought of seeing
you. Such was the effect upon me of an act on your part
which I should have considered heroic if my intelligence
had been equal to yours. I am beneath you in everything,
and at our first meeting I shall convince you of the
sincerity with which my repentant soul implores your
forgiveness. Except for this, I have no reason to wish
to recover my health. The stiffness which cripples me
did not allow me to write to you yesterday. I can assure
you that in the middle of the Murano canal, when I was
within inches of death, I thought that Heaven was punishing me for the fault I had committed in sending you
back the key to the casino, for when I found no boats at
the *traghetto* I should have returned there if I had had it
in my pocket; and, as you see, I should not now be ill and
unable to move. Is it not clear that, if I had perished, it
would only have been a just punishment for my crime in
sending you the keys? Praise be to the God who brought
me back to my senses, chastising me in a manner which
shows me all the error of my ways. In future I will keep
a better watch over myself, and nothing shall again have
power to make me doubt your love. But what do you
think of C. C.? She is an angel incarnate and she is like
you. You love us both, and she loves us equally. I am
the only weak and imperfect creature who cannot imitate
you both. Yet I think I would give my life for one of
you as freely as for the other. I feel a curiosity which I
dare not confide to paper; but you will satisfy it, I am
sure, the first time we see each other. It will be a miracle

if we can meet again before a week from today. Farewell, my angel."

The next day Laura found me sitting up and on the way to recovery. I asked her to tell it to C. C. when she gave her the letter I had written her, and she left after giving me a letter from C. C. which required no answer. Her letter contained one from M. M.; there was nothing in either of them but doubts and fears and desperately loving questions about my health.

It was before dinner six days later that I went to the casino in Murano, where the caretaker gave me a letter from M. M.

"Impatient," she wrote, "to know that your health has returned and that you have resumed possession of the casino where you now are and of all its privileges, I write you this note, my dear one, to ask you to let me know definitely when we shall meet again and where. Whether you want me to come here or to Venice is all one to me. In neither place will we have a witness."

I answered that I was in good health and that we would meet again on the next day but one at the usual hour in the place from which I was writing to her.

I was on fire to see her again. I considered myself at fault in a manner which made me ashamed. Knowing her character, I should have seen beyond doubt that what she had done, far from indicating scorn, had been the most refined exercise of a love whose aim was my pleasure rather than its own. She could not have guessed that I loved her alone. Just as her love for me did not prevent her from accommodating the Ambassador, so she supposed that I might accommodate C. C. She did not consider the different constitution of the two sexes and the privileges which Nature accords to women.

On the next day but one, the fourth day of February in the year 1754, I was again face to face with my beautiful angel. She was wearing her habit. Our mutual love declaring us equally guilty, we fell on our knees before each other at the same moment. We had both mistreated love, she treating it too childishly and I too Jansenistically.[9] Since the forgiveness which we were compelled to ask of each other could not be expressed in words it could only consist in a stream of kisses back and forth, all their power being felt by our loving souls, delighted for the moment that they needed no other language to express their desires and the joy with which they were flooded.

Transported with emotion, impatient to give each other proofs of the sincerity of our repentance and of the fire which urged us on, we rose without letting go of each other and we fell together on the sofa, where we remained inseparable until the time came for a long sigh which we would not have restrained even if we had been sure that it heralded our death. Such was the picture of the rekindling of our love, sketched out, executed in flesh and blood, and finished off by the great painter, all-wise Nature, who, inspired by love, could never paint another either truer or more interesting.

In the tranquillity in which perfect conviction leaves the soul, I laughed with M. M. when I saw that I had taken off neither my cloak nor my *bautta*.

"Is it certain," I asked as I took them off, "that our reconciliation has had no witness?"

At that she picked up a candlestick and, taking me by the hand, led me into the room which contained the large cupboard which I had concluded was the repository of the great secret. She opened it and, after she removed a board which covered the back of it, I saw a door, through which we entered a closet where I saw everything necessary for a person who had to spend a few hours in it. There were a sofa which became a bed when wanted, table, easy chair, desk, candles on flat candlesticks, in short, everything needed by a curious voluptuary one of whose principal pleasures must have been to remain there as the unknown spectator of others' pleasures. Beside the sofa I saw a movable board. M. M. drew it aside; and through twenty holes spaced a little way apart I saw the whole bedroom, in which the spectator must have seen dramas whose author had been Nature and in which he had had no reason to be dissatisfied with the actors.

"And now," said M. M., "I will satisfy the curiosity which you very prudently did not dare to commit to paper."

"You cannot know—"

"Be still. Love is divine, and a diviner; he knows all. Admit that you wish to know if our friend was here on the fatal night which cost me so many tears."

"I admit it."

"So there! He was; and you will not be sorry to learn that you enchanted him completely and that you have all his friendship. He admired your character, your love, your sentiments, and your probity; he approved of the passion you have inspired in me. It was he who consoled me that morning by telling me it was impossible that you would not come back to me as soon as I had acquainted you with my true feelings, my intention, and my good faith."

"But you and he must often have fallen asleep, for without something to interest it is impossible to spend eight hours in darkness and silence."

"His interest and mine were equally keen; besides, we were not in the dark except when you and she were on the sofa, where you could have seen the light coming through the holes in these flowers. We drew this curtain and we supped, listening closely to all your conversation while we were at table. His interest in it was even greater than mine. He told me that he had never known the human heart so well as on that occasion, and that you must never have suffered as much as you did that night; he pitied you for it; but C. C. astonished him as much as she did me, for it is impossible that a girl of fifteen

The Colleoni Monument near SS. Giovanni e Paolo, Venice

Amorous Encounter before Witnesses

should reason as she reasoned in her efforts to justify me, and should say all that she said with the help of no other art than that with which nature and truth supplied her, unless she has the soul of an angel. If you marry her you will have a divine wife. When I lose her I shall be miserable; but your happiness will make it up to me. I cannot understand either how you could fall in love with me when you loved her or how she can manage not to hate me when she knows that I stole your heart from her. C. C. is a goddess. She tells me that she told you of her sterile pleasures with me only to disburden her conscience of the crimes she thought she was committing against the loyalty she believed she owed you."

When we sat down at table M. M. remarked that I had become thinner. We grew merry recollecting past dangers, my masquerading as Pierrot, the Briati ball, where she had been told there was another Pierrot, and the extraordinary effect of the disguise, which made a person unrecognizable, for she thought the Pierrot in the visiting room was shorter and thinner than I. She reflected that if I had not happened to take the convent gondola and if I had not gone to the visiting room dressed as Pierrot, she would not have known who I was, for the nuns would not have been curious to know what happened to me; and she added that she breathed again when she learned that I was not a patrician as she feared, for otherwise she might in time have encountered a difficulty which would have driven her to despair.

I knew very well what she had to fear, but pretending not to know:

"I cannot imagine," I said, "what you might fear if I had been a patrician."

"My dear, the reason for my fear is such that I cannot tell it to you unless you give me your word of honor that you will do me the favor I will ask of you."

"What could prevent me from doing you any favor you could ask of me, provided it was in my power and did not jeopardize my honor, now that there are no more secrets between us? Speak, my dear one; tell me your reason and count upon my affection and hence on my willingness to do anything that would please you."

"Very well. I want you to give a supper at your casino. I will come to it with my friend, who is dying to make your acquaintance."

"And after supper you will leave with him?"

"You see that it must be so."

"And your friend already knows who I am?"

"I felt it necessary to tell him. Otherwise he would not have dared to sup with you."

"Now I have it! Your friend is a foreign ambassador." [10]

"Exactly."

"But when he does me the honor to sup with me he will not remain incognito."

"That would be outrageous. I will introduce him to you by his name and title."

"And could you suppose that I would hesitate to grant you this favor? Tell me if even you can do me a greater one. Set the day, and be sure that I shall await you impatiently."

"I should have been sure of your willingness if you had not taught me to doubt."

"I deserve your jibe."

"Please laugh at it. Now I am satisfied. The person who will sup with you is Monsieur de Bernis, the French Ambassador. Remember that he is aware that you must know he is my lover, but that you must not show that you are aware that he knows of our mutual affection."

"I know my duty, my love. This supper party crowns my wishes. You were right to be concerned over my rank, for if I were a patrician the State Inquisitors would have come prying in good earnest, and the terrible consequences of that make me tremble. If you had confided your uneasiness to me, I would have told you who I am, for the only reason for my secrecy was that, if I were known, C. C.'s father would put her in some other convent. Can you tell me the day for our supper? I am impatient.''

''Today is the fourth; we can sup together on the eighth. We shall come to your casino after the second ballet at the opera. Just give me the directions, so that we can find it without having to ask anyone the way.''

I thereupon wrote down for her all the directions for reaching the door of my casino either by water or, if they preferred, by the streets. Delighted with a prospect which would do me honor, I begged my angel to come to bed. I explained to her that I was recovering from an illness and that, having supped with a good appetite, once in bed I should no doubt offer my first homage to Morpheus. So she set the alarm for ten o'clock[11] and we went to bed in the alcove. From ten to twelve—for the nights were growing short—we made love.

We had fallen asleep not only without separating but with our mouths, which had treasured our last sighs, still clinging together. It was this position which kept us from cursing the alarm which six hours later warned us that we must finish the race which we had only interrupted. M. M. was a well-spring of light. Her cheeks, animated by joy, showed me the bright roses of Venus which heralded it. I told her so, and she, trying to understand me, urged me to look closely at her beautiful breasts, which by their unusual throbbing seemed to invite my lips to deliver them from the amorous spirits which were troubling them. After drinking in as much of them as I could, I hastened to her mouth, open to receive the kiss which signified her defeat and which I accompanied with mine.

Morpheus might perhaps have gained a second victory over us, if the clock had not warned us that we had only time enough left to dress.

She returned to the convent after confirming our engagement for the eighth. After sleeping until noon I went back to Venice, where I gave my cook orders for the supper, the thought of which brought me the greatest pleasure.

CHAPTER VII

*Supper for three with Monsieur de Bernis,
the French Ambassador, at my casino. M. M.'s
proposal; I accept it. Consequences. C. C. is
unfaithful to me but I cannot complain.*

IN SUCH a situation I thought that I should have
felt happy; but I was not. I loved gambling; and as I
could not deal I went and punted at the Ridotto and lost
day and night. My vexation over my losses made me
miserable. But why did I gamble? I did not need to, for
I had all the money I wanted to satisfy my wishes. Why
did I gamble when I felt my losses so keenly? What made
me gamble was avarice. I loved to spend, and my heart
bled when I could not do it with money won at cards.
In those four days I lost all the money M. M. had won
for me.

On the night of February 8th I went to my casino;
and at the appointed hour I saw M. M. with her distinguished gallant, whom she introduced to me by his name
and title as soon as he took off his mask. He said that he
had been most anxious to renew our acquaintance since
the Signora had told him that we had met in Paris.

While he spoke he looked at me attentively, as one

does when one is trying to remember a face. He complained of his poor memory. I put him at ease on that article by telling him that we had not spoken, so that he had not looked at me enough for my person to make an impression on his memory.

"The day," I said, "on which I had the honor to dine with Your Excellency at Signor Mocenigo's, your attention was entirely occupied by the Lord Marshal,[1] the Prussian Ambassador. You were to set off on your journey here four days later. After dinner you took your leave."

He remembered me then, recollecting that he had asked someone if I was the embassy secretary.

"But from this moment," he said, "we can never forget each other. The mysteries which unite us are of a nature to make us intimate friends."

After this remarkable couple had made themselves comfortable we sat down at table, where it was of course my part to do the honors. The Ambassador, an epicure, having highly approved of the Burgundy, the champagne, and the Graves, which I gave him after oysters from the Arsenal,[2] asked me where I had obtained them and was delighted to learn that it was from Count Algarotti.[3]

My whole supper was choice, and my attitude toward them both was that of a private citizen to whom a king in the company of his mistress should do the greatest of honors. I saw that M. M. was enchanted with my respectful behavior toward her and by all the things I said which induced the Ambassador to listen to me with the greatest attention. Seriousness never interfered with jesting on His Excellency's part, who in this was perfectly of the French temper. Everything was accompanied by an apt witticism; and M. M., skillfully turning the conversation, brought up the subject of the combination of circumstances which had led to her making my acquaintance.

Speaking of my passion for C. C., she gave him a most enticing description of her person and her character, to which he listened as if he had known nothing about the girl. It was the part he was obliged to play, for he was not aware that I knew he was in the hiding place. He told M. M. that she would have made me the most charming of presents if she had brought her to our supper. She answered that it would have been too risky for her.

"But," she added, addressing me in a tone of magnanimous condescension, "if you wish, I could arrange for you to sup with her at my casino, for she sleeps in my room."

The proposal greatly surprised me; but it was not the moment to show my surprise.

"It is impossible, Signora," I said, "to add anything to the pleasure one feels when one is with you; nevertheless, I could not but consider it a favor."

"Well, I will give it further thought."

"But," the Ambassador said to her, "if I am to be of the party I think you should warn her that a friend of yours will be present besides her lover."

"That will not be necessary, Your Excellency," I said, "for I will write to her to do whatever the Signora tells her to. I will make it my duty to do so tomorrow."

"Then I invite you to supper," said M. M., "day after tomorrow."

I then begged the Ambassador to be prepared to be indulgent to a girl of fifteen who had no experience of society.

It was then that I told them, in all its details, the story of O-Morphi.[4] My account gave him the greatest pleasure. He asked me to let him see her portrait. He said that she was still at the Parc aux Cerfs,[5] to the delight of the King, to whom she had already given a child.[6] They left at eight o'clock, well pleased; and I remained at the casino.

The next morning, in accordance with my promise to M. M., I wrote to C. C., not telling her that someone she did not know would be at the party. After giving my letter to Laura I went to the casino, where the caretaker gave me a letter from M. M., who wrote as follows:

"Ten o'clock has struck and I am going to bed; but if I am to have any hope of sleep I must first unburden my conscience. You may have consented to the supper with our young friend only out of politeness. Tell me the truth, my dear, and I will put an end to the whole thing without in any way implicating you; leave it to me. But if you like the idea of the supper, she shall come. I love your soul even more than I do your body."

Her fear was well justified, but I should have felt too ashamed if I had gone back on my word; and M. M. knew me too well to believe me capable of it. Here is my answer:

"Will you believe that I expected your letter? Yes, I was expecting it, for I know your mind and I know the idea that you must have of mine now that my sophisms have twice given you cause to fear me. I repent of it, my indulgent dear, when I think that my having made you suspect me must have lessened your love. So I beg you to forget my delusions and to believe in future that my soul is of the same stamp as yours. The supper which has been planned will give me real pleasure. My acceptance of it was prompted by gratitude rather than by politeness. Believe this. C. C. is inexperienced, and I am delighted that she should begin learning to appear in society. I commend her to you, and I beg you to show her even more of your kind attentions if that is possible. I am mortally afraid that you will persuade her to take the veil; but be sure that it would drive me to despair. Your friend is a king among men."

After thus cutting off my retreat, I allowed myself all the reflections which, knowing the human heart, I could not but make. I saw clearly that the Ambassador had become interested in C. C., that he had told M. M. so, and that, compelled by her part of the bargain to satisfy all his wishes, she had undertaken to do whatever she could to accomplish his purpose. This she could not do without my consent, nor would she have dared to suggest the arrangement to me. They had conspired to bring up the subject in such a way that politeness, my feelings, and my sense of propriety would force me to agree. The Ambassador, whose very profession demanded the skill to carry on an intrigue, had been successful in this one, and I had fallen into the trap. It was done; and it was now my part to accept whatever was to come with good grace, not only to keep from looking a fool but also not to seem ungrateful to a man who had granted me unparalleled privileges. But the consequence might well be a cooling of my feelings toward both M. M. and C. C.

M. M. had realized all this on her way home and she had hurried to set everything to rights, or at least to justify herself to me, by writing me that she would put an end to the whole thing without implicating me. She knew that I would not accept her offer. Self-esteem, which is stronger than jealousy, will not allow a man who aspires to be accounted intelligent to show that he is jealous, and especially if he is matched with another man who outshines him only by being free from every trace of that base passion.

The next morning, going to the casino a little earlier, I found no one but the Ambassador, who received me in the most friendly fashion. He said that if he had known me in Paris he would have found a way to introduce me at court, where, he insisted, I would have had the greatest success. "That may well be," I say to myself today when I think of it; "but to what would that success have led me?" I should have been one of the victims of the Revolution, as the Ambassador himself would have been if his position had not taken him to Rome to die in 1794. He died there unhappy though rich,[7] unless he changed his way of thinking before his death, which I consider unlikely.

I asked him if he enjoyed being in Venice, and he answered with a smile that he could not but enjoy it since he was in good health and, having money enough, could procure all the pleasures of life more easily there than anywhere else, but he added that he did not believe he would be allowed to remain the Ambassador there very long. He asked me to say nothing of this to M. M., for it might grieve her.

She arrived with C. C., whose surprise I saw when she found that I was not alone. I encouraged her by greeting her most lovingly, while the stranger showed every sign of pleasure when she answered his compliment in his own language. We applauded the skill of the mistress who had taught her so well.

But considering C. C. something which was to belong to me, my desire to see her shine drove out any base feeling of jealousy which might have preoccupied me. I brought her to a pitch of gaiety, making her talk on subjects on which I knew that she was charming. Applauded, listened to, flattered, and encouraged by the expression of satisfaction on my face, C. C. appeared a miracle to the man whom I nevertheless did not wish to see fall in love with her. What a contradiction! I myself did what anyone else would have earned my hatred by doing.

During supper the Ambassador showed C. C. all kinds of attentions. Wit and gaiety presided over our delightful party, and witticism followed witticism without the slightest lapse from decency.

If a critical observer, who knew nothing of the circumstances, had tried to guess if love made one of the company, he might perhaps have suspected it but he could never have been sure. M. M. never displayed anything but friendship toward the Ambassador, esteem toward me, and fond consideration toward C. C. The Ambassador, maintaining an attitude of respect mingled with gratitude toward M. M., showed the greatest interest in C. C.'s remarks, doing all that he could to draw attention to them yet referring everything to me with the most generous understanding. Of the four of us, the one who had least difficulty in playing her role was C. C., for, having no share in the conspiracy, she had only to follow her nature. So she played her role to perfection. Success is assured; but the nature must be beautiful—otherwise the tyro is certain to be hissed.

We had spent five equally happy hours; but the one who showed it the most was the Ambassador. M. M. looked like a person satisfied with her work, and I appeared to approve. C. C. seemed proud of having been able to delight all three of us, and vain that the stranger had appeared to bestow his greatest attention on her. She looked at me smiling, and I understood the language of her soul perfectly: she wanted to make me think of the difference between this company and that in which her brother had given her such an ugly example of society the year before.

At eight o'clock we talked of breaking up, and it was the Ambassador who expended himself in compliments. Thanking M. M. for having given him the pleasantest supper he had enjoyed in all his life, he obliged her to offer him its counterpart on the next day but one, keeping up appearances by asking me if I would attend it with equal pleasure. Could she doubt that I would accept? I do not think so. The appointment made, we parted.

Reflecting the next day on this exemplary supper, I had no difficulty in foreseeing how the thing would end. The Ambassador had not made women the stepping-stones to his successful career except by possessing and practicing the art of coddling love. Very voluptuous by nature, he made his nature serve his turn; pampering himself, he awakened desires, without which he was perfectly right not to want fruition. I saw that he was obviously in love with C. C.; and I could not believe that he was the man to enjoy no more than the light of her beautiful eyes. I was sure that he had a definite plan, which M. M., despite all her loyalty, was to manage, but with such delicacy and skill that I should see no evidence of it. Although I knew I was not one to push compliance too far, I nevertheless foresaw that I should end by being taken in and losing C. C. to them. I was not disposed either to fall in with the scheme or to raise obstacles to it. Knowing that my little wife was incapable of going to lengths which could displease me, I chose to shut my eyes, relying on the difficulty of seducing her. It was an intrigue of which I greatly feared the consequences yet whose end I was curious to see. I knew that this repetition of the supper did not mean that the same play would be performed again; I was certain that there would be vital changes.

I thought that all I need do was to adhere to the same line of conduct; thus enabled to set the tone, I promised myself that I should find a way to baffle them. But after all these reflections C. C.'s inexperience, which despite all that she had learned still kept her a novice, made me afraid. It would be easy to abuse her duty to be polite; but here the thought of M. M.'s innate delicacy reassured me. After she had seen how I had spent ten hours with the girl and convinced herself that I intended to marry her, I could not suppose her capable of such heinous treason. All these reflections, which were essentially only those of my weakness, jealousy, and shame, decided nothing. I could only let things take their course and look on.

At the usual hour I went to the casino and I found my two beauties before the fire.

"I greet you, my angels. Where is our Frenchman?"

I unmask; I sit down between them, showing that I loved them both equally by bestowing a full measure of kisses now on one, now on the other. Although I knew that they knew I had undeniable rights over them, I nevertheless remain strictly within the bounds prescribed by decency. I congratulate them on their attachment to each other, and I see that they are delighted to find that they need not blush for it. So we spent an hour, during which I never thought of permitting myself the slightest overt act, for, since M. M. was uppermost in my heart, C. C. could not but be insulted by any proof I might have given her of it.

Three o'clock having struck and the amiable Frenchman not making his appearance, M. M. was beginning to be uneasy, when the caretaker came up and gave her a letter which our friend had written her:

"A courier who arrived two hours ago prevents me from being happy tonight. I must spend the whole of it replying. I hope that you will not only forgive me but pity me too. May I hope that you will grant me on Friday the pleasure of which an adverse Fortune deprives me tonight? Let me know tomorrow. I hope I shall find you in the same company."

"We must bear our disappointment," said M. M., "it is not his fault; the three of us will eat supper. Will you come on Friday?"

"Yes, with pleasure. But what is the matter?" I said to C. C. "The news seems to have made you sad."

"Not sad; I feel sorry for my dear friend and for you, for I have scarcely ever met a man so polite and obliging."

"I congratulate you, my dear; I am delighted that he has made such an impression on you."

"What do you mean by that? Could anyone fail to be charmed by his behavior?"

"Better and better! I agree with you, my dear child. Now tell me that you are in love with him."

"Even if I loved him it doesn't follow that I would go and tell him so. Besides, I am sure that he loves my wife."

So saying, she rises and sits down on her lap, and the two fond friends begin giving each other caresses which make me laugh and which gradually arouse my interest. I am of a mind to excite and enjoy a spectacle with which I had long been familiar.

M. M. fetches the engravings for Meursius,[8] representing a fine series of amorous encounters between women, and, with a malicious glance at my face, asks me if I would like her to order a fire lighted in the room with the alcove; divining her idea, I answer that I should be glad of it, for since the bed was very big we could all three lie in it. She was afraid I might suspect that her friend was in the hiding place. So the table is placed in front of the alcove, and I am thus relieved of my fear that I might be seen. Supper is served, and we eat it hungrily. M. M. was teaching C. C. to make punch. Having them before me, I admired the progress C. C. had made in beauty.

"In nine months," I said, "your bosom will have achieved its utmost perfection."

"It is like mine," M. M. added. "Do you want to see?"

Whereupon she interrupts her punch to unfasten her dear friend's dress, who offers no resistance, then immediately unfastens her own to enable me to judge; at which I am instantly intoxicated with the desire to compare and judge everything. Keeping up the game, I put *L'Académie des dames*[9] on the table and show M. M. a posture I wanted to see. She asks C. C. if she is willing to demonstrate it for me, and she answers that they would have to undress and get into the bed. I beg them to do me the favor.

After laughing heartily over what they were going to show me, I set the alarm for eight o'clock and in less than five minutes we are all in a state of nature and prey to pleasure and love. They set to work with a fury like that of two tigresses which seem ready to devour each other.

The sight of my two beauties in combat making me ardent, I am at a loss how to begin. For the honor of sentiment I should have given the preference to C. C., but I feared M. M.'s jibes, for she was sure to crow over my love which I wanted her to believe was hers alone. C. C. was thinner than M. M., yet she had bigger hips and thighs; her ornaments were brown, the other's blonde, and they were both equally skilled in a combat which was tiring them without the possibility of their reaching a conclusion.

Unable to resist any longer, I fling myself on them, and, pretending to separate them, I put M. M. under me, but she escapes, throwing me onto C. C., who receives me with open arms and makes me give up my soul in less than a minute, accompanying my death by her own, with neither of us ever thinking of taking any precautions.

Recovered from our ecstasy, we attack M. M., C. C. animated by gratitude and I eager for the revenge which she owed me for having forced me to be unfaithful to her. I held her in subjection for a good hour, enjoying the sight of C. C., whose looks seemed to say that she was proud of having given her friend a lover worthy of her.

My heroines surrendered to my remonstrances. With one accord we succumbed to sleep until the chime should sound, certain that we would make good use of the two hours which would remain to us until we must leave.

Thus refreshed, the sight of one another in a state of nature gave us a new vigor. C. C. having complained with dignity that with her I had had only a last gasp of life, M. M. urged me to make it up to her, but she did not find me reluctant. After a long combat inspired by a formal resolve on both our parts to crown it by marriage if it should have consequences which we made it our duty to defy, M. M. wanted to run the same risk, surrendering completely to love. Braving whatever might come, she gave me an unqualified order not to spare her, and I obeyed her. All three of us, intoxicated by desire and *frustratoires* and transported by continual furies, played havoc with everything visible and palpable which Nature had bestowed on us, freely devouring whatever we saw and finding that we had all become of the same sex in all the trios which we performed. A half hour before dawn we parted, weary, exhausted, at the end of our strength, satisfied and humiliated that we had to admit it, but not surfeited.

Reflecting the next day upon this overanimated night, during which, as always, pleasure had conquered reason, I felt a certain remorse. M. M. wished to convince me that she loved me by combining her love with all the virtues which I made a part of mine: honor, probity, truth. But her temperament, which enslaved her mind, led her into excesses, and she made every preparation to indulge herself in them, meanwhile waiting for a chance to turn me into her accomplice. She pampered love and flattered it to make it compliant and thus gain the power to direct it as she would yet at the same time to feel that she was immune from reproach. She thought she had the right to demand my admiration. She chose to overlook the fact that I could complain of her having taken me by surprise. She knew that I could do that only by acknowledging that I was weaker or more cowardly than herself, which I must be ashamed to confess.

I was certain that the Ambassador's absence had been arranged between them. They had foreseen that I would guess it and that gratitude and my sense of honor would prompt me to be no less forward than they to sacrifice nature to sentiment and to the obligation I should feel to be as generous and polite as they had been.

The Ambassador having led off by procuring me a delicious night, how could I bring myself to oppose his wish for a night of the same kind? They had reasoned well. My mind resisted, but I knew that I must yield them the victory. They saw no obstacle to their plans in

C. C.; they were sure of her once they were not hindered by my presence; and I knew that they were right. It was M. M.'s part to make C. C. feel mortally ashamed if she should fail to imitate her. Poor C. C.! I saw her debauched, and it was my doing. Alas! I had not spared them. What was I to do if, a few months later, they proved to be pregnant? I saw them both on my hands. In this wretched struggle between reason and prejudice, nature and sentiment, I could not make up my mind either to go to the supper or to stay away. "If I go, the night will pass decently, and I shall show that I am ridiculous, jealous, niggardly, ungrateful, and impolite. If I stay away, C. C. will be lost, at least in my estimation. I feel that I will no longer love her and that I will certainly have no more thought of marrying her."

With this combat in my soul, I feel an absolute need for some certainty. I mask and I go straight to the French Embassy.[10] I tell the Swiss that I have a letter for Versailles and that he would do me a favor if he would give it to the courier who was to return there as soon as he had received His Excellency's dispatch. He answers that no special courier has been seen there for two months.

"What! Did not a courier arrive last evening?"

"Last evening His Excellency supped at the Spanish Ambassador's." [11]

Thus informed beyond peradventure, I saw that I must swallow the pill. I must abandon C. C. to her fate. If I write to the dear girl not to go, I shall be behaving like a churl.

Toward nightfall I go straight to the casino in Murano and I write M. M. a note in which I ask her to excuse me if unexpected and urgent business of Signor Bragadin's obliged me to spend the whole night with him. That done, I return to Venice in a very bad humor and go to pass the night at the Ridotto, where I lost my money three or four times over.

On the next day but one I went to the casino in Murano, certain that I should find a letter from M. M. The caretaker hands it to me; I open it and find another from C. C. Everything had become common between them. Here is C. C.'s letter:

"We were very sorry, my dear husband, when we learned that you could not come to supper. My dear M. M.'s friend, who arrived a quarter of an hour later, was not less disappointed. We expected that we should sup gloomily; but not a bit of it. The gentleman's charming comments put us in high spirits; and you cannot imagine, my dear, how gay we became when the champagne followed the punch; but he was as gay as we were. In our trios he did not tire us, but he made us laugh a lot. I assure you he is a charming man with every quality to make him loved; but he is in no way your equal. Be certain that I will never love anyone except you and that you will always be sole lord of my heart."

Despite my resentment, her letter could not but make me laugh. But M. M.'s was even stranger:

"I am certain, my angel, that you lied out of politeness; but you may be sure that I expected it. It was a splendid present which you generously made to our friend in exchange for his present to you in letting his M. M. give you her heart. It would be yours in any case, my dear, but it is sweet when one can season the pleasures of love with the charms of friendship. I was sorry not to see you; but I saw afterwards that if you had come we should not have had a very amusing evening, for despite his great intelligence our friend has some natural prejudices. C. C.'s mind is now as unprejudiced as ours; and she owes it to me. I can boast that I have completed her education for you. I wish you had been hidden in the observatory; I assure you that you would have spent delicious hours there. On Wednesday I shall be all alone, and all yours, at your casino in Venice. Send me word if you will be at the statue at the usual hour. If you cannot, fix another day."

I had to write to the two girls in the same spirit. I was bitter, and I must appear to be all sweetness: *Tu l'as voulu, Georges Dandin* ("It's what you asked for, Georges Dandin").[12] I have never been able to decide whether I was truly ashamed or merely embarrassed; and it would take me too long to thresh out the problem now. In my letter to C. C. I had the strength of mind to congratulate her and encourage her to imitate M. M. in all things as the true model of perfection.

I wrote to the latter that she would find me waiting obediently, as always, at the foot of the statue. In my letter, which was full of false congratulations on the education she was giving C. C., I told her only this one equivocal truth: *"I thank you for the place in the observatory which you wished I had occupied. I could not have held out there."*

On Wednesday I was at the meeting place in good time. She arrived dressed as a man. She declined both the opera and the theater.

"Let us go," she said, "to the Ridotto and either lose our money or double it."

She had six hundred zecchini and I had about a hundred. Fortune was against us. After losing everything, she went to a place where she knew she would find her friend and asked him for money. He came back an hour later and gave her a purse containing three hundred zecchini. She began punting again and she had recouped her losses; but not satisfied with that, she lost again, and after midnight we went to supper. She saw that I was sad, though I tried not to show it. For her part, she was beautiful, gay, playful, amorous, always the same.

She thought she would restore my spirits by telling me in detail the whole history of the night she had spent with C. C. and her friend. It was just what she ought not to do, but the mind only too often falls into the error of supposing that another's is as much at ease and as free as it is itself. I could not wait for us to get to bed and so put an end to a story whose voluptuous details did not have the effect on me they should have had. I feared that I should be in no condition to cut a good figure in bed; and to cut a bad one takes no more than the dread of it. A young man in love never fears that his love will be inadequate; if he does, love takes its revenge and abandons him.

But in bed my charming mistress's beauty, her caresses, and the purity of her soul banished all my bad humor. The nights having grown shorter, we had no time for sleep. After spending our two hours with love, we were still in love when we parted. She made me promise to go to the casino for money to play in partnership with her. I went there and took all the gold I found, and, determinedly doubling my stakes according to the system known as the martingale,[13] I won three or four times a day during the rest of the Carnival. I never lost the sixth card. If I had lost it, I should have been out of funds, which amounted to two thousand zecchini. In this way I was increasing my dear M. M.'s little capital, when she wrote to me that politeness demanded that the four of us should sup together on the last Monday in Carnival, and I agreed.

It was the last time that I supped with C. C. She was very gay; but having decided on my course I showed particular attention only to M. M. Not in the least embarrassed by my presence, the girl devoted hers entirely to her new suitor.

Foreseeing, however, that embarrassing moments were inevitable, I asked M. M. to arrange things so that the Ambassador could spend an uninterrupted night with C. C. and I with her, and she managed it very well.

After supper he talked of faro, which the two beauties

did not know,* and to show them what it was he called for cards and made a bank of a hundred double louis, which he saw to it that C. C. won. Not knowing what to do with so much money, she asked her dear friend to take care of it for her until she should leave the convent to be married.

After the game M. M. said that, having a headache, she would go to bed in the alcove and she asked me to go with her and put her to sleep. Thus we left the novice alone with the Ambassador. Six hours later, when the chime told us that we must end our orgy, we found them sleeping. For my part, I spent a night as amorous as it was peaceful with M. M. and with never a thought of C. C. So we finished out the Carnival.

---

* Because at the Ridotto only basset was played. (C.'s note.)

CHAPTER VIII

Monsieur de Bernis departs, leaving me his rights to the casino. Wise advice which he gives me; how little I follow it. Danger of perishing with M. M. Mr. Murray, the English envoy. We are without a casino and our meetings cease. M. M. dangerously ill. Zorzi and Condulmer. Tonina.

ON THE first Friday in Lent I found at her casino a letter from M. M. in which she gave me two sad pieces of news. The first was that C. C.'s mother having died,[1] the poor girl was in despair. The second was that, her lay sister having recovered from her cold, she had returned to her room and at the same time the nun who was C. C.'s aunt and who was especially fond of her had obtained permission from the Abbess for her to sleep in her apartment. This ended the Ambassador's hope of supping with her again. All these misfortunes seemed to me of little account in comparison with a greater which I feared. C. C. might be pregnant. Though the feelings which bound me to her were no longer love, they were still strong enough to keep me from ever abandoning her. M. M. invited me to supper with her friend on the following Monday. I went and I found both the Ambassador and M. M. very sad—he because he had lost C. C., she because she no longer had her in her

room and did not know what to do to console her for
the misfortune of losing her mother.

Toward midnight the Ambassador left us, saying
sadly that he believed he would have to spend some
months in Vienna on a matter of great importance. At
the same time we agreed to meet for fast-day suppers
every Friday.

As soon as we were alone she told me that the Ambassador would be grateful to me if in future I would come
to the casino two hours later. Rational though he was,
he could not abandon himself to love in the presence
of a third person. At all our suppers until he went to
Vienna[2] he always left us at midnight. It was no longer
in order to go and hide in the closet, for we always went
to bed in the alcove, and in any case, having made love
before I arrived, he had no desires left. M. M. found me
still in love and even more ardent, for since I could see
her only once a week I always waited impatiently for
Friday. C. C.'s letters, which she brought me, touched
me to tears. After losing her mother, she could no longer
count on friendliness in any of her relatives. She called
me her only friend and, speaking of the grief she felt
at the thought that as long as she remained in the convent she could not hope to see me, she begged me ever to
remain a faithful friend to M. M.

It was on Good Friday that, arriving at the casino at
suppertime, I found the couple very sad. They did not
eat, they scarcely spoke; it troubled me, and good
manners and discretion prevented me from asking the
reason. M. M. having gone somewhere, the Ambassador
told me that she was unhappy and that she well might
be since he had to leave for Vienna two weeks after
Easter.

"I will even tell you," he said, "that I may not come
back; but you must not say so to her, for she would be
in despair."

When she returned to the table I saw that her eyes were swollen. This is what he said to her:

"My departure is unavoidable, for I am not my own master; but my return is certain as soon as I finish the business which obliges me to go. The casino remains yours, but friendship and prudence oblige me to advise you, my dear, not to set foot in it during my absence, for once I am gone I can no longer count on the fidelity of the gondoliers I employ, and I doubt if our friend here can hope to find any who are incorruptible. I will tell you further that I not only believe our doings are known to the State Inquisitors, who dissimulate their knowledge from policy, but that I also cannot vouch for our secret's being kept at the convent once the nun whom you know becomes certain that your reason for going out can no longer be to sup with me. The persons for whose fidelity I can vouch are the caretaker and his wife. Before I leave I will order them to regard our friend as another myself. You can make arrangements with them, and all will be well until I return if you behave circumspectly.

"I will write to you through my caretaker, and his wife will convey my letters to you as she has been doing, and you will use the same means to answer me. I must go, my dear, but my heart remains with you. Until my return I leave you in the hands of a friend whom I am very glad to have met. He loves you, he has a heart, he knows the world, and he will not let you make any mistakes."

The news was such a blow to M. M. that she asked us to let her leave, as she felt she must go to bed. We set the Thursday after Easter for our next supper.

After she left, the Ambassador impressed upon me the absolute necessity of keeping it from her that he might not return.

"I am going to work," he said, "with the Vienna

cabinet on a project which will set all Europe talking.[3] Write me everything; and if you love her, protect her honor and, above all, if the necessity arises, have the strength to speak out against anything which could expose you to calamities which you could foresee and which would be fatal to you both. You know what happened to Signora da Riva, who was a nun in the convent of St. XXX.[4] She simply disappeared as soon as they discovered she was pregnant, and Monsieur de Froulay,[5] then the French Ambassador as I am now, soon afterward went mad and died. J. J. Rousseau[6] once told me that it was from poison; but he is a visionary. His poison was the grief he felt because he could do nothing for the unfortunate woman, whom the Pope finally dispensed from her vows, and she married and is now living in Parma.

"So let your feelings of friendship be stronger than your love, see her sometimes in the visiting room, and refrain from taking her to the casino, for the gondoliers will betray you. Our certainty that neither she nor her friend is pregnant lessens my grief a great deal; but admit that you have been very imprudent! You risked a terrible misfortune! Think of the desperate course you would have had to follow, for I am sure you could not have abandoned her. She believed that it was easy to bring on an abortion by taking certain drugs, but I disabused her. In God's name be prudent in future, and write me everything. It is my duty to be concerned for her fate."

He took me to Venice and went home. I spent a most uneasy night, and the next day I went back to the casino to write the sorrowing M. M. a letter designed to console her and to impress upon her how necessary it was for us to adopt a prudent course of conduct.

In her answer, which I received the next day, I saw the liveliest image of the despair which weighed on her soul. Nature had fostered in her a temperament which

made the cloister intolerable to her, and I foresaw the
terrible struggles, both with her and with myself, which
I must be prepared to undergo.

We saw one another on the Thursday after Easter.
I had sent her word that I would come at midnight. She
had spent four hours with her friend, sadly lamenting
her cruel destiny. After supper he left, asking me to
stay with her—which I did, certainly never thinking of
those pleasures which can find no place when the heart
is preoccupied by a great grief. She had grown thinner,
and she aroused a compassion in me which banished
every other feeling. I held her in my arms for an hour,
printing countless kisses on her appealing face, well
content to find that my soul was wholly concentrated on
respecting her grief. I should have thought I was insulting her if I had invited her to distract herself by frenzies
in which her soul, even as mine, could not have indulged.
She said when I left her that she had never felt so sure
that I loved her as she had that night, and she begged
me to remember that I was now her only friend.

The next week the Ambassador summoned the caretaker before supper and in his presence wrote out a
document, which he made him sign, in which he trans-
ferred to me all his rights to whatever was in the casino
and ordered him to serve me in everything just as he now
served him.

We were to sup together for the last time on the next
day but one; but I found M. M. alone, looking like a
statue of white Carrara marble.

"He is gone," she said, "and he commends M. M. to
you. Tomorrow evening he will leave Venice. Fatal being,
whom I shall perhaps not see again and whom I did not
know I loved! It is now when I lose him that I realize
it. I was not happy before I knew him; but I did not
think myself unhappy. I feel that I am so now."

I spent the whole night with her trying to calm her
grief. I knew the nature of her soul, as transported by

pleasures when she felt she was happy as it was sensible
to pain when grief overwhelmed her. She told me the
hour at which I should go to the visiting room on the
next day but one, and I was delighted to find her less
sad. She showed me a short letter which our friend had
written her from Treviso. Then she said that I must
come to see her two or three times a week and that she
would often come to the grating accompanied by another nun, and sometimes by still another, because she
foresaw that the visits I would pay her would become the
talk of the convent when it was discovered that I was the
same man who always went to mass at their church; so
she told me to have myself announced by a different
name to prevent any suspicion from arising in the mind
of C. C.'s aunt. But she said that this would not keep
her from coming to the grating alone when she needed to
talk to me without a witness. She asked me to do her
another favor, which I had no difficulty in granting. She
wanted me to promise her that I would sup and spend
the night at the casino at least once a week and after
supper write her a short letter, which the caretaker's
wife would convey to her as always.

In this way we spent two weeks quietly enough, until
she recovered her vivacity and her amorous inclinations
returned in full force. The news which she gave me,
and which was balm to my soul, was that C. C. no
longer had anything to fear.

Still in love and reduced to having no resource but
an awkward grating, we were inflamed. We racked our
brains to devise some way of meeting freely. M. M.
assured me that she could still count on the fidelity of
the gardener's wife for getting out and in without any
fear of being seen, since the little door close to the convent by which she entered the garden was not visible
from any window and indeed was thought to have been
walled up, and that no one could see her either when
she crossed the garden to reach the lodge on the little

quay, which was also thought to be unusable. We only
needed a one-oared gondola, and she thought it impossible
that, with the help of money, I could not find a gondolier
upon whom we could rely. I was unhappy to realize that
she suspected me of having very little love for her.

I proposed to go all alone in a boat of which I would
myself be the boatman and from which I would disembark, enter the garden, and then, shown the way by herself or the lay sister, her room, in which I would spend
the whole night and even the whole of the next day if
she was sure that she could keep me hidden; but the
plan made her tremble: she shuddered to think of the
risk I would run.

"But," she said, "since you can row, come in the boat,
let me know the hour and, if possible, the minute; the
faithful woman will be on the watch and you can be sure
you will not wait more than four minutes; I will get
into the boat, we will go to the casino, and we will be
happy for a time."

I promised her that I would consider it; and this was
the way I found to satisfy her:

I bought a small boat and, without telling her, I went
to the island alone at night and rowed around it to see
all the walls of the convent on the Lagoon side. A small
closed door which caught my eye could only be the one
onto the quay by which she habitually left. But to go
from there to the casino the necessary rounding of half
the island was no small matter, for the dry season forced
me to fetch a wide course. With only one oar it took me
at least a quarter of an hour.

As soon as I felt sure of it, I communicated my plan
to M. M., who greeted it joyously. We settled on Friday,
the day after Ascension Day, and on the same day I
went to the visiting room masked, and we set our watches
together; then I went to the casino to order supper for
two.

An hour after sunset I went to San Francesco della

Vigna,[7] where I had my boat in a *cavana*[8] which I rented. After having it bailed and put in good order I quickly dressed in the costume of the gondoliers and, stationed on the poop, I went directly to the little quay of the convent, the door of which opened at the very moment I arrived and where I did not have to wait the four minutes. Scarcely was the door open before M. M. came out, the door was shut again, and she got into the boat concealed in the hood of her cloak. Without in the least forcing my speed, in a quarter of an hour I reached the casino, where she got out at once and I followed two minutes later, for I had to fasten the boat to a chain and secure it with a padlock to safeguard it from thieves, who amuse themselves at night stealing as many boats as they can when they find them fastened only with rope. I was dripping sweat; but that did not prevent my angel from falling on my neck; gratitude challenged love; proud of my exploit, I smiled at the impulses of her soul. Since I had forgotten to bring a shirt with me, she gave me one of her shifts after drying me off and applying powder to absorb the sweat which covered my head. We did not sup until after we had spent two hours in prey to the flame which burned us even more violently than at the beginning of our acquaintance; but for all her protests I cheated her at the moment of danger, too greatly fearing the picture which our friend had drawn and which was ineffaceably imprinted on my mind. M. M., gay and wanton, finding me quite different in the guise of a gondolier, animated our encounters with the freest expressions; but she did not need to add anything to my ardor, for I loved her more than myself.

The nights were short. She had to return to the convent at six o'clock,[9] and four o'clock was just striking when we sat down at table. But what happened then not only to mar our joy but to make our hair stand on end was a storm coming up in the west. We could only console ourselves by counting on the nature of these storms,

which usually last no more than an hour; we hoped that
it would not be an unusual one and that it would not
leave behind it a wind which would be too strong for me,
who, though brave, had neither the experience nor the
strength of a gondolier.

In less than a half an hour the storm bursts with
thunder and lightning, the thunder roars incessantly,
and after a heavy rain the sky clears again, but without
a moon, which cannot shine during Ascension Week.[10]

Five o'clock strikes, but what I had foreseen happened.
After the storm the west wind, which was contrary for
me, was blowing hard: *ma tiranno del mar Libecchio
resta* ("but Libecchio remains the tyrant of the sea").[11]
This *libecchio*, which Ariosto rightly calls "the tyrant
of the sea," is the southwest; I said nothing, but it
terrified me. I tell M. M. that we must sacrifice an hour
of pleasure to prudence: we must leave at once, for if
the wind increases it will be impossible for me to round
the point. She listens to reason and she goes to the chest,
to which she also had a key, to take forty or fifty zecchini
which she needed. She was delighted when she saw four
times as much money as she had had at the end of Lent.
She thanked me for not having told her and, saying that
she wanted only my heart, she went down and lay at full
length in the bottom of the boat. I mounted the poop,
full of courage and fear at the same time, and in five
minutes I rounded the point. But beyond it I encountered
a resistance greater than my strength. Except for that
resistance, I should have needed only ten minutes. Without a rower at the prow I thought it impossible that I
could combat the wind and the current; I was rowing
with all my strength; but all I could do was to keep the
boat from going backward. After half an hour of this
trying effort I felt that I was losing my breath and I
dared say nothing; I could not think of resting, for the
least rest would instantly have driven me back. M. M.
lay there in silence, afraid to speak, for she knew that

I would not have the strength to answer her. Finally I felt sure that I was lost.

Far off I see a boat approaching rapidly; certain that I shall be rescued, I wait for it to pass me, for otherwise the wind would have prevented it from hearing my voice. As soon as I see it on my left, only two fathoms away, I cry:

"Help! for two zecchini!"

The boat at once lowers sail, rows to me with four oars, makes fast, and I ask only for one man to take me to the opposite point of the island. They demand a zecchino, which I hand over at once, promising another to whoever will get me to the point by manning the poop. In less than ten minutes, I rowing at the prow, we were off the little quay of the convent; but our secret was too precious to me to be risked. We reached the point, where I dismissed my man, giving him his zecchino. From there, with the wind in my favor, I easily reached the small port, where M. M. disembarked, saying only these words to me:

"Go and sleep at the casino."

I thought her advice very good, and I followed it. I had the wind in my favor, and if I had done the opposite I should have been in the same peril. I went to bed, I slept eight hours, I wrote to M. M. that I was well and that we would see each other at the grating; then I went to San Francesco, where, after having my boat put back in the *cavana,* I masked and went to the Liston.

The next day M. M. came to the grating alone so that I could share in the many reflections which her mind needed to make after all that had happened to us. But the result of our reflections was not to determine us never again to expose ourselves to such a danger; we only decided to anticipate the storm, if it should recur, by leaving everything the moment we saw it rising. It took us no more than a quarter of an hour. This was the only precaution which love allowed us to adopt. We fixed our second meeting for the Tuesday in Whitsun Week. Had we not encountered the boat bound for Torcello, I should have had to go back to the casino with M. M., who, it being then impossible for her to return to the convent, would have remained with me. I should have had to leave Venice with her and I could not have returned there, and, her fate being linked with mine, my life would have been governed by a destiny entirely different from the one whose vicissitudes have combined to bring me, at the age of seventy-two, to Dux, where I am today.

We continued for three months to see each other once a week, always in love and never troubled by the slightest mishap. M. M. could not keep from reporting it to the Ambassador, to whom I was also obliged to write an account of all that happened to us. He answered that he congratulated us on the happiness we were enjoying, but that he could foresee nothing but misfortunes if we did not resolve to make an end.

Mr. Murray,[12] the English Resident, a handsome man, full of wit, learned, and a prodigious lover of the fair sex, Bacchus, and good eating, was keeping the celebrated Ancilla,[13] who, encountering me in Padua, wanted me to make his acquaintance. After treating me to three or four suppers, this gallant man became my friend in the same way that the Ambassador had been, with only the difference that the latter liked to be the spectator and the former liked to provide the spectacle himself. I was never unwelcome at his amorous encounters, in which, to tell the truth, he acquitted himself well, the voluptuous Ancilla being delighted to have me for a witness; but I never gave them the satisfaction of joining in their bouts. I loved M. M.; but that was not the chief reason. Ancilla was always hoarse and constantly complained of a pain in her throat. I feared the pox, despite the fact that Murray was in good health. She died of it in the autumn,[14] and a quarter of an hour before she ex-

Masked Ball at the Ridotto

Callers in a Convent Visiting Room

pired her lover Murray, in my presence, yielded to her insistence and paid her the homage of a devoted lover despite a cancer which disfigured her. The thing became known all over the city, for it was he himself who told it, citing me as witness. It was one of the most striking spectacles I have seen in all my life. The cancer which ate away her nose and half of her beautiful face came up again from her esophagus two months after she believed she was cured of the pox by mercury ointment, which was administered to her by a surgeon named Lucchesi, who had undertaken to cure her for a hundred zecchini. She promised them to him in writing on condition that she would not pay them to him until after he had himself played the role of devoted lover to her. Lucchesi was unwilling to go so far, and since she obstinately refused to pay him unless he fulfilled the stipulated condition, the matter was taken before the magistrate. In England Ancilla would have won her case, but in Venice she lost it. The judge in his decision said that an unfulfilled criminal condition could not invalidate the contract. A very wise decision.

Two months before the cancer had eaten away the charming face of the celebrated courtesan and made it revolting, Signor Memmo,[15] my friend, later Procuratore di San Marco, asked me to take him to her house. At the height of the conversation a gondola arrives, and we see that the person getting out of it is Count Rosenberg,[16] Ambassador from the Court of Vienna. Signor Memmo was panic-stricken, for a Venetian nobleman cannot be in the company of an envoy of a foreign court without becoming guilty of a grave crime. So Signor Memmo rushes out of Ancilla's room and takes to his heels, and I follow him; but near the stairs he meets the Ambassador, who, seeing that he is trying to hide, bursts out laughing. I instantly board Signor Memmo's gondola with him and accompany him to the house of Signor Cavalli,[17] Secretary to the State Inquisitors, who lives a

hundred paces away on the same Grand Canal. The
only way Signor Memmo had of saving himself from at
least a serious reprimand was to go at once and tell the
story to the Secretary of the tribunal, who would see
that the thing was innocent; he was very glad that I
was with him to testify to the harmlessness of the occurrence.

Signor Cavalli receives Signor Memmo with a smile,
saying that he had done very well to come and confess
without losing any time. Signor Memmo, in the utmost
astonishment, then told him the brief story of the meeting, and the Secretary gravely said that he was informed of it and that he did not doubt the truth of his
account, since the circumstances were the same as those
which he already knew.

Leaving Signor Cavalli's we discussed the occurrence
sufficiently to decide that it could not possibly be known
to him; but the maxim of the tribunal was never to let
it be thought that it was in the dark concerning anything.

After Ancilla's death Resident Murray remained without an official mistress; but, changing from one to another, he always had the prettiest girls in Venice. This
amiable epicurean left two years later[18] for Constantinople, where he remained for twenty years as his
country's envoy. He returned to Venice in 1778, intending to settle down and end his days in peace there without
taking any further hand in politics; but he died in the
Lazaretto[19] a week before finishing his quarantine.

Fortune, which continued to treat me well at cards,
my meetings with M. M., the secret of which no one
could any longer betray since the nuns, who alone could
reveal it, were concerned to keep it inviolable, combined
to make my life very happy; but I foresaw that as soon
as the Ambassador should decide to disabuse M. M. of
her continued hope that she would see him back in
Venice, he would also recall the servants to whom he

was still paying wages in Venice and we should be without a casino. In addition I could no longer continue to go to Murano rowing alone in a small boat once the bad weather set in.

The first Monday in October—the day on which, with the opening of the theaters, masking began—I go to San Francesco, I mount the poop of my boat, and I go to Murano to fetch M. M., who was waiting for me; from there I go to the casino and, the nights having grown longer, we sup, then go to bed, and, at the sound of the alarm, prepare to exchange an amorous good morning, when a noise I seem to hear from the direction of the canal sends me to the window. I am greatly surprised to see a large boat row away, taking mine with it. I tell the robbers that I will give them ten zecchini if they will leave it for me; but they laugh, they refuse to believe me, and they make off, certain that at that hour I could neither raise a hue and cry nor go after them. The loss distresses me, and even M. M. is in despair, for she does not see how I can make it good. I quickly dress, thinking no more of love and with my only consolation the fact that I still had two hours in which to go and find a boat at all costs. I should have had no difficulty if I could have called a gondola; but the gondoliers would have been certain the next day to tell all Murano that they had taken a nun back to such-and-such a convent. So my only resource was to find a boat and buy it. I put pistols in my pocket and, after getting an oar and a row-lock, I leave, assuring M. M. that I will return with a boat even if I have to steal the first one I find. It was with this idea that I was taking the oar and the rowlock. The robbers had filed the chain of my boat with a smooth file. I had no files.

I go to the big bridge, where I knew that there were boats, and I see a quantity of them of all sorts, and tied, but there were people on the quay. Running like a madman I see a tavern open at the end of the quay. I go

in and ask the waiter if there are any boatmen there;
he answers that there are two who are drunk. I go and
speak to them and ask them which of them wants to
earn four lire to take me to Venice at once. My proposition sets them quarreling over which shall have the
preference. I quiet them by giving forty soldi to the
one who was the more drunk, and I go out with the other.

"You've drunk too much," I say, "lend me your
boat and I will return it to you tomorrow."

"I don't know you."

"I'll leave you a deposit. Here are ten zecchini; but
who will vouch for you, for your boat is not worth that
and you might leave it on my hands."

He then takes me back to the same tavern, and the
waiter stands surety that if I come back that day with
the boat the tavernkeeper will return me my money.
Very glad that he had succeeded, he takes me to his boat,
puts two rowlocks and another oar in it, and goes off
well satisfied to have cheated me, as I was to have submitted to being cheated. The whole business had cost
me an hour. I arrived at the casino, where M. M. was in
the greatest uneasiness; but as soon as she saw me all her
gaiety reappeared. I took her to the convent and I went
to San Francesco, where the man who rented me the
cavana thought I was making fun of him when I told
him that I had exchanged my boat for this one. I masked
and I went home to bed, for the strain had exhausted me.

At this same time my destiny decreed that I should
make the acquaintance of the patrician Marcantonio
Zorzi,[20] a great wit and famed for his skill at writing
couplets in the Venetian language. He also loved the
theater, and, aspiring to the honor of being an author,
he had written a comedy which the public had hissed.
Having taken it into his head that his play had failed
only because of a cabal mounted against him by the
Abate Chiari,[21] poet of the Teatro di Sant'Angelo,[22] he
became the declared enemy of all the Abate's comedies.

I had no difficulty in being accepted into the circle of this Signor Zorzi, who had a good cook and a pretty wife. He knew that I did not like Chiari as an author, and Signor Zorzi paid people who mercilessly hissed all his plays. My amusement consisted in criticizing them in Martellian verse,[23] a sort of doggerel then in fashion; Signor Zorzi circulated copies of my criticisms. These maneuvers made me a powerful enemy in the person of Signor Condulmer,[24] who also disliked me because I seemed to have monopolized the good graces of Signora Zorzi, whom he had been courting assiduously before my appearance. However, Signor Condulmer had good reason to dislike me because, since he owned a good share of the Teatro di Sant'Angelo, the failure of the poet's plays injured him. The boxes could only be sold at a very low price. He was sixty years of age, he loved women, gambling, and usury; but he passed for a saint because he showed himself every morning at mass at San Marco, weeping before a crucifix. He was made a Councilor[25] the following year and as such was for eight months a State Inquisitor. In that eminent position he did not find it difficult to suggest to his two colleagues that I should be put under the Leads as a disturber of the public peace. My reader will hear of this nine months hence.

The beginning of the winter[26] brought the astonishing news of the alliance concluded between the House of Austria and France. The political system of all Europe became entirely different in consequence of the unexpected treaty, which until then had seemed beyond probability to all thinking minds. The part of Europe which had the most reason to rejoice at it was Italy, because she was suddenly delivered from the fear of becoming the unhappy theater of war whenever the least difference should arise between the two courts. The celebrated treaty had sprung from the head of a young minister who until then had done nothing in politics

except play the role of wit. The surprising treaty, which
perished after forty years, was hatched in the year 1750
between Madame de Pompadour, Count (later Prince)
Kaunitz, the Viennese Ambassador, and the Abbé de
Bernis, who became known only the following year when
the King appointed him Ambassador to Venice. It re-
united the Houses of Austria and Bourbon in friendship
after two hundred and forty years of enmity. Count
Kaunitz, having returned to Vienna at the same time,
brought the Empress Maria Theresa a letter from the
Marquise de Pompadour which put the finishing touch
to the great negotiation. The Abbé de Bernis concluded
it at Vienna[27] the same year, still as Ambassador of
France to Venice. Three years later,[28] as Minister of
Foreign Affairs, he re-established the Parlement, after
which he was created a cardinal, then disgraced, then
given a post in Rome, then died. *Mors ultima linea rerum
est* ("Death is the final boundary line of all things").[29]

Nine months[30] after he left he announced his recall
to M. M., putting it as gently as possible; but if I had
not forestalled the blow by preparing her little by little
to rise above it, she would have succumbed under it.
It was to me that he gave his instructions. All the furnish-
ings of the casino were to be sold and whatever they
brought was to go to M. M., except the books and the
engravings, which the caretaker was to convey to him
in Paris.

While M. M. did nothing but weep, I carried out all
the instructions. By the middle of January 1755 we no
longer had a casino. She took away two thousand zecchini
and her diamonds and pearls, thinking she might sell
them some other time to buy herself an annuity, and
she left me our winnings at cards, in which we always
shared and shared alike. At this time I had three
thousand zecchini, and we no longer saw each other except
at the grating; but she fell ill and her life was in danger.
I saw her at the grating on February 2nd; her face dis-

played the signs of approaching death. She gave me the case with all her diamonds, all the money she had except a small sum, all the scandalous books, and all her letters, saying that I should return everything to her if she escaped from the illness on which she was entering and that everything would be mine if she died. She said that C. C. would be at pains to write me all her news and she begged me to have pity on her and continue to write to her, for she could look for no consolation except from my letters; she hoped to have the strength to read until the last moment of her life. I assured her, melting into tears, that I would stay in Murano until she had recovered her health. She said as she left me that she was sure C. C.'s aunt would let her be with her.

In the greatest grief, I had a sack full of books and packets of letters put into a gondola; and having pocketed the purses filled with money I returned to Venice, where I put everything in a safe place in the Palazzo Bragadin.[31] An hour later I went back to Murano to ask Laura to find me a furnished room in which I could live in complete freedom. She answered that she knew where there were two furnished rooms and a kitchen which I could have very cheaply and even without saying who I was if I would pay a month in advance to an old man who lived on the ground floor; he would give me all the keys, and if I liked I need never see anyone. She gave me the address, I went there at once, and finding everything more than satisfactory I paid for a month, he gave me the key to the street door and immediately made up the beds. It was a casino at the foot of a blind alley ending at the canal. I went back to Laura's and told her I needed a maidservant who would bring in meals for me and who could make my bed, and she promised me one for the next day.

I then returned to Venice, where I packed as if I had to make a long journey. After supper I took my leave of Signor Bragadin and my two other friends, telling them that I should be away for several weeks on very important business.

The next morning I took a *traghetto* gondola and went to my new little casino, where I was very much surprised to find Tonina, Laura's pretty fifteen-year-old daughter, who, blushing but with a presence of mind which I had not known she possessed, said that she would not be afraid to serve me with as much zeal as her mother herself could have shown.

In my afflicted state I could not be grateful to Laura for such a present, and I even decided at once that, since the thing could not lead where she wished it to, her daughter could not remain in my service. Meanwhile I treated her gently, I told her that I was certain of her good will, but that I wanted to talk with her mother. I said that as I wished to spend the whole day writing I would not eat until nightfall, and that I left it to her to see that adequate meals were brought in for me. After leaving my room she came back and gave me a letter, saying that she had forgotten to give it to me at once.

"You must never forget," I said, "for if you had waited another minute before giving me this letter a great misfortune might have resulted."

She blushed for shame. It was a short letter from C. C., in which she told me that her dear friend was in bed and that the convent physician had found that she had a fever. She promised me a long letter the next day. I spent the day setting my room in order, then writing to M. M. and to my poor C. C. Tonina came to bring me candles and say that my dinner was ready. I told her to serve it to me, and seeing that she had set only one place I made her set another, saying that she would always eat with me. I had very little appetite, but I found everything good except the wine. Tonina promised to find me some better wine, and she went off to bed in my anteroom.

After sealing my letters I went to see if Tonina had locked the door of her room on the stairway side, and I found it bolted. I sighed when I saw the girl, who was in a deep sleep or pretending to be, and whose idea I easily saw through; but I had never in my life felt so afflicted; I judged the intensity of my feeling by the indifference with which I looked at her and by my certainty that neither she nor I ran the slightest risk.

In the morning I called her very early, and she came in fully and neatly dressed. I gave her my letter for C. C., which contained one for M. M., and I told her to take it to her mother at once and return to make me coffee. At the same time I told her that I would dine at noon. She then said that she had cooked dinner for me the evening before, and that if I had been satisfied with it she would do the same every day. After telling her that it would please me if she did so, I gave her another zecchino. She said that she still had six lire left from the one I had given her the day before; but when I told her that I made her a present of the difference and that I would do the same thing every day, I could not prevent her from kissing my hand ten times. I was careful not to take it from her and embrace her, for I should but too easily have yielded to my natural inclination for amusement, which would have dishonored my grief. *Et faveo morbo cum juvat ipse dolor* ("I foster my sickness when the pain itself gives me pleasure").[32]

So the day passed like the one before. Tonina went to bed very glad that she had pleased me in her role of servant and that I had not again said that I wanted to talk with her mother. After sealing my letter, fearing that I should wake too late, I called the girl in a low voice, not wanting to wake her if she was asleep; but she heard me and came to find out what I wanted, wearing only a petticoat over her shift. Seeing too much, I at once turned my eyes away. Without looking at her I gave her the letter addressed to her mother, ordering

her always to take it to her in the morning before entering my room.

She went back to her bed, and aware of my weakness
I was saddened. I saw that Tonina was so pretty that,
thinking how easily she would have cured my grief, I
felt ashamed. My grief was precious to me. I fell asleep
resolved to tell Laura to rid me of her talisman, but in
the morning I could not bring myself to do it. I was
afraid of causing the kindhearted girl the most painful
of mortifications.

CHAPTER IX

Continuation of the preceding chapter. M. M. recovers. I return to Venice. Tonina consoles me. Weakening of my love for M. M. The physician Righelini. My strange conversation with him. Its consequences in regard to M. M. Mr. Murray undeceived and avenged.

DURING the following days she did not go off to bed until after receiving my letter, and I was grateful to her, because for two entire weeks M. M.'s illness grew so much worse that I expected every moment to receive word of her death. On the last day of the Carnival C. C. wrote me that her dear friend had not had the strength to read my letter, and that she was to receive the last sacraments the next day. Stricken by the news, I could neither get up nor eat. I spent the day writing and weeping, and Tonina did not leave my bedside until midnight; but I could not close my eyes.

The next morning Tonina gave me a letter from C. C., in which she told me that, between life and death, M. M. might live for another two or three weeks; a slow fever never left her, her weakness was extreme, she could take only broths, and her confessor was hastening her death by his boring sermons. I melted into tears. I could only soothe my grief by writing, and Tonina, with her sound

sense, said that I was fostering it and that I would die
of it. I myself saw that grief, staying in bed, eating
almost nothing, and writing all day would drive me mad.
I had imparted my sorrow to the poor girl, who no longer
knew what to say to me. Her occupation had become
drying my tears. I pitied her.

On the eighth or tenth day of the Carnival, after assuring C. C. that if M. M. died I should survive her by
only a few days, I begged her to tell her dying friend
that, if I was to live myself, I needed her promise that
she would let me carry her off if she recovered. I told
her that I had four thousand zecchini and her diamonds,
worth six thousand, amounting to a capital which would
give us enough to live well on anywhere in Europe.

C. C. wrote me the next day that the patient, after listening attentively while she read her my plan, had been
seized with spasmodic twitchings and that when they
subsided a high fever had risen into her brain, so that
for three whole hours she had raved in French in a way
which would have scandalized the nuns who were present
if they had understood what she was saying. This omi-
nous effect of my letter made me desperate.

I saw that I should die too if I did not go back to
Venice, for C. C.'s two letters, which I received morning
and night, made a mockery of my love twice a day. My
dear M. M.'s delirium lasted three days. C. C. wrote me
on the fourth that, after sleeping for three hours, she
had been able to reason and had told her to write me that
she was sure she would recover if she could be certain
that I would carry out the plan I had proposed to her. I
answered that she should have no doubt of it, and the
more so since my life depended upon my being certain
that she would consent to it. And so, both deceived by
our own hope, we recovered. Each letter from C. C. telling me that her friend was on the road to health was
balm to my soul; my appetite returned and I listened
with pleasure to the simple-minded Antonina, who had

got into the habit of not going to bed until she saw that I was asleep.

Toward the end of March M. M. herself wrote me that she thought she was out of danger and that, with the help of a proper diet, she hoped she would be able to leave her room after Easter. I replied that I would not leave Murano until after I had seen her at the grating, where we would agree in good time on the plan which would make us happy until death. On the same day I thought I should go to dine with Signor Bragadin, who, having heard no news of me for seven weeks, must be uneasy.

After telling Tonina not to expect me until about the fourth hour[1] of the night, I went to Venice without a cloak because, having gone to Murano masked, I had none. I had spent forty-eight days without ever leaving my room, forty of them in grief, and fifteen of those scarcely eating or sleeping. I had just conducted an experiment on myself which was highly flattering to my self-esteem. I had been waited on by a girl as pretty as they come, who had done everything to please me, gentle as a lamb, and whom, without any conceit on my part, I could believe to be, if not in love with me, at least inclined to grant me all the favors I might ask; and despite all that I had been able to resist all the power which her young charms had wielded over me during the first two weeks. I had reached the point, after the illness which had kept me prostrate for almost three weeks, of no longer fearing her. Being used to seeing her had dissipated my amorous sensations and had replaced them by feelings of friendship and gratitude, for her attentions to me had been most assiduous. She had spent whole nights in an armchair near my bed, and she had ministered to me as if she had been my mother.

It is true that I had never given her a single kiss, that I had been careful never to undress in her presence, and that, except for the first time, she had never entered my room less than decently dressed; nevertheless, I knew that I had fought. I felt proud of having gained the victory. What annoyed me was that neither M. M. nor C. C. would have believed the thing if they had heard of it, and that Laura herself, to whom her daughter must certainly have told everything, would only have pretended to believe it.

I arrived at Signor Bragadin's just as the soup was being served. He received me with cries of joy, laughing because he had always said that I would give them just such a surprise. Besides my two other friends, De La Haye, Bavois, and the physician Righelini[2] were at the table.

"What! without a cloak!" said Signor Dandolo.

"Because, having set out masked, I left it in my room."

The laughter redoubled, and I sat down. No one asked me where I had been for so long, since politeness demanded that it be left to me to bring up the subject; but the curious De La Haye could not refrain from making a little thrust at me, though with a smile.

"You have grown so thin," he said, "that evil tongues will be saying the worst about you."

"What will they say?"

"That you may well have spent the Carnival and nearly the whole of Lent in a warm room in the house of a skillful surgeon."

After allowing the company to laugh, I answered De La Haye that to escape such a hasty judgment I would leave that same evening. For all his saying "No, no," I told him that I thought too highly of his opinion not to act in accordance with it. Seeing that I was speaking seriously, my friends showed their displeasure, and the critic remained silent.

Righelini, who was an intimate friend of Murray's, said that he could not wait to bring him the news of my resuscitation and tell him that everything that had been said about my disappearance was nonsense. I said that we would sup at his house and that I would leave again after supper. To reassure Signor Bragadin and my other friends I promised to dine with them on April 25th, St. Mark's Day.

When the Englishman Murray saw me, he fell on my neck. He introduced me to his wife, a Lady Holderness,[3] who most obligingly invited me to supper. After telling me any number of stories which had been invented about me, Murray asked me if I knew a short novel [4] by the Abate Chiari which had been published at the end of the Carnival, and he made me a present of it, assuring me that it would interest me. He was right. It was a satire which tore Signor Marcantonio Zorzi's circle to shreds and in which the Abate made me cut a very poor figure; but I did not read it until some time afterward. Meanwhile I put it in my pocket. After supper I went to a *traghetto* to take a gondola and returned to Murano.

Midnight had struck, and, the sky being cloudy, I did not stop to see if the gondola was in good condition. It was raining just a little, and when the rain became heavier, I wanted to protect myself by drawing the blinds, but I found neither blinds nor the heavy cloth which usually covers the *felce*. A slight cross wind made the rain soak me. The harm was not great. I arrive at my little casino, I grope my way up the stairs, I knock at the door of my anteroom, where Tonina had already gone to bed. She had waited for me until four o'clock, and it was an hour after midnight.

As soon as Tonina heard my voice she came and opened the door. She had no light, I needed one, she fetches the tinderbox, and since I was in her room she gently warns me, with a little laugh, that she is in her shift. I answer offhandedly that unless she is dirty it does not matter. She does not reply and she lights a candle. She bursts out laughing when she sees me wetter from the rain than anyone has a right to be.

I said that all I needed her to do for me was to dry one

side of my hair, and she quickly brought powder and powder puff; but since her shift was very short and wide across the shoulders, I repented too late. I foresaw that I was lost, and all the more lost since she was laughing heartily because, having both hands encumbered with the powder puff and the powder box, she could not hold her shift up to prevent me from seeing a budding bosom whose power only a dead man would not feel. How was I to turn my eyes away? I fasten them there so openly that poor Tonina blushes.

"Come," I said, "take the front of your shift between your teeth and I will see nothing."

I put it there myself, but then I see half of two thighs which make me cry out. Not knowing how to hide her top and bottom from me at the same time, Tonina quickly sits down on the sofa, and I remain on fire, unable to make up my mind to anything.

"What now?" she says in an agitated voice. "Shall I go and get dressed to put on your nightcap?"

"No. Come sit on my lap and blindfold my eyes. Then I will blindfold yours, for I need you to help me undress."

She came; but I could bear it no longer, I clasped her in my arms, and there was no more thought of playing blindman's buff. I laid her on my bed, where, after I had covered her with kisses and sworn that I would be hers until death, she opened her arms in such a way that I saw she had long desired the moment. I picked the beautiful flower, finding it, as always, better than any of those I had picked during fourteen years.

At the end of our second encounter sleep overtook me and when I woke I found that I was in love with Tonina as I thought I had never been in love with any girl. She had got up without waking me. She came a quarter of an hour later, and giving her a thousand kisses I ask her why she had not waited for me to bid her good morning. Her only answer is to hand me C. C.'s letter. I thank her; I lay the letter aside, and I take her in my arms.

"What a wonder!" she said, laughing. "Are you in no hurry to read it? Inconstant man! Why would you not let me cure you six weeks ago? Blessed rain! But I do not reproach you. Love me as you have loved her who writes to you every day and I will be content."

"Do you know who she is?"

"She is a boarder, beautiful as an angel; but she is in there, and I am here. You are my master; and it rests only with you to be my master always."

Delighted that I could leave her in error, I promise her eternal love and ask her to come back to bed. She replies that, on the contrary, I ought to get up to dine, and she persuades me by describing a choice dinner in the Venetian fashion. I ask her who prepared it, and she answers that it was she herself, that it was an hour after noon, and that she had been up for five hours.

"You slept nine hours. We will go to bed tonight very early."

Tonina seemed to me to have become another person. Her face had the triumphant expression which is bestowed by satisfied love. I did not understand how I could have failed to perceive her rare qualities the first time I had seen her at her mother's house; but I was too much in love with C. C.; besides, she was not then mature. I got up, I drank coffee, and I asked her to put off our dinner for a couple of hours.

I found M. M.'s letter all tenderness, but not so interesting as the one of the day before. I at once set about answering her, and I was surprised to find it a burden. However, I filled four pages with the story of my short journey to Venice.

Tonina's company made my dinner delicious. Considering her at once my wife, my mistress, and my servant, I congratulated myself on being happy so easily. It was the first day on which I ate with her as her lover; so she found me all eagerness to give her unmistakable proofs of it. We spent the whole day at table talking of our love; nature does not afford a wider subject when the speakers are judge and plaintiff. She said, with enchanting sincerity, that, knowing very well that I could not fall in love with her because my heart and soul were filled with another, she only hoped to win me at some moment of surprise, and that she had seen that it was at hand when I had told her that she need not dress to light a candle. She said that until then she had told her mother the plain truth and that she had never believed her; but that now, to punish her, she would tell her nothing. Tonina was intelligent, and she could neither write nor read. She was delighted to have become rich without anyone in Murano being able to say the slightest thing about her which could reflect on her honor. I spent twenty-two days with the girl; and today, when I recall them, I count them among the happiest of my life. I did not return to Venice until toward the end of April, as soon as I had seen M. M. at the grating, finding her greatly changed; nevertheless, sentiment helped me to act toward her in such a way that she could not be aware either that I no longer loved her as I had before or that I had abandoned the plan which had restored her to life and on which she was still counting. I was too much afraid that she would fall ill again if I deprived her of that hope. I kept my casino, which cost me only three zecchini a month, going to see M. M. twice a week and sleeping there on those days with my dear Tonina.

After keeping my word to my friends and dining with them on St. Mark's Day I went with the physician Righelini to the visiting room of the Vergini[5] to attend a profession. The Convento delle Vergini is under the jurisdiction of the Doge of Venice; the nuns address him as "Most Serene Father"; they are all Venetian ladies from the leading families.

I having praised Mother M. E., who was a perfect

beauty, to Righelini, he whispered to me that he was sure he could arrange for me to see her if I was curious enough to pay for it. A hundred zecchini for her and ten for the go-between was the price; he assured me that Murray had had her and that he could have her again. Seeing my surprise, he said there was not a nun in Venice whom one could not have for money if one knew how to go about it. "Murray," he said, "had the liberality to pay five hundred zecchini to have a nun from Murano whose beauty is amazing. Her lover was the French Ambassador."

Though my passion for M. M. was declining, I felt my heart gripped as if by an icy hand. I had to resist all the power of sentiment in order to find the strength to seem indifferent to this piece of news. Despite my certainty that it was pure fiction, I was far from letting the subject drop without getting as much light on it as possible. I quietly answered Righelini, who was intelligent and a man of honor, that one might perhaps have some nun for money, but that it must happen very seldom because of the usual difficulties in convents; and as for the nun in Murano who was famous for her beauty, if it was M. M., a nun in the XXX convent, I told him that not only did I not believe Murray had had her but neither had even the French Ambassador, who must have confined himself to visiting her at the grating, where I did not know what one could accomplish.

Righelini answered coldly that the English Resident was a man of honor and that he had heard from his own lips that he had had her.

"If he had not confided it to me under the seal of secrecy," he said, "I would get him to tell you so himself. I beg you never to let him know what I have told you."

"You need say no more."

But the same evening, supping at Murray's casino with

Righelini, and only the three of us being present, I spoke enthusiastically of the beauty of Mother M. E. whom I had seen at the Vergini.

"Between Masons," the Resident said to me, "you can have her for a certain price, and not a very high one, if you want to; but you must know how to go about it."

"You have been talked into believing it."

"No, I am convinced of it. It is not as difficult as you think."

"If you are convinced I congratulate you and I no longer doubt it. I do not believe that a more perfect beauty is to be found in the convents of Venice."

"You are mistaken. Mother M. M., at the XXX in Murano, is still more beautiful."

"I have heard talk of her, after seeing her once; but is it possible to have her for money too?"

"I believe so," he said with a smile, "and when I believe something it is with good reason."

"You amaze me. Nevertheless, I would wager that you have been misled."

"You would lose. Since you have seen her only once, you would perhaps not recognize her from her portrait."

"I should indeed, for her face is striking."

"Wait a moment."

He gets up from the table, leaves the room, and comes back a minute later with a box in which there were eight or ten miniature portraits, all in the same costume. They were heads with hair down and bare bosoms.

"So those," I said, "are the rare beauties whom you have enjoyed."

"Yes, and if you recognize any of them be discreet."

"You may be sure of that. I know these three. This one looks like M. M.; but admit that you may have been deceived, unless you had her by going into the convent yourself or bringing her out yourself, for after all there are women who look alike."

"How on earth can I have been deceived? I had her

here, dressed in her habit, all one night. It was to herself that I gave a purse containing five hundred zecchini, and I gave the pimp another fifty.''

''You must, I suppose, have called on her in the visiting room before and after you had her here?''

''No, never, for she was afraid that her official lover would learn of it. You know that he was the French Ambassador.''

''She received him in the visiting room.''

''She went to his house dressed as a woman of fashion whenever he wished. I know it from the same man who brought her here to me.''

''Did you have her several times?''

''Once. That is enough. But I can have her when I please for a hundred zecchini.''

''This is no doubt all true, but I wager five hundred zecchini that you have been tricked.''

''I will answer you in three days.''

I did not believe a word of it; but I needed to be certain. I shuddered when I thought that it might be true. It would have been a crime which did not deserve to be forgiven, and which, moreover, would have relieved me of a number of obligations. I was sure that I should find her innocent; but if I was to find her guilty, I would gladly lose five hundred zecchini. In short, I needed to be certain; but on the most conclusive evidence. The uncertainty rent my soul. If Murray had been tricked, M. M.'s honor demanded that I find some way to undeceive the honest Englishman. Here is how Fortune helped me.

Three or four days later the Resident said to me, in Righelini's presence, that he was sure he could have the nun for a hundred zecchini, and that he would not wager more than that.

''If I win,'' he said, ''I shall have her for nothing; if I lose, I will give her nothing. My Mercury[6] tells me that I must wait until a masking day. The question now is to decide what we must do to be convinced, for otherwise neither of us will feel obliged to pay the wager; and to convince ourselves seems to me a difficult matter, for my honor will not permit me, if it is really M. M. who is with me, to let her know that I have betrayed her secret.''

''That would be unpardonable. Here is my plan, which cannot but satisfy us both, for after we have executed it we shall be convinced that we have fairly won or lost. As soon as you believe that you have secured the nun, you will leave her on some pretext and join me at a place where you can be sure I will be waiting for you. We will at once go to the convent, and I will have M. M. come down to the visiting room. When you have seen her, and even spoken with her, will you be convinced that the woman you have left in your house is nothing but a whore?''

''Completely convinced, and I shall never in my life have paid a wager more willingly.''

''I make you the same offer. If when I send for her the lay sister tells us that she is ill or busy, we will leave, and you will have won. You will go to supper with her and I will go where I please.''

''That is perfect. But since it can only be at night, it is possible that when you send for her the portress will answer that at that hour she does not announce visitors.''

''Then I shall have lost too.''

''So you are sure that if she is in the convent she will come down?''

''That is my concern. I repeat: if you do not speak with her, I declare myself satisfied that I have lost a hundred zecchini and even a thousand if you like.''

''No one can speak more plainly, my dear friend, and I thank you in advance.''

''I only insist that you come exactly on time, and that the hour is not too unusual for a convent.''

''An hour after sunset. Will that do?''

''Excellent.''

"I will also see to making the masker wait where I have her, even if it is the real M. M."

"She will not wait long if you can have her brought to you at a casino I have in Murano, where I secretly keep a girl with whom I am in love. I will arrange for her not to be there that day and I will give you the key to the casino. I will even have a little cold supper ready for you."

"That is perfect. I must know where the casino is so that I can tell my Mercury."

"Of course. I will have both of you to supper tomorrow evening, and all three of us will observe the greatest secrecy. We will go to my casino by gondola and we will leave after supper by a door onto the street; in that way you will learn how to go there by water and by land. You will only need to show M. M.'s guide the quay and the door. On the day he is to bring her to you, you will have the key and no one will be there except an old man who lives in a little room downstairs, from which he will see neither those who come in nor those who go out. My little girl will see nothing and will not show herself. Rest assured that I will arrange it all perfectly."

"I begin to believe," said the Resident, delighted with my arrangement, "that I have lost the wager; but I will see the thing out with the greatest pleasure."

I left them after making an appointment to meet them again the following evening.

In the morning I went to Murano, to tell Tonina that I would come to supper with her bringing two friends and to leave her some bottles of good wine, for my dear Englishman was a great and capable drinker. Tonina, delighted at the pleasure it would give her to do the honors of the table, only asked me if my two friends would leave after supper; and I saw that she was very happy when I said yes. After spending an hour in the visiting room with M. M., who was recovering her health and beauty every day, I went back to Venice and at the second hour of the night I returned to Murano with the Resident and Righelini, reaching my little casino by water.

The dinner was made delicious by the graces and the bearing of my dear Tonina. What a pleasure for me to see Righelini enchanted and the Resident reduced to silence by his admiration! When I was in love my manner did not encourage my friends to ingratiate themselves with the object of my love, though I was more obliging when time had cooled my flame.

After midnight we rose from table, and after showing Murray the way from the door of my casino to the place where I would wait for him on the night I was to take him to the convent, I went back to the casino to pay Tonina all the compliments she deserved both for the excellent plain supper she had prepared and for her charming behavior at table. She praised my friends, greatly astonished that the Resident had left fresh as a rose after emptying six bottles. Murray looked like a fine Bacchus painted by Rubens.

On Whitsunday Righelini came to tell me that Murray had arranged everything with M. M.'s alleged Mercury for the next day but one. I gave him the keys to the two doors of my casino, and told him to assure him that at the first hour of the night I would be at the door of the cathedral church.[7] My impatience brought on palpitations which would not subside; I spent two nights unable to sleep. Despite my being certain and more than certain that M. M. was innocent, I was nevertheless very uneasy. But what was the cause of my uneasiness? It seemed that it could only come from my impatience to see the Resident undeceived. In his mind M. M. must be nothing but a low hussy until the moment he became convinced that he had been tricked. The idea wrung my heart.

Murray was as impatient as I, but with the difference

that he, seeing the thing as a comedy, laughed over it, while I, seeing it as a tragedy, shuddered.

So on Tuesday morning I went to my casino in Murano to order Tonina to set out a cold supper, bottles, and everything necessary in my room and then to withdraw to the room of the old owner of the house, where she was to remain until after the guests had left. She assured me that I would be obeyed, without asking me a single question. After that I went to the visiting room and sent for M. M.

Not expecting my visit, she asks me why I had not gone to accompany the *Bucentaur,* which, the weather being fair, was to set out that day. After I had made several disconnected remarks, as she was quick to perceive, I finally came to the important matter.

"I must," I say, "ask you to do me a favor, and the peace of my soul demands that you grant it to me blindly without asking me for the reason."

"Command me, dear heart, I will refuse you nothing if only it is within my power."

"I will come this evening at the first hour of night, I will have you called to this grating, and you will come. You will stay with me only a moment. I shall be with someone. You will say two or three words to him, as politeness demands, then you will leave. Now let us try to find a pretext which will justify the unusual hour."

"It shall be done. But you cannot imagine how difficult it is in this convent to come down to the visiting room at night, for at twenty-four o'clock the visiting rooms are closed and the keys are with the Abbess. But since it is only a matter of five minutes I will tell the Abbess that I am expecting a letter from my brother which must be delivered to me this evening so that I can answer it at once. You will give me a letter, and the nun who will be with me will see it."

"You will not come alone?"

"No. I should not even dare to ask it."

"Very well. It makes no difference. Only try to come with some old nun whose sight is dim."

"I will leave the candle behind."

"No, no, my angel. On the contrary, you must set it on the rail of the grating, for it is important that the masker who will be with me sees your face."

"That is strange. But I have promised to obey you blindly. I will come down with two candles. May I hope that you will give me the answer to this enigma the first time we meet again?"

"I give you my word of honor that I will tell you all about it no later than tomorrow."

"I am curious to hear it."

After this agreement the reader will believe that my heart was at rest. Not a bit of it. I went back to Venice tormented by the fear that Murray would come to the door of the cathedral that evening only to tell me that his Mercury had informed him that the nun had been obliged to put it off. If that had happened I should certainly not have thought M. M. guilty; but I should have seen that the Resident had a right to think that I had been the reason why the nun had failed him. In that case I would certainly not have taken him to the visiting room. I would have gone there alone and very sad.

The day seemed extremely long to me. I put in my pocket a sham sealed letter, and at the hour agreed upon I took up my post at the door of the cathedral. Murray did not keep me waiting. I saw him a quarter of an hour later, masked as I was, hurrying toward the door.

"The nun," I said—"is she there?"

"Yes, my friend. Let us go to the visiting room if you wish, but you will see you will be told that she is ill or busy. We will call the wager off if you like."

"What are you saying? I will not call it off."

I go to the convent gate, I ask for M. M., and the portress restores me to life by saying that I was expected

and that I had only to go into the visiting room. I go
in with my friend, and I see that it is lighted by four
candles. Can I recollect those moments without loving
my life? It was not the innocence of the generous and
noble M. M. which I then acknowledged, but her divine
intelligence. Murray was no longer laughing. M. M.
enters, dazzling, with a lay sister, each of them carrying
a flat candlestick. She addresses a most flattering compliment to me in very good French. I hand her the letter; she looks at the address and the seal, then puts it in
her pocket. After thanking me, she says that she will
answer at once. She then looks at the Resident and says
that perhaps she has made him miss the first act of the
opera.

"The honor of seeing you, Signora, is worth all the
operas in the world."

"I have the impression that the Signore is English."

"Yes, Signora."

"The English nation is now the first in the world.
Signori, I am your very humble servant."

I had never seen M. M. so beautiful as she was at that
moment. I left the visiting room on fire with love and
feeling a contentment which was entirely new to me. I
made my way to the casino, paying no attention to the
Resident, who, no longer being in a hurry, followed me
slowly. I waited for him at the door.

"Well," I said, "are you convinced now that you were
tricked?"

"Be quiet. We shall have time enough to talk. Let us
go up."

"You want me to go up?"

"Please do. What do you expect me to do for four
hours with the whore who is upstairs? We will tan her
hide."

"Better turn her out."

"No, for at two hours after midnight her pimp is to
come for her. She would run and tell him, and he would

escape my vengeance. We'll throw them both out the window.''

"Calm yourself. M. M.'s honor demands that this matter be known to no one. Come, let us go up. We will have some fun. I am curious to see the slut.''

Murray enters first. As soon as she sees me she puts a handkerchief over her face and tells the Resident that his behavior is disgraceful. Murray does not answer.

She was standing, she was not as tall as M. M., she had spoken to him in bad French. Her *bautta,* her cloak, and her mask were on the bed; however, she was dressed as a nun. I could not wait to see her face. I gently ask her to do me the favor.

"Who are you?" she says.

"You are in my house and you do not know who I am?''

"I am here because I have been betrayed. I did not believe I was dealing with a scoundrel.''

Murray then tells her to be still, calling her by the name of her honorable trade, and the hussy got up to take her cloak, saying that she wanted to leave; but he pushed her back, telling her she must wait for her pimp and not make a noise if she did not want to go to prison instantly.

"I in prison!''

So saying she raised one hand to the opening of her dress; but I at once seized it and the Resident seized the other. We push her into a chair and we confiscate the pistols which she had in her pockets. Murray tears open the front of her sacred woolen robe and takes a stiletto eight inches long from her. The slut was weeping in torrents.

"Will you stay here quietly," said the Resident, "until Capsucefalo[8] comes, or do you want to go to prison?''

"And when Capsucefalo comes?''

"I promise to let you go.''

"With him?''

"Perhaps.''

"Well, I will stay here quietly."

"Have you any more weapons?"

At this question the hussy took off her dress and her petticoat and, if we had not stopped her, would have stripped naked, hoping to obtain from our animal nature what she could not hope from our reason.

What greatly astonished me during all this time was that I could see in her only a counterfeit resemblance to M. M. I said so to the Resident and he agreed with me; but, arguing with his usual astuteness, he made me admit that the power of a preconceived idea could have made many other men fall into the same trap.

CHAPTER X

*The affair of the sham nun ends amusingly.
M. M. learns that I have a mistress. She is
avenged on the infamous Capsucefalo. I ruin
myself at cards; urged on by M. M., I gradually sell all her diamonds to try my luck,
which doggedly runs against me. I surrender
Tonina to Murray, who provides for her. Her
sister Barberina takes her place.*

"SIX MONTHS ago," he said, "I happened to be
at the door of the convent with Smith,[1] our Consul;
I have forgotten what ceremony provided the occasion.
Having seen the nun in question among ten or twelve
others, I said to Smith that I would not hesitate an instant to pay five hundred zecchini to have her with me
for two or three hours. Count Capsucefalo heard me and
said nothing. Smith said that no one could have her except at the grating, like the French Ambassador, who
often visited her. Capsucefalo came the next morning
to tell me that if I had meant what I said he was sure he
could arrange for me to spend a night with the nun
wherever I pleased, provided she was sure the secret
would be kept. He said that he had just been speaking
with her and that when he had named me to her she had
answered that she had seen me with Smith and that she
would be very glad to sup with me, more from inclination

than for the five hundred zecchini. He said that he was the only person she trusted and that it was he who took her to Venice to a casino belonging to the French Ambassador whenever she ordered him to. He ended by saying that I need have no fear of being tricked, for it was to herself alone that I should give the money when I had her with me; after all that, he took from his pocket the portrait you have seen—here it is. I bought it from him two days after I believed I had slept with her. That came about two weeks after we agreed on the terms. Though masked, she arrived in her nun's habit; but I am vexed with myself for not at least suspecting the deceit when I saw her long hair, for I knew that nuns had their hair cut. She said that those who prefer to keep it under their caps are free to do so, and I believed her.''

The hussy was speaking the truth; but I did not feel it necessary to tell the Resident so just then. I examined her features with equal attention and surprise, holding the portrait, which was painted with the bosom bare. I said that so far as bosoms were concerned, painters invented them; and the shameless wench seized the occasion to show me that the copy was true to the original. I turned my back on her. The fact is that on that night I laughed at the axiom *Quae sunt aequalia uni tertio sunt aequalia inter se* (''Things which are equal to a third thing are equal to each other''), for the portrait resembled M. M. and it also resembled the strumpet, and the latter did not resemble M. M. Murray admitted it, and we spent an hour philosophizing. Since she insisted that she was innocent, we became curious to know how the rascal had induced her to consent to such a masquerade, and here is her story, which we saw bore the stamp of truth.

''It was two years ago that I became acquainted with Count Capsucefalo and his acquaintance was useful to

me. If he did not give me money himself, he put me in
the way of getting plenty of it from the people to whom
he introduced me. One day near the end of last autumn
he came to my house to tell me that if I was up to disguising myself as a nun in the clothes he would bring me
and pretending to be a nun with an Englishman who
would spend the night with me alone as my lover, I
should have a hundred zecchini. He assured me that I
had nothing to fear, that he would himself take me to
the casino where the gull would be waiting for me, and
that he would come at the end of the night to take me
back to my supposed convent. I liked the plot. I laughed
with anticipation. I said I was willing. On top of that,
I ask you if a woman of my trade can resist the temptation to earn a hundred zecchini. Finding the whole thing
very amusing, I begged to be allowed to do it; I assured
him that I would play my role perfectly. The bargain
was made. The only coaching I needed was in the dialogue. He said that the Englishman was bound to talk
to me of nothing but my convent, and, for form's sake,
ask me what lovers I had, and that I was to cut him off
short and answer that I didn't know what he was talking
about and even say lightly that the nearest I came to
being a nun was to dress up like one, and, to convince
him, I was to laugh and show him my hair. 'That,' he
said, 'will not keep him from believing you are the nun
he's in love with, since he will have made up his mind
that you can't be anyone else.' Seeing all the ingenuity
of the scheme, I did not stop to ask either the name of
the nun whose part I was to play or to what convent she
belonged. The only thing that interested me was the
hundred zecchini. And the proof is that, though I slept
with you and found you charming and even a man rather
to be paid than to pay, I never bothered to find out who
you are. Even now I don't know to whom I am talking.
You know how we spent the night, I found it delicious,

François Joachim de Pierre de Bernis

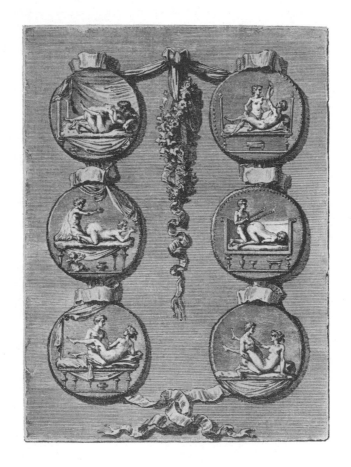

Scenes in Antique Style

and God knows with what pleasure I was promising myself another like it today. You gave me five hundred
zecchini, but I had to be satisfied with a hundred, as
Capsucefalo had told me I should and as he told me yesterday you would give me a hundred tonight which I
would share with him. You have discovered everything;
but I have no fear, for I can mask as I please and I
can't stop men who sleep with me from thinking I am a
saint if it amuses them. You found weapons on me; but
I can't be found guilty for that, because I only brought
them to defend my life in case any violence was offered
me. I cannot see that I am guilty of anything."

"Do you know me?" I asked.

"No. But I often see you passing under my windows.
I live in San Rocco,[2] in the first house on the left after
the bridge."

In the light of her story we concluded that Capsucefalo
deserved the iron collar and the galleys a hundred times
over; but we considered that the woman, being a whore,
was innocent. She must have been at least ten years older
than M. M., and she was pretty; but she was blonde and
my dear mistress was light chestnut and at least three
inches taller.

After midnight we sat down at table and ate what
Antonina had prepared for us with excellent appetites.
We had the firmness to leave the poor devil of a wench
where she was without offering her a single glass of wine.
We thought it our duty. In our conversation at table the
Resident treated me to commentaries both friendly and
witty on the eagerness I had shown to convince him that
he had not had M. M. He said it was not natural that I
should have done all I had done unless I was in love with
her. I replied that, being condemned and confined to the
visiting room, I was to be pitied; he answered that he
would gladly pay a hundred guineas a month merely for
the privilege of visiting her at the grating. So saying,

he gave me the hundred zecchini he owed me, thanking me for winning them from him. I simply put them in my pocket.

Two hours after midnight we heard a soft knocking at the street door.

"Here is our friend," I said. "Restrain yourself and be sure he will confess everything."

He enters and he sees Murray and the beauty. He does not notice that there is a third person until he hears the anteroom door being locked. He turns and sees me. He knew me. Not losing his self-possession, he says:

"Ah! It's you, is it? Very well. You are aware of the need for secrecy."

Murray laughs and tells him to sit down. Holding the hussy's pistols, he asks him where he will take her before dawn, and he replies that he will take her home.

"It is possible," said the Resident, "that you will both go to prison."

"No," he answered, "because there would be too much talk and you would be laughed at. Come," he said to the wench, "get dressed and we will go."

The Resident pours him a glass of Pontacq[3] and the pimp drinks to his health. Murray praises a fine cluster of white diamonds which he was wearing on his finger, and, pretending to be interested, draws it off. He declares it perfect and asks what it cost him.

"It is worth," said Capsucefalo, decidedly taken aback, "four hundred zecchini."

"I will keep it at that price," answers the Resident.

The other lowered his head. This display of modesty makes Murray laugh. He tells the woman to get dressed and be off with her friend. It took but a moment. They left after making us the lowest of bows and curtsies.

I thereupon embraced Murray, congratulating him and thanking him for having ended the matter so quietly, for making a noise about it could have injured three innocent people. He replied that the guilty parties would be punished and that no one would ever be able to find out the reason. I then sent down for Tonina, to whom the Englishman offered wine, but she excused herself. He looked at her with burning eyes. He left, thanking me most sincerely. After he was gone Tonina was convinced in my arms that I had not been in the least unfaithful to her. After sleeping for six hours and eating dinner with her I went to the visiting room to tell my noble M. M. the whole story.

The account which I gave her, not forgetting the smallest detail, the description of all my uneasiness, to which she listened without once blinking, brought to her face the various shades of feeling which could not but arise from the various sensations of her beautiful soul. Fear, anger, indignation, approval of the measures I had taken to clear everything up, her joy at seeing that everything I had done proved that I still loved her and was worthy of her—all this appeared before my eyes to reproach me with my deceitfulness in making her believe that my only thought was to carry out my plan of taking her to France.

She was delighted to learn that the masker who had been with me was the English Resident; but I saw her stung to noble disdain when I told her that he would give a hundred guineas a month to have the privilege of visiting her at the grating. She thought she had reason to be angry with him because he had enjoyed her in imagination and because he had found the portrait, which I had shown her, a good likeness. She could not recognize herself in it. She said, with a shrewd smile, that she was sure I had not let my little maid see the sham nun, because she might have been taken in.

"Then you know that I have a young maid?"

"And what's more, that she's pretty. She is Laura's daughter. And if you love her I am very glad and so is C. C.; but I hope you will find a way to show her to me; as for C. C., she knows her."

After promising to let her see the girl, I truthfully told her the whole story of my love affair and I saw that she was pleased. Just as I was about to leave she said she thought it was her duty to have Capsucefalo assassinated, for he had dishonored her. I swore that if the Resident did not avenge us within the week I would fulfill her wish myself.

Procurator Bragadin, the elder brother of my kind patron, died about this time. His brother's death made him quite rich. But as the family was on the verge of extinction, a woman who had been his mistress and who had given him a natural son who was still alive, took it into her head to become his wife. The marriage would have legitimatized the son and the family would not have died out. By dint of assembling the Collegio[4] she would have been granted citizenship, and all would have been well. She wrote me a note asking me to come and see her. We did not know each other. Just as I was leaving to go there, Signor Bragadin sent for me. He requested me to ask the oracle if he should follow De La Haye's advice in the matter which he had promised him he would not tell me about but which the oracle could not fail to know. The oracle answers that he should follow no advice except that of his own reason, and I at once go to call on the lady.

She tells me all the circumstances, she introduces her son to me, and she says that if the marriage could take place, a deed would be executed before a notary by virtue of which upon Signor Bragadin's death I would become the proprietor of an estate which yielded five thousand scudi a year.

Instantly understanding that the business must be the same as the one which De La Haye had proposed to Signor Bragadin, I reply without hesitating that since Monsieur de La Haye had already discussed the matter with Signor Bragadin I would have no part in it. After making this brief answer I bowed to them.

I thought it very strange in De La Haye that he should intrigue to marry off my friends without my knowledge. It was only two years earlier that, if I had not opposed it, he would have married off Signor Dandolo. I was not at all concerned over the extinction of the Bragadin family, but I was very much concerned for the life of my dear benefactor, whom the activity of marriage would have killed. He was sixty-three years old and he had had an apoplectic stroke.

I went to dine with Lady Murray. Englishwomen who are daughters of lords keep their title. After dinner the Resident told me that he had communicated the whole story of the sham nun to Signor Cavalli, Secretary to the State Inquisitors, and that the Secretary had informed him the day before that everything he could wish had been done; but here is what he had learned at the coffeehouse. Count Capsucefalo had been sent to Cephalonia,[5] his birthplace, with orders never to return to Venice. The courtesan had vanished.

What is admirable in these economical dispositions by the tribunal is that no one ever knows the reason for them. Secrecy is the soul of that redoubtable magistracy, which, though unconstitutional, is necessary to the preservation of the State. I saw that M. M. was overjoyed when I told her what had happened.

At this same time I was being ruined at cards. Playing by the martingale, I lost very large sums; urged on by M. M. herself, I sold all her diamonds, leaving her in possession of only five hundred zecchini. There was no more question of an elopement. I still played, but for small stakes, dealing at casinos against poor players. Thus I waited for my luck to come back.

The English Resident, after having me to supper at his casino with the celebrated Fanny Murray,[6] asked me to invite him to supper at my little casino in Murano, which I was still keeping only because of Tonina. I did him the favor, but without imitating his generosity; he found my little Tonina gay and polite, but within bounds which were not to his taste. The next morning he wrote me a note, of which this is a copy:

"I am irretrievably in love with your Tonina. If you will surrender her to me, this is the provision I am prepared to make for her. I will take a casino, which I will rent in her name, and I will furnish it for her, immediately making her a present of the furniture, on condition that I shall be free to go to see her whenever I please and shall have all the rights in her to which an accepted lover is entitled. I will give her a chambermaid and a cook, and thirty zecchini a month for a table for two persons, not including the wines, which I will furnish myself. In addition I will give her an annuity of two hundred scudi, which will become her property when we have known each other one year. I give you eight days to answer me."

I wrote him that I needed only three,[7] that Tonina had a mother whom she respected, and that judging by appearances I thought she was pregnant.

I at once saw that if I did not fall in with this proposal I should have cruelly ruined the girl's chances in life. I went to Murano the same day and told her everything.

"Then you want to leave me?" she said, weeping. "You no longer love me."

"I love you with all my heart, and I insist that the proposal I am making to you proves it."

"No, because I can't belong to two men."

"You will belong only to your new lover. Consider that you come into possession of a dowry which can bring you a very good marriage and that I am not in a position to make any such provision for you."

"Come to supper with me tomorrow."

The next day she said that the Englishman was handsome, that when he spoke Venetian he made her laugh, and that she could love him if her mother was willing.

"In case," she said, "our temperaments do not agree, we will separate at the end of a year, and I will be the gainer by an income of two hundred scudi. I am willing. Talk to my mother.''

Laura, whom I had not seen since she had given me her daughter, did not need to ask me for time to think it over. She said that Tonina would be in a position to support her and that she would leave Murano, where she was tired of serving. She showed me a hundred and thirty zecchini which Tonina had earned in my service and which she had entrusted to her. Her daughter Barberina, who was a year younger than Tonina, came to kiss my hand. I thought her striking, and I gave her all the silver money I had and told Laura that I would wait for her at her daughter's.

The good mother gave Tonina her maternal blessing, saying that she only asked her for three lire a day so that she could go to live in Venice with her family, and Tonina promised them to her. She had a boy whom she wanted to make a priest, and Barberina, who was to become a good seamstress. Her eldest daughter was already married. After concluding this important business I went to the visiting room, where M. M. made me the present of coming with C. C. I felt unfeigned pleasure in seeing her prettier than ever, though sad and in mourning because of her mother's death. She could stay with me only a quarter of an hour, being afraid that she might be seen and reprimanded, for she was still forbidden to go to the visiting room. I told M. M. the whole story of Tonina, who was going to live in Venice with the Resident, and I saw that the thing displeased her. She said that as long as I had Tonina she was sure of seeing me often, and that she would not see me often after she was gone. But the time of our eternal separation was drawing near.

It was on the same evening that I took Murray the news. He said that I could bring her with me to supper at the casino, which he designated to me, on the next day but one and leave her with him; and I did so.

In my presence the generous Englishman handed

Tonina the contract for an annuity of two hundred Venetian ducati drawn on the Bakers' Guild.[8] This is the equivalent of two hundred and forty florins. By another document he made her a present of everything in the casino except the china after she had lived with him for a year. He told her she would have a zecchino a day for the table and the servants and that if she was pregnant he would see to it that she was delivered with every comfort and that he would give me the child. In addition he told me that she would be free to receive me, and even to give me proofs of her affection until her pregnancy was over, and that she could receive her mother and also go to see her whenever she pleased. Tonina embraced him, expressing the most lively gratitude and assuring him that from that moment she would love no one but him and would only feel friendship for me. During all this scene she was able to hold back her tears; but I could not hold back mine. Murray made her happy; but I was not there to see it for long. The reason will be revealed a quarter of an hour hence.

Three days later Laura appeared in my house and, after telling me that she was already settled in Venice, asked me to take her to see her daughter. I did her the favor at once, and I was delighted to hear her alternately thanking God and me, not knowing to which of the two she was under the greater obligation. Tonina praised her lover to me in the highest terms, and did not complain that I had not come to see her, which greatly pleased me. Tonina's casino was in Cannaregio and her mother had gone to live in Castello.[9] I took her home and when we arrived there she asked me to get out of my gondola to see her little house, where she had a garden. I acceded, without remembering that I should find Barberina there.

The girl, who was as pretty as her sister though of a different type, began by arousing my curiosity. It is curiosity which makes a man who is inured to vice inconstant. If all women had the same looks and the same mental characteristics, a man would not only never become inconstant, he would never even fall in love. He would take some woman by instinct and remain content with her until he died. The economy of our world would be entirely different. Novelty is the tyrant of our soul; we know that what we do not see is more or less the same thing; but what they let us see makes us think the contrary; and that suffices them. Niggards by nature in letting us see what they have in common with other women, they force our imagination to suppose them something entirely different.

Young Barberina, who regarded me as an old acquaintance, whose own mother had taught her to kiss my hand, who had several times undressed down to her shift in my presence never supposing that there was anything about her to excite me, who knew that I had made her sister's fortune and the whole family's, and who of course thought she was the prettier because she had a whiter skin and darker eyes, realized that her only chance of conquering me was to take me by storm. Her good sense told her that, as I never went to her house, I could never fall in love with her unless she convinced me that she would grant me all the favors I could desire without its costing me the slightest effort. This reasoning was innate in her; her mother had not given her the slightest coaching.

After I had been shown her two rooms, her small kitchen, and the cleanliness of the housekeeping, Barberina asked me if I would like to go and see the garden. Her mother told her to give me some green figs if they were ripe.

In the little garden, which was twelve yards square, there was nothing but salad greens and a fig tree. I did not see any figs, but Barberina said that she saw some high up and that she would go for them if I would kindly hold the ladder for her. She climbs up, and to manage to reach some which are at a distance she stretches out one arm, throwing her body out of balance and holding to the ladder with the other hand.

"Ah, my charming Barberina! If you knew what I see!"

"What you've often seen of my sister's."

"True. But you are prettier."

Not troubling to answer me but pretending that she could not reach the figs, she puts one foot on a high branch, presenting me with a picture than which the most consummate experience could not have imagined one more seductive. She sees that I am in ecstasies, she does not hurry, and I am grateful for it. Helping her down, I ask her if the fig I was touching had been picked, and she lets me find out for myself, remaining in my arms with a smile and a sweetness which at once make me her captive. I give her an amorous kiss, which she returns with all the joy of soul which shone in her lovely eyes. I ask her if she will let me pick it, and she answers that her mother had to go to Murano the next morning and would stay there all day, that I would find her alone, and that she would refuse me nothing.

Such is the language which makes a man happy when it comes from the lips of a novice, for desires are really nothing but torments, they are positive pains, and we value enjoyment only because it frees us from them. From this we see that those who prefer a little resistance to a great receptivity are lacking in judgment.

I go upstairs again with the young darling, I embrace her in the presence of her mother, who laughs when she hears me say that she is a jewel beyond price. I give the sweet child ten zecchini, and I go away congratulating myself and at the same time berating Fortune for ill-treating me so that I could not immediately set Barberina up in the same style as her sister.

My dear Tonina had told me that politeness demanded

that I should sup with her, and that if I came that day I would find Righelini there.

What amused me at her supper was the perfect accord between Tonina and the Resident. I congratulated him on having lost a certain taste. He answered that he would be sorry to have lost any of his tastes.

"You used," I said, "to enjoy practicing love without veiling its mysteries."

"That was Ancilla's taste, not mine."

The answer pleased me, for I could not have watched him making love to Tonina except with great pain. When I happened to say that I was without a casino, Righelini told me that I could have two rooms on the Fondamenta Nuove[10] cheaply. This is a considerable quarter of Venice with a northern exposure, as pleasant in summer as it is unpleasant in winter. Murano is opposite to it, and I had to go there at least twice a week. So I told Righelini that I would be glad to look at the two rooms.

At midnight I said good-by to the rich and happy Resident, and went off to bed so that I could go early the next morning to San Giuseppe[11] in Castello, where I was to spend the day with Barberina.

"I am sure," she said at once, "that my mother will not be back until this evening, my brother eats dinner at school. Here is a cold fowl, ham, cheese, and two flagons of Scopolo wine.[12] We will dine soldier fashion whenever you please."

"How did you manage to get together such an appetizing dinner?"

"My mother did it all."

"Then you told her what we are going to do?"

"All I told her was that you said you would come to see me; and I gave her the ten zecchini. She said no harm would be done if you became my lover, since my sister was no longer living with you. The news surprised me and pleased me. Why did you leave my sister?"

"We haven't left each other, for I supped with her

last night; but we are no longer living together as lovers. I surrendered her to a friend of mine, who has provided for her handsomely.''

''Good! Please tell her that I have taken her place and that you found me such that you can swear I have never loved anybody.''

''And if the news grieves her?''

''So much the better. Will you do me the favor? It's the first one I've asked of you.''

''I promise to tell her everything.''

After this preamble we breakfasted, and then in perfect singleness of purpose went to bed, more as if we were going to sacrifice to Hymen than to Love.

The rite being a new experience for Barberina, her transports, her unformed ideas, which she expressed to me with the utmost ingenuousness, and her yieldings seasoned with the charms of inexperience would not have surprised me if I had not found that I was feeling inexperienced myself. I had the impression that I was enjoying a fruit whose sweetness I had never so fully tasted in the past. Barberina was ashamed to let me know that I had hurt her, and the same desire to dissimulate spurred her to do everything to convince me that the pleasure she felt was greater than the pleasure she really did feel. She was not yet a grown girl; the roses of her burgeoning breasts had not yet budded; her attainment of puberty as yet existed only in her young mind.

We got up for dinner, then we went back to bed, where we remained until evening. When Laura returned she found us dressed and happy. After making the beautiful child a present of twenty zecchini I left, assuring her of eternal love and certainly with no intention of deceiving her; but what destiny was preparing for me was incompatible with my plans.

The next day I went with the physician Righelini to see the two rooms; they were to my liking and I took them at once, paying three months in advance. The daughter of the mistress of the house, who was a widow, had been bled. She was a patient whom Righelini had been attending for nine months and whom he could not cure. I went into her room with him, and I thought I saw a statue of wax. I said it was beautiful but that the sculptor should give it some color; at which the statue smiled. Righelini said that I should not be surprised at her pallor, for she had just been bled for the hundred and fourth time. She was eighteen years old,[13] and having never had her menses she felt as if she were dying three or four times a week; and she would die, I was told, if a vein was not opened at once. He was thinking of sending her to the country, hoping much from the change of air. After telling the Signora that I would sleep in her house that night, I left with the physician. Talking to me of the girl's illness, he said that the real remedy to cure her would be a strong lover.

"As her physician," I answered, "you could also be her pharmacist."

"I should be risking too much, for I might be forced into marriage, which I fear more than death."

CHAPTER XI

*The beautiful patient. I cure her. Plot hatched
to ruin me. Incident at the house of the
young Countess Bonafede. The Erberia. House
search. My conversation with Signor Bragadin.
I am arrested by order of the State Inquisitors.*

SO AFTER supping early with Signor Bragadin I
go to my new casino to enjoy the cool air from the
balcony of my bedroom. On entering the balcony I am
surprised to find it occupied. A strikingly well-propor-
tioned young lady rises and asks me to forgive her for
the liberty she had taken.

"I am," she said, "she whom you took this morning for
a wax statue. We do not have a light as long as the windows are open, because of the gnats; but when you wish
to go to bed we will close them and go. This is my
younger sister, and my mother is in bed."

I replied that the balcony should be at her service,
that it was early, and that I only asked her permission
to put on a dressing gown and remain in her company.
She entertained me for two hours with remarks as intelligent as they were amusing, and at midnight she left.
Her young sister lit a candle for me, then went away,
wishing me a good sleep.

Getting into bed and thinking of the girl, it seemed to me impossible that she was ill. She spoke with energy, she was gay, cultivated, and very witty. I could not understand by what fatal mischance, if her illness required no remedy but what Righelini had said was the only one, she could still not be cured of it in a city like Venice, for despite her pallor she seemed to me perfectly deserving of an active lover and intelligent enough to make up her mind that, in one way or another, she would take a remedy than which nothing could be sweeter.

In the morning I ring to be got up, and it is the younger sister who enters; there were no servants in the house, and I did not want one of my own. I ask her for hot water to shave with and I ask her how her sister is feeling, and she says she is not ill, that her pallor is not a disease, but that she only needed to be bled every time her breath failed her.

"That does not keep her," she said, "from eating well and sleeping even better."

While the little girl was telling me all this I hear a violin.

"It's my sister," she said, "learning to dance the minuet."

I quickly dress to go and watch her, and I see a very pretty young lady whom an old dancing master was teaching to dance, though he let her turn in her toes. All that the girl lacked was the hue of the living soul. Her whiteness was too much like snow, it had no flush of rose.

The dancing master invites me to dance a minuet with his pupil, and I accept but I ask him to play *larghissimo*. He replies that it would tire the Signorina too much, but she tells him that she is not weak. After the minuet I saw her, with a touch of color in her cheeks, obliged to sink into a chair. However, she told the dancer that in future she wanted to dance only in that way. I said to her when we were alone that the lesson the man gave her was too short and that he did not correct her mistakes. I taught her to toe out, to offer her hand gracefully, to bend her knees in time, and when at the end of an hour I saw that she was a little overtired I asked her to forgive me and went to Murano to call on M. M.

I found her very sad. C. C.'s father having died,[1] she had been removed from the convent to marry an advocate.[2] She had left her a letter for me, in which she said that if I would again promise to marry her when I thought the time had come she would wait and persist in refusing the hand of any suitor who might appear. I answer her frankly that having no adequate income and there being no likelihood that I could expect to have one very soon, I left her at liberty, and I even advised her not to refuse anyone who asked for her hand and if she thought he could make her happy. Despite this sort of dismissal, C. C. did not marry XXX until after my escape from the Leads, when no one expected to see me back in Venice. I did not see her again until nineteen years later. For the past ten years she has been a widow and unhappy. If I were in Venice now I would not marry her, because marriage at my age is only a farce; but it is certain that I would unite her destiny with mine.

I laugh when I hear certain women calling men whom they accuse of inconstancy "perfidious." They would be right if they could prove that when we swear to be true to them we intend to fail them. Alas! *We love without consulting our reason, and our reason has no more to do with it when we stop loving.*

At this same time I received a letter from the Ambassador, who wrote another of the same purport to M. M. He told me that I should devote the powers of my mind to nothing but bringing M. M. to reason. He said that I could not be guilty of a greater imprudence than carrying her off to Paris, where despite all his influence she would not be safe. Charming even in her unhappiness, she infected me with her grief.

A small event caused us to reflect.

"We have just buried," she said, "a nun who died yesterday of consumption in the odor of sanctity at the age of twenty-eight. Her name was Maria Concetta. She knew you and she told C. C. your name when you used to come here to mass every feast day. C. C. could not help asking her to be discreet. The nun said you were a dangerous man of whom a girl should beware. C. C. told me all this after your masquerading as Pierrot disclosed your identity."

"What was her name when she was in the world?"

"Marta S." [3]

"Now I understand it all."

I then told M. M. the whole story of my love affair with Nanetta and Marta, ending with the letter she had written me in which she said that, though indirectly, she owed me her eternal salvation.

Within a week or ten days the conversations in which I engaged my hostess's daughter on my balcony until midnight and the lesson I gave her every morning had produced two very natural effects. The first was that she no longer lost her breath, and the second that I had fallen in love with her. Her menses had not come, but she had not needed to send for the surgeon. Righelini came to examine her, and finding that she was better he prognosticated that before autumn she would have the relief of nature, without which she could only be kept alive by art. Her mother considered me an angel whom God had sent her to cure her daughter, and the latter felt a gratitude which, in a woman, is distant from love by only the smallest of steps. I had persuaded her to dismiss her dancing master.

But at the end of ten or twelve days I thought I saw her dying before my eyes just as I was about to give her her dancing lesson. Her breath completely failed her; it was far worse than an attack of asthma. She dropped into my arms as if she were dead. Her mother, who was used to seeing her in this condition, at once sent for the surgeon, and her young sister fell to unlacing her dress and petticoat. The firmness of her bosom, which needed no color to be the perfection of beauty, surprised me. I covered it, telling her that the surgeon would bungle the bleeding if he saw it; but looking at me with expiring eyes she pushed my hand away with the greatest gentleness as soon as she realized that it was giving me pleasure to hold it there.

The surgeon arrived, quickly drew blood from her arm, and in an instant I saw her pass from death to life. He at once applied a compress, and it was over. Since he had drawn only a scant four ounces of blood and I learned from her mother that she never needed to have more drawn, I saw that the thing was not such a wonder as Righelini made it out to be. If he bled her in the same fashion twice a week he drew three pounds of blood from her in a month; it was what her menses ought to have given, and her vessels being obstructed in that direction, nature, always intent upon its own preservation, threatened her with death if she did not relieve it of the superfluity which denied it freedom of motion.

With the surgeon scarcely gone, she rather astonished me by saying that if I would wait a moment in the drawing room she would come and dance; and she came, feeling as well as if nothing had happened.

Her bosom, on which two of my senses could give a good report, had captivated my soul; she interested me so much that I returned at nightfall. I found her in her room with her sister. She said that she would come to enjoy the fresh air on my balcony at two o'clock[4] because she was expecting her godfather, who, having been an intimate friend of her father's, had come every evening to spend an hour and a half with her for the past eight years.

"How old is he?"

"Between fifty and sixty. He is married. He is Count S.[5] He is very fond of me, but like a father. He loves me today as he loved me in my earliest childhood. His wife even comes to see me sometimes and invites me to dinner. In the autumn I shall go to the country with her. He knows that you are lodging with us, and he has no objection to it. He does not know you, but if you wish you may make his acquaintance tonight."

This whole discourse, which told me everything there was to know without my having to ask indiscreet questions, delighted me. The Greek's[6] affection could only be of the flesh. He was the husband of the Countess with whom I had first seen M. M., two years earlier.

I found the Count most polite. He thanked me, adopting a fatherly tone, for the friendship I showed his goddaughter and asked me to come the next day and dine with her at his house, where he would have the pleasure of introducing me to his wife. I have always liked theatrical effects; and my meeting with the Countess should prove to be a quite interesting one. His invitation was most courteous, and I saw that the young lady was delighted when, after he left, I praised him. She said that he was in possession of all the documents necessary to obtain from the house of Persico[7] her family's entire inheritance, amounting to forty thousand scudi, one quarter of which belonged to her, not counting her mother's dowry, which she would make over to her daughters, so that she would bring the man she would marry a dowry of fifteen thousand ducati correnti, as would her sister.

The young lady was trying to make me fall in love with her and to ensure my constancy by being chary of her favors, for when I tried to gain any she checked me by remonstrances to which I dared not reply; but I was about to make her change her game.

The next day I accompanied her to the Count's house,

not informing her that I knew the Countess. I believed she would pretend not to know me; but not a bit of it. She gave me the warm greeting which is commonly bestowed on old acquaintances. When her husband, in some surprise, asked her where we had met she answered that we had seen each other at Mira[8] two years before. We spent the day very gaily.

Taking the young lady home in my gondola toward nightfall, I demanded some favors; but in their stead I received only reproaches which annoyed me so much that, after leaving her at her house, I went to sup with Tonina, where, the Resident coming in very late, I spent almost the entire night. So the next morning, having slept until noon, I did not give her a lesson. When I asked her to excuse me, she said that I must not put myself to any trouble. That evening she did not come to the balcony, and I was annoyed. The next morning I go out early, and no lesson; and that evening on the balcony I talk to her only of indifferent things; but in the morning a loud noise wakes me, I leave my room to see what it is, and my hostess tells me that her daughter cannot breathe. Quick, the surgeon!

I enter her room, and my heart bleeds to see her expiring. It was the beginning of July, she was in bed, covered with nothing but a sheet. She could speak to me only with her eyes. I ask her if she has palpitations, I put my hand on the place, I kiss the center, and she has not the strength to resist me. I kiss her lips, which are cold as ice, and my hand quickly moves a foot and a half lower and takes hold of what it finds. She pushed it weakly away, but with a great deal of strength in her eyes, which tell me enough to convince me that I am affronting her. At that moment the surgeon arrives, he opens her vein, and she immediately breathes. She wants to get up; I advise her to stay in bed and persuade her by saying that I will send for my dinner and eat it beside her. Her mother says that bed cannot but do her good. She puts on a corset and tells her sister to put a light coverlet over the sheet, for everyone could see her as if she were naked.

Burning with love because of what I had done, resolved to seize the moment of my good fortune if it came, I ask my hostess to send word to Signor Bragadin's kitchen to send me a dinner, and I sit down by the beautiful patient's bedside, assuring her that she would be cured if she could love.

"I am sure that I should be cured; but whom can I love when I am not sure that I am loved?"

The conversation becoming more animated, I slip my hand onto the thigh which is nearest to me and I beg her to let me stay there; instead, continuing to beg, I move upward and I arrive where I believe I am causing her a very pleasant sensation by tickling her. But she draws away, saying in a voice full of feeling that what I am about to do to her perhaps is the cause of her illness. I answer that it may be so, and from her confessing it I foresee that I shall arrive at what I desire and I feel inspired with the hope of curing her if what everyone says is true. I take care not to offend her modesty, by sparing her any indiscreet questions, and I declare myself her lover, promising to demand nothing from her except what she may see fit to bestow as food for my affection. She ate half of my dinner with a good appetite, she got up when I dressed to go out, and when I came back at two o'clock I found her sitting on my balcony.

On the balcony, where I sat down facing her, after a quarter of an hour of amorous talk she allowed my eyes to enjoy all her charms, which the starlight made even more interesting and which she let me cover with kisses. In the tumult which her overmastering passion raised in her soul, clinging to me in the closest of embraces, giving herself up to instinct, the enemy of every artifice, she made me happy with such fervor that I knew beyond doubt that she thought she was receiving more pleasure than she was giving me. I immolated the victim without steeping the altar in blood.

When her sister came to say that it was late and she was sleepy, she told her to go to bed; and as soon as we were alone we went to bed without the slightest preliminaries. We spent the whole night, I animated by love and the desire to cure her, she by gratitude and the most extraordinary degree of pleasure. Toward daybreak she went away to sleep in her room, leaving me very tired but not exhausted. The fear of making her pregnant had kept me from dying yet without ceasing to live. She slept with me for three whole weeks, and her breath never failed her and her menses came. I would have married her were it not that, toward the end of this same month, the catastrophe which will soon come out descended on me.

My reader may remember that I had reason to bear a grudge against the Abate Chiari on account of a satirical novel which Murray had given me to read and of which he was the author. A month before the time to which I have now come, I had expressed myself in terms from which it might well be believed that I would have my revenge, and the Abate was on his guard. About the same time I received an anonymous letter which said that, instead of thinking of having the Abate cudgeled, I would do better to think of myself, since the greatest of misfortunes was hanging over me. All people who write anonymous letters should be scorned, for they can only be traitors or fools; but one should never scorn the advice they give. That was my mistake.

About this same time a certain Manuzzi,[9] originally a jeweler by trade and then a spy for the State Inquisition, who was unknown to me, made my acquaintance, leading me to believe that he could get me diamonds on credit upon certain conditions which made it necessary for me to receive him where I was living. Looking at a number of books I had lying about, he paused over some manu-

scripts which dealt with magic. Enjoying his astonishment, I showed him those which taught the art of becoming acquainted with all the elemental spirits.[10]

The reader can well imagine that I scoffed at these
books, but I had them. Five or six days later the traitor
came to my house and said that a collector whom he could
not name was ready to give me a thousand zecchini for
my five books; but that he wanted to see them beforehand
to determine if they were genuine. Since he undertook to
return them to me twenty-four hours later, and I really
set no value on them, I entrusted them to him. He did
not fail to return them to me the next day, saying that
the person had found that they were forgeries; but I
learned some years later that he took them to the
Secretary to the State Inquisitors, who thus learned that
I was an arch-magician.

During the same fatal month Signora Memmo,[11] mother
of the Signori Andrea, Bernardo, and Lorenzo, having
taken it into her head that I was leading her sons
toward atheism, approached the old Cavaliere Antonio
Mocenigo,[12] Signor Bragadin's uncle, who bore me a
grudge because he said that I had led his nephew astray
by my cabala. Matters of this nature were under the
jurisdiction of the Holy Office,[13] but since it was difficult to have me locked up in the prisons of the ecclesiastical Inquisition, they decided to take the matter
to the State Inquisitors, who undertook to investigate
my behavior. It was the very thing to ruin me.

Signor Antonio Condulmer, the red[14] State Inquisitor
and my enemy because he was a friend of the Abate
Chiari, seized the opportunity to cast me in the role of
disturber of the public peace. An embassy secretary told
me some years later that an informer, with two witnesses,
had accused me of believing only in the devil. They
testified that when I lost my money at cards, a time at
which all true believers blasphemed God, no one heard
me curse anyone but the devil. I was accused of eating

meat every day, of going only to showy masses, and there were strong reasons for believing that I was a Freemason. To all this they added that I frequented foreign embassies and that since I lived with three patricians it was certain that, knowing everything that was done in the Senate, I revealed it for the large sums of money which I was seen to lose.

All these charges decided the all-powerful tribunal to treat me as an enemy of my country, a conspirator, and an arch-criminal. For two or three weeks several people in whom I could believe told me to take a journey abroad because the tribunal was looking into my affairs. No more was necessary; for the only people who can live happily in Venice are those whose existence is unknown to the formidable tribunal; but I made light of all their advice. Heeding them would have made me uneasy, and I detested uneasiness. I said that since I felt no remorse I could not be guilty, and that not being guilty I had nothing to fear. I was a fool. I reasoned like a free man. What also kept me from thinking seriously about an uncertain misfortune was the real misfortune which weighed on me day and night. I lost every day, I had debts everywhere, I had pawned all my jewels, even my portrait boxes,[15] though I had set those aside, putting them in the care of Signora Manzoni, with whom I had left all my important papers and my love letters. I saw that people were avoiding me. An old Senator told me that the tribunal knew that the young Countess Bonafede had gone insane from the drugs and love philters I had given her. She was still in the hospital and in her fits of madness she never failed to name me and heap curses on me. I must tell my reader this brief story. The young Countess, to whom I had given a few zecchini some days after my return to Venice, thought she could induce me to continue visits which could not but be profitable to her. Pestered by her letters, I had gone to see her a few more times, and I had always left her money; but except for the first time she had never found me willing to give her any proofs of love. At the end of a year she resolved upon a crime of which I could never convict her but of which I had very good reason to believe her guilty.

She wrote me a letter so couched as to persuade me to see her at such-and-such an hour on a matter of great importance. Curiosity took me there at the appointed hour. She at once fell on my neck, saying that the important matter was love. I laughed. I found her prettier than usual and cleaner. She talked of the Fortress of Sant'Andrea,[16] and she stimulated me to such effect that I was ready to satisfy her. I take off my cloak and I ask her if her father is at home; she answers that he has gone out. Needing to visit the privy I go out and, trying to return to her room, I lose my way and enter the room next to it, where I am surprised to see the Count with two villainous-looking men.

"My dear Count," I said, "your daughter the Countess just told me that you were not at home."

"I instructed her to say so myself, because I had business with these people, which I will finish some other day."

I make to leave; but he stops me; he sends away the two men and says he is delighted to see me. He tells me the story of his misfortunes. The State Inquisitors had suspended his pension, he was on the verge of being turned out into the street with his whole family and reduced to begging for charity. He was living in this house, managing by one device or another not to have paid the rent for three years; but that was all over, he was to be evicted. He said that if he only had enough to pay the first three months he would move at night and go into another house. As it is merely a matter of twenty ducati correnti, I take six zecchini from my pocket and give them to him. He embraces me, he weeps for joy, he calls his daughter, he tells her to keep me company, he takes his cloak, and he leaves.

I notice the door between the room I am in and the one I had been in with the girl, and I see that it is ajar.

"Your father," I say, "would have caught me in the act, and it is not hard to guess what he would have done with the two *sbirri* who were with him. The plot is obvious; it is God who saved me."

She denies it, she weeps, she falls on her knees, I do not look at her, I take my cloak, and I flee. I answered no more of her notes and I did not see her again. It was in the summer. The season, passion, hunger, and poverty addled her brains. She went mad to the point that one day at noon she went out stark naked, running about the Campo San Pietro[17] and asking whoever she met and the men who arrested her to take her to my house. This wretched story made the rounds of the city and was a great annoyance to me. The mad girl was locked up and did not recover her reason until five years later; but she only came out of the hospital to go begging for charity through the streets of Venice like all her brothers, except the eldest, whom twelve years later I found serving as a *garzón*[18] at Madrid in the bodyguard of His Catholic Majesty.

It was a year since the thing had happened, but it was dragged up again in the fatal month of July in this year 1755. All these black, heavy clouds gathered above my head to strike me with a thunderbolt. The tribunal ordered Messer Grande[19] to secure my person "alive or dead." This is the formula used in all the warrants for arrest issued by the redoubtable triumvirate. Its slightest order is never promulgated except on pain of death to him who infringes it.

Three or four days before the feast of St. James,[20] whose name I bear, M. M. presented me with several ells of silver lace which I was to wear on the eve of my name day. I went to see her, dressed in my fine coat, and said that I would come again the next day to ask her to lend me some money, since I was at my wits' end where to turn to find any more. She had set aside five hundred zecchini when I had sold her diamonds.

Certain that I would receive the amount on the morrow, I spent the day playing and losing, and that night I lost five hundred zecchini on my word. At daybreak, needing to calm myself, I went to the Erberia.[21] The place called the Erberia is on a quay on the Grand Canal, which crosses the city; and it is so named because it is in fact the market for herbs, fruits, and flowers.

The people who go to walk there so early say that they go for the innocent pleasure of seeing two or three hundred boats arriving with all sorts of greenstuff, fruits of all kinds, and flowers of the season, which the inhabitants of the small islands which surround the capital bring there and sell cheaply to the wholesalers, who sell them at a profit to middlemen, who sell them at a high price to retailers, who distribute them at a still higher price all over the city. But it is not true that the youth of Venice go to the Erberia before sunrise to enjoy that pleasure; it is only their pretext.

Those who go there are men and light women who have spent the night at casinos or inns or gardens, devoting themselves to the pleasures of the table or to the furies of gaming. The fashion of going to walk there proves that a nation can change its character.

The Venetians of an earlier age, as secretive in their love affairs as they were in their politics, are blotted from memory by the moderns, whose style is to make a secret of nothing. The men who go there with women want to arouse the envy of their fellows by advertising their conquests. The men who go alone try to make discoveries or to occasion jealousies; and the women go there more to be seen than to see. They are perfectly content to let everyone know that they are no prudes. Smartness is excluded by the havoc which has been wreaked upon dress. On the contrary, it seems that the women wish to display themselves as votaries of disorder, and that they want whoever sees them to draw conclusions from it. The men who escort them are expected to advertise the boredom inspired in them by a willingness too often repeated and to appear indifferent to anyone's guessing that the wrecks of an earlier smartness which their beauties flaunt are the proofs of their success. Everyone who walks there is expected to look tired out and to show every sign of needing to go to bed.

After strolling for half an hour I go to my casino, where everyone should still be in bed. I take the key from my pocket; but I did not need it. I see that the door stands open and, what is more, the lock has been broken. I go upstairs and I find all the family up and I hear my hostess lamenting. She tells me that Messer Grande with a band of *sbirri* had entered her house by force and turned everything upside down, saying that he was looking for a trunk full of salt, which was strictly contraband. He knew that the trunk had been brought in the evening before. She said that a trunk had in fact been unloaded from a gondola but that it belonged to Count S., who had nothing in it but his clothes. Messer Grande had seen it and had left without saying anything. He had also searched my room. She demanded reparation, and seeing that she was justified I promised to speak to Signor Bragadin about it that day; and I went to bed; but the insult which had been offered the house stuck in my gorge and I could sleep only three or four hours.

I go to Signor Bragadin's, I tell him the whole story, and I demand revenge. I forcibly put to him all the reasons my honest hostess had for insisting on a reparation proportionate to the offense, since the laws guaranteed the peace of every family whose conduct was irreproachable. After thus delivering myself to him, my two other friends being present, I saw all three of them sunk in thought. The wise old man said that he would answer me after dinner.

At dinner, during which De La Haye never said a word to me, I saw that they were all sad. I could only attribute the reason for it to their friendship for me. The intimacy between these three respectable and prominent persons and myself had always been the talk of the whole city. It was concluded that the thing could not be natural; hence it could only be the result of sorcery. They were pious in the highest degree, and there was not a greater libertine in Venice than I. Virtue, people said, could be indulgent to vice, but could not love it.

After dinner Signor Bragadin took me to his study with my two other friends, whose presence was never unwelcome. He said with the greatest calmness that instead of thinking of obtaining revenge for the insult Messer Grande had offered the house in which I lived, I should be thinking of escaping to a place of safety.

"The trunk filled with salt," he said, "is only a pretext. It was you whom they wanted and whom they thought they would find. Your angel made them miss you; run! I was a State Inquisitor for eight months,[22] and I know the kind of arrests the tribunal orders made. Doors are not broken down to seize a box of salt. It is also possible that they missed you on purpose. Believe me, my dear son—leave at once for Fusina and from there post day and night to Florence and stay there until I write you that you can come back. Have four rowers put to my gondola and go. If you have no money I will give you a hundred zecchini for the present. Prudence demands that you go."

I answer that since I know I am not guilty of anything I could not fear the tribunal and that consequently I could not follow his advice, though I saw that it was very prudent. He answers that the tribunal of the State

Inquisitors could find me guilty of crimes of which I had no knowledge. He urged me to ask my oracle whether I should follow his advice or not, and I declined, saying that I asked only when I was in doubt. As my final argument I put it to him that if I fled I should be showing a fear which would declare me guilty, for an innocent person, having no remorse, can have no fears either.

"If silence," I said, "is the soul of that great tribunal, you can never know after I leave whether I was right or wrong to go. The same prudence which, according to Your Excellency, orders me to go will also prevent me from returning. Must I then take an eternal leave of my country?"

He then tried to persuade me to sleep, at least that night, in my apartment in the palace, and I am still ashamed that I refused him the favor.

Constables cannot enter the palace of a patrician without a formal order from the tribunal; but such an order is never given.

I said that the precaution of sleeping in his palace would safeguard me only during the night and that I could be found anywhere during the day if the order was out to arrest me.

"They have the power if they want to use it," I said; "but it is not my part to be afraid."

The good old man then touched me by saying that perhaps we should not see each other again; and I begged him not to make me sad. In answer he thought for a moment, then smiled and embraced me, quoting the Stoic maxim, *Fata viam inveniunt* ("Destiny finds the way").[23]

I embraced him in tears, and I left. But his prediction was fulfilled. I did not see him again. He died eleven years later. I set out from the palace without the least shadow of fear in my soul, but in great distress because of my debts. I did not have the heart to go to

Murano to ask M. M. for the five hundred zecchini I should have paid immediately to the man who had won them from me the evening before; I preferred to go and ask him to wait for a week. After that I went home and, after consoling my hostess as well as I could and embracing her daughter, I went to bed. It was nightfall on the 25th of July 1755.

The next morning at daybreak Messer Grande entered my room. To wake, to see him, and to hear him ask if I was Giacomo Casanova took no more than the first moment. As soon as I answered that I was the person he had named, he ordered me to give him whatever papers I had, whether written by me or by anyone else, to dress, and to go with him. I having asked him by whose authority he gave me the order, he answered that it was by the authority of the tribunal.

CHAPTER XII
Under the Leads. Earthquake.

THE WORD "tribunal" petrified my soul, leaving me only the physical ability to obey him. My desk was open; all my papers were on the table at which I wrote, I told him he could take them; he filled a bag which one of his men brought him, and he said I must also surrender certain bound manuscripts which there was reason to suppose I possessed; I showed him where they were, and then I saw it: the jeweler Manuzzi had been the infamous spy who had accused me of having these books when he had gained entrance to my house, leading me to believe that he could arrange for me to buy diamonds and, as I said, that he could get me a purchaser for the books; they were the *Key of Solomon,*[1] the *Zecorben,*[2] a *Picatrix,*[3] a complete treatise on the planetary hours[4] favorable to making the necessary perfumes and conjurations for conversing with demons of all classes. Those who knew that I had these books thought I was a magician, and it rather pleased me. Messer Grande

Notebook with Pencil Case

Innocence Conquered

also took the books I had on my night table: Ariosto, Horace, Petrarch, the *Philosophe militaire*[5] in manuscript, which Mathilde[6] had given me, the *Portier des Chartreux*, and the little book of lubricious postures by Aretino which Manuzzi had also reported, for Messer Grande asked me for it too. The spy Manuzzi looked like an honest man, a necessary quality in his trade; his son made a fortune in Poland by marrying an Opeska[7] whom he did away with, or so they say, for I know nothing about it and even do not believe it, though I do know that he was capable of it.

While Messer Grande thus made a harvest of my manuscripts, my books, and my letters, I automatically got dressed, neither rapidly nor slowly; I made my toilet, I shaved, C. D.[8] dressed my hair, I put on a shirt with a lace ruff and my fine coat, all without thinking what I was doing and without saying a word, even as Messer Grande, who never took his eyes off me, did not dare to object to my dressing as though I were going to a wedding.

When I left my room I was surprised to find thirty or forty constables in the drawing room. They had done me the honor to think so many were needed to secure my person, whereas according to the axiom *ne Hercules quidem contra duos* ("not even Hercules against two"),[9] only two were necessary. It is strange that in London, where everyone is brave, only one man is used to arrest another, and that in my dear country, where people are cowards, thirty are sent. The reason may be that the coward who is forced to become an assailant must be more afraid than the man assailed, and the latter for that very reason may become brave; and in fact in Venice one often sees one man defend himself against twenty *sbirri* and get away after giving them a beating. In Paris I helped a friend of mine escape from forty bumbailiffs, whom we put to flight.

Messer Grande ordered me into a gondola, where he

sat down beside me, keeping only four men and sending
the rest away. Arrived at his headquarters, he locked
me into a room after offering me coffee, which I refused.
I spent four hours there during all of which I slept,
waking every quarter of an hour to make water—a
very strange phenomenon, for I had never suffered
from strangury, the heat was excessive, and I had not
supped; nevertheless I filled two large chamber pots
with urine. It had been my experience on other occasions
that surprise caused by an act of oppression produced
the effect of a strong narcotic on me, but it was only
now that I learned that it is highly diuretic. I leave it
to the physicians. I had a good laugh in Prague, where
I published my *Flight from the Leads*[10] six years ago,
when I learned that the fine ladies considered my account of the phenomenon a piece of swinishness which
I might well have omitted. I would perhaps have omitted
it in talking to a lady; but the public is not a lady, and
I like to be instructive. Furthermore it is not swinishness; there is nothing dirty or foul-smelling about it
despite the fact that we have it in common with swine,
just as we have eating and drinking, which no one has
ever dubbed swinishness.

It is likely that at the same time that my terrified
mind was reduced to displaying its weakness by the
collapse of its thinking faculty, my body, too, as if it
were in a wine press, had to expel a good part of the
fluids which, in their continual circulation, activate our
power to think; and that is how a terrifying surprise
can bring on sudden death and—God preserve us!—
send us to Paradise, for it can drive our soul from our
blood.

When the Terza[11] bell rang, the chief constable entered and said he had orders to put me "under the
Leads."[12] I followed him. We got into another gondola and, after taking a long way around through small
canals, we entered the Grand Canal and disembarked

at the Quay of the Prisons.[13] After going up several flights of stairs we crossed a high enclosed bridge[14] which provides the communication between the prisons and the Doge's Palace over the canal called the Rio del Palazzo.[15] Beyond this bridge we walked the length of a gallery, entered a room, then another, where he presented me to a man dressed in the robe of a patrician, who, after looking at me, said:

"*È quello; mettetelo in deposito.*" ("That is he; put him away.")

This personage was the Secretary to Their Excellencies the Inquisitors, the Circospetto[16] Domenico Cavalli, who apparently felt ashamed to speak Venetian in my presence, for he pronounced judgment on me in Tuscan. Messer Grande then turned me over to the warden of the Leads, who was there holding a bunch of keys and who, followed by two constables, made me go up two small flights of stairs, proceed through a gallery, then another separated from it by a locked door, then still another, at the end of which he used another key to open a door through which I entered a large, ugly, dirty garret, twelve yards long by two wide, badly lighted by a high dormer. I supposed this garret was my prison, but I was mistaken. The man, who was the jailer, took a thick key, he opened a heavy door lined with iron, three and a half feet high and with a round hole eight inches in diameter in the center of it, and ordered me to enter just as I was looking attentively at an iron mechanism which was fastened to the strong wall with nails and had the shape of a horseshoe; it was an inch thick and had a diameter of five inches from one of its parallel ends to the other. I was wondering what it could be when he said with a smile:

"I see, Signore, that you are trying to guess what this machine is for, and I can tell you. When Their Eminences order someone strangled, he is made to sit on a stool with his back to this collar and his head is placed so that the collar goes round half of his neck. The two ends of a skein of silk which goes round the other half of it pass through this hole leading to a winch to which they are fastened and a man turns it until the patient has rendered up his soul to Our Lord, for his confessor never leaves him—praise be to God!—until he is dead.''

"It is most ingenious, and I imagine, Signore, that it is you who have the honor of turning the winch.''

He did not answer. My height being five feet nine inches, I stooped low to enter; and he locked me in. Hearing him ask me through the grating what I wanted to eat, I answered that I had not yet thought about it. He went away, locking all his doors again.

Overwhelmed and bewildered, I put my elbows on the sill of the grating. It was two feet in all directions, crossed by six iron bars an inch thick which formed sixteen openings five inches square. It would have lighted my cell well enough if one of the main roof timbers, a square beam a foot and a half thick and entering the wall below the dormer, which was diagonally across from me, had not cut off what light came into the garret. Having made the round of this terrible prison, keeping my head down for it was only five and a half feet high, I found, chiefly by groping, that it formed three quarters of a square twelve feet by twelve. The quarter next to the missing one was to all intents and purposes an alcove large enough to contain a bed, but I found neither a bed nor a chair nor a table nor any kind of furniture except a bucket for the needs of nature and a board fastened to the wall, one foot wide and four feet above the floor. On it I put my beautiful floss-silk cloak, my fine coat which had started its life so badly, and my hat trimmed with Spanish point lace and a white feather. The heat was extreme. In my astonishment nature led me to the grating, the only place where I could rest leaning on my elbows; I could not see the dormer, but I saw the light which illuminated the garret and rats as big as rabbits which were walking about. These hideous animals, whose sight I loathed, came directly under my grating without showing the least sign of fear. I quickly drew the inner blind over the round hole in the center of the door, for a visit from them would have frozen my blood. Sunk in the deepest reverie, my arms still crossed on the sill, I spent eight hours there motionless, silent, and never leaving my post.

When twenty-one o'clock[17] struck, I began to feel uneasy because I saw no one appearing, not even to find out if I wanted to eat, not even to bring me a bed, a chair, or at least bread and water. I had no appetite, but I thought my jailers should not know it; never in my life had I had such a bitter taste in my mouth; yet I felt certain that before the day ended someone would appear; but when I heard twenty-four o'clock strike I succumbed to something very like madness, howling, stamping my feet, cursing, and accompanying all this useless noise which my strange situation drove me to make with loud cries. After half an hour of this exercise in fury, seeing no one come, with not the slightest sign to make me imagine that anyone could have heard my ravings, and shrouded in darkness, I closed the grating, fearing that the rats would jump into the cell. I threw myself at full length on the floor after wrapping my hair in a handkerchief. Such a pitiless desertion seemed to me unthinkable, even if I had been sentenced to death. My consideration of what I could have done to deserve treatment so cruel could continue no longer than a minute, for I found no cause for arresting me. As a great libertine, a bold talker, a man who thought of nothing but enjoying life I could not find myself guilty, but seeing that I was nevertheless treated as such, I spare my reader all that rage and indignation and despair made me say and think against the horrible despotism which was oppressing me. Yet my anger and the grief

which preyed on me and the hard floor on which I lay
did not keep me from falling asleep; my constitution
needed sleep; and when a person is young and healthy
his constitution can satisfy its need without his giving
it any thought.

The midnight bell woke me. That is a terrible awaken-
ing which brings regret for the nothingness or the
illusions of sleep. I could not believe that I had spent
three hours insensible of any discomfort. Not changing
my position but still lying as I was on my left side, I
put out my right arm to get my handkerchief, which
my memory assured me I had placed there. As I groped
along with my hand—God! what a surprise when I find
another hand as cold as ice! Terror electrified me from
head to foot and every one of my hairs stood on end.
Never in my life was I seized with such fear, and I had
never thought I was subject to it. I certainly spent
three or four minutes not only motionless but unable to
think. Recovering a little, I allowed myself the relief of
believing that what I had touched was only a figment
of my imagination; in this conviction I again stretch out
my arm to the same spot and I find the same hand, which,
frozen with horror and giving a piercing shriek, I grasp
and drop, drawing back my arm. I shudder; but regain-
ing control over my mind, I decide that while I was
asleep a corpse had been placed near me; for I was
certain that when I lay down on the floor nothing had
been there. I immediately imagine the body of some
innocent wretch, perhaps one of my friends, who had
been strangled and laid beside me so that when I woke
I should find an example of the fate which I must expect. The thought infuriates me; for the third time I
extend my arm to the hand, I grasp it, and at the same
moment get up, intending to pull the corpse toward me
and so ascertain the fact in all its atrocity; but as I
try to raise myself on my left elbow the same cold hand
which I am holding comes to life, draws away, and, to

my great surprise, I instantly realize that the hand in my right hand is none other than my left, which, numbed and stiffened, had lost motion, feeling, and warmth, the effect of the soft, yielding, cozy bed on which my poor self was lying.

The incident, though comic, did not cheer me. On the contrary it gave me cause to make the darkest reflections. I realized that I was in a place where if the false seemed true, realities must seem dreams; where the understanding must lose half of its privileges; where a distorted imagination must make reason the victim either of chimerical hopes or terrible despair. I at once put myself on guard against anything of that nature; and at the age of thirty years I for the first time in my life turned for help to philosophy, all the germs of which were in my soul and which I had never before had occasion either to value or to employ. I believe that the great majority of men die without ever having thought. I continued to sit where I was until eight o'clock;[18] the half-light of the new day appeared; the sun should rise at quarter past nine; I longed to see the day begin; a presentiment which I thought infallible assured me that I should be sent home; I was burning with desires for revenge which I did not conceal from myself. I seemed to be leading the people to exterminate the government and massacre the aristocrats; everything was to be brought to dust; I was not satisfied to leave the slaughter of my oppressors to executioners, it was I myself who should massacre them. Such is man: he does not suspect that what speaks such words in him is not his reason but his greatest enemy, anger.

I waited less time than I was prepared to wait; and that went some way toward calming my fury. At half past eight the profound silence of the place, the Hell of living humanity, was broken by the squeak of the bolts in the vestibules of the corridors which had to be traversed to reach my cell. I saw the jailer in front of my grating asking me if I had had "time to think about what I wanted to eat." One is lucky when the insolence of a villain assumes the mask of raillery. I answered that I wanted a rice soup, boiled beef, a roast, bread, water, and wine. I saw that the churl was surprised not to hear the lamentations he expected. He went away; but a quarter of an hour later he came back to say that he was astonished that I did not ask for a bed and whatever I needed because, said he,

"If you flatter yourself that you have been put here only for one night, you are mistaken."

"Then bring me everything you think I shall need."

"Where am I to go for it? Here is a pencil and paper. Write it all down."

I wrote him instructions where to go to get me a bed, shirts, stockings, dressing gown, slippers, nightcaps, an armchair, a table, combs, mirrors, razors, handkerchiefs, the books which Messer Grande had taken from me, ink and pens and paper. When I read him the list, for the rascal could not read, he told me to cross out books, ink, paper, mirror, razor, for they were all forbidden under the Leads by the regulations, and he asked me for money to buy my dinner. I had three zecchini and I gave him one of them. He left the garret and I heard him set off an hour later. During the hour, as I learned afterward, he waited on seven other prisoners who were confined up there in cells at a distance from one another to prevent any communication.

Toward noon the jailer appeared, followed by five constables appointed to serve the state prisoners. He opened my cell to bring in the furniture I had ordered and my dinner. The bed was put in the alcove, my dinner was set out on a small table. My table service consisted of an ivory spoon which he had bought with my money, knife and fork being forbidden as were all metal implements.

"Order what you want to eat tomorrow," he said,

"for I can only come here once a day at dawn. The most illustrious Secretary ordered me to tell you that he will send you suitable books, since those you want are forbidden."

"Thank him for his kindness in putting me in a cell by myself."

"I will give him your message, but you would do well not to make such jokes."

"I am not joking, for it is better, I think, to be alone than with the criminals who must be here."

"What, Signore? Criminals? I should resent that very much. There are only respectable people here, who, however, have to be sequestered from society for reasons which only Their Excellencies know. You have been put in a cell alone to increase your punishment, and you want me to convey your thanks for it?"

"I did not know that."

The ignoramus was right, as I had learned only too well a few days later. I discovered that a man shut up in solitude and deprived of any possibility of occupying himself, alone in an almost dark place, where he does not and cannot see anything except, once a day, the person who brings him food, and in which he cannot walk upright, is the most wretched of mortals. He longs for Hell, if he believes in it, only to have companionship. Confined there, I reached the point of longing for the company of a murderer, a maniac, a man with some stinking disease, a bear. Solitude under the Leads drives one to despair; but to know it one must have experienced it. If the prisoner is a man of letters, give him a writing desk and paper and his wretchedness will decrease by nine tenths.

After the jailer left I put the table near the hole to get a little light, and I sat down to dine by the glimmer which came from the skylight; but I could swallow only a little soup. Having had nothing to eat for forty-five hours, it is no wonder if I was ill. I spent the day in my armchair, without accesses of fury, longing for the morrow and preparing my mind to read the books which had been so graciously promised me. I passed a sleepless night to the disagreeable noise the rats made in the garret and in company with the clock of San Marco, which, when it struck the hours, seemed to be in the room with me. A kind of torture of which few of my readers will have any knowledge caused me intolerable pain: it was a million fleas romping all over my body, avid for my blood and my skin, and piercing them with a voracity of which I had no conception; the accursed insects gave me convulsions, made my muscles contract spasmodically, and poisoned my blood.

At the first light of dawn Lorenzo[19] (for such was the jailer's name) had my bed made and the place swept and dusted, and one of his *sbirri* brought me water to wash in. I wanted to go out into the garret, but Lorenzo told me it was not allowed. He gave me two thick books, which I refrained from opening, not being certain that I could control a first burst of indignation which they might arouse in me and which the spy would have reported. After leaving me my victuals and cutting two lemons for me, he went away.

After quickly eating my soup to eat it hot, I put one book under the light which reached the hole from the dormer, and I saw that I could easily read it. I look at the title, and I see *La Cité mystique de Soeur Marie de Jésus appelée d'Agreda*.[20] I had never heard of it. The second book was by a Jesuit whose name I have forgotten.[21] He instituted a new special adoration directed to the heart of Our Lord Jesus Christ. Of all the human parts of our divine mediator, it was the heart which, according to the author, should be especially adored— the strange idea of an ignorant fool, reading the first page of whose book was enough to revolt me, for I thought that the heart was an organ no worthier than the lungs. The *Cité mystique* interested me a little.

I read everything that the extravagance of the heated imagination of an extremely devout Spanish virgin, given to melancholy, shut up in a convent, and guided by ignorant and flattering confessors, could bring forth. All these chimerical and monstrous visions were adorned with the name of revelations; in love with the Holy Virgin and admitted to her intimate friendship, she had received a command from God himself to write the life of his divine mother; the information which she needed and which no one could have read anywhere had been supplied her by the Holy Spirit.

So she began the history of the mother of God not at her birth but at the moment of her most immaculate conception in the womb of St. Anne. This Sister María of Agreda was the Superior of a convent of Franciscan nuns[22] which she founded in her own house. After narrating in detail all that her great heroine did during the nine months before her birth, she said that at the age of three years she was sweeping her house, aided by nine hundred servants, all angels, whom God had bestowed on her, under the personal command of their own prince, Michael, who came and went between her and God and God and her on their reciprocal embassies. What is striking in this book is the certainty which is borne in upon the judicious reader that there is nothing in it which the more than fanatical author could think she had invented; invention cannot go so far; everything is told in perfect good faith; they are the visions of a sublimated cerebellum which, without a trace of pride, drunk with God, believes that it reveals nothing but what the Holy Spirit dictates to it. The book was printed with the permission of the Inquisition. I could not get over my astonishment. Far from increasing or exciting in my mind a fervor or a zeal for religion, the work tempted me to regard as fabulous all that we have in the way of mysticism and of dogma as well.

The nature of the book entails certain consequences.

A reader with a mind more susceptible to the miraculous and fonder of it than mine is in danger, when he reads it, of becoming a visionary and a maniacal scribbler like the virgin herself. The need to occupy myself with something led me to spend a week over this masterpiece of hyperexalted invention; I said nothing about it to the stupid jailer; but I could bear no more. As soon as I fell asleep I was aware of the plague with which Sister d'Agreda had infected my mind, weakened by melancholy and bad food. My extravagant dreams made me laugh when I recalled them in my waking hours, for I wanted to write them down, and if I had had writing materials I should perhaps have produced a work up there even madder than the one Signor Cavalli had sent me. From that time on I saw how mistaken they are who attribute a certain strength to the human mind; its strength is only relative, and a man who studied himself thoroughly would find nothing in him but weakness. I saw that though men do not often go mad, it is nevertheless true that the thing is easy. Our reason is like gunpowder, which, though very easy to ignite, nevertheless never catches fire unless fire is applied to it; or like a drinking glass, which never breaks unless it is broken. The Spanish woman's book is just what is needed to drive a man mad; but for the poison to take effect, he must be confined under the Leads alone and deprived of any other occupation.

In the month of November 1767, when I was traveling from Pamplona to Madrid, my driver Andrea Capello stopped for dinner in a town in Old Castille which was so gloomy and ugly that I felt curious to know its name. Oh, how I laughed when I was told that it was Agreda![23] "So it was here," I said to myself, "that the brain of that holy madwoman gave birth to her masterpiece, which, if I had never had anything to do with Signor Cavalli, I should never have known!" An old priest, who conceived the highest esteem for me as soon as I ques-

. tioned him about the life of that fortunate friend of the mother of her Creator, showed me the very place where she had written, assuring me that the father, mother, and sister of the divine biographer had all been saints. He told me, and it was true, that Spain had solicited Rome for her canonization together with that of the Venerable Palafox.[24] It was perhaps this mystical city[25] which gave Father Malagrida[26] the desire to write the life of St. Anne, which the Holy Spirit also dictated to him; but the poor Jesuit had to suffer martyrdom for it—all the more reason for securing his canonization when the Society revives and recovers its ancient splendor.[27]

At the end of nine or ten days I had no more money. Lorenzo asked me where he should go for some, and I laconically answered: "Nowhere." What offended this ignorant, curious, and talkative man was my silence. The next morning he told me that the tribunal granted me fifty soldi[28] a day, which he was to disburse and of which he would render me an account each month, and that he would use what I had left over as I instructed him. I told him to bring me the *Gazette de Leyde*[29] twice a week and he answered that it was not allowed. Seventy-five lire a month were more than I needed, since I could no longer eat. The extreme heat and the inanition brought on by lack of food had enervated me. It was the season of the pestilential dog days; the power of the sun's rays striking on the lead plates which covered the roof of my prison kept me as it were in a sweating room; the perspiration which oozed from my epidermis streamed onto the floor to left and right of my armchair, in which I sat stark naked.

Not having once gone to stool during the two weeks I had been there, I went and I thought I should die from pains of which I had no conception. They came from internal hemorrhoids. It was there that I acquired that tormenting malady, from which I have never recovered;

this keepsake, which now and again reminds me of its source, does nothing to make me cherish it. If natural philosophy does not teach us remedies to cure a number of diseases, it at least provides us with infallible means of acquiring them. However, my malady gained me compliments in Russia; it is so greatly esteemed that I did not dare to complain of it when I was there ten years later. The same thing happened to me in Constantinople, when I had a cold in the head and complained of it in the presence of a Turk; he said nothing, but he thought to himself that such a dog as I was unworthy of it.

On the same day violent chills showed me that I was attacked by fever. I stayed in bed and the next morning I said nothing about it; but on the day after, when Lorenzo found all my food still untouched, he asked me how I was.

"Perfectly well."

"No, Signore, for you do not eat. You are ill, and you will see the magnanimity of the tribunal, which will supply you with a physician, medicines, medicaments, and a surgeon, all for nothing."

Three hours later I saw him without any of his henchmen, carrying a candle, and preceding a grave personage whose imposing physiognomy informed me that he was a physician.[30] I was at the height of the fever which had been burning my blood for three days. He questioned me, and I answered that to my confessor and my physician I never spoke except without a witness. He told Lorenzo to leave. Lorenzo refused, and the learned doctor left, saying that I was in danger of death. It was what I wanted. I also felt some satisfaction in doing something which would show the pitiless tyrants who had confined me there the inhumanity of their proceedings.

Four hours later I heard the noise of bolts. The physician came in, holding a branched candlestick, and Lorenzo remained outside. I was in an extreme languor, which I found truly restful. A person who is really ill is free from the torment of boredom. I was delighted to see the villain left outside, for I could not bear him since he had explained the iron collar to me.

In a short quarter of an hour I told the learned doctor everything.

"If you want to recover your health," he said, "you must banish grief."

"Write me a prescription for that and take it to the only apothecary who can fill it. Signor Cavalli is the bad physician who gave me the *Heart of Jesus* and the *Mystical City*."

"Those two drugs may well have given you your fever and hemorrhoids; I will not abandon you."

He left after himself making me a large quantity of lemonade, which he asked me to drink frequently. I spent the night in exhaustion, dreaming of mystical extravagances.

The next morning, two hours later than usual, I saw him with Lorenzo and a surgeon who bled me. He left me a medicine which he told me to take in the evening and a bottle of broth.

"I have obtained permission," he said, "to have you moved to the garret, where it is not as hot as it is here, where the atmosphere is stifling."

"I decline the favor, for I loathe the rats, of whose existence you are not aware, and which will certainly get into my bed."

"How distressing! I told Signor Cavalli that he came very near to killing you with his books, and he said to return them to him and he would give you Boethius[31] instead. Here it is."

"He is an author who is superior to Seneca, and I thank you."

"I leave you a syringe and barley water; keep yourself amused with enemas."

He made me four visits and he pulled me through;

my appetite came back. By the beginning of September I was in good health. My only real afflictions were the extreme heat, the fleas, and the boredom, for I could not always read Boethius. Lorenzo told me that I had permission to leave my cell to bathe while I was waiting for my bed to be made and the place to be swept, the only way to reduce the number of the fleas which were eating me alive. It was a respite. I took advantage of the eight or ten minutes to walk energetically; the terrified rats did not dare to show themselves. The same day on which Lorenzo allowed me this relief, he gave me an accounting of my money. He was left owing me twenty-five or thirty lire, which I was not allowed to put in my purse. I let him keep them, telling him to have masses said for me. He thanked me as fulsomely as if he himself were the priest who was to celebrate them. I did the same every month, and I never saw any receipts from a priest; it is certain that the least injustice Lorenzo could do me was to appropriate my money and say my masses himself in some tavern.

I went on in this way, persuading myself every day that I should be sent home; I never went to bed without a sort of certainty that the next day someone would come to tell me that I was free; but when, always frustrated in my hope, I began thinking that a fixed term of imprisonment might have been meted out to me, I decided that it could not end later than October 1st, the day on which the reign of the new Inquisitors[32] began. I accordingly concluded that my imprisonment would continue as long as the present Inquisitors remained in office, and that was why I had never seen the Secretary, who, if the matter had not been decided, would come to examine me, convict me of my crimes, and pronounce my sentence:[33] I thought it could not fail to be so because it was only natural—a poor argument under the Leads, where nothing is done according to nature. I imagined that the Inquisitors must have recognized their injustice in my innocence and hence were keeping me there only as a matter of form and for the sake of their reputation, but that they would certainly have to set me free when their reign ended. I even felt that I could forgive them and forget the wrong they had done me. "How," I said to myself, "could they leave me here at the disposition of their successors, to whom they could have given no sufficient grounds for condemning me?" I thought it impossible that they could condemn me and write my sentence without communicating it to me and telling me the reason for it. That the right was on my side seemed to me incontestable, and I argued accordingly; but my argument had no currency in respect to the rules of a tribunal which differs from the legal tribunals of every government on earth. When this tribunal proceeds against a delinquent, it is already sure that he is such; so what need has it to talk with him? And when it has condemned him, what need is there to give him the bad news of his sentence? His consent is not necessary; it is better, they say, to let him hope; if he is told, that will not shorten his stay in prison by one hour; the wise man tells his business to no one; and the only business of the Venetian tribunal is to judge and to sentence; the guilty person is a machine which does not need to take any part in the business in order to co-operate in it; he is a nail which, to go into a plank, needs only to be hammered.

I knew something about these practices of the colossus under whose feet I lay; but there are things on earth which no one can ever say he knows well until he has experienced them. If among my readers there is one to whom these rules appear unjust, I forgive him because, to tell the truth, they certainly appear to be so; but he should know that, once established, they become necessary, for a tribunal of this sort could not continue to exist except by virtue of them. They who keep them in force are Senators chosen from among those who are best qualified and are known as the most virtuous.[34]

On September 30th I spent the night unable to sleep; I was impatient to see the new day appear, for I felt sure that I should be set free The pitiless men who had put me there had ended their reign. But day appeared, Lorenzo came with my food, and announced nothing new. I spent five or six days in rage and despair. I believed it was possible that, for reasons which I could not guess, it had been decided to keep me there the rest of my life. This terrible idea made me laugh, for I knew that I had the power to remain there only a very short time, once I had made up my mind to gain freedom at the risk of my life. Either they would kill me or I would succeed in it.

Deliberata morte ferocior ("Become more implacable by resolving to die"),[35] at the beginning of November I formed the plan of escaping by force from a place where I was being kept by force; it became my only thought. I began looking for, inventing, studying a hundred ways to succeed in an enterprise which many might have attempted before me but in which no one had succeeded.

During these same days a strange event showed me the pitiable state of mind to which I was reduced. I was standing in the garret looking up at the dormer; I also saw the very thick beam. Lorenzo was coming out of my cell with two of his men when I saw the enormous beam not quiver but turn toward its right side and then at once resume its original position by a slow, uninterrupted movement in the opposite direction; feeling at the same time that I had lost my balance, I was convinced that it was an earthquake shock, and the astonished constables said the same; delighted by the phenomenon, I did not say a word. Four or five seconds later the movement occurred again, and I could not keep from uttering these words: *"Un altra, un altra, gran*

Dio, ma più forte" ("Another, another, great God, but stronger"). The constables, terrified by what they considered the impiousness of a desperate and blaspheming madman, fled in horror. Examining myself afterward, I saw that I had counted it among possible events that the Doge's Palace could collapse and at the same time I could regain my freedom: the falling palace was to deposit me safe, sound, and free on the beautiful pavement of the Piazza San Marco. It was thus that I began to go mad. The shock came from the same earthquake which flattened Lisbon about the same time.[36]

CHAPTER XIII

*Various occurrences. Companions. I prepare
my escape. Change of cell.*

TO PREPARE my reader to understand my escape
from such a place I must describe the premises to him.
These prison cells, intended to hold state criminals, are
actually in what is known as the garret of the Doge's
Palace. The fact that its roof is covered not with tiles or
bricks but with lead plates three feet square and a line[1]
thick gives the name of the Leads to the prisons themselves. The only entrance to them is through the palace
doors or through the prison building, by which I was
brought in, crossing the Bridge of Sighs which I have already mentioned. One can go up to the prisons only by
passing through the room in which the State Inquisitors
meet; their secretary alone has the key to it, which the
warden of the Leads has to return to him as soon as he has
finished attending to the prisoners early in the morning.
This is done at daybreak, because later the constables
coming and going would be too much seen in a place filled
with all the people who have business with the heads of

the Council of Ten, who meet every day in the adjoining room known as the Bussola,[2] through which the constables must necessarily pass.

The prison cells are under the roof, and on opposite sides of the palace. Three are to the west, one of which was mine, and four are to the east. The gutter along the roof over those to the west gives onto the palace courtyard; the gutter to the east is perpendicularly above the canal called the Rio del Palazzo. On that side the cells are very light and one can stand upright in them, advantages lacking to the prison in which I was and which was called *il trave*.* The floor of my cell was directly above the ceiling of the Inquisitors' room, in which they usually assemble only at night after the daily session of the Council of Ten, of which all three of them are members.

Knowing all this as I did and having a perfect conception of the topography of the premises, the only way I could think of to escape which had any chance of succeeding was to make a hole in the floor of my prison; but I should need to have instruments, a difficult matter in a place where all outside communication was forbidden and neither visits nor corresponding with anyone were allowed. Having no money to bribe a constable, I could not count on any of them. Supposing that the jailer and the two underlings who accompanied him were obliging enough to let me strangle them, for I had no arms, another constable was stationed at the door of the locked gallery, which he opened only when one of his fellows who wanted to go out gave him the password. The one thought in my mind was to escape, and not finding the way in Boethius I stopped reading him. I thought of it constantly because I was certain that I should find it only by thinking of it. I have always believed that

---

* The word means beam. It was the enormous beam which deprived my cell of light. (C.'s note.)

when a man takes it into his head to accomplish some
project and pursues it to the exclusion of anything else,
he must succeed in it despite all difficulties; such a man
will become the Grand Vizier, he will become Pope, he
will overthrow a monarchy, provided that he begins
early; for the man who has reached the age which Fortune disdains no longer succeeds in any undertaking, and
without her help one can hope for nothing. The thing
is to count on her and at the same time to defy her
reverses. But this is one of the most difficult of political calculations.

In the middle of November Lorenzo told me that
Messer Grande had taken a prisoner and that Secretary
Businello,[3] the new Circospetto, had ordered him to put
him in the worst of all the cells, so he was going to put
him with me; he assured me that when he had explained
to him that I had regarded having been put by myself as
a favor he had answered that I must have become wiser
in the four months I had been there. The news did not
trouble me nor was I displeased to learn of the change
of Secretary. This Signor Pietro Businello was a worthy
man whom I had known in Paris when he was there on
his way to London as Resident for the Republic.

An hour after the Terza bell I heard the screech of
the bolts and I saw Lorenzo followed by two constables
holding a handcuffed young man who was weeping. They
locked him into my "home" and went off without even
a word. I was on my bed, where he could not see me. His
surprise amused me. Having the luck to be five feet tall,
he stood upright, looking closely at my armchair, which
he thought was for his own use. He sees the Boethius on
the sill of the grating. He dries his tears, opens it, and
disdainfully throws it down, perhaps disgusted by seeing
it was in Latin. He goes to the left side of the cell and
is amazed to find clothes; he approaches the alcove; he
thinks he sees a bed; he puts out his hand, he touches

me, and he begs my pardon; I tell him to sit down; and our acquaintance is made.

"Who are you?" I ask him.

"I am from Vicenza, my name is Maggiorin,[4] my father is coachman to the Poggiana[5] family, he kept me in school until I was eleven, where I learned to read and write, then I went to work in a wigmaker's shop, where I learned to dress hair very well. I became valet to Count XX. Two years later his only daughter came home from the convent and, dressing her hair, I fell in love with her as she did with me. After exchanging promises of marriage we surrendered to nature, and the Countess, who is eighteen as I am, became pregnant. A very devout maid discovered our relationship and the Countess's pregnancy and told her that her conscience obliged her to reveal all to her father; but my wife was able to make her keep quiet by assuring her that within a week she would have her confessor tell him the whole story. But instead of going to confession she warned me and we resolved to leave. She took a good sum of money and some diamonds which had belonged to her late mother, and we were to set off that night for Milan; but after dinner the Count sent for me, and, handing me a letter, ordered me to leave at once to deliver it directly to the person here in Venice to whom it was addressed. He spoke so kindly and calmly that I could never have suspected what happened to me. I went to fetch my cloak and in passing I said good-by to my wife, assuring her that there was nothing to fear and that she would see me back the next day. She fainted. As soon as I arrived here I took the letter to the person, who made me wait while he wrote the answer, after receiving which I went to a tavern to eat a bite and set off at once for Vicenza. But as I left the tavern the constables seized me and took me to the guardroom; I was there until the time they brought me here. I believe, Signore, that I can consider the young Countess my wife."

"You are mistaken."

"But nature—"

"Listening to nature leads a man from one folly to another until he is imprisoned under the Leads."

"Then I am under the Leads?"

"Even as I am."

He began to weep hot tears. He was a very good-looking young man, sincere, honest, and terribly in love, and I forgave the Countess, at the same time condemning the impudence of the Count, who could have had her hair dressed by a woman. In his tears and lamentations he talked of nothing but his poor Countess; he inspired me with the greatest pity. He thought someone would come back to bring him a bed and food, but I undeceived him, and I was right. I gave him some food, but he could swallow nothing. He spent the whole day complaining of his fate but only because he could not comfort his mistress and could not imagine what would become of her. She was already more than justified in my eyes, and I was sure that if the Inquisitors had been invisibly present in my cell, hearing everything the poor youth said to me, they would not only have sent him back but have married him to his mistress despite law or custom; and they might have locked up the Count her father, who had put the straw near the fire. I gave him my pallet, for though he was clean I could not but fear the dreams of a young man in love. He understood neither the magnitude of his crime nor the Count's need to have him punished in secret to save the family honor.

The next day he was brought a pallet and such a dinner as is to be had for fifteen soldi, which the tribunal allowed him "out of charity." I told the jailer that my dinner was enough for us both and that he could use what the tribunal allowed the young man to have three masses a week said for him. He gladly undertook the commission, congratulated him on being with me, and said we could walk in the garret for half an hour. I found the walking very good for my health and for my plan of escaping, which did not come to maturity until eleven months later. At the end of the rat-infested garret I saw a quantity of old household furniture lying on the floor to left and right of two chests and in front of a great pile of notebooks. I took ten or twelve of them to read for diversion. They were all criminal cases, which I found most entertaining reading, for I was free to read what in its time must have been highly secret. I saw strange answers to suggestive interrogations regarding seductions of virgins, attentions carried too far by men employed in girls' orphanages, facts about confessors who had abused their female penitents, schoolmasters convicted of pederasty, and guardians who had cheated their wards; some of them dated back two or three centuries, the style and the customs of which gave me a few hours of pleasure. Among the household implements lying about I saw a warming pan, a kitchen boiler, a fire shovel, tongs, old candelabra, earthenware pots, and a pewter syringe. I thought that some illustrious prisoner had been granted the privilege of using these implements. I also saw a sort of perfectly straight bolt as thick as my thumb and a foot and a half long. I did not touch them. The time had not yet come to look for a use for anything.

One fine day toward the end of the month my companion was taken away. Lorenzo told me he had been sentenced to the prisons known as "the Four." [6] They are within the precincts of the prison building. [7] They belong to the State Inquisitors. The prisoners who are there enjoy the privilege of calling the jailers whenever they need to; the cells are dark; but their inhabitants are provided with an oil lamp; everything is made of marble, and there is no fear of fire. I learned long afterward that poor Maggiorin remained there for five years and was afterward sent to Cerigo [8] for ten. I do not know if he died there. He was good company for me, and I realized it when, left alone again, I relapsed into melancholy. However, the privilege of walking in the garret for half an hour every day was still allowed me. I examined everything in it. One of the big chests was filled with fine paper, pieces of cardboard, untrimmed goose quills, and balls of string; the other was nailed shut. A piece of black polished marble an inch thick, six inches long, and three wide caught my eye; I took it with no particular purpose and put it under my shirts in my cell.

A week after Maggiorin left, Lorenzo told me I was likely to have a new companion. The fellow, who was by nature nothing but a gossip, began to be annoyed because I never asked him a question. His duty was not to gossip, and, having no chance to display his discretion to me, he imagined that I never interrogated him because I supposed he knew nothing; his self-esteem was hurt, and to show me that I was wrong he began to chatter without being questioned.

He told me he believed I should often have new visitors, for the six other cells each held two people who were not of a sort to be sent to "the Four." After a long time, seeing that I did not ask him what the distinction was, he said that in "the Four" there was a hodgepodge of all sorts of people whose sentences, though they did not know them, were recorded in writing; he added that those who, like myself, were in his charge "under the Leads" were all people of the greatest distinction and guilty of crimes which inquisitive persons could not guess.

"If you knew, Signore, what sort of people they are who share your fate! You would be astonished, for it's true they tell me you are intelligent; but, begging your pardon— You know there's no use your being intelligent only to be entertained here . . . You understand me . . . fifty soldi a day is something . . . they give a citi-

zen three lire,[9] a gentleman four, and a foreign Count
eight—I ought to know, for it all goes through my
hands.''

At this point he pronounced his own eulogy, made up
entirely of negative qualities:

''I am neither a thief nor a traitor nor a miser nor
cantankerous nor cruel like all my predecessors, and
when I've drunk an extra pint I grow kinder; if my
father had sent me to school I'd have learned to read
and write and perhaps I'd be Messer Grande; but it's
not my fault. Signor Andrea Diedo[10] thinks highly of
me, and my wife, who's only twenty-four and who pre-
pares your food every day, goes to speak with him whenever she likes and he has her shown right in even when
he's in bed, a favor he doesn't do to any Senator. I
promise you you'll have all the new arrivals with you,
though not for long, for as soon as the Secretary has
learned from their own lips what he needs to know he
sends them on to their destination, either to ''the Four''
or to some fort or to the Levant or, if they're foreigners,
to the frontiers of the State, for the government doesn't
consider itself free to deal with the subjects of other
princes unless they're in its service. The clemency of the
tribunal, Signore, has no equal; and there's not another
in the world which makes life so easy for its prisoners;
people say it is cruel because it won't let them write or
have visitors, but that's nonsense, because writing and
seeing people is a waste of time; you'll tell me you have
nothing to do, but we who work here can't say as much.''

Such, or very nearly such, was the first harangue with
which the scoundrel honored me and which, to tell the
truth, I found amusing. I saw that if the man had been
a little less stupid he would have been more malicious.
I decided to profit by his stupidity.

The next morning they brought my new cell-mate,
who was treated the first day as Maggiorin had been. I

learned that I needed a second ivory spoon, for the first day the newcomer was left with nothing to eat; it was up to me to treat him.

The man, to whom I showed myself at once, made me a deep bow. My beard, which was already four inches long, was even more imposing than my figure. Lorenzo often lent me his scissors to cut my toenails; but I was forbidden to cut my beard under threat of severe penalties. One gets used to everything.

My new companion was a man of fifty, of the same height as myself, slightly stooped, gaunt, with a big mouth and long dirty teeth; he had small hazel eyes and long red lashes, a round black wig which stank with oil, and a coat of coarse gray cloth. Despite accepting my dinner he was deliberately distant; he did not say a word to me all day and I did likewise; but he changed his tactics the next day. Early in the morning he was brought a bed which belonged to him and some linen in a bag. But for me, Maggiorin could not have changed his shirt. The jailer asked him what he wanted for dinner and for money to buy it with.

"I have no money."

"A rich man like you has no money?"

"I haven't a soldo."

"Very well. I will go at once and bring you a pound and a half of ration biscuits[11] and a jug of excellent water. Those are the regulations."

He brought them before he went away, leaving me with the scarecrow.

I hear him sigh, I feel sorry for him, and I break the silence.

"Do not sigh, Signore, you shall dine with me; but it seems to me you made a great mistake in coming here without money."

"I have some; but it's not the thing to tell these harpies."

"Most sagacious—if it didn't condemn you to bread

and water! May I ask you if you know the reason for your being in prison?''

"Yes, Signore, I know it; and to show you how pitiful it is I will tell you my story in a few words.

"My name is Sgualdo Nobili.[12] I am the son of a peasant, who had me taught to write and who at his death left me his little house and the patch of ground belonging to it. My birthplace is in Friuli, a day's journey from Udine. A swift stream called the Corno, which too often damaged my little property, determined me to sell it ten years ago and settle in Venice. I was paid eight thousand lire for it in fine gold zecchini. I had been told that in the capital of this glorious Republic everyone enjoyed an honorable freedom and that an industrious man with a capital such as mine could live there very comfortably by lending against pledges. Sure of my thrift, my judgment, and my knowledge of the world, I determined to practice that trade. I rented a small house in the Cannaregio quarter, I furnished it, and, living by myself, I spent two untroubled years which made me richer by ten thousand lire, for, wanting to live well, I spent a thousand on my household expenses. I was sure that I should soon be ten times as rich. About that time I lent a Jew two zecchini on a number of handsomely bound books, among which I found Charron's *Wisdom*.[13] I have never been fond of reading, I had never read anything but Christian doctrine; but Charron's *Wisdom* showed me how fortunate one is who can read. This book, Signore, which perhaps you do not know, is excellent. When one has read it one finds that one does not have to read any others; for it contains everything that a human being needs to know; it rids him of all the prejudices with which he was infected in childhood; it delivers him from the terrors of a future life; it opens his eyes, it shows him the road to happiness, it makes him wise. Find a way to read it and disregard the fools who will tell you that it is forbidden.''

From this discourse I knew my man, for I knew Charron, though I was not aware that he had been translated. But what books are not translated in Venice? Charron, a great admirer of Montaigne,[14] thought that he was outdoing his model, but he did not. He gave a methodical form to a number of things which Montaigne puts down without order and which, dropped here and there by that great man, did not seem liable to censure; but Charron, a priest and a theologian, was justly condemned. He has not been much read. The stupid Italian who translated him did not even know that the translation of the word *sagesse* is *sapienza*. Charron had the impertinence to give his book the title of Solomon's. My cell-mate continued:

"Freed by Charron from my scruples and all my old false impressions, I worked at my business to such effect that in six years I had nine thousand zecchini. You must not be surprised, for in this rich city gambling, debauchery, and idleness have everyone disorganized and needing money, and the wise profit by what the fools throw away.

"Three years ago a certain Count Seriman[15] made my acquaintance and, seeing what my thrift had made me, asked me to take five hundred zecchini from him, invest them in my business, and give him half the profits. He only asked a receipt, in which I undertook to return the amount to him on demand. At the end of the year I gave him seventy-five zecchini, which amounted to fifteen per cent, and he gave me a receipt, but he showed his dissatisfaction. He was wrong, for, having money enough, I did not use his in my transactions. The second year I did the same, out of pure generosity; but we went on to quarrel, so that he demanded the return of his money. I answered that I would deduct the hundred and fifty zecchini he had received; but that made him furious and he immediately served me with an extrajudiciary[16] demanding the return of the entire amount. A clever law-

yer undertook my defense and gained me two years;
three months ago I was offered a compromise, and I refused; but fearing violence I turned to the Abate Giustiniani, confidential agent of the Marchese di Montealegre,[17] the Spanish Ambassador, who rented me a
small house on the Lista,[18] where one is safe from surprises. I was perfectly willing to give Count Seriman
back his money, but I claimed the right to deduct the
hundred zecchini I had paid in legal costs for the suit he
had brought against me. My lawyer came to see me a
week ago with the Count's, and I showed them the two
hundred and fifty zecchini in a purse, which I was prepared to give them and not a soldo more. They left, both
dissatisfied. Three days ago the Abate Giustiniani sent
me word that the Ambassador had seen fit to permit the
State Inquisitors to send their men to my house to serve
a warrant. I did not know that it could be done. I
awaited their visit courageously, after putting all my
money in a safe place. I would never have believed that
the Ambassador would have let them arrest me as they
did. At daybreak Messer Grande came to my house, demanded three hundred and fifty zecchini, and, upon my
answering that I did not have a soldo, he carried me
off; and here I am.''

After this narrative I made my own reflections on the
infamous scoundrel who had been put in my company
and on the honor he had done me to think that I was a
scoundrel like himself, for otherwise he would not have
told me the whole story, supposing that I was one to applaud it. In all the stupid remarks he made to me for
three days on end, always quoting Charron, I saw the
truth of the proverb, *Guardati da colui che non ha letto
che un libro solo* (''Beware of the man who has read
only one book''). Charron had made him an atheist, and
he openly boasted of it. An hour after the Terza on the
fourth day Lorenzo came and told him to accompany
him downstairs to talk with the Secretary. He dressed

quickly, and instead of his own shoes he put on mine
without my noticing it. He went down with Lorenzo; a
half hour later he came upstairs again crying and took
from his shoes two purses in which he had three hundred
and fifty zecchini and which, preceded by Lorenzo, he
carried to the Secretary. He came up again afterward,
took his cloak, and left; Lorenzo told me later that he
had been released. The next morning his clothes were
sent for. I have always believed that the Secretary made
him confess that he had the money by threatening him
with torture—which, as a threat, may still be good for
something.

On the first day of the year 1756 I received my New
Year's gifts. Lorenzo brought me a dressing gown lined
with fox fur, a silk coverlet stuffed with cotton, and a
bearskin bag to put my legs into during the cold weather,
which was as extreme as the heat I had endured in August. As he gave them to me he said that, by order of the
Secretary, I could have the use of six zecchini a month
to buy all the books I wanted and the *Gazette* as well,
and that it was a present from Signor Bragadin. I asked
Lorenzo for a pencil and wrote on a scrap of paper:
*"I am grateful to the mercy of the tribunal and the
virtue of Signor Bragadin."*

One must have been in my situation to understand the
sentiments which this bounty aroused in my soul; in the
intensity of my gratitude I forgave my oppressors and
I almost abandoned my plan of escaping; so pliable is
man when misfortune degrades him. Lorenzo told me
that Signor Bragadin had come before the three Inquisitors and had gone down on his knees and wept as he
begged them for the favor of allowing me to receive this
proof of his constant affection if I was still among the
living; and that they had been so touched that they could
not refuse him. I immediately wrote down the titles of all
the books I wanted.

One fine morning as I was walking in the garret my

Conversation Outside the Caffè Florian, Venice

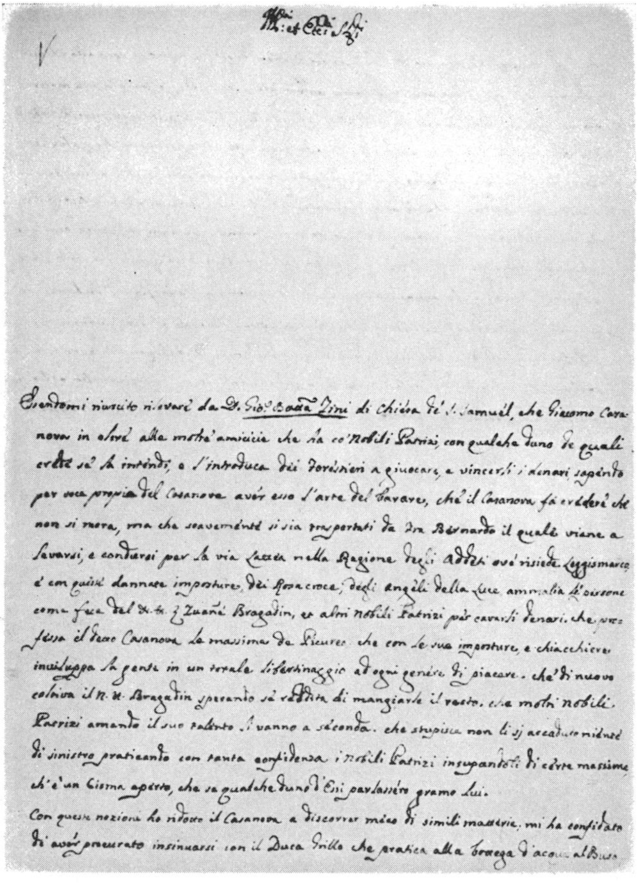

Ill.mi et Ecc.mi S.ri

Essendomi riuscito rilevare da D. Gio: Batta Zini di Chiesa de S. Samuel, che Giacomo Casanova in oltre alla molta amicizia che ha co' Nobili Patrizi, con qualcheduno de quali crede se la intendi, e s'introduca dei Forestieri a giuocare, e vincersi i denari, sapendo per voce propria del Casanova aver esso l'arte del barare, che il Casanova fa credere che non si mora, ma che soavemente si sia trasportati da Fra Bernardo il quale viene a levarsi, e condursi per la via Lattea nella Ragione degli Addeti ove risiede Loggismarco, e con queste dannate imposture, dei Rosacroce, degli angeli della Luce ammalia le persone come fece del N. H. S. Zuane Bragadin, ed altri Nobili Patrizi per cavarsi denari. che professa il detto Casanova la massima de Epicureo. che con le sue imposture, e chiacchiere inviluppa la gente in un totale libertinaggio ad ogni genere di piacere. che di nuovo coltiva il N. H. Bragadin sperando se reddita di mangiarle il resto. che molti Nobili Patrizi amando il suo talento si vanno a seconda. che stupisca non li sij accaduto niente di sinistro praticando con tanta confidenza i Nobili Patrizi insupandoli di certe massime ch'è un Cisma aperto, che se qualcheduno d'Essi parlassero gramo Lui.

Con queste nozioni ho ridotto il Casanova a discorrer meco di simili materie, mi ha confidato di aver procurato insinuarsi con il Duca Grillo che pratica alla bottega d'acqua al Buso [illegible]

G. B. Manuzzi's Report to the Inquisitors, July 17, 1775

eyes lingered over the long bolt which was there on the floor and I considered its possibilities as a weapon of attack and defense; I picked it up and took it into my cell, putting it under my coat with the piece of black marble; as soon as I was alone I found that the latter made a perfect whetstone, for, after rubbing the end of the bolt against the marble for a long time I saw that it showed a flat edge.

Interested in this strange kind of work, in which I was a novice, and to which I was inspired by the hope of possessing a tool which must be strictly forbidden up there, and further urged on by pride in managing to produce a weapon without the necessary instruments to make it with, even exasperated by the very difficulties— for I had to rub the bolt almost in darkness, working on the sill, only able to keep the stone from slipping with my left hand, and having no oil with which to wet and soften the iron on which I wanted to put a point—I used nothing but my saliva and I toiled for two weeks filing down eight triangular facets which at their apexes formed a perfect point; the facets were an inch and a half long. The result was an octagonal stiletto as well proportioned as one could have expected from a good cutler. It is impossible to imagine the pain and boredom I suffered and the patience I needed to accomplish this distasteful piece of work with not a tool except a loose piece of stone; for me it was torture of a kind *quam siculi non invenere tyranni* ("which even the Sicilian tyrants did not invent").[19] I could no longer move my right arm and my shoulder seemed to be out of joint. The palm of my hand had become one great sore after the vessels broke; despite my pain I did not stop my work; I was determined to see it perfected.

Proud of my production and not yet having decided how and for what I might use it, I thought about hiding it in some place where it would escape even a search; I hit upon the idea of putting it in the stuffing of my armchair, not on top, however, where, by taking up the cush-ion, anyone could see the unevenness it would cause in the surface, but by turning the chair upside down; I then pushed the bolt into it all the way, so that for any-one to find it he would have to know it was there. Thus did God provide me with what I needed for an escape which was to be a wonder if not a miracle. I admit that I am proud of it; but my pride does not come from my having succeeded, for luck had a good deal to do with that; it comes from my having concluded that the thing could be done and having had the courage to undertake it.

After three or four days spent in reflecting on the use to which I should put the bolt which I had transformed into a pike as thick as a walking stick and twenty inches[20] long, whose excellent sharp point showed me that it was not necessary to turn iron into steel in order to give it one, I saw that I had only to make a hole in the floor under my bed.

I was sure that the room below could only be the one in which I had seen Signor Cavalli; I was sure that it was opened every morning; and I was sure that I could easily let myself down, once the hole was made, by using my bedclothes, of which I would make a sort of rope and fasten the upper end of it to a trestle of my bed. Once in the room I would remain concealed under the tribunal's great table, and in the morning, as soon as I saw the door opened, I would go out by it and be in a place of safety before I could be pursued. I thought it probable that Lorenzo left one of his constables in the room as a guard, and if that were the case I would have killed the man at once by plunging my pike into his throat. Everything was well thought out; but since the floor might be double or even triple the work could have taken me one or two months; I thought it would be very difficult to keep the constables from sweeping my cell for so long. If I had forbidden them to do it I should have made them suspicious, and the more so since, to rid myself of the fleas, I had insisted that they sweep every day, so that the broom itself would have revealed the hole to them; I had to be absolutely certain that this misfortune would not befall me.

In the meanwhile I forbade them to sweep, at the same time not saying why I forbade it. A week or ten days later Lorenzo asked me why; I said that it was because the dust rising from the floor went into my lungs and might bring on tubercles.

"We will sprinkle water on the floor," he said.

"Certainly not, for the dampness can cause a plethora."

But a week later he ordered his men to sweep; he had them carry the bed out of my cell and, on the excuse of getting the place thoroughly cleaned, he lit a candle. I saw that it was suspicion which prompted this performance; but I showed indifference. I then hit on the way to advance my plan. The next morning I bloodied my handkerchief by pricking my finger and I waited for Lorenzo in bed.

"I had such a fit of coughing," I said, "that a vein in my chest broke and made me throw up all the blood you see; have the physician sent to me."

The learned physician came, he ordered me bled and wrote me a prescription. I told him that Lorenzo had brought on my trouble by insisting on sweeping. He reproached him and said that a young wigmaker[21] had just died of consumption from the same cause, for, according to him, dust once inhaled was never exhaled. Lorenzo swore he thought he was rendering me a service and that he would never have any sweeping done again as long as he lived. I laughed to myself, because the physician could not have spoken to better purpose if he had been my confederate. The constables who heard his doctrine were delighted to learn it and counted it among their acts of charity that henceforth they only swept the cells of those who were surly to them.

After the physician left, Lorenzo asked me to forgive him and assured me that all his other prisoners were in good health despite his having their rooms swept every day. He called them "rooms."

"But it is an important matter," he said, "and I will explain it to them, for I regard you all as my children."

I really needed the bleeding; it ended my sleepnessness and cured me of the spasmodic contractions which terrified me.

I had gained a great point; but the time to begin working had not yet come. The cold was intense and my hands could not hold the pike without freezing. My undertaking demanded a man foresighted enough to avoid anything which could easily be foreseen and a spirit bold and intrepid enough to resign itself to chance in case anything foreseen did not occur. The man who must act thus is most unfortunate; but a sound political calculation teaches that for the sake of all it is expedient[22] to risk all.

The overlong nights of winter distressed me. I had to spend nineteen mortal hours in absolute darkness; and on foggy days, which are not uncommon in Venice, the light which came in through the window and the hole in the door was not enough for me to read my book by. Since I could not read I went back to thinking of my escape, and a mind always fixed on one idea can go mad. Having an oil lamp would have made me happy; I thought about it, and I rejoiced when I believed I had found a way to obtain one by a ruse. To make the lamp I had to have the ingredients which would compose it. I needed a vessel, linen or cotton wicks, oil, a flint and steel, matches, and punk. The vessel could be a small earthenware pot, and I had the one in which my eggs were cooked in butter. I managed to get Lucca oil bought for me on the excuse that salad dressed with ordinary oil made me ill. From my quilt I pulled out enough cotton to make some wicks. I pretended to be tormented by a bad toothache, and I told Lorenzo I needed some pumice stone; he did not know what it was, and I substituted a gun flint, saying that it would produce the same effect if it was soaked in strong vinegar for a day and then applied to my tooth, when it would relieve the pain. Lorenzo said that my vinegar was of the best and that I could put a flint in it myself, and he threw me three or four. A buckle on the belt of my breeches would serve me as a steel; all I still needed was sulphur and tinder, but I had no idea how to go about getting them. But here is the way I found by dint of thinking about it, and the way Fortune took a hand in it.

I had a sort of measles which, after drying up, had left scabs on my arm that made me itch uncomfortably; and I told Lorenzo to ask the physician for a remedy. The next morning he brought me a note, which the Secretary had read, in which the physician had written: "One day of dieting and four ounces of oil of sweet almonds, and the skin will be cured; or application of an ointment of flowers of sulphur; but this topical remedy is dangerous."

"I don't care about the danger," I said to Lorenzo; "buy some of the ointment and bring it to me tomorrow; or give me some sulphur, I have butter and I will make the ointment myself; have you any matches? Give me some."

He took out all the matches he had in his pocket and gave them to me. How easily one is comforted when one is in distress!

I spent two or three hours considering what I could substitute for the punk, the only ingredient I did not have and which I could not imagine an excuse for obtaining, when I suddenly remembered that I had ordered my tailor to line my taffeta coat with punk under the arms and cover it with oilcloth, to prevent the stain from sweat which, chiefly in summer, spoils all coats at that particular place. My coat was there before me, it was brand-new, and my heart pounded; my tailor might have forgotten my order, and I was between hope and dread. I had to take only two steps to make sure, and I did not dare. I was afraid I should not find the punk and would have to give up so dear a hope. I finally make up my mind, I approach the board on which I had put my coat, and, suddenly feeling that I am unworthy of such a grace, I go down on my knees praying God that the tailor had not forgotten my order. After this fervent prayer I unfold my coat, I unsew the oilcloth, and I find the punk. My joy was great. It was natural that I should thank God, since I had looked for the punk confiding in his goodness; and I did so with an overflowing heart.

Examining my act of thanksgiving, I did not consider that I had been a fool, as I did when I reflected on the prayer I had offered to the master of all when I went to look for the punk. I would not have done it before I was put under the Leads, nor would I do it today; but being deprived of physical freedom stupefies the faculties of the soul. One should pray to God to grant graces, not to reverse the course of nature by miracles. If the tailor had not put the punk under the arms of my coat, I ought to have been sure that I should not find it; and if he had, I ought to have been sure that I should find it. So why was I troubling the master of nature? The meaning of my first prayer could only be: "Lord, let me find the punk even if the tailor forgot it, and if he put it in do not make it disappear." Some theologian might find my prayer pious, holy, and perfectly reasonable, for he would say it was based on the power of faith; and he would be right, just as I, who am not a theologian, am right to consider it absurd. In any case I do not need to be a great theologian to consider my act of thanksgiving praiseworthy. I thanked God that the tailor's memory had not failed him, and my gratitude was justified by the principles of a sound philosophy.

No sooner was I in possession of the punk I needed than I put oil into a pot, then a wick, and I saw a lamp. What a satisfaction it was to owe the boon only to myself and to break a most cruel regulation! For me, there were no more nights. Farewell salad! I was very fond of it, but I did not regret it; I thought that oil was created only to give us light. I decided to begin breaking the floor on the first Monday in Lent, for during the license of the Carnival I feared visitors from day to day; and I was right. On Quinquagesima Sunday at noon I heard the noise of the bolts, and I saw Lorenzo followed by a very fat man whom I at once recognized as the Jew Gabriel Schalon,[23] celebrated for his ability to raise money for young men by ruinous deals; we knew each other, so we exchanged the usual greetings the occasion demanded. The company of this man was not of a sort to please me, but I had to be patient; he was locked in. He told Lorenzo to go to his house to fetch his dinner, a bed, and everything he needed; and he answered that they would talk about it the next day.

This Jew, who was brainless, ignorant, talkative, and stupid except in his trade, began by congratulating me on my having been chosen above all others to share his company. My only answer was to offer him half of my dinner, which he refused, saying that he ate only food which was pure and that he had every expectation of eating his supper at home.

"When?"

"Tonight. You remember that when I asked him for my bed he said that we would talk about it tomorrow. That obviously means I do not need it. Can you suppose that they would leave a man like me without anything to eat?"

"That is how I was treated."

"No doubt; but there is some difference between you and me; and, strictly between ourselves, the State Inquisitors made a blunder when they had me arrested and they must now be wondering how to set their mistake right."

"They may give you a pension, for you are a man to be treated with consideration."

"Your conclusion is very sound; for there is not a broker on the Exchange more useful than myself to domestic trade, and the Five Savi[24] have profited greatly by the advice I have often given them. My imprisonment is a strange mistake, which may well be a lucky one for you."

"Lucky? How?"

"A month will not pass before I will have you out of here. I know to whom I must speak and what to say."

"Then I count on you."

The idiotic scoundrel thought he amounted to something. He insisted on telling me what people were saying about me; and since he only reported what the greatest fools in the city could find to say he bored me. I took up a book, and he had the impertinence to ask me not to read. His passion was talking, and always about himself.

I did not dare to light my lamp, and, when night drew on, he made up his mind to accept some bread and Cyprus wine and my pallet, which had become the bed for all new arrivals. The next morning he was brought food from his house and a bed. I had this stone around my neck for eight or nine weeks,[25] for before sentencing him to "the Four" the Secretary had to talk with him several times to bring to light his shady deals and to make him cancel some illegal contracts he had made. He confessed to me himself that he had bought certain revenues from Signor Domenico Micheli[26] which could not belong to the buyer until after the death of the Cavaliere Antonio, his father.

"It is true," he said, "that the seller lost a hundred per cent on the transaction, but it must be considered that the buyer would have lost everything if the son had died before the father."

When I saw that my unwelcome companion was not leaving, I resolved to light my lamp; he promised secrecy, but he kept quiet only as long as he remained with me; for, though there were no consequences, Lorenzo learned of it. In short the man was a burden to me and prevented me from working at my escape.

He also prevented me from the reading which kept me amused; demanding, ignorant, superstitious, blustering, timid, sometimes giving in to tears and despair, he tried to make me join in his noisy remonstrances by showing me that his imprisonment was ruining his reputation; I assured him that, so far as his reputation went, he had nothing to fear, and he took my gibe for a compliment. He refused to admit that he was avaricious, and to convince him that he was I demonstrated to him that if the State Inquisitors gave him a hundred zecchini a day and at the same time opened the gate of the prison for him, he would not leave in order not to lose the hundred zecchini. He had to agree, and he laughed over it.

He was a Talmudist, as all Jews are today; and he tried to make me believe that he was very much attached to his religion because of its wisdom. Being the son of a rabbi, he was learned in its ceremonies; but in my subsequent study of the human race I have seen that the majority of men believe that the most essential part of religion is discipline.

The Jew was excessively fat and, never leaving his bed and sleeping by day, he soon could not sleep at night, while he heard me sleeping quite well. Once he took it into his head to wake me when I was in my deepest sleep.

"In God's name," I said, "what do you want? Why did you wake me? If you die, I'll forgive you."

"Alas, my dear friend, I cannot sleep, have pity on me and let us talk a little."

"And you call me your dear friend? Hateful man! I believe that your insomnia is a real torture, and I am sorry for you; but if ever you dare again to relieve your misery by depriving me of the greatest good Nature allows me to enjoy in the misfortune which overwhelms me, I will get out of my bed and come and strangle you."

"Forgive me, I beg you, and be sure that I will never wake you in future."

It is possible that I would not have strangled him, but it is certain that he put the temptation in my way. A man in prison who is in the arms of sweet slumber is not in prison, and the sleeping slave does not feel the chains of slavery, just as kings do not reign in sleep. Hence the prisoner must regard the man thoughtless enough to wake him as an executioner come to deprive him of his freedom and plunge him back into wretchedness; add that the prisoner who sleeps usually dreams that he is free and that the illusion replaces the reality for him. I heartily congratulated myself on not having begun my work before the man arrived. He demanded that the place be swept, the constables whose task it was made me laugh when they told him that it brought me to death's door; he insisted. I pretended to be ill from it, and the constables would not have carried out his order if I had objected; but my interests demanded that I should be obliging.

On the Wednesday in Holy Week Lorenzo told us that after the Terza the Signor Circospetto would come up to pay us the customary Easter visit, which serves both to bring peace to the souls of those who wish to receive the Holy Sacrament and for him to learn if they have any complaint concerning the jailer's performance of his duties.

"And so, Signori," he said, "if you wish to complain

of me, complain; dress yourselves fully, for that is the rule.''

I ordered Lorenzo to have a confessor sent to me the next day.

So I dressed up, and the Jew did likewise, at the same time taking his leave of me because he felt sure that the Circospetto would set him free as soon as he had talked with him; he said that his presentiment was of a kind which had never deceived him. I congratulated him. The Secretary arrived, the cell was opened, the Jew emerged and fell on his knees; I heard nothing but tears and cries, which continued for four or five minutes without a word from the Secretary. He came back, and Lorenzo told me to go out. With my eight-months beard and wearing a coat designed by love and intended for the heat of July on that very cold day, I was a figure fit to inspire laughter and not to arouse pity. The terrible cold made me shake like the edge of the shadow cast by the darkness which the setting sun brings on—which annoyed me only because the Secretary might think I was shaking with fear. Since I came out of the cell stooped over, my bow was already made; I drew myself up, I looked at him neither proudly nor cringingly, without speaking or moving; the Circospetto, equally motionless, remained silent too; the mute scene between us continued for two minutes. Seeing that I said nothing, he bent his head half an inch and left. I returned to my cell, undressed, and got into bed to revive my natural heat. The Jew was astonished that I had not spoken to the Secretary, whereas my silence had said much more than he had thought he was telling him with his cowardly cries. A prisoner of my sort in the presence of his judge should never open his mouth except to answer questions.

The next day a Jesuit came to confess me, and on Holy Saturday a priest from San Marco came to give me the

Holy Eucharist. Since my confession appeared too la-
conic to the missionary priest who heard it he saw fit to
remonstrate with me before he absolved me.

"Do you pray to God?" he asked.

"I pray to him from morning to night and from night
to morning, even when I am eating and sleeping, for in
the situation in which I am, everything that takes place
in me, even my moments of agitation or impatience or
folly, can only be prayer before the divine wisdom, which
alone sees my heart."

The Jesuit heard my specious sermon on prayer with
a slight smile and repaid it by a metaphysical discourse
of a nature quite incompatible with mine. I would have
refuted it completely if, wise in his profession, he had
not had the skill to astonish me and reduce me to less
than the size of a flea by a sort of prophecy which
awed me.

"Since it was from us," he said, "that you learned
the religion you profess, practice it as we practice it,
and pray to God as we taught you to do, and know that
you will never leave here except on the day dedicated
to the saint who is your patron."

After speaking these words he gave me absolution and
left. The impression they made on me was incredible;
try as I would, I could not get them out of my head. I
considered all the saints I found in the calendar.

The Jesuit was the spiritual director of Signor Flaminio Corner,[27] the old Senator, then a State Inquisitor.
The Senator was a famous man of letters, a great politi-
cian, very devout, and the author of works all of which
were pious, extraordinary, and written in Latin.[28] His
reputation was spotless.

Informed that I was to leave the place on my patron
saint's day by a man who might well know, I rejoiced
to have learned that I had a patron saint and to understand that he was concerned for me; but since I had to
pray to him, I had to know him. Who was he? The

Jesuit himself could not have told me if he knew, for he would have betrayed the secret; but "Come," I said to myself, "let's see if I can guess." It could not be St. James of Compostela,[29] whose name I bore; for it was precisely on his feast day that my door had been broken down by Messer Grande. I took the calendar and, looking for the nearest saint's day, I came to St. George,[30] a saint of some renown, but of whom I had never thought. So I settled on St. Mark, whose day came on the twenty-fifth of the month, and to whose protection I, as a Venetian, could lay some claim; so I addressed my prayers to him, but in vain. His feast day went by, and I was still there. I took the other St. James,[31] the brother of Jesus Christ, who comes with St. Philip, but I was wrong again; so I settled on St. Anthony,[32] who, or so they say in Padua, performs thirteen miracles a day; but no less in vain. In this way I passed from one to another and insensibly became accustomed to hoping in vain for protection from the saints. I was convinced that the saint in whom I should trust was my pointed bolt. Nevertheless, the Jesuit's prophecy came true. I got out of there on All Saints' Day, as my reader will see, and it is certain that, if I had one, my protector must be honored on that day, for they are all included.

Two or three weeks after Easter I was delivered from the Jew; but the poor man was not sent home; he was sentenced to "the Four," where he remained for two years, and afterwards went and finished his days in Trieste.

As soon as I was alone I went to work with the greatest eagerness. I needed to hurry before the arrival of some new guest who would insist that the place be swept. I pulled out my bed, lighted my lamp, and flung myself on the floor pike in hand, after spreading out a napkin beside me to receive the bits of wood which I excavated with the point of the bolt; the thing was to break away the board by driving the iron into it; at the beginning of my labors the fragments were no bigger than a grain of wheat, but later they became good-sized pieces. The board was of larch and sixteen inches wide; I began to dig into it where it joined the next one; there was neither a nail nor an iron clamp, and my job was perfectly straightforward. After working six hours I tied my napkin up and set it aside so that I could go and empty it the next morning behind the pile of notebooks at the end of the garret. The fragments I had broken off were four or five times bigger in bulk than the hole from which I had taken them; its circumference was roughly thirty degrees of a circle, its diameter[33] about ten inches. I put my bed back in place, and in the morning when I emptied my napkin I had no reasons to fear that my fragments would be seen.

On the second day I found under the first board, which was two inches thick, a second board which I supposed was of the same size. Never having suffered the misfortune of visitors, and always tormented by fear of it, in three weeks I succeeded in breaking completely through three boards, under which I found the kind of flooring incrusted with small bits of marble which is known in Venice as *terrazzo marmorin*.[34] It is the usual flooring of rooms in all houses in Venice which do not belong to poor people. The great noblemen even prefer *terrazzo* to parquetry. I was appalled when I saw that my bolt was not biting into it; it was in vain that I bore down and pushed; my point slipped. It discouraged me completely. Then I remembered Hannibal, who, according to Livy,[35] had opened a passage through the Alps by chopping away the rock which he had softened through the action of vinegar—a thing I had considered incredible, not so much because of the power of the acid but because of the prodigious quantity of vinegar he must have had. I thought Hannibal had succeeded in it not *aceto* ("by vinegar") but *asceta*, which in the Latin of Padua might be the same as *ascia*[36] ("ax"), and that the error might stem from the copyists. Nevertheless I poured into my excavation a bottle of strong vinegar which I had; and the next morning, whether as the result of the vinegar or of greater patience, I saw that I should succeed, for it was not a matter of breaking the small pieces of marble but of pulverizing the cement between them with the point of my implement; and I was greatly relieved when I found that the great difficulty occurred only at the surface; in four days I destroyed the entire piece of paving without damaging the point of my pike. Its facets shone even more brightly.

Under the *marmorin* flooring I found another board, as I expected; it must be the last, that is, the first counting up in the roofing of any room whose beams support its ceiling. I began my work on this board with somewhat greater difficulty because my hole had become ten inches deep. I constantly commended myself to the mercy of God. Those freethinkers who say that prayer is of no use do not know what they are talking about. I know that after praying to God I always felt stronger; and that is enough to prove its usefulness, whether the increase in strength comes directly from God or is a physical result of one's confidence in him.

On June 25th, the day on which only the Republic of Venice celebrates the prodigy of the Evangelist St. Mark's appearing in the emblematic form of a winged lion in the ducal church toward the end of the eleventh century, an event which showed the Senate in its wisdom that it was time to dismiss St. Theodore,[37] whose credit was no longer powerful enough to aid it in its plans of aggrandizement, and to take for its patron the sainted disciple of St. Paul (or, according to Eusebius,[38] St. Peter) whom God now sent it—at three hours past noon on that day, when, stark naked, running with sweat, and lying flat on my stomach, I was working at the hole, in which, in order to see, I had set my lighted lamp, I was mortally terrified to hear the shrill grating of the bolt

in the door to the first corridor. What a moment! I blow
out my lamp, I leave my pike in the hole, throw my napkin into it, I rise, I hastily put the trestles and the boards
of my bed in the alcove, I throw the pallet and the mattresses on top of it; and not having time to put on the
sheets, I fall on it as if dead just as Lorenzo is opening
my cell. One minute earlier, and he would have caught me
in the act. Lorenzo would have stepped on me if a cry I
gave had not made him crouch back into the doorway,
saying emphatically:

"My God, I pity you, Signore, for it is as hot here as
in an oven. Get up and thank God, who sends you excellent company. Come in, come in, Illustrissimo Signore,"
he said to the unfortunate who was following him. The
churl pays no attention to my nakedness, and the Illustrissimo enters, making his way around me, while, not
knowing what I was doing, I gather up my bedclothes,
throw them on the bed, and can nowhere find the shirt
which decency demands that I put on. The newcomer
thought he was entering Hell. He exclaimed:

"Where am I? Where are they putting me? What
heat! What a stench! With whom am I?"

At that Lorenzo called him out, asking me to put on a
shirt and come into the garret; he told him that he had
orders to bring him a bed from his house and everything
he asked for, and that until his return he could walk in
the garret and that meanwhile the cell would be purged
of the stench, which was only the smell of oil. What a
surprise for me to hear him say that the stench was only
oil! As a matter of fact it came from the lamp, which I
had extinguished without snuffing it. Lorenzo did not ask
me a single question about it; so he knew everything;
the Jew had told him. How lucky I was that he could
not have told him more! At that moment I began to feel
somewhat kindly toward Lorenzo.

After quickly putting on a fresh shirt and a dressing
gown, I came out. The new prisoner was writing in pen-

cil a list of what he wanted. He was the first to speak when he saw me:

"It's Casanova!"

I at once recognized the Abate Count Fenaroli,[39] of Brescia, a man of fifty years, amiable, rich, and a favorite in the choicest society. He came and embraced me, and when I said I would have expected to see anyone else on earth up there except himself, he could not hold back his tears, which provoked mine.

As soon as we were alone I said to him that when his bed arrived I would offer him the alcove but that he should do me the favor of refusing it and that he should not ask for the cell to be swept, adding that I would tell him the reasons when there was more time. I explained the reason for the stench of oil, and after assuring me that he would keep everything secret he said that he considered himself fortunate to have been put with me. He said that no one knew what my crime was, so everyone was trying to guess it. Some said I was the head of a new religion; others said Signora Memmo had convinced the tribunal that I was teaching her sons atheism. Still others said that Signor Antonio Condulmer, one of the State Inquisitors, had had me imprisoned as a disturber of the public peace because I hissed the Abate Chiari's comedies and was planning to go to Padua on purpose to kill him.

All these accusations had some basis which gave them an air of probability, but they were all fabrications. I did not care enough about religion to be interested in founding a new one. Signora Memmo's three sons, all of them highly intelligent, were more the sort to lead others astray than to be led astray themselves, and Signor Condulmer would have been kept too busy if he had tried to lock up everyone who hissed the Abate Chiari. As for the Abate, who had been a Jesuit, I had forgiven him. The celebrated Father Origo,[40] likewise a Jesuit, had taught me how to avenge myself on him by speaking well of him at large gatherings. My praises provoked my hearers to satires, and I was avenged without any trouble to myself.

Toward evening a bed was brought, together with an armchair, linen, scented waters, a good dinner, and good wines. The Abate could eat nothing; but I did not imitate him. His bed was set up without moving mine and we were locked in.

I began by taking from the hole my lamp and my napkin, which, having fallen into the lamp, had become soaked with oil. I laughed heartily. An accident which has no consequences and which is occasioned by causes which could have tragic ones is a good reason for laughter. I put everything in order; and I lit my lamp, the story of which made the Abate laugh. We spent a sleepless night, not so much because of the million fleas which were devouring us as because our talk was so interesting that we could not bring ourselves to end it. Here is the story of his arrest, as he himself told it to me:

"Yesterday at twenty o'clock[41] a party consisting of Signora Alessandri,[42] Count Paolo Martinengo,[43] and myself boarded a gondola; we reached Fusina at twenty-one and Padua at twenty-four, intending to see the opera and return here immediately afterward. During the second act my evil genius sent me to the gaming room, where I saw Count Rosenberg, the Ambassador from Vienna, with his mask off, and ten paces from him Signora Ruzzini,[44] whose husband is about to leave for the same court as Ambassador of the Republic. I bowed to them both and I was going to leave when the Ambassador said to me loudly: '*You are very fortunate to be able to pay your court to so charming a lady; it is only at moments like this that the part I play in the most beautiful country in the world becomes my torment. Tell her, I beg you, that the laws which prevent me from speaking to her here have no power in Vienna, where I shall see her next year and where I shall make war on her.*' Signora Ruzzini, who saw that we were speaking

of her, asked me what the Count had said and I repeated
it to her word for word. 'Answer him,' she said, 'that
*I accept his declaration of war and that we shall see
which of us two is the better warrior.*' I did not think
I was committing a crime by repeating her answer, which
was merely a compliment. After the opera we ate a fowl
and we were back here at fourteen o'clock. I was going
to bed to sleep until twenty, when a *fante* brought me
a note which ordered me to be at the Bussola at nineteen
o'clock to hear what the Circospetto Businello, Secretary
to the Council of Ten, had to say to me. Astonished by
the order, which is always an ill omen, and much troubled that I had to obey it, at the appointed hour I appeared before the minister, who, without saying even a
word to me, ordered me put here.''

Nothing was more innocent than his offense; but there
are laws in the world which one can break innocently and
the transgressors of which are no less guilty for that. I
congratulated him on knowing what his crime was, on
his crime itself, and on the manner of his arrest, and
since his offense was a very slight one I told him that he
would remain with me only a week and then be ordered
to go and live on his estate in Brescia for six months.
He answered sincerely that he did not believe he would
be left there a week—a perfect example of the man who,
feeling no guilt, cannot conceive that he will be punished.
I let him keep his illusion; but what I told him proved
to be the case.[45] I made up my mind to be a good companion to him in order to give him as much comfort as
I could in the great distress his imprisonment caused
him. I sympathized in his misfortune to such a point
that I entirely forgot my own during all the time he was
with me.

The next morning at daybreak Lorenzo brought coffee
and a big basket containing dinner for the Count-Abate,
who did not understand how anyone could suppose a
man would want to eat at such an hour. We were allowed

to walk for an hour and then were locked in. The fleas which tormented us made him ask me why I did not have the place swept. I could not bear to have him either think me a swine or believe that my skin was thicker than his; I told him, and even showed him, everything. I saw that he was surprised, and indeed mortified because he had in a sense forced me to entrust him with so weighty a secret. He encouraged me to work and to finish the hole that day if possible, so that he could himself let me down and afterward pull up my rope; for his part, he did not wish to make his crime more serious by flight. I showed him the model of a device by which I was sure that when I had got down I could pull the sheet I had used as a rope down after me; it was a bit of stick fastened at one end to a long string. My sheet was to be secured to the trestle of my bed only by this stick, which would go into the two halves of a loop in the rope under the trestle; the string which operated the stick was to go to the floor of the Inquisitors' room, where, as soon as I found myself on my feet, I would pull on it. He had no doubt of its working, and he congratulated me on it, the more so since the precaution was absolutely necessary, since if the sheet had stayed there it would be the first thing to catch the eyes of Lorenzo, who could not come up to where we were except by passing through that room; he would look for me at once, find me, and arrest me. My noble companion was convinced that I should give up my work, since there was great danger of my being caught at it and the more so as it would take me several more days to finish the hole, which was to cost Lorenzo his life. But could the thought of purchasing freedom at the price of his life lessen my eagerness to obtain my freedom? I should have done what I did if the consequence of my escape would have been the death of all the constables in the Republic and even of the State itself. Love of country becomes nothing but a phantasm in the mind of the man whom his country is oppressing.

But my good humor did not prevent my dear companion from succumbing to moments of melancholy. He was in love with Signora Alessandri, who had been a singer and who was the mistress or the wife of his friend Martinengo, and he must have had her favors; but the more a lover is in favor, the more miserable he becomes if he is torn from the arms of the woman he loves. He sighed, tears flowed from his eyes, and he admitted that he loved a woman who combined all the virtues. I sincerely condoled with him, taking care not to comfort him by saying that love is only a trifle, a distressing sort of consolation which only fools offer to lovers; it is not even true that love is nothing but a trifle.

The week which I had predicted passed very quickly; I lost his precious companionship; but I did not give myself time to regret it. I took good care never to ask this honorable man to keep my secret; the least doubt on my part would have been an insult to his noble soul.

On July 3rd Lorenzo told him to be ready to leave at the Terza, which during that month rings at twelve o'clock. For this reason he did not bring him his dinner. During the whole week the only nourishment he took was soup, fruits, and Canary wine.[46] It was I who ate well, to the great satisfaction of my friend, who admired my cheerful temperament. We spent the last three hours vowing the tenderest friendship. Lorenzo appeared, went down with him, and reappeared a quarter of an hour later to take away all of this most amiable man's possessions.

On the next day Lorenzo gave me an accounting of his expenditures during the month of June, and I saw that he was touched when, finding that I had a balance of four zecchini, I told him that I made his wife a present of them. I did not tell him that it was the recompense for my lamp; but he may have thought so.

Devoting myself entirely to my work, I saw it reach perfection on August 23rd. The delay was caused by a very natural mishap. When, digging into the last board, always with the greatest care to make it only extremely thin, I got very close to its opposite surface, I put my eye to a small hole through which I ought to see the Inquisitors' room, as in fact I did see it; but at the same time I saw, at a very short distance from the same hole, which was no bigger than a fly, a perpendicular surface about eight inches across. This was what I had always feared: it was one of the beams supporting the ceiling. I saw that I should have to make the hole bigger in the direction away from the beam; for the latter made the space so narrow that my rather portly person could never have got through it. I had to enlarge the opening by a fourth, still always fearing that the space between the two beams would not be enough. After the enlargement a second little hole of the same size showed me that God had blessed my work. I stopped up the little holes, both to prevent the small fragments from dropping into the room and to make it impossible for a ray from my lamp to pass through and so reveal my operation to anyone who might have seen it.

I set the night before St. Augustine's Day[47] as the time for my escape, because I knew that the Great Council met on that feast and hence there would be no one in the Bussola, which was next door to the room through which I must necessarily pass on my way out. I therefore decided to leave on the night of the 27th.

At noon on the 25th something happened to me which makes me tremble even now as I record it. At noon precisely, I heard the screech of the bolts; I thought I should die. A violent palpitation of my heart, which was beating three or four inches below its proper place, made me fear that my last hour had come. I dropped into my armchair in panic. Coming into the garret, Lorenzo put his head to the grating and said in joyous tones:

"I congratulate you, Signore, on the good news I bring you."

Instantly supposing that he meant my freedom, for I knew of no other news which could be good, I saw that I was lost. The discovery of the hole would have led to my pardon being revoked.

Lorenzo enters and tells me to come with him.

"Wait till I get dressed."

"It doesn't matter, for you are only going from this vile cell to another which is light and brand-new, where you will see half of Venice from two windows, where you can stand upright, where—"

But I could bear no more, I felt that I was dying.

"Give me some vinegar," I said. "Go and tell the Signor Secretary that I thank the tribunal for this kindness and that I beg him in God's name to leave me here."

"You make me laugh. Have you gone mad? You are to be taken out of Hell and put in Paradise, and you refuse? Come, come, you must obey; stand up. I will give you my arm and I will have your clothes and your books brought you."

Astonished and in no position to say another word, I rose, I left the cell, and I instantly felt a slight relief when I heard him order one of his men to follow him with my armchair. As always, my pike was hidden in its stuffing, and that was at least something. I wished I were also being followed by the fine hole I had made with such effort, and which I had to abandon; but it was impossible. My body moved on; but my soul remained behind.

Supporting myself on Lorenzo's shoulder, while the fellow supposed he was giving me courage with his jokes, I passed through two narrow corridors and, after going down three steps, entered a large and very light room, at the far left-hand corner of which I went through a small door into a corridor which was two feet wide and twelve long and had two grated windows to my right, through which I clearly saw the upper part of the whole section of the great city which lay on that side, as far as the Lido. But I was in no state to be consoled by a fine view.

The door of the cell was in the corner of this corridor; I saw a grated window which was opposite one of the two which lighted the corridor, so that the prisoner, though shut in, could enjoy much of the pleasant prospect. Most important of all, since the window was open, it let in a gentle, cool wind which tempered the unbearable heat and which was veritably balm to the poor creature who had to breathe in the cell, especially during this season.

I did not make these observations at the time, as the reader can well imagine. As soon as Lorenzo saw me in the cell, he had my armchair brought, and I instantly flung myself into it; then he left, saying that he would have my bed and all my belongings fetched at once.

The stoicism of Zeno,[48] the ataraxia of the Pyrrhonists,[49] present our judgment with most extraordinary images. They are praised, they are derided, they are admired, they are laughed at, and the wise admit their possibility only with restrictions. Any man who is called upon to judge of a moral possibility or impossibility has every reason to start only from himself, for if he is honest he cannot admit an inner power in anyone unless he feels the seed of it in himself. What I find in myself on this subject is that, through a power gained by great application, a man can succeed in keeping from crying out in his sufferings and can resist being swept away by his first impulses. That is all. *Abstine* ("abstain") and *sustine*[50] ("bear") are the tokens of a good philosopher, but the material sufferings which afflict the Stoic will not be less than those which torment the Epicurean, and grief will be more painful for him who conceals it than for him who obtains a real relief by complaining.

The man who tries to seem indifferent to an event which determines his condition only appears to be so, unless he is an idiot or in a frenzy. He who boasts of perfect tranquillity lies, and I beg Socrates' pardon a thousand times. I will believe in Zeno completely if he will tell me that he has found the secret of preventing nature from turning pale, blushing, laughing, and crying.

I sat in my armchair like a man in a stupor; motionless as a statue, I saw that I had wasted all the efforts I had made, and I could not repent of them. I felt that I had nothing to hope for, and the only relief left to me was not to think of the future.

My thoughts rising up to God, the state in which I was seemed to me a punishment visited on me directly by him because, though he had left me time to finish my whole task, I had abused his mercy by putting off my escape for three days. It was true that I could have gone down three days earlier, but I did not think I deserved so severe a punishment for having delayed in consequence of the most prudent consideration possible, or for exercising a caution enforced on me by a forethought which, on the contrary, deserved to be rewarded, since if I had obeyed only my natural impatience I would have defied every danger.

To fly in the face of the reasoning which had made me put off my escape until August 27th, I should have had to receive a revelation; and reading Maria de Agreda had not turned me into an idiot.

CHAPTER XIV

Underground prisons called "the Wells."
Lorenzo's revenge. I enter into a correspond-
ence with another prisoner, Father Balbi; his
character. I plan my escape with him. The
method. My stratagem for sending him my
pike. Success. I am given an infamous com-
panion; portrait of him.

A MINUTE later two *sbirri* brought me my bed and
left, only to return at once with all my clothes; but two
hours passed during which I saw no one, though the
doors to my cell were open. The delay caused me much
thought but I could reach no conclusion. Having everything to fear, I tried to attain a state of tranquillity
such that I could resist whatever tribulation might come.

Besides "the Leads" and "the Four," the State
Inquisitors had nineteen other terrible prison cells underground in the Doge's Palace; to these they sentenced
criminals who had deserved death. All the highest judges
on earth have always believed that by sparing the life
of him who has deserved death they have shown him
mercy, no matter how horrible a punishment they mete
out to him instead. In my opinion it can only be mercy
if it seems so to the criminal; but they do it without consulting him. It becomes injustice.

These nineteen underground prisons have every re-

semblance to tombs but they are called "wells"[1] because they are always flooded by two feet of sea water,
which comes in through the same grated hole by which
they receive a little light; these holes are only a square
foot in size. The prisoner, unless he enjoys being in a
salt bath up to his knees all day, has to sit on a platform
where he also has his pallet and on which at dawn a
jailer puts his water, his soup, and his ration biscuit,
which he has to eat at once, for if he delays enormous
sea rats would tear it from his hands. In this horrible
prison, to which the prisoners are usually condemned
for the remainder of their days, and with such food, a
number of them live to extreme old age. A criminal who
died about that time had been sent there at the age of
forty-four. Convinced that he had deserved death, he
may have thought his prison a merciful reprieve. There
are those who fear nothing but death. The man's name
was Beguelin;[2] he was French. He had served with the
rank of captain in the troops of the Republic during
her last war with the Turks in the year 1716, and in
Corfu under Field Marshal Count Schulenburg,[3] who
forced the Grand Vizier to raise the siege. Beguelin
served the Marshal as a spy, disguising himself as a
Turk and boldly entering the enemy army; but at the
same time he was spying for the Grand Vizier. Found
guilty of his double espionage, he deserved death, and
it was certain that the judges who sent him to die in
"the Wells" showed him mercy; and the fact is that
he lived for thirty-seven years. He can only have been
bored and always hungry. He may have said: *Dum vita
superest bene est* ("So long as life remains, it is well").[4]
But the prisons I saw at Spielberg[5] in Moravia, to which
clemency consigned prisoners sentenced to death and
which the criminal never managed to survive for a year,
are such that the death they bring *siculi non invenere
tyranni* ("even Sicilian tyrants did not invent").[6]

During the two hours I waited I did not fail to imagine

that I was perhaps to be taken to "the Wells." In a place where the poor wretch who is condemned to it feeds on chimerical hopes he must also feel unreasonable panic terrors. The tribunal, master of the garrets and the cellars of the great palace, might well have decreed Hell for anyone who had tried to run away from Purgatory.

I finally heard furious steps approaching. I saw Lorenzo, his face distorted by anger. Frothing with rage, blaspheming God and all the saints, he began by ordering me to give him the ax and the tools I had used to make a hole in the floor and to tell him which of his *sbirri* had brought them to me. Not stirring even a finger, I replied that I did not know what he was talking about. He orders me searched. But at that I quickly get up, I threaten the scoundrels, and, stripping naked, I told them to do their duty. He had my mattresses searched and my pallet emptied, he even made his men search the stinking chamber pot. He picked up the cushion of my armchair, and finding nothing hard in it, he threw it angrily on the floor.

"You refuse," he said, "to tell me where the tools with which you made the hole are, but someone will make you talk."

"If it is true that I made a hole in the floor, I will say that I received the tools from you and have given them back to you."

At this answer, which his men, whom he seemed to have angered, received with approbation, he shouted, he banged his head against the wall, he stamped his feet; I thought he was going mad. He went out, and his men brought my clothes, my books, my bottles, and everything except my lamp and my stone. That done, before leaving the corridor he closed the two windows through which I got a little air. I was now shut up in a small space with no opening by which the air could enter. I confess that after he left I thought I had got off cheaply. Despite his training in his trade he did not think of

turning my armchair upside down. Finding that I was
still in possession of my bolt, I adored Providence and
I saw that I could still count on making it the means of
my escape.

The intense heat and the shock of the day's events
kept me from sleeping. Early the next morning he
brought me wine which had turned to vinegar, stinking
water, rotting salad, spoiled meat, and very hard bread;
he did not have the place swept, and when I asked him
to open the windows he did not even answer. An extraordinary ceremony which was begun that day consisted
in a constable making the round of my cell carrying an
iron bar with which he pounded the entire floor and the
walls and especially under the bed. I noticed that the
constable who was doing the pounding never struck
the ceiling. This observation gave me the idea that I
could get out by way of the roof; but to succeed in such
a project demanded a combination of circumstances
which did not depend upon me; for I could do nothing
which was not visible. The cell was brand-new; the least
scratch would have been instantly seen by all the constables when they came in.

I spent a terrible day. The intense heat began toward
noon. I really believed I should be stifled. I was in
nothing short of a sweating room. I could neither eat
nor drink, for everything was spoiled. The weakness
caused by the heat and by the sweat which came out in
great drops all over my body made it impossible for me
either to walk or to read. My dinner the next day was
the same; the stench of the veal he brought me reached
my nose at once. I asked him if he had been ordered to
kill me off by hunger and heat, and he went away without
answering. He did the same thing the next day. I told
him to give me a pencil because I wanted to write something to the Secretary, and again he did not answer and
left. I ate the soup out of spite and dipped some bread
in Cyprus wine to preserve my strength and kill him the

next day by plunging my pike into his throat; things
had become so bad that I thought I had no other course;
but the next day instead of carrying out my plan I
satisfied myself with swearing to him that I would kill
him when I was set free; he laughed, and left without
answering. I began to believe he was acting as he did by
order of the Secretary, to whom he had perhaps reported
the hole. I did not know what to do; my patience
struggled against despair; I felt that I was dying of
inanition.

It was on the eighth day that, in the presence of his
constables, I demanded in a voice of thunder that he
give me an accounting of my money, calling him an
infamous hangman. He answered that I should have it
the next day; but before he locked my cell I grabbed up
the bucket of filth and showed him by my posture that
I meant to throw it into the corridor; at that he told
a constable to take it and, the air having become foul,
he opened a window; but after the constable gave me a
clean bucket he shut the window again and left, paying
no attention to my outcries. Such was my situation; but
seeing that what I had obtained had been the result of
the insults to which I had treated him, I prepared to
talk to him even more roughly the next day.

The next day my rage cooled. Before giving me my
account he presented me with a basket of lemons which
Signor Bragadin had sent me and I saw a large bottle
of water which I thought was fit to drink and in my
dinner a chicken which looked promising; moreover, a
constable opened the two windows. When he handed
me my account I merely glanced at the total and told
him to give the balance to his wife, except for a zecchino
which I ordered him to distribute among his men, who
were there and who thanked me. Left alone with me, he
proceeded to deliver the following discourse calmly
enough:

"You have already told me, Signore, that it was from

me you obtained what you needed to make the enormous hole you made in the other cell, so I am no longer in doubt about it. But would you be so good as to tell me who gave you what you needed to make the lamp?''

''You did.''

''What, again? I did not believe that intelligence consisted in audacity.''

''I am not lying. It is you, and with your own hands, who gave me everything I needed: oil, gun flint, and matches—all the rest I had.''

''You are right. Can you as easily convince me that I also gave you what you needed to make the hole?''

''Yes, just as easily. I received nothing except from you.''

''God have mercy on me! What are you saying? Please tell me how I gave you an ax?''

''I will tell you everything if you like, but in the Secretary's presence.''

''I do not wish to hear more, and I believe you. Say nothing, and remember that I am a poor man and have children.''

He went away, holding his head in his hands.

I was very glad I had found the way to instill fear into the rascal, for whom it was decreed that I should cost him his life. I now realized that his own interest forbade his telling the minister anything that I had done.

I had ordered Lorenzo to buy me the complete works of the Marchese Maffei;[7] he did not want to spend the money, and he did not dare tell me so. He asked me what I could need with books when I had so many.

''I have read them all and I need new ones.''

''I will arrange to have someone who is here lend you books if you will lend him yours, and so you will save your money.''

''They are novels, which I do not like.''

''They are learned books; and if you think you are the only one with brains here, you are wrong.''

"Very well. We shall see. Here is a book I will lend to the man with brains. Bring me one too."

I gave him Pétau's *Rationarium*[8] and four minutes later he brought me the first volume of Wolff.[9] Pleased, I canceled my order to buy me Maffei; and even more pleased that he had made me listen to reason on such an important subject, he left.

Less tempted by the prospect of reading the learned work than by seizing the opportunity to begin a correspondence with someone who could perhaps help me in the plan for escaping which I had already sketched out in my mind, upon opening the book I found a piece of paper on which I read, in six well-turned verses, a paraphrase of Seneca's saying: *Calamitosus est animus futuri anxius* ("It is misery for the mind to be anxious about the future").[10] I immediately made six more verses. I had let the nail of the little finger of my right hand grow in order to clean my ears with it, I cut it to a point and made a pen of it, in place of ink I used the juice of black mulberries, and I wrote my six verses on the same piece of paper. In addition I wrote a list of the books I had, and I put it behind the spine of the same book. All books bound in boards in Italy have a sort of pocket under the binding at the back. On the spine of the same book, where the title is put, I wrote *latet*[11] ("something is hidden"). Impatient to receive an answer, the next morning I at once told Lorenzo that I had read the book through and that the person would do me a favor if he would send me another. He immediately brought me the second volume.

A loose note between the pages of the book ran as follows: "We who are together in this prison are both greatly pleased that the ignorance of a miser procures us an unparalleled privilege. I who write am Marin Balbi,[12] a Venetian nobleman and a monk of the Somaschian Order. My companion is Count Andrea Asquin,[13] of Udine, the capital of Friuli. He commands

The Doge and Council Sitting as a Tribunal

The Rio Side of the Doge's Palace, Venice

me to tell you that you are at liberty to make use of all
his books, a catalogue of which you will find in the hollow
of the binding. We must, Signore, employ every precaution to keep our little correspondence from Lorenzo.''

That we had both hit upon the idea of sending each
other catalogues and the idea of concealing a written
message in the aperture at the back of the book did not
surprise me, for it seemed to me to require nothing but
common sense; but I thought his warning to exercise
caution very strange when the letter which told all was
a loose sheet. Lorenzo not only might open the book, it
was his duty to do so, and, seeing the letter and unable
to read, he would have put it in his pocket to get it read
to him in Italian by the first priest he came upon in the
street, and everything would have been discovered at
its very beginning. I at once decided that this Father
Balbi must be a blockhead.

I read the catalogue and on the other half of the
sheet I wrote them who I was, how I had been arrested,
my ignorance of my crime, and my hope that I would
soon be sent home. On receiving another book, Father
Balbi wrote me a letter which covered sixteen pages.
Count Asquin never wrote to me. The monk entertained
himself by writing me the whole story of his misfortunes.
He had been under the Leads for four years[14] because,
having had three bastards by three indigent girls, all
of them virgins, he had had them baptized under his own
name. His Father Superior[15] had admonished him the
first time, threatened him the second, and the third time
had lodged a complaint with the tribunal, which had
imprisoned him; and the Father Superior sent him his
dinner every day. His defense took up half of his letter,
in which he amply displayed the poverty of his intelligence. Both his Superior, he said, and the tribunal were
nothing short of tyrants, for they had no jurisdiction
over his conscience. He said that, since he was sure that
the bastards were his, he could not deprive them of the

advantages they could derive from his name; and that their mothers were respectable though poor, for before him they had had commerce with no man. He ended by saying that his conscience obliged him to recognize publicly that the children these honest young women had given him were his, thus forestalling the slander that they were the children of others, and that in any case he could not deny nature or the fatherly love which he felt for the poor innocents. "There is no danger," he said, "that my Superior will fall into the same fault, since his pious affection is shown only to his boy pupils."

I needed no more to know my man: eccentric, sensual, a poor reasoner, malicious, imprudent, and ungrateful. After saying in his letter that he would be very unfortunate without the company of Count Asquin, who was seventy years of age and had books and money, he used up two pages abusing him to me and describing his faults and absurdities. Out of prison I would not have answered a man of his character; but up there I had to make use of everything. In the back of the book I found pencil, pens, and paper, which made it possible for me to write at my ease.

All the rest of his long letter contained the histories of all the prisoners who were under the Leads and who had been there during the four years he had spent there himself. He told me that Niccolò was the constable who secretly bought him whatever he wanted and who told him the names of all the prisoners and everything that went on in the other cells, and to convince me of it he told me all he knew about the hole I had made. "You were taken from there," he said, "to make room for the patrician Priuli Gran Can,[16] and Lorenzo spent two hours having the hole you made stopped up by a carpenter and an ironsmith, on whom he enjoined silence upon pain of their lives, as he did on all his constables. Niccolò assured me that only one day later you would have left by a method which would have caused a great scandal, and that Lorenzo could have been strangled because it was perfectly clear that, though he tried to show surprise when he saw the hole and pretended to be furious with you, it could only be he who had given you the tools to break open the floor, which you must have given back to him. Niccolò also told me that Signor Bragadin promised him a thousand zecchini if he can make it possible for you to leave and that Lorenzo is confident that he can earn them without losing his post through the protection of Signor Diedo, who is his wife's lover. He also said that none of the constables dared tell the Secretary what had happened for fear that Lorenzo would get out of it with clean hands and would then avenge himself on the informer by having him discharged. I beg you to have confidence in me and to tell me all the particulars of this business and especially how you managed to procure the necessary tools. I promise you that my discretion will be equal to my curiosity.''

I had no doubt of his curiosity but much doubt of his discretion, since his very question proved him to be the most indiscreet of men. However, I saw that I had to humor him, for I thought that a creature of his sort would be just the one to do everything I told him to do and to help me regain my freedom. I spent the whole day answering him; but a strong feeling of suspicion made me put off sending him my answer; I saw that our exchange of letters might be a trick of Lorenzo's to find out who had given me the tools to break the floor and where I was keeping them. I wrote him in a few words that a big knife with which I had made the hole was under the sill of the window in the corridor leading to the cell where I now was, I having myself put it there when I came in. This spurious confidence set my mind at rest in less than three days, for Lorenzo did not search the sill and he would have searched it if he had intercepted my letter.

Father Balbi wrote me that he knew I could have the big knife, for Niccolò had told him I had not been searched before I was locked in; Lorenzo had known this, and the circumstance might have saved him if I had succeeded in escaping, for he claimed that when he received a man from the hands of Messer Grande he could not but suppose that he had already been searched. Messer Grande would have said that, having seen me get out of my bed, he was sure that I had no weapons about me. He ended his letter by asking me to send him my knife by Niccolò, whom I could trust.

The monk's rashness surprised me. When I felt sure that my letters were not being intercepted I wrote him that I was not able to repose any confidence in his Niccolò and that I could not even entrust my secret to paper. Meanwhile his letters amused me. In one of them he told me the reason why Count Asquin was confined under the Leads even though he could not move, since, in addition to his being seventy years of age, he was hampered by a big belly and by a leg he had broken long ago and which had been badly set. He said that, not being rich, the Count practiced law as an advocate at Udine and that in the city council he defended the peasantry against the nobility, who were seeking to deprive them of the right to vote in the provincial assemblies. Because the demands of the peasants disturbed the public peace the nobles had recourse to the tribunal of the State Inquisitors, which ordered Count Asquin to abandon his clients. Count Asquin replied that the municipal code authorized him to defend the constitution, and he disobeyed; but the Inquisitors had him carried off, despite the code, and confined him under the Leads, where he had been for five years.[17] Like me, he had fifty soldi a day, but he had the privilege of handling his money himself. In this connection the monk, who never had a soldo, freely denigrated his companion to me, especially on the score of avarice. He said that in the cell on the other side of the hall there were two gentle-men[18] from the Sette Comuni, also in prison for dis-obedience, the elder of whom had gone mad and was kept tied up. In another cell there were two notaries.[19]

About this time a Veronese Marchese,[20] of the Pinde-monte family, had been imprisoned for disobeying a summons to appear. This nobleman had enjoyed great privileges, perhaps the most important of them being that his servants were allowed to deliver his letters into his own hands. He was there only a week.

When my suspicions were set at rest, my state of mind led me to reason as follows. I wanted my freedom. The pike I had was excellent; but I could not use it because each morning every corner of my cell was sounded with an iron bar, except the ceiling. So I could only hope to escape through the ceiling by having it broken from outside. Whoever was to break it could escape with me by helping me to make a hole in the great roof of the palace the same night. Once on the roof I would see what needed to be done; so the thing was to resolve and begin. I could see no resource except the monk, who, at the age of thirty-eight, though he was lacking in judgment, could carry out my instructions. So I must make up my mind to confide everything to him and think of some way to send him my bolt. I began by asking him if he wanted his freedom and if he was prepared to do everything to gain it by escaping with me. He replied that both he and his companion would be ready to do everything to break their chains; but that there was no use thinking about what was impossible; here he made me a long list of the difficulties, with which he filled four pages and which would have kept me occupied for the rest of my life if I had tried to circumvent them. I answered that I was not concerned about the general difficulties and that, having made my plan, I had thought only of solving the particular ones, which I could not entrust to paper. I promised him freedom if he would give me his word of honor to carry out my orders blindly. He promised me he would do everything.

I then wrote him that I had a pointed iron bar twenty inches long, which he was to use to break open the ceiling of his cell so that he could get out of it; and that once out, he was to break through the wall which separated us, pass through the opening he had made to a point above my cell, break it open above, and pull me out. "Once you have done all this," I said, "you will have nothing more to do, for I will do all the rest. I will get you both out, you and Count Asquin."

He answered that when he had got me out of my cell I would at best be in a prison which would differ from the first only in size. "We shall be in the garrets," he wrote, "still confined behind three locked doors." "I know that, Reverend Father," I replied, "and it is not by way of the doors that I intend we shall escape. My plan is made and I am sure of it, and all that I ask from you is carrying it out to the letter, and no objections. Think only of some way by which my twenty-inch bar can reach your hands without whoever is to bring it to you knowing that he is bringing it; and send me your ideas on the subject. In the meanwhile have Lorenzo buy you forty or fifty images of saints big enough to paper the whole inside of your cell. All these prints of religious subjects will give Lorenzo no occasion for suspecting that their only use will be to cover the hole which you will make in the ceiling and by which you will get out. It will take you several days to make the hole; and in the morning Lorenzo will see nothing of what you have accomplished the day before, for you will put the print back where it was and your work will pass unnoticed. I cannot do this, for I am under suspicion and no one would believe that I have any great reverence for prints. Do this, and think of some way to get my bar."

Thinking about it too, I ordered Lorenzo to buy me a

folio Bible which had recently been printed and which contained the Vulgate[21] and the Septuagint.[22] I thought of this book, the size of which led me to hope that I could put my pike in the back of the binding and so send it to the monk; but when I received it I found that the bolt was two inches longer than the Bible, which measured exactly a foot and a half. The monk had written me that his cell was already papered with prints; and I had written him my idea about the Bible and the great difficulty due to the length of my bar, which I could not shorten except with a forge. He answered, deriding the poverty of my imagination, that I had only to send him the bolt in my fox-skin cloak. He said Lorenzo had told him that I had this fine cloak, and it would give no cause for suspicion if Count Asquin asked to see it in order to have one like it bought for him. I had only, he said, to send it to them folded up; but I was sure that Lorenzo would unfold it on the way, for a folded cloak was more awkward to carry than if it were unfolded; but in order not to discourage him and at the same time to convince him that I was less stupid than himself, I wrote him that he need only send for the cloak. The next morning Lorenzo asked me for it, and I gave it to him folded up but without the bolt. A quarter of an hour later he brought it back to me, saying that they had admired it.

The next day the monk wrote me a letter in which he admitted that he had been guilty of giving me bad advice; but he added that I had been wrong to take it. According to him, the pike was lost, for Lorenzo had brought the cloak unfolded and he must have put the bar in his pocket. So all hope was lost. I consoled him by telling him the truth, at the same time asking him to give his advice less rashly in the future. I then decided to send the monk my bolt in the Bible, but taking a precaution which would infallibly prevent Lorenzo from looking at the ends of the big volume. So I told him that I wanted to celebrate St. Michael's Day[23] with two big dishes of macaroni[24] with butter and Parmesan cheese; I wanted two dishes of it because I wanted to make a present of one to the worthy personage who lent me books. Lorenzo said that the same worthy personage wished to read the big book which had cost three zecchini. I answered that I would send it to him with a dish of macaroni; but I said that I needed the largest dish he had in his house and that I wanted to season it myself; he promised to do everything to the letter. In the meanwhile I wrapped the bolt in paper and I put it in the back of the binding of the Bible. I divided the two inches; each end of the bolt protruded from the Bible by one inch. By placing a big dish of macaroni filled with butter on the Bible, I was sure that Lorenzo's eyes would remain fixed on the butter for fear of spilling it on the Bible, and that thus he would not have time to look at the two ends of the back of the volume. I informed Father Balbi of all this beforehand, urging him to be deft when he received the macaroni from Lorenzo and to be careful not to take first the dish and then the Bible but both together, for taking the dish would expose the Bible and then Lorenzo could easily see the two protruding ends.

On St. Michael's Day Lorenzo appeared very early in the morning with a great kettle in which the macaroni were boiling; I at once put the butter on a portable stove to melt it and I got my two dishes ready, sprinkling them with Parmesan cheese, which he had brought me all grated. I took the pierced spoon and I began to fill them, adding butter and cheese with each spoonful and not stopping until the big dish meant for the monk could hold no more. The macaroni were swimming in butter, which came up to the very edge of the dish. Its diameter was almost twice the width of the Bible.[25] I picked it up and set it on the big book, which I had put beside the door of my cell, and holding it on the palms

of my hands with the spine toward Lorenzo I told him
to put out his arms and spread his fingers, and I
admonished him to carry it with the greatest care and
slowly so that the butter would not spill out of the dish
and run over the Bible. As I admonished him to be
careful of this most important burden, I kept my eyes
fixed on his, which I was most happy to see never moved
from the butter, which he was afraid of spilling. He
wanted to take the macaroni and come back for the
Bible afterward; but I laughed and said that if he did
that, my present would lose all its beauty. He finally
took it, complaining that I had put in too much butter
and protesting that if it spilled on my Bible it would
not be his fault. I knew that I was certain of victory as
soon as I saw the Bible on his arms, for the two ends
of the pike, which were now at a distance from my eyes
equal to the width of the book, had become invisible
for him now that he was holding it; they were next to
his shoulders and there was no reason for him to raise
his eyes to look at either of the ends, which had not
the slightest interest for him. He could only be concerned to keep his dish horizontal. I followed him with
my eyes until I saw him go down three steps to enter
the corridor in front of the monk's cell, who, by blowing
his nose three times, gave me the prearranged signal
that everything had reached his hands in good order.
Lorenzo came back and said that everything had been
delivered according to my instructions. Father Balbi
took a week to make a big enough opening in his ceiling,
easily hiding it each day with a print which he removed
and pasted up again with bread.

On October 8th he wrote me that he had spent the
whole night working at the wall which separated us and
that he had only managed to remove one brick; he exaggerated the difficulty of breaking out bricks held
together by mortar which was too solid; he promised to
continue, and in all his letters he repeated that we should

make our situation worse, for we could not succeed. I answered that I was certain of the contrary.

Alas! I was certain of nothing; but I had to do as I was doing or give up my whole plan. How could I have told him that I did not know? I wanted to be out of there—that was all I knew; and the only thing in my mind was to take what steps I could to forward my escape, and not to stop until I was confronted with something insurmountable. I had read the great book of experience and I had learned from it that great enterprises were not to be talked about but executed, though with due regard for the power which Fortune exercises over all the undertakings of men. If I had imparted these lofty mysteries of moral philosophy to Father Balbi he would have said that I was mad.

His work proved to be difficult only on the first night; during those which followed, the more bricks he took out the easier it was to get out more. At the end of his work he found that he had removed thirty-six bricks from the wall.

On October 16th at eighteen o'clock,[26] just as I was amusing myself translating one of Horace's odes, I heard footsteps above my cell and then three knocks; I at once replied with another three; it was the signal we had arranged to inform each other that we had not been mistaken. He worked until evening, and the next day he wrote me that if my ceiling was only two boards thick his work would be completed that day, for each board was only an inch thick. He assured me that he would make the small circular entrance-way as I had told him to do, and that he would take great care never to go completely through the last board; this I had strongly urged on him because the least sign of a break in my cell would have raised the suspicion that it originated outside of it. He assured me that he would carry his excavation to the point at which it could be completed in a quarter of an hour. I had already settled on the next day but one as the time when I would leave my cell by night and not return to it, for with a companion I felt sure that in three or four hours I could make an opening in the great roof of the Doge's Palace and get up onto it, and then take the best means which chance offered me of getting down.

Two hours after noon on that day, which was a Monday,[27] while Father Balbi was still at work, I heard the sound of the door to the room next to my cell being opened; my blood froze; but I had strength enough left to knock twice, the alarm signal we had agreed to use, on hearing which Father Balbi was to hurry back through the hole in the wall and regain his cell. A moment later I saw Lorenzo, who asked my pardon for giving me the company of a "beggarly scoundrel." I saw a man between forty and fifty years of age, short, thin, badly dressed, with a round black wig, whom two constables proceeded to unbind. I had no doubt that he was a rogue, since Lorenzo had so characterized him in my presence and he had taken no offense at the title. I answered Lorenzo that the tribunal was lord and master; after having a pallet brought for him, he left, telling him that the tribunal allowed him ten soldi a day. My new cellmate replied:

"May God repay them!"

Overwhelmed by this fatal obstacle, I looked at the scoundrel, whose face betrayed him. I was thinking of getting him to talk, when he began himself by thanking me for the pallet which I had had brought for him. I told him that he would eat with me, and he kissed my hand, asking me if even so he could have the ten soldi the tribunal allowed him, and I said that he could. He then went down on his knees, took a rosary from his pocket, and began peering all around the cell.

"What are you looking for, my friend?"

"I am looking, if you will forgive me, for some image *dell'immacolata Vergine Maria,* since I am a Christian, or at least for some poor crucifix, for I was never in such need of commending myself to St. Francis of Assisi, whose name I unworthily bear, as I am at this moment.''

I could hardly keep from bursting into laughter, not at his Christian piety, which I revered, but at the way in which he had defended himself; his asking my pardon made me think he took me for a Jew; I hastened to give him the Office of the Holy Virgin,[28] whose image he kissed, then handed it back to me, modestly saying that his father, warden of a galley, had failed to have him taught to read. He said that he was a devotee of the most holy Rosary and told me a quantity of its miracles, to which I listened with the patience of an angel, and he asked my permission to recite it looking at the holy image which was the frontispiece to my Book of Hours. After the Rosary, which I recited with him, I asked him if he had dined and he said he was dying of hunger. I gave him everything I had; he devoured it all ravenously, drank all the wine I had, and when he was tipsy he began first crying and then babbling without rhyme or reason. I asked him the cause of his misfortune, and here is his story:

''My one and only passion in this world, dear master, has always been the glory of this sacred Republic and strict obedience to its laws; always attentive to the evil practices of the wicked, whose sole occupation is to deceive their prince and cheat him out of his dues and to keep their own activities concealed, and I have tried to discover their secrets and I have always faithfully reported to Messer Grande whatever I have been able to discover; it is true that I have always been paid; but the money I have received has never given me as much pleasure as the satisfaction I have felt in seeing that I was useful to the glorious Evangelist St. Mark. I have always scorned the prejudice of those who attach an evil meaning to the designation 'spy'; that name is ill-sounding only in the ears of those who do not love the government, for a spy is nothing but one who fosters the good of the State, the scourge of criminals, and the loyal subject of his prince. When I have been called upon to put my zeal into action, the feeling of friendship, which may have some weight with others, has never had any with me, still less what is called gratitude, and I have often vowed silence to wrest from someone an important secret which, as soon as I learned it, I punctually reported, assured by my confessor that I could reveal it not only because I had had no intention of keeping my oath of silence when I took it but because, where the public welfare is concerned, no oath is binding. I feel that, the slave of my zeal, I would have betrayed my father and I would have stilled the promptings of nature.

"Three weeks ago, then, I observed at Isola,[29] a small island where I was living, a great intimacy among four or five notable personages of the city whom I knew to be dissatisfied with the government because of the discovery and confiscation of a certain contraband shipment, which the principals had been obliged to expiate by imprisonment. The First Chaplain[30] of the parish, born a subject of the Empress-Queen, was in the plot, whose secret I determined to unravel. The plotters met in the evening at an inn, in a room where there was a bed; and after drinking and talking together they left. I boldly determined to hide under the bed one day when, sure that I was unobserved, I found the room open and empty. Toward evening my plotters arrived and talked about the city of Isola which they said was not under the jurisdiction of St. Mark but under that of the principality of Trieste, for it could not be regarded as a part of Venetian Istria. The Chaplain said to the leader of the plot, whose name was Pietro Paolo, that if he would sign a document and the others would do the same, he would himself wait on the Imperial Ambassador[31] and that the Empress would not only seize the city but would reward them. They all told the Chaplain they were ready, and he promised to bring the document the next day and leave at once and come here to bring it to the Ambassador. I decided to make their infamous project miscarry, despite the fact that one of the conspirators was my godfather, a spiritual relationship which gave him a claim on me more sacred and inviolable than if he had been my brother.

"After they left I had plenty of time to get away, thinking it useless to run a second risk by hiding myself the next day under the same bed. I had discovered enough. I left at midnight in a boat, and the next day before noon I was here, where I had someone write down the names of the six rebels for me, then took them to the Secretary to the State Inquisitors, telling him the facts. He ordered me to go early the next morning to Messer, who would give me a man with whom I should go to Isola to point out the Chaplain to him, for it seemed that the Chaplain would not have left by then, and after that I was to let the matter alone. I carried out his order. Messer gave me the man, I took him to Isola, I showed him the Chaplain, and I went about my business.

"After dinner my godfather sent for me to come and shave him, for I am a barber. After I had shaved him he gave me an excellent glass of refosco[32] and some slices of garlic sausage and he ate with me in good fellowship. My love for him as my godfather then filled my soul, I took his hand and, with heartfelt tears, advised him to end his acquaintance with the Chaplain and above all not to sign the document of which he knew; upon this he said to me that he was no more friendly with the Chaplain than with anyone else and he swore he had no idea what document I was referring to. I then began to laugh, I said I had been joking, and I left him, repenting that I had listened to the voice of my heart.

"The next day I saw neither the man nor the Chaplain,

and a week later I left Isola and came here. I went to see Messer Grande, who instantly had me locked up; and here I am with you, dear master. I thank St. Francis that I am in the company of a good Christian who is here for reasons which I do not seek to know, for I am not curious. My name is Soradaci,[33] and my wife is a Legrenzi, daughter of a Secretary to the Council of Ten, who trampled on prejudice in order to marry me. She will be in despair not to know what has become of me; but I hope I shall stay here only a few days; I can be here only for the convenience of the Secretary, who presumably will need to question me.''

After this brazen narrative, which showed me what kind of monster he was, I pretended to condole with him and, lauding his patriotism, predicted that he would be free in a few days. A half hour later he went to sleep, and I wrote the whole story to Father Balbi, urging upon him the necessity of suspending our work to await a favorable opportunity. The next day I ordered Lorenzo to buy me a wooden crucifix and a print of the Holy Virgin, and to bring me a flask of holy water. Soradaci asked him for his ten soldi, and Lorenzo scornfully gave him twenty. I ordered him to bring me four times as much wine and some garlic, for my cell-mate delighted in it. After he left I deftly took Father Balbi's letter from the book; he described his fright to me. He had returned to his cell more dead than alive and had quickly put the print back over the hole. He reflected that all would have been lost if Lorenzo had taken it into his head to put Soradaci in his garret instead of putting him with me. Lorenzo would not have seen him in the cell and he would have seen the hole.

The account Soradaci gave me of his activities led me to conclude that he would certainly have to undergo questioning, for the Secretary could not have had him locked up except on suspicion of slander or because his report was not clear. I therefore decided to entrust him with two letters which, if he had taken them to those to whom they were addressed, would have done me neither good nor harm, and which would have done me good if the traitor gave them to the Secretary in proof of his fidelity. I spent two hours writing the letters in pencil. The next morning Lorenzo brought me the image of the Virgin, the bottle of holy water, and all that I had ordered.

After feeding the scoundrel well I told him that I was under the necessity of asking him to do me a favor upon which my happiness depended.

"I count, my dear Soradaci, on your friendship and your courage. Here are two letters which I beg you to take to their addresses as soon as you regain your freedom. My happiness depends on your fidelity; but you must hide them, for if they are found on you when you leave here we are both lost. You must swear to me by this crucifix and by this Holy Virgin that you will not betray me."

"I am ready, master, to swear whatever you ask; I am under too great an obligation to you to betray you."

He began crying and protesting that he was wretched enough without my supposing him capable of treachery. After giving him a shirt and a nightcap, I took my nightcap off, I sprinkled the cell with holy water, and in the presence of the two sacred images I intoned an oath accompanied by imprecations which had no sense but were horrifying, and after several signs of the cross I made him get down on his knees and swear with imprecations which set him trembling that he would deliver the letters. After that I gave them to him, and it was he who insisted on sewing them into the back of his vest between the cloth and the lining.

I was morally certain that he would give them to the Secretary; so I used every art to write in such a style that no one would ever discover my ruse. My letters were of a nature to gain me the indulgence of the tribunal and even its esteem. I wrote to Signor Bragadin and to the Abate Grimani and I told them to set their minds at rest and not to repine over my fate, for I had reason to hope that I would soon be released. I told them that when I came out they would find that my punishment had done me more good than harm, because no one in Venice had stood in greater need of reformation than I. I asked Signor Bragadin to send me a pair of lined boots for the winter, since my cell was high enough for me to stand upright and walk about in. I did not want Soradaci to know that my letters were so innocent, for he might have taken it into his head to act like an honest man and deliver them.

CHAPTER XV

Soradaci turns traitor. How I overawe him.
Father Balbi successfully completes his work.
I leave my cell. Count Asquin's untimely
observations. The moment of departure.

TWO OR three days later Lorenzo came up at the
Terza and took Soradaci down with him. Not seeing him
return, I thought I should see no more of him; but he
was brought back toward the end of the day, which rather
surprised me. After Lorenzo left he told me that the
Secretary suspected him of having warned the Chaplain,
since the priest had never gone to see the Ambassador
and no document had been found on him. He said that
after a long interrogation he had been put all alone in
a very small cell where he had been left for seven hours
and that afterward he had been fettered again and
taken to the Secretary, who tried to make him confess
that he had told someone in Isola that the priest would
not return there; this he could not confess, for he had
never said it to anyone. The Secretary had finally rung
and he had been brought back to my cell.[1]

In bitterness of soul I realized that he might well be
left with me for a long time. During the night I wrote

all this to Father Balbi. It was under the Leads that I learned to write in the dark.

The next morning after swallowing my broth, I wanted to make sure of what I already suspected.

"I wish," I said to the spy, "to add something to the letter I wrote Signor Bragadin; give it to me; you can sew it back in afterward."

"It is dangerous," he answered, "for someone might come in just at that moment and catch us at it."

"Let them come. Give me back my letters."

The monster then fell on his knees before me and swore that when he appeared before the terrible Secretary for the second time he was seized with a violent shaking and felt an intolerable pressure on his back just where the letters were, and the Secretary asking him what it was, he could not keep from telling him the truth, and Lorenzo having taken off his fetters and then his vest, he had unsewn the letters, which the Secretary had put in a drawer after reading them. He added that the Secretary had said that if he had delivered the letters it would have been known and his crime would have cost him his life.

I then pretended to feel ill. I covered my face with my hands and flung myself on the bed on my knees before the crucifix and the Virgin demanding vengeance upon the monster who had betrayed me by violating the most solemn of all oaths. After that I lay down on my side with my face to the wall, and I had the firmness to remain there all that day without uttering a word, pretending not to hear the villain's tears and cries and protestations of repentance. I played my role wonderfully well in a comedy of which I already had the whole plot sketched out in my head. During the night I wrote Father Balbi to come at exactly nineteen o'clock,[2] and not one minute earlier or later, to finish his work, and to work for only four hours, so that he should leave without fail exactly when he heard twenty-three o'clock strike. I told him that our freedom depended on this absolute precision on his part and that he had nothing to fear.

It was the 25th of October, and the days were nearing when I must either carry out my project or abandon it forever. The State Inquisitors and even the Secretary went every year to spend the first three days of November[3] in some village on the mainland. During these three days when his masters were on vacation Lorenzo got drunk in the evening, slept until the Terza, and did not appear under the Leads until very late. It was a year earlier that I had learned all this. Prudence demanded that, if I was to escape, I must choose one of these three nights, in order to be certain that my flight would not be discovered until fairly late in the morning. Another reason for my eagerness, and one which led me to take the resolve at a time when I could no longer doubt that my companion was a scoundrel, was extremely powerful, and I think it deserves to be recorded.

The greatest relief a man in misfortune can have is the hope of soon escaping from it; he thinks of the happy moment when he will see the end of his misery, he persuades himself that it will not be long in coming, and he would do anything on earth to know exactly when it will come; but no one can know at what time something which depends on the will of another will happen, unless that other has announced it. However, in his impatience and weakness, the man comes to believe that by some occult means he can discover the time. "God," he says, "must know it, and God may permit it to be revealed to me by some omen." As soon as his curiosity has led him to this reasoning he does not hesitate to consult the omens, whether he is ready or not to believe all that they may tell him. Such was the state of mind of those who in past ages consulted oracles; such is the state of mind of those who today still question cabalas and who seek revelations in a verse of the Bible or a verse of

Vergil, which has brought such fame to the *sortes vir-gilianae*[4] of which so many writers tell us.

Not knowing what method to use to make Destiny reveal to me through the Bible the moment at which I was to regain my freedom, I decided to consult the divine poem of *Orlando furioso* by Messer Lodovico Ariosto, which I had read countless times and which was still my delight up there. I worshiped his genius and I thought him far better suited than Vergil to foretell my good fortune.

With this idea in mind, I composed a short question in which I asked the supposed Intelligence which canto of Ariosto contained the prediction of my day of deliverance. After that I constructed an inverted pyramid made up of the numbers which resulted from the words of my question, and by subtracting nine from each pair of digits I finally came out with the number *nine*. I therefore concluded that the prediction I sought was in the ninth canto. I used the same method to discover in which stanza the prediction occurred and the resulting number was *seven*. Now eager to learn which verse of the stanza contained the oracle, the same method gave me the number *one*. So having the numbers 9, 7, 1 I took up the poem and, with my heart palpitating, found canto *nine,* stanza *seven,* first verse:

Tra il fin d'Ottobre, e il capo di Novembre

("Between the end of October and the beginning of November").[5]

The clarity of the verse and its appropriateness struck me as so amazing that I will not say I had complete faith in it, but my reader will forgive me if, for my part, I prepared to do all that I could to help verify the oracle. The strange thing is that "between the end of October and the beginning of November" there is only midnight, and it was in fact at the stroke of midnight on October 31st that I left there, as the reader will see. I beg him, after this faithful account, not to dismiss me as more superstitious than anyone else, for he would be wrong. I recount the thing because it is true and extraordinary, and because if I had disregarded it I should perhaps not have escaped. The incident will teach all those who have not yet attained wisdom that but for predictions many things that have happened would never have happened. The event does the prediction the service of verifying it. If the event does not occur the prediction becomes nul and void; but I refer my kind reader to universal history, where he will find many events which would never have occurred if they had not been predicted. Forgive the digression.

And now for the way I spent the day until nineteen o'clock, meaning to strike awe into the soul of the stupid, vicious brute who was my companion, to confuse his feeble mind by astonishing images, and so make him powerless to harm me. When Lorenzo left us that morning I told Soradaci to come and eat his soup. The villain was in bed and he had told Lorenzo that he was ill. He would not have dared to come to me if I had not summoned him. He got up and, groveling on his belly at my feet, kissed them and, bursting into tears, said that unless I forgave him he would be a dead man that same day and that he already felt the beginning of the curse laid on him by the vengeance of the Holy Virgin, whom I had invoked against him; he felt griping pains tormenting his entrails and his tongue was covered with ulcers; he showed it to me and I saw that it was really covered with aphtha; I do not know if he had them the day before. I was not interested in examining him to see if he was telling me the truth; my interest was to pretend that I believed him and even to make him hope for forgiveness. I had next to make him eat and drink. The traitor might be intending to deceive me; but determined as I was to deceive him, it was a matter of finding out which of us was the cleverer. I had prepared an attack against which I was certain he could not defend himself.

I instantly assumed the countenance of a man inspired and I ordered him to sit down.

"Let us eat this soup," I said, *"and afterward I will declare your good fortune to you. Know that the Holy Virgin of the Rosary appeared to me at daybreak and commanded me to forgive you. You will not die and you will leave this place with me."*

Lost in wonder, he ate the soup with me, kneeling on the floor because there were no stools, then he sat on his pallet to hear me out. This is what I said:

"The grief which your treachery caused me kept me awake all night, because my letters, which you gave to the Secretary, would have been read by the State Inquisitors and have led to my being sentenced to stay here the rest of my life. My only consolation, I confess to you, was my certainty that you would die before my eyes within three days. With my mind full of this thought unworthy of a Christian, for God commands us to forgive, a slumber at daybreak brought me a vision. I saw this Holy Virgin, whose image you see, come to life, move, stand before me, open her mouth, and speak to me in these words: *'Soradaci is a devotee of my holy Rosary, I protect him, it is my will that you forgive him; and the curse he drew upon himself will now cease to operate. As the reward of your generous act I will command one of my angels to put on human form and at once come down from Heaven to break open the roof of this cell and take you from it in five or six days. The angel will set to work today at nineteen o'clock and he will work until half an hour before sunset, for he must return to Heaven by daylight. When you leave here with my angel you will take Soradaci with you, and you will look after him on condition that he gives up his trade of spy. You will tell him all this.'* After saying these words the Holy Virgin vanished, and I found that I was awake.''

Maintaining all the gravity I could muster, I studied the countenance of the traitor, who appeared to be petrified. I then took my Book of Hours, I sprinkled the cell with holy water, and I began pretending to pray to God, from time to time kissing the image of the Virgin. An hour later the beast, who had never said a word, asked me point-blank at what hour the angel was to come down from Heaven and if he would hear him breaking open the cell.

''I am certain that he will come at nineteen o'clock, that we will hear him working, and that he will leave at twenty-three; and it seems to me that four hours of work is enough for an angel.''

''You may have been dreaming.''

''I am sure I was not. Are you prepared to swear to me that you will renounce being a spy?''

Instead of answering he went to sleep and did not wake until two hours later, when he asked me if he could put off giving me his oath that he would renounce his trade.

''You can put it off,'' I said, ''until the moment the angel enters this cell to take me away with him; but I warn you that if you do not swear to give up your evil trade I will leave you here, for such is the order I received from the Holy Virgin.''

I then saw his relief, for he felt sure that the angel would not come. He seemed to pity me. I could not wait to hear the nineteenth hour strike, and the comedy entertained me vastly, for I was sure that the arrival of the angel would set the brute's miserable reason tottering. The thing was infallible unless, to my great regret, Lorenzo had forgotten to deliver the book.

At eighteen o'clock I began eating dinner, and I drank water. Soradaci drank all the wine and for dessert ate

all the garlic I had; it was his sweetmeat. When I heard
nineteen o'clock I fell on my knees, ordering him to do
likewise in a voice which made him tremble. He obeyed,
looking at me like an idiot with unseeing eyes. When I
heard the little noise which told me that my accomplice
was passing through the wall,

"The angel is coming," I said.

I then lay down on my stomach, at the same time
giving him a push between the shoulders which made
him fall into the same position. The noise from the breaking was loud, and I remained there prostrate for a good
quarter of an hour. Did I not have reason enough to
laugh when I saw that the scoundrel had remained
motionless in the same position? But I did not laugh. I
was engaged in the noble work of driving him mad or at
least frantic. His accursed soul could not become human
except by being steeped in terror. I spent three and a
half hours reading while he told the Rosary, falling
asleep from time to time and never daring to open his
mouth, only looking up at the ceiling when he heard
the noise of the monk splitting a board. In his stupor he
kept bowing to the image of the Virgin in the most comical way imaginable. At the stroke of twenty-three o'clock
I told him to do as I would do, since it was time for the
angel to leave; we prostrated ourselves, Father Balbi
left, and we heard not another sound. When I rose the
expression I saw on the villain's face betokened dread
and terror rather than rational surprise.

I amused myself for a while talking with him to hear
how he would reason. He said things, always weeping,
the connection between which was little short of absurdity; it was a hodgepodge of ideas none of which
was pursued. He talked of his sins, of his special devo-
tions, of his zeal for St. Mark, of his duties to his prince,
and it was to this merit in him that he attributed the
grace which the Holy Virgin was granting him, and I
had to put up with a long tale of the miracles of the

Rosary which his wife, whose confessor was a Dominican, had told him. He said that he could not guess what I would do with him, ignorant as he was.

"You will be in my service and you will have everything you need, without pursuing your vile and dangerous trade of spying."

"But we cannot stay in Venice."

"Of course not. The angel will lead us to a state which does not belong to St. Mark. Are you ready to swear to me that you will renounce your trade? And if you swear, will you perjure yourself again?"

"If I swear, I will not break my oath, that is sure; but admit that if I had not perjured myself you would not have obtained the grace which the Holy Virgin has granted you. So you must be grateful to me and love me for betraying you."

"Do you love Judas, who betrayed Jesus Christ?"

"No."

"Then you see that one must loathe the traitor and at the same time adore Providence, which makes good come out of evil. You have been a scoundrel, my dear man, until now. You have offended God and the Holy Virgin, and at present I will no longer accept your oath unless you expiate your sin."

"What sin have I committed?"

"Your sin of pride in supposing that I should feel obliged to you for giving my letters to the Secretary."

"Then what must I do to expiate my sin?"

"You must do this. Tomorrow when Lorenzo comes you must remain motionless on your pallet with your face to the wall and never look at Lorenzo. If he speaks to you you must answer him, without looking at him, that you could not sleep. Do you promise to obey me?"

"I promise you that I will do all that you say."

"Promise it to this holy image. Quick!"

"I promise you, most holy Virgin, that when Lorenzo

comes I will not look at him and that I will not stir from
my pallet.''

''And I, most holy Virgin, swear to you by the bowels
of Jesus Christ your God and son, that as soon as I see
Soradaci turn to Lorenzo I will run and strangle him
to your honor and glory.''

I asked him if he had anything to object to my oath,
and he said he was satisfied with it. I then gave him
something to eat and told him to go to bed because I
needed sleep. I spent two hours writing an account of
all this to the monk and I said that if the work was almost completed he need come to the roof of my cell again
only to break through the board and enter. I told him
that we would leave on the night of October 31st, and
that we would be four, counting his companion and
mine. It was the 28th. Early the next day the monk
informed me that the small entrance-way was finished and
that he needed to get on the roof of my cell again only to
open it, which he was sure he could do in four minutes.
Soradaci obeyed his orders perfectly. He pretended to be
asleep, and Lorenzo did not even speak to him. I kept my
eyes on him and I believe I should really have strangled
him if I had seen him turn his head toward Lorenzo,
for to betray me he would have had to do no more than
give him a wink.

I spent the day treating him to sublime discourses
calculated to inspire fanaticism, leaving him in peace
only when I saw that he was drunk and ready to fall
asleep or on the point of going into convulsions under the
impact of a metaphysics equally foreign and new to his
mind, which had never applied its faculties to anything
but inventing some trick of his spying trade.

He gave me pause for a moment by saying that he
could not understand how an angel would need to work
so long to open my cell; but I at once regained the upper
hand by saying that he was not working as an angel but

as a man, and I added that his evil thought must have instantly offended the Holy Virgin.

"And you will see," I said, "that because of your sin the angel will not come today. You always think not like an honest, pious, devout man but like a wicked sinner who supposes he is dealing with Messer Grande and the *sbirri*."

He then began weeping, and I was delighted to see that he was in despair when nineteen o'clock struck and there was no sound of the angel arriving. I then broke into lamentations which distressed him, and I left him to suffer all day. The next day he did not fail to obey, and when Lorenzo asked after his health he answered without looking at him. He maintained the same behavior on the following day, until I finally saw Lorenzo for the last time on the morning of the 31st, having given him the book in which I told the monk to come and make the opening. This time I feared no more obstacles, having learned from Lorenzo himself that not only the Inquisitors but the Secretary too had gone to the country. I had no reason to fear the arrival of any other guest; and I no longer needed to humor my infamous companion.

But now for an apology which I should perhaps make to some reader who might think unfavorably of my religion and morals because of the way I abused our holy mysteries and the oath which I made the idiot swear and the lies I told him about the appearance of the Holy Virgin.

Since my purpose was to tell the story of my escape with all its circumstances as they really happened, I considered it my duty to conceal nothing. I cannot say that I am confessing, for I feel no sting of repentance; nor can I say that I am proud of what I did, for it was with the utmost reluctance that I made use of the imposture. If I had disposed of any better means I would certainly have given them the preference. To regain my freedom I feel that I would still do the same thing today, and perhaps a great deal more.

Nature commanded me to escape, and religion could not forbid me to do it; I had no time to lose; having a spy with me who had given me an indubitable example of his perfidy, I must make it morally impossible for him to inform Lorenzo that the roof of the cell was being broken in. What was I to do? I had only two possibilities, and I must choose. Either I must bind the villain's soul by terror, or silence him by strangling him, as any other reasonable man more cruel than I would have done. It would have been much easier for me, and I should even have had nothing to fear, for I would have said that he died a natural death and no one would have taken much trouble to discover if it was true or not. Now where is the reader who can think that I would have done better to strangle him? If there is one such, may God enlighten him; his religion will never be mine. I believe that I did my duty; and the victory which crowned my exploit may be proof that eternal Providence did not disapprove of the means I employed. As for the oath I made him that I would always look after him, thank God he himself freed me from it, for he did not have the courage to escape with me; but even if he had found the courage I confess to my reader that I should not have thought I was perjuring myself if I had not kept it. I would have got rid of the monster at the first opportunity, even if I had had to hang him from a tree. When I swore that I would always help him, I knew that his loyalty would last only as long as the frenzy of his fanaticism, which was bound to disappear as soon as he saw that the angel was a monk. *Non merta fè chi non la serba altrui* ("He does not deserve loyalty who does not observe it").[6] A man has far more right to sacrifice everything to his own self-preservation than sovereigns have to do the same to preserve the State.

After Lorenzo left I told Soradaci that the angel would come to make an opening in the roof of my cell at seventeen o'clock; "he will bring a pair of scissors," I said, "and you shall cut my beard and the angel's."

"Does the angel wear a beard?"

"Yes, you will see it. After that we will leave and go to break open the roof of the palace; and at night we will get down into the Piazza San Marco and go to Germany."

He did not answer; he ate by himself, for my heart and mind were too much occupied with my escape to leave me capable of eating. I had not even been able to sleep.

Seventeen o'clock strikes, and the angel is there! Soradaci made to prostrate himself, but I said it was no longer necessary. In less than three minutes he broke through, the perfectly round piece of board dropped at my feet, Father Balbi slid into my arms.

"Your work," I said as I embraced him, *"is done; mine begins."*

He delivered the pike to me and gave me a pair of scissors, which I handed to Soradaci so that he could cut off our beards at once. This time I could not keep from laughing when I saw the utter astonishment with which the brute was staring at the angel, who looked like a devil. Beside himself, he cut our beards perfectly with the points of the scissors.

Impatient to see the topography of the place, I told the monk to stay there with Soradaci, for I did not want to leave him alone; I climbed out and found that the hole in the wall was narrow, but I got through it; I came to the roof of the Count's cell, I entered it and cordially embraced the unfortunate old man. I saw a figure not fitted to encounter the difficulties and dangers which such a flight was sure to bring us on an immense sloping roof covered with lead plates. He at once asked me what my plan was, saying that he thought the steps I had taken were not sufficiently considered.

"All I ask," I replied, "is to go forward until I find freedom or death."

He said, grasping my hand, that if my idea was to make a hole in the roof and try to find a way down over the lead plates, he did not see how I could do it unless I had wings.

"I have not," he added, "the courage to go with you; I will stay here and pray to God for you."

I then went out to investigate the great roof, getting as close as I could to the sides of the loft. Managing to touch the under side of the roof at the narrowest point of the angle, I sat down among the roof timbering, with which the lofts of all great palaces are filled. I sounded the boards with the point of my bolt and I found that they were as if rotting away. At each blow I made with my pike everything it entered fell to pieces. Seeing that I could certainly make a big enough opening in less than an hour, I went back to my cell, where I spent four hours cutting up sheets, napkins, mattresses, and everything I had which would make a rope. I insisted on knotting the pieces together myself with weaver's knots, for a badly made knot could have come undone and whoever was hanging from the rope at that moment would have fallen to the ground. I saw myself in possession of a hundred *braccia*[7] of rope. In great enterprises there are certain points which decide the issue and in regard to which the leader who deserves to succeed is he who trusts no one.

After finishing the rope I made a bundle of my coat, my floss-silk cloak, some shirts, stockings, and handkerchiefs, and the three of us went to the Count's cell carrying all this with us. The Count first congratulated Soradaci on having had the luck to be put with me and to be about to follow me. His look of confusion gave me an almost irresistible desire to laugh. I no longer restrained myself; I had cast off the mask of Tartufe[8] which I had worn all day for the past week to prevent the two-faced scoundrel from betraying me. I saw that he was sure I had deceived him, but otherwise he was completely bewildered; for he could not guess how I could have corresponded with the supposed angel to make him come and go at the hour I pleased. He heard the Count saying that we were braving the most obvious danger of perishing, and coward as he could not but be, he was already turning over a plan to excuse himself from the perilous journey. I told the monk to bundle up his things while I went to make the hole at the edge of the loft.

I needed no help to complete my opening by two o'clock[9] that night. I pulverized the boards. My aperture was twice as big as necessary, and I was able to touch the entire plate of lead. The monk helped me get it out of the way, for it either curved around the edge of the marble gutter or was riveted to it; but by pushing my pike between the gutter and the plate I got it loose, and then with our shoulders we bent it back until the opening through which we would have to pass was large enough. Putting my head out of the hole, I was distressed to see the bright light of the crescent moon, which would reach its first quarter the following day. It was an obstacle which we had to bear with patience, putting off our departure until midnight, when the moon would have gone to light the antipodes. On a splendid night, when everyone of any account would be strolling in the Piazza San Marco, I could not risk being seen walking about up there. Our shadows, stretching far over the pavement of the square, would have been seen by the strollers, they would have looked up, and our persons would have provided a most unusual spectacle which would have aroused curiosity, especially on the part of Messer Grande, whose *sbirri,* the only guardians of the great city of Venice, keep watch all night. He would in-

The Doge Francesco Loredan

The Canale della Giudecca, Venice

stantly have found a way to send a troop of them up there, which would have ruined all my fine plans. I therefore imperiously decreed that we were not to go out until after the moon had set. I called on God for help, and I did not ask for miracles. Exposed to the whims of Fortune, I must give her as little scope as I could. If my enterprise failed, I must not have the slightest miscalculation to reproach myself with. The moon was certain to set at five, and the sun would rise at half past thirteen; we would have seven hours of total darkness in which to act.

I told Father Balbi that we would spend three hours conversing with Count Asquin; and to go to him by himself at once and let him know that I was in need of his lending me thirty zecchini which might be as indispensable to me as my pike had been in accomplishing all I had done. He did my errand and four minutes later came back and told me to go alone because the Count wanted to speak to me without witnesses. The poor old man began by gently telling me that I did not need money to make good my escape, that he had none, that he had a large family, that if I died the money he gave me would be lost, adding a great many other reasons, all calculated to hide his avarice. My answer took half an hour. I used excellent arguments but ones which have never had any power since the world began, for no orator can extirpate a passion. It was a case of *nolenti baculus* ("for him who is unwilling, the rod"), but I was not hardhearted enough to use force on the unfortunate old man. I ended by saying that if he wanted to flee with me I would carry him on my shoulders as Aeneas did Anchises;[10] but that if he wanted to remain and pray to God for us his prayer would achieve nothing, for he would be asking God to bring success to an undertaking to which he had not contributed by ordinary means. The sound of his voice called my attention to his tears, which tried my temper; he asked me if two *zecchini* would satisfy me, and I answered that I had to be satisfied with anything. He gave them to me, begging me to return them if after making a round of the great roof of the palace I took the sensible course of going back to my cell. I promised him I would do so, a little surprised that he supposed I could decide to return. I was certain that I would never go back there.

I called my companions, and we put all our equipment near the hole. I divided the hundred *braccia* of rope into two coils and we spent two hours talking and not unpleasurably recalling all our vicissitudes. The first sample Father Balbi gave me of his excellent character was to tell me ten times over that I had broken my word to him, since I had assured him in my letters that my plan was all laid and infallible, whereas it was nothing of the kind; and he brazenly told me that if he had known this beforehand he would not have got me out of my cell. The Count, with all the gravity of his seventy years, told me that my wisest course was not to go on, for the impossibility of getting down from the roof was as obvious as the danger, which might cost me my life. I said mildly that the two things which were obvious to him were far from obvious to me; but since he was an advocate by profession, here is the harangue with which he tried to convince me. What spurred him on was the two zecchini which I should have had to return to him if he had persuaded me to stay.

"The slope of the roof, covered as it is with lead plates, will not allow you to walk over it for you can scarcely stand upright on it. The roof has seven or eight dormers, but they are all barred with iron and there is no way of reaching them to stand in front of them for they are all distant from the edges. The ropes you have will be of no use to you, because you will find no place to which you could fasten one end securely, and even if you found it, a man descending from such a height cannot remain suspended by his arms or manage his own descent. So one of you three would have to put a rope around the other two,

one at a time, and let them down as you let a bucket
down into a well; and whoever did this would have to
stay behind and go back to his cell. Which of the three
of you feels inclined to perform this act of charity? And
supposing that one of you is hero enough to be willing
to remain behind, pray tell me on which side you will
go down. Not on the side toward the square and the pillars, for you would be seen. Not on the side toward the
church, for you would still be shut in. Not on the side
toward the courtyard of the palace, for the Arsenalotti[11]
make constant rounds there. You can only go down on
the side toward the canal. You have no gondola and no
boat waiting for you; so you would have to throw yourselves into the water and swim as far as Sant'Apollonia,[12] which you would reach in a deplorable state, not
knowing where to go at night to put yourselves in fit
condition to continue your flight. Consider that it is
slippery on the leads, and if you fall into the canal you
cannot hope to escape death even if you can swim, for
the height is so great and the canal so shallow that the
fall would crush you to death before you could drown.
Three or four feet of water are not a volume of fluid
sufficient to lessen the violence of the descent of a solid
body falling into it. The least that could happen to you
would be to find you had broken your legs or arms.''

I listened to this harangue, inappropriate as it was to
the exigencies of the situation, with a patience which was
not like me. The monk's reproaches, hurled at me with no
consideration, made me indignant and provoked me to
refute them harshly; but I would have ruined what I
had built up, for I was dealing with a coward quite
capable of answering that he was not desperate enough
to brave death and so I had only to set off by myself; and
by myself I could not hope to succeed. I humored these
grudging spirits by mildness. I said that I was sure I
would save us though I was not in a position to tell them
my plans in detail. I told Count Asquin that his sensible

considerations would make me act with prudence and that my trust in God was so great that it stood me in stead of all else.

I frequently put out my hands to discover if Soradaci was still there, for he never said a word; I laughed as I thought of what he might be turning over in his malicious mind, which must know that I had deceived him. At half past four I told him to go and see where the crescent moon was in the sky. He came back and said that in a half hour it would no longer be visible, and that an unusually thick fog must be making the leads very dangerous.

"It is enough for me, my man, if the fog is not oil. Make a bundle of your cloak and some of our ropes, which we must divide equally between us."

I was then surprised to find the man at my knees, taking my hands and kissing them, and saying with tears that he begged me not to ask his death.

"I am certain," he said, "to fall into the canal; I can be of no use to you. Alas! Leave me here and I will spend the whole night praying to St. Francis for you. It is in your power to kill me; but I will never make up my mind to come with you."

The fool did not know that I thought his company would bring me misfortune.

"You are right," I said, "stay; but on condition that you will pray to St. Francis and go at once and bring all my books, which I wish to leave to the Count."

He obeyed me instantly. My books were worth a hundred scudi[13] at least. The Count said he would return them to me when I came back.

"Be sure," I answered, "that you will not see me here again, and that I am very glad this base coward has not courage enough to follow me. He would be in my way, and in any case such a coward is unworthy to share the honor of so signal an escape with Father Balbi and me. Is not that so, my brave companion?" I said to the monk, another coward in whom I hoped to arouse some sense of honor.

"Very true," he said, "always provided that he does not have cause to congratulate himself tomorrow."

I then asked the Count for pens, ink, and paper, all of which he had despite the prohibition, for prohibitions were nothing to Lorenzo, who would have sold St. Mark himself for a scudo. I then wrote the following letter, which I left in the care of Soradaci without being able to read it over, for I wrote it in the dark. I began it with a visionary motto, which under the circumstances I thought very appropriate.

Non moriar sed vivam, et narrabo opera Domini.

("I shall not die, but live, and declare the works of the Lord.")[14]

"Our Lords the State Inquisitors are bound to do everything to keep a culprit in prison by force; but the culprit fortunate enough not to be on parole must also do everything he can to gain his freedom. Their right is founded upon justice; the culprit's upon nature. Just as they did not need his consent to lock him up, so he cannot need theirs to flee.

"Giacomo Casanova who writes this in the bitterness of his heart knows that he is liable to the misfortune of being caught before he leaves the State and returned to the hands of those whose sword he seeks to flee, and in that case he appeals on his knees to the humanity of his generous judges, begging them not to make his fate still more cruel by punishing him for what he has done only at the prompting of reason and nature. He begs them, if he is taken, to return to him all his belongings which he leaves in the cell he has vacated. But if he has the good fortune to escape, he gives all that he leaves here to Francesco Soradaci, who remains a prisoner because he fears the danger to which I am about to expose myself and does not, as I do, love his freedom more than his life. Casanova begs the magnanimous virtue of Their Excellencies not to deny the wretch the gift he has made him. Written an hour before midnight without light in the cell of Count Asquin this 31st day of October 1756.''

Castigans castigavit me Deus, et morti non tradidit me.

("The Lord hath chastened me sore: but he hath not given me over unto death.")[15]

I gave him the letter, warning him not to give it to Lorenzo but only to the Secretary himself, who certainly would not fail to come up. The Count told him that my letter would infallibly produce the intended effect, but that he must give everything back to me if I reappeared. The idiot answered that he hoped to see me again and return everything to me.

But it was time to leave. The moon was no longer visible. I tied half the ropes to Father Balbi's neck on one side and the bundle of his wretched clothing on his other shoulder. I did the same to myself. Both of us in our vests, with our hats on our heads, we set forth to what we might find.

E quindi uscimmo a rimirar le stelle (Dante).

("And from there we went out to see the stars again.")[16]

CHAPTER XVI

*I leave the prison. I am in danger of losing my
life on the roof. I leave the Doge's Palace, I
embark, and I reach the mainland. Danger to
which Father Balbi exposes me. Stratagem I
am obliged to use to get rid of him for a time.*

I WENT out first; Father Balbi followed me. I told
Soradaci to put the lead plate back where it had been
and dismissed him to pray to his St. Francis. Down on
my hands and knees, I got a good grip on my pike and,
extending my arm, I pushed it slantwise into the joints
between the plates, with the result that by using my four
fingers to grasp the edge of the plate I had raised, I was
able to help myself along to the top of the roof. To follow me the monk had put the four fingers of his right
hand into the belt of my breeches near the buckle, so that
I was in the unhappy position of a beast of burden at
once carrying and drawing, and what is more while
climbing a slope wet from the fog.

Halfway up this rather dangerous ascent the monk
told me to stop because one of his bundles had come loose
from his neck and rolled down, perhaps no farther than
the gutter. My first response was the temptation to give
him a good kick; it would have been more than enough

to send him hurrying after his bundle; but God granted me the strength to resist it; the punishment would have been too great both for him and for me, since all by myself I simply could not have got away. I asked him if it was the bundle of ropes; but when he said that it was the one in which he had put his black redingote, two shirts, and a precious manuscript he had found under the Leads and which, he insisted, would make his fortune, I calmly told him that he must bear it patiently and go on. He sighed, and, still clinging to my behind, he followed me.

After passing over fifteen or sixteen plates, I found that I had reached the ridge of the roof, on which, spreading my legs, I sat comfortably astride. The monk did likewise behind me. We had our backs turned to the small island of San Giorgio Maggiore,[1] and two hundred paces ahead of us were the numerous domes of the Church of San Marco, which forms part of the Doge's Palace; it is the Doge's chapel; no monarch on earth can boast of having one equal to it. I at once got rid of my burdens and told my accomplice that he might do likewise. He managed well enough to put his bundle of ropes between his thighs, but his hat, which he tried to put there too, lost its balance and, after turning all the somersaults necessary to bring it to the gutter, dropped into the canal. My companion instantly succumbed to despair.

"A bad omen," he said. "Here I am, at the beginning of our enterprise, without a shirt, without a hat, and without a manuscript which contained the precious and completely unknown history of all the festivals celebrated in the palace of the Republic."

Less savage than I had been when I was climbing, I told him that the two accidents he had just experienced were far too natural for even a superstitious person to call them auguries, that I did not consider them such, and that they did not discourage me; but that they should serve him as a last warning to be prudent and obedient and to reflect that if his hat had fallen off to his right instead of to his left we should have been lost, for it would have dropped into the palace courtyard, where the Arsenalotti would have picked it up, and, concluding that there must be someone on the roof of the Doge's Palace, they would certainly have done their duty and found some way to pay us a visit.

After spending several minutes looking to right and left, I told the monk to stay there with the bundles and not to move until I returned. I set out carrying only my pike, moving along on my behind, still straddling the angle without any difficulty. I spent nearly an hour going everywhere, stopping, observing, examining; but, seeing nothing in any direction to which I could fasten one end of my rope to let myself down into a place where I should be safe, I was in the greatest perplexity. There was no use giving further thought either to the canal or to the palace courtyard. On the top of the church I could see only precipitous slopes between the domes, none of them leading anywhere which was not locked. To get beyond the church in the direction of La Canonica² I should have had to climb over steep curved surfaces; it was natural that I dismissed as impossible what I saw no way of doing. I had to be *bold but not foolhardy*. The exact point between them is, I believe, one of the most imperceptible middle points in philosophy.

My eyes and my thought began to dwell on a dormer which was on the side toward the Rio del Palazzo,³ about two thirds of the way down the slope. It was far enough from the place at which I had made my exit to assure me that the loft which it lighted did not belong to the guarded precincts of the cells I had broken open. It could only furnish light to some garret, inhabited or not, above one of the palace apartments, in which when day began I should naturally find the doors open. As for the palace servants, or those of the Doge's family,⁴ I was morally

certain that they would have hastened to get us away and
done anything except put us back in the hands of in-
quisitorial justice, even if they had known us to be the
greatest criminals in the State. With this idea in mind,
I felt impelled to inspect the front of the dormer, and I
proceeded there at once by raising one leg and letting
myself slide until I was more or less sitting on its small
horizontal roof, which was three feet long and a foot and
a half wide. I then bent well over, holding firmly to its
sides, and bringing my head as close to it as I could. I
saw, or rather, managed to feel, a light iron grating and
behind it a window with round panes joined together by
narrow slotted strips of lead. I thought nothing of the
window, though it was shut; but the grating, light as it
was, demanded a file, and the only tool I had was my
pike.

Thoughtful, gloomy, and baffled, I did not know what
to do when a very natural occurrence had the effect of
an extraordinary prodigy on my astonished soul. I hope
that my sincere avowal will not lower me in the eyes of
my philosophical reader, if he considers that a man in
a state of anxiety and distress is only half of what he
can be in a state of tranquillity. The midnight bell sound-
ing from San Marco just at that moment was the phenomenon which seized upon my mind and which, by a
violent shock, delivered it from the dangerous doubt
under which it was laboring. The bell reminded me that
the day which was just then to begin was All Saints'
Day; if I had a patron saint, he must be among them.
But what raised my courage still more and actually increased my physical powers was the profane oracle I had
received from my dear Ariosto: *Tra il fin d'Ottobre, e
il capo di Novembre*. If a great misfortune makes a freethinker pious, it is almost impossible for him not also to
become in some degree superstitious. The sound of the
bell spoke to me, told me to act, and promised me victory. Lying prone up to my neck and bending my head

down toward the small grating, I pushed my bolt into the frame which held it and I determined to break it and remove the grating in one piece. It took me only a quarter of an hour to smash all the wood which made up the four sides of the frame. The grating being now in my hands in one piece, I put it beside the dormer. I found it no more difficult to break away the glazed window, paying no attention to the blood flowing from my left hand, which was slightly cut by a pane I pulled out.

With the help of my bolt I used my original method to return to my position astride the pyramidal summit[5] of the roof, and I made my way to the place where I had left my companion. I found him desperate, furious, and in an atrocious humor; he reviled me because I had left him all alone for two long hours. He assured me that he was only waiting for seven o'clock to go back to his cell.

"What did you think I was doing?"

"I thought you had fallen into some chasm."

"And aren't you glad to see that I didn't?"

"What were you up to all this time?"

"You'll see. Follow me."

I tied my belongings and my rope to my neck and proceeded toward the dormer. When we came to the place where it was to our right I gave him a detailed account of all that I had done, consulting him as to how we could both get into the loft. I saw that it would be easy for one of us, because the other could let him down by means of the rope; but I did not know what means the other could employ to get down too, for I did not see how I could make the cord fast so that I could tie myself to it. If I got in and let myself go, I might break a leg, for I did not know if the jump down was too long to risk. To these sound considerations, delivered in friendly tones, the monk replied that I had only to let him down, and that then I would have all the time I needed to think out how I could rejoin him in the place to which I had lowered him. I controlled myself enough not to reproach

him with all the cowardice of his answer but not enough
to defer setting his mind at rest. I instantly undid my
bundle of ropes; I put a loop around his chest under the
armpits, I made him lie down on his belly, and I let him
down feet first to the small roof of the dormer, where,
still controlling the rope from my position astride the
summit, I told him to get his legs inside up to the hips,
supporting himself with his elbows on the roof. I then
slid down the slope as I had done the first time and, lying
down on my belly, I told him to let his body go without
any fear for I had a firm hold of the rope. When he
reached the floor of the loft he untied himself, and pulling the rope back I found that the distance from the
dormer to the floor was ten times the length of my arm.
It was too long a jump to risk. He said that I could throw
the ropes inside; but I took good care not to follow his
stupid advice. I went back to the summit, and not knowing what to do, I made my way to a place near a cupola
which I had not inspected. I saw a flat terrace, paved
with lead plates, next to a large dormer window closed
by a pair of blinds, and in a vat I saw a heap of quick-
lime and beside it a trowel and a ladder long enough for
me to use it to climb down to where my companion was;
only the ladder interested me. I passed my rope under
the top rung and, resuming my position astride the roof,
I dragged the ladder to the dormer. It was now a matter
of getting it in. The ladder was twelve times the length
of my arm.

The difficulties I had to overcome in the process of getting the ladder in were so great that I heartily repented
of having deprived myself of the monk's help. I had
pushed the ladder in the direction of the gutter so that
one end of it touched the opening in the dormer and the
other end protruded beyond the gutter by a third of the
length of the ladder. I then slid down to the roof of the
dormer, I dragged the ladder sidewise and, pulling it to
me, I fastened the rope to the eighth rung. I then pushed

it down again and got it back in line with the dormer; then I pulled the rope toward me; but the ladder could only go in as far as the fifth rung, its top struck against the roof of the dormer and no amount of force could have made it go in any farther. It was absolutely necessary to raise the other end; raising it would lower the opposite end, and the whole ladder could be put in. I could have set the ladder across the opening, tied my rope to it, and let myself down without any risk; but the ladder would have remained where it was, and in the morning it would have shown the *sbirri* and Lorenzo the place where I might well still be.

Somehow, then, the entire ladder had to be brought into the dormer, and having no one with me I was left with no choice except making up my mind to go down to the gutter myself and raise the end of it. This is what I did, exposing myself to a danger which, but for an extraordinary intervention of Providence, would have cost me my life. I had no hesitation about letting the ladder go by slackening the rope, for there was no fear that it would drop into the canal since it was hooked to the gutter by its third rung. Holding my pike, I slid slowly to a point in the gutter beside the ladder; I put down the pike and nimbly turned so that I was directly facing the dormer and had my right hand on the ladder. The gutter sustained the tips of my toes, for I was not standing but lying on my belly. In this position I mustered strength enough to raise the ladder half a foot, at the same time pushing it forward. I had the satisfaction of seeing it go in a good foot. The reader will understand that its weight must have diminished considerably. It was now necessary to raise it two more feet to make it go in that much farther; with that done, I was sure I could get it all the way in by at once returning to the roof of the dormer and pulling on the cord which I had tied to the rung. To elevate it two feet, I rose to my knees, but the force I tried to use to push it up made the toes of my two feet slip, so that my body dropped off into space as far as my chest, till it hung from my two elbows. It was in the same terrible instant that I used all my strength and all the aid of my elbows to press my body forward and check my further descent by my ribs; and I succeeded. Taking care not to slip, I managed with the help of the rest of my arms as far as the wrists to hold myself against the gutter with my whole belly. I had no fear for the ladder, since, my two efforts having pushed it in three feet, it could not move from where it was. So, finding that I now had my wrists and my groins from my lower belly to the top of my thighs actually on the gutter, I saw that by raising my right thigh so that I could put first one knee and then the other on the gutter, I should be out of my great danger. The effort I made to carry out my plan brought on a nervous spasm, the pain from which is enough to fell the strongest of men. It seized me just as my right knee was already touching the gutter; but the painful spasm, which is called a "cramp," not only practically paralyzed me in every limb, it necessitated my remaining motionless to wait for it to go away of itself, as previous experience had taught me it would do. Terrible moment! Two minutes later I made the attempt and—thank God!—I brought one knee to the gutter, then the other, and as soon as I thought I had sufficiently recovered my breath I straightened up, though still on my knees, and raised the ladder as far as I could, and I managed to get it high enough to be on a level with the opening in the dormer. Sufficiently well acquainted with the laws of the lever and of equilibrium, I then took my bolt and, following my usual method, climbed to the dormer, where I had no difficulty getting the ladder in, my companion receiving the end of it in his arms. I threw the ropes, my clothes, and all the debris from breaking the window down into the loft and then entered it, warmly greeted by the monk, who saw to pulling in the ladder. Arm in arm, we made the round of the dark place we were in, which might have been thirty feet long and ten wide.

At one end of it we found a double door made of iron bars; turning the latch at the center, I opened it. We groped our way around the walls, and, starting to cross the place, we found a large table surrounded by stools and armchairs. We went back to where we had touched windows; I opened one, then the blinds, and by the starlight we saw chasms between domes. I did not for a moment think of climbing down; I wanted to know where I was going, and I knew nothing of this part of the palace. I closed the blinds, we left the room, and returned to the place where we had left our baggage. At the end of my strength, I dropped onto the floor, stretched out with a bundle of ropes under my head, and in my utter exhaustion of body and mind a very sweet slumber took complete possession of me; I fell so irresistibly asleep that I thought I was yielding to death, and even had I been sure that it was so, I would have made no resistance, for the pleasure I felt in falling asleep was unbelievable.

My sleep lasted three hours and a half. The piercing cries and rough shaking of the monk were what waked me. He said that twelve o'clock[6] had just struck and that it was inconceivable I should sleep in our situation. It was inconceivable to him; but my sleep had not been voluntary; it was my constitution at bay which had brought it on, and the inanition due to my having neither eaten nor slept for two days. But the sleep had restored all my vigor, and I was delighted to see that the darkness of the loft had lessened a little.

I rose, saying:

"This place is not a prison; there must be a perfectly simple way of getting out of it, which will be easy to find."

We then made our way to the end opposite the door made of iron bars and in a very narrow corner I thought

I felt a door, I feel a keyhole, I thrust my bolt into it, hoping that it is not a closet. After three or four pushes I open it, I see a small room, and I find a key on a table. I try the key in the door, and I see that I have locked it. I open it and I tell the monk to go quickly for our bundles, and as soon as he brings them I lock the small door again and put the key back where it was. I leave the small room and find that I am in a gallery lined with niches full of notebooks. They were archives. I find a short, narrow stone stairway and I go down it; I find another with a glazed door at the end; I open it and I see that I am at last in a room I knew; we were in the ducal chancellery.[7] I open a window, and I see that I could easily get down, but I would be in the labyrinth of little courtyards which surround the Church of San Marco. God forfend! On a desk I see an iron instrument with a wooden handle and a round point, which the chancellery secretaries use to make holes in parchments, to which they then attach the lead seals[8] with thread; I take it. I open the desk and find a copy of a letter informing the Proveditor-General[9] in Corfu of the dispatch of three thousand zecchini for restoring the old fortress. I look to see if I can find the money, but it is not there. God knows with what pleasure I would have appropriated it, and how I would have laughed at the monk if he had dared to tell me that it was robbery. I would have considered it a gift from Providence, to say nothing of appropriating it by right of conquest.

I go to the door of the chancellery, I put my bolt into the lock, but convinced in less than a minute that my pike could not force it, I quickly decide to make a hole in one of the two leaves of the door. I choose the place where there are the fewest knots in the wood. I go to work on the board at the point where its junction with the other leaf affords me a crack, and all goes well. I made the monk force the wooden-handled instrument into the cracks I opened with the pike; then, pushing the latter as hard as I could to left and right, I broke and split and shattered the wood, heedless of the tremendous noise which my method of attack produced; the monk was trembling, for someone must be hearing it far away. I knew the danger, but I had to risk it.

In half an hour the hole was large enough, and so much the better for us that it was, for I should have had great difficulty making it any bigger. Knots to left, right, above, and below would have made it necessary for me to use a saw. The circumference of the hole was frightening, for it bristled all round with points jagged enough to tear our clothes and lacerate our skins. It was five feet up; under it I set a stool, onto which the monk climbed. He put his joined arms and his head into the hole, and I, standing behind him on another stool and taking him first by the thighs and then by the legs, managed to push him out into a dense darkness; but I did not care how dark it was, for I knew the place. When my companion was out, I threw him all my belongings, leaving nothing but the ropes in the chancellery.

I then set two stools side by side below the hole, and adding a third on top of them I climbed up on it; in this way the hole was opposite my thighs. I pushed myself into it up to the lower part of my abdomen with considerable difficulty and lacerating myself, for it was narrow; then, having no one behind to help me get farther, I told the monk to take me around the chest and pull me through without mercy and even in pieces if necessary. He obeyed my order, and I silently bore all the pain which my badly scratched flanks and thighs caused me.

As soon as I was out I quickly gathered up my clothes, went down two stairways, and had no difficulty in opening the door onto the passage in which is the great door to the Royal Stairs[10] and, beside it, the office of the Savio alla Scrittura.[11] The great door was locked, as was the one to the Hall of the Four Doors.[12] The door to the stairs was as big as a city gate; it took only a glance to show me that without a ram or a petard it was inviolable; at that moment my bolt seemed to be saying to me: *"Hic fines posuit* ['Here he has set the bounds'];[13] you have no more use for me." Precious instrument of my freedom, worthy to be hung *ex voto* on the altar of my tutelary divinity! Serene and calm, I sat down, saying to the monk that my work was ended and it was now for God or Fortune to do the rest:

> *Abbia chi regge il ciel cura del resto*
> *O la Fortuna se non tocca a lui.*

> ("Let him who rules the heavens see to the rest, or Fortune if it is not his concern.")[14]

"I do not know," I said, "if the palace sweepers will come here today, which is All Saints' Day, or tomorrow, All Souls' Day. If anyone comes I will run out as soon as I see the door opened, and do you follow in my tracks; but if no one comes I will not stir from here; and if I die of hunger I don't know what I can do about it."

At these words the poor man became furious. He called me a madman, desperate, a deceiver, a liar, and I know not what else. My patience was heroic. Thirteen o'clock[15] struck. From the moment I awoke in the loft under the dormer until that moment, only an hour had passed. The important thing which now occupied me was changing all my clothes. Father Balbi looked like a peasant, but he was unscathed: he was neither in rags nor bleeding; his red flannel vest and his violet leather breeches were not torn. But my figure inspired pity and horror. I was torn and scratched from head to foot and covered with blood. When I pulled my silk stockings off of two wounds I had, one on each knee, they both bled. The gutter and the lead plates had put me in this state. The hole in the chancellery door had torn my vest, my shirt, my breeches, my hips, and my thighs; I had terrible scratches everywhere. I ripped up some handkerchiefs and made such bandages as I could, tying them on with string, of which I had a ball in my pocket. I put on my fine coat, which on that cold day became laughable; I dressed my hair as well as I could and tied it up in the net; and, having no others, I put on white stockings, a shirt trimmed with lace, and put two more shirts, handkerchiefs, and stockings in my pocket, and I threw my breeches, my torn shirt, and everything else behind an armchair. I put my fine cloak on the monk's shoulders, which made him appear to have stolen it. I had the look of a man who, after attending a ball, has gone to some place of ill fame and there been roughed up. The bandages visible on my knees were the only thing which marred the elegance of my attire.

Thus decked out and wearing my fine hat trimmed with gold Spanish lace and a plume, I opened a window. My presence was at once noticed by some idlers in the palace courtyard, who, not understanding how a person of my appearance could be at that window at such an early hour, went and told the man who had the key to the place. Thinking he might have locked someone in the evening before without noticing it, he fetched his keys and came. I did not learn this until I was in Paris five or six months later.

Sorry that I had shown myself at the window, I sat down beside the monk, who was proceeding to treat me to some untimely remarks when I heard the sound of keys and of someone coming up the Royal Stairs. In the greatest perturbation I get up, I look through a crack in the great door, and I see a man alone,[16] wearing a black wig and no hat, calmly coming up carrying a bunch of keys in both hands. I told the monk in the most impressive tone not to open his mouth, to stand behind me, and follow me. I took hold of my pike, keeping it concealed under my coat, and I stationed myself by the door in such a position that, as soon as it was opened, I could start down the stairs. I prayed to God that the man would offer no resistance, for, otherwise, I should have to cut his throat. I was resolved to do it.

As soon as the door opened I saw that he was as if turned to stone by my appearance. Never pausing or saying a word to him, I went down as fast as I could, followed by the monk. Neither dawdling nor running, I took the magnificent "Stairway of the Giants," as it is called, disregarding the voice of Father Balbi who followed me repeating over and over:

"Let us go to the church!"

The door to the church was on the right, twenty paces beyond the stairs.

The churches of Venice do not enjoy the slightest immunity as asylums for any wrongdoer, be his offense criminal or civil; so no one goes there any more to stave off the constables who have a warrant to capture him. The monk knew this; but his knowledge was not enough to overcome the temptation. He told me afterward that what prompted him to take refuge at the altar was a religious feeling which I ought to respect.

"Why didn't you go by yourself?"

"Because I did not have the heart to abandon you."

The immunity I sought was beyond the boundaries of the Most Serene Republic;[17] I was already beginning even then to make my way to it; I was there in spirit, and I had to get my body there. I went straight to the Porta della Carta,[18] which is the royal entrance to the Doge's Palace; and looking at no one (a way to avoid being looked at), I crossed the Piazzetta, reached the quay, and got into the first gondola I found there, saying loudly to the gondolier on the poop:

"I want to go to *Fusina*, call another man quickly."

The other man came on board at once; I drop nonchalantly onto the cushion in the middle, the monk sits down on the bench, and the gondola at once leaves the quay. The person of the hatless monk wrapped in my cloak contributed not a little to my being taken for a charlatan or an astrologer.

No sooner had we rounded the Customs House[19] than my gondoliers began vigorously cutting through the waters of the great Giudecca Canal, which has to be traversed to reach either Fusina or Mestre, the place to which I really wanted to go. When I saw that we were halfway down the canal, I said to the gondolier on the poop:

"Do you think we shall be at Mestre before fourteen o'clock?"

"You told me to go to *Fusina*."

"You are mad; I said *Mestre*."

The other gondolier said I was wrong; and Father Balbi, as a good Christian zealous for the truth, told me I was wrong too. I then laughed, admitting that I might have made a mistake but that I had intended to say "to Mestre." No one answered. My gondolier said that he was ready to take me to England.

"We shall be at Mestre," he said, "in three quarters of an hour, for *we have the current and the wind in our favor.*"

I then turned and looked down the splendid canal; and seeing not a single boat and admiring the most beautiful day one could hope for, the first rays of a magnificent sun just rising above the horizon, the two young gondoliers rowing at top speed, and thinking at the same time of the cruel night I had spent, of the place where I had been the day before, and of all the coincidences which had been favorable to me, feeling took possession of my soul, which rose up to a merciful God, setting the springs of my gratitude in motion, touching me with extraordinary power and so profoundly that my tears suddenly found fullest vent to relieve my heart, which was choking from excess of joy; I sobbed, I cried like a child forced to go to school.

My charming companion, who until then had not
spoken except to side with the gondoliers, thought it his
duty to calm my tears, of whose noble source he was unaware; and the way he went about it did indeed make
me pass in an instant from tears to a laugh so strange
that, baffled by it, he confessed to me some days later
that he thought I had gone mad. The monk was stupid,
and his malice came from his stupidity. I saw that I was
in the difficult position of having to turn it to advantage;
but he came very near to being my ruin, though unin-
tentionally, because he was stupid. He would never believe that I had ordered the gondoliers to go to Fusina
when I intended to go to Mestre; he said that the idea
could not have come to me until I was on the Grand
Canal.

We reached Mestre. I found no horses at the posthouse; but at the Osteria della Campana[20] there were
plenty of *vetturini,* who serve as well as the post. I
went into the stable, and seeing that the horses were good
I agreed to give the *vetturino* what he asked to be at
Treviso in an hour and a quarter. Within three minutes
the horses were put in, and supposing that Father Balbi
was behind me, I turned to say "Get in—"

But I did not see him. I look about, I ask where he is,
nobody knows. I tell the stableboy to go and look for
him, determined to reprimand him even if he had gone to
attend to his natural needs; for we were under the necessity of putting that off too. I am told that he is not to be
found. I was like a soul in torment. I think of leaving by
myself, it was the thing to do; but I listen to a weak feeling instead of to my strong reason, and I run out. I ask
for him, everyone says he has been seen but no one can
tell me where he may have gone; I search the arcades of
the principal street, it occurs to me to stick my head into
a coffeehouse, and there I see him, standing at the
counter drinking chocolate and talking with the waitress.
He sees me, he says she is charming and urges me to drink

a cup of chocolate too; he says I must pay, for he has no money. I control myself and answer that I do not want any, telling him to hurry and gripping his arm so hard he thought I had broken it. I paid, he followed me. I was shaking with anger. I start off toward the carriage, which is waiting for me at the door of the inn; but I have scarcely taken ten steps before I meet a citizen of Mestre named Balbo Tomasi, a good man but who had the reputation of being a spy for the tribunal of the Inquisitors. He sees me, he comes up, and he exclaims:

"You here, Signore! I am delighted to see you. So you have just escaped. How did you manage it?"

"I did not escape, Signore, I was set free."

"That is impossible, for I was at the Grimani palace in San Polo last evening and I should have heard of it."

The reader can imagine the state of my soul at that moment: here I was, discovered by a man who I believed had been hired to have me arrested, which he could do by merely winking at the first *sbirro,* of which Mestre was full. I told him to speak in a whisper and to follow me behind the inn. He came, and when I saw that we were out of anyone's sight and that I was close to a little ditch beyond which there was nothing but open country, I put my right hand on my pike and my left on his collar; but he nimbly escaped me, jumped the ditch, and began running as fast as he could away from the city of Mestre, turning every now and again to kiss his hand to me by way of saying: "A good journey to you, have no fear!" I lost sight of him; and I thanked God that the man's being able to escape from my hands had prevented me from committing a crime, for I was on the verge of cutting his throat and he had no evil intentions. My situation was dreadful. I was alone, and at open war with all the forces of the Republic. I had to sacrifice everything to foresight and caution. I put my pike back in my pocket.

In all the dejection of a man who has just escaped

from a great danger, I cast a look of scorn on the base coward who had seen to what a pass he had brought me, and I got into the carriage. He sat down beside me and never dared to say a word. I thought of how I could rid myself of the wretch. We reached Treviso, where I ordered the post master to have two horses ready to leave at seventeen o'clock;[21] but I did not intend to continue my journey by the post—first because I had no money, and second because I feared I should be followed. The innkeeper asked me if I wanted breakfast, and I needed it to stay alive, for I was dying of inanition; but I did not have the courage to say yes. A quarter of an hour lost could be fatal to me. I dreaded being caught and feeling ashamed of it all the rest of my life, for a man with his wits about him and a clear field should be able to defy four hundred thousand men to find him. If he does not know how to hide, he is a fool.

I went out by the San Tomasso[22] gate like a man who is going for a stroll, and after walking a mile along the highroad I made off into the fields, not intending to leave them until I was out of the Venetian State. The shortest road out of it was by way of Bassano, but I took the longest because there might be men waiting for me at the nearest point of exit and I was sure that no one would suppose that, to leave the State, I would take the road to Feltre, which was the longest way round to reach the jurisdiction of the Bishop of Trento.

After walking for three hours I sank onto the hard ground, absolutely at the end of my strength. I either had to take some nourishment or prepare to die there. I told the monk to put the cloak beside me and to go to a farmhouse which I saw and buy something to eat and bring it all to me where I was. I gave him money enough. After saying he thought I had more courage, he went off on my errand. The wretch was stronger than I was. He had not slept; but he had eaten well the day before, he had

drunk a cup of chocolate, he was thin, caution and honor
were not harrowing his soul, and he was a monk.

Though the house was not an inn the farmer's kindly
wife sent me a peasant girl with an adequate dinner,
which cost me only thirty soldi. When I felt sleep about
to overtake me I started off again, with a good sense of
my direction. Four hours later I stopped behind a village
and learned that I was twenty-four miles[23] from Treviso.
I was done in; my ankles were swollen and my shoes
broken. Daylight would end in an hour. I lay down in the
middle of a clump of trees and made the monk sit down
beside me.

"We must go," I said, "to Borgo di Valsugana,[24] the
first town beyond the borders of the Venetian State. We
shall be as safe there as in London, and we will rest, but
to reach the town, which belongs to the Prince-Bishop of
Trento, we must take some unavoidable precautions, the
first of which is that we must separate. You will go by
way of the forest of Mantello,[25] I through the mountains,
you by the easiest and shortest way, I by the hardest and
longest, you with money, I without a soldo. I make you
a present of my cloak, which you will exchange for a cape
and a hat, and then everyone will take you for a peasant,
for fortunately you have the look of one. Here is all the
money I have left from the two zecchini I got from Count
Asquin, it comes to seventeen lire, take them; you will
be at Borgo tomorrow evening, and I twenty-four hours
later. You will wait for me at the first inn on the left.
I need to sleep in a good bed tonight, and Providence
will show me the way to one, but I need to be in it peacefully, and with you I cannot be at peace. I am sure that
we are now being searched for everywhere and that our
descriptions have been circulated so accurately that we
should be arrested at any inn which we dared to enter
together. You see my deplorable condition and my absolute need to rest for ten hours. So farewell. Go, and leave

me to set about finding myself a refuge somewhere nearby.''

''I was already expecting,'' he replied, ''all that you have just said to me; but my only answer is to remind you of what you promised me when I let you persuade me to break open your cell. You promised that we would never separate; so do not hope that I will leave you, your fate shall be mine and mine shall be yours. We will find a good refuge for our money and we will not go to inns; we will not be arrested.''

''So you are determined not to follow the good advice I have given you.''

''Absolutely determined.''

''We shall see.''

So saying I got up, not without effort; I took his measure and marked it out on the ground, then I drew the pike from my pocket, lay down on my left side, and began to make a small excavation, maintaining the utmost calm and answering not a word to all the questions he asked me. After working for a quarter of an hour I looked at him sadly and said that, as a Christian, I considered it my duty to warn him that he should commend his soul to God.

''For,'' I said, ''I am going to bury you alive in this hole, and if you are stronger than I am, you shall bury me in it. This is the only course which your brute stubbornness leaves open to me. However, you can run away if you choose, for I will not run after you.''

Seeing that he did not answer I went on working. I began to fear that the sorry beast, of whom I was determined to rid myself, would drive me to extremes.

Finally, whether deliberately or in terror, he came hurtling toward me. Not knowing his intention, I advanced the point of the pike; but there was nothing to fear. He said that he would do everything I wished. I then embraced him; I gave him all the money I had, and I repeated my promise to join him at Borgo. Though

left without a soldo, and having two rivers to cross, I
heartily congratulated myself on having been able to
shake off the burden of such a man's company. With
that done, I was certain that I should succeed in getting
out of the State.

VOLUME 4 • NOTES

CHAPTER I

1. *Gritti:* Zuan Antonio Gritti, surnamed Sgombro (1702-1768), Venetian patrician, banished to Cattaro ca. 1753.
2. *Sgombro:* The word means "mackerel"; C. may be using it here in the sense of French *maquereau,* slang for "pimp."
3. *Two sons:* Gritti had three sons, Domenico, Francesco, and Camillo Bernardo (born 1736); the reference here is probably to the last.
4. *Cattaro:* Venetian town and fortress on the gulf of the same name; it had belonged to Venice from 1420. Now the Yugoslavian city of Kotor.
5. *End of the year:* Gritti died in Cattaro, but not until 1768.
6. *Council of Ten:* The Consiglio dei Dieci, the highest judicial authority of the Venetian Republic, consisted of the Doge, his Councilors, and ten elected patricians.
7. *Contarini:* Carlo Contarini (1732-1781), Venetian patrician and advocate, was banished in 1780 for advocating radical reforms and died in 1781.
8. *Great Council:* The Gran Consiglio (also Maggior Consiglio) was the highest authority in Venice; it originally consisted of all citizens and was given a constitution in 1172. This was altered in 1297, and from then on only patricians over twenty-five years of age were members of the Great Council.
9. *Cornelia Gritti:* Née Barbaro (ca. 1719-1808); she was a poetess and a friend of Metastasio, Algarotti, and Goldoni and a member of the Arcadian Academy under the name of Aurisbe Tarsense.
10. *Ghetto:* From 1516 the Jews who lived in Venice were confined to the Ghetto Vecchio (Old Ghetto) and the Ghetto Nuovo (New Ghetto); in the 17th century the Ghetto

Nuovissimo (Newest Ghetto) was added. All three were in
Cannaregio, north of the Grand Canal and northeast of
the present railway station.

11. *Profession:* When a nun made her profession ("took the
veil"), her relatives and friends were permitted to be present
at the solemn ceremony. If she belonged to a prominent
family in the city, the attendant festivities attracted many
curious onlookers.

12. *Traghetto gondola:* A designated station at which a certain
number of gondolas were required by law to be in readiness
to take passengers was called a *traghetto*. Originally these
gondolas only made particular crossings, especially on the
Grand Canal.

13. *Casino:* C. uses the Italianism *casin,* in the sense of country house, pleasure house, garden house.

14. *Aventurine:* A brownish colored glass flecked with gold,
first manufactured at Murano; also, a variety of quartz of
the same color.

15. *San Canziano:* Church northeast of the Rialto Bridge,
near the Church of Santa Maria dei Miracoli.

16. *Countess S.:* C. wrote Seguro, but crossed it out and substituted the initial. Countess F. or T. Seguro, wife of Count
Seguro, probably came, like the whole Seguro (Sigouros)
family, from the island of Zante in the Ionian Sea.

17. *Riva del Rio Marin:* Original, *quai du Romarin* ("Rose-
mary Quay"). C. undoubtedly means one of the streets on
either side of the Rio Marin (directly opposite the present
railway station, south of the Grand Canal).

18. *Convent of the XXX:* Presumably the convent of San
Giacomo di Galizzia, on the island of Murano.

19. *M. M.:* It has not yet been possible to identify M. M.
with certainty. Earlier Casanova scholars (Gugitz) believed
she was a certain Maria Lorenza Pasini, whose name in religion was Maria Maddalena; as she was of the citizen class
and nothing has yet been discovered which would indicate
that she enjoyed any celebrity, the possibility must be excluded. Further on in the manuscript C. several times first
wrote "Mathilde," then substituted "M. M." Probably she
is Maria Eleonora Michiel (or Micheli), of a Venetian
patrician family, who had become a nun in the convent of

Santa Maria degli Angeli in Murano in 1752. Her mother was born a Bragadin. This fact would explain not only M. M.'s acquaintance with Countess S. and her references to her high birth but also her turning to C., of whom she had presumably heard from the Bragadin family.

CHAPTER II

1. *Countess Coronini:* Maria Theresia, Countess Coronini-Cronberg (died 1761), married to Johann Anton, Count Coronini-Cronberg, in 1700, lady in waiting at the Bavarian court and later at the Imperial Court of Charles VII.

2. *Santa Giustina:* A very old Venetian church, property of the nuns of the Augustinian Order from 1448; it no longer exists.

3. *Nun of the Celsi family:* This nun has not yet been identified beyond doubt; she may have been the abbess of the convent of San Sepolcro, whose name was Celsi and who died in 1785 at the age of sixty-nine.

4. *Nun of the Micheli family:* This reference to a nun bearing this family name speaks against the assumption that she is the mysterious M. M. (cf. note 19 to Chapter I of this volume). Yet C. may here have been deliberately trying to mislead.

5. Horace, *Satires*, II, 2, 79.

6. Horace, *Epistles*, I, 2, 54.

7. *Friulian:* Friuli (the name is derived from the Roman settlement Forum Julii) is a district south of the Carnic Alps; it belonged to the Venetian Republic from 1420. Friulians often served as porters, lantern-carriers, and messengers in Venice, and had a reputation for reliability.

8. *Savoyards:* Many inhabitants of Savoy, which was a part of Italy in the 18th century, emigrated to Paris and had a similar reputation for reliability in their more or less menial occupations.

9. *Zecchini:* 1 soldo = 1/20 of a Venetian lira; 1 lira = 1/22 of a zecchino.

10. *Honor:* The Brockhaus-Plon edition reads *honneur*. Laforgue gives *bonheur* ("happiness," "good fortune"), which is more probably right.

11. *Montealegre:* José Joaquín, Duke of Montealegre (died 1771), was Spanish Ambassador in Naples from 1740 to 1746 and in Venice from 1748. C. probably met him in Naples rather than in Parma.

12. *Rosenberg:* Philipp Joseph, Count Orsini-Rosenberg (1691-1765), was Austrian Ambassador in Venice from 1754 to 1764.

13. *French Ambassador:* François Joachim de Pierre de Bernis (1715-1794) was French Ambassador in Venice from 1752 to 1755. See note 10 to the following chapter.

14. *Vestal:* Vesta, the Roman goddess of the hearth fire, had a circular temple in the Forum in which the perpetually burning hearth of the State was tended by six vestals. These priestesses lived a cloistered life near the temple; they had to take a vow of chastity, the penalty for breaking which was death.

15. *Augustine:* Aurelius Augustinus (354-430), saint and celebrated Father of the Latin Church. Casanova here refers to his *De civitate Dei,* Book XXII, Chap. 24.

16. Slightly altered from Horace, *Epistles,* I, 2, 62-63.

CHAPTER III

1. *Julius Florus:* Roman historian who accompanied the Emperor Tiberius (A.D. 14-37) to the Near East.

2. Horace, *Epistles,* II, 2, 191-192.

3. *Casino:* The exact location of the Abbé de Bernis's pleasure house (according to C. he was M. M.'s lover) is not known. (Cf. note 10 to this chapter and Chaps. IV-VIII).

4. *Half past the first hour of night:* According to the Italian reckoning the first hour of the day of twenty-four hours began at the Angelus, a half hour after sunset. As the season was winter the time mentioned would be about 8:00 P.M.

5. *Four o'clock:* I.e., about 11:00 P.M.

6. *Sèvres porcelain:* The famous manufactory, which was originally in Vincennes, was moved to Sèvres in 1753.

7. *Cook:* The cook employed by the Abbé de Bernis from 1753 to 1755 was named Durosier.

8. *"Oeil de perdrix" champagne:* A pink champagne from

Villes-Allerand. Its color resembles that of a partridge's eye; hence the name.

9. *Signor Mocenigo:* Alvise II Zuan Mocenigo (1710-1756), Venetian patrician; he was Venetian Ambassador in Paris from 1751 to 1756.

10. *The A. de B.:* Here the Abbé de Bernis is first referred to by his initials. His full name does not appear until Chapter VI. François Joachim de Pierre de Bernis (1715-1794), abbé from 1727, writer, member of the French Academy and the Arcadian Academy. French Ambassador in Turin 1752, in Venice from Oct. 1752 to Oct. 1755, made a cardinal in 1758; later held other high diplomatic posts. Some of C.'s biographers consider his account of De Bernis slanderous, especially since the Cardinal's own memoirs mention no such adventures. However, contemporary sources tend to show that C.'s portrait is accurate on the whole.

11. *Count of Lyons:* Members of the Cathedral Chapter of Lyons bore this title. To be received into the chapter candidates had to show descent from sixteen noble ancestors. De Bernis received the title in 1748.

12. *Belle-Babet:* After a Parisian flower vendress whose beauty was greatly admired. Voltaire called De Bernis "the flower girl of Parnassus."

13. *His poems: Poésies de M.L.D.B.,* Paris, 1744.

14. *St. Catherine's Day:* The feast of St. Catherine of Alexandria was celebrated on November 25th.

15. *Palazzo Morosini del Giardino:* This palace of the Morosini family near the Church of the Santi Apostoli took its name from an especially beautiful and elaborate garden, which disappeared at the beginning of the present century.

16. *Flanders post:* The imperial post, operated by the Thurn und Taxis family.

17. *Here:* C. appears to have forgotten that the conversation is taking place not at M. M.'s casino but in the convent visiting room.

18. *Bartolomeo da Bergamo:* Bartolomeo Colleoni (1400-1475), from 1455 Captain-General of the Venetian Republic. The famous equestrian statue of him by Verrocchio (1436-1488) stands in the square in front of the Church of SS. Giovanni e Paolo.

19. *Lord Holderness:* Robert d'Arcy, fourth Earl of Holderness (1718-1778), was English Ambassador in Venice from 1744 to 1746.

20. *Second hour:* Cf. note 4 to this chapter.

21. *Alençon point:* A kind of lace. Laces played a great part in 18th-century fashion. After Venetian laces, those from Alençon, in northern France, were most highly esteemed.

22. *Saxon porcelain:* From the manufactory at Meissen, founded in 1710.

23. *First hour:* Cf. note 4 to this chapter.

24. *Bautta:* See Vol. 3, Chap. XIII, n. 25.

25. *Henriette:* Cf. Vol. III, Chaps. 1-5.

26. *L'Étorière:* Marquis de l'Étorière (died 1774), French general staff officer, was considered one of the handsomest men in Paris.

27. *Antinoüs:* A beautiful Bithynian youth, favorite of the Emperor Hadrian; he accompanied him to Egypt and was drowned in the Nile in A.D. 130. Hadrian paid him divine honors after his death. He is represented in countless antique statues and bas-reliefs.

28. *Third Heaven:* According to the Ptolemaic system, the Heaven of Venus.

29. *The Mother and the Son:* Venus and Love.

CHAPTER IV

1. *No masking:* Going masked was forbidden in Venice from December 16th to December 25th because of the novena (see note 5) before Christmas.

2. *Lord Bolingbroke:* Henry St. John, Viscount Bolingbroke (1678-1751), English statesman and writer. His collected works (*On Authority in Matters of Religion, Concerning the Nature, Extent and Reality of Human Knowledge, On the Rise and Progress of Monotheism*, etc.) were published in 1754.

3. *Charron:* Pierre Charron (1541-1603), French moralist and disciple of Montaigne. His *Traité de la sagesse* was published at Bordeaux in 1601. Charron's advocacy of the Stoic

philosophy and his skepticism made it a handbook for the freethinkers of the 18th century.

4. *Bishop Diedo:* Vincenzo Maria Diedo (died 1753), Carmelite monk and Bishop of Altino-Torcello; the nuns of Murano were under his jurisdiction.

5. *Novena:* In the Roman Catholic Church, nine days of devotion for any religious object. C. here refers to the novena preceding Christmas.

6. *Portier des Chartreux: Histoire de Dom Bougre, portier des Chartreux, écrite par lui-même* ("History of Dom Bugger, Porter of the Carthusians, written by himself") by J. C. Gervaise de Latouche; it was first published at Rome in 1745.

7. *Meursius:* Johannes Meursius (1579-1639), Dutch antiquary; he wrote his essays in Latin. The obscene book *Joannis Meursii Elegantiae latini sermonis, seu Aloisiae Sigeae Toletanae Satyra Sotadica de Arcanis Amoris et Veneris* (first published in Holland in 1680) at first passed as a Latin translation by Meursius from a Spanish text by Luisa Sigea of Toledo. Its real author was Nicolas Chorier (1609-1692).

8. *Opera:* The feast of St. Stephen is celebrated on December 26th. The theaters in Venice reopened on that date.

9. *Ridotto:* Gambling casino in the San Moisè quarter. All its patrons had to be masked unless they were patricians. It was closed in 1774.

10. *Robe:* The obligatory dress for Venetian patricians was a black robe. Senators wore red.

11. *Corrector:* The Correttori delle Leggi e del Palazzo were the members of a magistracy make up of five patricians and established in 1553; their chief duty was to amend laws.

12. *Lucca oil:* Olive oil from the Lucca district in Tuscany was considered especially good.

13. *Four Thieves vinegar:* Acetum quattuor latronum, a vinegar with herbs.

14. *Frustratoires:* From Latin *frustratio*, "frustration," but in slang use (see note 16 to this chapter) apparently meaning "stimulant."

15. *Muff:* In the 18th century men also carried muffs in winter.

332 History of My Life

16. *À gogo,* etc.: *À gogo,* slang "going to it hard"; *frustratoire,* see note 14; *dorloter,* "to coddle." The last is a perfectly ordinary word but apparently M. M. had not heard it until C. used it, like the others, in an obscene sense.

17. *Madame de Boufflers:* Marie Louise, Marquise de Boufflers-Rouverel.

18. *Con rond:* In French it has the obscene meaning "round cunt," but what letters of the Italian alphabet Madame de Boufflers had in mind remains a mystery. Cf. Count Lamberg writing to C. in 1792: "I do not understand how Mme. de Boufflers can have asked you why one says *con rond* in the Italian alphabet. What are the letters which are thus pronounced?" (*Casanova und Graf Lamberg, Briefe,* ed. G. Gugitz, Vienna and Leipzig, 1935, p. 234).

19. *Condoms:* Contraceptive sheaths, then made of fine linen.

20. *Masulipatam:* An Indian cotton cloth, so named from the city in which it was woven.

21. *St. Andrew's cross:* A cross in the shape of the letter X.

22. *Straight tree:* One of the thirty-two erotic positions described by Pietro Aretino (1492-1556) in his *Sonetti lussuriosi* composed for engravings by Raimondi after drawings by Giulio Romano (1492-1546).

23. *Annunciation:* Mengs painted his Annunciation in the Royal Chapel at Madrid in 1768.

CHAPTER V

1. *Sappho:* The Greek poetess Sappho (ca. 600 B.C.) lived on the island of Lesbos and gathered girls about her as votaries of Aphrodite and the Muses. The community was later misunderstood, so that Sappho came to be regarded as the most celebrated representative of Lesbian love.

2. *Correggio's Magdalen:* Antonio Allegri da Correggio (1494-1534), Italian Renaissance painter; C. probably saw his Mary Magdalen (painted ca. 1520) in Dresden (according to some experts, the painting at Dresden is a copy of the original).

3. *Poisoned:* There is no historical support for C.'s allegation that Bartolomeo Colleoni (see note 18 to Chapter III of this volume) was poisoned. In fact C. himself refutes it in the

third volume of his *Confutazione della Storia del Governo Veneto d'Amelot de La Houssaie* (1769).

4. The saying is attributed to the Emperor Caracalla (188-217) after the murder of his brother Geta.

5. *Two o'clock:* About two and a half hours after sunset.

6. *Mocenigo:* Alvise II Girolamo (called Momolo) Mocenigo (born 1721), Venetian patrician.

7. *Signora Marina Pisani:* Marina Pisani, née Sagredo, married to the patrician Almorò II Andrea Pisani in 1741; passionately addicted to gambling, in 1751 she was forbidden to enter the Ridotto. The prohibition was later withdrawn.

8. *Marcello:* Piero Marcello di San Polo (1719-1790), of a Venetian patrician family, sentenced to six years of imprisonment under the Leads in 1755 and later banished to Corfu. However, it is possible that the reference is to a Piero Marcello di San Caterina (born 1720).

9. *Signora Venier:* Elisabetta Venier, née Mocenigo, married to the patrician Sebastiano Venier in 1741.

10. *Pierrot:* Pierrot wore white and powdered his face with flour. The masks named later on are from the *commedia dell'arte* or its French derivatives.

11. *Furlanas:* The furlana was a lively dance from Friuli; it was always danced by a couple.

CHAPTER VI

1. *Filippi:* The filippo was originally a Milanese coin struck after a Spanish model. The filippo minted under Charles VI and later under Maria Theresa was worth 7½ Milanese and 10½ Venetian lire.

2. *San Michele:* Small island between Murano and Venice, originally the property of the Camaldolite Order; in the early 19th century it became the cemetery for Venice.

3. *Rio dei Gesuiti:* A wide canal in the northern part of Venice, near the Fondamenta Nuove.

4. *Felce:* Originally the cloth which covered the cabin of a gondola, later the cabin itself.

5. *Aeolus:* In classical mythology, the god of the winds.

6. *Rio dei Mendicanti:* A canal in the northern part of Venice

which opened onto the Lagoon some 1200 feet east of the
Rio dei Gesuiti.

7. *Santa Marina:* The district took its name from the old
parish church of Santa Marina in the Castello quarter, in
the northern part of Venice; the church was closed in 1818
and now serves as a storehouse for wine.

8. *Briati ball:* Named after a famous Muranese glass-blowing
family, it was a charity affair which took place every year
on March 19th.

9. *Jansenistically:* Jansenism was a reformist movement within
the Catholic Church, based on the teachings of Cornelis
Jansen (1585-1638), Bishop of Ypres. Stressing the Augustinian doctrines of original sin and freedom and grace, it ended
in a rigorism not far from Calvinism. It was very influential
in France in the 17th century.

10. *Foreign ambassador:* For fear of espionage the Venetian
Republic forbade patricians the slightest contact with foreigners, especially with the envoys of other states. Though
C., as a nonpatrician, was not subject to the same strict
regulations, his acquaintance with the French Ambassador
de Bernis may well have been the final reason for his imprisonment under the Leads.

11. *Ten o'clock:* About 3:00 A.M.

CHAPTER VII

1. *Lord Marshal:* George Keith, 10th Earl Marischal of
Scotland (ca. 1693-1778), exiled from Great Britain in 1716;
settled in Berlin in 1745 and was Prussian Ambassador in
Paris from 1751 to 1754 and in Madrid from 1758 to 1760;
he was one of the most intimate friends of Frederick the
Great and lived in Potsdam from 1764 until his death.

2. *Arsenal:* The name was extended to the adjacent fishing
port.

3. *Algarotti:* Count Bonomo Algarotti (born before 1712) was
the owner of a celebrated mercantile establishment in Venice;
he was the brother of the better-known writer Francesco
Algarotti (1712-1764). They had both received the title of
Count from Frederick the Great.

4. *O-Morphi:* See note 4 to Vol. 3, Chap. XI.

5. *Parc aux Cerfs:* See note 11 to Vol. 3, Chap. XI.
6. *A child:* She bore a girl in 1754, who lived in a convent under the name and title of Demoiselle de Saint-Antoine de Saint-André. See also Vol. 3, Chap. XI, n. 12.
7. *Rich:* Cardinal de Bernis was the French Ambassador in Rome from 1769 to 1791 and died there in 1794; he lost the greater part of his fortune during the Revolution.
8. *Mersius:* C. refers to the so-called *Meursius français*, a French version of the obscene work by Nicolas Chorier (cf. note 7 to Chap. IV of this volume).
9. *L'Académie des dames:* Alternative title of the *Meursius français*.
10. *French Embassy:* Near the Church of La Madonna dell' Orto, in Cannaregio.
11. *Spanish Ambassador's:* The Spanish Ambassador in Venice at the time was José Joaquín, Duke of Montealegre.
12. After Molière's *Georges Dandin*, Act I, Scene 9, where the reading is: *"Vous l'avez voulu, Georges Dandin."* The phrase had become proverbial in France.
13. *Martingale:* A system of betting according to which the stake is successively doubled.

CHAPTER VIII

1. *Having died:* The date of C. C.'s mother's death is not known. But since in a letter written to Casanova in 1779 his friend Francesca Buschini conveys greetings to him from Caterina Marsigli (née Capretta) and her mother, he is probably in error here; it is possible that the death was that of Caterina's father, which he mentions at the beginning of Chapter XI of this volume.
2. *Went to Vienna:* The Kirg's original plan to send De Bernis to the Imperial Court at Vienna was abandoned. However, he did finally leave Venice in October 1755 and had been in Parma from January to April of that year. In any case, C. is here in error concerning both dates and events.
3. *Set all Europe talking:* The reference is to the treaty concluded at Versailles (not Vienna) on May 1, 1756. Austria pledged neutrality in the war between France and England

(1756-1763). De Bernis negotiated for France, Prince Star-
hemberg for Austria. In his memoirs Cardinal de Bernis does
not mention the idea of the treaty until 1754; but in all
probability it was already under discussion in 1750-1752,
when Count Kaunitz was Austrian Ambassador in Paris.

4. *XXX:* Maria da Riva, a nun in the Benedictine convent of
San Lorenzo in Venice, was sent in 1742 to a convent of the
same order in Parma on account of her love affair with the
then French Ambassador in Venice; she fled from Parma
with a new lover, a certain Colonel Novara, to Switzerland,
and there married, but died soon afterward.

5. *Froulay:* Charles François, Count de Froulay or Froullay
(1673-1744), French Ambassador in Venice from 1732 to
1743; he did go mad.

6. *Rousseau:* Jean Jacques Rousseau (1712-1778) was secretary to Count Montaigu and accompanied him to Venice
when he went there to succeed De Froulay as French Ambassador; however, he remained in Venice only a year and
returned to Paris in 1744.

7. *San Francesco della Vigna:* Old parish church in the northern part of the city near the Fondamenta Nuove; originally
surrounded by vineyards, whence the name.

8. *Cavana:* A small boat basin, often roofed over.

9. *Six o'clock:* About 3:00 A.M.

10. *Ascension Week:* C. is right in this astronomical observation so far as the night hours are concerned. Since Easter
is always the first Sunday after the first full moon after the
vernal equinox (March 21st), and Ascension Day is 40 days
later, the moon is then in its last quarter and does not rise
until morning.

11. Ariosto, *Orlando furioso,* XIX, 51, 8, where the reading
is: *"e sol del mar tiran Libecchio resta."*

12. *Murray:* John Murray (ca. 1714-1755), English diplomat,
from 1754 to 1766 Resident in Venice, from 1766 to 1775 in
Constantinople; he died in quarantine at Venice on his way
from Constantinople to London.

13. *Ancilla:* Venetian dancer and courtesan, married to the
dancer Vincenzo Campioni.

14. *Autumn:* Since C.'s account of her death is that of an

eyewitness she must have died earlier, as he was already in prison at the end of July 1755.

15. *Memmo:* Andrea Memmo (1729-1793), Venetian patrician and Senator, Ambassador to Rome and Constantinople (1777), Procuratore from 1785.

16. *Rosenberg:* See Vol. 4, Chap. II, n. 12.

17. *Cavalli:* Domenico Maria Cavalli, Venetian diplomat, Resident in Milan, Turin, and Naples from 1741 to 1753; from 1755 Secretary to the Council of Ten.

18. *Two years later:* Murray did not leave Venice until 1766 (cf. note 12).

19. *Lazaretto:* On the small island of San Lazzaro, between Venice and the Lido; it was used as a quarantine station into the 19th century.

20. *Zorzi:* Marcantonio Zorzi (1703-1787), Venetian patrician, diplomat, and poet.

21. *Chiari:* Pietro Chiari (1711-1785), Jesuit, Professor of Oratory at Modena (1736-1737), then lived in Venice as a writer, was director of the *Gazetta Veneta* from 1761 to 1762, later became court poet in Parma.

22. *Teatro di Sant'Angelo:* Built in 1676 on the Grand Canal, closed at the beginning of the 19th century. In 1753 Chiari succeeded Goldoni as playwright for the theater.

23. *Martellian verse:* Pier Jacopo Martelli (1665-1727) was the first to use this fourteen-syllable verse, which took its name (*verso martelliano*) from him.

24. *Condulmer:* Antonio Condulmer (1701 - after 1755), Venetian patrician, served as Councilor and State Inquisitor in 1755.

25. *Councilor:* The Doge was assisted by a Council of six members; one of the three State Inquisitors was chosen from among them, the other two from the Council of Ten.

26. *Beginning of the winter:* The treaty was not concluded and published until May 1, 1756 (cf. note 3).

27. *At Vienna:* Another error (cf. note 3). There is no evidence that De Bernis went to Vienna.

28. *Three years later:* De Bernis was appointed Minister of Foreign Affairs on June 26, 1757.

29. Horace, *Epistles,* I, 16, 79.

30. *Nine months:* Another error in date (cf. note 2).
31. *Palazzo Bragadin:* In Vol. 3, Chap. XVI, Casanova says that he was living in the parish of Santa Maria Formosa. The Bragadin palace was in the parish of Santa Marina. Presumably C. had moved on account of his friendship with De Bernis, to avoid creating difficulties for Signor Bragadin. However, it is entirely possible that he would store valuable possessions in the old Senator's palace.
32. Tibullus, II, 5, 110.

CHAPTER IX

1. *Fourth hour:* About 11:00 P.M.
2. *Righelini:* Giano Righelini, also Righellini, Reghellini, of Scio; he practiced medicine in Venice and there published his medical work *Osservazioni sopra alcuni casi rari medici e chirurgici* (1764).
3. *Lady Holderness:* Lady Bridget Murray, daughter of Sir Ralph Milbank and Elisabeth d'Arcy, sister of the Earl of Holderness (died 1774).
4. *Short novel:* The reference is to Chiari's *La commediante in Fortuna*, published at Venice in 1755.
5. *Vergini:* The Augustinian convent of Santa Maria delle Vergini, in the Castello quarter, was founded in 1224 exclusively for Venetian ladies of patrician rank. It was demolished in 1806.
6. *Mercury:* The Roman equivalent of the Greek god Hermes, the messenger of the gods, here used ironically for "pimp."
7. *Cathedral church:* The Basilica of SS. Maria e Donato, in Murano, probably begun in the 7th century, owes its present form chiefly to the 12th; it was restored in the 19th century.
8. *Capsucefalo:* Francesco, Count Capsucefalo (also Capsochiefalo), had been governor of the Venetian island of Zante; he was later known in patrician circles as a procurer, and on March 29, 1755, was sentenced for espionage and relations with a foreign ambassador to three years' imprisonment in Corfu, followed by perpetual banishment to the Ionian Islands.

CHAPTER X

1. *Smith:* Joseph Smith (1682-1770), English merchant, English Consul in Venice from 1744 to 1760; he was well known in the 18th century as a bibliophile and patron of the arts.
2. *San Rocco:* District taking its name from the Church of San Rocco, built in 1489, rebuilt in 1725 and 1766.
3. *Pontacq:* A French wine from the town of the same name in the Basses-Pyrénées.
4. *Collegio:* The college of the Savi (Pien Collegio or Collegio Eccellentissimo), composed of twenty-six patricians: the Doge, his six Councilors, the three heads of the Quarantia Criminale, the six Grandi Savi, the five Savi di Terraferma, and the five Savi degli Ordini.
5. *Cephalonia:* Large island in the Ionian group, which then belonged to the Venetian Republic; modern Greek Kephallenía. However, Capsucefalo was banished to Zante (cf. Chap. IX, n. 8).
6. *Fanny Murray:* Real name Rudman (ca. 1729-1798), daughter of a musician, celebrated English courtesan, mistress of Sir Richard Atkins, who died in 1756; she soon afterward married the actor David Ross. Atkins planned a journey to Italy in 1755 and may have taken her there.
7. *Three:* At this point in his manuscript C. wrote and then canceled *jours pour lui répondre que Henriette* ("days to tell him that Henriette"), which may show that Tonina's name was really Enrichetta.
8. *Bakers' Guild:* One of the Scuole delle arti (corporations of artisans) which existed in Venice from the 13th century. They often had charge of considerable funds and so could act as bankers.
9. *Castello:* Venice was divided into six wards (*sestieri*): Castello, San Marco, and Cannaregio northeast of the Grand Canal, and Dorsoduro, San Polo, and Santa Croce southwest of it.
10. *Fondamenta Nuove:* Quayside at the northeastern edge of the city. C. was then living in the present Calle della Gorna, near the Church of SS. Giovanni e Paolo.

11. *San Giuseppe:* District taking its name from the small Church of San Giuseppe di Castello.
12. *Scopolo wine:* A then popular Greek wine from the island of Skópelos, one of the Sporades, in the Aegean Sea.
13. *Eighteen years old:* The girl in question may be a certain Anna Maria dal Pozzo, who, however, was born in 1725. Her father was a worker in mosaic.

CHAPTER XI

1. *Father having died:* C.'s statements are confusing, for in Chapter VIII he refers to her mother's death (cf. Chap. VIII, n. 1).
2. *Advocate:* Probably the advocate Sebastiano Marsigli (died ca. 1783); the date of the marriage is not known.
3. *Marta S.:* Countess Marta Savorgnan; under the name of Maria Concetta she was a nun in the convent of Santa Maria degli Angeli in Murano. Her father was Count Giacomo Savorgnan, who was related to the Grimani family. Her sister, Countess Nanetta, married a Count Rambaldi in 1745. (For the two sisters, see especially Vol. 1, Chaps. IV ff.)
4. *Two o'clock:* About 10:00 P.M.
5. *Count S.:* The name "Seguro" is crossed out in the manuscript. The Seguro (Sigouros) family was noble and came from the island of Zante. The later statements by the "beautiful patient" are incomprehensible. How could a mosaic worker be the friend of a Count, and how could his widow have claims to the inheritance of a patrician family?
6. *Greek:* C. almost always applies the term "Greek" (*grec*) to a sharper. But in this case he probably refers to the Count's origin.
7. *Persico:* The Persicos were a family of rich Venetian merchants who bought their way into the nobility. It is not clear whether "house" (*maison*) is used here to designate the house in which the family resided or the family itself.
8. *Mira:* On the Brenta between Venice and Padua; it was the site of numerous patrician summer residences.
9. *Manuzzi:* Giovanni Battista Manuzzi (died after 1774),

dealer in gems, from ca. 1740 to 1774 spy (*confidente*) for the Venetian Inquisitors. See also Appendix.

10. *Elemental spirits:* According to the doctrine of the cabala, the spirits assigned to the four elements (cf. Vol. 2, Chap. VII, n. 22).

11. *Signora Memmo:* Lucia Memmo, married to the patrician Pietro Memmo in 1719. Their sons became high officers of the Republic. Andrea Memmo was a friend of C.'s (cf. Chap. VIII, n. 15, in this volume).

12. *Mocenigo:* Alvise Antonio Mocenigo (born 1667), Venetian patrician, Cavaliere della Stola d'Oro, brother of Andrea Bragadin's wife Chiara.

13. *Holy Office:* Established by Pope Paul III in 1542 as the Congregation of the Inquisition, it was the highest court for offenses against the faith; suspended by Napoleon in 1808, but not finally abolished until 1859.

14. *Red:* The State Inquisitor appointed from the Doge's Council wore a red toga. The tribunal consisted of three Inquisitors.

15. *Portrait boxes:* Boxes with portraits inside them were very fashionable from the 17th century; in the 18th century they were most commonly snuffboxes, which were a favorite gift.

16. *Sant'Andrea:* Fortress built in 1544 on an island between Venice and the northern point of Malamocco. It was at Sant'Andrea that C. had first met the young Countess Bonafede.

17. *Campo San Pietro:* Square on the island of San Pietro in the Castello district in the eastern part of the city; it was the prostitutes' quarter.

18. *Garzón:* Title of an adjutant in the Spanish bodyguard. The Kings of Spain bore the title "Catholic Majesty" by papal permission.

19. *Messer Grande:* Also Missier Grande or Capitan Grande; title of the Venetian Chief of Police. The office had been held by Matteo Varutti from 1750.

20. *St. James:* Italian, Giacomo. He was revered in the West as the "first martyr." His tomb in Santiago de Compostela in northern Spain was and still is a famous place of pilgrimage. His feast is celebrated on July 25th.

21. *Erberia:* The fruit and vegetable market of Venice from the twelfth century, located in a square near the Rialto bridge.

22. *Eight months:* This was the regular term of office of a State Inquisitor.

23. Vergil, *Aeneid*, III, 395, and again X, 113. C. frequently cites it.

CHAPTER XII

1. *Key of Solomon: Clavicula Salomonis*, a book of magic lore; first printed in Hebrew, then in Latin, and finally translated into the modern languages. King Solomon was regarded in the East and in the Christian Middle Ages as a great magician.

2. *Zecor-ben:* Otherwise *Zohar*, also known in earlier literature as *Midrasch-Na-Zohar;* it professed to contain the divine revelation of a certain Rabbi Ben Yohai to his pupils. The book is composed partly in Hebrew and partly in Aramaic; first published in Spain in the 13th century by Moses de León; printed in Italy in 1558. It is considered a key work of cabalism.

3. *Picatrix:* A medieval treatise on conjuring up the devil; the original manuscript is in the Bibliothèque de l'Arsenal, Paris. It was mentioned by Rabelais in his *Pantagruel*, Book 3, Chapter 23.

4. *Treatise on the planetary hours:* It is impossible to determine to which of the many books on the subject current in the 18th century C. here refers.

5. *Philosophe militaire:* "The Philosophical Soldier"; the manuscript was published at London in 1768 by Jacques André Naigeon under the title *Le Militaire philosophe ou difficultés sur la Religion proposées au R. P. Malebranche prêtre de l'Oratoire par un ancien officier.* The book is outspokenly antireligious.

6. *Mathilde:* This name appears here for the first time. It is possible that it is M. M.'s real name; more probably, however, C. was still concealing her real name here. In any case, the reading represents words which C. crossed out in his manuscript.

7. *Opeska:* Antonio Niccolò Manuzzi was created a count by Stanislas Poniatowski when he married the latter's mistress Countess Opeska.

8. *C. D.:* Perhaps Clotilda Cornelia Dal Pozzo, daughter of the widow in whose house C. was then lodging and younger sister of the "beautiful patient"; she married Giovanni G. Gabrieli in 1768.

9. Greek proverb, based on Hercules' fight with the Hydra; quoted by Plato in his *Phaedo.*

10. *Flight from the Leads:* C.'s account was printed at Prague in 1788 under the title *Histoire de ma fuite des prisons de la République de Venise qu'on appelle les Plombs écrite à Dux en Bohême l'année 1787,* and published at Leipzig.

11. *Terza:* Name of a bell in the campanile of San Marco; it was rung only to summon the members of the magistracy to their regular afternoon sessions. According to the season, the hour varied from noon to 5:00 P.M.

12. *Under the Leads:* The prison was installed under the lead roof of the Doge's Palace in 1561. According to C.'s account it contained 7 cells, according to other sources only 4. The cells disappeared sometime in the 19th century.

13. *Quay of the Prisons:* C. writes *quai des prisons,* which might correspond to the Fondamenta delle Prigioni, which was on the Rialto in front of the prisons on the ground floor of the Palazzo dei Camerlenghi. But he can here only refer to the quayside on the Rio delle Prigioni, officially the Rio del Palazzo, next to the Doge's Palace.

14. *Enclosed bridge:* The famous Ponte dei Sospiri ("Bridge of Sighs") which connected the Doge's Palace with the Prigioni Nuove (see note 7 to Chap. XIII); the bridge and the Prigioni Nuove were built in 1589.

15. *Rio del Palazzo:* Also called Rio delle Prigioni (cf. n. 13).

16. *Circospetto:* Title of the Secretary to the Senate and the Council of Ten.

17. *Twenty-one o'clock:* 2½ hours before sunset.

18. *Eight o'clock:* 8½ hours after sunset; about 5:30 A.M. in July.

19. *Lorenzo:* Lorenzo Basadonna, warden from 1755. After C.'s escape he was imprisoned and in 1757 was sentenced to ten years in jail for murder.

20. *La Cité mystique . . . : La mística ciudad de Dios* ("The Mystical City of God") was written by the nun María de Agreda, by her civil name María Coronel (died 1665) and first published at Madrid in 1670. A French translation appeared in 1729 at Brussels. The work, which was in three volumes, was heavily attacked in the 17th and 18th centuries and until 1748 was on the Index. It has enjoyed a sort of renaissance in the 20th century.

21. *Forgotten:* C. later added the name Caravita in the margin. However, Vincenzo Caravita (1681-1734), a learned Neapolitan Jesuit, did not write a book on this subject. C. perhaps refers to *La Dévotion au Sacré Coeur,* by the Jesuit Jean Croiset (1656-1738), which was first published in 1689 and instituted the adoration of the Sacred Heart.

22. *Franciscan nuns:* The name of the convent was La Inmaculada Concepción.

23. *Agreda:* A small town some sixty miles east of Soria.

24. *Palafox:* Juan de Palafox y Mendoza (1600-1659) was made Bishop of Puebla de Los Angeles in America, served as Vice-Regent of Mexico from 1640 to 1642, and was made Bishop of Osma (Spain) in 1653. Proceedings to canonize him were begun in 1726 but were definitively abandoned in 1777.

25. *Mystical city:* Original, *cette cité mystique.* This is probably a reference to Agreda; but as C. is more than careless about capitals and underlinings he may have been referring to the title of the book.

26. *Malagrida:* Gabriele Malagrida (1689-1761), Italian Jesuit and missionary in Brazil, later confessor to a convent in Lisbon. He wrote his *La vida de gloriosa Santa Anna* in prison from 1759 to 1761. The book was put on the Index and in 1761 Malagrida was strangled and burned by order of the Inquisition. But the real reason for his condemnation would appear to have been that in 1758 he urged the assassination of the King of Portugal and prophesied his death.

27. *Ancient splendor:* In the course of the 18th century the Society of Jesus was outlawed in several European countries (Portugal 1759, France 1764, Spain and the Kingdom of Naples 1767) and was finally suppressed by Pope Clement XIV in 1773. It was restored in 1814 by Pope Pius VII.

28. *Fifty soldi:* Contemporary sources confirm that Basadonna was authorized to expend 48 soldi a day for C. The amount was later reduced to 30 soldi.

29. *Gazette de Leyde:* So named from its place of publication (Leiden, Holland), it bore the subtitle *Nouvelles extraordinaires de divers endroits.* It had been published regularly from 1680.

30. *Physician:* The archives of the Venetian Inquisition show that his name was Bellotto or Bellotti.

31. *Boethius:* Anicius Manlius Severinus Boethius (480-524), minister to Theodoric the Great, wrote his famous treatise *De consolatione philosophiae* in prison.

32. *New Inquisitors:* The three Inquisitors who sentenced C. were Andrea Diedo, Antonio Condulmer, and Antonio da Mula. On October 1, 1755, they were succeeded by Alvise Barbarigo, Lorenzo Grimani, and Francesco Sagredo (the latter pardoned C. in 1774).

33. *Sentence:* C. was actually sentenced to five years' imprisonment under the Leads for atheism on September 12, 1755.

34. At this point C. crossed out nearly a whole page of his manuscript so heavily that what he wrote cannot be deciphered.

35. Horace, *Odes,* I, 37, 29.

36. *The same time:* The great Lisbon earthquake occurred on November 1, 1755.

CHAPTER XIII

1. *Line:* One-twelfth of an inch.

2. *Bussola:* Name of the anteroom of the Council of Ten and the State Inquisitors (cf. Vol. 3, Chap. VI).

3. *Businello:* Pietro Businello, also Busenello, was the Venetian Resident in London from 1748 to 1751, then became Secretary to the Council of Ten. The Venetian Republic appointed ambassadors, who were always patricians, only to Constantinople, Rome, Paris, Vienna, and Madrid. To all other countries it sent residents appointed from among the secretaries to the Senate and the Council of Ten; they belonged to the class of *cittadini*. C. presumably met Busi-

nello in Paris in 1751, when Businello was on his way from London to Venice.

4. *Maggiorin:* C. is either mistaken or is purposely concealing his companion's name. The man was Lorenzo Mazzetta, of Milan; he was valet to Count Giorgio Marchesini, of Vicenza.

5. *Poggiana:* A patrician family of Vicenza.

6. *"The Four":* I Quattro, four prison cells in the Doge's Palace which were at the disposition of the State Inquisitors. The same name was also applied to cells in the so-called "New Prisons" (see the following note) which were connected with the Doge's Palace by the Bridge of Sighs.

7. *Prison building:* Built by Antonio da Ponte, separated from the Doge's Palace by the Rio del Palazzo.

8. *Cerigo:* Mazzetta escaped from prison in January 1762. It is not known if he was recaptured. There is no record of his having been exiled to Cerigo.

9. *Lire:* One Venetian lira was worth 20 soldi.

10. *Diedo:* Andrea Diedo (born 1691), Senator, State Inquisitor from October 1754 to October 1755.

11. *Ration biscuits:* Venetian ration biscuit was famous for its keeping qualities; it was prepared for soldiers and prisoners.

12. *Nobili:* According to the documents in the case his name was Carlo (not Sgualdo) Nobili.

13. *Charron's* Wisdom: See note 3 to Chap. IV of this volume. The first Italian translation of *De la sagesse* appeared in 1698 and a second in 1768.

14. *Montaigne:* Michel de Montaigne (1533-1592), author of the world-famous *Essais*.

15. *Seriman:* Roberto, Count Seriman, of Persian descent, diamond dealer in Venice, known in his day as a great gambler.

16. *Extrajudiciary:* A document drawn up by a notary for the purpose of settling a suit without going to court, that is, "extrajudicially," whence the name.

17. *Montealegre:* See note 11 to Chap. II.

18. *Lista:* The zone around and belonging to a foreign embassy; the embassy's right of asylum usually extended to it. For reasons of surveillance the foreign embassies were all in one part of the city (near the present railway station).

The street now named the Lista di Spagna points back to this circumstance.

19. Adapted from Horace, *Epistles,* I, 2, 58-59.

20. *Twenty inches:* Earlier in this chapter C. gave its length as two feet.

21. *Young wigmaker:* Probably a certain Giacomo Gobbato, who died on November 25, 1755, at the age of twenty-one.

22. *Is expedient:* C. uses the Latin verb *expedit.*

23. *Schalon:* Gabriel Schalon, also Schalom, Salom, of Padua. According to the documents in the case he became C.'s cellmate as early as December 19, 1755.

24. *Five Savi:* The Cinque Savi alla Mercanzia constituted a sort of ministry of commerce (established in 1506).

25. *Eight or nine weeks:* C. first wrote "nearly three months," then canceled it.

26. *Micheli:* Domenico Micheli (1732-1782), Venetian patrician, Senator from 1745; he may have been M. M.'s brother.

27. *Corner:* Flaminio Corner, also Cornaro (1692-1779), Venetian patrician, Senator, and author.

28. *In Latin:* His principal work was a history of the Church in Venice and Torcello, *Ecclesiae venetae et torcellanae antiquis monumentis,* etc., Venice, 1749.

29. *St. James of Compostela:* See Chap. XI, n. 20.

30. *St. George:* His feast is celebrated on April 23rd.

31. *The other St. James:* His feast is celebrated on May 1st, with that of St. Philip.

32. *St. Anthony:* His feast is celebrated on June 13th.

33. *Diameter:* C. must mean "radius"; he could not get through a hole only ten inches across.

34. *Terrazzo marmorin:* A flooring made of small pieces of marble held together by lime.

35. *Livy:* Book XXI, Chap. 37.

36. *Asceta . . . ascia:* C.'s hypothesis is completely unfounded. Livy wrote *infuso aceto* ("after vinegar had been poured in").

37. *St. Theodore:* St. Theodore of Euchaita, martyred during the reign of the Emperor Diocletian, was the first patron saint of Venice. Since tension between Venice and the Patriarchate of Aquileia, whose patron saint was St. Hermagoras, a pupil of St. Mark the Evangelist, had already begun in the early Middle Ages, the Venetians sought an

348 History of My Life

opportunity to outdo the neighboring State. In 828 the
relics of St. Mark were secretly brought from Alexandria to
Venice, and installed in a chapel which was later replaced
by the church of San Marco. Thereafter the winged lion,
St. Mark's emblem, became the emblem of the Venetian
Republic.

38. *Eusebius:* Eusebius, Bishop of Caesarea (died 339), court
theologian to the Emperor Constantine the Great, wrote the
first history of the Church. He describes St. Mark as St.
Peter's companion in Book II, Chap. 15 of his history.

39. *Fenaroli:* Count Tommaso Fenaroli, known in his day as
a great gambler, was imprisoned under the Leads July 22-30,
1755.

40. *Origo:* Father Origo, earlier a Jesuit, was in the service of
the Abbé de Bernis during his term as ambassador in Venice.

41. *Twenty o'clock:* About three and a half hours before
sunset.

42. *Signora Alessandri:* Margherita Alessandri, Italian singer,
born in Bologna.

43. *Martinengo:* Paolo Emilio, Count of Martinengo da Barco
(1704 - after 1795), Venetian patrician.

44. *Signora Ruzzini:* Arpalice Ruzzini, née Manin, married to
Giovanni Antonio Ruzzini (1713 - after 1766) in 1746; he was
a Venetian patrician and diplomat, ambassador in Madrid
1750-1754, in Vienna 1755-1761, in Constantinople 1766.

45. *Proved to be the case:* Count Fenaroli had broken the
strict Venetian law which forbade any conversation between
patricians and foreign ambassadors except in connection
with official business.

46. *Canary wine:* Wine from the Canary Islands, especially
from Tenerife, had long been esteemed.

47. *St. Augustine's Day:* His feast is celebrated on August 28th.

48. *Zeno:* Greek philosopher (late 4th - early 3rd century B.C.),
founder of the Stoic school.

49. *Pyrrhonists:* Disciples of the Greek philosopher Pyrrho
(360-271[?] B.C.), founder of the Skeptic school. The Greek
word *ataraxia* means complete tranquillity of soul; according to the doctrine of Epicurus and the Pyrrhonists, achieving it is the highest moral duty of man.

50. *Abstine . . . sustine:* From a maxim of Epictetus, quoted in Aulus Gellius, *Noctes atticae,* XVII, 19.

CHAPTER XIV

1. *"Wells":* I Pozzi; the prison cells so named were eighteen in number, located in the Doge's Palace under the offices of the State Inquisitors and the Council of Ten, and could be reached only from there by a secret stairway. It is possible that the nine lower cells were occasionally flooded; but the condition was certainly not constant.

2. *Beguelin:* Probably Domenico Lodovico Beghelin, also Bighelin (ca. 1696 - after 1775), of Mantua, captain in the service of the Venetian Republic; he was first sentenced to the "pozzi" and later to the "camerotti" (cells without windows).

3. *Count Schulenburg:* Johann Mathias, Count von der Schulenburg (1661-1747), first in the service of Poland, from ca. 1715 Venetian Field Marshal; he distinguished himself by his defense of Corfu against the Turks.

4. Seneca, *Epistles,* CI, where the saying is attributed to Maecenas.

5. *Spielberg:* The citadel of Spielberg in Brünn (now Brno) was the state prison of the Austro-Hungarian monarchy; it was destroyed by the French in 1809.

6. After Horace, *Epistles,* I, 2, 58.

7. *Maffei:* See Vol. 3, Chap. VIII, n. 4. His collected works were not published until 1790; so it was a matter of buying various books of his, some of them in several volumes.

8. *Rationarium:* The *Rationarium temporum,* a work on chronology by Denys Pétau, called Petavius (1583-1652); it was published at Paris in 1633-1634.

9. *Wolff:* Baron Christian von Wolff, also Wolf (1679-1754), German philosopher of the Age of Reason. Since there was no edition of his collected works, it is not possible to determine to which of his writings C. refers; possibly to his latest book at the time, *Philosophia moralis sive ethica,* 5 vols., Halle, 1750-1753.

10. Seneca, *Epistles,* XCVIII.

11. *Latet:* C. first wrote *quaere* ("seek"), then crossed it out and substituted *latet*.

12. *Balbi:* Marin Balbi (1719-1783), Venetian patrician and monk of the Somaschian Order (founded in 1532 and confirmed by Pope Paul IV in 1540; it exists only in Italy).

13. *Asquin:* Count Andrea Asquin, also Asquini (died after 1762), of Udine.

14. *Four years:* According to the Venetian judicial archives Balbi was not arrested until November 5, 1754.

15. *Father Superior:* Either Girolamo Barbarigo (1723-1782), Somaschian monk and professor at the University of Padua, or his brother Luigi Barbarigo, who was Superior of the Somaschian monastery of Santa Maria della Salute.

16. *Priuli Gran Can:* Alvise Priuli (1718 - after 1763), Venetian patrician; sentenced to the Leads in August 1755. His sobriquet may have been derived from the famous representative of the Veronese family of Scaliger, Can Grande della Scala (1291-1329).

17. *Five years:* Count Asquin was sentenced to life imprisonment on September 20, 1753, but in 1762 he managed to escape with sixteen other prisoners.

18. *Two gentlemen:* They were the brothers Bernardo and Domenico Marcolongo. The Sette Comuni is a German-language enclave in upper Italy, between the Astico and the Brenta Rivers.

19. *Two notaries:* They were Giovanni and Pietro Zuccoli, sentenced to the Leads on April 2, 1756.

20. *Veronese Marchese:* Count (not Marchese) Desiderato Pindemonte, of Verona, sentenced to the Leads in 1756.

21. *Vulgate:* The official Latin text of the Bible approved by the Roman Catholic Church, in large part translated by St. Jerome. A Venetian printer did bring out an edition of the Bible in an unusually large format about this time; it is nearly 18 inches high.

22. *Septuagint:* A Greek translation of the Old Testament made, according to tradition, by order of Ptolemy Philadelphus II (284-247 B.C.) by 72 Egyptian Jewish scholars (*septuaginta* means seventy, hence the name).

23. *St. Michael's Day:* The feast of St. Michael is celebrated on September 29th.

24. *Macaroni:* The name did not mean the form of pasta to which it is applied today but what are now known as "gnocchi."

25. *Twice the width of the Bible:* The Bible was a folio, so its width was some 13 inches.

26. *Eighteen o'clock:* About 1:00 P.M.

27. *Monday:* Reckoning from the last date given by C.— October 16th—Soradaci became his cell-mate on October 18th; but in 1756 October 18th was a Saturday.

28. *Office of the Holy Virgin:* The *Officium parvum*, a book of prayers in honor of the Virgin Mary, used in the Roman Catholic Church from the 11th century.

29. *Isola:* Town on the north coast of the Istrian peninsula (now Izola); it is an island connected with the mainland, hence the name.

30. *First Chaplain:* Probably the priest Pietro Madecich, who was born in Mantua and hence was a subject of the Empress Maria Theresa.

31. *Ambassador:* See vol. 3, Chap. IX, n. 84.

32. *Refosco:* A well-known wine from the vicinity of Udine.

33. *Soradaci:* Francesco Soradaci, barber and wigmaker, of Isola in Istria.

CHAPTER XV

1. *Brought back to my cell:* According to the extant documents in his case, Francesco Soradaci had already been arrested on September 1, 1756, but was probably kept in another prison until October 18th and was set free on December 31, 1756. The account given in the documents does not correspond with the story C. puts in his mouth.

2. *Nineteen o'clock:* About 2:00 P.M.

3. *First three days of November:* The first days of November were official holidays in Venice; many patricians spent them in their country houses in the Terra Ferma (the parts of the mainland ruled by the Republic), especially in the celebrated villas along the Brenta between Venice and Padua.

4. *Sortes virgilianae:* A form of divination in which an inquirer opened the works of Vergil at random and read a

meaning applicable to his situation in the first verse that met his eye.

5. Ariosto, *Orlando furioso*, IX, 7, 1.

6. In his first account of his escape (published in 1788), C. added *dit le Tasse* ("says Tasso") after this quotation. However, the line is not found in Tasso. It occurs in Metastasio's *Didone abbandonata*, Act I, Scene 4.

7. *Braccia:* A Venetian measure of length, equivalent to about 26 inches.

8. *Tartufe:* Type of the pious hypocrite, from the famous comedy by Molière (1622-1673).

9. *Two o'clock:* About 8:00 P.M.

10. *Aeneas . . . Anchises:* According to Vergil, *Aeneid*, II, 707 ff., Aeneas carried his father Anchises out of burning Troy on his shoulders.

11. *Arsenalotti:* Workers in the Arsenal, the military port of Venice. They also formed the guard of the Great Council; their weapons were a sword and a red stick.

12. *Sant'Apollonia:* District of the city taking its name from a confraternity dedicated to St. Apollonia. It is in the Sestiere di San Marco, near the Ponte della Canonica.

13. *Scudi:* The scudo was a gold coin which had been minted in Venice from the 16th century; its value was 8 lire or 160 soldi. One hundred scudi were worth about 46 zecchini.

14. Vulgate, Psalm 117, verse 17.

15. Vulgate, Psalm 117, verse 18.

16. Dante, *Divina commedia*, "Inferno," XXXIV, 139. It is the last line of the "Inferno."

CHAPTER XVI

1. *San Giorgio Maggiore:* This island, on which is the domed church of the same name (begun by Palladio in 1565 but not completed until 1610, by V. Scamozzi), lies south of the Piazzetta, some 1500 feet from the Doge's Palace.

2. *La Canonica:* Street immediately north of San Marco. The canons of the church lived there, hence its name.

3. *Rio del Palazzo:* C. provides a French translation of the name in the margin.

4. *Doge's family:* The Doge in office lived in the palace with

his family; the Doge at the time was Francesco Loredan.

5. *Pyramidal summit:* So C. (*sommet pyramidal*), though his previous description—to say nothing of the existing monument—shows that the roof was not a pyramid.

6. *Twelve o'clock:* About 6:00 A.M.

7. *Ducal chancellery:* The Cancelleria ducale chiefly served the purpose of an archive; laws, decrees, and ordinances were preserved there.

8. *Lead seals:* At the time only the Republic of Venice, the Roman Curia, and the Grand Master of the Teutonic Order had the privilege of sealing with lead; in general wax was used.

9. *Proveditor-General:* The Provveditor General di Mar was to all intents and purposes supreme commander of the Venetian naval forces; he resided in Corfu.

10. *Royal Stairs:* This stairway, commonly called the Scala dei Giganti, took its name from large statues of Mars and Neptune by J. Sansovino (1554). The Doges were crowned on the highest landing. The stairs lead from the north side of the inner courtyard to the lobby on the second floor of the palace.

11. *Savio alla Scrittura:* The closest counterpart to this official in other countries is the Minister of War.

12. *Hall of the Four Doors:* The Sala delle Quattro Porte is on the third floor and takes its name from four symmetrically placed doors. C.'s topography is not entirely accurate.

13. Perhaps after Psalm 147, 14, in the Vulgate version.

14. Ariosto, *Orlando furioso*, XXII, 57, 3-4.

15. *Thirteen o'clock:* About 7:00 A.M.

16. *A man alone:* His name was Andreoli. At the inquiry he testified that the two fugitives knocked him down.

17. *Most Serene Republic:* Venice had assumed the sobriquet of La Serenissima, as her great rival Genoa had assumed that of La Superba.

18. *Porta della Carta:* The official entrance to the Doge's Palace from the Piazzetta (directly beside the Church of San Marco). Built from 1438 to 1443, it took its name from the fact that the government posted all laws and ordinances on it.

19. *Customs House:* The Dogana da Mare, the Venetian cus-

toms office, is situated on the point in the southern part of the city formed by the confluence of the Grand Canal and the Giudecca Canal, near the Church of Santa Maria della Salute.

20. *Osteria della Campana:* So called in the 18th century; in the 19th it was known as the Albergo della Campana ("The Bell") and was a much frequented hotel (in 1825 the Austrian Emperor Franz I stayed there with his family). It was in the center of the city.

21. *Seventeen o'clock:* About 11:00 A.M.

22. *San Tomasso:* C. seems to have used the wrong name. The reference should be to the Porta San Teonisto (now Porta Cavour).

23. *Twenty-four miles:* It appears from what follows that C. was really only about half that distance northwest of Treviso.

24. *Borgo di Valsugana:* The principal town of the Val Sugana, between Trento and Bassano del Grappa, some seventy miles from Mestre (Venice). It belonged to the Bishopric of Trento and so was not under the rule of the Venetian Republic.

25. *Forest of Mantello:* Bosco del Mantello, an oak forest north of Treviso belonging to the Republic, which harvested timber there for shipbuilding.

APPENDIX

Giovanni Battista Manuzzi's Report to the Inquisitors
Concerning Casanova's Activities, July 17, 1755.*

Most Illustrious and Most Excellent Lords:

Having succeeded in learning from D[on] Gio[vanni]
Batt[ist]a Zini, of the parish of San Samuel[e], concerning Giacomo Casanova that, in addition to the many
friendships which he has with Noble Patricians, he believes that he has an understanding with some of them
and brings them foreigners to gamble, to win their
money, knowing from Casanova's own mouth that he has
the art of cheating at cards, that Casanova makes [peo-
ple] believe that they will not die but that they will be
gently carried away by Fra Bernardo, who comes to
raise them up and take them by the Milky Way to the
Land of the Adepts, where Leggismarco lives; and with
these damnable impostures of Rosicrucians and Angels
of Light he bewitches people, as he did N. H. [the Noble-
man] Ser Zuanne [Giovanni] Bragadin and other Noble
Patricians to get money out of them. That the said Casanova professes the maxims of Picurec [Epicurus]. That
with his impostures and chatter he entices people into
a complete libertinism in all kinds of pleasure. That he
is again cultivating N. H. Bragadin hoping to inherit
from him and eat up all the rest; that many Noble Patri-

* *The first page of the original report in Manuzzi's handwriting
is reproduced facing page 209.*

cians, admiring his talents, lend him their support. That
he is amazed [or: it is amazing] that nothing evil has
happened to him in his so intimate association with Noble
Patricians into whom he inculcates [?] certain maxims;
that there is open war if one of them speaks ill of him.

Having all these things in mind, I brought Casanova
to talk with me on similar subjects; he confided to me
that he has managed to ingratiate himself with Duke
Grillo who frequents the Al Buso drinkshop; that he
made him several discourses on numbers with the idea
of gradually bringing him to Chemistry [Alchemy] and
deceiving him into believing that he knows how to compound the universal powder, and then persuade him that
he will not die but pass gently over to the adepts; that
from the answers he received from Grillo on the subject
of the powder he saw that it would be a difficult undertaking since he had refuted his principles but that even
so he could make him spend a treasure, which would almost all go into his own purse, without Grillo's being
aware of it; that he had succeeded in bewitching others,
especially Ser Zuanne Bragadin; that in view of the intimate friendship between them about seven years ago
it had been bruited throughout the Country that both
N. H. Bragadin and he talked with the spirits, that
Bragadin having been warned that Masonry had been
laid before This Most High Tribunal, in order not to be
imprisoned or exiled he had left Venice. The said Casanova boasts that he is a cheater at cards, a freethinker,
and believes in nothing in matters of Religion, that he
has all the suppleness necessary to ingratiate himself
with people and deceive them, that in the past he was
often on the verge of ruin from lack of consideration,
but that now he operates with the greatest caution, because this is a Country in which it is impossible to talk
of Government or Religion without great danger, protesting that he believes nothing of our Religion, just as
certain Noble Patricians of his acquaintance do not be-

lieve. That his frequentations are with Ser Zuanne
Bragadin, Ser M[ar]co Ant[oni]o Zorzi, Ser Alvise
Grimani, Ser Marco Donado, Ser Bernardo Mem[m]o,
Ser Pro[curatore] Alvise Barbaro and very many other
Noble Patricians who love him; that in the case of some
of them he goes to their houses to dinner, since they all
ask him, with others he goes to coffeehouses, to the wineshop called "da Lissandro" in Frezzaria, where he tells
me that sometimes, but not often, they gamble. That he
has many acquaintances among foreigners and among
the noblest youths, that he frequents the houses of very
many unmarried and married ladies and of women of
another sort, that he tries to amuse himself in every way,
and is always attempting great coups to improve his
fortune; that he does not lack money to satisfy his desires, that some days ago he lost more than sixty zecchini
in Padua. This loss I learned from Giacomo Canal, and
I also heard of it from a certain Cesarino, a faro player
who frequents the Mondo d'Oro; in the presence of
the said Cesarino on Monday night in the drinkshop Al
Rinaldo Trionfante Casanova read aloud an impious
piece in verse, in the Venetian language, which he is now
composing. I do not know if anything can be more monstrous than his thoughts and his talk on the subject of
Religion, since Casanova holds that those who believe in
Jesus Christ are feeble-minded. Conversing with and
becoming intimate with the said Casanova one sees truly
united in him misbelief, imposture, lasciviousness, volup-
tuousness in a manner to inspire horror. N. H. Ser Bene-
detto Pisano has knowledge of the imposture practiced
on N. H. Ser Zuanne Bragadin by Casanova and that he
made him believe that the Angel of Light would come to
him, which made Casanova the ruin of the said N. H.
Bragadin.

Giacomo Canal, who also knows N. H. Ser Bernardo
Mem[m]o, tells me that Casanova is highly intelligent,
that he is on intimate terms with Noble Patricians, that

he believes that on occasion he serves them as a pimp,
that Ser Bernardo Mem[m]o, though he is often with
Casanova, sometimes loves him and sometimes despises
him.

From Giacomo Berti I learn that one of the boys at
the wineshop in Frezzaria told him that Casanova frequents it in the evening and that he retired to an inner
room to talk with Ser Bernardo Mem[m]o and with
Barbaro, and that some of them have seen Casanova in
the past few days with a purse full of gold and that he
always has money.

Venice, June 17, 1755.

[Your] most devoted, most humble,
and most obedient Servant.

Gio[vanni] Batt[ist]a Manuzzi